◀ 30TH ANNUAL EDITION ▶

CHILDREN'S WRITER'S & ILLUSTRATOR'S MARKET

2018

Cris Freese, Editor

WD
WRITER'S DIGEST
BOOKS

WritersDigest.com
Cincinnati, Ohio

Children's Writer's & Illustrator's Market 2018. Copyright © 2017 F + W Media, Inc. Published by Writer's Digest Books, an imprint of F+W Media, Inc., 10151 Carver Road, Suite 200, Blue Ash, Ohio 45242. Printed and bound in the United States of America.

Writer's Market website: www.writersmarket.com
Writer's Digest website: www.writersdigest.com

Distributed in Canada by Fraser Direct
100 Armstrong Avenue
Georgetown, Ontario, Canada L7G 5S4
Tel: (905) 877-4411

Distributed in the U.K. and Europe by F&W Media International
Brunel House, Newton Abbot, Devon, TQ12 4PU, England
Tel: (+44) 1626-323200, Fax: (+44) 1626-323319
E-mail: postmaster@davidandcharles.co.uk

ISSN: 0897-9790
ISBN-13: 978-1-4403-5268-3
ISBN-10: 1-4403-5268-3

Attention Booksellers: This is an annual directory of F + W Media, Inc. Return deadline for this edition is December 31, 2018.

fw

Edited by: Cris Freese
Designed by: Alexis Estoye
Production coordinated by: Debbie Thomas

CONTENTS

FROM THE EDITOR 1

GETTING STARTED

HOW TO USE *CHILDREN'S WRITER'S & ILLUSTRATOR'S MARKET*....2

QUICK TIPS FOR WRITERS & ILLUSTRATORS 5

BEFORE YOUR FIRST SALE 8

ARTICLES

CREATING UNFORGETTABLE CHARACTERS,
    by Debbie Dadey 15

FINDING YOUR WRITING SUPERPOWER,
    by Laurel Snyder.. 21

WRITING EFFECTIVE DIALOGUE,
    by Kerrie Flanagan... 27

AUDIENCES & ADVOCATES,
    by Suzanne Morgan Williams.. 31

TEN MARKETS FOR YOUR SHORT FICTION,
    by Windy Lynn Harris 37

INTERVIEWS

KWAME ALEXANDER,
    by Kerrie Flanagan... 44

KENNETH OPPEL,
    by David McPherson... 48

DANDI DALEY MACKALL,
    by Jean Daigneau 55

MINDY MCGINNIS,
    by Gloria G. Adams.. 61

KIRBY LARSON,
    by Suzanne Morgan Williams.. 65

CAROLYN CRIMI,
    by Carmela A. Martino... 70

ROUNDUPS

THE EVER-CHANGING PICTURE BOOK MARKET,
by Lana Wayne Koehler...77

WORKING WITH SMALL PRESSES,
by Carmela A. Martino...83

WHAT ARE AGENTS REALLY LOOKING FOR?,
by Kerrie Flanagan...89

BREAKING INTO NONFICTION,
by Nancy Parish..97

DEBUT AUTHORS TELL ALL,
compiled by Cris Freese...104

RESOURCES

GLOSSARY OF INDUSTRY TERMS *128*

MARKETS

BOOK PUBLISHERS 135

CANADIAN & INTERNATIONAL BOOK PUBLISHERS 194

MAGAZINES.. 205

AGENTS & ART REPS 224

CLUBS & ORGANIZATIONS 294

CONFERENCES & WORKSHOPS 302

CONTESTS, AWARDS, & GRANTS 324

INDEXES

SUBJECT INDEX.. 352

EDITOR & AGENT NAMES INDEX.. 371

AGE-LEVEL INDEX... 391

PHOTOGRAPHY INDEX 393

ILLUSTRATION INDEX 395

GENERAL INDEX 397

Photo: Al Parrish

FROM
THE EDITOR

///

When tackling my first edition of *Children's Writer's & Illustrator's Market* as the new editor, I wanted to keep readers informed with loads of information about breaking in and what it means to be a writer. I often hear from writers about how *CWIM* helped them find an agent, land a deal with a publisher, or inspire their career as a writer/illustrator. To that end, I hope you'll find this latest edition as inspiring as ever!

I loaded up the Debut Authors Tell All feature with 21 different writers, spread near-evenly between picture book writers, middle-grade authors, and young adult novelists who have all broken in over the past year. They're here to share a wealth of information about how they got their agent, what they would have done differently in the process, and what they did before they wrote their first book. And I'm excited to tell you that we're featuring the wonderful Angie Thomas and her *New York Times* best-selling novel, *The Hate U Give*, in these pages.

There's interviews aplenty—from Newberry Medal-winning author Kwame Alexander to Dandi Daley MacKall, author of over 500 books—and roundups featuring agents, writers who focus exclusively on nonfiction, and authors who have worked with small presses.

I'd like to think this is the most comprehensive edition of *CWIM* to date. There's a little something in here for you, no matter what you're writing. I hope you'll take the time to read these helpful articles before diving into the newly-updated listings. And, if you'd like to stay in touch, please send me a note at cris.freese@fwmedia.com, check out my blog at guidetoliteraryagents.com/blog, and follow me on Twitter (@crisfreese). And don't forget to check out the free webinar from amazing agent Jennifer De Chiara on breaking into the children's literature market at www.writersmarket.com/2018-cwim-webinar!

Cris Freese
Managing Editor, Writer's Digest Books & Writer's Market Series

HOW TO USE *CHILDREN'S WRITER'S & ILLUSTRATOR'S MARKET*

As a writer, illustrator, or photographer first picking up *Children's Writer's & Illustrator's Market*, you may not know quite how to start using the book. Your impulse may be to flip through the book and quickly make a mailing list, then submit to everyone in hopes that someone will take interest in your work. Well, there's more to it. Finding the right market takes research. The more you know about a market that interests you, the better chance you have of getting work accepted. We've made your job a little easier by putting a wealth of information at your fingertips. Besides providing listings, this directory has a number of tools to help you determine which markets are the best ones for your work. By using these tools, as well as researching on your own, you raise your odds of being published.

USING THE INDEXES

This book lists hundreds of potential buyers of material. To learn which companies want the type of material you're interested in submitting, start with the indexes.

Subject Index

But let's narrow the search further. Take your list of young adult magazines, turn to the **Subject Index**, and find the **Fashion** subheading. Then highlight the names that appear on both lists (**Young Adult** and **Fashion**). Now you have a smaller list of all the magazines that would be interested in your teen fashion article. Read through those listings and decide which seem (or look) best for your work.

Illustrators and photographers can use the **Subject Index** as well. If you specialize in painting animals, for instance, consider sending samples to book and magazine publishers listed under **Animals** and, perhaps, **Nature/Environment**. Because illustrators can simply send general examples of their style to art directors to keep on file, the indexes may be more helpful to artists sending manuscript/illustration packages who need to search for a specific subject. Always read the listings for the potential markets to see the type of work art directors prefer and what type of samples they'll keep on file, and obtain art or photo guidelines if they're available online.

Editor & Agent Names Index

This index lists book editors, magazine editors, art directors, agents, and art reps—indicating the companies they work for. Use this specific index to find company and contact information for individual publishing professionals.

Age-Level Index

Age groups are broken down into these categories in the Age-Level Index:

- **PICTURE BOOKS OR PICTURE-ORIENTED MATERIAL** are written and illustrated for preschoolers to eight-year-olds.
- **YOUNG READERS** are for five- to eight-year-olds.
- **MIDDLE READERS** are for nine- to eleven-year-olds.
- **YOUNG ADULT** is for ages twelve and up.

Age breakdowns may vary slightly from publisher to publisher, but using them as general guidelines will help you target appropriate markets. For example, if you've written an article about trends in teen fashion, check the **Magazines Age-Level Index** under the **Young Adult** subheading.

Photography Index

In this index, you'll find lists of book and magazine publishers that buy photos from freelancers. Refer to the list and read the listings for companies' specific photography needs. Obtain photo guidelines if they're offered online.

USING THE LISTINGS

Some listings begin with symbols. Many listings indicate whether submission guidelines are indeed available. If a publisher you're interested in offers guidelines, get them and read them. The same is true with catalogs. Sending for and reading catalogs or browsing them online gives you a better idea of whether your work would fit in with the books a publisher produces. (You should also look at a few of the books in the catalog at a library or bookstore to get a feel for the publisher's material.)

A Note for Artists & Photographers

Along with information for writers, listings provide information for illustrators and photographers. Illustrators will find numerous markets that maintain files of samples for possible future assignments. If you're both a writer and an illustrator, look for markets that accept manuscript/illustration packages and read the information offered under the **Illustration** subhead within the listings.

If you're a photographer, after consulting the **Photography Index**, read the information under the **Photography** subhead within listings to see what format buyers prefer. For example, some want the highest resolution .jpg available of an image. Note the type of photos a buyer wants to purchase and the procedures for submitting. It's not uncommon for a market to want a résumé and promotional literature, as well as sample URLs linking to previous work. Listings also note whether model releases and/or captions are required.

QUICK TIPS FOR WRITERS & ILLUSTRATORS

//

If you're new to the world of children's publishing, reviewing this edition of *Children's Writer's & Illustrator's Market* may have been one of the first steps in your journey to publication. What follows is a list of suggestions and resources that can help make that journey a smooth and swift one:

1. MAKE THE MOST OF *CHILDREN'S WRITER'S & ILLUSTRATOR'S MARKET*. Be sure to take advantage of the articles and interviews in the book. The insights of the authors, illustrators, editors, and agents we've interviewed will inform and inspire you.

2. JOIN THE SOCIETY OF CHILDREN'S BOOK WRITERS AND ILLUSTRATORS. SCBWI, more than 22,000 members strong, is an organization for both beginners and professionals interested in writing and illustrating for children, with more than seventy active regional chapters worldwide. It offers members a slew of information and support through publications, a website, and a host of Regional Advisors overseeing chapters in almost every state in the U.S. and a growing number of locations around the globe. SCBWI puts on a number of conferences, workshops, and events on the regional and national levels (many listed in the **Conferences & Workshops** section of this book). For more information, visit www.scbwi.org.

3. READ NEWSLETTERS. Newsletters, such as *Children's Book Insider*, *Children's Writer*, and the *SCBWI Bulletin*, offer updates and new information about publishers on a timely basis and are relatively inexpensive. Many local chapters of SCBWI offer regional newsletters as well.

4. READ TRADE AND REVIEW PUBLICATIONS. Magazines such as *Publishers Weekly* (which offers two special issues each year devoted to children's publishing and is available on newsstands as well as through a digital subscription) offer news, articles, reviews of newly published titles, and ads featuring upcoming and current releases. Referring to them will help you get a feel for what's happening in children's publishing.

5. READ GUIDELINES. Most publishers and magazines offer writers' and artists' guidelines that provide detailed information on needs and submission requirements, and some magazines offer theme lists for upcoming issues. Many publishers and magazines state the availability of guidelines within their listings. You'll often find submission information on publishers' and magazines' websites.

6. LOOK AT PUBLISHERS' CATALOGS. Perusing publishers' catalogs can give you a feel for their line of books and help you decide where your work might fit in. If catalogs are available, visit publishers' websites, which often contain their full catalogs. You can also ask librarians to look at catalogs they have on hand. You can even search Amazon.com by publisher and year. (Click on "book search" then "publisher, date" and plug in, for example, "Lee & Low" under *publisher* and "2016" under *year*. You'll get a list of Lee & Low titles published in 2016, which you can peruse.)

7. VISIT BOOKSTORES. It's not only informative to spend time in bookstores—it's fun, too! Frequently visit the children's section of your local bookstore (whether a chain or an independent) to see the latest from a variety of publishers and the most current issues of children's magazines. Look for books in the genre you're writing or with illustrations similar in style to yours, and spend some time studying them. It's also wise to get to know your local booksellers; they can tell you what's new in the store and provide insight into what kids and adults are buying.

8. READ, READ, READ! While you're at that bookstore, pick up a few things, or keep a list of the books that interest you and check them out of your library. Read and study the latest releases, the award-winners and the classics. You'll learn from other writers, get ideas, and get a feel for what's being published. Think about what works and doesn't work in a story. Pay attention to how plots are constructed and how characters are developed, or the rhythm and pacing of picture book text. It's certainly enjoyable research!

9. TAKE ADVANTAGE OF INTERNET RESOURCES. There are innumerable sources of information available online about writing for children (and anything else you could possibly think of). It's also a great resource for getting (and staying) in touch with other writers and illustrators through listservs, blogs, social networking sites, and e-mail, and it can serve as a vehicle for self-promotion.

10. CONSIDER ATTENDING A CONFERENCE. If time and finances allow, attending a writers conference is a great way to meet peers and network with professionals in the field of children's publishing. As mentioned earlier, SCBWI offers conferences in various locations year round. (See scbwi.org and click on "Events" for a full conference calendar.) General writers' conferences often offer specialized sessions just for those interested in children's writing. Many conferences offer optional manuscript and portfolio critiques as well, giving you feedback from seasoned professionals. See the **Conferences** section of this book for information on conferences.

11. NETWORK, NETWORK, NETWORK! Don't work in a vacuum. You can meet other writers and illustrators through a number of the things listed earlier—SCBWI, conferences, online. Attend local meetings for writers and illustrators whenever you can. Befriend other writers in your area (SCBWI offers members a roster broken down by state)—share guidelines, share subscriptions, be conference buddies and roommates, join a critique group or writing group, exchange information, and offer support. Get online—subscribe to listservs, post on message boards and blogs, visit social networking sites and chatrooms. Exchange addresses, phone numbers, and e-mail addresses with writers or illustrators you meet at events. And at conferences, don't be afraid to talk to people, ask strangers to join you for lunch, approach speakers and introduce yourself, or chat in elevators and hallways.

12. PERFECT YOUR CRAFT AND DON'T SUBMIT UNTIL YOUR WORK IS AT ITS BEST. It's often been said that a writer should try to write every day. Great manuscripts don't happen overnight; there's time, research, and revision involved. As you visit bookstores and study what others have written and illustrated, really step back and look at your own work and ask yourself, *How does my work measure up? Is it ready for editors or art directors to see?* If it's not, keep working. Join a critique group or get a professional manuscript or portfolio critique.

13. BE PATIENT, LEARN FROM REJECTION, AND DON'T GIVE UP! Thousands of manuscripts land on editors' desks; thousands of illustration samples line art directors' file drawers. There are so many factors that come into play when evaluating submissions. Keep in mind that you might not hear back from publishers promptly. Persistence and patience are important qualities in writers and illustrators working toward publication. Keep at it—it will come. It can take a while, but when you get that first book contract or first assignment, you'll know it was worth the wait. (For proof, read the "Debut Authors Tell All" article later in this book!)

BEFORE YOUR
FIRST SALE

//

If you're just beginning to pursue your career as a children's book writer or illustrator, it's important to learn the proper procedures, formats, and protocol for the publishing industry. This article outlines the basics you need to know before you submit your work to a market.

FINDING THE BEST MARKETS FOR YOUR WORK

Researching markets thoroughly is a basic element of submitting your work successfully. Editors and art directors hate to receive inappropriate submissions; handling them wastes a lot of their time, not to mention your time and money, and they are the main reason some publishers have chosen not to accept material over the transom. By randomly sending out material without knowing a company's needs, you're sure to meet with rejection.

If you're interested in submitting to a particular magazine, see if it's available in your local library or bookstore, or read past articles online. For a book publisher, obtain a book catalog and check a library or bookstore for titles produced by that publisher. Most publishers and magazines have websites that include catalogs or sample articles (websites are given within the listings). Studying such materials carefully will better acquaint you with a publisher's or magazine's writing, illustration, and photography styles and formats.

Many of the book publishers and magazines listed in this book offer some sort of writers', artists', or photographers' guidelines on their websites. It's important to read and study guidelines before submitting work. You'll get a better understanding of what a particular publisher wants. You may even decide, after reading the submission guidelines, that your work isn't right for a company you considered.

SUBMITTING YOUR WORK

Throughout the listings, you'll read requests for particular elements to include when contacting markets. Here are explanations of some of these important submission components.

Queries, Cover Letters, & Proposals

A query is a no-more-than-one-page, well-written letter meant to arouse an editor's interest in your work. Query letters briefly outline the work you're proposing and include facts, anecdotes, interviews, or other pertinent information that give the editor a feel for the manuscript's premise—enticing her to want to know more. End your letter with a straightforward request to submit the work, and include information on its approximate length, date it could be completed, and whether accompanying photos or artwork are available.

In a query letter, think about presenting your book as a publisher's catalog would present it. Read through a good catalog and examine how the publishers give enticing summaries of their books in a spare amount of words. It's also important that query letters give editors a taste of your writing style. For good advice and samples of queries, cover letters, and other correspondence, consult *Guide to Literary Agents 2018*, as well as *Formatting & Submitting Your Manuscript, 3rd Ed.* and *The Writer's Digest Guide to Query Letters* (all published by Writer's Digest Books).

- **QUERY LETTERS FOR NONFICTION.** Queries are usually required when submitting nonfiction material to a publisher. The goal of a nonfiction query is to convince the editor your idea is perfect for her readership and that you're qualified to do the job. Note any previous writing experience and include published samples to prove your credentials, especially samples related to the subject matter you're querying about.
- **QUERY LETTERS FOR FICTION.** For a fiction query, explain the story's plot, main characters, conflict, and resolution. Just as in nonfiction queries, make the editor eager to see more.
- **COVER LETTERS FOR WRITERS.** Some editors prefer to review complete manuscripts, especially for picture books or fiction. In such cases, the cover letter (which should be no longer than one page) serves as your introduction, establishes your credentials as a writer, and gives the editor an overview of the manuscript. If the editor asked for the manuscript because of a query, note this in your cover letter.
- **COVER LETTERS FOR ILLUSTRATORS AND PHOTOGRAPHERS.** For an illustrator or photographer, the cover letter serves as an introduction to the art director and establishes professional credentials when submitting samples. Explain what services you can provide as well as what type of follow-up contact you plan to make, if any. Be sure to include the URL of your online portfolio if you have one.

- **RÉSUMÉS.** Often writers, illustrators, and photographers submit résumés with cover letters and samples. They can be created in a variety of formats, from a single page listing information to color brochures featuring your work. Keep your résumé brief, and focus on your achievements, including your clients and the work you've done for them, as well as your educational background and any awards you've received. Do not use the same résumé you'd use for a typical job application.
- **BOOK PROPOSALS.** Throughout the listings in the **Book Publishers** section, listings refer to submitting a synopsis, outline, and sample chapters. Depending on an editor's preference, some or all of these components, along with a cover letter, make up a book proposal.

    A *synopsis* summarizes the book, covering the basic plot (including the ending). It should be easy to read and flow well. The gold standard for synopsis length is one page, single-spaced.

    An *outline* covers your book chapter by chapter and provides highlights of each. If you're developing an outline for fiction, include major characters, plots, and subplots, and book length. Requesting an outline is uncommon, and the word is somewhat interchangeable with *synopsis*.

    Sample chapters give a more comprehensive idea of your writing skill. Some editors may request the first two or three chapters to determine if they're interested in seeing the whole book. Some may request a set number of pages.

Manuscript Formats

When submitting a complete manuscript, follow some basic guidelines. In the upper-left corner of your title page, type your legal name (not pseudonym), address, and phone number. In the upper-right corner, type the approximate word count. All material in the upper corners should be single-spaced. Then type the title (centered) almost halfway down that page, the word "by" two lines under that, and your name or pseudonym two lines under "by."

The first page should also include the title (centered) one-third of the way down. Two lines under that, type "by" and your name or pseudonym. To begin the body of your manuscript, drop down two double spaces and indent five spaces for each new paragraph. There should be one-inch margins around all sides of a full page. (Manuscripts with wide margins are more readable and easier to edit.)

Set your computer to double-space the manuscript body. From page two to the end of the manuscript, include your last name followed by a comma and the title (or key words of the title) in the upper-left corner. The page number should go in the top right corner. Drop down two double spaces to begin the body of each page. If you're submitting a novel, type each chapter title one-third of the way down the page. For more information on manuscript formats, read *Formatting & Submitting Your Manuscript, 3rd Ed.* (Writer's Digest Books).

Picture Book Formats

The majority of editors prefer to see complete manuscripts for picture books. When typing the text of a picture book, don't indicate page breaks and don't type each page of text on a new sheet of paper. And unless you are an illustrator, don't worry about supplying art. Editors will find their own illustrators for picture books. Most of the time, a writer and an illustrator who work on the same book never meet or interact. The editor acts as a go-between who works with the writer and illustrator throughout the publishing process. *How to Write and Sell Children's Picture Books* by Jean E. Karl (Writer's Digest Books) offers advice on preparing text and marketing your work.

If you're an illustrator who has written your own book, consider creating a dummy or storyboard containing both art and text, and then submit it along with your complete manuscript and sample pieces of final art (hi-res PDFs or JPGs—never originals). Publishers interested in picture books specify in their listings what should be submitted. For tips on creating a dummy, refer to *How to Write and Illustrate Children's Books and Get Them Published*, edited by Treld Pelkey Bicknell and Felicity Trotman (North Light Books), or *How to Write, Illustrate, and Design Children's Books* by Frieda Gates (Lloyd-Simone Publishing Company).

Writers may also want to learn the art of dummy-making to help them through the writing process with things like pacing, rhythm, and length. For a great explanation and helpful hints, see *You Can Write Children's Books*, by Tracey E. Dils (Writer's Digest Books).

Mailing Submissions

Your main concern when packaging material is to be sure it arrives undamaged. If your manuscript is fewer than six pages, simply fold it in thirds and send it in a #10 (business-size) envelope. For a SASE, either fold another #10 envelope in thirds or insert a #9 (reply) envelope, which fits in a #10 neatly without folding.

Another option is folding your manuscript in half in a 6x9 envelope, with a #9 or #10 SASE enclosed. For larger manuscripts, use a 9x12 envelope both for mailing the submission and as a SASE (which can be folded in half). Book manuscripts require sturdy packaging for mailing. Include a self-addressed mailing label and return postage. If asked to send artwork and photographs, remember they require a bit more care in packaging to guarantee they arrive in good condition. Sandwich illustrations and photos between heavy cardboard that is slightly larger than the work. The cardboard can be secured by rubber bands or with tape. If you tape the cardboard together, check that the artwork doesn't stick to the tape. Be sure your name and address appear on the back of each piece of art or each photo in case the material becomes separated. For the packaging, use either a manila envelope, a foam-padded envelope, or a mailer lined with plastic air bubbles. Bind nonjoined edges with reinforced mailing tape and affix a typed mailing label or clearly write your address.

Mailing materials first class ensures quick delivery. Also, first-class mail is forwarded for one year if the addressee has moved, and it can be returned if undeliverable. If you're concerned about your original material reaching its destination, consider other mailing options such as UPS. No matter which way you send material, never send it in a way that requires a signature for receipt. Agents and editors are too busy to sign for packages.

Remember, companies outside your own country can't use your country's postage when returning a manuscript to you. When mailing a submission to another country, include a self-addressed envelope and International Reply Coupons, or IRCs. (You'll see this term in many listings in the Canadian & International Book Publishers section.) Your postmaster can tell you, based on a package's weight, the correct number of IRCs to include to ensure its return. If it's not necessary for an editor to return your work (such as with photocopies), don't include return postage.

Unless requested, it's never a good idea to use a company's fax number to send manuscript submissions. This can disrupt a company's internal business. Study the listings for specifics and visit publisher and market websites for more information.

E-mailing Submissions

Most correspondence with editors today is handled over e-mail. This type of communication is usually preferred by publishing professionals because it is easier to deal with as well as free. When sending an e-mailed submission, make sure to follow submission guidelines. Double-check the recipient's e-mail address. Make sure your subject line has the proper wording, if specific wording is requested. Keep your introduction letter short and sweet. Also, editors and agents usually do not like opening unsolicited attachments, which makes for an awkward situation for illustrators who want to attach .jpgs. One easy way around this is to post some sample illustrations on your website. That way, you can simply paste URL hyperlinks to your work. Editors can click through to look over your illustration samples, and there is no way your submission will be deleted because of attachments. That said, if editors are asking for illustration samples, they are most likely used to receiving unsolicited attachments.

Keeping Submission Records

It's important to keep track of the material you submit. When recording each submission, include the date it was sent, the business and contact name, and any enclosures (such as samples of writing, artwork or photography). You can create a record-keeping system of your own or look for record-keeping software in your area computer store.

Keep copies of articles or manuscripts you send together with related correspondence to make follow-up easier. When you sell rights to a manuscript, artwork, or photos, you can "close" your file on a particular submission by noting the date the material was accepted, what rights were purchased, the publication date, and payment.

Often writers, illustrators, and photographers fail to follow up on overdue responses. If you don't hear from a publisher within their stated response time, wait another month or so and follow up with an e-mail asking about the status of your submission. Include the title or description, date sent, and a SASE (if applicable) for response. Ask the contact person when she anticipates making a decision. You may refresh the memory of a buyer who temporarily forgot about your submission. At the very least, you will receive a definite "no" and free yourself to send the material to another publisher.

Simultaneous submissions

Writers and illustrators are encouraged to simultaneously submit—sending the same material to several markets at the same time. Almost all markets are open to this type of communication; those that do not take simultaneous submissions will directly say so in their submission guidelines.

It's especially important to keep track of simultaneous submissions, so if you get an offer on a manuscript sent to more than one publisher, you can instruct other publishers to withdraw your work from consideration. (Or, you can always use the initial offer as a way to ignite interest from other agents and editors. It's very possible to procure multiple offers on your book using this technique.)

AGENTS & ART REPS

Most children's writers, illustrators, and photographers, especially those just beginning, are confused about whether to enlist the services of an agent or representative. The decision is strictly one that each writer, illustrator, or photographer must make for herself. Some are confident with their own negotiation skills and believe acquiring an agent or rep is not in their best interest. Others feel uncomfortable in the business arena or are not willing to sacrifice valuable creative time for marketing.

About half of children's publishers accept unagented work, so it's possible to break into children's publishing without an agent. Writers targeting magazine markets don't need the services of an agent. In fact, it's practically impossible to find an agent interested in marketing articles and short stories—there simply isn't enough financial incentive.

One benefit of having an agent, though, is it may speed up the process of getting your work reviewed, especially by publishers who don't accept unagented submissions. If an agent has a good reputation and submits your manuscript to an editor, that manuscript will likely bypass the first-read stage (which is generally done by editorial assistants and junior editors) and end up on the editor's desk sooner.

When agreeing to have a reputable agent represent you, remember that she should be familiar with the needs of the current market and evaluate your manuscript/artwork/ photos accordingly. She should also determine the quality of your piece and whether it is salable. When your manuscript sells, your agent should negotiate a favorable contract and clear up any questions you have about payments.

Keep in mind that no matter how reputable the agent or rep is, she has limitations. Representation does not guarantee sale of your work. It just means an agent or rep sees potential in your writing, art, or photos. Though an agent or rep may offer criticism or advice on how to improve your work, she cannot make you a better writer, artist, or photographer.

Literary agents typically charge a fifteen percent commission from the sale of writing; art and photo representatives usually charge a twenty five or thirty percent commission. Such fees are taken from advances and royalty earnings. If your agent sells foreign rights or film rights to your work, she will deduct a higher percentage because she will most likely be dealing with an overseas agent with whom she must split the fee.

Be advised that not every agent is open to representing a writer, artist, or photographer who lacks an established track record. Just as when approaching a publisher, the manuscript, artwork, or photos, and query or cover letter you submit to a potential agent must be attractive and professional looking. Your first impression must be as an organized, articulate person. For listings of agents and reps, turn to the **Literary Agents & Art Reps** section.

For additional listings of art reps, consult *Artist's Market*; for photo reps, see *Photographer's Market*; for more information and additional listings of literary agents, see *Guide to Literary Agents* (Writer's Digest Books).

CREATING UNFORGETTABLE CHARACTERS

Create characters that stick with your readers long after the story is over.

....

Debbie Dadey

Some things you never forget. Even though I've spoken at thousands of venues during the twenty-seven years since the release of my first book, *Vampires Don't Wear Polka Dots*, one school and one little boy in Evansville, Indiana, stand out in my mind. The child was sobbing in the hallway. The librarian said he was upset because I was visiting. Not exactly the thing you want to hear when you are preparing to speak to hundreds of kids. But then she followed up with, "He thought he was going to see Eddie, Melody, Howie, and Liza."

I have to admit, that made me feel much better. He wanted to meet the characters in The Adventures of the Bailey School Kids series that I wrote with Marcia Thornton Jones. To him, those characters were *real*. And isn't that what we, as writers, have to do? We have to make our characters leap off the page—we have to make them come alive to our readers. That's easy to say, but so hard to do.

Creating unforgettable characters is a pretty tall order. How is it done? Or, how can you do it better? This is something we could spend a lifetime perfecting, so let's get started learning more about developing characters together.

WHO ARE GREAT CHARACTERS?

Characters answer the question, who is this story about? Robert Newton Peck said that "When the question is 'What am I going to write about?' the answer is 'Who?'"

I believe that stories develop from characters and their reactions to a problem. In his writing reference, *On Writing*, Stephen King says, "I want to put a group of characters (perhaps a pair; perhaps even just one) in some sort of predicament and then watch them try to work themselves free."

Characters drive a story. It is through the characters' eyes, ears, words, behaviors, and emotions that readers move through the story. If we do it well, the reader will, in essence, become that character and feel his desires and pain.

There are basically three kinds of characters: the protagonist, the antagonist, and secondary characters. The *protagonist* is the main character in the story. This is the one you want to root for. This is the one everyone needs to like. The protagonist is often an ordinary person dropped into an unusual predicament. Think of normal Harry Potter, who is suddenly introduced to a world of magic.

Something to consider in creating a great protagonist: They often don't follow the rules! They also have big hearts and dreams. They want or need something universal—something that everyone can understand. They almost always have deep flaws. Why? Because *real* people have flaws. If we want our characters to become real, they can't be perfect.

The easy way to look at the *antagonist* is that he is the bad guy. He is the adversary of our main character. In some way, the antagonist makes life difficult for our main character.

And since we don't live by ourselves in the real world, our imaginary world is made up of *secondary characters*, such as co-workers, teachers, parents, and friends.

All of these characters must have a personality to come alive to our readers. They all need flaws because a good guy is not always perfect and a bad guy may have some redeeming qualities. They are more real this way. And real is what we are going for, isn't it?

It's helpful to limit the number of characters and vary the character's names and personalities. It can get confusing for any reader to read about Kim, Kane, and Kurt. Keep in mind that your characters should solve their own problems, even if you are writing for children. Adults should not ride in on a white horse and save the day. Something that helps me quite a bit are character sketches and charts.

HOW CAN WE MAKE GREAT CHARACTERS?

A simple character chart can be found on the writing page of my website, www.debbiedadey.com. The basics involve jotting down what you know about your characters so you'll have a reference. The point is to learn about your characters. You need to know what they want most, where they live, their innermost thoughts, and their best friends. You need to know how old they are, what scares them, what they hate, and what they love. You need to know their birthdays and what they do with their fingers when they are bored. You need to know if they've ever had a pet and the secrets they keep buried.

Do your characters have a favorite word or unique saying? Dialogue is very important and readers should be able to tell which character is speaking without tags. Be careful to avoid slang, but strive to make each character unique.

Before Marcia Thornton Jones and I wrote the Keyholder series for Tor, we worked for a solid year coming up with character sketches and world building. I did the same thing for six months with my newest series, Mermaid Tales. I'm currently doing character sketches for my next idea. Keep in mind that when you are filling out character charts you will not use every bit of information in your story. Some of it is for you and only you to know.

You must love your characters enough to live with them for years, perhaps even decades. My first series, The Adventures of the Bailey School Kids, spawned fifty-one numbered books, Super and Holiday specials, as well as two spin-off series. I still get fan mail, even though we are no longer adding to the series. As writers, we need to love those little guys because we may live with them for a long time. We'll be taking them with us wherever we go!

In fact, that is exactly what you should do. Take your characters throughout your day with you to see how they would react. Have a little notebook and jot down what they would pick up at the grocery store. What would scare them at the dentist office? What is their favorite tree on your street? Which house would they always avoid rather than walk past? Do they want a Hershey bar every afternoon at three o'clock? Add these to your character sketches.

HOW CAN WE MAKE CHARACTERS BETTER?

Now we know about characters and how to create them, but perhaps you've received a rejection letter that says these dreaded words: *your characters are flat* or *your characters are not developed enough* or *I don't feel like I know your characters*. One important thing to make sure that you haven't overlooked is a dogma in writing: *show don't tell*. What does this mean for characters? It is terribly easy for us to say that *Andy hated his math teacher*. That's telling. Instead, it is often better for us to show it: *Andy threw his math book across the room and screamed, "You can't tell me what to do!"*

Another example of telling is *Sara was tired*. This would be showing: *Sara propped her chin in her hand. She tried to pay attention to her history teacher's lecture on ancient Greece, but her eyes kept closing and more than once she jerked herself awake.* Which one can you visualize more: *Sara is tired* or the scene in history class?

Take a look at your story and find places of telling. See if you can bring that scene and your character to life by showing. Most of the time showing will require having your character in some sort of action. Readers love action in stories (and so do editors!). This will also keep your writing from becoming passive.

Once you've finished your character sketch and written a rough draft, you should begin to go over your story with a fine-tooth comb. It won't be easy, but it will be worth it. This can take some time, but it could be the difference between a so-so character and one that is unforgettable.

While using that fine-tooth comb, consider your character's inner conflict. You need to know what is tearing your main character apart. Aside from the main problem of the story, give them an internal problem that conflicts with the main plot, if possible. An example of internal conflict in the *Hunger Games* is that Katniss is unsure about her feelings for both Peeta and Gale. To keep her family safe she must pretend to have feelings for Peeta, which hurts Gale because he cares for her. At the same time, she isn't sure if her feelings for Peeta are real. As you can see, the reader feels for Katniss because she feels so much.

Look back at your character sketches. Have you included physical, emotional, and social traits? Is your character embarrassed by her frizzy hair or the big freckle at the end of his nose? His meddling mom? Her deadbeat dad? What does he do when he's nervous or scared?

This is also the time to be a little over the top. Have some fun with your characters and let them shine. Pick a scene to make your protagonist larger than life. You may have so much fun that you'll do it again. One way to get started is to think of something that they would never do and have them do it. Then, they have to deal with the aftermath.

While you're making your main character more realistic, don't forget about your bad guy. Give your antagonist a good quality. Even the Penguin in Batman had feelings.

Find a place where you can show feelings. Find four! Show readers what's inside, what makes your characters tick. Put yourself in their shoes—literally (find a picture or some real shoes that match your character's to put on your desk as inspiration). I once went to a Pam Conrad workshop and never forgot her lesson: Try the same exercise by thinking about your character's shoes. Or are they barefoot? Are their bare feet filthy? Bloody and bruised? Or perhaps your character has shiny brand-new patent leather shoes with a black bow on top. Shoes can tell a lot about a person's character. Are they uptight, or are their parents? Now, go up your character's legs. Are their socks dirty and scrunched around their ankles? Or pink with little sea horses dancing on them? Now, keep going to see if their knees are scratched. Is there a Sponge Bob adhesive bandage? Or perhaps your character's knees are covered with perfectly pressed pants? Don't stop now. Is your character wearing their favorite jeans or a frilly dress? Keep going. Are their elbows skinned? Fingernails bitten? Keep getting higher. Pimples? Snotty nose? Keep going higher. Are there tangles in her hair? Did she accidently singe the right side in a candle while reading late at night, like in *The Hired Girl*? If you do this with your main character, you'll know them better. But guess what? You need to do it with each person in your story.

Once when my friend Marcia Thornton Jones and I were struggling while writing a scene for a Bailey School Kids book, we peeked inside a student's desk. We wanted to know what Eddie would do when he was sitting behind Liza and her long blond ponytail. Eddie has a well-deserved reputation for creating mischief. We pulled paper wads and pencil stubs out of the desk, which went into our story. But then, eureka! Inspiration was right there as we pulled out a pair of scissors. Acting out your character's actions may just help bring them to life.

Look at all your characters—make a list of them. Which one can you get rid of? Can you combine two to make one stronger character? Relationships are important. How is your main character related to each of the supporting characters? Make sure all your characters have hobbies or quirks. This is how secondary characters can shine.

Something important must be at stake in a story for us to care. And the more heart-breakingly important it is to our character, the more we care. Look at your story to see what is at stake.

Newbery Honor winner Marion Dane Bauer said that "to find good story ideas, you must understand what makes a story. A story involves someone who has a problem he must struggle to solve or who wants something he must struggle to get. (Character and plot are inseparable. As has often been said, plot is simply character in action.) The important word in that definition is *struggle*. If your character isn't struggling—if he's simply sitting around looking at, thinking about his problem the way most of us do in real life— you don't have a story. So to find a good idea, you first have to find someone whose problem or desire feels compelling to you. Then you have to carry that someone around with you long enough to begin to know how he or she will solve his problem."

Not surprisingly, the first section in Donald Maass's *Writing the Breakout Novel Workbook* is about character development. I highly recommend this workbook—I just finished using it for my most recent revision. It isn't easy, but if you wanted easy, you wouldn't be a writer, right?

We've discussed characters, how to make them, and how to make them better. But sadly, those three things are not enough to create characters that readers can't forget.

One more thing is critical: We must do the work. We can't write a story on ideas and thinking. Those are important steps, of course, but not enough. We must be more than dreamers. We must put our rears in a chair and stay there. We must do the work. Newbery Award winner Neil Gaiman said, "This is how you do it: You sit down at the keyboard and you put one word after another until it is done. It's that easy and that hard."

....

DEBBIE DADEY has authored and co-authored 166 traditionally-published children's books, with sales of more than 42 million. Her newest series is called Mermaid Tales from Simon and Schuster and her newest chapter book is *Ready, Set, Goal!* This STEM friendly series is about four diverse characters and their adventures in a school under the sea. You can Like Debbie at Facebook.com/debbiedadey and follow her on Twitter.

....

FINDING YOUR WRITING SUPERPOWER

Want to write a unique story? It's all about finding your voice, and writing *your* story.

....

Laurel Snyder

There's a big difference between wanting to become a writer and wanting to become an author. And while it is possible to simultaneously strive to become both a writer *and* an author, I've found that it's difficult to focus on both goals at the same time.

In fact, I discovered, at one critical moment in my own career, that all the useful books and websites and classes designed to help me submit my work and get published actually made it much harder for me to sit down and write. This is because there is a common belief that the "best practices" of publishing (querying, formatting, submitting, etc.) are the same for everyone. And maybe they are.

But the "best practices" of writing? The best practices of writing are individual, personal. Because *you* are the only person who knows what story you have to tell, what voice you're going to use, and how to find it.

Think about it like this—imagine you're going to a party. Really picture it. Go on. Close your eyes. Okay, so you pull up to the house like everyone else. You walk in the door, clutching a bottle of wine, like everyone else. Right? Maybe you're looking around, trying to figure out where to put your coat?

So far, we're all sitting here, our eyes closed, pretty much having the same experience. So far, the "best practices for party-going" might apply to us all.

But now you step into the room, and open your mouth, and in that magical moment, you are *not* like anyone else. Because the minute you begin to speak, you're *you*—a particular person with a specific voice, and something to say. Nobody could mistake you!

Your voice might be drunk, or too loud. Your voice might be planning to make an excuse to leave early, because parties make you nervous and your favorite TV show is coming on in an hour. But the point is that on some level, you *can't* really change who you are. You can't take advice from other people on how to be *you* at the party.

What happens when you try to use a voice that isn't yours, at a party? What happens if you try to mimic someone "cool" in a way that doesn't feel natural to you? How well does that go over?

When we take a class in writing, or read a book on craft, or search helpful blogs for advice on how to get published, we are looking for advice on how to be successful. But also, we're yearning for information about what's worked for people who *aren't* us. We want to believe these things are universal, and so we talk about trends. We talk about "what's against the rules." We hear the same inspirational bits of advice. *Glue your butt to the chair. Show don't tell. Build your platform. Try to be yourself on social media.* There's so much advice.

The problem is that when we listen to those rules, we're searching for the lowest common denominators. The things that work for everyone. And that's fine. It makes us feel less alone, less lost. We all get something out of those conversations, for sure. We like the tips and best practices. We feel a sense of community, a sense of hope.

But lately, surrounded by so many of these conversations, I've been feeling the need to discuss something else—the lonely process of figuring things out by myself. I want to talk about authenticity, and finding my singular voice. Because *that* is the one thing nobody can teach you to do. You have to teach yourself to find your voice, to hunt for your own distinct story. Lowest common denominators won't get you there.

That said, while nobody can tell you what your voice is, or how to use it, I've been wondering if maybe it's possible to think of best practices for *prioritizing* that search. Maybe it's possible to set ourselves up to do that individual thinking. Maybe it's worth an essay like this to shift the focus away from the publishing "best practices" and onto the solitary act of writing.

Which begins with a sort of meditation, a reflection on *who we are*. Because it is my personal belief that *what we write* most authentically extends from *who we are*.

Take me. Who am I? *I'm Laurel, a woman who grew up with a Jewish dad and a Catholic mom, raised in Baltimore. I was the oldest kid, went through a divorce, rode lots of public buses. I had epilepsy. (Still do.) As a kid I believed in fairies and unicorns firmly, but also in progressive politics. As an adult, I waited tables for 15 years, and then had two kids, and stopped waiting tables. I went to a small public southern college, but then a very fancy-pants graduate program with a huge chip on my shoulder about how deep down I was really a waitress. I used to be a vegetarian, but I'm not anymore. I'm kind of a slob, but my worst personal trait is that I'm a bad interrupter. I love country music and I am honest, to a fault. Though sometimes I lie by accident. (It can be hard to remember facts.)*

Now, this is a fairly random list of things about me, but when I add them all together like that, they feel defining. The fact that I chose to put each detail on the list *makes* them defining. I've sculpted something here, my own personal narrative, my history. It could be much longer. It could go on forever. But even in this brief form, it's particular. Nobody else has a list quite like mine, and whether or not I write *about* the details from this list, I am always, in some way, writing *from* that set of experiences.

Am I southern? Am I religious? Am I still a waitress at heart? Sure! When it's useful. But I'm so much more complicated than any of those terms. This list is so much more useful to me than being a "Jewish poet" or a "woman writer" or anything else generalized. "Who you are" defies categorization. If you can categorize it, by definition you got it wrong.

The thing to know is that *you* have a list like that too. You should be aware of that. It's a magical device, a superpower. It's the antidote to the lowest common denominators that may never feel like they fit you. It's how you remember you're a specific person. How you understand when "The Rules" don't apply to you. And I think that maybe you'll find your best, most distinct, bravest work will come from somewhere deep in that list, if you dig down.

Here's an interesting tidbit: Did you know that Maurice Sendak's original manuscript for *Where the Wild Things Are* was called *Where the Wild Horses Are*? You should look it up. It's an odd, oddly-shaped creation, that original book. Sendak said of it:

> "I couldn't really draw horses. And I didn't, for the longest time, know what to use as a substitute. I tried lots of different animals in the title, but they just didn't sound right. Finally I lit on things. But what would 'things' look like? I wanted my wild things to be frightening. But why? It was probably at this point that I remembered how I detested my Brooklyn relatives as a small child. They came almost every Sunday. My mother always cooked for them, and, as I saw it, they were eating up all our food. We had to wear good clothes for these aunts, uncles, and assorted cousins, and ugly plastic covers were put over furniture. About the relatives themselves, I remember how inept they were at making small talk with children. There you'd be, sitting on a kitchen chair, totally helpless, while they cooed over you and pinched your cheeks. Or they'd lean way over with their bad teeth and hairy noses, and say something threatening like, 'You're so cute I could eat you up.' And I knew if my mother didn't hurry up with the cooking, they probably would. So, on one level at least, you could say the wild things are Jewish relatives."
> (from *The Art of Sendak*, Selma G. Lanes)

Now, you may not have Jewish relatives who want to eat you up like Sendak, but Sendak's "things" came from his list, for sure. Nobody else's "best practices" could have suggested them.

And somewhere on your list are the things you can dig down into, to find the brave work. The work that taps into your specific story. That vulnerable place. The story only you can tell. Which is, honestly, the only story worth your time.

So the question is … where's your vulnerable place? What are the bits of your life that make you shiver, laugh, worry, and rage? And how do you remember them, find them? How do you figure out where you should start?

The really great books, the ones we love best, dig down into the personal story. They employ that individual superpower. They bring something new, something personal. This is probably true of your favorite book, even if you don't know it. Even when it isn't obvious.

Now we think of books in the Chronicles of Narnia series as "types" of books, don't we? We think of *The Wonderful Wizard of Oz* the same way. But those books were written out of C. S. Lewis's religious journey, as a Christian convert, and also out of his memories from World War I. Baum, a newspaperman, wrote *Oz* with strong feelings about women's rights. Both of them created what now feels like a "type" of book, out of their own lists.

More recently, Rick Riordan gave us Percy Jackson, drawing on his own personal and familial experiences with learning disabilities. And Suzanne Collins has explained that *The Hunger Games* grew out of her memories of watching footage from the Vietnam War, while her father was overseas, fighting. Because this is how we produce truly innovative, startling, meaningful work—the work that connects most deeply with readers. By mining our lists, our memories, and finding our truest voices.

Which brings us to the big question—what's your story, your superpower, your voice? What's the story only you can tell? And how do you find it? Below, I've tried to generate some ideas for ways you can connect with your superpower. They may not work for everyone (or anyone), but I hope they'll yield something useful. There is no succeeding or failing here. Only a goal—that we shift away from thinking about "what worked" for other people, and into a mode of thinking deeply about ourselves.

1. **YOUR LIST.** Try making a list like mine. Keep it going, indefinitely. Think about who you are, what turf you have that's just yours. The book nobody else but you can write.

2. **JOURNALING.** It's always good to do some daily writing. One fun idea is to write down the stories you retell often. "The one about the camping trip." Or "That time you had chicken pox in Chicago." We all have stories we tell. Write them down! (Related: If you have old journals or blogs, dig them out and spend time with them.

Make photocopies and revise them. Play!)

3. **OLD PHOTOS.** What makes you cry or laugh? Who is missing from your life, and why? What happened? Take some time to free-write about the old photos you find. You might be surprised at the memories that resurface.

4. **FAVORITE BOOKS.** Not just popular trendy books, but the books that really set you on fire or spoke to you as a kid. Revisiting these old texts is a remarkable way to "wake up" childhood memories.

5. **RAW EMOTION.** When you have a big feeling, don't try to fix it. Rather, have the feeling. Let it wash over you. Heighten it if you can. Sit in the darkness, shut out the noise. You don't want to get depressed, but in a safe way, explore the feeling.

6. **DREAM BOOK.** Keep a notebook by your bed for writing down dreams, which can uncork powerful emotions. I often find that writing first thing in the morning feels dreamy and different too.

7. **OTHER SENSES.** Music is powerful for me—especially music from other chapters of my life. But for some people, baking or cooking or gardening can do this too. The trick is to be present with the senses. Be alone with them, and isolate them. (If you're listening to podcasts while you bake, or emailing while you listen to old records, it won't work the same way)

8. **KIDS.** Get some! And then listen to them. Really focus on what they say and how they say it! If you have kids, or access to kids you love, steal from them. Our feelings about children tend to be so big and authentic, and kids can awaken things in us, our own memories of childhood.

9. **DRAW (OR PAINT OR SCULPT).** Get out your art supplies. Sometimes, what you can't seem to access with words you can reach in another way. But again, you need to isolate yourself with the visual or tactile experience. The idea is to uncork something, and that won't happen if you're watching TV at the same time.

10. **IMAGINARY READER.** Sit and think about the person who will read this book. To go back to the party I talked about earlier, think about how, when you walk into the party, you look for someone you know, because it's easier to talk to them. Seriously think about this—about the audience for your book, your ideal reader. Sometimes, simply thinking about this will change your tone completely.

11. **WRITE OUT LOUD.** Keep a tape recorder in the car or your purse or backpack. Sometimes, the way you talk your words out is different, and more natural, than the way you write them down. You can go back later, and transcribe, and sometimes you'll be very surprised.

12. **GET BORED.** I think this is perhaps the single biggest thing any of us can do in this day and age. When we are consuming external voices, it's extremely hard to

channel something authentic from within. So boredom is an important part of the creative process for me. I often "work" in the bath. Or I take a walk with a notebook and pen. The critical thing is to leave my phone at home. Distraction is death to real insight. You have to spend time with yourself, and flounder and dream, to get to something good.

LAUREL SNYDER is the author of six novels for children: *Orphan Island, Bigger than a Bread Box, Penny Dreadful, Any Which Wall, Up and Down the Scratchy Mountains OR The Search for a Suitable Princess,* and *Seven Stories UP.* She has also written many picture books, two books of poems, and edited an anthology of nonfiction. A graduate of the Iowa Writers' Workshop and a former Michener-Engle Fellow, Laurel has published work in the *Utne Reader, Chicago Sun-Times, Revealer, Salon, The Iowa Review, American Letters and Commentary,* and more.

WRITING EFFECTIVE DIALOGUE

Learn the differences between writing dialogue for early readers, middle grade, and young adult.

....

Kerrie Flanagan

Dialogue is the backbone of every great children's story. But the nuances of dialogue in different age groups are very different. When children are young and learning to read, dialogue is simple. As children get older, the conversations—and the techniques for writing dialogue—become more complex.

Dialogue serves a larger purpose than simply showing a conversation between people or characters. It creates mood, enhances setting, unveils backstory, provides insights into the characters, and propels a story forward. It adds substance to the story; the way dialogue is formatted, adds white space to a page, making the text visually appealing and easier to read.

Tag lines are important as they show the reader who is speaking: *"I wish I had a magic wand,"* Claire said. The phrase "Claire said" is the tag. Understanding how to use these effectively for various age groups will help you be more successful when writing for children.

EARLY READERS

For young children who are beginning to learn how to read, dialogue is especially important. Ellen Javernick, kindergarten teacher and author of more than 100 books for early readers including, *What if Everybody Did That?* and *The Birthday Pet* says, "With little people, you want to have a lot of dialogue; very little text otherwise. It carries the story for the children and can take the place of the showing."

Say you have the following:

> Johnny saw a bowl of chocolates on the table. He got excited. He asked his mother if he could have one.

Instead of simply telling the reader what's happening, you can put it into dialogue:

> "Look at those yummy chocolates on the table," Johnny said. "Mom, can I have one?"

By making this dialogue instead of narrative, it became more active and engaging for the reader.

The tags used for young readers should be simple. Stick to the basics. "Ninety-percent of the time it will be, *said*," Javernick explains. "You can occasionally weave in a couple of others like *asked* or *yelled*, but remember, these children are just learning to read. The word said is common and one of the first one-hundred sight words taught in school."

MIDDLE-GRADE

As children grow up and move toward middle-grade books, they learn to read more words and expand their vocabulary. Laura Backes, publisher of Children's Book Insider (www.writeforkids.org), *The Children's Writing Monthly*, and co-creator of Writing-Blueprints.com, says, "You can get more sophisticated with the speech tags and verbs of speech, using words like *murmured*, *intoned*, *proclaimed* as long as they fit the dialogue and tone of the scene."

The danger can happen when writers want to avoid using the word *said* and then overuse other tags. The truth is, the word *said* becomes invisible to readers. When you begin adding too many different words, like *demanded*, *articulated*, *lamented*, it can slow down readers and distract them from the conversation. Use these types of tags sparingly, otherwise you end up with something like this:

> "Are you awake?" Chuck inquired.
> "Of course, I'm awake," Eddie chortled. "I'm talking. Are you awake?"
> "Duh. I'm talking, too," Chuck confirmed. "I wonder if the bear came back."
> "Maybe it snuck into our van and ate all our food. Let's go look!" Eddie exclaimed.

Dialogue can show how a character is feeling and even reveal something about his personality, and the choice of speech tags can go a long way toward showing state of mind:

> "Of course I'll help," Sam mumbled.

> "Of course I'll help!" Sam exclaimed.

Adding action also gives us information about that character.

> "Of course I'll help," Sam said, rolling his eyes.

> "Of course I'll help." Sam sprang off the couch, knocking over his tray table and sending his dinner flying across the living room floor.

In all of these examples, what the character is saying hasn't change, but how he is saying it, or his action following the statement, give more insight.

YOUNG ADULT

When kids become teens, their needs as readers become more sophisticated. They are looking for characters and storylines with more depth, and dialogue can play a big role in that.

Todd Mitchell, YA author of *Backwards* and *The Secret to Lying*, says dialogue should also reveal your characters' desires, especially with older readers. Your characters must want something different out of the dialogue, and work hard to get that. "Dialogue is a dance where two characters are each working to achieve their desires without directly speaking them. When done well, characters show who they are and what they really want through the words and gestures they try to hide behind."

When you move into the young adult genre, tags can be left out as long as it is clear who is talking. Adding action instead of a tag can help make that clear as well.

Here is an example from Mitchell's *Secret to Lying*. This is a phone conversation between the main character, fifteen-year-old James, who is away at boarding school, and his parents. This example not only shows that you don't need tags on every line, it also refers back to what Mitchell said about the characters wanting something different from the dialogue. Plus, we get a glimpse of the relationship between James and his mom.

> I scrambled to change the subject. "Look, about this weekend. I've got a lot of work to do. There's a chemistry study group and I need to get the notes."
> "Wouldn't you rather come home?"
> "I can't."
> Mom paused. "What's wrong with you?"
> "Nothing's wrong."
> "You don't sound right to me."
> "What am I supposed to say to that?" I asked. "I mean, really, do I sound 'right' now?"
> "No. You don't." She addressed my dad: "Does he sound right to you?"
> "How about this, Mother? Is this better? It's lovely weather out."
> "Honestly, you don't sound like yourself," she said.
> "Too bad. This is me."

Great dialogue does so much more than relay a conversation. Go to a bookstore or library and study the way authors use dialogue for various age groups. Pay attention to the tags, the type of action, and think about what each scene conveys and how it moves the story along.

A memorable book includes compelling characters and an intriguing storyline. Dialogue is a great vehicle to achieve both. Understanding how to write effective dialogue for your target age group will allow you to create stronger, more interesting stories that will resonate with readers of all ages.

KERRIE FLANAGAN is an author, writing consultant, publisher, and accomplished freelance writer with more than 18 years' experience. Her work has appeared in publications such as *Writer's Digest*, *Alaska Magazine*, *The Writer*, and six *Chicken Soup for the Soul* books. She is the author of seven books, including two children's books, *Claire's Christmas Catastrophe* and *Claire's Unbearable Campout*, all published under her label, Hot Chocolate Press. She was the founder and former director of Northern Colorado Writers and now does individual consulting with writers. Her background in teaching and enjoyment of helping writers has led her to present at writing conferences across the country, including the Writer's Digest Annual Conference, the Willamette Writer's Conference, and the Writer's Digest Novel Writing Conference. You can find her online at www.KerrieFlanagan.com, www.hotchocolatepress.com, and on Twitter at @Kerrie_Flanagan.

AUDIENCES & ADVOCATES

The importance of connecting with librarians, readers, and teachers.

Suzanne Morgan Williams

After you sign that book contract you've dreamed of, your publisher may contact you with a list of questions. They'll want to know what contacts you have in the school, library, and blogging communities; what awards you may qualify for; if you have a social media presence; and how comfortable you are with doing school and library visits. At this point, it's not unusual to hear a newly published author say, "I wrote the book, why do I have to sell it too?"

True, larger publishers have marketing and school and library departments. True, many introverted writers would rather have a root canal than stand in front of an audience to speak. But it's also true that this push for contacts and speaking isn't just about selling one book. It's about connecting you and your work to readers. There's a reason you spent all that time writing or illustrating your unique story. And it probably wasn't totally about the money. You had something to say. Reaching out to teachers and librarians creates opportunities to gain readers. When kids read your work, they'll hear your message. And that's valuable.

Newbery Medal winner Linda Sue Park says, "How do we reach readers? Through teachers, librarians, and booksellers. These "superheroes" have always been the ones who urge readers to pick up books they might not choose on their own. Teachers and librarians are the *only* way we have to reach readers who come from homes that lack a reading culture." Those same "superheroes" will spread the word about you and your books. They may recommend you as a presenter to other libraries or schools. Often, they are the first ones to nominate your books for awards. You'll have no better allies in your publishing career than librarians, teachers, and enthusiastic booksellers. They share your goal—get kids to read wonderful books. They know the power of story.

You have something to offer them too. Betsy Bird, Collection Development Manager at the Evanston Public Library in Evanston, Illinois, author, and *School Library Journal*'s A Fuse #8 Production blogger says, "One of the most important things you can do as a writer is show kids that you actually exist. That may sound kind of funny, but when I was a kid, I didn't think of writing as a 'real job.' Writers were like opera singers or presidents—not something you'd actually aspire to be in a realistic way. Meeting a writer can make a huge difference in a kid's life. By showing them you're a living breathing human being capable of producing thoughts on a page ... well, that's worth all the money in the world." Don't sell yourself short. Just the act of showing up gives you the possibility of being a role model.

But as such, you have responsibilities. You owe it to your audiences, whether they are children or adults, to share something they'll find worthwhile. You owe it to the people who are arranging your events to be professional and polite. After all, they're using their time to help you. Don't assume it's the other way around. Bird continues, "Some authors make it sound as if it's the library's lucky day that they'd deign to speak to the children there. Not cool." Whether you like it or not, when you visit a library or school, you're representing a lot of other authors and illustrators. If your event goes well, that librarian will be anxious to host another author. If it's boring or difficult, she may not want to spend her time or money like that again.

Don't let this put you off. You don't have to start by jumping into giving huge presentations. In fact, maybe you shouldn't. Maybe you don't know how to give a presentation, or you're still waiting for that elusive contract. What can you do now to prepare?

Start by making contacts in your community or renewing those you already have. Author and school presenter, Alexis O'Neill, recommends you join organizations such as your PTO or International Literacy Association. If you don't already belong, join the Society of Children's Book Writers and Illustrators (SCBWI) and a local writers' group. Get to know the published writers and illustrators in your area. Your professional peers are a great resource—many are willing to share connections. Ask them who the literary movers and shakers are in your town and if they'll introduce you to them when it's appropriate.

Armed with these names and positions—the owner of the independent bookstore, the director of the local writers' conference, the youth librarian who's on all the state library committees—make appointments to meet them. Don't ask *for* anything. Find out what they do and how you might help. Support *them*. Something positive may come naturally from these discussions.

Once your book is under contract, or even while you're working seriously on a project, begin planning for future presentations. Bruce Hale, author and frequent school presenter, suggests that before offering paid presentations you get some practice. "Volunteer in schools and libraries, read stories and spend time with kids (if you don't have your own). It helps to know what young readers respond to and what their issues are—and it will serve you in good stead when it comes time to charge for your visits."

Author Terri Farley calls this "going to the well" and suggests that being around children or teens will refresh your writing too. So invite a children's librarian to lunch. Ask how you can help them reach new readers. Volunteer to host a school book club, offer a writing workshop at your library, speak at a high school career day, or just ask teachers, librarians, and booksellers to recommend books in your genre that they think you should read. Nothing opens up a relationship between book lovers like reading.

When your book comes out, imagine how cool it will be to show it off to the teachers and librarians who've been part of your journey. These are the people who will remember your name as a conference speaker or for awards, blogs, and book clubs. They'll be proud to hand your book to young readers and recommend it to other professionals. They'll build your word of mouth, opening doors you didn't know were there. Book sales make money; connections make opportunities. But, relationships are a two-way street. You should reciprocate when you can, and you must do your best to live up to their recommendations.

When you have a published or soon-to-be-published book, it's time to get on social media. It's not necessary to spend hours there, but a presence will help. You'll develop a network of friends and followers who will support your work and cheer for you on those important book birthdays. You'll be there for them to pass the word along about their books and events. You'll have a platform for asking questions of other book people. "What are you reading? What do your students know about the Cold War? Would a preschooler be interested in gemstones?" Remember, social media isn't a billboard for sales. It's about conversation and community. You'll get out of it what you give back.

Online, community, and in person connections all lead to one thing—more readers. It's time to prepare for school and library presentations and to step out in front of your audience. First, who *is* your audience? You'll have very different things to say to a room of school librarians than to two dozen kindergarteners. Who do you want to talk to? Who is your book appropriate for? Not sure? Visit with those book people you now know well. Take a class. If you will mainly be presenting to children and teens, a drama class may suit you better than an adult public speaking group. Some SCBWI Regions offer sessions on school visits. The key to great school visits is practice and preparation. A well-designed program will take you far. Nonfiction author Kelly Milner Halls says, "I observed every author I could to learn what works and what doesn't work for them. There is no need to reinvent every part of this wheel. Learn from the best, then make your presentation your own."

RESOURCES

- American Library Association, www.ala.org
- Your State Library Association and State Association of School Librarians
- International Literacy Association, www.literacyworldwide.org
- Library of Congress Center for the Book, www.read.gov; list of state affiliates, www.read.gov/cfb/state-affiliates.php
- Your PTA and public library
- Your local independent bookstore, IndieBound, American Bookseller Association, www.bookweb.org/professional-bookselling/indiebound
- Society of Children's Book Writers and Illustrators, www.scbwi.org
- KidLitosphere, Society of Bloggers in Children's and Young Adult Literature, www.kidlitosphere.org/bloggers
- Elizabeth Bird's A Fuse#8 Production; School Library Journal Blog, http://blogs.slj.com/afuse8production
- Terri Farley's website, www.terrifarley.com
- Bruce Hale's website, www.brucehale.com
- Kelly Milner Halls's website, www.wondersofweird.com
- Alexis O'Neill's School Visit Experts website, www.schoolvisitexperts.com

---

Jane Kulow, Director of Virginia Center for the Book, says, "Not all excellent writers present well in person. We would like to know that the author can be an engaging presenter. Providing credible feedback from librarians or teachers may aid our decision. Providing non-contextual quotes from entertained children doesn't persuade us." How do you get feedback when you're starting out? Enlist your posse of supporters. Ask if you can present to their class or library group. Charge a *small* fee—this is for your practice and confidence building after all—but ask them to provide a recommendation that you can include in publicity materials and on your website. It's a fair trade—a win-win. And as you move along in your speaking career, be sure to ask for new recommendations. These build your credibility.

Once you have an idea of what you would do in a presentation, turn your attention to your website. Retired school librarian and coordinator of Nevada Reading Week Conference, Ellen Fockler, says, "The more complete an author's website is, the more likely I would be to consider inviting him to present at a conference." She suggests your site include intriguing bits of your background, photos, recommendations, and a short outline of the presentations you plan to offer. Fockler says, "But ultimately, it's their work and its popularity with kids that attracts me."

When you have a new book, use *all* your connections to gain readers. Start with your publisher. Ask if they will send Advance Reader Copies to the book professionals and bloggers you've gotten to know. Share your own ARCs or author's copies with local librarians, teachers, and conference planners. Ask for recommendations of conferences you might go to or submit proposals to speak at. Attending teacher and librarian conferences is a great way to meet the gatekeepers who will hand your books to children or hire you to speak.

At the conference, take business cards, postcards, or bookmarks—something small and representative with your contact information—that you can hand out. This expands your circle of connections. Be professional. If you are speaking, don't just peddle your book, but be sure your topic adds value to the attendees' professional lives. Remember, you are building relationships, not sales. Those will come. If you are in a social setting, don't pounce. Most librarians and teachers will be truly interested in your books once they find out you're an author or illustrator. Collect their cards and make notes on who you met and what they need. If it makes sense, send a follow up e-mail saying how nice it was to meet them and that you hope to see them in the future. Keep a list or spreadsheet of these people. You don't know when or how you may connect again, but now they are part of your "team."

Whenever you speak, there may be opportunities to sell books. If not, your presence still encourages readers to buy books later. And don't assume that because you didn't get book sales or speaking invitations *right then* that it won't happen. Someone may remember you years later and ask to feature you on their blog or to give a keynote at their conference.

Now think big. You have connections. You have a web presence. You have new supporters. What can you do to touch readers in ways you are passionate about? What will your outreach be? Yes, some people will contact you, especially if your book is getting good sales and reviews, but there's nothing to keep you from reaching out to them too. Add value. Share your passion. Create excitement. Terri Farley, who writes fiction and nonfiction about wild horses, sometimes follows her elementary school presentations by introducing students to an adopted (and tamed) wild mustang. Kelly Milner Halls writes about kid friendly topics like aliens and sasquatches. She says, "Because my books are high-interest topics—subjects often overlooked—they are of huge interest to reluctant and autistic readers. I find that fact incredibly rewarding." She comes prepared with visuals and props of creepy things. Her passion shines through and the kids want to read her work. That was the point to begin with, right?

Betsy Bird says, "We have an organization that ... selected six authors to speak during a single week to every child in every public school in Evanston, Illinois. The result was amazing. Every child in our city got to see firsthand what it was like to be an author, to ask them questions, and to generally find out more about these people and their lives. It didn't just touch one or two kids. It touched a whole town. If more cities adopted this idea, it could do wonders for children, authors, and the communities as well." You are a writer or an illustrator. Your stories can change the children who read your work.

Just remember, writing and illustrating, making connections, planning, booking, and delivering presentations—it's not all about you. Bruce Hale reminds us, "I wish [authors and illustrators] knew to make their presentation about their audience, even while they're talking about themselves. Kids ... want to be entertained, and they want to know how the talk applies to their own lives." Alexis O'Neill sums it up: "New authors should understand that their presentation is not about them, *per se*. Rather, it's about what 'gift' they can give to kids to make their lives better. That gift can come through the stories they write, the stories about their personal lives they share, the struggles they admit to, and the knowledge they impart that kids can apply in their own lives."

What can really happen when librarians and teachers bring authors and readers together? A teen reaches out to a suicide prevention hotline, a fourth grader writes to his congressman about animal cruelty, an Iraqi-born girl translates a novel about the impact of war into Arabic for her family, a child who rarely reads is inspired to write her own 70-page story. The examples are numerous. Ask most authors and illustrators what they value most about their business and chances are they'll say connecting with, and touching their readers. Now step out. It's your turn.

SUZANNE MORGAN WILLIAMS is the author of the middle-grade novel *Bull Rider* and eleven nonfiction books for children. *Bull Rider* is a Junior Library Guild Selection, is on several state award lists and won a Western Heritage Award from the National Cowboy Museum in Oklahoma City. Suzanne has presented and taught writing workshops at dozens of schools, libraries and professional conferences across the U.S. and Canada. She was SCBWI Member of the Year in 2012. A writer for more than twenty years, she has found connections with other book people to be pivotal in both her professional and personal life. She is currently working on a historical novel of her own. Visit www.suzannemorganwilliams.com.

TEN MARKETS FOR YOUR SHORT FICTION

Sometimes the best way to break in is by writing short. Learn about some markets that are currently looking for submissions.

Windy Lynn Harris

Whether you're writing picture books, middle grade stories, or young adult novels, showcasing your writing in children's magazines is a great way to garner attention in the industry. Great news: You don't need an agent to help you through this process! You can submit stories and land bylines all by yourself. Here's how:

MAKE THE RIGHT MATCH

The first step to seeing your work in print is to make the right match with a magazine. Every children's magazine will have a list of requirements, usually called writer's guidelines (you can find some of these in this article, in the listings sections, and at the magazine's website). Writer's guidelines will tell you the age of the magazine's intended reading audience, the length of the pieces they publish, and the payment they offer, among other things.

Sometimes you'll see the terms "simultaneous submissions" and "multiple submissions" mentioned in the guidelines. When a magazine is open to simultaneous submissions, it means that you can send that same story to other editors at the same time, with the caveat that you'll let them know if your story gets picked up elsewhere. When a magazine is open to multiple submissions, they mean that you can send them more than one story in your submission document—usually up to five—as long as they're short.

Compare the polished stories you'd like to publish to what you read in each magazine's writer's guidelines. Really examine the age groups they target. Does your story also target these age groups? Is your language appropriate for the vocabulary level intended? And what about the topics each magazine is looking for? If you don't see an authentic match to your own work, move on to another magazine. Don't send editors something they don't actually acquire. It's a waste of your time, and theirs.

Let's take a look a closer look at ten well-respected children's magazines and what they're looking for from writers like you. Maybe there's a perfect match right here in this list.

LADYBUG

Audience: 3–6 years old.

Ladybug publishes contemporary stories, original folk and fairy tales, and funny pieces with human characters or anthropomorphic animals. City settings and stories that take place outside the United States are especially welcome, as well as subject matter that appeals to both boys and girls. When reviewing submissions, the editors look for clear and beautiful language, a sense of joy and wonder, and a genuinely childlike point of view.

Length: Up to 800 words, but significantly shorter manuscripts are often accepted.

SPIDER

Audience: 6–9 years old.

Spider editors want energetic, beautifully crafted stories with strong "kid appeal" (an elusive, yet recognizable quality, often tied to high-interest elements such as humor, adventure, and suspense). They have particular interests in stories that explore themes of identity (gender, race and ethnicity, neighborhoods, beliefs and traditions); citizenship and global cultures; scientific and technological exploration; and the creative spirit.

Length: 300–1,000 words.

HIGHLIGHTS MAGAZINE

Audience: 6–12 years old.

The *Highlights* motto is "Fun with a Purpose." The editors have a mission to help children grow in basic skills and knowledge, in creativeness, in ability to think and reason, in sensitivity to others, and in worthy ways of living. They are looking for short fiction in these areas: graphic stories (provide text only), humor, mystery, world cultures, contemporary, urban, historical, sports, adventure.

Length: Up to 750 words for independent readers, 475 words for beginning readers.

THE CATERPILLAR
Audience: 7–11 years old.
The Caterpillar is a literary magazine that publishes four times per year. Every issue contains fiction and poetry, as well as other hard-to-categorize pieces of writing. This magazine has showcased some great writing by the likes of Michael Morpurgo, Meshack Asare, Julie O'Callaghan, Chrissie Gittins, Frank Cottrell Boyce, and Mo O'Hara. Bonus: Check out the annual *Caterpillar* Story For Children's Prize.
Length: Up to 1,000 words.

COBBLESTONE
Audience: 8–14 years old.
Cobblestone is a classroom distributed Parent's Choice Award Winning magazine. Editors are interested in stories with historical accuracy in these categories: biographical fiction, adventure, and retold legends relating to the current theme. Monthly themes are available online several months in advance.
Length: Up to 800 words.

CRICKET
Audience: 9–14 years old.
Cricket seeks contemporary middle-grade fiction appropriate for the 9- to 14-year-old audience. Strong submissions will feature a protagonist who is actively engaged in the challenges and adventures of being a kid—taking on new responsibilities, discovering hidden talents, overcoming fears, or meeting new and surprising people. Editors consider unsolicited submissions from writers of every experience level. Since 1973, *Cricket* has published some of the most respected writers of children's literature.
Length: 1,200–1,800 words.

LUNCH TICKET
Audience: 13 years old and up.
Lunch Ticket strives to balance cutting edge literary and visual art with conversations about social justice and community activism. Editors are seeking fiction and flash fiction in any genre. This magazine is geared entirely toward the YA market, making it a terrific place to gain exposure with your YA stories.
Length: Up to 5,000 words.

CICADA
Audience: 14 years and up
Cicada is a one of the finest YA lit/comics magazines out there. Editors appreciate the lyric and strange, and are committed to showcasing work that speaks to teens' truths. They

publish realistic and genre fiction, including flash fiction. Special interests include magical realism, SF/fantasy, historical fiction. Especially welcome: works by people of color, people with disabilities, LGBTQAI+ folks, genderqueer folks, and other marginalized peoples. Not welcome: cultural appropriation.

Length: Up to 1,000 words for flash fiction, up to 9,000 words.

HUNGER MOUNTAIN

Audience: 14 years and up.

Hunger Mountain is an annual print journal of the arts. They publish both YA and children's fiction. Past contributors include Pinckney Benedict, Ron Carlson, Hayden Carruth, Kwame Dawes, Matthew Dickman, Mark Doty, Rita Dove, Terrance Hayes, Alice Hoffman, Pam Houston, Maxine Kumin, Dorianne Laux, Bret Lott, and many other well-known writers, but the editors emphasize that they love to feature never-before-published authors as well. *Hunger Mountain* also hosts the annual Katherine Paterson Prize for Young Adult and Children's Writing for Young Adult, Middle Grade, or Picture Book manuscripts, up to 10,000 words.

Length: up to 10,000 words.

SUCKER LITERARY

Audience: 14 years and up.

Sucker Literary publishes provocative and hopeful YA fiction. Editors want writing that is literary and sharp, but gritty and authentic, too. A tip for breaking into this magazine: Connect with your protagonist deeply. Think character-driven, most of all. All protagonists need to be between 14 and 19 years old.

Length: 1,500–2,000 words usually, but will consider stories up to 10,000.

WRITE A COVER LETTER

Once you've selected a few magazines that match your stories, you'll need to write an introductory letter to accompany your submission. Cover letters for short creative works are called such because of their brevity. It's just a few sentences in a one-page business letter.

In the first paragraph, introduce your story with the title and word count. If you have a reason to submit to the magazine, you should add that, too. Maybe you liked a certain piece they published last month, or maybe you know a friend who was published there.

Your writing credentials come next. Before you have publishing credits, mention a few writing groups or writing classes you've attended. After you've been published, list your publishing credits instead.

Last, thank the editor for her time considering your work.

To construct your cover letter:

1. Use 12-point font. Times New Roman or Courier (or something similar).
2. Use block paragraphs (single space paragraphs with an extra space between paragraphs—no indents).
3. Use 1- to 1-½-inch margins.
4. Address your letter to the proper editor and spell her name correctly.

When you send your query letter by snail mail, you have some additional steps:

5. At the top left corner, add your name, address, e-mail address, website, and phone number. These items are single-spaced.
6. Add the date of your submission below your information.
7. Add the magazine's contact information below the date.
8. Leave three extra lines after your salutation so that you have room to sign your name.
9. Tell the editor what you've sent in a short enclosure line (Encl: Manuscript and SASE). SASE stands for Self Addressed Stamped Envelope, which you will need to provide.

Cover Letter Example

Dear Ms. Burke,

I'm sending you my 400-word beginning reader story, "Leaves I Left On The Pond," for your consideration. This story is based on my small Northwestern town childhood. I think it would be a good fit with the other funny stories you print in *Highlights*.

I am a member of SCBWI and The Children's Writer's Guild.

Thank you for your time considering "Leaves I Left On The Pond." I have attached the completed manuscript, per your request.

Sincerely,

This Writer

Once you create a custom cover letter for a story, you can send that same letter to as many editors as it takes to find your work a home—just remember to change the editor's name and the magazine information.

FORMAT YOUR MANUSCRIPT

Before you send that story out the door, you need to format your work to current professional standards. Here's your guide:

1. Print manuscripts on 8½ x 11", white paper.
2. 1- to 1-½-inch margins all around.
3. Use 12-point standard typeface: Times New Roman or Courier (or similar).
4. No end-of-the-line hyphenated words or justified right margin.

5. Double-space the entire manuscript.

6. Indent paragraphs five spaces.

7. No additional spacing between paragraphs.

Next, add identifying information, your byline, and the header:

8. Type your name, address, phone number, and e-mail in the upper left corner, single-spaced. In the upper right corner, type the word count.

9. Drop down about halfway on the first page and center your title. Your byline goes beneath that. These are double-spaced. You can capitalize your title, or not. Your choice.

10. On page two and subsequent pages, add a header that includes your title and last name.

STAY ORGANIZED

One more thing: You need to stay organized. Keep track of the dates you submit your stories, who you send work to, and what kind of response you get. As soon as your story is accepted by a magazine, contact the other editors and let them know the story is no longer available. Then celebrate your success!

Writing for children's magazines can be a rewarding and career-launching experience. Judy Burke, editor of *Highlights for Children* has this advice to share: "Fiction is the most competitive category to enter. If you're just getting started in the business, study recent issues and try writing a 'short'—a craft, puzzle, activity, recipe, or game. Before submitting, test out your content on real kids, and observe without interfering. Are they having fun? Are any of the instructions tripping them up? Did they finish the activity, and did they seem happy with the end result? Edit your work further as needed, then submit it. If you don't have success at first, keep working at it, let kids inspire you, and be persistent!"

BREAK INTO MAGAZINES WITH NONFICTION ARTICLES!

Cricket Media is seeking nonfiction from writers like you!

From the editorial team at Cricket Media: "Our science, social studies, and discovery magazines seek writers with subject expertise. Those interested in writing for these magazines should submit a resume and several writing samples." Send your résumé and writing samples to:

Cricket Media, Inc.

7926 Jones Branch Drive

Suite 870

McLean, Virginia 22102

Cricket is currently seeking nonfiction submissions for these magazines:

- **CLICK SCIENCE AND DISCOVERY** for ages 3–7. *CLICK* introduces young children to ideas and concepts in the natural, physical, or social sciences; the arts; technology; math; and history.
- **ASK SCIENCE AND DISCOVERY** for ages 7-10. *ASK* is a nonfiction magazine for children 7–10 years old who are curious about science and the world they live in. Each edition of *ASK* is built around a central theme on some question or concept in the natural, physical, or social sciences; technology; mathematics; history; or the arts.
- **MUSE SCIENCE AND DISCOVERY** for ages 10 and up. *MUSE* is a discovery magazine for children and teens. The editors seek fresh, entertaining stories from the fields of science, technology, engineering, art, and math. Timeliness is essential, but humor, irreverence, and atypical angles are also hallmarks of *MUSE*.
- **DIG INTO HISTORY WORLD HISTORY AND ARCHAEOLOGY** for ages 9–14. *DIG Into History* focuses on world history with a 10- to 14-page section that focuses on an archaeological discovery or topic related to the issue's theme. Each issue is theme-related. Accuracy is essential.
- **FACES WORLD CULTURES AND GEOGRAPHY** for ages 9–14. Lively, original approaches to the subject are the primary concerns of the editors of *FACES* in choosing material. All material must relate to the theme of a specific upcoming edition in order to be considered.

WINDY LYNN HARRIS is a prolific writer with more than 70 bylines in literary, women's, and trade magazines across the U.S. and Canada, in places like *The Literary Review*, *The Review Review*, *Arcadia*, and *Literary Mama*, among many others. She is the founder of Marketing Coaching for Creative Writers, a mentoring program that teaches writers how to get their short stories, poems, and essays published in magazines, and the author of *Writing & Selling Short Stories & Personal Essays: The Essential Guide to Getting Your Work Published* (Writer's Digest Books). Windy teaches the craft of writing online and in person. She is a frequent speaker at literary events. Find her online at windylynnharris.com

KWAME ALEXANDER

In this profile, the *New York Times* best-selling author shares how his career has been launched by a simple word: yes.

....

Kerrie Flanagan

Kwame Alexander is the *New York Times* best-selling author of 24 books, including *The Crossover*, *The Playbook*, *Surfs Up*, and *Booked*. Kwame believes that poetry can change the world, and he uses it to inspire and empower young people through his Page to Stage Writing and Publishing Program. A regular speaker at schools and conferences in the U.S., he also travels the world planting seeds of literary love. He co-founded LEAP for Ghana, an International literacy program that has established student scholarship opportunities, provided literacy training for teachers, facilitated girls' empowerment workshops, and facilitated career development projects in conjunction with Ashesi University and the U.S. Embassy in Ghana.

Alexander's 23-year journey to the 2015 Newberry Medal Award for his book, *The Crossover*, was filled with many ups and downs. But his willingness to say *yes* to potential opportunities and take control over his own destiny enabled his success.

Growing up, Alexander was surrounded by books. His father was a publisher and his mother an English teacher. Despite his parents' influences, by middle school, he fell out of love with reading and his passion for books became dormant.

"I grew up with a man who had written 16 books, gotten his Ph.D. from Columbia University, forced me to read the encyclopedia and the dictionary, made me read books

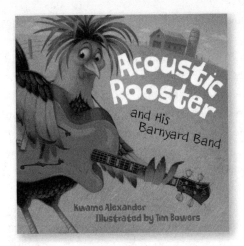

from the time I could walk," Alexander says. "By the time I was 12, I knew *Pedagogy of the Oppressed* by Paulo Freire, I knew *The Three Musketeers*; I knew literature, but I hated it."

When he went to college at Virginia Tech, he wanted nothing to do with literature, so he pursued a biochemistry major with the hopes of becoming a doctor. During his sophomore year, his life took a new direction down a familiar path. He enrolled in a poetry class taught by professor and award-winning poet, Nikki Giovanni.

"Taking Nikki's class woke me up and reminded me of the joy, and what can happen when you read a poem that knocks you off your feet. It was also at a time when I was meeting a lot of girls on campus. I may not know how to talk to them, but I can certainly write them a poem. Those two things conspired together and I was off to the races."

He changed his major to English and immersed himself back into the world of literature. During his junior year, he started down the road to becoming a writer, saying *yes* to new opportunities.

In addition to writing love poems to some of the campus co-eds (including one whom is now his wife), he wrote a play. Alexander wanted to produce it, but needed a venue and an audience. After learning about a student leadership conference that was being held at the College of William and Mary, he called the organizer to ask if she was interested in having entertainment during the event. She agreed to his terms—including payment—and the play was performed for about 800 students.

"After the play, during the Q&A, one of the students asked, 'Is your play going on tour?' [pause] *Yes!* Of course, it's going on tour. At the end of that night, I had bookings for eight colleges including Rutgers, Princeton, Temple, Hampton University, and so forth," Alexander recalls. "I am a junior in college, and I am understanding what this idea of saying *yes* means; of walking through a door and figuring out what is on the other side, and figuring out how to make it happen."

He continued with his writing—including another play—trying his hand at novels, poetry, and staying open to new opportunities. If someone asked him, "Kwame, have you ever thought about …?" and even if he hadn't, he would say, *yes*. This led to a children's show for television, reciting poetry to a church congregation in L.A., and successfully selling his children's book *Acoustic Rooster and his Barnyard Band* at farmers markets.

If opportunities he hoped for didn't pan out, Alexander didn't let that stop him. When publishers rejected his books, he self-published; when he wasn't invited to book festivals, he organized his own; and when he was turned down for a three-month writing fellowship in Brazil, he created his own, inviting eight accomplished, authors to join him for three weeks in Tuscany.

"There will be opportunities in life we don't get," Alexander says, "and we are going to feel sad and disappointed. But even when people are telling us no, we can say *yes* to ourselves."

And that is exactly what he kept doing. At an event in New York City, an editor suggested Alexander write a novel in verse for middle school boys about basketball. After 17 books and 20-plus years of writing, he went to his office (at Panera Bread) and began working on this project. He felt it was the best thing he had ever written. Alexander submitted the manuscript three times to the same agent who suggested the idea. She turned him down each time.

After sending it out and getting rejected by twenty different publishers, he decided he was going to publish it himself. But before he could start that process, he got one more response. An editor at Houghton Mifflin said she would be honored to publish *The Crossover*. The book was released in March 2014. On February 2, 2015, Alexander received a call: It had won the Newbery Medal Award.

"For 23 years of my writing career, I was a jet plane on a runway," Alexander says. "With each book and each year, I picked up speed. When I won the Newberry, the plane took off. And it soared 30,000 feet, and I haven't come down since. I don't know if I will ever get used to it. Sometimes I wake up and laugh and pinch myself. There is a new normal now."

Winning the award has provided him more opportunities to reach students and publish the books that are important to him.

"I want to save the world. I believe that words can do that, that books can do that. I believe the mind of an adult begins in the imagination of a child. And so, I want to create the most well-rounded, informed, honest, empathetic, connected imagination for children that I can. So that when they become adults, they have truly become more human."

Alexander proves persistence and openness can lead to reaching your dreams. He believes writers should always be prepared to walk through the door, because a *yes* will be there somewhere. It might not be in the way originally anticipated, but it will come.

He has noticed most writers are more than willing to put in the work to be successful at a job for an employer, but when it comes to putting in the work for themselves *as a writer*, it becomes more challenging and difficult.

"If you want to take destiny into your own hands, I think you have to treat your dream like you would a job. You have to put in work for it, you have to be consistent, and you have to be unwavering in your commitment."

He says a good support system is important: Make sure the people around you are going to be encouraging, supportive, and at least as smart, if not smarter than you. Surround yourself with other business minded people who are going to propel you forward.

During a keynote address to writers Alexander shared the following:

> I was the guy who self-published poetry.
>> I was the guy who was told time and time again, poetry doesn't sell.
>> I was the guy who went to farmers markets.
>> I was you—I am you.
>> The only difference between you and me is that I just happened to win this medal thing and I got lucky. You don't get lucky unless you put yourself in a situation to get lucky. I mean, I think I wrote a good book, but we all write good books. This idea of saying *yes*—it works.

His best advice: "Do it! Tap into your life as a child. Remember what you went through. Pull from those experiences. Write about things that you want to write. Don't try to write to the audience. Remember what it was like to *be* the audience and write something you think is real and authentic and beautiful and compelling. I say do it."

KENNETH OPPEL

On finding your voice, setting the scene, and lessons from the writing life.

....

David McPherson

When inspiration hits Kenneth Oppel, it's like standing on a horizon and seeing all the possibilities. Inspiration first struck the award-winning children's author during his formative years; thankfully for him—and his readers—the well of creativity has flowed frequently ever since. Sure, like all authors, there are times it feels like the well is ready to run dry, but then—often inspired by a setting—his imagination takes flight and Oppel is off on a new adventure—discovering and inventing characters and the wonderful worlds they inhabit.

From an early age, Oppel chose the writing life. By the time he was 12, he knew his calling was crafting fiction. He wrote sci-fi epics, which he calls his "*Star Wars* phase"; then, he progressed to swords and sorcery tales, his "*Dungeons & Dragons* phase"; finally, during the summer holidays when he was 14, Oppel started writing a humorous story about a boy addicted to video games. The following summer, he rewrote the tale and the resulting novel—*Colin's Fantastic Video Adventure*—was published in 1985 in Britain, Canada, the U.S., and later in France.

Since this teenage debut, Oppel, 50, has written and published 20 books, many of which have won awards. His most popular titles are: The Silverwing Trilogy (*Sunwing, Firewing, Darkwing*), which sold more than 1 million copies around the world; *Airborn*, which won the Michael L Printz Honor Book (2005, ALA), Ruth and Sylvia Schwartz Children's Book Award (2005), Red Maple Award (2004, OLA), and The Governor General's Award for Children's Literature; *Half Brother*; *The Nest*; *Skybreaker*; *The Boundless*; and *Starclimber*. The author's latest, *Every Hidden Thing*, was published in the fall of 2016.

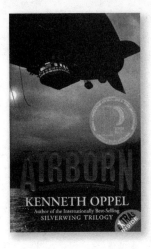

Born in Port Alberni, British Columbia—a mill town on Vancouver Island—Oppel spent his formative years in Victoria, B.C., and on the opposite coast, in Halifax, Nova Scotia. Today, the author lives in Toronto with his wife and three children, writing away the days, looking to discover new horizons, and taking readers with him on these inspirational journeys.

Here, Oppel talks about finding your voice, the role setting plays in sending his muse on creative flight, and other life lessons from a writer's life well lived.

Your story is pretty unique. Tell me about how you published your first novel back in 1985?

Yes, I was incredibly lucky. A family friend knew a famous writer, Roald Dahl, who liked my story enough to pass it on to an agent who liked it and passed it on and got me a publishing deal. It took me a while after that though to find my own voice, because I was only 14, and I was really trying to imitate Dahl's style, cadence, and dialogue. It was an apprentice piece for me, and definitely took a few years after that to really discover what kind of stories I wanted to write and to find my voice.

How does a writer find his voice?

Mimicry is how you begin. When I was starting, I wrote like Roald Dahl, [tried] *Star Wars* fan fiction, and I copied stories about video games and stories based on *Dungeons & Dragons* that I loved reading. The good thing about imitation is that it develops your skill as a writer by mimicking … you get to try out all these different styles and eventually, by practice and perseverance, you learn what is comfortable for you. It's like trying on a pair of shoes.

I'm sure that once you've found your voice, it constantly changes and evolves?

For sure your voice evolves. A writer's voice changes from book to book and over the course of a career … it's not fixed; most writers are chameleons.

Where do you get your ideas? I understand you once said that the inspiration/starting point for one of your books was from a photograph. Describe this process.

Sure, a photograph is a good way to jumpstart a creative writing workshop, but my ideas mostly come from things that I get passionate about or I'm curious about. There is no rhyme or reason to how I come across these ideas. It usually takes me about one to two years to write a book, so I need to be really engaged in the subject matter.

I understand that often a setting propels your muse and starts you on that creative journey?

Definitely. Settings inspire me. For example, the interior of the longest train in the world (*The Boundless*) or the inside of a hot air balloon (*Airborn*); these settings give me visual spaces that I can invent, populate, and play with, and that's what is most inspiring for me.

What happens once you inhabit this place?

I start thinking about who lives in these places and what characters might emerge. After I get a premise and a setting, then my mind gets to work thinking about all the possibilities that can conglomerate around this one idea. There are no rules to where the ideas come from. I write down all my ideas in a notebook—most of them are not good, but I know quickly which ones *are* good. I test them and they start sending out tendrils and shoots, that's when you know you are onto something.

I know songwriter Chip Taylor talks about how he gets chills when inspiration hits. As an author, do you experience a similar feeling when you discover a special idea?

Yes. I never tire of that moment of excitement you feel when you are on to something big. It's like standing on a horizon and seeing all these possibilities in front of you. You have those moments when you come up with an idea and you have them while writing a book. I always hope that they are frequent occurrences.

Talk about your latest novel *Every Hidden Thing*. On your website, you describe it as, "*Romeo and Juliet* meets *Indiana Jones* in this epic tale that combines the hunt for a dinosaur skeleton, bitter rivalries and a forbidden romance." Right away you've got the reader hooked. Tell us more.

It's a novel about two teenage paleontologists whose fathers are famous fossil hunters that hate each other; they've had a professional feud their entire lives and always want to destroy the others' reputation. Their kids meet at a lecture and then later out in the field in Wyoming and fall in love while searching for the same fossil they've called The Rex. They just have a tooth—but it's enormous—and that indicates the owner will have the biggest fossil find ever. I remember wondering who the first person was that found a dinosaur bone and how exciting that must have been and all the ways they used to describe what they had found: a mythological creature, biblical, etc. That excitement and mystery was my initial inspiration. Then, I read about the first paleontologists [Edward] Marsh & [Charles] Cope in the U.S. and this huge feud and rivalry they had. Those two real scientists were a huge inspiration. They were larger than life characters and I thought, "Wouldn't it be great if they each had a kid who fell in love with each other?" The story is part scientific fact, part history based on these larger-than-life figures, all mixed with a fictitious pair of star-crossed lovers.

What advice do you have for authors trying to break into children's literature?

Write the book that you most want to write and try to avoid that powerful magnetic pull to write something that might be popular, trendy, or moneymaking, because in the end no one really knows what type of book will be popular. Write the one that makes you the most excited and that you have the most to bring to … the story should call up something inside you and call up all your passions and be something only you can write. You have a far better chance of winning a publisher, agent, and audience through that strategy versus the approach of, *I'm going to write another dystopian novel.* Sure, some are successful, but I believe there are too many copycats out there, and books that are trendsetters and classics are always original.

What's the biggest lesson you've learned throughout your writing career?

The fact is, you will, as an aspiring/emerging writer, get a lot of rejections and you have to resign yourself to a certain statistical rejection. You will send your story out to many places before you get an offer of publication. Know that the reaction to your work is so subjective; it's really about lining your book up with the right reader. For a writer to achieve a certain level of expertise, you need talent, and you need to produce a polished piece of work to even get into the running. Even then, it's incredibly difficult. I know people who've written novels and sent them to 75 places before they get one offer, and the book goes on to be critically acclaimed.

Do you think it's still possible for someone to have a career as a children's author?

There is no guarantee anymore for someone to have a "writing career." It's tougher than ever to sustain a career and keep it going for a long time. There is a lot of energy in publishing dedicated to first-time novelists, but most of those don't fulfill their expectations. Then, it's hard to publish a second, third, or fourth book. It takes a lot of perseverance and discipline to write regularly.

Walk me through your typical day, knowing that no day is the same in a writer's life?

The writer's life is divided into compartments like any job. Some of it is brainstorming, note taking, researching, and fleshing out ideas to see how far they go. Once you have an idea, some writers just dive in, but I outline and try to figure out as much as possible … I need a road map. Once I start the actual writing, I try to write 1,000 words per day. The first draft is always horrible and it's torture. I skip around a lot, jump forward and backwards in the story to just get through it, then I suture it all together into a rough first draft.

What comes next after you've got a solid, rough first draft?

Revision, revision, revision. That's when the story really comes together: the breadth of the characters and what the story is really about. I never know what the story is about when I start. I just start with a premise, some characters, and a setting, which is usually the catalyst. The story comes to me in writing and rewriting. The rest of my days are spent editing, copyediting, and doing administrative stuff. I also do a lot of public speaking. Overall, it's an interesting and varied diet.

Really, when it comes down to it, you really have to want it, don't you?

For sure, you've got to want it. Like anything else that is off the typical path in terms of a career, it has to be this type of thing. First you have to think: Is there anything else I would rather be doing? Most artists say no. You have to be committed to even get to the starting line. It requires your full attention and energy; it can be, and often is, poorly paid, plus there's no pension plan, no benefits, or no matching contributions from a benevolent employer! You need to feel like this is really your calling. Basically, do not become a writer if you have another secret passion like wanting to be a dentist.

Did you always want it?

Yes. I was lucky. I decided early what I wanted to do and I didn't sway from that. I kept being what I most wanted to do. That told me that that was the thing.

What's the most rewarding part of being an author?

For me, the early stages of creation are still the most exciting and rewarding. That sense when you have this beautiful shiny thing in your hands—in your brain— and you are excited … you see all the places your story can go, just that sense of excitement of exploring it and mapping it out and creating this experience for a reader. The actual structure in creating it I find difficult, but the sense of satisfaction of holding the finished book is still a thrill for me: looking at the spine, the cover, the dust jacket, and smelling it … holding my own books and saying, "look, I made this, I brought this into the world." I love when I talk to a kid, or get a letter from an adult, and they remember what one of my books meant to them and how it was transporting, comforting, and educational. For example, when I hear from doctors, marine biologists, or pilots, who tell me my books inspired them to pursue their chosen career. To think you were this early ember in someone's imagination that sent him or her on this journey is pretty incredible.

Do you think today's do-it-yourself world of self-publishing has made it easier for new authors to break in and/or do you think there is still value in the traditional route of getting an agent/finding a publisher for your work?

I think the traditional route is still the most ideal route. I know of several notable examples where people self-published, their book caught on through word-of-mouth, attracted interest later from a legacy publisher, and then it was published traditionally, but those stories are rare. I've heard of some who do incredibly well who publish to Amazon/Kindle, etc. There are just so many options today and places to go; the market is so fragmented.

After having your own children, did fatherhood change and/or alter/influence your writing? Are they and your wife beta readers for your manuscripts these days?

Sure. I was writing well before I had kids and I have two in college now, but they were often excellent test audiences. I always read my first draft to them. They are great because they vote with their body language. You could always tell when they were bored, when they were interested, and those moments when you had them, as they would lean closer to me. When I would read aloud to them, I would make notes in the margin.

Reading your draft manuscript aloud sounds like another good tip for aspiring children's authors.

Definitely. When you read your stuff aloud you hear it and immediately know where it's sloppy or where the language is slack; it's a really good tool for editing and tightening.

For me, as a writer, reading is one of the best ways to improve and hone my skills. Do you agree? If so, do you read with an analytical mind, and who are some of your influences?

Reading. Oh yeah. Your style is inevitably influenced and tugged and pulled at by all the books you are reading. Early in my life—and throughout my life—I've learned tricks and techniques from other writers, and I steal techniques when I can. I'm now trying to read more non-fiction. As a fiction writer, I get way more ideas from nonfiction and way more stuff I can be inspired by. It's just another way to learn about the world in all its breadth and wonder. Reading about real things is more inspiring. That said, I still love fiction and I can always inhale a good story.

DAVID MCPHERSON is a Canadian writer and editor. As a freelance writer for the past 20 years, he's contributed to many publications, including *The National Post*, *Golf Canada*, *CAA Magazine*, *Hamilton Magazine*, PGATOUR.com, *Words + Music*, *Canadian Retailer*, and more. Reach him at david@mcphersoncommunications.com and follow him on Twitter (@mcphersoncomm).

DANDI DALEY MACKALL

An interview with an award-winning author of more than 500 books.

....

Jean Daigneau

As an author, Dandi Daley Mackall has done things many writers only dream about. Besides being a prolific writer, with more than 500 children and adult books to her credit, Dandi has appeared on a number of shows on radio and national television; she's won an impressive number of awards, including the Helen Keating Ott Award for Contributions to Children's Literature; and she has her own imprints. Dandi is much sought after as a presenter at conferences and workshops and at schools throughout the United States. She has penned several series, including Winnie the Horse Gentler and Starlight Animal Rescue.

You've been writing for some time now. How has the industry changed since you started, specifically as it relates to authors?

We have fewer publishing possibilities, thanks to mergers and downsizing. Most editors no longer have time to "groom" a new author, so authors must arrive with nearly finished manuscripts. Most houses expect an author to play the biggest role in marketing. When I started out, there was no such thing as social media. Now, many [publishing] houses won't consider manuscripts if the author's presence isn't strong enough out there in cyberspace. On the other hand, I think editors still want to discover a new author, the next big name. Sometimes it's better to be a first-time

author than a mid-list author—one who sells okay, but not great. And a drastic change has occurred in the last couple of years, as "self-publishing" has become "independent publishing," without the former stigma attached to a DIY book. Many well-established authors are now going independent or bringing back out-of-print books. And new authors have an alternative.

How does your writing process work? Are you a plotter or a pantser?

I honestly wish I knew how my writing process works. Some books, like *Larger-Than-Life Lara*, take off on their own, and I type as fast as I can to keep up. Others, like *The Silence of Murder*, begin as a thought, an idea. Then as I write, I know I need to plot. Sometimes I'll write the climax, as I see it, or the ending, which will probably change. Then I can work toward it. Other times, I begin by asking a major dramatic question, such as, "Will she or won't she solve the murder? Get the guy?" Then a major character-development question: "Will she discover that love means sacrifice? That she has the stamina and faith to become what she wants?" Then I might ask a "minor dramatic question" for each chapter, a plot question that can be answered yes or no. "Will he come up with a convincing lie to get out of detention?" "Will he steal the abused horse?"

For picture books, I'm a pure pantster, and my own severe and demanding editor. Editor Dandi will take Creative Dandi's manuscript and work it until there's a plot, a narrative, a good reason why page 3 isn't page 8, an arc.

You've said that it's okay to write a *#@&$) first draft. Can you share your revision process?

First drafts are fun, but hard. My first draft is usually twice as long as the final draft, (much like honing the vomit draft for the chunks). I give myself something to work with so, like a sculptor, I can find the real story inside that junky draft. I revise and rewrite (not at all the same thing) more than anyone I know. I *love* rewriting. You can only make it better, which is why I don't read the books when they come out, unless I have to do a public reading. I can always find something I'd rewrite.

I write a lot and usually have a couple of manuscripts going, hopefully in different stages. I like to "fresh-write" in the mornings and rewrite in the afternoons.

You are one of the most prolific writers I know. Where do all of these ideas come from and how do you know which ones are worth pursuing?

I am so thankful that I've never run out of ideas. Those sparks are everywhere: a cardinal lands on your car; you hear a song that gets to you; a broken-down chair sits in a cornfield; you hear a child ask where stars go in the day; you wonder what it would have been like to live in a different era. Keep those sparks. Write them down in a blank book you carry everywhere. Maybe nothing works out now, but in ten years, you may understand why that old spark moved you. When an idea pulls at you, play with it. Then work with it by researching. Not everything you write will sell, but everything you write will make you a better writer.

Now that you have your own imprint, how does the submission process work for you? Do you still go through edits with an editor, art director, etc.?

Don't kid yourself. I've been fortunate enough to have a couple of imprints with a couple of publishers, and that's been fun. But I've never written anything that wasn't edited. Like crazy. The one exception might be a few of the rhyming books because I'm a stickler for rhythm and true rhyme, and a one-word edit can throw off everything. When I have a good editor, I love the whole editing process. I have some fantastic editors who make me much better than I really am.

What keeps you excited about a new idea, when you've already written so many books?

You know, I never thought about it. But you're right—I am excited about everything I write. If an idea grows cold and uninteresting, I put it away. But when you know you're onto something real, something that makes you feel inside, it's a rush. I could write for hours, and it seems like minutes. Each book still feels like the first, like I can't believe I'm holding this book in my hands, proudly giving copies to family and friends.

What was it like finding out you won the Edgar Award for *The Silence of Murder*? Has that changed your life in any way?

What a wonderful experience! I couldn't believe it when *The Silence of Murder* made it as a finalist, with four authors I've read and loved. It meant I got to go to New York City for the big Mystery Writers of America banquet, which is kind of like the mystery book's Academy Awards. They open the envelope and everything. My husband

and I got all gussied up and joined my Knopf/Random House team and my agent for the festivities. I was so sure I wouldn't win that my sweet husband visited pawn shops all day while I was meeting with editors. He bought me a 100-year-old necklace with a charm of an old typewriter, had it wrapped, tucked in his pocket, ready to surprise me with it when I didn't win. When they called my name, my agent had to push me up to the mike, where I babbled because I hadn't prepared a talk (like they told me to). When I stepped down, I muttered that I had no idea what I'd just said. The M.C., Sandra Brown, said, "Well, Sugar, your first two words were 'Holy cow.'"

How much input did you have when your book *My Boyfriends' Dogs* was made into a made-for-television movie? Is there anything you would have changed?

The whole thing was just so cool. I'd actually written this as an adult novel, but my Dutton/Penguin editor asked me to turn it into a YA because I'd had good sales with YAs. But my agent shopped around the adult version, and that's what sold. The producers were great and wanted the screenplay to be close to the book. I got to go to Vancouver for the last week of filming. I was afraid I'd feel like an intruder, but directors, actors, producers were so welcoming and wonderful—like living in a fairytale. They'd actually read the book and asked me about their characters. And I loved those dogs!

What advice do you have for a writer just starting out?

Write your heart—whatever keeps you up at night and invades your mind during the day. Read new books by publishers you're targeting, but don't worry much about trends because they'll change before your book comes out. Go to SCBWI conferences, and join your local group. The best way to break into print is by meeting an editor at your SCBWI conference. Above all, enjoy the process. If you don't love writing, do something else. But if you love to write, a sentiment not shared with about 95 percent of humans, then pay attention to that. And write!

Can you share with us some of your experience with rejections and what you would suggest a writer do when going through that process?

I could share so many rejections with you! Even my first acceptance turned out to be a rejection after 6 months because my editor died and they refused to honor his acceptance letters and verbal contracts. But, it was okay because I thought I was a writer and I'd kept writing and snagged two contracts. That first book became my third, and it was so much better than it would have been.

Yep, with five-hundred books under my belt, I'll bet I have that many in my attic or my trash bin. I still get rejections that make me feel like I must be a horrible writer and everything that went before was one giant sham. Rejections hurt! They can undermine confidence in ourselves as writers. But we can't let rejections govern our lives. Here are some thoughts to get you through rejection:

- Realize that there are many reasons for rejecting a manuscript, and some of those reasons have nothing to do with your manuscript. That editor might not like the genre; she may have a similar book in progress; she might have her list filled until 2037; she might have rejected it without a fair shot because she doesn't know you and has a stable of authors she's hoping for.
- If you get a personal rejection from an editor, thank him or her for it. That editor will probably remember you the next time.
- Join a good critique group and ask them for their honest opinions to help you if you undertake a rewrite.
- If you get a series of rejections, or a couple that say the same thing, then you've been given a terrific learning experience. With the help of how-to books and critique groups, you can make your book even better.
- Don't carry a basket with only one egg in it. As soon as you're finished with your manuscript—or simultaneously, if that works for you—start another writing project. And another. Rejections don't hurt as much when you have other eggs in your basket.

If you were just starting out as a writer today, what, if anything, would you do differently?

I'm not sure, but I doubt I'd do things much differently. In the beginning, writing was my hobby and my dream, as I taught English and writing at a university. Eventually, I was able to stop teaching and write full-time. Today, I'd probably opt for a safe start too. But I think I am as excited and grateful as I was way back then.

We can't have an interview with you without discussing your much-loved adult book, *With Love, Wherever You Are*, based on your parents' war-time letters. How much different was that for you writing from such a personal place? Did that make it easier or harder in any way?

Thank you for asking about this novel. It has a big chunk of my heart, and I worked on it for a few decades as I listened to my parents' stories growing up. I knew they'd met in basic training after Pearl Harbor—a young Army doctor and Army nurse. I knew they'd married after a few weeks and then were shipped to different countries for the rest of the war. What I didn't know until Dad died was that they'd written each other two to three times a day during the war and that those letters were in their attic, inside an old Army trunk, stacks of over six hundred letters, tied with boot strings and untouched since 1945. The letters would show me the struggles they had to keep their marriage alive, while trying to survive the dangers and the horrors of war. I knew I had to write their story, but it was so hard to read their letters at first. I put it off, turning to WWII research until I could get through a letter without crying. What a privilege to get to know my parents when they were newlyweds! I treasured everything in those letters, every experience, every "character." My first draft was about 900 pages. I sent it to my editor/friend, who returned it with praise and encouragement, but said: "And now, revise it and show us Helen and Frank, rather than Mom and Dad." I knew she was right, though it took me a year to accomplish.

To answer the question, writing this novel wasn't like anything else I've written. I'm so grateful and pray that I've honored my parents and everyone who sacrificed as part of the "greatest generation." If you have two minutes, you can peek at the video clip about the book—two minutes, and they only had to film for five hours to get it: https://youtu.be/LJL59-UsAyo.

JEAN DAIGNEAU has been published in the adult and children's newspaper and magazine markets, including *Highlights for Children*, and has sold education testing material, craft ideas, and greeting card text. Her work has appeared in *Guide to Literary Agents* and *Children's Writer's & Illustrator's Market*. Jean has appeared on local radio and television and currently writes a column called "Genre Spotlight" for the *Children's Book Insider*. She serves on the board of SCBWI Ohio North.

MINDY MCGINNIS

On POV, science fiction, and theme.

....

Gloria G. Adams

With complex stories and beautiful writing, Mindy McGinnis has built an award-winning career. She crafts compelling narratives with fluid, easy storytelling, and shows the skill to paint characters with hard edges, unstoppable courage, broken hearts, and desperate situations. Her characters put you through the emotional ringer—you'll fall in love, want to scream at them, root for them during trying times, cry during hardships, experience the pang of despair, and triumph in their successes.

And they stay with you. For a long time.

McGinnis grew up with the kind of hands-on experience that has translated into her very hands-on method of crafting stories. She grew up on a farm in rural Ohio and still cans her own food and heats her house with wood. McGinnis can shoot and field dress a deer.

It doesn't get much more hands-on than that.

Her experiences served her well while crafting the backdrop for her dystopian, science-fiction novel, *Not a Drop to Drink*, which is currently being adapted into a movie.

Her writing also reflects fearlessness—McGinnis tackles multiple genres, points of view, and some of the darkest experiences of the human condition. Her gothic, historical fiction, *A Madness So Discreet*—for which she won the coveted Edgar Allan Poe Award for Young Adult Fiction in 2016—takes place within the walls of insane asylums in Boston and Ohio.

And McGinnis has found a place to give back to the writing community—she spent 15 years working in a school library, and working with her target audience. She still enjoys connecting with kids using books, interacting with readers, offering guest posts, and interviewing authors, agents, and editors. She also helps other writers by critiquing query letters.

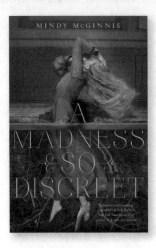  

McGinnis took a break from her busy schedule—she travels thousands of miles each year to speak, sign books, and interact with fans—to speak with *Children's Writer's & Illustrator's Market*.

As writers, one of our goals/challenges is to make our readers care so much about our characters and what happens to them that they can't put the book down. You are incredibly skillful at this; how do you create your characters?

It may seem like a simplistic answer, but I allow them to be real people. Using an archetype can help get you started as a writer, but it's important to remember that archetypes aren't always easy to relate to. Make them real. Give them space.

Before landing an agent with *Not a Drop to Drink*, you had been writing and trying to get published for ten years. What did you learn from that experience that you can share as advice to new and pre-published authors?

I think aspiring authors don't like the idea of having to do research and homework in order to become published. I know I didn't. I balked at having to be anything other than a creative in order to succeed, but that's the reality of the situation.

What is it like working with an agent?

Pretty wonderful! I have an excellent agent in Adriann Ranta of Foundry Literary, and she does a great job of not only selling my books, but also being a career shaper. She helps me decide which work should come next, to capitalize on readership. That's not always easy [as] a genre-jumper.

What is your writing process?

I really don't have one. I sit down and write the book linearly, usually not knowing what's going to happen next. I've had many people ask me, "How do you write a book?" And the answer is that I don't know. I just do it.

What are the best strategies that have worked for you on social media?

Remember that the worst part about TV is the commercials, and make sure you're not constantly selling your stuff. Be personable. Be yourself.

How did winning the Edgar Allan Poe Award impact your writing career?

It was unexpected. So much so that I just sat at my table for a moment before I realized I needed to get up and go get the award. As far as an impact, awards are lovely and help distinguish your work, but in the end they ultimately don't boost sales. What it does do—and what is more important—is that it does rededicate the author to what they are doing, and provide the encouragement to keep going.

How much time do you spend doing speaking engagements, book signings, etc.? Does your publisher set them up, or do you?

In general, I set them up myself. Larger, national events and book signings are handled through the publisher, but the vast majority of my appearances are from networking. I couldn't really put a time amount on it, but I drove about 7,000 miles in 2016 for appearances.

Your first three books were told from one character's point of view, _The Female of the Species_ was told from three, and _Given to the Sea_, four. What were the challenges in using multiple POVs? What would you recommend for new writers?

I think you have to write whatever POV the story itself wants. For both _Female_ and _Sea_ there was no way to deliver the stories without having multiple perspectives. The trick with it is to make sure that each character has a distinct voice for their sections. If the reader has to check the chapter header to figure out who is speaking, then you haven't delivered. New writers should follow whatever the story needs to work, but they have to be aware of the challenges of multiple POV.

You've written in a wide range of genres, including dystopian sci-fi, historical fiction, contemporary, and fantasy. Which have you enjoyed writing the most and why?

Contemporary is the easiest to write, simply because there was little research involved. When I was writing historical, I would have moments when 15 minutes of research was necessary to finish a line of dialogue. With contemporary I know my world. I know how teens speak and what goes on at parties. It freed me up to do more organic flow while writing.

Describe the world-building process for your fantasy book, _Given to the Sea_.

I don't really know a lot about world-building, I simply knew I had to deliver something different than our world. So I took familiar things (trees, cats, humans) and made them slightly different than what we have.

You write honestly and fearlessly about some very heavy aspects of the human experience—rape, murder, sexual abuse, mental illness, revenge, sacrifice, love, death. What are the takeaways from your books that you want for your readers?

I want my books to remain with the reader, to be something they can read ten years later and have it still resonate—even if in a different way. You can read my books as a teen and feel solidarity, or read them as an adult and feel pain for the suffering of the characters, or both. I think each subsequent change in the reader will be reflected in the text, which is what good fiction should do.

What kinds of feedback have you gotten from your teen readers about *The Female of the Species*?

A lot of personal outreach, girls letting me know what it's meant to them, given their own experiences. It's not easy to read some of the letters and emails that I get, but I do, because I know my book wasn't easy for them, either.

What was it like landing the movie deal for *Not a Drop to Drink*? How much input do you have? Anything else you can tell us about it?

It was surreal, and continues to be. I'm lucky to be fairly involved in the process, but I can't really say a whole lot about it at this point. Secrets make things cooler.

What makes you happiest about writing? What drives you crazy about it?

Writing is an escape from reality, and given the way 2016 went, I'm all for any kind of escape I can find. What drives me crazy about it is how damn hard it is. Technically, anyone can write. Move your pen across paper, tap your fingers across keys and you're doing it. But can you make your readers care about things that never happened to people that don't exist? That's hard.

What's down the road for Mindy McGinnis? What kinds of books from you might we expect in the future?

I had *Given to the Sea* release in April of 2017, as well as a fall contemporary thriller titled *This Darkness Mine*. In 2018 you'll get the sequel to *Given to the Sea*, as well as another (probably) contemporary in the fall.

. . . .

GLORIA G. ADAMS spent most of her career as a children's librarian and is now a freelance writer living in Stow, Ohio. She has been published in several magazines, including *Turtle* and *Girlworks*, and has won prizes in children's and adult literary contests. Her picture book, *Ah-Choo!* (Sterling Publishing), written with co-author Lana Koehler, was released in March 2016. Another book, *My Underpants Are Made From Plants* (co-author, Vera J. Hurst) is part of the Schoolwide, Inc. digital library. Gloria is a member of the Society of Children's Book Writers and Illustrators.

. . . .

KIRBY LARSON

On collaboration, writing historical fiction, and reaching out in the children's writing community.

Suzanne Morgan Williams

Kirby Larson says she "owns a tiara and is not afraid to use it!" (Surely if we crowned children's literature royalty, she'd be a princess from the House of Historical Fiction.) But you can almost see her grinning as she says this. Kirby's not an intimidating princess type and she hasn't always loved history. "I went from history-phobe to history fanatic while writing the 2007 Newbery Honor Book, *Hattie Big Sky*, and its sequel, *Hattie Ever After*." Larson continued her passion for historical fiction with her WWII Dogs series, *Liberty*, *Duke*, and *Dash* (winner of the 2015 Scott O'Dell Historical Fiction Prize), and the Audacity Jones books, *Audacity Jones to the Rescue* and *Audacity Jones Steals the Show*.

But like most successful writers, this list of awards and books doesn't tell Larson's whole story. She began writing for children in 1990 and her first book, *Second Grade Pig Pals*, was published in 1994. A quick look at her credits shows a hiatus of six years between the publication of her first three chapter books and the Newberry Honor book, *Hattie Big Sky*. Kirby says, "Cling to those dreams no matter what." She doesn't give up.

And there's more to Kirby than her books. She's active in the children's writers' community. She's often invited to speak at conferences or festivals and she often credits the writers who inspire her and her peers who share her passion for creating books. She seems truly surprised and grateful to stand in front of the audiences who admire her work. Kirby is a giver.

Have you always written historical fiction? What else have you dabbled in?

Inspired by the amazing Patricia Reilly Giff, I started my career writing chapter books, geared to the first to third grade reader. I adore this genre, which I call the soap operas of kid lit—all drama and action! My dream is to someday write historical fiction chapter books along the lines of the powerful books written by Ann Turner (*Nettie's Trip South, Dakota Dugout*).

How do you choose your topics? Do you ever abandon a topic? Why?

I am drawn to stories about underdogs (and plain old dogs! Thus my WWII dog series) and to stories about people who accomplished incredible things but never made the headlines. To date, I have not abandoned a topic. As someone who accumulated over 250 rejection letters before ever getting published, I suspect I am too stubborn to give up on a story.

How do you know when you've found something special or important to write about?

If I come across something that makes me stop whatever else I'm doing to dig deeper, that's a pretty sure sign. For example, when I read a line in a book about kids on the U.S. home front during WWII that said: "Some kids even loaned their dogs to the war effort," I threw myself into the project of finding out if that statement was true. And it was! Approximately 25,000 family pets were donated to Uncle Sam, a stunning fact that led to the writing of my novel, *Duke*.

How do you decide when to approach a topic as nonfiction and when to create historical fiction? Are there pros and cons to these choices?

I have only written two books of nonfiction (*Nubs: The True Story of a Mutt, a Marine and a Miracle* and *Two Bobbies: A True Story of Hurricane Katrina, Friendship and Sur-*

vival, both co-written with Mary Nethery); in those cases, the real life stories were intensely compelling and needed to be told as is.

History is rarely neat and tidy, following a perfect story arc. Thus, when I am inspired by historical events, I generally need to bridge those events with scenes and actions that could have happened, to create a sense of forward movement and resolution.

You mention Mary Nethery, your co-author on some of your projects. What are the positives of collaboration? Any tips for making it work?

The biggest blessings of my writing life have come from my collaboration with my darling friend, Mary Nethery. We decided to tackle a book together during a time when neither of us were getting published; we figured we might change our luck by partnering up! One of our first decisions was to choose a genre that neither of us individually had attempted: narrative nonfiction. And our firm and fast guiding rule was that nothing would go in one of our books unless we both agreed to it. There is a joy and energy in collaborating that cannot be experienced in solo work. Mary and I are especially proud of finding a voice that is neither Mary nor Kirby. Honestly, it is impossible for us to remember who wrote what in our two books.

Speaking of voice, your characters' voices seem both grounded in their times and accessible to modern readers. Is there anything special you do to achieve this blend?

I read old newspapers, diaries, and journals to get the sense of typical speech during a particular era. If you notice, I also employ vocabulary from the time period in which a book is set (dungarees instead of jeans, or valise for suitcase, for example). To get into a character, I often write letters as that character to other players in a book (these letters are typically for my use only) which helps to ground me. The rest, as they say, is magic.

Research is a mainstay of historical fiction. Do you have any research tips you'd like to share?

Two words: primary resources. Do whatever it takes to get those in your hot little hands! I dig up historic recipes, songs, newspapers, photographs; I even scour eBay and Etsy for old journals, postcards, and letters. For *Dash*, I wanted—no, *needed*—a map of Camp Harmony (one of the assembly centers to which persons of Japanese descent were sent in Washington state) and I could not find a complete one anywhere. So, I put on my armor of bravery and reached out to Dr. Louis Fiset, who had written a book on the topic, asking if he could share where he'd found the map used in his book. It turns out, it was a one of a kind—he had stitched it together from maps he'd dug out of archives I had neither the time nor money to visit. To my astonishment and, without my asking, he mailed me *his only copy*! I was touched, elated, and panicked—what if my dog chewed it up? His generous action is only one example of the ways in which I've been helped by experts while researching my books.

Historical fiction isn't always seen as an "easy sale." Why do you continue to write it?

I am very weary of hearing this "fact." My books have earned dozens of state young readers' choice awards. That means *kids* read the books, voting on their favorites. Look: Kids love good stories. They don't care *when* a story takes place, as long as the character and/or the problems that character is facing speak to them. Think back to when you were a kid. Of course, you would have balked if a caring adult handed you a book and said, "This will teach you something about history." *Boring!* Too much like schoolwork. But if that caring adult said, "This book is about an 11-year-old orphan who rescues the President's kidnapped niece," you would likely grab the book and sit right down to read. Frankly, I am impassioned about writing historical fiction because I am terrified at the prospect of a future where we don't have a clue about where we've come from.

What do you wish readers knew about historical fiction?

History is about ordinary people like you and me, not about dates and wars and famous generals. Historical fiction is our chance to read other peoples' letters and diaries; it's our chance to step back into another time and place. It's a chance to increase our capacity for empathy.

So far, can you describe a high point in your career?

High points of my career: That first published book. That first fan letter. Taking my mechanical contractor father to the Newbery banquet in Washington, D.C., and hearing him say, "This is a big deal, isn't it?" Getting an e-mail from a woman who was sent to Camp Harmony (and Minidoka) telling me that *Dash* was written as if I'd been in those places. Having a foster kid write a song inspired by *Duke*. Counting among my friends such amazing writers as Karen Cushman, Susan Hill Long, Mary Nethery, Barbara O'Connor, Ann Whitford Paul, Augusta Scattergood, and so many, many more.

You have a reputation of being generous with other authors. What part does the community of children's writers and illustrators play in your career and experiences?

The thing is, I would not be writing today without the support and encouragement of fellow book creators. The creative life can be lonely and discouraging. Countless kind and generous book creators have kept me from giving up along the way! My gratitude has led me to pay back those kindnesses. But, honestly, the finest people I know have dedicated their lives to writing books for children and young adults. Why wouldn't I do everything I could to celebrate them and share their good news? (One of my favorite things is the Friend Friday feature on my blog, where I shine the spotlight on friends' new books. Do check it out: kirbylarson.com/blog.)

What is the best advice you received as a writer? What advice would you give to writers starting out? What advice would you give to, in particular, historical fiction writers?

The best advice I got was from Karen Cushman, during a keynote she gave to a thousand-plus people at an SCBWI conference in Los Angeles, but I swear she was speaking directly to me: "Find your passion." And I knew in that instant that the crazy idea I had about writing a story inspired by my family history was worth the effort it would take. And how can I top advice from Karen Cushman? One thing I might add is to cling to those dreams, no matter what.

What one or two things do you wish you'd known when you started?

I wish I'd known about Scrivener (which didn't even exist back then!) and I wish I'd known it was okay to ask for help. But I am glad I didn't know how many times I would have to revise a manuscript before I got it just right.

You've won a Newberry Honor and a Scott O'Dell Award as well as many state awards and other honors. Have these awards changed your writing life?

I am still a bit bewildered that an ordinary person like me has received such amazing honors. They have changed my life for the better—more people know my books!—*and* for the worse—what if I never measure up again? Such a mixed blessing, but one I would wish for all my talented writing friends.

CAROLYN CRIMI

How a best-selling picture book author turned novelist engages young readers with humor.

Carmela A. Martino

Carolyn Crimi is the award-winning author of more than a dozen picture books, including the best-selling *Henry and the Buccaneer Bunnies* and its sequel, *Henry and the Crazed Chicken Pirates*, both illustrated by John Manders and both from Candlewick Press. She has an uncanny ability to craft stories that touch on universal themes while making readers laugh out loud. Her most recent, *There Might Be Lobsters* (Candlewick Press), illustrated by Laurel Molk, is described as a "funny and honest read-aloud about how overwhelming the world can be when you're worried."

Crimi says she dreamed of being a writer from an early age. "As a child, I was always writing and illustrating little handmade books for my family, mostly because I was a cheap kid and these gifts didn't cost me a dime. I told any adult who asked that I wanted to be the next L. Frank Baum." Crimi grew up on Long Island in a house surrounded by woods. She spent many hours reading outside, whether in a homemade fort in the woods or on a blanket in her own backyard. Baum's Oz books were among her favorites. With the publication of her forthcoming middle-grade novel, *Weird Little Robots* (Candlewick Press), Crimi will soon join Baum as an author of illustrated children's novels.

Despite her childhood dream, Crimi followed a roundabout route to publication. An art history major in college, she worked in retail sales and in advertising before spotting an ad on a grocery store bulletin board for the Institute of Children's Literature. Crimi

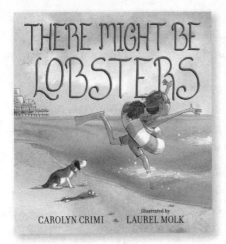

enrolled and began submitting her work while still in the program. Her first sale was a short story to *Child Life* magazine. In 1995, Simon & Schuster published her first picture book, *Outside, Inside*, illustrated by Linnea Asplind Riley. Crimi later received an MFA in Writing for Children and Young Adults from Vermont College. She highly recommends the Vermont College program "for anyone who is seriously committed to writing children's literature."

Crimi still loves the outdoors and reading for hours on end, but she now lives in the busy college town of Evanston, Illinois. In 2012, she received the Prairie State Award, an annual award that honors an Illinois author whose body of work for children/young adults "demonstrates excellence, engenders a love of literature, and embraces an important part of the mission of the Illinois Reading Council—to promote lifelong literacy." Her books have also received numerous state awards across the country. For more about her, see www.carolyncrimi.com.

Given your early interest in writing, why did you take such a roundabout route to becoming a published author?

While being an author was a dream of mine, I didn't really think it was possible. The "getting paid" part seemed tricky. I didn't know any authors when I first began, which made the whole thing that much more vague and unattainable. So, I sold pantyhose at a department store instead, since that is anything but vague and unattainable.

Can you tell us about how you wrote and sold your first picture book, *Outside, Inside*?

It's funny to look back on the writing of that book. It seems like ages ago because it was ages ago. I wrote the manuscript in 1992-ish? Thereabouts. It was one of many manuscripts I was working on and submitting at the time. It's a very quiet story and

I didn't have much hope for it. In fact, after receiving seven rejections, I had decided to put it away. The eighth publisher, Simon and Schuster, said yes. I will never forget that phone call from my future editor. She called me in the morning while I was getting dressed. I remember looking in the mirror thinking, "This is the biggest moment in my life, and I'm in my underwear."

Back in ye olden days, you didn't need an agent. Like all of my submissions back then, *Outside, Inside* was an unsolicited submission. I usually had about ten or twelve manuscripts circulating at one time. I was all about the throwing-spaghetti-at-the-wall technique. Something had to stick, and it did.

Publishers Weekly called your second picture book, *Don't Need Friends* (Random House), a "slyly funny and deeply touching story." Your picture books often focus on important themes while making readers laugh out loud, which is probably why they end up on so many children's choice award lists. How do you weave warmth and humor together so effectively in your writing?

I don't try to write something funny. I just try to tell a story. If it happens to be funny, great. But as soon as I try to be funny, I stop enjoying the process. The jokes wind up sounding forced. For me, the best way to do it is to tell the story first and let the humor grow out of the situation or character.

Warmth comes naturally to me because I believe in books with heart. If some poor parent is going to read my book over and over and over, it better be more than just a punch line. It's the heart of the story that draws the reader back to it.

I'm so pleased that that book has been in print since 1999. It's still one of my favorites.

Your picture book *Henry and the Buccaneer Bunnies* (Candlewick Press) was so popular it made *Publishers Weekly*'s Bestseller List. It's your only book with a sequel, *Henry and the Crazed Chicken Pirates*. What was it like to write a sequel to a bestseller?

Ugh! I didn't like writing a sequel one bit! In fact, that was my least favorite book to write. Henry, my main character, had already solved his biggest problem in the first book. I wasn't sure how to give him another problem to solve without changing his character too much. I really struggled before coming up with a solution. I still get a little itchy just looking at the cover.

Editors and agents often discourage submissions of holiday-themed picture books because the market is generally saturated. Yet you have not one, but two, Halloween-themed titles: *Boris and Bella* (Harcourt) and *Where's My Mummy?* (Candlewick Press). Can you explain your success with these titles? What advice do you have for writers who want to write holiday stories?

I happen to love Halloween, so that helps. I think about it a lot and I look forward to it all year. I couldn't write about, say, President's Day. It's just not my jam. But if you love President's Day the way I love Halloween, and you think about it and count the days until it happens, by all means, write a President's Day book! I don't believe in writing for the market. Getting published is such a crapshoot. You might as well write what you love.

Reviewers often comment on your marvelous use of wordplay, snappy prose, and rhythmic language in your picture books. Do you have any advice for writers who want to sharpen their use of language?

My advice to writers is to read your work out loud. I always, always read my manuscripts out loud and consider it one of the most important steps in the process. After you've read it out loud to yourself, read it to a friend. You'll be a lot more aware of all the little hiccups if you have an audience. I once read a story out loud to a friend and discovered, much to my dismay, that I had used the word "bunnies" roughly ten thousand times in one short story. Finally, have someone else read it to you. You'll hear which sentences, words, or phrases she stumbles over.

I think of picture books as a script and the adult reading the book as the actor. I know a lot of busy parents and teachers may grab a book without fully reading it first, so I try to make it easy for that person to convey what's in the story on a cold read. For instance, I'll show them where to pause by using a lot of white space around the words.

Like this.

And this.

I try not to have difficult alliteration. Some alliteration is fine, but if it turns into a tongue twister your adult reader is going to hate you. Sentences like "Bodacious bunnies bop while wearing big blue bonnets" are scary.

Can you tell us about your forthcoming novel, *Weird Little Robots* (Candlewick Press)? What was the inspiration behind the story?

I saw a picture one day on Facebook of a tiny handmade robot. I happen to love miniatures, so the idea of a miniature robot was very appealing to me. Also, it made me think of these little robot toys I wanted when I was about eight years old. They walked if you wound them up, and I remember thinking how fun it would be if they would follow me around all day. I'd watch the commercial for them and imagine what it would be like to have them follow me through the mall or down the school hallways. When I finally got one it was extremely disappointing. It wasn't alive, like a pet, which was basically what I wanted it to be. It simply whirred along like a match-box car.

I got to thinking about what it would be like if a tiny robot did come to life. Or a couple of tiny robots. What if the girl who made them was a little bit shy and lonely like I was? I tossed the idea out to my writer's group and they loved it. I was off and running!

Weird Little Robots was announced as your "debut" middle-grade novel. But you published two earlier novels as a ghostwriter for R. L. Stine's Ghosts of Fear Street series. Can you tell us how you got the assignment to write those books and what the process was like?

I had submitted a novel about a ghost to this one publisher without realizing that they were actually a packager. They didn't want to publish my novel, but they were interested in having me write for their series. It's fast and furious work, and I learned a lot, especially about plot. Those books move along at a brisk pace! The deadlines are tight, so there's no room for procrastination or writer's block. It was a great experience.

What is your typical writing process? Is it different for novels versus picture books?

I think in many ways my process for both is the same. I thrash around a lot in the beginning of the story. I usually start out by writing notes using good old-fashioned pencil and paper. I jot down everything I know, or think I know, about the story. Strange, cryptic notes that I often don't understand later. A lot of my ideas start with images, either pictures that I've seen or ones that have popped into my head out of the blue. For a novel, I write a very brief chapter outline. For a picture book, I might write a summary. When I think I know enough about the story I open up a file on my computer and start typing.

You have a degree in art history. Have you taken any illustration classes? Have you considered illustrating your own work?

Yes, I have taken illustration classes and I would like to illustrate my own work! I have always loved to draw and actually find it to be very relaxing. I totally get the appeal of those adult coloring books, although I prefer to color in my own images.

You enjoy taking acting and improv classes. How have those classes influenced your writing and/or your school visit presentations?

The advice I often give to new writers is to take acting classes. Nobody tells you when you are a beginner that you will probably earn most of your income doing presentations. I actually thought I would make all my money from my writing!

I did Second City here in Chicago. It taught me how to fail miserably on stage and survive. After you've failed a couple of hundred times it's really not so daunting. It teaches you to get over yourself.

Scene work is important, too. I take lots of acting classes, mainly because I'm a ham, but also because they teach me about character. How am I moving my body when I say this line, and how would I write that into a scene? What is my character thinking about when she says that line? What was the "moment before" the play/story began, and how does that affect the tone and mood of each scene?

My acting feeds my writing and my writing feeds my acting. It's a very cannibalistic relationship.

You're known for presenting entertaining and engaging school visits. What do you think is the key to a successful author visit?

My school visits are 90 percent entertaining and 10 percent educational. If I'm making them laugh I have their attention, and if I have their attention I can slip in a little something educational.

It's similar to my stories. I want them to be fun and entertaining. I want kids to want to read them. I see some writers create stories that feel like a big plate of broccoli. They've put the educational value or the "lesson" first. I want my books and my presentations to be the chocolate cake of children's lit.

Can you share any stories of especially memorable school visits?

Well, let's see. I've been thrown up on, sneezed on, and coughed on. I've been asked my weight, my income, and my age. But perhaps my most memorable school visit experience was from a few years ago. During my talk, I saw a little boy in the front row wiggling around in that distinctive way children do when they have to go to the bathroom. Before I could catch the teacher's eye, he stood up quickly with this alarmed look on his face. Suddenly there was a stream of urine heading my way. Luckily, I was able to dodge it. The moral of the story is you have to be quick on your feet when you're doing a school visit.

You also do presentations to teachers on a variety of topics, including the value of humor in the classroom. What advice do you give teachers on adding humor into the curriculum?

I encourage teachers to incorporate "Funny Fridays" into their curriculum. I tell them to take the last ten minutes of the day on Friday and use it for funny activities. During this time, kids can read funny books, tell jokes, vote for their favorite funny book, write stories based on a funny picture—the list goes on.

I remember giving a talk to teachers about this. As I walked away I thought grumpy thoughts about how no one will ever do this in their classroom and why did

I even bother and so on. Seconds after I had these grumpy thoughts a teacher came running up to me. She told me that she had heard my lecture the year before and that since then her entire school had incorporated Funny Fridays into their curriculum. Apparently, both the teachers and students loved it and they will continue doing it every year.

I swooned with happiness!

What's next for you? Are you working on a sequel to *Weird Little Robots*? Do you plan to continue writing picture books or will you switch to novels?

I will always write picture books but right now I'm writing another middle-grade novel that I started seventeen years ago! I'm also toying with the idea of turning *Don't Need Friends* into a musical and having my actor friends perform it.

CARMELA A. MARTINO has an MFA in Writing for Children and Young Adults from Vermont College. Her middle-grade novel, *Rosa, Sola* (Candlewick Press) was named a Booklist "Top Ten First Novel for Youth." This fall, Vinspire Publishing published her young adult novel, *Playing by Heart*, a historical romance inspired by the lives of Maria Teresa Agnesi, one of the first women to compose a serious opera, and her older sister, Maria Gaetana Agnesi, a mathematician and linguist. Carmela teaches writing workshops for children and adults, and co-founded TeachingAuthors.com, a blog by six children's authors who are also writing teachers. For more information, see www.carmelamartino.com.

THE EVER-CHANGING PICTURE BOOK MARKET

Three accomplished authors share their thoughts on what a successful picture book looks like, and the future of the industry as they see it.

....

Lana Wayne Koehler

///

Never before has the children's market seen such an influx of writing—the middle-grade and young adult genres are scorching hot right now. And the picture book market continues to be as profitable as ever. In this roundtable, we have three accomplished picture book authors to share their thoughts on the future of the market, the changes we've seen in picture books, those authors who are pulling off classic works now, and much more.

MEET THE AUTHORS

LISA J. AMSTUTZ is the author of more than 50 children's books. Her work has also appeared in a wide variety of magazines and newspapers. A former outdoor educator, Lisa specializes in topics related to science, nature, and agriculture. Her background includes a B.A. in Biology from Goshen College and an M.S. in Environmental Science/Ecology from the University of Virginia.

LAURIE LAZZARO KNOWLTON's first published work was a note passed to a boy in third grade. Laurie has gone on to write forty books and is the author/illustrator of two more. *Why Cowboys Sleep with Their Boots On* won the Premier Print Award given by Eastman Kodak and has sold more than 45,000 copies since publication. Laurie is an international speaker, addressing students, educators, and writers throughout the United States and Mexico.

DANDI DALEY MACKALL won her first writing contest as a ten-year-old tomboy. Her 50 words on "Why I Want to Be Batboy for the Kansas City A's" won first place, but the team wouldn't let a girl be batboy. It was her first taste of rejection. Since then, she has become an award-winning author of about 500 books for all ages, with sales of 4 million copies in 22 countries. Dandi is a national speaker and has made dozens of appearances on local and national television.

How has the picture book market changed over the last 10 years?

AMSTUTZ: I started writing for children at the end of the recession, when publishers were slashing their budgets and the market was extremely tight. While I don't know the numbers, the market is definitely expanding again. As a nonfiction writer, I particularly see a lot of growth and opportunity in that area. Common Core and Next Generation Science Standards call for increasing amounts of informational text, and nonfiction picture books fit the bill.

KNOWLTON: Since 2007 I have noticed three major trends. In 2007, the economy was still pretty much intact. In 2008, the United States encountered a major economic shift and spendable cash dried up everywhere, including the publishing market. What I saw as a result was that publishers were being more cautious about what they were going to publish. The marketing people began to have a bigger say in what books would be chosen for publication. The numbers had to justify the investment to publish a book.

Before 2008, publishers were more willing to accept a quiet book, or a book with longer text, or perhaps a book about an important topic that might not be a bestseller but did offer a unique perspective on a topic. After 2008 it was all about numbers and cash.

Another milestone since 2007 is that the majority of states adopted the Core Curriculum State Standards. Teachers are now given a standard that all students across the U.S. are to be learning the same thing during the same grade year. This idea is based on wanting all students to have the same universal education after completing each grade.

The main difference in the education is that the teachers are to help the students develop better critical and abstract thinking skills and center less on rote learning and memorization.

Publishers were quick to get on board. The schools needed books on specific topics, nonfiction publishing grew in leaps and bounds, and even fiction required back matter to get the reader involved in deeper levels of comprehension.

One last thing I noticed about the market in the past few years is that many publishers want shorter text. When I started getting published, picture books ran anywhere up to 1000 words. Now, less is more. The publishers are looking for tight, fast-moving text under 500 words.

MACKALL: Whoa! Let me count the ways.

1. Topics: Not only are the cultural edges accepted now—they're desired.
2. Picture book editors seem to be more specialized. We hear "Not a good fit" more often, I think.
3. Money is tighter, so editors can't afford to take a manuscript they're in love with if they know the sales will be limited.
4. It follows that celebrities and famous name authors can get mediocre books published, when our masterpieces get returned.
5. In many cases, text has grown sparser, and the fewer the words the better, unless a specialized publisher takes on picture books for older readers.
6. Independent publishing has changed everything. "Self-published" books were discounted as wannabe books that couldn't get a real publisher. That's changed. as many authors have turned out successful books.

Finally, I'd say picture books are the hardest books to sell to a publisher.

What do you see as the focus in today's picture book market?

AMSTUTZ: There has been a recent, much-needed push for diversity in children's books, popularized in part by the We Need Diverse Books campaign. Strong characters and humor are perennial favorites, and metafictive books are increasingly popular as well. In nonfiction, I see a strong focus on STEM topics and tightly focused biographies for young readers.

In general, today's picture books are much shorter and tighter than in years past. The recommended word count for a fiction picture book has steadily dropped since I started writing, from 800–1000 to around 500 today. The limits are not as strict for nonfiction, however, and longer nonfiction picture books for an older market have found a niche as well.

KNOWLTON: The focus is as it has always been, providing quality books that expand a child's world in a fun and interesting way. With technology part of every child's world, literature has to keep up in keeping the child engaged. The one thing that keeps picture books relevant in a technical world is that nothing can replace the presence of an adult reading to a child. It is the relationship that is built while engaged in that one-on-one experience that makes them irreplaceable.

MACKALL: Doing fewer books and only books that fit their target audience. Knopf tends toward literary, light-text picture books that tug heartstrings or make the reader smile. Sleeping Bear prefers longer, often historical picture books, and they market them successfully to fifth-grade readers. Authors need to study each publisher's recent picture books and send a manuscript to the right one—the perfect fit.

Who do you think is doing this well and why?

AMSTUTZ: It's hard to pick just a few, but Jane O'Connor's Fancy Nancy, Ian Falconer's Olivia, and Kevin Henkes's Lilly are examples of strong characters that have spawned successful series. Metafictive titles such as Mo Willems' Pigeon books and Bill Cotter's *Don't Push the Button* interact with the reader in a direct and humorous way.

Two of my favorite recent biographies for young readers are Deborah Heiligman's *The Boy Who Loved Math: The Improbable Life of Paul Erdos* and Stephanie Roth Sisson's *Star Stuff: Carl Sagan and the Mysteries of the Cosmos*. Creative takes on nonfiction topics include Melissa Stewart's *Feathers: Not Just for Flying* and Candace Fleming's *Giant Squid*.

KNOWLTON: I think books that challenge children are the drive in the market today. In 2016, we saw a picture book, *Last Stop on Market Street*, win the Newbery Award for the second time in the history of the award. In Matt de la Pena's text, the main character asks question after question. Nana's answers are sometimes given, sometimes answered with a question, and sometimes inferred; all in all the book is meant to get the main character and the reader to open their heart and minds and witness the beauty around them.

MACKALL: For the sake of time, I'm using my own experience.

- **TYNDALE HOUSE PUBLISHERS:** They specialize in fun and meaningful Christian picture books that don't preach, and they spend up, in order to get good illustrators and designers. This year I started a picture book series, Flipside Stories, showing the same story twice, from two points of view. I've wanted this for ten years, so it's been a good year.

- **HARPERCOLLINS CHRISTIAN/ZONDERKIDZ AND TOMMY NELSON:** Both put out terrific picture books that sell in mainstream and Christian markets. I love my holiday books with ZonderKidz: *The Legend of Saint Nicolas*, *The Legend of the Christmas Cookie*, *17 Christmases*, *The Legend of the Easter Robin*. And Tommy Nelson published my Christmas book this year, simultaneous versions in classic picture book and streamlined board book: *One Small Donkey*. All of them sold well and earned out fast.
- **SKYHORSE PUBLISHING:** This publisher has grown like crazy, with a wide range of fun and funky picture books, like my *Rock Away Granny*, a rock and roll ride.
- **RANDOM HOUSE/PENGUIN/DUTTON:** I did a picture book for Dutton that may have been their only Nativity, first-Christmas book. It didn't do well, and I suspected their buyers weren't used to the genre. I also wrote a funny picture book for them, *Are We There Yet?*, and it sold well.

What do you see as the future of picture books?

AMSTUTZ: While e-books have their place, I don't see picture books going away anytime soon. At least, I hope not! There is something special about reading aloud to a child, turning the pages and looking at the pictures together, that can't be replaced with technology.

KNOWLTON: When Kindles and other reading material became the rage, everyone said, "Oh no! It's the end of the printed book!"

But as you can see, people still love the feel of the book; they love the intimate relationship of the turning of a page, the smell of the paper, and the ability to hand a book to another person and say, "You have to read this book!"

I think having a personal library is an important aspect of teaching a child responsibility and respect in caring for something. Books are physical things that require gentle hands. To have a collection of books on a shelf is like always having a friendly face ready to spend time with you. What more can anyone ask?

I believe picture books are here to stay.

MACKALL: We'll always have them. The pendulum swings between feast and famine, but the world needs books children can hold while seated on someone's lap.

Any advice for new authors/illustrators of picture books?

AMSTUTZ: If you're interested in writing and/or illustrating picture books, start by visiting your public library or a bookstore and reading all the recent picture books you can get your hands on. This will give you an idea of what's selling in today's market. Study books about writing/illustrating for children and check out some of the many classes and resources available online. Get involved in the kidlit community by joining SCBWI, attending conferences and workshops, and connecting with other writers on social media. A good critique group is essential—if you don't have a local group, join or start an online group. Most of all, hang in there! The path to publication can be long, so celebrate your successes along the way, and enjoy the journey!

KNOWLTON: My advice for new authors and or illustrators is to be active in the marketing of your book. Build an Internet presence. Offer school visits, library visits, and speaking engagements. No one is going to be as enthusiastic as you about your new book, and you know what they say about enthusiasm—it's contagious!

MACKALL: Write your heart out! If you don't cry or laugh or feel deeply, an editor won't, and the reader won't either. Study other picture books for length, form, and other conventions. But write your heart.

LANA WAYNE KOEHLER (www.lanakoehler.com) is a regular contributor to A Song of Six Pens blog, Today's Little Ditty, and The Mighty. Her debut picture book, *Ah-Choo!*, is co-written with Gloria G. Adams.

WORKING WITH SMALL PRESSES

A roundup of authors share the advantages and challenges of working with a small press

....

Carmela A. Martino

Many authors and illustrators dream of being published by an imprint of one of the "Big 5" United States trade publishers: Penguin Random House, HarperCollins, Simon & Schuster, Macmillan, and Hachette. But these imprints tend to accept only agented submissions. Those that do accept unsolicited submissions can be excruciatingly slow to respond.

Small presses aren't always open to unsolicited submissions, and they can be slow to respond, too, but they tend to take on a greater variety of projects than the Big 5, often focusing on niche markets. My new young adult novel, *Playing by Heart*, is an example of a book with niche appeal. The manuscript won the young adult category of the 2013 Four Seasons Romance Writing Contest and was a finalist in three other writing competitions. As my prize, I received feedback from the editors and agents who judged these contests. They all commended the writing, but they told me the book would be a "tough sell" because it was a young adult historical romance without paranormal or fantasy aspects. My "hook" was that the novel was based on the lives of two amazing sisters who lived in 18th-century Milan—one a composer and the other a mathematician. Unfortunately, that wasn't enough of a hook for the larger houses I queried. However, it was enough for Vinspire Publishing, a small press that specializes in historical and inspirational romance.

In researching the topic of small presses, I consulted several industry professionals for a definition of "small press" when it comes to children's publishing. The term is generally used to describe any publisher who isn't one of the Big 5. By that definition, publishers like Candlewick and Scholastic would be considered "small presses," even though they produce a large number of books. For this article, I interviewed three authors about their experiences working with even smaller presses—publishers that aren't imprints of the Big 5, and that typically release fewer than 50 books per year.

MEET THE AUTHORS:

LAURA ATKINS (www.lauraatkins.com) grew up in an activist family and learned the power of telling stories from a young age. She is an author, teacher, and independent children's book editor who worked at Children's Book Press, Orchard Books, and Lee & Low Books. She has an MA in Children's Literature from Roehampton University in London and an MFA in Writing for Children and Young Adults from Vermont College of Fine Arts. The co-author of the middle-grade biography, *Fred Korematsu Speaks Up* (Heyday Books), and author of the picture book, *Sled Dog Dachshund* (Minted Prose Press), Laura lives in Berkeley, California.

NANCY BO FLOOD (www.nancyboflood.com) has always loved stories, whether as a fish-brain surgeon at the University of Minnesota or as a rodeo poem wrangler. She has authored more than a dozen books, mostly with small presses. *Navajo Year, Walk Through Many Seasons* (Salinas Bookshelf) was an ALA Notable Social Studies book and an Arizona Book of the Year. *Warriors in the Crossfire* (Boyds Mills) received Colorado Book of the Year. *Cowboy Up! Ride the Navajo Rodeo*, (Wordsong), was a Junior Library Guild selection. *Water Runs Through This Book* (Fulcrum Publishers) received the Sigurd Olson Environmental Writing Award. Her most recent release is *Soldier Sister, Fly Home* (Charlesbridge).

CLAUDIA GUADALUPE MARTÍNEZ (www.claudiaguadalupemartinez.com) grew up in sunny El Paso, Texas, where she learned that letters form words from reading the subtitles of old westerns with her father. Her debut novel, *The Smell of Old Lady Perfume* (Cinco Puntos), received the 2009 Paterson Prize for Books for Young People, the 2008 Texas Institute of Letters Best Young Adult Book Award, and a 2009 Americas Award Commendation. Her sophomore novel, *Pig Park* (Cinco Puntos), won the 2015 Texas Institute of Letters Best Young Adult Book and the 2015 NACCS Tejas Foco Young Adult Fiction Award. Claudia now lives and writes in Chicago.

I turned to a small press when I realized my novel, *Playing by Heart*, wouldn't work for mainstream publishers. Vinspire Publishing typically accepts only agented submissions, but I was able to pitch to them at an online conference. What made you decide to go with a small press? How did you connect with them?

MARTÍNEZ: Cinco Puntos Press was actually the first press I submitted my debut novel to. I didn't submit it to a whole lot of places. Mostly, I kept working on it and kept resubmitting to the same press. I'd heard about Cinco Puntos because they are headquartered in my hometown of El Paso, Texas. I liked that we had that connection. When I wrote my second novel, I submitted it to a few agents who passed on it. In my heart, I knew that I should just submit to Cinco Puntos, so I did. I really loved my editor, Lee Byrd, and I knew I would have a positive experience.

ATKINS: I love small presses, having worked primarily in editorial departments at small publishers. When I finished my MFA, I had to think about where I wanted to submit my work. While I've felt tempted to approach bigger publishers, and have some contacts to do so, I feel more comfortable and happy working with small presses. Heyday Books in Berkeley published *Fred Korematsu Speaks Up*, which I co-wrote with Stan Yogi. Our editor gave her heart and soul to the project, and I loved that going in for meetings, I knew almost every person at the publisher. While they may not have the budget of larger publishers, they are deeply committed to each title they publish. This relationship works for me. It's personal, and they are accessible and passionate. I would expect to be more lost in the large mainstream model.

FLOOD: A regional press seemed to be the best choice for my manuscripts that had a more regional focus. I looked carefully at the quality and type of books being produced by regional publishing houses. I asked myself, did I want my book to have that "look," that quality of paper, illustration, print, etc.? Good distribution was also an important consideration. A successful regional publisher knows their readership—what topics and types of books they are interested in reading and where they will look for new books. I knew if teachers, librarians, and readers could not find my book, they certainly wouldn't buy my book. My overall experience with connecting with small presses is very positive. Usually, one can email or call and communicate with the publisher or editor directly and promptly.

One other big plus for small presses: most support their backlist, which means your book will stay in print for years rather than disappearing after six months. The backlist will be part of each catalog and sometimes grouped with newer books about a similar topic or a similar genre.

One of the advantages I experienced with a small press is a quick turnaround. Vinspire asked to acquire the novel seven weeks after I submitted the full manuscript and published it within a year of finalizing the contract. What do you see as advantages of working with small presses?

FLOOD: Editorial time and attention is a key advantage. An editor at a small press has chosen your book because she felt a connection, an interest, a passion to work with your book for a year or more because she believed in your work.

Yes, faster turnaround is usually a plus, but not too fast. Quality of editing and design is more important than speed.

ATKINS: I see lots of advantages. You are dealing with a smaller group of people who are deeply committed to each title they publish. Things move more quickly, and I feel like I have great access to all levels of publishing, from my editor to the people in sales and marketing. I have a good understanding of how the process works, can ask questions, and feel like I've got a real and personal relationship with the people at the publisher. It all feels so much more human than I imagine working with a larger corporate publisher would feel.

MARTÍNEZ: I think you get a lot of creative freedom with small presses. When I published my first novel, I actually got an offer from an agent, too. I decided on Cinco Puntos because of the editorial attention I'd already gotten even in my initial rejection letters from them. They didn't try to change my voice to sell more books; it was really just about honing the story. Cinco Puntos made me feel very welcomed and like I was joining their family, and they believed in what I was trying to do.

Have you experienced any challenges or disadvantages by being published with a small press? How have you dealt with these issues?

ATKINS: Small presses have tight budgets, so that can be an issue. While planning the launch event for the Fred Korematsu book, we needed to think creatively about finding co-sponsors for keeping costs down. Small publishers don't necessarily have the same level of access to the marketplace and distribution channels. In my case, Heyday hasn't done a lot of work with the school and library market, so we are all doing our best on that front. Really, I think money and distribution are the main issues. Bookstores and other book sources may not be as familiar with the publisher. It can also be difficult for small publishers to get reviews from the mainstream journals, and get recognized with awards. That said, Heyday has a fantastic relationship with local publishers and other resources, which is the advantage of their primarily regional model.

MARTÍNEZ: I've never been published by a big press, so I'm not sure that I can compare in that way. However, with a small press, you will be doing a lot of your own marketing, and distribution might not be as wide as with a Big 5. If you want to see your small press book in bookstores, you're going to have to work hard yourself to make that happen. Small presses have limited staff and resources for promotion.

FLOOD: One challenge I've encountered is having a small press that has a small line of children's books understand the nuances/politics specific to children's and YA trade books. Reviews are important if libraries are going to purchase a book, especially nonfiction, and libraries (public and school) are the biggest/largest source of customers. This is less true for fiction, especially YA novels. Teens learn about great books to read from other teens, especially via teen blogs and social media.

Another huge challenge can happen if your editor leaves the company. This is devastating no matter what size the publisher, but with small houses, if one editor leaves, it may take months before another is hired. Yes, I've faced that challenge and I'm very happy to say that story had a happy ending—hurrah for Boyds Mills and *Warriors in the Crossfire*. Some authors don't like the small advances that are usually part of working with a small press. I prefer having a small advance, which is fulfilled, and thus the book is economically successful, which contributes to my track record as an author.

Authors published with large presses often complain of having little or no input on their cover art. What has the cover design process been like for your books? Have you been pleased with the results?

MARTÍNEZ: I had the exact opposite experience with my cover art. I was allowed to give substantial feedback and I was given the option of approval. Honestly, their designer did a great job. My niece is actually on the cover for my first book as the model for my character Chela, which is rather cool.

ATKINS: My co-author and I both had input not just on the cover art, but on the interior art in the book as well. The process was very collaborative. And yes, I am pleased with the results.

FLOOD: With each small press the design of the cover—and the title—has been a collaboration. I was asked by Charlesbridge to suggest Navajo artists. We were all excited when Shonto Begay, after reading the manuscript, agreed to create the cover for *Soldier Sister, Fly Home*. Boyds Mills sent three possible covers for *Warriors in the Crossfire* and asked for my comments. One cover highlighted an almost-naked sumo wrestler, which would have felt totally inappropriate! The editors had a good laugh at my reaction and agreed to design a different cover. *Water Runs Through This*

Book initially had a cover with a river raft nearly splashing off the page, an exciting image but not consistent with the tone of the book. We worked together to select a different picture. My experience has been that this collaboration between author and editor regarding the visual representation of a book's content has been positive for all involved. My bottom line—the editor and art director know best, but don't be afraid to offer your opinion!

I've heard of writers signing with small presses that turned out to be vanity presses or even scams, so I researched my publisher thoroughly. What advice do you have for writers and illustrators considering small presses?

MARTÍNEZ: I think the SCBWI handbook is a great resource (www.scbwi.org/online-resources/the-book). They list small publishers. I think if you have doubts about a publisher it's probably a good idea to look at their list and reach out to others they've published.

FLOOD: Look at their products—their books—carefully. What is the quality of editing, of illustrations, of overall layout and design? You want a reader to reach for your book because the cover is intriguing and attractive. When the reader opens your book, the first reaction should be "yes, this looks interesting." Go to the press's website. Is it professional, easy to navigate, easy to place an order? Look at recent publications. Are awards and recognitions listed? Does the publisher get copies of the books to important review sources? Choose a few of the publications and look for them on Amazon. Are they available? How are they selling? Are reviews and awards listed? For a book to succeed, no matter how good it is, librarians, teachers, and readers need to know about the book. Does the publisher market and distribute books effectively? Effective distribution and focused marketing mean your book thrives and your author wish comes true. A reader opens the cover to your book and begins reading, turning the pages, and steps into the world you have created, the story you have told.

ATKINS: It's all about doing your research. Read online, dig deep, and make sure the publisher is reputable. Most of the time, they shouldn't ask you for money, unless the business model is as a hybrid press (such as my impression of something like She Writes Press). See what other books they have published, and ask if you can contact other authors. If they don't want to put you in touch, that could be a red flag. Ask the publisher questions about how they produce and market books, with specifics to take you through the process. Don't be afraid to ask lots of questions. This should be a partnership, and if you even have a negative feeling in communication, think hard before committing to this relationship. Small presses can be your best friends, but you want to make sure it's a good match before committing!

WHAT ARE AGENTS REALLY LOOKING FOR?

Four literary agents who rep children's authors and illustrators explain what they're looking for in today's landscape.

....

Kerrie Flanagan

///

Earning a contract with a major publisher requires finding representation with a literary agent first. They are the gatekeepers. Your agent will be your advocate; she will want to see your book succeed as much as you do. She will help strengthen your manuscript before pitching it to editors, negotiate the contract with the publisher, act as a liaison between you and the editor, sell sub-rights (audio, dramatic, translation rights), and process the money due to you.

But what are agents really looking for? Four agents who represent children's literature, took time out of their busy day to share their insight and wisdom on queries, platform, what makes an engaging story, ideal clients, and writing for young audiences. By understanding what agents want to see in their submissions inbox and in their clients, you will have a better idea of how to approach them, and ultimately find representation.

MEET THE AGENTS

KELLY SONNACK (Andrea Brown Literary Agency) represents illustrators and writers for all age groups within children's literature: picture books, middle grade, chapter book, young adult, and graphic novels. Kelly is on the Advisory Board and faculty for UCSD's certificate in Writing and Illustrating for Children, and is a frequent speaker at conferences, including SCBWI's national and regional conferences, and can be found talking about all things children's books on Facebook (/agentsonnack) and Twitter (@KSonnack).

JOHN RUDOLPH's (Dystel, Goderich & Bourret LLC) list started out as mostly children's books, it has evolved to the point where it is now half adult, half children's authors—and he's looking to maintain that balance. On the children's side, John is keenly interested in middle-grade and young adult fiction and would love to find the next great picture book author/illustrator.

SARA MEGIBOW (KT Literary) is a literary agent with nine years of experience in publishing. Sara specializes in working with authors in middle grade, young adult, romance, erotica, science fiction, and fantasy. She represents *New York Times* best-selling authors, Roni Loren and Jason Hough, and international best-selling authors, Stefan Bachmann and Tiffany Reisz. Sara is LGBTQ-friendly and presents regularly at SCBWI and RWA events around the country. She tries to answer professional questions on twitter (@SaraMegibow) as time allows.

JENNIFER MARCH SOLOWAY (Andrea Brown Literary Agency) represents authors and illustrators of picture book, middle grade, and YA stories, and is actively building her list. For picture books, she is drawn to a wide range of stories from silly to sweet, but she always appreciates a strong dose of humor and some kind of surprise at the end. When it comes to middle grade, she likes all kinds of genres, including adventures, mysteries, spooky-but-not-too-scary ghost stories, humor, realistic contemporary, and fantasy. Jennifer regularly presents at writing conferences all over the country, including the San Francisco Writers Conference, the Northern Colorado Writers Conference, and regional SCBWI conferences. For her latest conference schedule, craft tips, and more, follow Jennifer on Twitter at @marchsoloway.

In a writer's world, once a manuscript is complete, writing a good query can be all-consuming, knowing it is the key to getting representation. But in your world, reading queries are a small part of how you spend your time. What catches your eyes when it comes to a query and what do you like to see in an effective query?

> **SONNACK:** I prefer my queries straightforward, simple, and professional. Tell me why you're querying me, what your book is about, and a little relevant information about

yourself. I never mind a compliment about something I've said that resonated with you or made you want to query me, or hearing about a client's book that you loved (if it's honest; I can smell a fake claim a mile away). Don't go overboard; think of this as a job application. And always follow the directions on the agent's website!

RUDOLPH: Professionalism. When I started out in publishing, I was taught to think of queries like a job application to work at a bank: If the manuscript is your résumé, the query letter is your cover letter. And just as you wouldn't try to be overly clever or silly when you apply for a bank job, your query should be equally serious, straightforward, and brief. If it helps, all I'm really looking for is a brief introduction stating genre and length, a one or two paragraph description of the work, and any relevant writing credits the author might have. No need to add any whistles or bells!

MEGIBOW: In short, a query catches my eye when it is well-written and succinctly describes an interesting story. To move from query to full manuscript to an offer of representation, I'm looking for submissions that I love and think I can sell.

However, let's back up a bit. You said "knowing it is the key to getting representation" and I want to clarify something—the query isn't the key to getting representation. The manuscript itself is the key to getting representation and (hopefully) a book deal. It may sound crazy, but in my 11-plus years' experience, I've found that a strong query accurately represents a strong manuscript. So, before jumping into the query slush pile, write, edit, polish, re-read, re-edit, and re-polish that manuscript!

So, how do we write an effective query? First, write a one-sentence description of your book—the pitch—and really nail it! This is the elevator pitch—the short, high-level description of your story, as you would explain it to a reader who is considering buying your book. Second, write a one paragraph description of the book and make that paragraph sound just like the back cover of a novel. That's it! A strong pitch plus an engaging paragraph of description is what makes an effective query.

Our website hosts a series of blog posts called "About My Query" in which our literary agents read and critique query letters (*with* the authors' permission). Read this blog: www.ktliterary.com/category/ask-daphne/about-my-query. Also, check out the Writer's Digest Successful Queries posts on the Guide to Literary Agents blog: (www.writersdigest.com/editor-blogs/guide-to-literary-agents/successful-queries), as well as the info on Query Shark (www.queryshark.blogspot.com). These resources are excellent for helping a writer see what works and what doesn't work in a query letter.

SOLOWAY: Because we receive so many submissions, unfortunately, we don't have that much time to spend on each one. We only get to see a small sample of the work, and we have to make a decision fast. Our submission guidelines ask for a query letter with a short pitch about the project and the first ten pages of a manuscript—or the complete text of a picture book. I personally am most interested in the writing and will often read the pages first before I read the query letter.

I find the projects that capture my interest have at least three of the following traits:

- A strong, engaging voice.
- An intriguing premise that somehow feels different from anything else I've seen.
- A dynamic opening scene filled with drama that has enough context to immediately ground me in the world and suck me into the story.
- An irresistible character with high stakes and agency.
- An additional story thread that is also compelling.

The best ones have all of the above!

However, I do think it's important to be able to pitch a project. I've found the best pitches raise a question in my mind (or better yet, two or three questions), the kind of question that is so intriguing, I just have to know the answer—so much so, that I will request the manuscript right away and stay up reading until three in the morning to find out what happens!

Let's say a writer has written a great query and you request the full manuscript. What typically keeps you reading and what is something that will stop you right away?

SONNACK: A great premise will keep me reading because I want to see where it goes. I start reading a manuscript wanting to love it and I read until I lose interest. Sometimes that's because I'm not connecting to a character. Sometimes it's because the stakes aren't high enough. Sometimes it's because the premise doesn't feel original or unique enough for today's market.

RUDOLPH: I don't think there's any one poison pill that will make me stop. Often, it's either a weak voice, a misunderstanding of the proposed genre, a plot that takes too long to get off the ground, or any and all combinations thereof—but it could also be something totally arbitrary, which is why I don't discourage multiple submissions. What keeps me reading? A good story well told.

MEGIBOW: I'm looking for a full manuscript that demonstrates superior craft. Yes, that's a tall order but (to reassure you all), the vast majority of my clients came to me via the query slush pile with a great query and superior manuscript. So, write and query—you're in great company!

Let's break it down a bit though. In a full manuscript, I want to see superior writing and a compelling story. I evaluate manuscripts by looking for strong characters, authentic narrative voice, organic world building, engaging conflict, compelling backstory, and an exciting plot. Typically, I stop reading if the manuscript starts to feel generic or the writing becomes less polished.

Need some examples? Check out the Books page on the KT Literary website: www.ktliterary.com/books. I'd point to any of these books and say, "here is an example of superior craft."

It can be hard to tell when your book is polished enough to keep an agent reading. My best suggestion is to read widely in the genre you're writing. Read recent titles (published in the past two years), especially by debut authors. Read books published by major publishing houses and ones that have won awards. Read widely and keep writing!

SOLOWAY: I love a good story, and if a project has a great hook—something that raises a question that I find compelling, I must read on—chances are I will read the entire manuscript. Most of the manuscripts I see have great potential, but those same drafts tend to be too raw and in need of more work. In those cases, I can tell the author is still writing to discover, or if they have discovered the end, they have yet to rework the beginning and middle.

Similarly, I find that many authors write for story but gloss over thoughts, feelings, and emotional depth in order to pursue the action, and I will find myself wondering how the character feels or thinks about a turn of events or other character. Those layers are often missing from the early draft, and it's those layers that make a good story great, or make an interesting character fascinating.

That's not to say the submission needs to be perfect, but it needs to be revised and reworked enough for me to help the author ready and polish the work for an editor. I am looking for projects that I feel I can provide value editorially and champion. I also want to feel a deep connection with the story, the characters, and the writing.

If I have trouble connecting with the character or the story, I will likely stop reading and pass. Rejections are the worst part of my job. I love writers, and I truly want everyone to achieve.

What is the biggest mistake adult writers make when writing for young audiences (up through middle grade)?

SONNACK: Sounding like they've been listening in on their kids' conversations. It's really obvious when a writer approaches a story because they want to teach their kids a lesson versus really remembering what it was like to be that age and writing from a kid's perspective.

RUDOLPH: Likewise, misunderstanding the proposed genre. For picture books, that could mean a text that's way too long, vocabulary and sentence structure way above age level, or adult characters without any kid appeal. Chapter books and middle grade are more flexible, but I still turn down a lot of those projects where the voice and characters are too advanced—or too young.

MEGIBOW: Great question! In my opinion, the biggest mistake adult writers make when writing for young readers is they use a narrative voice that sounds like an adult writing for a child. Young readers demand authentic books! Some adult writers "talk down" to young audiences by using silly language or by not fleshing out complex conflicts or characters. Avoid these mistakes! Write complex characters, real conflict, and always use an authentic voice.

SOLOWAY: Crafting a voice that sounds adult instead of having the perspective of a child.

There is lots of talk at conferences and in writing magazines about platform. How important is it to you that a writer has an established platform?

SONNACK: Platform is something that means a lot more for the adult nonfiction market where readers are looking for advice/information from an established source (say, you want a book about finance—you're probably going to want to buy a book written by someone who has some expertise in that field). In nonfiction for kids, this can be important too, but for kids' fiction, your readers don't really care who you are. This really only comes into play when an author has been successful and established a fan base. At that point, the child reader may follow the writer and want to read their next book(s).

Instead of platform, I like to see market awareness and engagement with the kid lit community. These things indicate that a prospective writer is more prepared for a career as a writer/illustrator. And that they're giving back and participating in the community we hope will support them once they publish.

RUDOLPH: I don't think platform is as important in children's books, or at least not at the point when I sign a client. I do like to see authors engage with the world, whether through social media, being a member of SCBWI, or writing in other genres. But that's very much secondary to the quality of the work. Once a client is signed, though, I do ask them to work on all of those things, and continue that work once their book is sold.

MEGIBOW: For a debut fiction writer, I'm not worried about platform at the point I read a query letter. Some writers query with no platform at all and some come to the slush pile with an extensive social media campaign already in place. Both of these writers' manuscripts will be reviewed equally. If a writer has an author website at the point they submit, I like to see that in the query letter—but it's not a deal-maker or a deal-breaker. If we go on to work together, there is time to build platform and branding after we get a book deal.

A smart platform is important to have in place once the publishing house starts shopping a novel to its retailers and once the agent starts shopping subsidiary rights, but that platform should be tailored to the author's personality and the genre in which they write. These are things that can be done after the query phase.

SOLOWAY: For me, a platform is less important than the quality of the writing and story, but good platforms never hurt!

What characteristics make up your ideal client?

SONNACK: Professional, creative, aware, kind, thoughtful, keyed in to the kid lit community, and in it for the long haul.

RUDOLPH: Optimism, patience, flexibility, and reasonable expectations. A good sense of humor doesn't hurt, either.

MEGIBOW: My clients are all amazing! They differ tremendously in personality and that's natural—I am honored to work for each and every one of them.

I represent introverts (lots of them!) and extroverts (a couple of them). I represent authors who write slowly and authors who write very, very quickly. I represent debut authors and experienced, multi-published authors and everything in between.

In general, when I offer representation to a writer they usually say, "I want to write a lot of books and keep writing for a long time." In my experience there are two characteristics that help authors survive for a long time in this competitive, crazy, unpredictable business. Those two characteristics are patience and discipline. Many successful authors have the patience to put up with publishing's ups and downs and the discipline to keep writing. But, those characteristics are not deal-breakers or deal-makers. At the end of the day I'm looking in the slush pile for incredible books that I fall head-over-heels in love with and think I can sell.

SOLOWAY: I am very editorial with my clients. I am looking for authors and illustrators who are open to revision and willing to put in the work necessary to make the project the best it can be. My style is detailed and encouraging; I don't like to be harsh or blunt. I see myself as their cheerleader and champion of their work. So I am looking for someone who appreciates that style and wants to work with me. I like to be transparent with my clients, and I hope they will do the same with me.

Because picture books are short, some writers think they are easy to write. What is the biggest mistake writers make when writing for this market and what makes a great picture book?

SONNACK: I think they're one of the hardest forms to execute, especially for new writers. Many writers don't take the time to explore the current landscape of picture books and what is succeeding today (which is quite different than when they were a picture book reader). They also often think the illustrations need to be a part of the submission package (which isn't true; the publisher usually selects an illustrator once they purchase the text). I also see a lot of manuscripts that aren't full stories (with a beginning, middle, and end, including conflict and resolution), or that aren't doing anything special with the writing.

RUDOLPH: I don't know if this is the biggest mistake, but not telling a story is up there. I get a ton of picture book manuscripts that aren't stories—they're glorified lists or concept books or poems—and I pass on almost all of them. Want to write a great picture book? Tell a great story!

SOLOWAY: The best picture books have wonderful language at the line level that is fun to read aloud, a full story arc, a full character arc, an additional story thread, and an unexpected twist at the end that is either funny or sweet or both—and all of that needs to happen in 500 words or less. It's quite a task, and the people who write great picture books are masters at their craft!

BREAKING INTO NONFICTION

A roundup of children's writers, who write primarily nonfiction, talk about breaking into their respective market.

....

Nancy Parish

//

Whether it's learning about moments in history, exploring the lives of famous people, or finding out how scientists spend their days, reading nonfiction literature is an important part of children's lives. We've gathered together three successful nonfiction writers to learn more about what it's like writing in this research-driven category.

MEET THE AUTHORS

BRANDON MILLER: Brandon was a stay-at-home mom with a history degree from Purdue University when she got her start writing for a history-themed magazine, *Cobblestone*. Her first article was accepted and later published for the magazine. Then an editor for *Cobblestone* passed her name on to an editor at Lerner Publishing. Lerner was about to start a new book series titled People's History and was looking for projects. Brandon submitted a query, wrote an outline and sample chapter, and that led to her first book, *Buffalo Gals: Women of the Old West*. Brandon has published nine more books since then with at least one more on the way. Her books have been honored by the International Reading Association (IRA), The National Council for Social Studies, Voices of Youth Advocates (VOYA), and the Junior Library Guild. She blogs at: www.hands-on-books.blogspot.com.

KERRIE LOGAN HOLLIHAN: When her children were grown, Kerrie wrote a middle-grade biography of Percy Lavon Julian, an African American chemist who synthesized cortisone from soybeans. She joined the Cincinnati SCBWI group in hopes of learning how to get that book published. While that book is still in a drawer, she forged some valuable friendships with the other SCBWI members. Two such members, Brandon Miller and Mary Kay Carson put her in touch with their editor at Chicago Review Press. He was looking for a biography of Isaac Newton—a subject Kerrie happened to be researching at the time. Six books have followed with one more in production. Her books have been honored by VOYA, *Smithsonian Magazine*, The Junior Library Guild, the Children's Book Council, and the National Council for the Social Studies. She blogs at: www.hands-on-books.blogspot.com.

MARY KAY CARSON: Armed with a biology degree from the University of Kansas, Mary Kay worked in the Peace Corp, as a fisheries observer in Alaska, and has taught ESL in Spain and in Kansas. After studying science writing in New York, she landed a job with Scholastic's science magazine, *SuperScience*. Within the first few months, she interviewed scientists, wrote and sketched out a four-paneled cartoon that explained center of mass, and helped choose photos to accompany a feature article. The creativity of the job hooked her for writing for kids. She eventually moved onto freelancing and has written more than fifty books for kids about wildlife, space, weather, nature, and other science and history topics. Her book, *Exploring the Solar System*, won the American Institute of Aeronautics and Astronautics 2009 Children's Literature Award. Other honors include: 2015 Ohioana Book Award Finalist for *PARK SCIENTISTS: Gila Monsters, Geysers*, and *Grizzly Bears in America's Own Backyard* and ALA Notable book for *The Bat Scientist*. She blogs at: www.hands-on-books.blogspot.com.

When starting a new project, how do you approach your research?

MILLER: I usually start with the big picture, reading adult books on my topic. I use the bibliographies and source notes in those books to find new resources. After I have a good handle on things, I narrow down my research, looking at individual topics in more depth that are part of the "whole pie." I look at scholarly journals online and use collections of digitized primary sources from libraries, historic societies, national historic parks, and universities. I use my computer to take virtual tours. If possible, I travel to sites to see things for myself, and you also find great books and other resources to buy! But I only travel after doing enough research that I can ask the right questions and have a sense of knowing what I'm seeing.

HOLLIHAN: For biographies, I begin by reading several adult bios to gain a sense of both my subjects' lives and how history has regarded him or her. Then I narrow my focus and read more about specific events and people that I will include in my own book. For fact checking, I maintain a subscription to Britannica.com. I cannot emphasize enough how much Internet research makes my work so much easier—when I first wrote my college senior thesis, I had to order a full, Xeroxed copy of a book I needed because it couldn't leave its home library!

My WIP is a middle-grade book about mummies, heavy in content but light in tone. Again I started with adult books on the subject that range from Howard Carter's memoir about his discovery of King Tut to fairly recent books that focus on other mummy discoveries. From there I moved to both academic and popular journals and magazines, because scientific research underscores so much of modern mummy study. I also contact experts in the field—sometimes a few questions, sometimes more in depth.

CARSON: If it's an assigned book, like *What Sank the World's Biggest Ship?*, then I often start by checking out kid books from the library on that topic (i.e. the Titanic). Going through them really helps me recognize what's been done to death, what's been done poorly, and what could be done even better. Then I can draft a working outline before digging into primary sources. Things change, of course, as I research and stumble on awesome tidbits or come up against contested facts.

Research is different with longer, in-depth books, like the Scientists in the Field books—*Mission to Pluto*, for example. These are books about people working and are organized around in-person interviews done while tagging along on a storm chase or rhino ultrasound. I usually don't have any sort of structure before I start spending time with the scientist(s). I do prepare for the interviews by reading what the scientists have written or what's been written about them, as well as general reading on the topic. But the scientists themselves are the primary sources.

What's your most useful writing tool?

MILLER: Besides my reading glasses? My computer—I research, write, and revise on the computer and couldn't do without it. Also, my main revisions are always done on paper with pencil—still great tools. I use a camera if I travel for research and take photos of every little detail. And I always carry a notebook when I travel to write everything down—facts, impressions of places, names of people I want to contact.

HOLLIHAN: There are two: Evernote and Microsoft OneNote. I like both. Evernote is a quick app that clips my Internet research into files that I set up as I research a book. I especially like Evernote for dictation. As I read books, I dictate notes and page numbers and [note] if a passage is a direct quote. Having both is a great help when I go back to find a direct quote. If I happen to come up with a fresh idea, then I also dictate that into a note—this helps me keep straight when I'm quoting a source, paraphrasing it, or making my own statement.

OneNote is very useful for storing research. I set up folders by subject or chapter, depending on my WIP. I clip bits and pieces of information from web pages into separate sub files in each folder. Then I go back and highlight what's useful. I sometimes write in OneNote and then transfer the info into my draft document.

CARSON: The Internet! I'm not someone who wants to go write in a cabin in the woods. I need access to lots of information when I write. And while lots of my research involves books, notes, interview transcripts, etc., I often don't necessarily know everything that I'm going to need until I'm writing. Being able to access a YouTube video explaining electromagnetism, an online graphic thesaurus, or make a Google search for something vague can really help me get unstuck. Of course, you have to be ever vigilant against all the distraction online. I pretty much work in Word, though I've used Scrivener for the past few Scientists in the Field books. It's especially handy for keeping track of citations, etc.

What surprised you the most about writing for kids?

MILLER: The publishing industry can be harsh, difficult to break into, and even more difficult to earn a living as a writer. But, I've met so many wonderful, kind, and supportive people in the kidlit universe—writers, editors, agents. I also love how much truth you can give kids without adding sugary sweetness or watered down information. Give them facts, give them stories, encourage them, and hopefully inspire them.

HOLLIHAN: Two things, I'd never read much juvenile nonfiction until I got into writing it. It's extraordinary how the best authors capture the essence of people and the past and distill that into a readable text.

So much research goes into one 35- to 40,000 word book! I tell people all the time that one of my books is like an iceberg: ten percent book floating on top with 90 percent research supporting it.

CARSON: How even though you're writing about history or science, editors don't seem to care if you're a historian or a scientist! And it's okay to be a generalist. You're judged as a writer based on what you've written. That's it. My friends who are science writers for adults need to specialize to build credibility. I'm often juggling projects about very different things at the same time. Right now, it's a rework of an Alexander

Graham Bell biography, a middle grade book about a tornado scientist who tweets as @Tornatrix, and a folk tale picture book about wolves.

How did you develop your platform as a writer?

MILLER: I think my platform, such as it is, has developed over time as I've gained experience and published more books. It has been about building relationships, even forging friendships, both in person and via social media. It is something I can always improve upon. I don't (as of now) have a newsletter, for instance, which is recommended. I have a website, and I'm on FB and Twitter. I enjoy FB, but I'm not as fond of Twitter. I know that new social mediums appear all the time. The three of us share a blog, Hands-On-Books, where we offer interesting posts about science and history with activities. But I don't sweat about my number of followers or how many likes I get. Platform is a tricky thing and you can't just go by numbers. How many people will really buy your book without that personal relationship?

HOLLIHAN: Hmm … social media arose just as I joined the nonfiction kid lit world. We hear "platform, platform, platform" all the time. Sure, having a platform is a necessary part of authoring these days. I use Twitter to promote my books when current events relate to them, but I try to be careful to provide stuff that's "useful" or amusing, rather than hard-selling. I do a bit with Facebook, as well. All of that said, I try to promote myself as "an author who writes library books for kids." That's how I explain what I do. Some of my books have adult crossover, so I also place myself as a speaker for groups of older adults.

I'd caution someone starting out in this field not to worry much about platform. Writing is what matters. Start small—get published in something local—get into a critique group and network when you can.

CARSON: I'm not really sure I have one, but I think it's mostly through subject matter. I've written a *bunch* of books about space, I keep in contact with those I've interviewed, stay up on what's going on in space science, share what's cool to me to social media, and give school visit presentations about the solar system. *Ding!* A platform. Same thing for bats and rhinos and the Wright brothers. …

What's your best advice for writers wanting to write nonfiction for kids?

MILLER: It's still a story, but it all has to be true and verified. So dig in and take your time to do the research—you never know what you'll find. Look for details, but don't forget the big picture. Develop interesting back matter for the book—here you can tell more of the story, or what happened afterwards, or explain something in more detail. Also, a pet peeve of mine—*do not make up* dialogue for historical persons.

HOLLIHAN: Find what interests you and go for it! Read widely. If your topic is controversial, read up on both sides of the argument. Read old books and newer ones—views change over time and space. Talk to people. Read what's hot on the market in kids' nonfiction—you can find out by reading *School Library Journal*, *Publishers Weekly*, and so on. Join a critique group—you'll learn a ton and make some great friends, too. Get on list-serves: NFforKids on Yahoo is a good one. Join SCBWI and attend conferences. And study this very book!

CARSON: Writing for articles and educational publishers is a great way to gain experience and hone skills writing for different reading levels, doing research, and meeting deadlines. Much of nonfiction is published in series, so you can look at series and find topics not yet written about and then pitch them to the editor. Trade nonfiction is trickier and requires a hook of some sort—a unique twist, different angle, newsworthiness. Spend time reading, dissecting, and reverse-engineering the kinds of books you'd like to write.

Final thoughts?

MILLER: History books for kids are so much more inclusive than when I was growing up. And the books have great appeal with fantastic design and illustrations—which can be created by artists or with period photographs, paintings and maps. Kid books have back matter, source notes, bibliographies, and indexes. Adult readers can enjoy these books, too, just because the research and quality is so high. It's a great time to be writing history!

HOLLIHAN: Nonfiction is under-appreciated in today's popular culture where it seems that every editor is awaiting the next Harry Potter or *Hunger Games* to land on her desk. But in my view, a well-written and imaged work of nonfiction is a work of art. I write for children—and adults—who want to learn more about something that interests them. Or to interest them in something new. I figure that if my books launch my readers into further exploration of a topic, then I've done my job. And I love my job!

CARSON: Children's book publishing is a hard business—and getting harder in my opinion. Not only to break in, but to keep going even after being traditionally published. So be honest with yourself! Make sure you know why you want to do it, set specific goals, start ticking them off. If you don't need to make money and have a passion for writing about elephants, then follow that passion wherever it goes! If you want to make a living as a writer, then cultivate a balance of projects—some for money and others for love. If being a rich and famous author is your motivation, write YA fiction instead!

NANCY PARISH is a Cincinnati-based freelance writer and the founder of the Cincinnati SCBWI group. Her column, "Footnotes," appeared on the Guide to Literary Agents blog for several years. Her writing has also appeared in *Snatch Magazine* and *Children's Writer's & Illustrator's Market*. She is currently working on a young adult novel. When she is not working or writing, she is teaching her cats to fetch their own toys.

DEBUT AUTHORS TELL ALL

Learn how 21 first-time authors got published.

compiled by Cris Freese

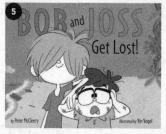

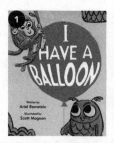

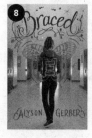

PICTURE BOOKS

1 Ariel Bernstein

ARIELBERNSTEINBOOKS.COM

I Have a Balloon (September 2017, Paula Wiseman Books, illustrations by Scott Magoon)

QUICK TAKE: When Monkey sees Owl's shiny red balloon, he offers to trade everything he has, including his sock. But when Owl points out that Monkey's sock has a star and a perfectly shaped hole, Monkey has a pretty tough decision to make. **WRITES FROM:** I grew up outside of Philadelphia, and I currently live in Northern New Jersey. **PRE-BOOK:** I was a stay-at-home mom when I started writing children's books. **TIME FRAME:** I first thought of the idea for my book during the 2015 SCBWI Winter Conference in New York. A couple days later, I sat down and wrote the story. Revisions usually take me a few months, but this story was ready after a couple weeks. **ENTER THE AGENT:** I submitted my story to Mary Cummings at Betsy Amster Literary Agency by email, so I was found in the slush pile. We talked on the phone and I really liked the editorial feedback she gave me. I've been signed with Mary for about two years now and it's been great working with her. **BIG-GEST SURPRISE:** The biggest surprise is how different each book deal is. I've learned from my own book deals (one for the picture book, one for my chapter book series) with two different publishers, and from hearing what book deals have been like for other authors of children's books. Sometimes the process can be relatively smooth, but there can be plenty of unexpected delays and hiccups along the way. Publishing requires a never-ending supply of patience! **WHAT I DID RIGHT:** I don't think every author or illustrator needs to attend a conference, but I know that attending the 2015 Winter SCBWI Conference is what pushed me in the right direction. Hearing from agents, editors, and published authors gave me a ton of insight into the current publishing world. I came out of the conference feeling much more informed, energized, and confident about where to go with my writing. What I'm doing right today is that I work with a wonderful critique group that helps me improve each manuscript over many, many revisions. **WHAT I WISH I WOULD HAVE DONE DIFFERENTLY:** I would have found critique partners right away. I spent too much time in the beginning trying to revise on my own. **PLATFORM:** I can be found at www.ArielBernsteinBooks.com and on Twitter at @ArielBBooks. I'm also a member of Picture The Books, a group of 2017 debut authors and illustrators (@PictureTheBooks, www.PictureTheBooks.com). **ADVICE FOR WRITERS:** Criticism can be hard to hear, but seriously taking in constructive feedback is one of the best ways to improve your manuscript. **NEXT UP:** I'm currently working on picture book manuscripts and a new chapter book.

② Rebecca Green

REBECCAGREENILLUSTRATION.COM

How To Make Friends With A Ghost (September 2017, Tundra Books)

QUICK TAKE: A whimsical guide to ghost care and supernatural friendships, this book celebrates the sweet bond between a young girl, Bellis, and her new ghost friend. **WRITES FROM:** Nashville, TN. **PRE-BOOK:** I'm a full-time illustrator for children's and young adult books. **TIME FRAME:** I wrote and illustrated the first draft as a personal project in the fall of 2015 and printed 125 "dummy" books to sell. I also posted the content online and the book was picked up by my publisher shortly after. Once I began working with the editor, there were many changes, extensions and revisions to the book. It took two years to complete from the spark of the initial idea to the publishing date. **ENTER THE AGENT:** I'm represented by Nicole Tugeau of Tugeau2 Agency, which represents illustrators and illustrator/authors. We connected about five years ago when one of her artists recommended me. My work was not ready for the children's market at the time as I was focusing on gallery and editorial work. We stayed in touch for the next couple of years and once I settled on publishing and prepared my portfolio, we spoke again and signed on to work together. It's been a tremendous experience—I don't know what I'd do without her! **BIGGEST SURPRISE:** Since my work is generally compulsive, it was surprising to me how many drafts have to be edited again and again. Even for this particular book, which has minimal text, there were endless suggestions, edits, and improvements to polish the final product. I feel extremely lucky to be working with the entire team at Tundra—they've helped me push this book to its full potential. It's been eye opening just how many people it takes to bring a book to fruition. **WHAT I DID RIGHT:** My intention was true. I did not set out to write a book, much less think of myself as an author. My goal wasn't to get a book published. Instead, my only desire in the beginning was to capture this little story that celebrates Autumn and friendship. Had the process ended after the initial dummy books had been made, I would have been content (not to say I'm not beyond thrilled that it's a published book!). Now that I'm dreaming of my next picture book, I am conscious of not creating a book for publishing's sake, but I'm waiting for that intuitive spark, where I have to tell a story. **WHAT I WISH I WOULD HAVE DONE DIFFERENTLY:** After any large project is done, I always want to redo the illustrations! By the end of the project, I've discovered so much about the process of the artwork, that I always have an itch to recreate the whole thing so I can use what I've learned on each piece. **PLATFORM:** The majority of the time, I use Instagram as my main platform. I think it's unique because it appeals to different industries and different ages. **ADVICE FOR WRITERS:** While I would not consider myself a writer per se, I am a storyteller. My advice regarding narrative work is that you should tell stories that burn you up inside if you don't tell them. Also, instead of focusing on the goal of getting a book—any book—published, the goal should be to tell your story honestly amidst vulnerability. When your strong, unique voice shines though, people will notice and will want to emotionally invest in your world. **NEXT UP:** I'm currently working on an illustrated novel, which is extremely intimidating given that I'm not a writer. As a storyteller though, I have a story that I have to tell, so I'm working bit by bit on an attempt to put a longer book together. The progress has been quite slow due to the fact that I spend the majority of my time illustrating and painting.

3 Andrea J Loney

ANDREAJLONEY.COM

Bunnybear (January 2017, Albert Whitman & Company, illustrated by Carmen Saldaña)

Take a Picture of Me, James VanDerZee! (May 2017, Lee & Low Books, illustrated by Keith Mallett)

QUICK TAKE: *Take a Picture of Me, James VanDerZee!* is a picture book biography about a famous black photographer of the Harlem Renaissance who used innovative photo retouching techniques to photograph the black middle class. *Bunnybear* is about a bear who believes in his heart that he is actually a bunny. The bears don't believe him and the bunnies won't accept him, but everything changes when he finds a special friend who adores him just the way he is. **WRITES FROM:** Inglewood, CA. **PRE-BOOK:** Before I wrote for children, I worked in film and television. I wrote for the *Chicken Soup for the Soul* television series and for other shows and movies. I also performed stand-up comedy, and worked on captions and subtitles for feature films. **TIME FRAME:** While I'd loved James VanDerZee's photos since I was a child, it took me about 11 years of research before I finally summoned the courage to write his story. Once I started, it took about two months and 12 drafts to complete the draft that won the 2014 Lee & Low Books New Voices Award. The idea for Bunnybear arrived while brainstorming with a friend in December of 2013, but I didn't write it until October of 2014. It took about six months and eight drafts to complete the version that my agent sold to Albert Whitman & Company in September 2015. **ENTER THE AGENT:** I actually met my agent, Jill Corcoran, at a local writers' event, but was far too shy to actually speak to her. Months later, in March 2015, I sent *Bunnybear* to her through an online writing program—the 12x12 Challenge—where we wrote 12 picture books a month and submitted a manuscript to one agent each month. Jill loved *Bunnybear* so much that she asked to see my other work, so I sent her five more manuscripts. **BIGGEST SURPRISE:** I had no idea that my debut book would sell without an agent and would eventually become my second debut book. I was also surprised that both book publication dates were pushed to 2017, although it has definitely been worth the wait. I was especially surprised to learn that it can take over two years to publish a picture book. **WHAT I DID RIGHT:** I am so grateful to have joined the Society of Children's Book Writers and Illustrators (SCBWI), as well as some other organizations for children's authors. Getting information and feedback from working professionals, sharing my work with critique groups, and immersing myself in the kid lit world made all the difference for me. **WHAT I WISH I WOULD HAVE DONE DIFFERENTLY:** When I first tried to write children's books, I became overwhelmed by rejection, isolation, and lack of confidence. I wish I'd joined SCBWI sooner. **PLATFORM:** You can find me @andreajloney on Twitter, Instagram, Pinterest, and Author Andrea J Loney on Facebook. **ADVICE FOR WRITERS:** Write as much as you can, read as much as you can, join a critique group, submit your very best work, and keep going until someone says "Yes!" **NEXT UP:** My next picture book, *Double Bass Blues*, illustrated by Rudy Gutierrez, will be published by Knopf in 2017. And I'm always working on more stories.

4 Mike Malbrough

MIKEMALBROUGH.COM

Marigold Bakes A Cake (July 2017, Philomel Books)

QUICK TAKE: A fastidious, excitable cat who loves to bake is driven to distraction by some busybody birds. **WRITES FROM:** Orange, NJ. **PRE-BOOK:** I freelanced as an illustrator and graphic designer for many years. I was a teacher and created silly puppet shows for children. **TIME FRAME:** Super-fast! I created Marigold the Cat for my portfolio in January of 2016. I wrote and revised the script over the next few months. I took a dummy of *Marigold Bakes a Cake* to a conference in April of that year. An art director at the conference liked the book and took it back to her publisher. By the end of spring I was offered a book deal and before the end of 2017, I had turned in the final art. A total whirlwind! **ENTER THE AGENT:** I was introduced to my agent through a friend who had recently signed with her. She liked my work, which opened the door to possible future representation. From there I cultivated a relationship with her by checking in every few months, asking questions and sharing my work. I made a checklist of all of the steps that she suggested I take and kept her informed of my progress. Eventually, about a year and a half later, I officially sought representation and she said yes! That agent is Lori Kilkelly at Rodeen Literary Management. **BIGGEST SURPRISE:** I have been surprised by how much is up to me. Trying to find an agent/publisher can feel very reactionary. You have to figure out what they are looking for. You can't be too precious about your work. You have to be flexible and adaptive. Then, suddenly, you have an agent, or a deal, and the buck stops with you. It's your book, your career. **WHAT I DID RIGHT:** Having a long career in the creative arts has been a huge help. I have had my work rejected so many times in the past in fields nowhere near as supportive and collaborative as the Children's Literary Market. I also think that building good relationships from face-to-face introductions has served well. **WHAT I WISH I WOULD HAVE DONE DIFFERENTLY:** I wish I would have met the fine people in this industry much earlier in my career. I would have more hair left … I think. **PLATFORM:** I am on Facebook, Instagram, and Twitter. I treat those spaces like other relationships, professional or otherwise. Play nice, listen to others, and don't always talk about yourself. **ADVICE FOR WRITERS:** Big Picture: Jog. Don't sprint. Find a pace that you can sustain and keep a level head. Write consistently. Send out your work and grow from feedback. A practical picture book tidbit: As an author/illustrator I can submit my books in dummy form. This gives me more control over pacing and page turns, and I can demonstrate the thought put into these important reading elements. Writers who are submitting manuscripts should consider how they choose line breaks in a similar way. **NEXT UP:** I am currently writing and illustrating the sequel to *Marigold Bakes a Cake* with Philomel. Look for it in Summer 2018. I am also illustrating a chapter book series called Warren and Dragon written by Ariel Bernstein, published by Viking. The first two books will be released in 2018!

⑤ Peter McCleery
PETERMCCLEERY.COM
Bob and Joss Get Lost! (February 2017, HarperCollins, illustrated by Vin Vogel)

QUICK TAKE: *Bob and Joss Get Lost!* is a fun, comical escapade where two best friends get more excitement than they bargained for when they are shipwrecked on what may or may not be a deserted island. **WRITES FROM:** Portland, OR. **PRE-BOOK:** Before I became a writer I had many different creative pursuits. I studied architecture and then later got an MFA in sculpture. I was a conceptual installation artist for a while. After that I worked in advertising as a copywriter. I was all over the map, literally and figuratively. Then I started writing children's books and it just clicked. **TIME FRAME:** The first draft of this book came rather quickly. The characters and their dialogue poured out of me in about one morning. I ended up putting it in a drawer for years but pulled it out one day and started revising it over the course of a few weeks. **ENTER THE AGENT:** At the moment I'm not represented by anyone, since my first agent left the agenting side of the business. Which proves you never know what will happen! But I originally got my agent through the slush pile. It does happen! I submitted. She liked it. We talked. Contracts were signed. **BIGGEST SURPRISE:** Every step of the process has new challenges. You think once I get "this" or "that," maybe it's an agent or a book contract, whatever, the rest will be easy. Nope. There is always something new to learn, or another challenge. But also many new and unexpected rewards. It works both ways. You never know what's ahead! **WHAT I DID RIGHT:** I think I was patient and knew that I should only submit my very best work. My approach was if I focused on learning the craft and finding my unique voice the rest will take care of itself. **WHAT I WISH I WOULD HAVE DONE DIF-FERENTLY:** I probably would trust myself more. I perhaps shelved the first draft of this book for too long because I thought it wasn't what agents and editors were looking for. That was the wrong instinct. **PLATFORM:** I'm currently on Twitter, Facebook, Instagram, and I have a website. But, honestly, I have no idea what I'm doing. **ADVICE FOR WRITERS:** People want unique and new things. So be unique and new; which translated means, write the thing that you want to read. Be true to yourself. **NEXT UP:** I have several picture books in the works. And I also hope to get some middle grade and graphic novel ideas onto bookshelves.

6 Annie Silvestro

ANNIESILVESTRO.COM

Bunny's Book Club (February 2017, Doubleday Books for Young Readers, illustrated by Tatjana Mai-Wyss)

QUICK TAKE: *Bunny's Book Club* tells the story of a book-loving bunny who sneaks books from the library and shares them with his forest friends. Join Bunny on an adventure that celebrates the power of books, libraries, and the one-of-a-kind magic of reading. **WRITES FROM:** Rumson, NJ. **PRE-BOOK:** Before I began writing I worked as an Assistant Editor at *Harper's Bazaar, Talk,* and *Allure* magazines. **TIME FRAME:** I joined the SCBWI in 2009 and started writing in earnest soon after my first conference. I wrote *Bunny's Book Club* in 2013. It sold in 2014, and was published in 2017. **ENTER THE AGENT:** I am represented by Liza Voges of Eden Street LLC. We met at a New Jersey SCBWI event in November of 2013. We hit it off at dinner, and when I told her what I was working on, she asked me to send her the manuscripts. I happily signed with her soon after. **BIGGEST SURPRISE:** The biggest surprise about the process has been how differently each publishing house works. I've learned something new each time. The absolute best surprise, though, has been seeing the art in process. It's an amazing feeling to see each character come to life in ways

I could never have imagined! **WHAT I DID RIGHT:** Getting involved with the SCBWI was the best thing I ever did. It led me to a network of people who have been invaluable in every step of the process. Making like-minded friends, attending conferences, joining a critique group, volunteering—all of it has helped me immeasurably. **WHAT I WISH I WOULD HAVE DONE DIFFERENTLY:** In the very beginning I definitely rushed too much. I wrote two stories and sent them out before they were ready, before I was ready. It's all part of the learning process but I wish I had had more stories under my belt before I started sharing them. **PLATFORM:** I love Twitter. There is an incredible network of educators, authors, illustrators, librarians, and kidlit enthusiasts on Twitter. I have found it to be a very supportive community and so informative as well. Hashtags help to organize information as well as the various chats or groups writers may want to get involved with. I'm slowly starting to learn Instagram, too. (I'm @anniesilvestro on both.) **ADVICE FOR WRITERS:** Join the SCBWI. Take your time. Read as much as you can. Write as much as you can. Always read your work aloud. And, most importantly, try not to compare yourself to others. **NEXT UP:** I'm working on some new picture books and a chapter book as well. I'm looking forward to the release of my next picture books, *Mice Skating*, illustrated by Teagan White (Sterling, Fall 2017) and *The Christmas Tree Who Loved Trains*, illustrated by Paola Zakimi (HarperCollins, Fall 2018).

7 Jessie Sima

JESSIESIMA.COM

Not Quite Narwhal (February 2017, Simon & Schuster Books for Young Readers)

QUICK TAKE: Kelp, a unicorn, grows up under the sea believing himself to be a narwhal. He doesn't mind being different from his friends, but when a strong current carries him away, Kelp encounters some mysterious, sparkling creatures who leave him wondering if maybe he isn't a narwhal at all. **WRITES FROM:** New York City. **PRE-BOOK:** Before I was agented, I was designing graphics for a women's apparel company. Specifically, we created merchandise for sci-fi and fantasy licenses, such as *Star Wars*, *Doctor Who*, and Marvel. I also picked up freelance illustration and design work when I could. **TIME FRAME:** It's hard to say exactly how long this book took to write. It came together in bits and pieces over time. The original idea came to me when I was in college, but I had no intention of writing or illustrating a book. Years later, after the idea had begun to become a story in the back of my mind, I took a chance on writing it. I write and sketch at the same time, and in this case they came together pretty quickly. Maybe in about a week. That is before it was sent to agents or a publishing house. The process of taking a picture book "dummy" and turning it into an actual book is, of course, much longer. **ENTER THE AGENT:** My agent, Thao Le, and I found each other during a Twitter pitch party. Basically, there's a designated date and time frame during which authors pitch their books in 140 characters or less, and agents (and sometimes editors) look through and "like" the posts that they would like to see more of. In my case, Thao liked one of my *Not Quite Narwhal* pitch posts and I followed up with a query email. She was very enthusiastic and we signed fairly quickly after that. **BIGGEST SURPRISE:** I was surprised at just how collaborative the process is and how much I enjoy that collaboration. My agent is editorial, and we work on my stories a bit before sending them out to editors. Once the book is bought by a publishing house, there are many rounds of sketches before going to final art. Even final art isn't final. All along the way, you work with other people who are trying to help you make the book the best it can be. If you trust each other and communicate well, this can be a wonderful experience. **WHAT I DID RIGHT:** Something I did right, which isn't directly connected with my writing or art skill, was to form positive relationships with my agent, editor, and art director. By keeping communication open, making sure to meet deadlines, and asking questions, I laid a foundation for respect and trust that has made the entire publishing experience better. **WHAT I WISH I WOULD HAVE DONE DIFFERENTLY:** I don't think I would do anything differently. There are definitely things I have learned and that I'm taking into future projects. For example, now I know that there are many opportunities for changing art and text throughout the publication process, so I am less concerned about having things be "perfect" the first time around. It's better to have them be finished, and to go back and make them better afterwards. **PLATFORM:** The only social media I really use is Twitter. My handle is @jessiesima. I don't think my platform was particularly unique. I was sharing drawings and sketches sometimes, but otherwise I just used it to get to know people in the industry. Since my book deal, I've also used it to share news about what is going on with my book, and as a way to connect with parents, teachers, librarians, and booksellers. **ADVICE FOR WRITERS:** Be willing to listen and compromise when it is in the service of the story. Decide early on what parts of your story are most important to you, and be able to defend them. This is useful anywhere from critique groups to replying to editorial notes. **NEXT UP:** I'm currently finishing up the artwork for my second book, *Harriet Gets Carried Away*, which is set to publish in Spring 2018 with Simon & Schuster BFYR.

MIDDLE-GRADE

8 Alyson Gerber
ALYSONGERBER.COM
Braced (March 2017, Arthur A. Levine Books)

QUICK TAKE: Soccer star Rachel has friends, a crush, and … scoliosis. When her doctor prescribes a back brace, she feels trapped and mortified. Will it break her—or make her stronger? **WRITES FROM:** Brooklyn, NY. **PRE-BOOK:** I worked in corporate marketing and communications. **TIME FRAME:** I started writing *Braced* a few months after I graduated from The New School in 2012. It took me about a year to write the first draft and then I edited the manuscript with the help of beta readers before I finally got the courage to start querying agents. **ENTER THE AGENT**: I searched Publishers Marketplace and Twitter for agents who represented contemporary middle-grade books that I thought were similar to *Braced* in voice and/or content and queried about twenty agents. I had a few offers, and ultimately I chose the amazing Kate McKean to represent me! **WHAT I DID RIGHT**: When I first started writing, I would try to incorporate everyone's feedback into my revisions. I wrote as if there were a right answer. It was sort of a disaster. The thing I did right was that I learned to filter feedback and trust myself. **WHAT I WISH I WOULD HAVE DONE DIF-FERENTLY**: I didn't try writing middle-grade (or chapter or picture) books until my second year of graduate school, because I was so sure I wanted to write contemporary YA. I wish I had tried writing for different ages earlier. Experimenting in other genres helped me find my voice and identify the type of stories I wanted to be writing. **PLATFORM**: Instagram (alysongerber), Facebook (/alysongerberbooks), Twitter (@alysongerber), and Snapchat (alysongerber). Like the main character in *Braced*, I wore a back brace during middle school to treat my scoliosis. I use social media to share my experience and challenges, because I want my readers to know they're not alone. **ADVICE FOR WRITERS**: Keep writing! It takes time to learn how to write a book. It's okay if you don't figure it out right away. I didn't. And most authors write a few books before they get published. **NEXT UP**: My next two middle-grade novels are going to be published by Scholastic in 2018 and 2019. I'm currently working on *Focused*, where the world of competitive chess meets *Fish in a Tree*. In the book, seventh grader Clea comes to terms with her ADHD diagnosis and discovers the different ways she can succeed.

9 Kristin L. Gray
KRISTINLGRAY.COM
Vilonia Beebe Takes Charge (March 2017, Paula Wiseman Books)

QUICK TAKE: Fourth-grader Vilonia must prove she's responsible enough to adopt a dog to help her mother overcome her grief. Also starring runaway hens and one precarious goldfish. **WRITES FROM:** Northwest Arkansas. **PRE-BOOK:** I was a pediatric RN turned stay-at-home mom. **TIME FRAME:** *Vilonia Beebe Takes Charge* is my second completed middle-grade novel but first sale. I wrote it during 2014 (the first year my five children were all in school). Amazingly, it sold in January 2015 to Simon Kids. I did spend a few years prior to this writing picture books, but my longer work was picked up first. **ENTER THE AGENT:** To back up a bit, I took the opening pages of *Vilonia* to two writing conferences in 2013 for feedback. One was a local SCBWI conference, and the other was the Andrea Brown Literary Agency's Big Sur Writing Conference set in beautiful Big Sur, California. There, I was lucky enough to be assigned to Caryn Wiseman's roundtable. Caryn simply got Vilonia's heart and humor from those early pages. That was a huge boost to me as a writer, to have an industry professional connect with my work. I returned home and finished drafting. Thankfully, Caryn still loved the manuscript. **BIGGEST SURPRISE:** The amount of waiting ... until you don't. So much of publishing is waiting and more waiting until ... just kidding, now! This is why it's a good idea to have projects in various stages, so while you are waiting on an edit letter for one project, you are also drafting something new. Though I'm still figuring this balance out. **WHAT I DID RIGHT:** Attend Big Sur. I was both excited and terrified to fly across the country to attend this writing conference where I knew no one. But I remembered a quote that stated life expands in proportion to one's courage. So, I went, and doors opened. Having just enough courage for the moment and then following through to finish the manuscript were key for me. **WHAT I WISH I WOULD HAVE DONE DIFFERENTLY:** I regret taking so long to write my first drafts. Days go by where I am filled with doubt and afraid to write even a line. I have to summon courage every time I sit at my desk. I remind myself that everything can be rewritten. Nothing is sacred. Writing is rewriting. **PLATFORM:** You can find me online at kristinlgray.com, on Twitter (@kristinlgray), and on Instagram (kristinlgray). Chatting with other writers is my favorite form of procrastination. **ADVICE FOR WRITERS:** You cannot fix what is not written. Get your words on the page. Read widely. Protect your time. And have fun. If you enjoy your work, it will show. **NEXT UP:** A quirky middle-grade mystery titled *The Amelia Six* and a few picture book texts that I'm super excited about.

10 Carter Higgins

DESIGNOFTHEPICTUREBOOK.COM

A Rambler Steals Home (February 2017, HMH Books for Young Readers)

QUICK TAKE: *A Rambler Steals Home* is about 11-year-old Derby, a loyal and messy friend who wants nothing more than to put hope back into the community she loves most. There's a little baseball, a little brother, lipstick, turtles, and a shoebox banjo, too. **WRITES FROM:** Los Angeles, CA. **PRE-BOOK:** Before I began writing for kids, I was a school librarian and a major book lover. When I moved to Los Angeles, I shifted to a career in motion graphics. Although that seems like a bit of a stretch, it was a continuing thread of visual storytelling. Ultimately, I moved back to the school library where I've stayed throughout the editorial process and publication of *A Rambler Steals Home*. **TIME FRAME:** The first seed of this story was planted in late 2011, and I began drafting the book in 2012. It took about one year for me to finish the first draft. **ENTER THE AGENT:** I first saw my agent, Rubin Pfeffer, speak at an SCBWI summer conference in 2012, and I felt a connection to his style of working and his vision for what kind of work he wanted to show the world. After that conference, I queried him with a few picture book manuscripts and the beginning of what became *A Rambler Steals Home*. After many months of learning from his expertise and fantastic editorial support, we began working together in 2013. **BIGGEST SURPRISE:**

The most surprising thing to me has been how collaborative a process it is. Writing itself is very solitary, but the process of bringing a book into the world involves so many people. That has been so satisfying, and good practice for giving the book to its readers. **WHAT I DID RIGHT:** Because publishing moves so slowly, sometimes the waiting can get excruciating. I'm glad I didn't rush the process, and that I focused on the writing and the story before I was worried about the rest of a publishing path. **WHAT I WISH I WOULD HAVE DONE DIFFERENTLY:** I wish I had kept better records of drafts and changes and edits and ideas as proof of the story's evolution, and encouragement that *yes, you can do this again*. **PLATFORM:** I've been blogging at Design of the Picture Book for about six years. I like to look at picture books through a graphic design story, but it's certainly been a great place for me to study the form over the years as well. I've also been active on Twitter for a while, which has been a great place to connect to other librarians and teachers. None of my social media outreach or planning has been book-specific, which I think helps it remain authentic and friendly. **ADVICE FOR WRITERS:** Watch and listen to everything, because it takes many small moments to make up a story. Pay less attention to the technicalities of the craft and more attention to what might be a seed for the story you want to share. Also, read. The best writing lessons are on the pages of books. **NEXT UP:** My debut picture book with Chronicle Books, *This is Not a Valentine*. Lucy Ruth Cummins is illustrating. It's a look at love in en elementary school classroom, and I can't wait for people to get their hands on this one.

11 Jodi Kendall
JODIKENDALL.COM
The Unlikely Story of a Pig in the City (October 2017, HarperCollins)

QUICK TAKE: Eleven-year-old Josie makes it her mission to save the piglet named Hamlet that her brother brings home from college, as she and Hamlet each struggle to find their place in a crowded, chaotic family. Pitched as *Charlotte's Web* meets *The Penderwicks*. Sequel to follow in Fall 2018. **WRITES FROM:** New York City. **PRE-BOOK:** Freelance writer and digital/social media marketing consultant. **TIME FRAME:** I first-drafted my book over about six or seven months, back in early 2014. The earliest version first posted on a digital storytelling platform. A year later, I revised the story with my agent before submitting to publishers, and within weeks it sold at auction in a two-book deal. I spent the majority of 2016 deep in edits. **ENTER THE AGENT:** It took six different manuscripts, seven years, and *over a hundred* rejection letters before I received four offers of literary representation back in 2014, when I queried with a picture book. Even though I've been an active member of SCBWI for many years, with all the agents that offered me rep, I was discovered in the slush pile of query letters. I signed with Alexander Slater at Trident Media Group, and it was one of the best decisions I've made thus far in my writing career. **BIGGEST SURPRISE:** I didn't anticipate the close author friendships I'd make in my debut year. Sometimes you just need someone to "get" what you're going through—and through shared experiences, I'm lucky to have bonded with several kind, positive, supportive, and talented kidlit authors. **WHAT I DID RIGHT:** No matter how rocky my emotions got during my debut journey (editing is scary and *hard*), I always felt gratitude above it all. **WHAT I WISH I WOULD HAVE DONE DIFFERENTLY:** No regrets … yet. But I'm still seven months out from my pub date! I'm taking it all one step at a time.

PLATFORM: My favorite social media platform—and where I focus most of my social media time, by far—is Instagram. Be thoughtful and creative in your imagery while staying true to who you are. Don't just promote your book over and over again. Try to share something valuable with your followers, whether that's a writing tip, behind-the-scenes pics at events, current favorite books/authors, but also be authentically *you*—not just another person trying to sell something. Ask yourself, why do you love following so-and-so? Some of my favorite writer-ly accounts on Instagram are @taherehmafi, @firstdraftpod, @ransomriggs, @kwamealexander, @inkygirl, @Class2k17Books, and @WriteInBk. All use this platform so effectively. On my account, @Jodi_Kendall, I post about all sorts of things, but if you look at my top nine images, you'll see a snapshot of what I'm all about. In my professional and personal life, I've learned that visual storytelling on this social channel is more an art than a science. Don't spontaneously post a low-light, grainy photograph with a long-winded caption. People are swiping through Instagram on elevators, while waiting in restaurant lines, during television commercials—your photograph needs to grab their attention first and make them stop swiping down the screen. You don't need an expensive camera. Phone cameras are fabulous these days, and there are tons of stellar photo editing apps, like VSCO. Be smart with selected hashtag use on Instagram. Don't just slap fifteen generic hashtags onto your caption, such as #books #happy #writer #smile, in an attempt to up your follower count—these hashtags on Instagram are way too broad and oversaturated with content. Consider instead #mglit #kidlit #yalit to narrow your audience and attract meaningful followers who will engage with you and your content (and it's important to engage back). Having a robust social media presence is great for any debut author, but I wouldn't personally stress over social media too much in the beginning—wonderful books will find the right home, and you can evaluate social platform later on in your journey. Just having an account on each channel, and listening and learning from the conversations that take place, is a good start. **ADVICE FOR WRITERS:** Join SCBWI, be brave, don't give up, and keep working on the next thing. If you're struggling with focus and productivity (story of my life!) then time your writing sessions. I follow the Pomodoro Technique (I like the website www.grooveotter.com). I set the timer for twenty-five minutes for a distraction-free, highly focused writing session. Then I take a five-minute break to stretch, respond to a quick email, etc, but when those five minutes are up, it's back to work. I repeat this three or four times, and then take a longer break to walk the dog or eat lunch or something. I'm always surprised by how much I can accomplish in just twenty-five minutes when I really commit. **NEXT UP:** I'm currently writing the untitled sequel to my debut novel (which will publish in Fall 2018) and I'm outlining another middle-grade idea inspired by my past wildlife work. I've also been dabbling with a movie script.

 12 Corabel Shofner
CORABELSHOFNER.COM
Almost Paradise (July 2017, Macmillan)

QUICK TAKE: How about a blurb from Augusta Scattergood? "A rescued pig, an identical twin mix-up, and a girl with determination and a personality to match her cowboy boots make this a totally delightful debut novel. What a joy to meet a spirited heroine like Ruby Clyde Henderson and to linger over Corabel Shofner's glorious words." **WRITES FROM:** Nashville, TN (also lived in Mississippi, Texas, and New York.). **PRE-BOOK:** Actress, lawyer, wife, mother. **TIME FRAME:** 857 days (2 years, 4 months, 4 days) from sale of the book to FSG to launch. Four months to find an agent. Six months to get the book out of the drawer, revive, and spruce it up. Ten years to write the book in fits and starts. **ENTER THE AGENT:** Elizabeth Copps with Maria Carvainis Agency, through cold call e-mail. Magic. **BIGGEST SURPRISE:** That I could do things that seemed impossible, like make serious editorial changes without killing the book. **WHAT I DID RIGHT:** Kept on writing, kept on learning, kept on trying. **WHAT I WISH I WOULD HAVE DONE DIFFERENTLY:** Nothing, don't mess with "what-ifs." **PLATFORM:** Facebook, Twitter, Instagram under my name. I also have a Backroads Bookstores account on each of those platforms where I post all my photos of indie bookstores. I adore indie bookstores. When we travel, my husband goes to museums; I go to bookstores. Each of them is unique and heartwarming and the people are the best. **ADVICE FOR WRITERS:** Live and write, observe and learn, these are good for everybody. If you want to make a career of it, then treat it like a profession. There is much to learn, much to do. **NEXT UP:** Secret! But it has a lot of swirling colors and heartbreak.

 13 Ali Standish
ALISTANDISH.COM
The Ethan I Was Before (January 2017, HarperCollins)

QUICK TAKE: After losing his best friend in a terrible accident, Ethan Truitt and his family move from Boston to the tiny coastal town of Palm Knot, Georgia, where Ethan simply wants to escape his memories of Kacey. But he finds more than he bargained for in this quiet little town, including mystery, adventure, a new best friend, and maybe even the second chance he so desperately needs. **WRITES FROM:** Raleigh, NC. **PRE-BOOK:** I had been working in a Title I school in Washington, D.C., and worrying about the lack of titles that dealt with tough issues in a way that was authentic but also accessible and, ultimately, uplifting. At the same time, I had started to think about the nature of lying and storytelling, and how one is seen as immoral, while the other is seen as artistic expression. I became really interested in the gray area in between, and in writing a character who existed in that gray space. Those two lines of thought collided, and *boom!* Ethan was born. **TIME FRAME:** I began writing in 2014 after moving to the U.K. with my husband. I didn't yet have a work visa, so I thought, why not write this novel? I had a first draft in two months, a better draft in another two months, and I started querying it in November. I signed with Greenhouse in January 2015, and in April we announced the book deal with HarperCollins. It was a whirlwind! **ENTER THE AGENT:** I'm represented by the lovely Polly Nolan and Sarah Davies at Greenhouse. My agent match story is actually quite unique. I had queried Polly in November, and in January, she asked me to come in and meet with her and Sarah. That same week, I was starting an internship with a book packager in London. The first day of my internship, I walked in to find that the book packager shared an open office space with Greenhouse (they're actually owned by the same media company). I was completely freaked out. I thought Polly or Sarah would see me there and think I was stalking them. I actually ended up being told to sit at Polly's desk (who was, thankfully, not in the office that day). I had to write an email to her from *her* computer to tell her what had happened. I was so nervous she would think I was completely bonkers, that she wouldn't believe this could possibly be a coincidence. But Polly and Sarah both thought it was hilarious. I signed with them a week later. **BIGGEST SURPRISE:** I don't think anyone can prepare you for the challenges that come with this job and this career path. It's unlike anything else. You spend months or years writing down a piece of your soul, you work with your team to make it perfect, and then you just have to let go. It's a bit like sending a child out into the world. You hope the world will be good to them. You hope you did enough to prepare them for it. Writing is a job you do in private for a long time, and then suddenly it's in the public sphere. And that is exhilarating and terrifying and gratifying all in one. **WHAT I DID RIGHT:** I put in the work. I wrote for years before I wrote *Ethan*, but it was the first book I really queried because I knew the work I had done before then wasn't ready for publication. And then I went over every word of the manuscript with a fine-toothed comb before I queried it. I didn't put it out into the world until I knew it was the best I could possibly make it on my own. And I think that saved me a lot of challenges and grief later on. **WHAT I WISH I WOULD HAVE DONE DIFFERENTLY:** Worried a little less. Maybe a lot less. **PLATFORM:** You can find me on Twitter (@alistandish) and Facebook (/alistandishbooks). I also keep a blog on my website where I ruminate about different parts of the writing and publishing process. **ADVICE FOR WRITERS:** Don't confuse rejection with failure. They are not the same thing. All writers get rejected. It comes with the territory. Remember that word count is not everything. You also have to give yourself time and space to daydream, to imagine, to really connect with your story on a deeper level. And, above all, remember that you are your story's greatest advocate. You have to absolutely fall in love with it and be willing to fight for it before anyone else will. You owe that to your story. **NEXT UP:** I'm working on a couple of middle-grade projects with similar themes to *The Ethan I Was Before*, but very different premises! We'll see what happens.

 Ellie Terry
ELLIETERRY.COM
Forget Me Not (March 2017, Feiwel & Friends)

QUICK TAKE: *Forget Me Not* is a dual-POV, verse novel about a girl named Calliope who tries to hide her Tourette syndrome from her new school, while trying to convince her mother not to move them yet again, especially after she meets Jinsong—the boy next door—who happens to be the school's popular student body president. **WRITES FROM:** St. George, UT. **PRE-BOOK:** I've worked at two different chiropractor's offices (as a receptionist), a sourdough pizza joint, a family fun center, and a jewelry store. I was also a cheerleading coach and a baton twirling coach. Now I just write. **TIME FRAME:** I started drafting *Forget Me Not* in August 2013. It took about six months to get that first draft down and then another six months to revise it. In August 2014 I entered a contest called Pitch Wars and was chosen to be mentored by Joy McCullough-Carranza. I spent two intense months cutting out an entire POV and then I began querying agents with the manuscript. **ENTER THE AGENT:** In January 2015, I queried Steven Chudney. After he read the manuscript, we spoke on the phone and he gave me a lot of insights and suggestions on how to improve the plot and characters. I spent six weeks deleting and re-writing the last quarter of the novel, among other things, and I must have done a good job, because Steven emailed four days after I sent it with an offer of representation. **BIGGEST SURPRISE:** That there would be so much waiting. It was a long road to signing with an agent (eleven years of querying five middle-grade novels and forty picture books) but my debut sold very quickly (two-and-a-half weeks). So I assumed that once I had a book deal, things would just speed up! The truth is, you're always waiting on something. Hearing back from an agent, waiting on edit notes from your editor, waiting to see the draft of the cover, etc. It's best to sit back and enjoy the journey (and always be working on the next project, or two.) **WHAT I DID RIGHT:** Connecting with other authors. Being able to talk to other debut authors as well as those further in their publishing journey proved to be invaluable for me. **WHAT I WISH I WOULD HAVE DONE DIFFERENTLY:** Worried less. There are so many things in publishing that are out of an author's control, and therefore provide plenty of opportunity for anxiety issues to grow. I wish I would have learned earlier that it's best to focus on the one thing I do have control over: writing the best stories I can.

PLATFORM: I hang out on Facebook and Twitter, mostly. There aren't a whole lot of books for the middle-grade market that deal with characters who have Tourette syndrome. My platform is unique in that my debut novel deals with Tourette syndrome and I myself am diagnosed with the condition. **ADVICE FOR WRITERS:** Read. Join a critique group. Read. Never give up. Read. Write lots of stories. Read. Take yourself seriously and those around you will follow suit. Read. Don't be afraid to try new things. Also ... read. **NEXT UP:** I am currently working on two MG projects—both verse novels—and both boy main characters, so we'll see how that goes!

15 Kim Ventrella

KIMVENTRELLA.COM

Skeleton Tree (September 2017, Scholastic Press)

QUICK TAKE: When twelve-year-old Stanly finds a bone growing in his backyard, he thinks he can use it to win the Young Discoverer's Prize and convince his father to come home. He doesn't expect the bone to grow into a full-sized skeleton that calls into question everything he knows about life, love, and the mysterious forces that connect us. **WRITES FROM:** Oklahoma City. **PRE-BOOK:** In my previous lives, I have worked as the Children's Manager at a public library, the overnight staff person at a women's shelter, a French teacher, and a Peace Corps Volunteer in Kyrgyzstan. **TIME FRAME:** I wrote the first draft of *Skeleton Tree* sitting in a dog bed, while my dog sat on the couch looking over my shoulder. It took two weeks. What can I say? Dog beds are really comfy. The journey from first draft to final pass pages, though, took over a year. **ENTER THE AGENT:** My agent, Brianne Johnson of Writers House, is a fearless defender of weird, wonderful books of all kinds. I chose to query her after reading about her love of Roald Dahl in her Publishers Marketplace listing. She said the first story I sent her was a little too creepy for middle grade, but she gave me the option of revising and resubmitting or sending her a different manuscript. I sent her *Skeleton Tree*. **BIGGEST SURPRISE:** It is wonderful and strange and surreal to hear actual people tell you how much they loved your book. **WHAT I DID RIGHT:** I chose a fabulous editor in Mallory Kass who wholeheartedly believes in me and my story. **WHAT I WISH I WOULD HAVE DONE DIFFERENTLY:** I wish I would have been able to chill out a little and enjoy the process of going to auction. Seriously, though, it's one of those things that's awesome in retrospect but terrifying when it's actually happening. **PLATFORM:** I'm on Twitter, Instagram, and Facebook. On my feed you will find: snazzy skeletons and pictures of my dog, along with occasional book updates, writing advice, and giveaways. But mostly dog pics. **ADVICE FOR WRITERS:** When you're searching for new story ideas, start with emotion. Ask yourself what feeling or new insight you want readers to come away with after reading your book, and work backwards from there. Once you finish a first draft, it's time to revise. I read through a manuscript at least five times before sending it off, each time focusing on improving one aspect of the story. Start with big picture issues, like voice and pacing, and then hone in on the smaller stuff. After you submit, keep writing. If I hadn't started writing *Skeleton Tree* as soon as I'd submitted my previous novel, it wouldn't have been ready to submit to my agent when she asked for it. Finally, be resilient. If one story doesn't work for the audience, the market, or the moment, take a deep breath and write another. **NEXT UP:** I'm working on a second standalone middle-grade novel. No details yet, but I can guarantee it will be one part whimsy, two parts wonder, and just a little weird.

YOUNG ADULT

  **16** Cale Dietrich

CALEDIETRICH.COM

The Love Interest (May 2017, Feiwel & Friends)

QUICK TAKE: *The Love Interest* is about two spies who are competing for the affections of the same girl, but who end up falling for each other instead. **WRITES FROM:** Brisbane, Australia. **PRE-BOOK:** I studied creative writing at university, and then post-graduation I worked a variety of part-time retail jobs while I was writing. **TIME FRAME:** From memory, the first draft took about two months. I revised for around a month, and got feedback from my critique partners. Once I felt it was ready, I queried, and managed to snag an agent offer in under two weeks. I still feel really lucky about that. The road was far from over though, as I revised for about a year before I got a book deal. **ENTER THE AGENT:** Pretty much as soon as I started writing it, I knew I wanted to query this manuscript, so I did a lot of research about agents as I was writing. During this time, I saw an article in *Writer's Digest* announcing that Leon Husock had been hired at the L. Perkins Agency. I'd also read that new agents are a great opportunity for writers, so I wrote his name down, and when I was ready to query, I pitched him. Luckily he liked the pitch and the manuscript, and he offered to represent me. **BIGGEST SURPRISE:** I think I've been really surprised by how nice and welcoming everyone in the YA community has been. I honestly haven't had a bad experience yet, as everyone has been so kind, welcoming and helpful. **WHAT I DID RIGHT:** I think one of the best things I did was work really hard on my query letter. I spent countless hours working on it, and it was critiqued by so many people. I think having a solid query really helped me not only when I was querying, but also with editor submissions, as that same query was pretty much the same one that my agent used to pitch editors. **WHAT I WISH I WOULD HAVE DONE DIFFERENTLY:** This is a hard one to answer! I think it would've been smart to revise the manuscript more before going out on submission for the first time. But then again, the feedback I received from that ultimately unsuccessful first round enabled me to revise and turn it into a manuscript that sold. So it all worked out, but I learned the lesson that a lot of work over a long period of time is the best thing for a manuscript. **PLATFORM:** Twitter is my main social media account, as it's by far my favorite. I also have a website with a blog and an Instagram, but I'm much less active on those. **ADVICE FOR WRITERS:** I think it's really important for writers to listen to their own instincts! And to pursue passion projects even if they aren't sure they'll sell, because those end up being the best books. Plus, I think they're way more likely to sell more than something you don't love that you only wrote because you think it fits the market. **NEXT UP:** I'm working on two new YA books at the moment, and I'm really excited about both of them.

17 Tiffany D. Jackson

WRITEINBK.COM

Allegedly (January 2017, Katherine Tegen Books)

QUICK TAKE: *Orange Is the New Black* meets Walter Dean Myer's *Monster* in this gritty, twisty, and haunting debut about a girl convicted of murder seeking the truth while surviving life in a group home. **WRITES FROM:** Brooklyn, NY. **PRE-BOOK:** TV production manager/line producer (BBC America, FUSE, BET, National Geographic TV). **TIME FRAME:** I wrote the first draft during Hurricane Sandy back in 2012, took another year to research and complete the story, and then I hired a developmental editor to help polish and fix any plot issues. By April 2014 I was ready to query, signed with my agent June 2014, and received an offer January 2015. **ENTER THE AGENT:** Good, old-fashion cold querying to Natalie Lakosil sealed the deal, but I had been following her amazingly helpful website, Adventure's In Agent Land, for almost two years prior. It was listed in *Writer's Digest* as one of the top 100 websites for authors and has a ton of query/industry tips. **BIGGEST SURPRISE:** How *long* the publishing process is! Waiting two years for a book to hit shelves that took years to write is painful. Patience is key but not easily mastered. **WHAT I DID RIGHT:** I'm actually most proud of my determination to find an agent! I set a goal for myself that I would query 100 agents before reevaluating my novel. I bought the yearly *Guide to Literary Agents*, combed through it with a highlighter and sticky tabs, targeting agencies by genre and specific request. Then, I set up an excel spreadsheet and organized the agents in tiers, keeping track of queries sent, and following up every two weeks. I still have the marked up edition under my desk. **WHAT I WISH I WOULD HAVE DONE DIFFERENTLY:** I wish I had found my writing support system much earlier. I signed my contract in January 2015, but didn't truly know the YA author community until April 2016. Until then, it felt like I lived on my own island with no one to talk to about the issues I faced. **PLATFORM:** Twitter (@writeinbk) is key! You can forge relationships with your readers, make connections with authors you admire, and learn about the industry. Several of my best marketing opportunities happened through Twitter. **ADVICE FOR WRITERS:** As *soon* as you're done with your book, work on the next one. The key to a long writing career is having more books for people to read. **NEXT UP:** My second book should be out next spring (Title TBD), and I'm working on proposals for my third and fourth.

⓲ S. Jae-Jones
SJAEJONES.COM

Wintersong (February 2017, Thomas Dunne Books)

QUICK TAKE: When the Goblin King steals Liesl's younger sister to be his bride, she must journey Underground to rescue her. **WRITES FROM:** North Carolina. **PRE-BOOK:** I worked in editorial at a Big 5 publishing house before moving to North Carolina with my partner. I currently work in a financial services position at a large corporation. **TIME FRAME:** *Wintersong* was the fastest thing I've ever written. From start to finish, I drafted 100,000 words in 59 days. It began as a NaNoWriMo project and I just kept writing until I finished. **ENTER THE AGENT:** Right, so when I tell my representation story, I always warn writers, *Do as I say, not as I do!* After my first draft, I let the manuscript rest for a grand total of a week before combing through it for typos and sending it out to agents. I queried a very small, select number, and those with whom I had some sort of relationship. I had the advantage of having worked in editorial, so I was acquainted with agents through work. But the experience of working as an acquiring editor gave me another advantage: an instinct for a commercial (salable) idea. **BIGGEST SURPRISE:** To be honest, not much has surprised me; I've seen it all from the other side of the desk, so to speak. **WHAT I DID RIGHT:** *Wintersong* was not the first book I've ever written, but it was the first novel I attempted to get published. I'd written four books before *Wintersong*, and it took me that long to write something worth publishing. **WHAT I WISH I WOULD HAVE DONE DIFFERENTLY:** I'm not sure I would have necessarily done anything differently. I have been extraordinarily lucky in my publishing journey, and I don't take any of that for granted. **PLATFORM:** I am more or less on all the social media platforms, but I use Twitter (@sjaejones), Instagram (@sjaejones), and Tumblr (@sjaejoneswriter) the most. **ADVICE FOR WRITERS:** Finish your book. **NEXT UP:** I'm currently working on the sequel to *Wintersong*, which will be out in 2018.

⓳ Tricia Levenseller
TRICIALEVENSELLER.COM

Daughter of the Pirate King (February 2017, Feiwel & Friends)

QUICK TAKE: *Daughter of the Pirate King* is about a seventeen-year-old female pirate captain who gets herself kidnapped by enemy pirates on purpose so she can steal a treasure map from off their ship. **WRITES FROM:** Utah. **PRE-BOOK:** I was working on my undergrad degree before selling my book. I was also doing internships with publishers and literary agencies. I knew I wanted to work in publishing already, and I was learning everything I could about being an editor and an agent in case the writing didn't work out. I'm so glad it did! **TIME FRAME:** I wrote my first novel during the summer of 2010. By 2011, I had an agent. I wrote two more books with that agent, none of which sold. I wrote the first 50,000 words of *DotPK* (my fourth book) during National Novel Writing Month in 2013. I finished writing and editing the book somewhere in the middle of 2014. Then I ended up parting ways with my first agent and signing on with a new agent. By November 2014, my book went on submission with editors. It sold in July of 2015. **ENTER THE AGENT:** I signed with Rachel Brooks after going through the querying process. The best resources I found to help with querying were agentquery.com and querytracker.com. **BIGGEST SURPRISE:** At first I thought (and in my defense, I was only nineteen) that signing on with an agent meant my book would sell. I'd never heard any stories of authors with agents who didn't have books published, but I think that was because people weren't so open about books that weren't successes. I wish I had known that having an agent wasn't a guaranteed success. I still needed to work hard and write more books to finally get that contract. **WHAT I DID RIGHT:** I think the best thing I did was to never stop writing. No matter how disheartening it was to find out book after book didn't sell, I'm so glad I stuck with writing and never gave up. **WHAT I WISH I WOULD HAVE DONE DIFFERENTLY:** After I finished my first book, I started working on the sequel for that book. Bad idea. Until you sell the first book in a series, start a new series. Don't work on a sequel. If publishing is your goal, working on a sequel is a waste of time until you have a contract. **PLATFORM:** I have a blog (www.tricialevenseller.com/blog), Facebook (/tricialevensellerbooks), Twitter (@Tricia-Levensell), Pinterest (TriciaLevensell), and Instagram (tricialevenseller). I built (and am still building) my platform by doing two things. I talk frequently about books other than my own. Booklovers are drawn to book talk. I also talk about all things pirates, which brings fellow pirate lovers to my social media sites. **ADVICE FOR WRITERS:** Never give up. I firmly believe that anyone who wants to be published, will be published if they do two things: never stop writing and never stop trying to improve. **NEXT UP:** I'm working on a brand-new YA fantasy with a viking-esque feel to it.

㉙ Angie Thomas
ANGIETHOMAS.COM
The Hate U Give (February 2017, Balzer + Bray)

QUICK TAKE: Sixteen-year-old Starr Carter navigates between the poverty-stricken neighborhood she has grown up in and the upper-crust suburban prep school she attends. Her life is up-ended when she is the sole witness to a police officer shooting her best friend, Khalil, who turns out to have been unarmed during the confrontation. **WRITES FROM:** Mississippi. **PRE-BOOK:** I was an assistant to a Bishop at a local mega church. **TIME FRAME:** I first wrote the book as a short story back in 2010/2011, and I put it aside for a few years. I started working on it as a full-length novel in December 2014/January 2015. It took me about five months of drafting and revising before I queried it. **ENTER THE AGENT:** I surprisingly got my agent through Twitter. The Bent Agency held a question and answer session. I was afraid to query my book because of the topic, so I asked if it was an appropriate book to query. Brooks Sherman responded and said not only was it appropriate, but he asked to see it when I finished. I queried him a few weeks later. Not long after that, he made an offer of representation. Not too long after signing with him, we went on submission and ended up in a thirteen-publishing house auction. Not bad for a process that started with Twitter. **BIGGEST SURPRISE:** One of the biggest surprises about this process has been that waiting never ends. When you're sending queries and waiting for responses, you may think that once you get an agent, everything happens quickly. Not so much. Even once you get a publishing contract, there's more waiting. You soon learn that patience truly is key. **WHAT I DID RIGHT:** For years, I revised and queried a middle-grade project only to get rejection after rejection after rejection. During my third round of submissions, I decided to work on something new. That "something new" became *The Hate U Give*. Sometimes the next book is *the* book. **WHAT I WISH I WOULD HAVE DONE DIFFERENTLY:** I wish I would have moved on from my MG project sooner. Not that there's anything wrong with it, but sometimes when we're querying we can get so caught up in one project that we don't allow ourselves to even consider other options. Allow yourself to write other things. **PLATFORM:** I love Twitter (@acthomasbooks), and I am trying to use Instagram (acwrites) a bit more. **ADVICE FOR WRITERS:** Don't fret over all of the "nos" (and there will be plenty of them)—all it takes is one "yes." **NEXT UP:** I'm working on my second book. It's a YA contemporary, set in the same neighborhood as *The Hate U Give*, but it is not a sequel. That's all I can say for now.

21 Peternelle van Arsdale

PETERNELLEVANARSDALE.COM

The Beast Is An Animal (February 2017, Margaret K. McElderry Books)

QUICK TAKE: A dark fairy tale about how fear makes monsters, and fear makes us into monsters. **WRITES FROM:** New York City. **PRE-BOOK:** A book editor for various publishers for 20-plus years, and then a freelance book editor. **TIME FRAME:** I wrote the prologue for *The Beast Is an Animal* at the end of 2011, but at that time it was for an entirely different novel. That novel was a middle-grade contemporary fantasy and was intended to be one in a series. To put it mildly, it was not the book I was destined to write. I struggled, and struggled, and struggled with it. I shelved it permanently in early 2012, not long after I wrote the prologue that would become the start of *The Beast Is an Animal*. I didn't put the finishing touches on *The Beast Is an Animal* until January of 2016, which is when my agent began submitting it to publishers. During the four years between writing the prologue and finishing the novel, I was also freelance editing and ghostwriting, which absorbed a lot of my time and creative energy. At the same time I was working on the novel in spurts between projects, generating multiple drafts that were never quite right. **ENTER THE AGENT:** The answer to this is very much tied up with the answer to the question about time frame. My agent, Rebecca Sherman of Writers House, is the person who read that middle-grade fantasy with the prologue attached and said, essentially: "How about you dump everything but the prologue?" This meant discarding 250 pages—an entire novel—that were the result of possibly five years of work. I think both Rebecca and Simon Lipskar, who had referred me to her, thought there was a very good chance I'd say "no way," but instead I was relieved. I knew that other novel wasn't working, and I'd lost love for it. But I passionately loved my prologue, and Rebecca freed me to write the kind of novel that I would want to read, the one that really came from my heart and gut. Over the course of three more years and many drafts, she and her associate at Writers House, Andrea Morrison, were ceaselessly patient with me. They constantly challenged and inspired me with their edits to make *The Beast Is an Animal* as strong and satisfying as it could possibly be. **BIGGEST SURPRISE:** It's very difficult for anything to surprise me, because I've been in the book business for so long, and I'm anxious and a creature of dread by nature, so I'm constantly imagining what might happen (or go wrong). That said, I suppose that one thing this process has taught me is that as knowledgeable as I might think I am, I can still have that feeling that authors are so familiar with—that they're on the outside of the process looking in. We're left with so much to wonder about. Are people going to buy my book? Are they buying my book right now? Will they ever buy my book? These are things the author doesn't really have any control over, and yet what is more important to the author's writing career than that? Of course we can always write, whether people buy our books or not—but the career part, that's the tricky thing. And that feeling of helplessness is something I've known authors of mine to have, but you can't *really* know what it's like until you experience it yourself. **WHAT I DID RIGHT:** I persisted. Because I loved my book and it meant so much to me to see it through to completion, I just kept going. Even when draft after draft wasn't right, I took the edits and I found new inspiration. I don't give myself credit for a whole lot, but I do give myself credit for that. **WHAT I WISH I WOULD HAVE DONE DIFFERENTLY:** I might have been easier on myself when it took so long to make the book right. I had this idea that I should have needed less help—particularly since I'm an editor myself. I wept when I heard yet again that it wasn't quite there. But it took the time it took, and I think in the end the novel benefited from all the living I did while I was working on it. **PLATFORM:** I have no unique platform whatsoever! I'm just another person with a story that I hope others might like. I particularly enjoy Twitter (@peternelleva), Instagram (@peternellevanarsdale), and Facebook (peternellevanarsdale/author). **ADVICE FOR WRITERS:** I hesitate to advise other writers, because I think that what works for one won't necessarily work for another. But if you're like me, then you cannot write well what you do not passionately love. So my first bit of advice is to make sure that what you're writing is something you would be delighted to read. If you hate what you're working on, even because you're just tired of it, then stick it in a drawer and work on something else. I don't mean you should give up on it if you're simply frustrated, but if you really are only working on it because you don't want to feel that you've failed to complete it—that's not a good enough reason. And my second piece of advice would be that if you really love it, then you should take as long as you need to make it right. There's no correct amount of time one should work on a book. Good books take as long as they take. **NEXT UP:** I'm working on my second novel, which is also a dark fairytale, but is not a sequel. I'm also writing essays and short stories, and I continue to freelance edit, because editing is and always will be my first and lasting love.

CRIS FREESE is the managing editor of Writer's Digest Books, the editor of *Children's Writer's & Illustrator's Market,* and the editor of *Guide to Literary Agents* (both online and in print).

GLOSSARY OF INDUSTRY TERMS
Common terminology and lingo.

///

AAR. Association of Authors' Representatives.

ABA. American Booksellers Association.

ABC. Association of Booksellers for Children.

ADVANCE. A sum of money a publisher pays a writer or illustrator prior to the publication of a book. It is usually paid in installments, such as one half on signing the contract, one half on delivery of a complete and satisfactory manuscript. The advance is paid against the royalty money that will be earned by the book.

ALA. American Library Association.

ALL RIGHTS. The rights contracted to a publisher permitting the use of material anywhere and in any form, including movie and book club sales, without additional payment to the creator.

ANTHOLOGY. A collection of selected writings by various authors or gatherings of works by one author.

ANTHROPOMORPHIZATION. The act of attributing human form and personality to things not human (such as animals).

ASAP. As soon as possible.

ASSIGNMENT. An editor or art director asks a writer, illustrator, or photographer to produce a specific piece for an agreed-upon fee.

B&W. Black and white.

BACKLIST. A publisher's list of books not published during the current season but still in print.

BEA. BookExpo America.

BIENNIALLY. Occurring once every two years.

BIMONTHLY. Occurring once every two months.

BIWEEKLY. Occurring once every two weeks.

BOOK PACKAGER. A company that draws all elements of a book together, from the initial concept to writing and marketing strategies, then sells the book package to a book publisher and/or movie producer. Also known as book producer or book developer.

BOOK PROPOSAL. Package submitted to a publisher for consideration, usually consisting of a synopsis and outline as well as sample chapters.

BUSINESS-SIZE ENVELOPE. Also known as a #10 envelope. The standard size used in sending business correspondence.

CAMERA-READY. Refers to art that is completely prepared for copy camera platemaking.

CAPTION. A description of the subject matter of an illustration or photograph; photo captions include persons' names where appropriate. Also called cutline.

CBC. Children's Book Council.

CLEAN-COPY. A manuscript free of errors that needs no editing; it is ready for typesetting.

CLIPS. Samples, usually from newspapers or magazines, of a writer's published work.

CONCEPT BOOKS. Books that deal with ideas, concepts and large-scale problems, promoting an understanding of what's happening in a child's world. Most prevalent are alphabet and counting books, but also includes books dealing with specific concerns facing young people (such as divorce, birth of a sibling, friendship, or moving).

CONTRACT. A written agreement stating the rights to be purchased by an editor, art director, or producer and the amount of payment the writer, illustrator, or photographer will receive for that sale.

CONTRIBUTOR'S COPIES. The magazine issues sent to an author, illustrator, or photographer in which her work appears.

CO-OP PUBLISHER. A publisher that shares production costs with an author but, unlike subsidy publishers, handles all marketing and distribution. An author receives a high percentage of royalties until her initial investment is recouped, then standard royalties. (Children's Writer's & Illustrator's Market does not include co-op publishers.)

COPY. The actual written material of a manuscript.

COPYEDITING. Editing a manuscript for grammar usage, spelling, punctuation, and other general style.

COPYRIGHT. A means to legally protect an author's/illustrator's/photographer's work. This can be shown by writing the creator's name and the year of the work's creation.

COVER LETTER. A brief letter, accompanying a complete manuscript, especially useful if responding to an editor's request for a manuscript. May also accompany a book proposal.

CUTLINE. See caption.

DIVISION. An unincorporated branch of a company.

DUMMY. A loose mock-up of a book showing placement of text and artwork.

ELECTRONIC SUBMISSION. A submission of material by e-mail or Web form.

FINAL DRAFT. The last version of a polished manuscript ready for submission to an editor.

FIRST NORTH AMERICAN SERIAL RIGHTS. The right to publish material in a periodical for the first time, in the U.S. or Canada.

F&GS. Folded and gathered sheets. An early, not-yet-bound copy of a picture book.

FLAT FEE. A one-time payment.

GALLEYS. The first typeset version of a manuscript that has not yet been divided into pages.

GENRE. A formulaic type of fiction, such as horror, mystery, romance, fantasy, suspense, thriller, science fiction, or western.

GLOSSY. A photograph with a shiny surface, as opposed to one with a matte finish.

GOUACHE. Opaque watercolor with an appreciable film thickness and an actual paint layer.

HALFTONE. Reproduction of a continuous tone illustration with the image formed by dots produced by a camera lens screen.

HARD COPY. The printed copy of a computer's output.

HARDWARE. Refers to all the mechanically integrated components of a computer that are not software—circuit boards, transistors and the machines that are the actual computer.

HI-LO. High interest, low reading level.

HOME PAGE. The first page of a website.

IBBY. International Board on Books for Young People.

IMPRINT. Name applied to a publisher's specific line of books.

IRA. International Reading Association.

IRC. International Reply Coupon. Sold at the post office to enclose with text or artwork sent to a recipient outside your own country to cover postage costs when replying or returning work.

KEYLINE. Identification of the positions of illustrations and copy for the printer.

LAYOUT. Arrangement of illustrations, photographs, text and headlines for printed material.

LGBTQ. Lesbian/gay/bisexual/trans/queer.

LINE DRAWING. Illustration done with pencil or ink using no wash or other shading.

MASS MARKET BOOKS. Paperback books directed toward an extremely large audience sold in supermarkets, drugstores, airports, newsstands, online retailers, and bookstores.

MECHANICALS. Paste-up or preparation of work for printing.

MIDDLE-GRADE OR MID-GRADE. See middle reader.

MIDDLE READER. The general classification of books written for readers approximately ages nine to twelve. Often called middle-grade or mid-grade.

MS (MSS). Manuscript(s).

MULTIPLE SUBMISSIONS. See simultaneous submissions.

NCTE. National Council of Teachers of English.

NEW ADULT (NA). Novels with characters in their late teens or early twenties who are exploring what it means to be an adult.

ONE-TIME RIGHTS. Permission to publish a story in periodical or book form one time only.

PACKAGE SALE. The sale of a manuscript and illustrations/photos as a "package" paid for with one check.

PAYMENT ON ACCEPTANCE. The writer, artist, or photographer is paid for her work at the time the editor or art director decides to buy it.

PAYMENT ON PUBLICATION. The writer, artist, or photographer is paid for her work when it is published.

PICTURE BOOK. A type of book aimed at preschoolers to eight-year-olds that tells a story using a combination of text and artwork, or artwork only.

PRINT. An impression pulled from an original plate, stone, block, screen, or negative; also a positive made from a photographic negative.

PROOFREADING. Reading text to correct typographical errors.

QUERY. A letter to an editor or agent designed to capture interest in an article or book you have written or propose to write. (See the article "Before Your First Sale.")

READING FEE. Money charged by some agents and publishers to read a submitted manuscript. (Children's Writer's & Illustrator's Market does not include agencies that charge reading fees.)

REPRINT RIGHTS. Permission to print an already published work whose first rights have been sold to another magazine or book publisher.

RESPONSE TIME. The average length of time it takes an editor or art director to accept or reject a query or submission, and inform the creator of the decision.

RIGHTS. The bundle of permissions offered to an editor or art director in exchange for printing a manuscript, artwork, or photographs.

ROUGH DRAFT. A manuscript that has not been checked for errors in grammar, punctuation, spelling, or content.

ROUGHS. Preliminary sketches or drawings.

ROYALTY. An agreed percentage paid by a publisher to a writer, illustrator, or photographer for each copy of her work sold.

SAE. Self-addressed envelope.

SASE. Self-addressed, stamped envelope.

SCBWI. The Society of Children's Book Writers and Illustrators.

SECOND SERIAL RIGHTS. Permission for the reprinting of a work in another periodical after its first publication in book or magazine form.

SEMIANNUAL. Occurring every six months or twice a year.

SEMIMONTHLY. Occurring twice a month.

SEMIWEEKLY. Occurring twice a week.

SERIAL RIGHTS. The rights given by an author to a publisher to print a piece in one or more periodicals.

SIMULTANEOUS SUBMISSIONS. Queries or proposals sent to several publishers at the same time. Also called multiple submissions. (See the article "Before Your First Sale.")

SLANT. The approach to a story or piece of artwork that will appeal to readers of a particular publication.

SLUSH PILE. Editors' term for their collections of unsolicited manuscripts.

SOFTWARE. Programs and related documentation for use with a computer.

SOLICITED MANUSCRIPT. Material that an editor has asked for or agreed to consider before being sent by a writer.

SPAR. Society of Photographers and Artists Representatives.

SPECULATION (SPEC). Creating a piece with no assurance from an editor or art director that it will be purchased or any reimbursements for material or labor paid.

SUBSIDIARY RIGHTS. All rights other than book publishing rights included in a book contract, such as paperback, book club, and movie rights.

SUBSIDY PUBLISHER. A book publisher that charges the author for the cost of typesetting, printing and promoting a book. Also called a vanity publisher. (Note: Children's Writer's & Illustrator's Market does not include subsidy publishers.)

SYNOPSIS. A summary of a story or novel. Usually a page to a page and a half, single-spaced, if part of a book submission.

TABLOID. Publication printed on an ordinary newspaper page turned sideways and folded in half.

TEARSHEET. Page from a magazine or newspaper containing your printed art, story, article, poem or photo.

THUMBNAIL. A rough layout in miniature.

TRADE BOOKS. Books sold in bookstores and through online retailers, aimed at a smaller audience than mass market books, and printed in smaller quantities by publishers.

TRANSPARENCIES. Positive color slides; not color prints.

UNSOLICITED MANUSCRIPT. Material sent without an editor's, art director's, or agent's request.

VANITY PUBLISHER. See subsidy publisher.

WORK-FOR-HIRE. An arrangement between a writer, illustrator, or photographer and a company under which the company retains complete control of the work's copyright.

YA. See young adult.

YOUNG ADULT. The general classification of books written for readers approximately ages twelve to sixteen. Often referred to as YA.

YOUNG READER. The general classification of books written for readers approximately ages five to eight.

BOOK PUBLISHERS

///

There's no magic formula for getting published. It's a matter of getting the right manuscript on the right editor's desk at the right time. Before you submit it's important to learn publishers' needs, see what kind of books they're producing, and decide which publishers your work is best suited for. *Children's Writer's & Illustrator's Market* is but one tool in this process. (Those just starting out, turn to the article "Quick Tips for Writers & Illustrators" in this book.)

To help you narrow down the list of possible publishers for your work, we've included several indexes at the back of this book. The **Subject Index** lists book and magazine publishers according to their fiction and nonfiction needs or interests. The **Age-Level Index** indicates which age groups publishers cater to. The **Photography Index** indicates which markets buy photography for children's publications. The **Poetry Index** lists publishers accepting poetry.

If you write contemporary fiction for young adults, for example, and you're trying to place a book manuscript, go first to the Subject Index. Locate the fiction categories under Book Publishers and copy the list under Contemporary. Then go to the Age-Level Index and highlight the publishers on the Contemporary list that are included under the Young Adults heading. Read the listings for the highlighted publishers to see if your work matches their needs.

Remember, *Children's Writer's & Illustrator's Market* should not be your only source for researching publishers. Here are a few other sources of information:

- The Society of Children's Book Writers and Illustrators (SCBWI) offers members an annual market survey of children's book publishers for the cost of postage or free online at www.scbwi.org. (SCBWI membership information can also be found at www.scbwi.org.)
- The Children's Book Council website (www.cbcbooks.org) gives information on member publishers.
- If a publisher interests you, send a SASE for submission guidelines or check publishers' websites for guidelines *before* submitting. To quickly find guidelines online, visit The Colossal Directory of Children's Publishers at www.signaleader.com.

- Check publishers' websites. Many include their complete catalogs, which you can browse. Web addresses are included in many publishers' listings.
- Spend time at your local bookstore to see who's publishing what. While you're there, browse through *Publishers Weekly* and *The Horn Book*.

SUBSIDY & SELF-PUBLISHING

Some determined writers who receive rejections from royalty publishers may look to subsidy and co-op publishers as an option for getting their work into print. These publishers ask writers to pay all or part of the costs of producing a book. We strongly advise writers and illustrators to work only with publishers who pay them. For this reason, we've adopted a policy not to include any subsidy or co-op publishers in *Children's Writer's & Illustrator's Market* (or any other Writer's Digest Books market book).

If you're interested in publishing your book just to share it with friends and relatives, self-publishing is a viable option, but it involves time, energy, and money. You oversee all book production details. Check with a local printer for advice and information on cost or check online for print-on-demand publishing options (which are often more affordable).

Whatever path you choose, keep in mind that the market is flooded with submissions, so it's important for you to hone your craft and submit the best work possible. Competition from thousands of other writers and illustrators makes it more important than ever to research publishers before submitting—read their guidelines, look at their catalogs, check out a few of their titles, and visit their websites.

ABBEVILLE FAMILY

Abbeville Press, 116 W. 23rd St., New York NY 10011. (646)375-2136. **Fax:** (646)375-2359. **E-mail:** abbeville@abbeville.com. **Website:** www.abbeville.com. Our list is full for the next several seasons. *Not accepting unsolicited book proposals at this time.* **Publishes 8 titles/year. 10% of books from first-time authors.**

FICTION Picture books: animal, anthology, concept, contemporary, fantasy, folktales, health, hi-lo, history, humor, multicultural, nature/environment, poetry, science fiction, special needs, sports, suspense. Average word length 300-1,000 words.

HOW TO CONTACT Please refer to website for submission policy.

ILLUSTRATION Works with approx 2-4 illustrators/year. Uses color artwork only.

PHOTOGRAPHY Buys stock and assigns work.

ABDO PUBLISHING CO.

8000 W. 78th St., Suite 310, Edina MN 55439. (800)800-1312. **Fax:** (952)831-1632. **E-mail:** nonfiction@abdopublishing.com. **Website:** www.abdopublishing.com. ABDO publishes nonfiction children's books (pre-kindergarten to 8th grade) for school and public libraries—mainly history, sports, biography, geography, science, and social studies. "Please specify each submission as either nonfiction, fiction, or illustration. Publishes hardcover originals. **Publishes 300 titles/year.**

TERMS Guidelines online.

ABRAMS

115 W. 18th St., 6th Floor, New York NY 10011. (212)206-7715. **Fax:** (212)519-1210. **E-mail:** abrams@abramsbooks.com. **Website:** www.abramsbooks.com. **Contact:** Managing Editor. Publishes hardcover and a few paperback originals. **Publishes 250 titles/year.**

Does not accept unsolicited materials.

FICTION Publishes hardcover and "a few" paperback originals. Averages 150 total titles/year.

TIPS "We are one of the few publishers who publish almost exclusively illustrated books. We consider ourselves the leading publishers of art books and high-quality artwork in the U.S. Once the author has signed a contract to write a book for our firm the author must finish the manuscript to agreed-upon high standards within the schedule agreed upon in the contract."

ABRAMS BOOKS FOR YOUNG READERS

115 W. 18th St., New York NY 10011. **Website:** www.abramsyoungreaders.com.

Abrams no longer accepts unsolicited mss or queries.

ILLUSTRATION Illustrations only: Do not submit original material; copies only. Contact: Chad Beckerman, art director.

ALADDIN

Simon & Schuster, 1230 Avenue of the Americas, 4th Floor, New York NY 10020. (212)698-7000. **Website:** www.simonandschuster.com. Aladdin also publishes Aladdin M!X, for those readers too old for kids' books, but not quite ready for adult or young adult novels. **Contact:** Acquisitions Editor. Aladdin publishes picture books, beginning readers, chapter books, middle grade and tween fiction and nonfiction, and graphic novels and nonfiction in hardcover and paperback, with an emphasis on commercial, kid-friendly titles. Publishes hardcover/paperback originals and imprints of Simon & Schuster Children's Publishing Children's Division.

HOW TO CONTACT Simon & Schuster does not review, retain, or return unsolicited materials or artwork. "We suggest prospective authors and illustrators submit their mss through a professional literary agent."

ALGONQUIN YOUNG READERS

P.O. Box 2225, Chapel Hill NC 27515. **Website:** algonquinyoungreaders.com. Algonquin Young Readers is a new imprint that features books for readers 7-17. "From short illustrated novels for the youngest independent readers to timely and topical crossover young adult fiction, what ties our books together are unforgettable characters, absorbing stories, and superior writing.

FICTION Algonquin Young Readers publishes ficiton and a limited number of narrative nonfiction titles for middle grade and young adult readers. "We don't publish poetry, picture books, or genre fiction."

HOW TO CONTACT Query with 15-20 sample pages and SASE.

ILLUSTRATION "At this time, we do not accept unsolicited submissions for illustration."

TERMS Guidelines online.

AMBERJACK PUBLISHING

P.O. Box 4668 #89611, New York NY 10163. (888)959-3352. **Website:** www.amberjackpublishing.com. Amberjack Publishing offers authors the freedom to write without burdening them with having to promote the work themselves. They retain all rights. "You will have no rights left to exploit, so you cannot resell, republish, or use your story again."

FICTION Amberjack Publishing is always on the lookout for the next great story. "We are interested in fiction, children's books, graphic novels, science fiction, fantasy, humor, and everything in between."

HOW TO CONTACT Submit via online query form with book proposal and first 10 pages of ms.

Ⓐ AMULET BOOKS

Imprint of Abrams, 115 W. 18th St., 6th Floor, New York NY 10001. **Website:** www.amuletbooks.com. *Does not accept unsolicited mss or queries.* **10% of books from first-time authors.**

FICTION Middle readers: adventure, contemporary, fantasy, history, science fiction, sports. Young adults/teens: adventure, contemporary, fantasy, history, science fiction, sports, suspense.

ILLUSTRATION Works with 10-12 illustrators/year. Uses both color and b&w. Query with samples. Contact: Chad Beckerman, art director. Samples filed.

PHOTOGRAPHY Buys stock images and assigns work.

ANDREWS MCMEEL PUBLISHING

1130 Walnut St., Kansas City MO 64106 (816)581-8921 or (800) 851-8923. **E-mail:** tlynch@amuniversal.com; marketing@amuniversal.com. **Website:** www.andrewsmcmeel.com. **Contact:** Tim Lynch, Creative Director. Our company's core publication categories include: cook books, comics & humor, puzzles & games, and illustrated middle grade. We're always looking for new authors and new book ideas.

💬 See also listings for Universal Press Syndicate and uclick (other divisions of Andrews McMeel Universal) in the Syndicates & Cartoon Features section.

HOW TO CONTACT Send cover letter with bio along with outline and first two chapters. We are happy to consider submissions from both literary agents and directly from authors. Full submission guidelines listed on site. "Please allow at least 90 days to receive a response. We get many submissions a day and we may not get to yours immediately."

TIPS "We want designers who can read a manuscript and design a concept for the best possible cover. Communicate well and be flexible with design."

ARBORDALE PUBLISHING

612 Johnnie Dodds, Suite A2, Mt. Pleasant SC 29464. (843)971-6722. **Fax:** (843)216-3804. **E-mail:** katie@arbordalepublishing.com. **Website:** www.arbordalepublishing.com. **Contact:** Katie Hall. "The picture books we publish are usually, but not always, fictional stories with nonfiction woven into the story that relate to science or math. All books should subtly convey an educational theme through a warm story that is fun to read and that will grab a child's attention. Each book has a 4-page *'For Creative Minds'* section to reinforce the educational component. This section will have a craft and/or game as well as 'fun facts' to be shared by the parent, teacher, or other adult. Authors do not need to supply this information with their submission, but if their ms is accepted, they may be asked to provide additional information for this section. Mss should be less than 1,000 words and meet all of the following 4 criteria: fun to read—mostly fiction with nonfiction facts woven into the story; national or regional in scope; must tie into early elementary school curriculum; must be marketable through a niche market such as a zoo, aquarium, or museum gift shop." Publishes hardcover, trade paperback, and electronic originals. **Publishes 12 titles/year. 50% of books from first-time authors. 100% from unagented writers.**

FICTION Picture books: animal, folktales, nature/environment, science- or math-related. No more than 1,000 words.

NONFICTION Prefer fiction, but will consider nonfiction as well

HOW TO CONTACT All mss should be submitted via e-mail to Katie Hall. Mss should be less than 1,000 words. 1,000 mss received/year. Accepts electronic submissions only. Snail mail submissions are discarded without being opened. Acknowledges receipt of ms submission within 1 month. Publishes book 18 months after acceptance. May hold onto mss of interest for 1 year until acceptance.

ILLUSTRATION Works with 20 illustrators/year. Prefers to work with illustrators from the US and Canada. Uses color artwork only. Submit Web link or 2-3 electronic images. Contact: Katie Hall.

TERMS Pays 6-8% royalty on wholesale price. Pays small advance. Book catalog and guidelines online.

TIPS "Please make sure that you have looked at our website to read our complete submission guidelines and to see if we are looking for a particular subject. Manuscripts must meet all four of our stated criteria. We look for fairly realistic, bright and colorful art—no cartoons. We want the children excited about the books. We envision the books being used at home and in the classroom."

ARTISAN BOOKS

Workman Publishing, 225 Varick Street, New York NY 10014. 10020. **Website:** workman.com/im-prints/artisan. **Contact:** Editoral Department. See website for full details and list of published titles. Publishes the BrainQuest series.

TERMS "Before submitting a proposal, please review this site to learn more about our current list and the type of books we typically publish. When submitting a proposal, please keep in mind that it may take up to 3 months for editors to review it." Please review full submission guidelines on website.

Ⓐ ATHENEUM BOOKS FOR YOUNG READERS

Simon & Schuster, 1230 Avenue of the Americas, New York NY 10020. **Website:** kids.simonand-schuster.com. Publishes hardcover originals.

FICTION All in juvenile versions. "We have few specific needs except for books that are fresh, interesting, and well written. Fad topics are dangerous, as are works you haven't polished to the best of your ability. We also don't need safety pamphlets, ABC books, coloring books, and board books. In writing picture book texts, avoid the coy and 'cutesy,' such as stories about characters with alliterative names." Agented submissions only. No paperback romance-type fiction.

NONFICTION Publishes hardcover originals, picture books for young kids, nonfiction for ages 8-12, and novels for middle-grade and young adults. 100% require freelance illustration. Agented submissions only.

TERMS Guidelines for #10 SASE.

TIPS "Study our titles."

BAILIWICK PRESS

309 East Mulberry St., Fort Collins CO 80524. (970)672-4878. **Fax:** (970)672-4731. **E-mail:** info@bailiwickpress.com. **Website:** www.bailiwickpress.com. "We're a micro-press that produces books and other products that inspire and tell great stories. Our motto is 'books with something to say.' We are now considering submissions, agented and unagented, for children's and young adult fiction. We're looking for smart, funny, and layered writing that kids will clamor for. Authors who already have a following have a leg up. We are only looking for humorous children's fiction. Please do not submit work for adults. Illustrated fiction is desired but not required. (Illustrators are also invited to send samples.) Make us laugh out loud, ooh and aah, and cry, 'Eureka!'"

HOW TO CONTACT "Please read the Aldo Zelnick series to determine if we might be on the same page, then fill out our submission form. Please do not send submissions via snail mail or phone calls. You must complete the online submission form to be considered. If, after completing and submitting the form, you also need to send us an e-mail attachment (such as sample illustrations or excerpts of graphics), you may e-mail them to aldozelnick@gmail.com." Responds in 6 months.

ILLUSTRATION Illustrated fiction desired but not required. Send samples.

Ⓐ BALZER & BRAY

HarperCollins Children's Books, 10 E. 53rd St., New York NY 10022. **Website:** www.harpercollinschildrens.com. "We publish bold, creative, groundbreaking picture books and novels that appeal directly to kids in a fresh way." **Publishes 10 titles/year.**

FICTION Picture Books, Young Readers: adventure, animal, anthology, concept, contemporary, fantasy, history, humor, multicultural, nature/environment, poetry, science fiction, special needs, sports, suspense. Middle readers, young adults/teens: adventure, animal, anthology, contemporary, fantasy, history, humor, multicultural, nature/environment, poetry, science fiction, special needs, sports, suspense.

NONFICTION "We will publish very few nonfiction titles, maybe 1-2 per year."

HOW TO CONTACT Contact editor. Agented submissions only. Publishes book 18 months after acceptance.

ILLUSTRATION Works with 10 illustrators/year. Uses both color and b&w. Illustrations only: send tearsheets to be kept on file. Responds only if interested. Samples are not returned.

PHOTOGRAPHY Works on assignment only.

TERMS Offers advances. Pays illustrators by the project.

Ⓐ BANCROFT PRESS

P.O. Box 65360, Baltimore MD 21209-9945. (410)358-0658. **Fax:** (410)764-1967. **E-mail:** bruceb@bancroftpress.com. **Website:** www.bancroftpress.com. **Contact:** Bruce Bortz, editor/publisher (memoirs, health, investment, politics, history, humor, literary novels, mystery/thrillers, chick lit, young adult). "Bancroft Press is a general trade publisher. Our only mandate is 'books that enlighten.' Our most recent emphasis, with 'The Missing Kennedy' and 'Both Sides of the Line,' has been on memoirs." Publishes hardcover and trade paperback originals as well as e-books and audiobooks. **Publishes 4-6 titles/year. 50% of books from first-time authors. 80% from unagented writers.**

NONFICTION "We advise writers to visit the website." All quality books on any subject of interest to the publisher.

HOW TO CONTACT Submit complete ms. Submit proposal package, outline, 5 sample chapters, competition/market survey. Responds in 6-12 months. Publishes book up to 3 years after acceptance of ms.

TERMS Pays 8-15% royalty on retail price. Pays $750-2,500 advances. Guidelines online.

TIPS "We advise writers to visit our website and to be familiar with our previous work. Patience is the number one attribute contributors must have. It takes us a very long time to get through submitted material, because we are such a small company. Also, we only publish 4-6 books per year, so it may take a long time for your optioned book to be published. We like to be able to market our books to be used in schools and in libraries. We prefer fiction that bucks trends and moves in a new direction. We are especially interested in mysteries and humor (especially humorous mysteries)."

Ⓐ BANTAM BOOKS

Imprint of Penguin Random House, Inc., 1745 Broadway, New York NY 10019. (212)782-9000. **Website:** www.randomhousebooks.com. *Not seeking mss at this time.*

BAREFOOT BOOKS

2067 Massachusettes Ave., 5th Floor, Cambridge MA 02140. (617)576-0660. **Fax:** (617)576-0049. **E-mail:** help@barefootbooks.com. **Website:** www.barefootbooks.com. **Contact:** Acquisitions Editor. "We are a small, independent publishing company that publishes high-quality picture books for children of all ages and specializes in the work of artists and writers from many cultures. We focus on themes that support independence of spirit, encourage openness to others, and foster a life-long love of learning. Prefers full manuscript." Publishes hardcover and trade paperback originals. **Publishes 30 titles/year. 35% of books from first-time authors. 60% from unagented writers.**

FICTION "Barefoot Books only publishes children's picture books and anthologies of folktales. We do not publish novels."

HOW TO CONTACT Barefoot Books is not currently accepting ms queries or submissions. 2,000 queries received/year. 3,000 mss received/year.

ILLUSTRATION Works with 20 illustrators/year. Uses color artwork only. Reviews ms/illustration packages from artists. Send query and art samples or dummy for picture books. Query with samples or send promo sheet and tearsheets. Responds only if interested. Samples returned with SASE. Pays authors royalty of 5% based on retail price. Offers advances. Sends galleys to authors. Originals returned to artist at job's completion.

TERMS Pays advance. Book catalog for 9x12 SAE stamped with $1.80 postage.

BARRON'S EDUCATIONAL SERIES, INC.

250 Wireless Boulevard, Hauppauge NY 11788. **E-mail:** waynebarr@barronseduc.com. **Contact:** Wayne Barr, Acquisitions Manager. "Barron's Educational Series, Inc. rapidly became America's leading publisher of test preparation manuals and school directories." **Publishes 300+ titles/year.**

NONFICTION "We are currently interested in children and young adult fiction and nonfiction books, foreign language learning books, New Age books, cookbooks, business and financial advice books, parenting advice books, art instruction books, sports, fashion, crafts, and study guides. We do not publish poems, and we are not interested in books that have already been published. We would also like to hear from established authors of Test Prep books."

HOW TO CONTACT When submitting a proposal for a children's fiction book: Please include an outline summary; you may include sample pages (please do not include the manuscript in its entirety); artwork is not necessary, but is helpful if author is also the illustrator (please only include a sample); author's credentials must be included. When submitting a work of adult or Juvenile Nonfiction: Include a Table of Contents, along with two sample chapters; a brief description of the work should be included in the cover letter, as well as an overview citing the market being targeted (e.g., children, ages 2-4; secondary school teachers, etc.); please include sample illustrations if the book is to be illustrated; author's credentials must also be included. Due to the large volume of unsolicited submissions received, a complete evaluation of a proposal may take 4-6 weeks. Please do not call about the status of individual submissions.

TERMS "A large, self-addressed, stamped envelope, with enough postage, must be included if you want your material returned. Only *queries* are accepted by email."

BARRONS EDUCATIONAL SERIES

250 Wireless Blvd., Hauppauge NY 11788. **Fax:** (631)434-3723. **Website:** www.barronseduc.com. **Contact:** Wayne R. Barr, manuscript acquisitions.

FICTION Picture books: animal, concept, multicultural, nature/environment. Young readers: adventure, multicultural, nature/environment, fantasy, suspense/mystery. Middle readers: adventure, fantasy, multicultural, nature/environment, problem novels, suspense/mystery. Young adults: problem novels. "Stories with an educational element are appealing."

NONFICTION Picture books: concept, reference. Young readers: biography, how-to, reference, self-help, social issues. Middle readers: hi-lo, how-to, reference, self-help, social issues. Young adults: reference, self-help, social issues, sports.

HOW TO CONTACT Query via e-mail with no attached files. Full guidelines are listed on the website. Submit outline/synopsis and sample chapters. "Nonfiction submissions must be accompanied by SASE for response." Due to the large volume of unsolicited submissions received, a complete evaluation of a proposal may take 4-6 weeks. Please do not call about the status of individual submissions. Publishes book 1 year after acceptance.

ILLUSTRATION Works with 20 illustrators/year. Reviews ms/illustration packages from artists. Query first; 3 chapters of ms with 1 piece of final art, remainder roughs. Illustrations only: Submit tearsheets or slides plus résumé. Responds in 2 months.

TERMS Pays authors royalty of 10-12% based on net price or buys ms outright for $2,000 minimum. Pays illustrators by the project based on retail price. Catalog available for 9x12 SASE. Guidelines available on website.

TIPS Writers: "We publish pre-school storybooks, concept books and middle grade and YA chapter books. No romance novels. Those with an educational element." Illustrators: "We are happy to receive a sample illustration to keep on file for future consideration. Periodic notes reminding us of your work are acceptable." Children's book themes "are becoming much more contemporary and relevant to a child's day-to-day activities, fewer talking animals. We are interested in fiction (ages 7-11 and ages 12-16) dealing with modern problems."

BEHRMAN HOUSE INC.

11 Edison Place, Springfield NJ 07081. (973)379-7200. **Fax:** (973)379-7280. **E-mail:** customersupport@behrmanhouse.com. **Website:** www.behrmanhouse.com. **Contact:** Editorial Committee. Publishes books on all aspects of Judaism: history, cultural, textbooks, holidays. "Behrman House publishes quality books of Jewish content—history, Bible, philosophy, holidays, ethics—for children and adults." **12% of books from first-time authors.**

NONFICTION All levels: Judaism, Jewish educational textbooks. Average word length: young reader: 1,200; middle reader: 2,000; young adult: 4,000.

HOW TO CONTACT Submit outline/synopsis and sample chapters. Responds in 1 month to queries; 2 months to mss. Publishes book 18 months after acceptance.

ILLUSTRATION Works with 6 children's illustrators/year. Reviews ms/illustration packages from artists. "Query first." Illustrations only: Query with samples; send unsolicited art samples by mail. Responds to queries in 1 month; mss in 2 months.

PHOTOGRAPHY Purchases photos from freelancers. Buys stock and assigns work. Uses photos of families involved in Jewish activities. Uses color and b&w prints. Photographers should query with samples. Send unsolicited photos by mail. Submit portfolio for review.

TERMS Pays authors royalty of 3-10% based on retail price or buys ms outright for $1,000-5,000. Offers advance. Pays illustrators by the project (range: $500-5,000). Book catalog free on request. Guidelines online.

BELLEBOOKS

P.O. Box 300921, Memphis TN 38130. (901)344-9024. **Fax:** (901)344-9068. **E-mail:** bellebooks@bellebooks.com. **Website:** www.bellebooks.com. BelleBooks began by publishing Southern fiction. It has become a "second home" for many established authors, who also continue to publish with major publishing houses. **Publishes 30-40 titles/year.**

FICTION "Yes, we'd love to find the next Harry Potter, but our primary focus for the moment is publishing for the teen market."

HOW TO CONTACT Query e-mail with brief synopsis and credentials/credits with full ms attached (RTF format preferred).

TERMS Guidelines online.

TIPS "Our list aims for the teen reader and the crossover market. If you're a 'Southern Louise Rennison,' that would catch our attention. Humor is always a plus. We'd love to see books featuring teen boys as protagonists. We're happy to see dark edgy books on serious subjects."

Ⓐ BERKLEY

Penguin Group (USA) Inc., 375 Hudson St., New York NY 10014. **Website:** penguin.com. The Berkley Publishing Group publishes a variety of general nonfiction and fiction including the traditional categories of romance, mystery, and science fiction. Publishes paperback and mass market originals and reprints. **Publishes 700 titles/year.**

"Due to the high volume of manuscripts received, most Penguin Group (USA) Inc. imprints do not normally accept unsolicited mss. The preferred and standard method for having mss considered for publication by a major publisher is to submit them through an established literary agent."

FICTION No occult fiction.

NONFICTION No memoirs or personal stories.

HOW TO CONTACT Prefers agented submissions.

Ⓞ BESS PRESS

3565 Harding Ave., Honolulu HI 96816. (808)734-7159. **Fax:** (808)732-3627. **Website:** www.besspress.com. Bess Press is a family-owned independent book publishing company based in Honolulu. For over 30 years, Bess Press has been producing both educational and popular general interest titles about Hawai'i and the Pacific.

NONFICTION "We are constantly seeking to work with authors, artists, photographers, and organizations that are developing works concentrating on Hawai'i and the Pacific. Our goal is to regularly provide customers with new, creative, informative, educational, and entertaining publications that are directly connected to or flowing from Hawai'i and other islands in the Pacific region." Not interested in material that is unassociated with Hawai'i or the greater Pacific in theme. Please do not submit work if it does not fall into this regional category.

HOW TO CONTACT Submit your name, contact information, working title, genre, target audience, short (4-6 sentences) description of your work, target audience(s), how your work differs from other books already publishing on the same subject, and discussion of any additional material with samples. All submissions via e-mail. Responds in 4 months.

TERMS Catalog online. Guidelines online.

TIPS "As a regional publisher, we are looking for material specific to the region (Hawai'i and Micronesia), preferably from writers and illustrators living within (or very familiar with) the region."

BETHANY HOUSE PUBLISHERS

Division of Baker Publishing Group, 6030 E. Fulton Rd., Ada MI 49301. (616)676-9185. **Fax:** (616)676-9573. **Website:** bakerpublishinggroup.com/bethanyhouse. Bethany House Publishers specializes in books that communicate Biblical truth and assist people in both spiritual and practical areas of life. Considers unsolicited work only through a professional literary agent or through manuscript submission services, Authonomy or Christian Manuscript Submissions. Guidelines online. *All unsolicited mss returned unopened.* Publishes hardcover and trade paperback originals, mass market paperback reprints. **Publishes 90-100 titles/year. 2% of books from first-time authors. 50% from unagented writers.**

HOW TO CONTACT Responds in 3 months to queries. Publishes a book 1 year after acceptance.

TERMS Pays royalty on net price. Pays advance. Book catalog for 9x12 envelope and 5 first-class stamps.

TIPS "Bethany House Publishers' publishing program relates Biblical truth to all areas of life—whether in the framework of a well-told story, of a challenging book for spiritual growth, or of a Bible reference work. We are seeking high-quality fiction and nonfiction that will inspire and challenge our audience."

ⓐ BEYOND WORDS PUBLISHING, INC.
20827 NW Cornell Rd., Suite 500, Hillsboro OR 97124. (503)531-8700. **Fax:** (503)531-8773. **E-mail:** info@beyondword.com. **Website:** www.beyondword.com. **Contact:** Submissions Department (for agents only). "At this time, we are not accepting any unsolicited queries or proposals, and recommend that all authors work with a literary agent in submitting their work." Publishes hardcover and trade paperback originals and paperback reprints. **Publishes 10-15 titles/year.**

NONFICTION For adult nonfiction, wants whole body health, the evolving human, and transformation. For children and young adult, wants health, titles that inspire kids' power to incite change, and titles that allow young readers to explore and/or question traditional wisdom and spiritual practices. Does not want children's picture books, adult fiction, cookbooks, textbooks, reference books, photography books, or illustrated coffee table books.

HOW TO CONTACT Agent should submit query letter with proposal, including author bio, 5 sample chapters, complete synopsis of book, market analysis, SASE.

BLACK ROSE WRITING
P.O. Box 1540, Castroville TX 78009. **E-mail:** creator@blackrosewriting.com. **Website:** www.blackrosewriting.com. Author provides illustrations, fully-illustrated or samples. **Contact:** Reagan Rothe. Black Rose Writing is an independent publishing house that strongly believes in developing a personal relationship with their authors. The Texas-based publishing company doesn't see authors as clients

or just another number on a page, but rather as individual people. who deserve an honest review of their material and to be paid traditional royalties without ever paying any fees to be published. Publishes fiction and nonfiction. **Publishes 150+ titles/year. 75% of books from first-time authors. 80% from unagented writers.**

HOW TO CONTACT "Our preferred submission method is via Authors.me, please click 'Submit Here' on our website." 3,500 submissions received/year. Responds in 3-6 weeks on queries; 1-2 months on mss. Publishes ms 3-6 months after acceptance.

ILLUSTRATION Must be provided by author.

TERMS Royalties start at 10%, e-book royalties 15% (25-30% net). Catalog online. Guidelines online.

ⓐ BLOOMSBURY CHILDREN'S BOOKS
Imprint of Bloomsbury USA, 1385 Broadway, 5th Floor, New York NY 10018. **Website:** www.bloomsbury.com/us/childrens. No phone calls or e-mails. *Agented submissions only.* **Publishes 60 titles/year. 25% of books from first-time authors.**

HOW TO CONTACT *Agented submissions only.* Responds in 6 months.

TERMS Pays royalty. Pays advance. Book catalog online. Guidelines online.

BLOOMSBURY SPARK
Website: www.bloomsbury.com/us/bloomsbury-spark. "Bloomsbury Spark is a one-of-a-kind, global, digital imprint from Bloomsbury Publishing dedicated to publishing a wide array of exciting fiction eBooks to teen, YA, and new adult readers. Our outstanding list features multiple genres: romance, contemporary, dystopian, paranormal, science fiction, mystery, thriller, and more."

FICTION "We're always in the market for fast-paced, unputdownable Young Adult novels on the older end of the spectrum. Whether it's a pulse-pounding adventure set in a post-apocalyptic future or a heart-wrenching romance, we want it! Bring on the fantasy! Anything that puts a fresh spin on magic, wizards, and far-off lands will always grab our attention." Full wishlist available on website.

HOW TO CONTACT "Due to the volume of e-mails we receive, we unfortunately cannot respond to each individual submission, but we will let you know within two months if we would like to read more of your fantastic manuscript!"

TERMS If you have a manuscript between 25 and 100k words in one (or more!) of our wishlist categories, please send us: A query letter, the first three chapters of your manuscript pasted into the body of the message, a brief biography, and links to your online presence."

BOOKFISH BOOKS

E-mail: bookfishbooks@gmail.com. **Website:** bookfishbooks.com. **Contact:** Tammy McKee, acquisitions editor. BookFish Books is looking for novel-length young adult, new adult, and middle grade works in all subgenres. Both published and unpublished, agented or unagented authors are welcome to submit. "Sorry, but we do not publish novellas, picture books, early reader/chapter books or adult novels." Responds to every query.

HOW TO CONTACT Query via e-mail with a brief synopsis and first 3 chapters of ms.

TERMS Guidelines online.

TIPS "We only accept complete manuscripts. Please do not query us with partial manuscripts or proposals."

BOYDS MILLS PRESS

Highlights for Children, Inc., 815 Church St., Honesdale PA 18431. (570)253-1164. **Website:** www.boydsmillspress.com. Boyds Mills Press publishes picture books, nonfiction, activity books, and paperback reprints. Their titles have been named notable books by the International Reading Association, the American Library Association, and the National Council of Teachers of English. They've earned numerous awards, including the National Jewish Book Award, the Christopher Medal, the NCTE Orbis Pictus Honor, and the Golden Kite Honor. Boyds Mills Press welcomes unsolicited submissions from published and unpublished writers and artists. Submit a ms with a cover letter of relevant information, including experience with writing and publishing. Label the package "Manuscript Submission" and include a SASE. For art samples, label the package "Art Sample Submission." All submissions will be evaluated for all imprints.

FICTION Interested in picture books and middle grade fiction. Do not send a query first. Send the entire ms of picture book or the first 3 chapters and a plot summary for middle grade fiction (will request the balance of ms if interested).

NONFICTION Include a detailed bibliography with submission. Highly recommends including an expert's review of your ms and a detailed explanation of the books in the marketplace that are similar to the one you propose. References to the need for this book (by the National Academy of Sciences or by similar subject-specific organizations) will strengthen your proposal. If you intend for the book to be illustrated with photos or other graphic elements (charts, graphs, etc.), it is your responsibility to find or create those elements and to include with the submission a permissions budget, if applicable. Finally, keep in mind that good children's nonfiction has a narrative quality—a story line—that encyclopedias do not; please consider whether both the subject and the language will appeal to children.

HOW TO CONTACT Responds to mss within 3 months.

ILLUSTRATION Illustrators submitting a picture book should include the ms, a dummy, and a sample reproduction of the final artwork that reflects the style and technique you intend to use. Do not send original artwork.

TERMS Catalog online. Guidelines online.

CALKINS CREEK

Boyds Mills Press, 815 Church St., Honesdale PA 18431. **Website:** www.boydsmillspress.com. "We aim to publish books that are a well-written blend of creative writing and extensive research, which emphasize important events, people, and places in US history."

HOW TO CONTACT Submit outline/synopsis and 3 sample chapters.

ILLUSTRATION Accepts material from international illustrators. Works with 25 (for all Boyds Mills Press imprints) illustrators/year. Uses both color and b&w. Reviews ms/illustration packages. For ms/illustration packages: Submit ms with 2 pieces of final art. Submit ms/illustration packages to address above, label package "Manuscript Submission." Reviews work for future assignments. If interested in illustrating future titles, query with samples. Submit samples to address above. Label package "Art Sample Submission."

PHOTOGRAPHY Buys stock images and assigns work. Submit photos to: address above, label package "Art Sample Submission." Uses color or b&w 8×10 prints. For first contact, send promo piece (color or b&w).

TERMS Pays authors royalty or work purchased outright. Guidelines online.

TIPS "Read through our recently published titles and review our catalog. When selecting titles to publish, our emphasis will be on important events, people, and places in US history. Writers are encouraged to submit a detailed bibliography, including secondary and primary sources, and expert reviews with their submissions."

Ⓐ CANDLEWICK PRESS

99 Dover St., Somerville MA 02144. (617) 661-3330. **Fax:** (617) 661-0565. **E-mail:** bigbear@candlewick.com. **Website:** www.candlewick.com. "Candlewick Press publishes high-quality, illustrated children's books for ages infant through young adult. We are a truly child-centered publisher." Publishes hardcover and trade paperback originals, and reprints. **Publishes 200 titles/year. 5% of books from first-time authors.**

Ⓞ *Candlewick Press is not accepting queries or unsolicited mss at this time.*

FICTION Picture books: animal, concept, contemporary, fantasy, history, humor, multicultural, nature/environment, poetry. Middle readers, young adults: contemporary, fantasy, history, humor, multicultural, poetry, science fiction, sports, suspense/mystery.

NONFICTION Picture books: concept, biography, geography, nature/environment. Young readers: biography, geography, nature/environment.

HOW TO CONTACT "We currently do not accept unsolicited editorial queries or submissions. If you are an author or illustrator and would like us to consider your work, please read our submissions policy (online) to learn more."

ILLUSTRATION "Candlewick prefers to see a range of styles from artists along with samples showing strong characters (human or animals) in various settings with various emotions."

TERMS Pays authors royalty of 2.5-10% based on retail price. Offers advance.

TIPS *"We no longer accept unsolicited mss. See our website for further information about us."*

CAPSTONE PRESS

Capstone Young Readers, 1710 Roe Crest Dr., North Mankato MN 56003. **E-mail:** author.sub@capstonepub.com; il.sub@capstonepub.com. **Website:** www.capstonepub.com. The Capstone Press imprint publishes nonfiction with accessible text on topics kids love to capture interest and build confidence and skill in beginning, struggling, and reluctant readers, grades pre-K-9.

FICTION Send fiction submissions via e-mail (author.sub@capstonepub.com). Include the following, in the body of the e-mail: sample chapters, résumé, and a list of previous publishing credits.

NONFICTION Send nonfiction submissions via postal mail. Include the following: résumé, cover letter, and up to 3 writing samples.

HOW TO CONTACT Responds only if submissions fit needs. Mss and writing samples will not be returned. "If you receive no reply within 6 months, you should assume the editors are not interested."

ILLUSTRATION Send fiction illustration submissions via e-mail (il.sub@capstonepub.com). Include the following, in the body of the e-mail: sample artwork, résumé, and a list of previous publishing credits. For nonfiction illustrations, send via e-mail (nf.il.sub@capstonepub.com) sample artwork (2-4 pieces) and a list of previous publishing credits.

TERMS Catalog available upon request. Guidelines online.

Ⓞ CAPSTONE PROFESSIONAL

Maupin House, Capstone, 1710 Roe Crest Dr., North Mankato MN 56003. (312)324-5200. **Fax:** (312)324-5201. **E-mail:** author.sub@capstonepub.com. **Website:** www.capstonepd.com. Capstone Professional publishes professional learning resources for K-12 educators under the imprint of Maupin House. **Publishes 6-8 titles/year. 60% of books from first-time authors. 100% from unagented writers.**

NONFICTION Professional development offerings by Capstone Professional range from webinars and workshops to conference speakers and author visits. Submissions for products that speak to the needs of educators today are always accepted. "We continue to look for professional development resources that support grades K–8 classroom teachers in areas, such as these: Literacy, Language Arts, Content-Area Literacy, Research-Based Practices, Assessment, Inquiry, Technology, Differentiation, Standards-Based Instruction, School Safety, Classroom Management, and School Community."

HOW TO CONTACT Receives 25 submissions/year. Responds in less than 1 month. Publishes 6 months after acceptance.

TERMS Pays royalty. Catalog and guidelines online.

CAROLRHODA BOOKS, INC.

1251 Washington Ave. N., Minneapolis MN 55401. **Website:** www.lernerbooks.com. "We will continue to seek targeted solicitations at specific reading levels and in specific subject areas. The company will list these targeted solicitations on our website and in national newsletters, such as the SCBWI Bulletin." Interested in "boundary-pushing" teen fiction. *Lerner Publishing Group no longer accepts submissions to any of their imprints except for Kar-Ben Publishing.*

Ⓐ CARTWHEEL BOOKS

Imprint of Scholastic Trade Division, 557 Broadway, New York NY 10012. (212)343-6100. **Website:** www.scholastic.com. Cartwheel Books publishes innovative books for children, up to age 8. "We are looking for 'novelties' that are books first, play objects second. Even without its gimmick, a Cartwheel Book should stand alone as a valid piece of children's literature." Publishes novelty books, easy readers, board books, hardcover, and trade paperback originals.

FICTION Again, the subject should have mass market appeal for very young children. Humor can be helpful, but not necessary. Mistakes writers make are a reading level that is too difficult, a topic of no interest or too narrow, or mss that are too long.

NONFICTION Cartwheel Books publishes for the very young, therefore nonfiction should be written in a manner that is accessible to preschoolers through 2nd grade. Often writers choose topics that are too narrow or "special" and do not appeal to the mass market. Also, the text and vocabulary are frequently too difficult for our young audience.

HOW TO CONTACT *Accepts mss from agents only.*

TERMS Guidelines available free.

CEDAR FORT, INC.

2373 W. 700 S, Springville UT 84663. (801)489-4084. **Website:** www.cedarfort.com. "Each year we publish well over 100 books, and many of those are by first-time authors. At the same time, we love to see books from established authors. As one of the largest book publishers in Utah, we have the capability and enthusiasm to make your book a success, whether you are a new author or a returning one. We want to publish uplifting and edifying books that help people think about what is important in life, books people enjoy reading to relax and feel better about themselves, and books to help improve lives. Although we do put out several children's books each year, we are extremely selective. Our children's books must have strong religious or moral values, and must contain outstanding writing and an excellent storyline." Publishes hardcover, trade paperback originals and reprints, mass market paperback and electronic reprints. **Publishes 150 titles/year. 60% of books from first-time authors. 95% from unagented writers.**

HOW TO CONTACT Submit completed ms. Query with SASE; submit proposal package, including outline, 2 sample chapters; or submit completed ms. Receives 200 queries/year; 600 mss/year. Responds in 1 month on queries; 2 months on proposals; 4 months on mss. Publishes book 10-14 months after acceptance.

TERMS Pays 10-12% royalty on wholesale price. Pays $2,000-50,000 advance. Catalog and guidelines online.

TIPS "Our audience is rural, conservative, mainstream. The first page of your ms is very important because we start reading every submission, but good writing and plot keep us reading."

Ⓒ CHARLESBRIDGE PUBLISHING

85 Main St., Watertown MA 02472. (617)926-0329. **Fax:** (617)926-5720. **E-mail:** tradeeditorial@charlesbridge.com. **Website:** www.charlesbridge.com. "Charlesbridge publishes high-quality books for children, with a goal of creating lifelong readers and lifelong learners. Our books encourage reading and discovery in the classroom, library, and home. We believe that books for children should offer accurate information, promote a positive worldview, and embrace a child's innate sense of wonder and fun. To this end, we continually strive to seek new voices, new visions, and new directions in children's literature. As of September 2015, we are now accepting young adult novels for consideration." Publishes hardcover and trade paperback nonfiction and fiction, children's books for the trade and library markets. **Publishes 45 titles/year. 10-20% of books from first-time authors. 50% from unagented writers.**

FICTION Strong stories with enduring themes. Charlesbridge publishes both picture books and transitional bridge books (books ranging from early readers to middle-grade chapter books). Our fiction titles include lively, plot-driven stories with strong, engaging characters. No alphabet books, board books, coloring books, activity books, or books with audiotapes or CD-ROMs.

NONFICTION Strong interest in nature, environment, social studies, and other topics for trade and library markets.

HOW TO CONTACT Please submit only 1 ms at a time. For picture books and shorter bridge books, please send a complete ms. For fiction books longer than 30 ms pages, please send a detailed plot synopsis, a chapter outline, and 3 chapters of text. If sending a young adult novel, mark the front of the envelope with "YA novel enclosed." Please note, for young adult, e-mail submissions are preferred to the following address; yasubs@charlesbridge.com. Only responds if interested. Full guidelines on site. Please submit only 1 or 2 chapters at a time. For nonfiction books longer than 30 ms pages, send a detailed proposal, a chapter outline, and 1-3 chapters of text. 2,000 submissions/year. Responds in 3 months. Publishes ms 2-4 years after acceptance.

TERMS Pays royalty. Pays advance. Guidelines online.

TIPS "To become acquainted with our publishing program, we encourage you to review our books and visit our website where you will find our catalog."

CHICAGO REVIEW PRESS

814 N. Franklin St., Chicago IL 60610. (312)337-0747. **Fax:** (312)337-5110. **E-mail:** csherry@chicagoreviewpress.com; jpohlen@chicagoreviewpress.com; lreardon@chicagoreviewpress.com; ytaylor@chicagoreviewpress.com. **Website:** www.chicagoreviewpress.com. **Contact:** Cynthia Sherry, publisher; Yuval Taylor, senior editor; Jerome Pohlen, senior editor; Lisa Reardon, senior editor. "Chicago Review Press publishes high-quality, nonfiction, educational activity books that extend the learning process through hands-on projects and accurate and interesting text. We look for activity books that are as much fun as they are constructive and informative."

FICTION Guidelines now available on website.

NONFICTION Young readers, middle readers and young adults: activity books, arts/crafts, multicultural, history, nature/environment, science. "We're interested in hands-on, educational books; anything else probably will be rejected." Average length: young readers and young adults, 144-160 pages.

HOW TO CONTACT Enclose cover letter and a brief synopsis of book in 1-2 paragraphs, table of contents and first 3 sample chapters; prefers not to receive e-mail queries. For children's activity books include a few sample activities with a list of the others. Full guidelines available on site. Responds in 2 months. Publishes a book 1-2 years after acceptance.

ILLUSTRATION Works with 6 illustrators/year. Uses primarily b&w artwork. Reviews ms/illustration packages from artists. Submit 1-2 chapters of ms with corresponding pieces of final art. Illustrations only: Query with samples, résumé. Responds only if interested. Samples returned with SASE.

PHOTOGRAPHY Buys photos from freelancers ("but not often"). Buys stock and assigns work. Wants "instructive photos. We consult our files when we know what we're looking for on a book-by-book basis." Uses b&w prints.

TERMS Pays authors royalty of 7.5-12.5% based on retail price. Offers advances of $3,000-6,000. Pays illustrators and photographers by the project (range varies considerably). Book catalog available for $3. Ms guidelines available for $3.

TIPS "We're looking for original activity books for small children and the adults caring for them—new themes and enticing projects to occupy kids' imaginations and promote their sense of personal creativity. We like activity books that are as much fun as they are constructive. Please write for guidelines so you'll know what we're looking for."

CHILDREN'S BRAINS ARE YUMMY (CBAY) BOOKS

P.O. Box 670296, Dallas TX 75367. **E-mail:** submissions@cbaybooks.com. **Website:** www.cbaybooks.com. **Contact:** Madeline Smoot, publisher. "CBAY Books currently focuses on quality fantasy and science fiction books for the middle grade and teen markets. We are not currently accepting unsolicited submissions. We do not publish picture books." **Publishes 3-6 titles/year. 30% of books from first-time authors. 80% from unagented writers.**

HOW TO CONTACT Responds in 2 months. Publishes ms 24 months after acceptance.

ILLUSTRATION Accepts international material. Works with 0-1 illustrators/year. Uses color artwork only. Reviews artwork. Send manuscripts with dummy. Send résumé and tearsheets. Send samples to Madeline Smoot. Responds to queries only if interested.

PHOTOGRAPHY Buys stock images.

TERMS Pays authors royalty 10-15% based on wholesale price. Offers advances against royalties. Average amount $500. Pays advance. "We are distributed by IPG. Our books can be found in their catalog at www.ipgbooks.com." Brochure and guidelines online.

CHOOSECO, LLC

P.O. Box 46, Waitsfield VT 05673. 1-800-564-3468; (802)496-2595. **Fax:** (802) 496-7965. **Website:** www.cyoa.com/pages/manuscript-submissions. **Contact:** Submissions. "Chooseco LLC was formed in 2003 by series founder R.A. Montgomery to republish some of the best-selling titles in the original Choose Your Own Adventure® series. We have also published 19 CYOA books for younger readers under our Dragonlarks imprint. These books are shorter, with a larger page format and vibrant color artwork (aimed at readers aged 5-8). Chooseco has introduced CYOA: The Golden Path, an original three volume hardcover series written by Anson Montgomery. The Golden Path series is our experiment with a 'longer form' version of interactive fiction for slightly older readers (Age 12+)."

HOW TO CONTACT "While Chooseco works with a team of very talented writers, we are able to review manuscripts or writing samples from potential new writers. We receive many submissions each year, so please be patient awaiting a response."

ILLUSTRATION We are always interested in hearing from artists. Please email a link to a portfolio to art@chooseco.com.

TERMS Chooseco, LLC does not accept online submissions of manuscripts. If you are interested in submitting a manuscript, please print and fill out the Submissions Contract available online, and mail it to our address with a cover letter describing your manuscript. You will be notified if they are interested in pursuing your submission. Any submissions not adhering to these guidelines will not be reviewed.

CHRONICLE BOOKS

680 Second St., San Francisco CA 94107. **E-mail:** submissions@chroniclebooks.com. **Website:** www.chroniclebooks.com. "We publish an exciting range of books, stationery, kits, calendars, and novelty formats. Our list includes children's books and interactive formats; young adult books; cookbooks; fine art, design, and photography; pop culture; craft, fashion, beauty, and home decor; relationships, mind-body-spirit; innovative formats such as interactive journals, kits, decks, and stationery; and much, much more." **Publishes 90 titles/year.**

FICTION Only interested in fiction for children and young adults. No adult fiction.

NONFICTION "We're always looking for the new and unusual. We do accept unsolicited manuscripts and we review all proposals. However, given the volume of proposals we receive, we are not able to personally respond to unsolicited proposals unless we are interested in pursuing the project."

HOW TO CONTACT Submit complete ms (picture books); submit outline/synopsis and 3 sample chapters (for older readers). Will not respond to submissions unless interested. Will not consider submissions by fax, e-mail, or disk. Do not include SASE; do not send original materials. No submissions will be returned. Submit via mail or e-mail (prefers e-mail for adult submissions; only by mail for children's submissions). Submit proposal (guidelines online) and allow 3 months for editors to review and for children's submissions, allow 6 months. If submitting by mail, do not include SASE since our staff will not return materials. Responds to queries in 1 month. Publishes a book 1-3 years after acceptance.

ILLUSTRATION Works with 40-50 illustrators/year. Wants "unusual art, graphically strong, something that will stand out on the shelves. Fine art, not mass market." Reviews ms/illustration packages from artists. "Indicate if project *must* be considered jointly, or if editor may consider text and art separately." Illustrations only: Submit samples of artist's work (not necessarily from book, but in the envisioned style). Slides, tearsheets and color photocopies OK. (No original art.) Dummies helpful. Résumé helpful. Samples suited to our needs are filed for future reference. Samples not suited to our needs will be recycled. Queries and project proposals responded to in same time frame as author query/proposals."

PHOTOGRAPHY Purchases photos from freelancers. Works on assignment only.

TERMS Generally pays authors in royalties based on retail price, "though we do occasionally work on a flat fee basis." Advance varies. Illustrators paid royalty based on retail price or flat fee. Book catalog for 9x12 SAE and 8 first-class stamps. Ms guidelines for #10 SASE.

CHRONICLE BOOKS FOR CHILDREN

680 Second St., San Francisco CA 94107. (415)537-4200. **Fax:** (415)537-4460. **Website:** www.chronicle-kids.com. "Chronicle Books for Children publishes an eclectic mixture of traditional and innovative children's books. Our aim is to publish books that inspire young readers to learn and grow creatively while helping them discover the joy of reading. We're looking for quirky, bold artwork and subject matter." Publishes hardcover and trade paperback originals. **Publishes 100-110 titles/year. 6% of books from first-time authors. 25% from unagented writers.**

FICTION Does not accept proposals by fax, via e-mail, or on disk. When submitting artwork, either as a part of a project or as samples for review, do not send original art.

HOW TO CONTACT Query with synopsis. 30,000 queries received/year. Responds in 2-4 weeks to queries; 6 months to mss. Publishes a book 18-24 months after acceptance.

TERMS Pays variable advance. Book catalog for 9x12 envelope and 3 first-class stamps. Guidelines online.

TIPS "We are interested in projects that have a unique bent to them—be it in subject matter, writing style, or illustrative technique. As a small list, we are looking for books that will lend our list a distinctive flavor. Primarily we are interested in fiction and nonfiction picture books for children ages up to 8 years, and nonfiction books for children ages up to 12 years. We publish board, pop-up, and other novelty formats as well as picture books. We are also interested in early chapter books, middle grade fiction, and young adult projects."

CLARION BOOKS

Houghton Mifflin Co., 215 Park Ave. S., New York NY 10003. **Website:** www.hmhco.com. "Clarion Books publishes picture books, nonfiction, and fiction for infants through grade 12. Avoid telling your stories in verse unless you are a professional poet. *We are no longer responding to your unsolic-ited submission unless we are interested in publishing it. Please do not include a SASE. Submissions will be recycled, and you will not hear from us regarding the status of your submission unless we are interested. We regret that we cannot respond personally to each submission, but we do consider each and every submission we receive.*" Publishes hardcover originals for children. **Publishes 50 titles/year.**

FICTION "Clarion is highly selective in the areas of historical fiction, fantasy, and science fiction. A novel must be superlatively written in order to find a place on the list. Mss that arrive without an SASE of adequate size will *not* be responded to or returned. Accepts fiction translations."

NONFICTION No unsolicited mss.

HOW TO CONTACT Submit complete ms. No queries, please. Send to only *one* Clarion editor. Submit proposal package and sample chapters. Responds in 2 months to queries. Publishes a book 2 years after acceptance.

ILLUSTRATION Pays illustrators royalty; flat fee for jacket illustration.

TERMS Pays 5-10% royalty on retail price. Pays minimum of $4,000 advance. Guidelines online.

TIPS "Looks for freshness, enthusiasm—in short, life."

CRAIGMORE CREATIONS

PMB 114, 4110 SE Hawthorne Blvd., Portland OR 97124. (503)477-9562. **E-mail:** info@craigmorecre-ations.com. **Website:** www.craigmorecreations.com.

NONFICTION "We publish books that make time travel seem possible: nonfiction that explores prehistory and Earth sciences for children."

HOW TO CONTACT Submit proposal package. See website for detailed submission guidelines.

CREATIVE COMPANY

P.O. Box 227, Mankato MN 56002. (800)445-6209. **Fax:** (507)388-2746. **E-mail:** info@thecreativecom-pany.us. **Website:** www.thecreativecompany.us. "We are currently not accepting fiction submissions." **Publishes 140 titles/year.**

NONFICTION Picture books, young readers, young adults: animal, arts/crafts, biography, careers, geography, health, history, hobbies, multicultural, music/dance, nature/environment, religion, science, social issues, special needs, sports. Average word length: young readers: 500; young adults: 6,000.

HOW TO CONTACT Submit outline/synopsis and 2 sample chapters, along with division of titles within the series. Responds in 3-6 months. Publishes a book 2 years after acceptance.

PHOTOGRAPHY Buys stock. Contact: Photo Editor. Model/property releases not required; captions required. Uses b&w prints. Submit cover letter, promo piece. Ms and photographer guidelines available for SAE.

TERMS Guidelines available for SAE.

TIPS "We are accepting nonfiction, series submissions only. Fiction submissions will not be reviewed or returned. Nonfiction submissions should be presented in series (4, 6, or 8) rather than single."

CRESTON BOOKS

P.O. Box 9369, Berkeley CA 94709. **E-mail:** submissions@crestonbooks.co. **Website:** crestonbooks.co. Creston Books is author-illustrator driven, with talented, award-winning creators given more editorial freedom and control than in a typical New York house. **50% of books from first-time authors. 50% from unagented writers.**

HOW TO CONTACT Please paste text of picture books or first chapters of novels in the body of e-mail. Words of Advice for submitting authors listed on the site.

TERMS Pays advance. Catalog online. Guidelines online.

CURIOSITY QUILLS

Whampa, LLC, P.O. Box 2160, Reston VA 20195. (800)998-2509. **Fax:** (800)998-2509. **E-mail:** editor@curiosityquills.com. **Website:** curiosityquills.com. **Contact:** Alisa Gus. Curiosity Quills is a publisher of hard-hitting dark science-fiction, speculative fiction, and paranormal works aimed at adults, young adults, and new adults. Firm publishes science-fiction, speculative fiction, steampunk, paranormal, and urban fantasy, and corresponding romance titles under its new Rebel Romance imprint. **Publishes 75 titles/year. 60% of books from first-time authors. 65% from unagented writers.**

FICTION Looking for "thought-provoking, mind-twisting rollercoasters—challenge our mind, turn our world upside down, and make us question. Those are the makings of a true literary marauder."

NONFICTION Writer's guides, on a strictly limited basis.

HOW TO CONTACT Submit ms using online submission form or e-mail to acquisitions@curiosityquills.com. 1,000 submissions/year. Responds

in 1-6 weeks. Publishes ms 9-12 months after acceptance.

TERMS Pays variable royalty. Does not pay advance. Catalog available. Guidelines online.

DARBY CREEK PUBLISHING

Lerner Publishing Group, 1251 Washington Ave. N., Minneapolis MN 55401. (612)332-3344. **Fax:** (612)332-7615. **Website:** www.lernerbooks.com. "Darby Creek publishes series fiction titles for emerging, striving, and reluctant readers ages 7 to 18 (grades 2-12). From beginning chapter books to intermediate fiction and page-turning YA titles, Darby Creek books engage readers with strong characters and formats they'll want to pursue." Darby Creek does not publish picture books. Publishes children's chapter books, middle readers, young adult. Mostly series. **Publishes 25 titles/year.**

○ "We are currently not accepting any submissions. If that changes, we will provide all children's writing publications with our new info."

FICTION Middle readers, young adult. Recently published: *The Surviving Southside* series, by various authors; *The Agent Amelia* series, by Michael Broad; *The Mallory McDonald* series, by Laurie B. Friedman; and *The Alien Agent* series, by Pam Service.

NONFICTION Middle readers: biography, history, science, sports. Recently published *Albino Animals*, by Kelly Milner Halls, illustrated by Rick Spears; *Miracle: The True Story of the Wreck of the Sea Venture*, by Gail Karwoski.

ILLUSTRATION Illustrations only: Send photocopies and résumé with publishing history. "Indicate which samples we may keep on file and include SASE and appropriate packing materials for any samples you wish to have returned."

TERMS Offers advance-against-royalty contracts.

DAWN PUBLICATIONS

12402 Bitney Springs Rd., Nevada City CA 95959. (530)274-7775. **Fax:** (530)274-7778. **Website:** www. dawnpub.com. **Contact:** Carol Malnor, associate editor. "Dawn Publications is dedicated to inspiring in children a sense of appreciation for all life on earth. Dawn looks for nature awareness and appreciation titles that promote a relationship with the natural world and specific habitats, usually through inspiring treatment and nonfiction." Dawn accepts mss submissions by e-mail; follow instructions posted on website. Submissions by mail OK. Publishes hardcover and trade paperback originals. **Publishes 6 titles/year. 15% of books from first-time authors. 90% from unagented writers.**

HOW TO CONTACT 2,500 queries or mss received/year. Automated confirmation of submission sent upon receipt. Followup in 2 months if interested. Publishes book 1-2 years after acceptance.

ILLUSTRATION Works with 5 illustrators/year. Will review ms/illustration packages from artists. Query; send ms with dummy. Illustrations only: Query with samples, résumé.

TERMS Pays advance. Book catalog and guidelines online.

TIPS "Publishes mostly creative nonfiction with lightness and inspiration." Looking for "picture books expressing nature awareness with inspirational quality leading to enhanced self-awareness." Does not publish anthropomorphic works; no animal dialogue.

ⓐ DELACORTE PRESS

1745 Broadway, New York NY 10019. (212)782-9000. **Website:** randomhousekids.com; randomhouseteens.com. An imprint of Random House Children's Books, a division of Penguin Random House LLC, New York. Publishes middle grade and young adult fiction in hard cover, trade paperback, mass market and digest formats.

- All query letters and manuscript submissions must be submitted through an agent or at the request of an editor.

DIAL BOOKS FOR YOUNG READERS

Imprint of Penguin Group (USA), 345 Hudson St., New York NY 10014. (212)366-2000. **Website:** www.penguin.com/children. "Dial Books for Young Readers publishes quality picture books for ages 18 months-6 years; lively, believable novels for middle readers and young adults; and occasional nonfiction for middle readers and young adults." Publishes hardcover originals. **Publishes 50 titles/year. 20% of books from first-time authors.**

FICTION Especially looking for lively and well-written novels for middle grade and young adult children involving a convincing plot and believable characters. The subject matter or theme should not already be overworked in previously published books. The approach must not be demeaning to any minority group, nor should the roles of female

characters (or others) be stereotyped, though we don't think books should be didactic, or in any way message-y. No topics inappropriate for the juvenile, young adult, and middle grade audiences. No plays.

HOW TO CONTACT Accepts unsolicited queries and up to 10 pages for longer works and unsolicited mss for picture books. Will only respond if interested. "We accept entire picture book manuscripts and a maximum of 10 pages for longer works (novels, easy-to-reads). When submitting a portion of a longer work, please provide an accompanying cover letter that briefly describes your manuscript's plot, genre (i.e. easy-to-read, middle grade, or YA novel), the intended age group, and your publishing credits, if any." 5,000 queries received/year. Responds in 4-6 months to queries.

ILLUSTRATION Send nonreturnable samples, no originals, to Lily Malcolm. Show children and animals.

TERMS Pays royalty. Pays varied advances. Book catalog and guidelines online.

TIPS "Our readers are anywhere from preschool age to teenage. Picture books must have strong plots, lots of action, unusual premises, or universal themes treated with freshness and originality. Humor works well in these books. A very well-thought-out and intelligently presented book has the best chance of being taken on. Genre isn't as much of a factor as presentation."

ⓒ EDUPRESS, INC.

Teacher Created Resources, 12621 Western Ave., Garden Grove CA 92841. (800)662-4321. **Fax:** (800)525-1254. **Website:** www.edupress.com. **Contact:** Editor-in-Chief. Edupress, Inc., publishes supplemental curriculum resources for PK-6th grade. Currently emphasizing Common Core reading and math games and materials.

- "Our mission is to create products that make kids want to go to school."

HOW TO CONTACT Submit complete ms via mail or e-mail with "Manuscript Submission" as the subject line. Responds in 2-4 months. Publishes ms 1-2 years after acceptance.

ILLUSTRATION Query with samples. Contact: Cathy Baker, product development manager. Responds only if interested. Samples returned with SASE.

PHOTOGRAPHY Buys stock.

TERMS Work purchased outright from authors. Catalog online.

TIPS "We are looking for unique, research-based, quality supplemental materials for Pre-K through 6th grade. We publish mainly reading and math materials in many different formats, including games. Our materials are intended for classroom and home schooling use. We do not publish picture books."

WILLIAM B. EERDMANS PUBLISHING CO.

2140 Oak Industrial Dr. NE, Grand Rapids MI 49505. (616)459-4591. **Fax:** (616)459-6540. **E-mail:** info@eerdmans.com. **Website:** www.eerdmans.com. "The majority of our adult publications are religious and most of these are academic or semi-academic in character (as opposed to inspirational or celebrity books), though we also publish general trade books on the Christian life. Our nonreligious titles, most of them in regional history or on social issues, aim, similarly, at an educated audience." Publishes hardcover and paperback originals and reprints.

NONFICTION "We prefer that writers take the time to notice if we have published anything at all in the same category as their manuscript before sending it to us."

HOW TO CONTACT Query with SASE. Query with TOC, 2-3 sample chapters, and SASE for return of ms. Responds in 4 weeks.

TERMS Book catalog and ms guidelines free.

ELLYSIAN PRESS

E-mail: publisher@ellysianpress.com. **Website:** www.ellysianpress.com. **Contact:** Maer Wilson. "At Ellysian Press, we seek to create a sense of home for our authors, a place where they can find fulfillment as artists. Just as exceptional mortals once sought a place in the Elysian Fields, now exceptional authors can find a place here at Ellysian Press. We are accepting submissions in the following genres: fantasy, science fiction, paranormal, paranormal romance, horror, along with young/new adult in these genres. Please submit polished manuscripts. It's best to have work read by critique groups or beta readers prior to submission." **25%% of books from first-time authors. 100% from unagented writers.**

HOW TO CONTACT "We accept online submissions only. Please submit a query letter, a synopsis, and the first ten pages of your manuscript in the body of your e-mail. The subject line should be as follows: QUERY – Your Last Name, TITLE, Genre."

If we choose to request more, we will request the full manuscript in standard format. This means your manuscript should be formatted as follows: One inch margins on all sides and a nonjustified right margin; 12 pt Times New Roman font; double spaced; either .doc or .docx is fine; ensure that your paragraph indentations are done via the ruler. Please do not use the "Tab" key. There are many online guides that explain how to use the ruler. We accept simultaneous submissions. We accept submissions directly from the author or from an agent. We answer every query and submission. If you do not hear back from us within one week, we most likely did not receive your query. Please feel free to check with us. Please do not submit queries for any genres not previously listed. You may e-mail queries to submissions@ellysianpress.com. Responds in 1 week for queries; 4-6 weeks for partials and fulls. Publishes ms 12+ months after acceptance.

TERMS Pays quarterly. Does not pay advance. Catalog online. Guidelines online.

ELM BOOKS

1175 Hwy. 130, Laramie WY 82070. (610)529-0460. **E-mail:** leila.monaghan@gmail.com. **Website:** www.elm-books.com. **Contact:** Leila Monaghan, publisher. "We are eager to publish stories by new writers that have real stories to tell. We are looking for short stories (5,000-10,000 words) with real characters and true-to-life stories. Whether your story is fictionalized autobiography, or other stories of real-life mayhem and debauchery, we are interested in reading them!"

FICTION "We are looking for short stories (1,000-5,000 words) about kids of color that will grab readers' attentions—mysteries, adventures, humor, suspense, set in the present, near past, or near future that reflect the realities and hopes of life in diverse communities." Also looking for middle grade novels (20,000-50,000 words).

HOW TO CONTACT Send complete ms for short stories; synopsis and 3 sample chapters for novels.

TERMS Pays royalties.

ENTANGLED TEEN

Website: www.entangledteen.com. "Entangled Teen and Entangled digiTeen, our young adult imprints publish the swoonworthy young adult romances readers crave. Whether they're dark and angsty or fun and sassy, contemporary, fantastical, or futuristic. We are seeking fresh voices with interesting twists on popular genres."

FICTION "We are seeking novels in the subgenres of romantic fiction for contemporary, upper young adult with crossover appeal."

HOW TO CONTACT E-mail using site. "All submissions must have strong romantic elements. YA novels should be 50K to 100K in length. Revised backlist titles will be considered on a case by case basis." Agented and unagented considered.

TERMS Pays royalty.

EVIL JESTER PRESS

46 Gull Dipp Rd., Attn: Charles Day, Ridge NY 11961. **Website:** http://eviljesterpress.com/for-authors/novel-submissions/. **Contact:** Charles Day. "..a respected small press committed to publishing the best in dark fiction and comics. Horror, thrillers, dark fantasy and science fiction—that's our game."

FICTION "We are looking for dark and thoughtful novels between 40,000 and 100,000 words for our selected tomes will fall somewhere in the horror, thriller, dark fantasy, or science-fiction genres. Mash ups are fine, but we're tired of zombies." Starting to publish MG and YA.

TERMS "Send the entire manuscript (no partials) to EJP's Acquisitions Editor, charles@eviljester-press.com. Include the following in the subject line: Novel or Comic Submission/Title/Author's last name/Word Count. Include a short bio in the body of the email, but do not send a synopsis. We want to discover the story as a reader would, and knowing where things are going will remove the element of surprise. Sell us with your prose, your craft, not your marketing copy." Send complete manuscript as one RTF file, double-spaced, Times New Roman (size 12). Page headers (in the upper right hand of every page except the title page) should include: Author name/Title/Page #.

○ FACTS ON FILE, INC.

Infobase Learning, 132 W. 31st St., 16th Floor, New York NY 10001. (800)322-8755. **Fax:** (800)678-3633. **E-mail:** llikoff@infobaselearning.com; custserv@infobaselearning.com. **Website:** www.infobase-learning.com. **Contact:** Laurie Likoff. Facts On File produces high-quality reference materials in print and digital format on a broad range of subjects for the school and public library market and the general nonfiction trade. Publishes hardcover originals and reprints and e-books as well as reference databases. **Publishes 150-200 titles/year. 10% of books from first-time authors. 45% from unagented writers.**

NONFICTION "We publish serious, informational books and e-books for a targeted audience. All our books must have strong library interest, but we also distribute books effectively to the trade. Our library books fit the junior and senior high school curriculum." No computer books, technical books, cookbooks, biographies (except YA), pop psychology, humor, fiction, or poetry.

HOW TO CONTACT Query or submit outline and sample chapter with SASE. No submissions returned without SASE. Responds in 2 months to queries.

ILLUSTRATION Commissions line art only.

TERMS Pays 10% royalty on retail price. Pays $3,000-5,000 advance. Reference catalog available free. Guidelines online.

TIPS "Our audience is school and public libraries for our more reference-oriented books and libraries, schools and bookstores for our less reference-oriented informational titles."

FAMILIUS

1254 Commerce Way, Sanger CA 93657. (559)876-2170. **Fax:** (559)876-2180. **E-mail:** bookideas@familius.com. **Website:** familius.com. **Contact:** Acquisitions. Familius is all about strengthening families. Collective, the authors and staff have experienced a wide slice of the family-life spectrum. Some come from broken homes. Some are married and in the throes of managing a bursting household. Some are preparing to start families of their own. Together, they publish books and articles that help families be happy. Publishes hardcover, trade paperback, and electronic originals and reprints. **Publishes 40 titles/year. 30% of books from first-time authors. 70% from unagented writers.**

FICTION All picture books must align with Familius values statement listed on the website footer.

NONFICTION All mss must align with Familius mission statement to help families succeed.

HOW TO CONTACT Submit a proposal package, including a synopsis, 3 sample chapters, and your author platform. Submit a proposal package, including an outline, 1 sample chapter, competition evaluation, and your author platform. 200 queries; 100

mss received/year. Responds in 1 month to queries and proposals; 2 months to mss. Publishes book 12 months after acceptance.

TERMS Authors are paid 10-30% royalty on wholesale price. Catalog online and print. Guidelines online.

FARRAR, STRAUS & GIROUX FOR YOUNG READERS

Macmillan Children's Publishing Group, 175 Fifth Ave., New York NY 10010. (212)741-6900. **Fax:** (212)633-2427. **Website:** www.fsgkidsbooks.com.

FICTION All levels: all categories. "Original and well-written material for all ages."

NONFICTION All levels: all categories. "We publish only literary nonfiction."

HOW TO CONTACT Submit cover letter, first 50 pages by mail only. Submit cover letter, first 50 pages by mail only.

ILLUSTRATION Works with 30-60 illustrators/year. Reviews ms/illustration packages from artists. Submit ms with 1 example of final art, remainder roughs. Do not send originals. Illustrations only: Query with tearsheets. Responds if interested in 3 months. Samples returned with SASE; samples sometimes filed.

TERMS Book catalog available by request. Ms guidelines online.

TIPS "Study our catalog before submitting. We will see illustrators' portfolios by appointment. Don't ask for criticism and/or advice—due to the volume of submissions we receive, it's just not possible. Never send originals. Always enclose SASE."

FATHER'S PRESS

590 N.W. 1921 St. Rd., Kingsville MO 64063. (816) 550-1138. **Website:** www.fatherspress.com. **Contact:** Mike Smitley, owner (fiction, nonfiction). Publishes hardcover, trade paperback, and mass market paperback originals and reprints. **Publishes 6-10 titles/year.**

HOW TO CONTACT Query with SASE. Unsolicited mss returned unopened. Call or e-mail first. Responds in 1-3 months. Publishes ms 6 months after acceptance.

TERMS Pays 10-15% royalty on wholesale price. Guidelines online.

Ⓐ FEIWEL AND FRIENDS

Macmillan Children's Publishing Group, 175 Fifth Ave., New York NY 10010. (646)307-5151. **Website:** us.macmillan.com. Feiwel and Friends is a publisher of innovative children's fiction and nonfiction literature, including hardcover, paperback series, and individual titles. The list is eclectic and combines quality and commercial appeal for readers ages 0-16. The imprint is dedicated to "book by book" publishing, bringing the work of distinctive and oustanding authors, illustrators, and ideas to the marketplace. This market does not accept unsolicited mss due to the volume of submissions; they also do not accept unsolicited queries for interior art. The best way to submit a ms is through an agent.

TERMS Catalog online.

FEY PUBLISHING

Website: www.feypublishing.com/submissions. html. "Young Fey is everything you've come to expect from Fey Publishing—quality science fiction, fantasy, horror, and speculative fiction, but written with a younger audience in mind. Young and old alike will love these tales of whimsy and triumph from some of the best up-and-coming authors of young adult and middle-grade fiction."

FICTION "We'd love to see more YA books without romance as a focus, or if there is romance, we'd prefer it to be nontraditional and not the focus of the story. We want strong characters, characters that teens can look up to. We'd love to find more stories with friendship, not just romance, as the focus. We also prefer YA books with science fiction and fantasy elements, but it's not required. YA stories can feature darker stories and introduce some adult concepts within reason (issues that the age range may experience as they grow up). Middle-grade stories should be age appropriate."

HOW TO CONTACT Usually responds within 3 months.

TERMS "We are looking for full-length and completed manuscripts only. No short story collections, just novels. We ask that they be at least 50,000 words in length, no novellas please. There is no maximum length, however, books that go over 100,000 will have to be exceptional to be considered. We will accept series, but ask that the series be completed or be near completed before submission." Submit cover letter along with full manuscript. See website for formatting instructions and brands. Submit via link on website.

A FIRST SECOND

Macmillan Children's Publishing Group, 175 Fifth Ave., New York NY 10010. **E-mail:** mail@firstsecondbooks.com. **Website:** www.firstsecondbooks.com. First Second is a publisher of graphic novels and an imprint of Macmillan Children's Publishing Group. First Second does not accept unsolicited submissions.

HOW TO CONTACT Responds in about 6 weeks.

TERMS Catalog online.

FLASHLIGHT PRESS

(718)288-8300. **Fax:** (718)972-6307. **Website:** www.flashlightpress.com. **Contact:** Shari Dash Greenspan, editor. Publishes hardcover original children's picture books for 4-8 year olds. **Publishes 2-3 titles/year. 50% of books from first-time authors. 50% from unagented writers.**

FICTION Average word length: 1,000 words. Picture books: contemporary, humor, multicultural.

HOW TO CONTACT "Query by e-mail only, after carefully reading our submission guidelines online. Do not send anything by snail mail." 2,000 queries received/year. "Only accepts e-mail queries according to submission guidelines." Publishes ms up to 3 years after acceptance.

TERMS Pays 8-10% royalty on net. Pays advance. Book catalog online. Guidelines online.

FORWARD MOVEMENT

412 Sycamore St., Cincinnati OH 45202. (513)721-6659; (800)543-1813. **Fax:** (513)721-0729. **E-mail:** editorial@forwardmovement.org. **Website:** www.forwardmovement.org. "Forward Movement was established to help reinvigorate the life of the church. Many titles focus on the life of prayer, where our relationship with God is centered, death, marriage, baptism, recovery, joy, the Episcopal Church and more. Currently emphasizing prayer/spirituality." **Publishes 30 titles/year.**

NONFICTION "We are an agency of the Episcopal Church. There is a special need for tracts of under 8 pages. (A page usually runs about 200 words.) On rare occasions, we publish a full-length book."

HOW TO CONTACT Query with SASE or by e-mail with complete ms attached. Responds in 1 month.

TERMS Book catalog free. Guidelines online.

TIPS "Audience is primarily Episcopalians and other Christians."

WALTER FOSTER, JR.

Quarto Publishing, 6 Orchard, Suite 100, Lake Forest CA 92630. (949)380-7510. **Fax:** (949)380-7575. **E-mail:** pauline.molinari@quartous.com. **Website:** www.quartoknows.com/Walter-Foster-Jr. **Contact:** Pauline Molinari, Editorial Director. Building on the success of Walter Foster Publishing, a leader in the art instruction field for more than 90 years, Walter Foster, Jr. develops high-quality, affordable books that spark excitement and curiosity. As a creator of content for children and families, Walter Foster, Jr. strives to bring out that childlike wonderment in all of us and inspire lifelong interests. Walter Foster, Jr. publishes fun and imaginative books and kits for children of all ages. Encouraging learning and exploring, Walter Foster, Jr. titles cover a wide range of subjects, including art, transportation, history, craft, gardening, and more.

TERMS "Walter Foster Publishing is always on the lookout for authors and artists with creative ideas that enhance and broaden our publishing list. Our topics span everything from traditional oil painting to newer art techniques like tangling and mixed media. See our submissions guidelines online if you are interested in submitting your ideas for consideration. Asks authors to sign a submission agreement."

FREE SPIRIT PUBLISHING, INC.

6325 Sandburg Rd., Suite 100, Minneapolis MN 55427-3674. (612)338-2068. **Fax:** (612)337-5050. **E-mail:** acquisitions@freespirit.com. **Website:** www.freespirit.com. "Free Spirit is the leading publisher of learning tools that support young people's social-emotional health and educational needs. We help children and teens think for themselves, overcome challenges, and make a difference in the world." Free Spirit does not accept general fiction, poetry, or storybook submissions. Publishes trade paperback originals and reprints. **Publishes 25-30 titles/year.**

FICTION "Please review catalog and author guidelines (both available online) for details before submitting proposal. If you'd like material returned, enclose a SASE with sufficient postage."

NONFICTION "Many of our authors are educators, mental health professionals, and youth workers involved in helping kids and teens." No general fiction or picture storybooks, poetry, single biographies or autobiographies, books with mythical or animal characters, or books with religious or New

Age content. "We are not looking for academic or religious materials, or books that analyze problems with the nation's school systems."

HOW TO CONTACT Query with cover letter stating qualifications, intent, and intended audience and market analysis (comprehensive list of similar titles and detailed explanation of how your book stands out from the field), along with your promotional plan, outline, 2 sample chapters (note: for early childhood submissions, the entire text is required for evaluation), résumé, SASE. Do not send original copies of work. Responds to proposals in 2-6 months.

ILLUSTRATION Works with 5 illustrators/year. Submit samples to creative director for consideration. If appropriate, samples will be kept on file and artist will be contacted if a suitable project comes up. Enclose SASE if you'd like materials returned.

PHOTOGRAPHY Uses stock photos. Does not accept photography submissions.

TERMS Book catalog and guidelines online.

TIPS "Our books are issue-oriented, jargon-free, and solution-focused. Our audience is children, teens, teachers, parents, and youth counselors. We are especially concerned with kids' social and emotional well-being and look for books with ready-to-use strategies for coping with today's issues at home or in school—written in everyday language. We are not looking for academic or religious materials, or books that analyze problems with the nation's school systems. Instead, we want books that offer practical, positive advice so kids can help themselves, and parents and teachers can help kids succeed."

FULCRUM PUBLISHING

4690 Table Mountain Dr., Suite 100, Golden CO 80403. **E-mail:** acquisitions@fulcrumbooks.com. **Website:** www.fulcrum-books.com. **Contact:** T. Baker, acquisitions editor.

NONFICTION Looking for nonfiction-based graphic novels and comics, US history and culture, Native American history or culture studies, conservation-oriented materials. "We do not accept memoir or fiction manuscripts."

HOW TO CONTACT "Your submission must include: a proposal of your work, including a brief synopsis, 2-3 sample chapters, brief biography of yourself, description of your audience, your assessment of the market for the book, list of competing ti-

tles, and what you can do to help market your book. We are a green company and therefore only accept e-mailed submissions. Paper queries submitted via US Mail or any other means (including fax, FedEx/UPS, and even door-to-door delivery) will not be reviewed or returned. Please help us support the preservation of the environment by e-mailing your query to acquisitions@fulcrumbooks.com."

PHOTOGRAPHY Works on assignment only.

TERMS Pays authors royalty based on wholesale price. Offers advances. Catalog for SASE. Guidelines online.

TIPS "Research our line first. We look for books that appeal to the school market and trade."

GIBBS SMITH

P.O. Box 667, Layton UT 84041. (801)544-9800. **Fax:** (801)544-8853. **E-mail:** debbie.uribe@gibbs-smith.com. **Website:** www.gibbs-smith.com. **Publishes 3 titles/year. 50% of books from first-time authors. 50% from unagented writers.**

NONFICTION Middle readers: activity, arts/crafts, cooking, how-to, nature/environment, science. Average word length: picture books: under 1,000 words; activity books: under 15,000 words.

HOW TO CONTACT Submit an outline and writing samples for activity books; query for other types of books. Responds in 2 months. Publishes ms 1-2 years after acceptance.

ILLUSTRATION Works with 2 illustrators/year. Reviews ms/illustration packages from artists. Query. Submit ms with 3-5 pieces of final art. Illustrations only: Query with samples; provide résumé, promo sheet, slides (duplicate slides, not originals). Responds only if interested. Samples returned with SASE; samples filed.

TERMS Pays illustrators by the project or royalty of 2% based on retail price. Sends galleys to authors; color proofs to illustrators. Original artwork returned at job's completion. Pays authors royalty of 2% based on retail price or work purchased outright ($500 minimum). Offers advances (average amount: $2,000). Book catalog available for 9×12 SAE and $2.30 postage. Ms guidelines available by e-mail.

TIPS "We target ages 5-11. We do not publish young adult novels or chapter books."

THE GLENCANNON PRESS

P.O. Box 1428, El Cerrito CA 94530. (510)528-4216. **E-mail:** merships@yahoo.com. **Website:** www.

glencannon.com. **Contact:** Bill Harris (maritime, maritime children's). "We publish quality books about ships and the sea." Average print order: 500. Member PMA, BAIPA. Distributes titles through Baker & Taylor. Promotes titles through direct mail, magazine advertising, and word of mouth. Accepts unsolicited mss. Often comments on rejected mss. Publishes hardcover and paperback originals and hardcover reprints. **Publishes 4-5 titles/year. 25% of books from first-time authors. 100% from unagented writers.**

HOW TO CONTACT Submit complete ms. Include brief bio, list of publishing credits. Send SASE for return of ms or send a disposable ms and SASE for reply only. Responds in 1 month to queries; 2 months to mss. Publishes ms 6-24 months after acceptance.

TERMS Pays 10-20% royalty.

TIPS "Write a good story in a compelling style."

Ⓐ DAVID R. GODINE, PUBLISHER

15 Court Square, Suite 320, Boston MA 02108. (617)451-9600. **Fax:** (617)350-0250. **E-mail:** info@godine.com. **Website:** www.godine.com. "We publish books that matter for people who care." This publisher is no longer considering unsolicited mss of any type. Only interested in agented material.

HOW TO CONTACT Only interested in agented material.

ILLUSTRATION Only interested in agented material. Works with 1-3 illustrators/year. "Please do not send original artwork unless solicited. Almost all of the children's books we accept for publication come to us with the author and illustrator already paired up. Therefore, we rarely use freelance illustrators."

Ⓐ Ⓒ GOLDEN BOOKS FOR YOUNG READERS GROUP

1745 Broadway, New York NY 10019. **Website:** www.penguinrandomhouse.com. "Random House Books aims to create books that nurture the hearts and minds of children, providing and promoting quality books and a rich variety of media that entertain and educate readers from 6 months to 12 years." Random House-Golden Books does not accept unsolicited mss, only agented material. They reserve the right not to return unsolicited material. **2% of books from first-time authors.**

TERMS Pays authors in royalties; sometimes buys mss outright. Book catalog free on request.

GOOSEBOTTOM BOOKS

Fax: (888)407-5286. **E-mail:** submissions@goosebottombooks.com. **Website:** goosebottombooks.com. **Contact:** Shirin Bridges. Goosebottom Books is a small press dedicated to "fun nonfiction" founded by Shirin Yim Bridges, author of *Ruby's Wish*. *The Thinking Girl's Treasury of Dastardly Dames* was named by *Booklist* as one of the Top 10 Nonfiction Series for Youth of 2012. *Horrible Hauntings* made the IRA Children's Choices list with a mention that it "motivated even the most reluctant reader." And *Call Me Ixchel, Goddess of the Moon* was named one of the Top 10 Middle Grade Novels 2013 by Foreword Reviews. Middle grade nonfiction and fiction. **Publishes less than 6 titles/year. 50% of books from first-time authors. 100% from unagented writers.**

FICTION Gosling Press is a new partnership publishing imprint for children's middle grade fiction. Any fiction for adults.

HOW TO CONTACT 1,000 submissions received/year. Responds in 1 month. Publishes ms 18 months after acceptance.

ILLUSTRATION Considers samples.

TERMS Goosebottom Books: Pays advance plus royalties; Gosling Press: Pays royalties only. Catalog online. Goosebottom Books is not accepting submissions at this time. Goosebottom Books never accepts hard copy submissions. "We like trees."

GREENHAVEN PRESS

27500 Drake Rd., Farmington Hills MI 48331. (800)877-4523. **Website:** www.gale.com/greenhaven. Publishes 220 young adult academic reference titles/year. 50% of books by first-time authors. Greenhaven continues to print quality nonfiction anthologies for libraries and classrooms. "Our well-known Opposing Viewpoints series is highly respected by students and librarians in need of material on controversial social issues." Greenhaven accepts no unsolicited mss. Send query, resume, and list of published works by e-mail. Work purchased outright from authors; write-for-hire, flat fee.

NONFICTION Young adults (high school): controversial issues, social issues, history, literature, science, environment, health.

Ⓐ GREENWILLOW BOOKS

HarperCollins Publishers, 10 E. 53rd St., New York NY 10022. (212)207-7000. **Website:** www.greenwillowblog.com. *Does not accept unsolicited mss.* "Unsolicited mail will not be opened and will not be returned." Publishes hardcover originals, paperbacks, e-books, and reprints. **Publishes 40-50 titles/year.**

HOW TO CONTACT *Agented submissions only.* Publishes ms 2 years after acceptance.

TERMS Pays 10% royalty on wholesale price for first-time authors. Offers variable advance.

Ⓐ GROSSET & DUNLAP PUBLISHERS

Penguin Random House, 345 Hudson St., New York NY 10014. **Website:** www.penguin.com. Grosset & Dunlap publishes children's books that show children that reading is fun, with books that speak to their interests, and that are affordable so that children can build a home library of their own. Focus on licensed properties, series, and readers. "Grosset & Dunlap publishes high-interest, affordable books for children ages 0-10 years. We focus on original series, licensed properties, readers, and novelty books." Publishes hardcover (few) and mass market paperback originals. **Publishes 140 titles/year.**

HOW TO CONTACT *Agented submissions only.*

TERMS Pays royalty. Pays advance.

Ⓞ GRYPHON HOUSE, INC.

P.O. Box 10, 6848 Leon's Way, Lewisville NC 27023. (800)638-0928. **E-mail:** info@ghbooks.com. **Website:** www.gryphonhouse.com. "At Gryphon House, our goal is to publish books that help teachers and parents enrich the lives of children from birth through age 8. We strive to make our books useful for teachers at all levels of experience, as well as for parents, caregivers, and anyone interested in working with children." Publishes trade paperback originals. **Publishes 12-15 titles/year.**

NONFICTION Currently emphasizing social-emotional intelligence and classroom management; de-emphasizing literacy after-school activities.

HOW TO CONTACT "We prefer to receive a letter of inquiry and/or a proposal, rather than the entire manuscript. Please include: the proposed title, the purpose of the book, table of contents, introductory material, 20-40 sample pages of the actual book. In addition, please describe the book, including the intended audience, why teachers will want to buy it, how it is different from other similar books already published, and what qualifications you possess that make you the appropriate person to write the book. If you have a writing sample that demonstrates that you write clear, compelling prose, please include it with your letter." Query. Submit outline/synopsis and 2 sample chapters. Responds to queries/mss in 6 months. Publishes a book 18 months after acceptance. Will consider simultaneous submissions, e-mail submissions. Book catalog and ms guidelines available via website or with SASE.

ILLUSTRATION Works with 4-5 illustrators/year. Uses b&w realistic artwork only. Query with samples, promo sheet. Responds in 2 months. Samples returned with SASE; samples filed. Pays illustrators by the project.

PHOTOGRAPHY Pays photographers by the project or per photo. Original artwork returned at job's completion.

TERMS Pays royalty on wholesale price. Guidelines available online.

TIPS "We are looking for books of creative, participatory learning experiences that have a common conceptual theme to tie them together. The books should be on subjects that parents or teachers want to do on a daily basis."

HACHAI PUBLISHING

527 Empire Blvd., Brooklyn NY 11225. (718)633-0100. **Fax:** (718)633-0103. **E-mail:** info@hachai.com; dlr@hachai.com. **Website:** www.hachai.com. **Contact:** Devorah Leah Rosenfeld, editor. Hachai is dedicated to producing high quality Jewish children's literature, ages 2-10. Story should promote universal values such as sharing, kindness, etc. Publishes hardcover originals. **Publishes 5 titles/year. 75% of books from first-time authors.**

Ⓞ "All books have spiritual/religious themes, specifically traditional Jewish content. We're seeking books about morals and values; the Jewish experience in current and Biblical times; and Jewish observance, Sabbath and holidays."

FICTION Picture books and young readers: contemporary, historical fiction, religion. Middle readers: adventure, contemporary, problem novels, religion. Does not want to see fantasy, animal stories, romance, problem novels depicting drug use or violence.

HOW TO CONTACT Submit complete ms. Submit complete ms. Responds in 2 months to mss.

ILLUSTRATION Works with 4 illustrators/year. Uses primary color artwork, some b&w illustration.

Reviews ms/illustration packages from authors. Submit ms with 1 piece of final art. Illustrations only: Query with samples; arrange personal portfolio review. Responds in 6 weeks. Samples returned with SASE; samples filed.

TERMS Work purchased outright from authors for $800-1,000. Guidelines online.

TIPS "We are looking for books that convey the traditional Jewish experience in modern times or long ago; traditional Jewish observance such as Sabbath and holidays and mitzvos such as mezuzah, blessings etc.; positive character traits (middos) such as honesty, charity, respect, sharing, etc. We are also interested in historical fiction for young readers (7-10) written with a traditional Jewish perspective and highlighting the relevance of Torah in making important choices. Please, no animal stories, romance, violence, preachy sermonizing. Write a story that incorporates a moral, not a preachy morality tale. Originality is the key. We feel Hachai publications will appeal to a wider readership as parents become more interested in positive values for their children."

HARMONY INK PRESS

Dreamspinner Press, 5032 Capital Circle SW, Suite 2 PMB 279, Tallahassee FL 32305. (850)632-4648. **Fax:** (888)308-3739. **E-mail:** submissions@harmonyinkpress.com. **Website:** harmonyinkpress.com. **Contact:** Anne Regan. Teen and new adult fiction featuring at least 1 strong LGBTQ+ main character who shows significant personal growth through the course of the story. **Publishes 26 titles/year.**

FICTION "We are looking for stories in all subgenres, featuring primary characters across the whole LGBTQ+ spectrum between the ages of 14 and 21 that explore all the facets of young adult, teen, and new adult life. Sexual content should be appropriate for the characters and the story."

HOW TO CONTACT Submit complete ms.

TERMS Pays royalty. Pays $500-1,000 advance.

Ⓐ HARPERCOLLINS CHILDREN'S BOOKS/ HARPERCOLLINS PUBLISHERS

195 Broadway, New York NY 10007. (212)207-7000. **Website:** www.harpercollins.com. HarperCollins, one of the largest English language publishers in the world, is a broad-based publisher with strengths in academic, business and professional, children's, educational, general interest, and religious and spiritual books, as well as multimedia titles. Publishes hardcover and paperback originals and paperback reprints. **Publishes 500 titles/year.**

FICTION "We look for a strong story line and exceptional literary talent."

NONFICTION No unsolicited mss or queries.

HOW TO CONTACT Agented submissions only. All unsolicited mss returned. Agented submissions only. Unsolicited mss returned unopened. Responds in 1 month, will contact only if interested. Does not accept any unsolicted texts.

TERMS Negotiates payment upon acceptance. Catalog online.

TIPS "We do not accept any unsolicited material."

HENDRICK-LONG PUBLISHING CO., INC.

10635 Tower Oaks, Suite D, Houston TX 77070. (832)912-READ. **Fax:** (832)912-7353. **E-mail:** hendrick-long@att.net. **Website:** hendricklongpublishing.com. "Hendrick-Long publishes historical fiction and nonfiction about Texas and the Southwest for children and young adults." Publishes hardcover and trade paperback originals and hardcover reprints. **Publishes 4 titles/year. 90% from unagented writers.**

NONFICTION Subject must be Texas related; other subjects cannot be considered. "We are particularly interested in material from educators that can be used in the classroom as workbooks, math, science, history with a Texas theme or twist."

HOW TO CONTACT Query with SASE. Submit outline, clips, 2 sample chapters. Query, or submit outline and 2 sample chapters. Responds in 3 months to queries. Publishes ms 18 months after acceptance.

TERMS Pays royalty on selling price. Pays advance. Book catalog available. Guidelines online.

HEYDAY BOOKS

c/o Acquisitions Editor, Box 9145, Berkeley CA 94709. **Fax:** (510)549-1889. **E-mail:** heyday@heydaybooks.com. **Website:** www.heydaybooks.com. **Contact:** Gayle Wattawa, acquisitions and editorial director. "Heyday Books publishes nonfiction books and literary anthologies with a strong California focus. We publish books about Native Americans, natural history, history, literature, and recreation, with a strong California focus." Publishes hardcover originals, trade paperback originals, and reprints.

Publishes 12-15 titles/year. 50% of books from first-time authors. 90% from unagented writers.
FICTION Publishes picture books, beginning readers, and young adult literature.
NONFICTION Books about California only.
HOW TO CONTACT Submit complete ms for picture books; proposal with sample chapters for longer works, include a chapter by chapter summary. Mark attention: Children's Submission. Reviews manuscript/illustration packages; but may consider art and text separately. Tries to respond to query within 12 weeks. Query with outline and synopsis. "Query or proposal by traditional post. Include a cover letter introducing yourself and your qualifications, a brief description of your project, a table of contents and list of illustrations, notes on the market you are trying to reach and why your book will appeal to them, a sample chapter, and a SASE if you would like us to return these materials to you." Responds in 3 months. Publishes book 18 months after acceptance.
TERMS Pays 8% royalty on net price. Book catalog online. Guidelines online.

⊘ HOLIDAY HOUSE, INC.

425 Madison Ave., New York NY 10017. (212)688-0085. **Fax:** (212)421-6134. **E-mail:** info@holidayhouse.com. **Website:** holidayhouse.com. "Holiday House publishes children's and young adult books for the school and library markets. We have a commitment to publishing first-time authors and illustrators. We specialize in quality hardcovers from picture books to young adult, both fiction and nonfiction, primarily for the school and library market." Publishes hardcover originals and paperback reprints. **Publishes 50 titles/year. 5% of books from first-time authors. 50% from unagented writers.**
FICTION Children's books only.
HOW TO CONTACT Query with SASE. No phone calls, please. Please send the entire ms, whether submitting a picture book or novel. "All submissions should be directed to the Editorial Department, Holiday House. We do not accept certified or registered mail. There is no need to include a SASE. We do not consider submissions by e-mail or fax. Please note that you do not have to supply illustrations. However, if you have illustrations you would like to include with your submission, you may send detailed sketches or photocopies of the original art. Do not send original art." Responds in 4 months. Publishes 1-2 years after acceptance.
ILLUSTRATION Accepting art samples, not returned.
TERMS Pays royalty on list price, range varies. Guidelines for #10 SASE.
TIPS "We need manuscripts with strong stories and writing."

HOUGHTON MIFFLIN HARCOURT BOOKS FOR CHILDREN

Imprint of Houghton Mifflin Trade & Reference Division, 222 Berkeley St., Boston MA 02116. (617)351-5000. **Fax:** (617)351-1111. **Website:** www.houghtonmifflinbooks.com. Houghton Mifflin Harcourt gives shape to ideas that educate, inform, and above all, delight. Does not respond to or return mss unless interested. Publishes hardcover originals and trade paperback originals and reprints. **Publishes 100 titles/year. 10% of books from first-time authors. 60% from unagented writers.**
NONFICTION Interested in innovative books and subjects about which the author is passionate.
HOW TO CONTACT Submit complete ms. Query with SASE. Submit sample chapters, synopsis. 5,000 queries received/year. 14,000 mss received/year. Responds in 4-6 months to queries. Publishes ms 2 years after acceptance.
TERMS Pays 5-10% royalty on retail price. Pays variable advance. Guidelines online.

IMMEDIUM

P.O. Box 31846, San Francisco CA 94131. (415)452-8546. **Fax:** (360)937-6272. **Website:** www.immedium.com. **Contact:** Submissions Editor. "Immedium focuses on publishing eye-catching children's picture books, Asian-American topics, and contemporary arts, popular culture, and multicultural issues." Publishes hardcover and trade paperback originals. **Publishes 4 titles/year. 50% of books from first-time authors. 90% from unagented writers.**
HOW TO CONTACT Submit complete ms. Submit complete ms. 50 queries received/year. 25 mss received/year. Responds in 1-3 months. Publishes book 2 years after acceptance.
TERMS Pays 5% royalty on wholesale price. Pays on publication. Catalog online. Guidelines online.
TIPS "Our audience is children and parents. Please visit our site."

IMPACT PUBLISHERS, INC.

5674 Shattuck Ave., Oakland CA 94609. **E-mail:** proposals@newharbinger.com. **Website:** www.newharbinger.com/imprint/impact-publishers. **Contact:** Acquisitions Department. "Our purpose is to make the best human services expertise available to the widest possible audience. We publish only popular psychology and self-help materials written in everyday language by professionals with advanced degrees and significant experience in the human services." **Publishes 3-5 titles/year. 20% of books from first-time authors.**

NONFICTION Young readers, middle readers, young adults: self-help.

HOW TO CONTACT Query or submit complete ms, cover letter, résumé. Responds in 3 months.

ILLUSTRATION Works with 1 illustrator/year. Not accepting freelance illustrator queries.

TERMS Pays authors royalty of 10-12%. Offers advances. Book catalog for #10 SASE with 2 first-class stamps. Guidelines for SASE.

TIPS "Please do not submit fiction, poetry, or narratives."

ISLANDPORT

P.O. Box 10, Yarmouth ME 04096. **Website:** http://www.islandportpress.com/submission-guidelines/. **Contact:** Acquisitions Editor, Children's/YA.

FICTION "We will consider picture books, story books, middle grade chapter books, and young adult titles. We are not currently publishing poetry or early readers. As with our adult titles, all our children's books have New England sensibilities, and we do prefer to work with authors and illustrators who are connected to New England or the Northeast United States."

HOW TO CONTACT Three to six months

ILLUSTRATION "We are committed to supporting artists who live and/or work in New England. We are always interested in seeing work from new illustrators. If you would like to send us samples of your portfolio, please send us copies (never send originals) to: Melissa Kim, Senior Editor, Children's Books, Islandport Press, P.O. Box 10, Yarmouth, Maine 04096. Please include a cover letter, artist bio, and full contact information including your e-mail address. You are also welcome to send a CD or send a link to an online portfolio."

TERMS "We prefer paper copies of manuscripts and written submissions (please do not submit children's books by e-mail). If you are submitting a children's book that you have illustrated, please include copies of your illustrations, but keep in mind that if we accept your manuscript, we still may decide to choose our own illustrator." Please include the following with your proposal: Cover letter with the date and contact information, author bio, a copy of your manuscript, relevant marketing information, and publicity and social media contracts. Include SASE to have materials returned. Publisher cannot guarantee return of manuscript. Include e-mail address with materials as publisher will acknowledge receipt via email . Note in query letter if your submission is a simultaneous submission. **Please do not submit your only copy!**

JEWISH LIGHTS PUBLISHING

LongHill Partners, Inc., Sunset Farm Offices, Rt. 4, P.O. Box 237, Woodstock VT 05091. (802)457-4000. **Fax:** (802)457-4004. **E-mail:** submissions@turner-publishing.com. **Website:** www.jewishlights.com. "Jewish Lights publishes books for people of all faiths and all backgrounds who yearn for books that attract, engage, educate, and spiritually inspire. Our authors are at the forefront of spiritual thought and deal with the quest for the self and for meaning in life by drawing on the Jewish wisdom tradition. Our books cover topics including history, spirituality, life cycle, children, self-help, recovery, theology, and philosophy. We do not publish autobiography, biography, fiction, haggadot, poetry, or cookbooks. At this point we plan to do only two books for children annually, and one will be for younger children (ages 4-10)." Publishes hardcover and trade paperback originals, trade paperback reprints. **Publishes 30 titles/year. 50% of books from first-time authors. 75% from unagented writers.**

FICTION Picture books, young readers, middle readers: spirituality. "We are not interested in anything other than spirituality."

NONFICTION Picture book, young readers, middle readers: activity books, spirituality. "We do *not* publish haggadot, biography, poetry, memoirs, or cookbooks."

HOW TO CONTACT Query with outline/synopsis and 2 sample chapters; submit complete ms for picture books. Query. Responds in 6 months to queries. Publishes ms 1 year after acceptance.

TERMS Pays authors royalty of 10% of revenue received; 15% royalty for subsequent printings. Book catalog and guidelines online.

TIPS "We publish books for all faiths and backgrounds that also reflect the Jewish wisdom tradition. Explain in your cover letter why you're submitting your project to us in particular. Make sure you know what we publish."

JOURNEYFORTH

Imprint of BJU Press, 1700 Wade Hampton Blvd., Greenville SC 29614. (864)770-1317. **E-mail:** journeyforth@bjupress.com. **Website:** www.journeyforth.com. **Contact:** Nancy Lohr. JourneyForth Books publishes fiction and nonfiction that reflects a worldview based solidly on the Bible and that encourages Christians to live out their faith. JourneyForth is an imprint of BJU Press. Publishes paperback originals. **Publishes 8-10 titles/year. 30% of books from first-time authors. 80% from unagented writers.**

FICTION "Our fiction is all based on a Christian worldview." Does not want short stories, poetry, picture books, or fiction for the adult market.

NONFICTION Christian living, Bible studies, church and ministry, church history. "We produce books for the adult Christian market that are from a conservative Christian worldview."

HOW TO CONTACT Submit proposal with synopsis, market analysis of competing works, and first 5 chapters. Receives 400+ queries/year. Responds in 1 month to queries; 3 months to mss. Publishes book 12-18 months after acceptance.

TERMS Pays authors royalty based on wholesale price. Book catalog available free or online. Guidelines online.

TIPS "Study the publisher's guidelines. We are looking for engaging text and a biblical worldview. Will read hard copy submissions, but prefer e-mail queries/proposals/submissions."

JUST US BOOKS, INC.

P.O. Box 5306, East Orange NJ 07019. (973)672-7701. **Fax:** (973)677-7570. **Website:** justusbooks.com. "Just Us Books is the nation's premier independent publisher of Black-interest books for young people. Our books focus primarily on the culture, history, and contemporary experiences of African Americans."

FICTION Just Us Books is currently accepting queries for chapter books and middle reader titles only. "We are not considering any other works at this time."

HOW TO CONTACT Query with synopsis and 3-5 sample pages.

TERMS Guidelines online.

TIPS "We are looking for realistic, contemporary characters; stories and interesting plots that introduce both conflict and resolution. We will consider various themes and story-lines, but before an author submits a query we urge them to become familiar with our books."

⏻ KAEDEN BOOKS

P.O. Box 16190, Rocky River OH 44116. **Website:** www.kaeden.com. "Children's book publisher for education K-3 market: reading stories, fiction/nonfiction, chapter books, science, and social studies materials." Publishes paperback originals. **Publishes 12-20 titles/year. 30% of books from first-time authors. 95% from unagented writers.**

FICTION "We are looking for stories with humor, surprise endings, and interesting characters that will appeal to children in kindergarten through third grade." No sentence fragments. Please do not submit: queries, ms summaries, or résumés, mss that stereotype or demean individuals or groups, mss that present violence as acceptable behavior.

NONFICTION Mss should have interesting topics and information presented in language comprehensible to young students. Content should be supported with details and accurate facts.

HOW TO CONTACT Submit complete ms. "Can be as minimal as 25 words for the earliest reader or as much as 2,000 words for the fluent reader. Beginning chapter books are welcome. Our readers are in kindergarten to 3rd grade, so vocabulary and sentence structure must be appropriate for young readers. Make sure that all language used in the story is of an appropriate level for the students to read independently. Sentences should be complete and grammatically correct." 1,000 mss received/year. Responds only if interested. Publishes ms 6-9 months after acceptance.

ILLUSTRATION Work with 8-10 illustrators per year. Looking for samples that are appropriate for children's literature. Submit color samples no larger than 8 1/2×11. Samples kept on file. Responds only if interested. "No originals, disks or slides please." Samples not returned.

TERMS Work purchased outright from authors. Pays royalties to previous authors. Book catalog and guidelines online.

TIPS "Our audience ranges from kindergarten-third grade school children. We are an educational publisher. We are particularly interested in humorous stories with surprise endings and beginning chapter books."

Ⓐ KANE/MILLER BOOK PUBLISHERS

4901 Morena Blvd., Suite 213, San Diego CA 92117. (858)456-0540. **Fax:** (858)456-9641. **Website:** www.kanemiller.com. **Contact:** Editorial Department. "Kane/Miller Book Publishers is a division of EDC Publishing, specializing in award-winning children's books from around the world. Our books bring the children of the world closer to each other, sharing stories and ideas, while exploring cultural differences and similarities. Although we continue to look for books from other countries, we are now actively seeking works that convey cultures and communities within the US. We are committed to expanding our picture book list and are interested in great stories with engaging characters, especially those with particularly American subjects. When writing about the experiences of a particular community, we will express a preference for stories written from a firsthand experience." Submission guidelines on site.

FICTION Picture Books: concept, contemporary, health, humor, multicultural. Young Readers: contemporary, multicultural, suspense. Middle Readers: contemporary, humor, multicultural, suspense. "At this time, we are not considering holiday stories (in any age range) or self-published works."

HOW TO CONTACT If interested, responds in 90 days to queries.

TIPS "We like to think that a child reading a Kane/Miller book will see parallels between his own life and what might be the unfamiliar setting and characters of the story. And that by seeing how a character who is somehow or in some way dissimilar—an outsider—finds a way to fit comfortably into a culture or community or situation while maintaining a healthy sense of self and self-dignity, she might be empowered to do the same."

KAR-BEN PUBLISHING

Lerner Publishing Group, 1251 Washington Ave. N., Minneapolis MN 55401. **E-mail:** editorial@karben.com. **Website:** www.karben.com. Kar-Ben publishes exclusively children's books on Jewish themes. Publishes hardcover, trade paperback, and e-books. **Publishes 20 titles/year. 20% of books from first-time authors. 70% from unagented writers.**

FICTION "We seek picture book mss 800-1,000 words on Jewish-themed topics for children." Picture books: Adventure, concept, folktales, history, humor, multicultural, religion, special needs; must be on a Jewish theme. Average word length: picture books: 1,000. Recently published titles: *The Count's Hanukkah Countdown*, *Sammy Spider's First Book of Jewish Holidays*, *The Cats of Ben Yehuda Street.*

NONFICTION "In addition to traditional Jewish-themed stories about Jewish holidays, history, folktales and other subjects, we especially seek stories that reflect the rich diversity of the contemporary Jewish community." Picture books, young readers; Jewish history, Israel, Holocaust, folktales, religion, social issues, special needs; must be of Jewish interest. No textbooks, games, or educational materials.

HOW TO CONTACT Submit full ms. Picture books only. Submit completed ms. 800 mss received/year. Responds in 12 weeks. Most mss published within 2 years.

TERMS Pays 5% royalty on NET sale. Pays $500-2,500 advance. Book catalog online; free upon request. Guidelines online.

TIPS "Authors: Do a literature search to make sure similar title doesn't already exist. Illustrators: Look at our online catalog for a sense of what we like—bright colors and lively composition."

KREGEL PUBLICATIONS

2450 Oak Industrial Dr. NE, Grand Rapids MI 49505. (616)451-4775. **Fax:** (616)451-9330. **E-mail:** kregelbooks@kregel.com. **Website:** www.kregel-publications.com. "Our mission as an evangelical Christian publisher is to provide—with integrity and excellence—trusted, Biblically based resources that challenge and encourage individuals in their Christian lives. Works in theology and Biblical studies should reflect the historic, orthodox Protestant tradition." Publishes hardcover and trade paperback originals and reprints. **Publishes 90 titles/**

year. **20% of books from first-time authors. 10% from unagented writers.**

FICTION Fiction should be geared toward the evangelical Christian market. Wants books with fast-paced, contemporary storylines presenting a strong Christian message in an engaging, entertaining style.

NONFICTION "We serve evangelical Christian readers and those in career Christian service."

HOW TO CONTACT Finds works through The Writer's Edge and Christian Manuscript Submissions ms screening services. Responds in 2-3 months. Publishes ms 12-16 months after acceptance.

TERMS Pays royalty on wholesale price. Pays negotiable advance. Guidelines online.

TIPS "Our audience consists of conservative, evangelical Christians, including pastors and ministry students."

LEE & LOW BOOKS

95 Madison Ave., #1205, New York NY 10016. (212)779-4400. **E-mail:** general@leeandlow.com. **Website:** www.leeandlow.com. "Our goals are to meet a growing need for books that address children of color, and to present literature that all children can identify with. We only consider multicultural children's books. Sponsors a yearly New Voices Award for first-time picture book authors of color. Contest rules online at website or for SASE." Publishes hardcover originals and trade paperback reprints. **Publishes 12-14 titles/year. 20% of books from first-time authors. 50% from unagented writers.**

FICTION Picture books, young readers: anthology, contemporary, history, multicultural, poetry. Picture book, middle reader: contemporary, history, multicultural, nature/environment, poetry, sports. Average word length: picture books: 1,000-1,500 words. "We do not publish folklore or animal stories."

NONFICTION Picture books: concept. Picture books, middle readers: biography, history, multicultural, science and sports. Average word length: picture books: 1,500-3,000.

HOW TO CONTACT Submit complete ms. Receives 100 queries/year; 1,200 mss/year. Responds in 6 months to mss if interested. Publishes book 2 years after acceptance.

ILLUSTRATION Works with 12-14 illustrators/year. Uses color artwork only. Reviews ms/illustration packages from artists. Contact: Louise May. Illustrations only: Query with samples, résumé, promo sheet, and tearsheets. Responds only if interested. Samples returned with SASE; samples filed. Original artwork returned at job's completion.

PHOTOGRAPHY Buys photos from freelancers. Works on assignment only. Model/property releases required. Submit cover letter, résumé, promo piece, and book dummy.

TERMS Pays net royalty. Pays authors advances against royalty. Pays illustrators advance against royalty. Photographers paid advance against royalty. Book catalog available online. Guidelines available online or by written request with SASE.

TIPS "Check our website to see the kinds of books we publish. Do not send mss that don't fit our mission."

ARTHUR A. LEVINE BOOKS

Scholastic, Inc., 557 Broadway, New York NY 10012. (212)343-4436. **Fax:** (212)343-6143. **Website:** www.arthuralevinebooks.com. Publishes hardcover, paperback, and e-book editions.

FICTION "Arthur A. Levine is looking for distinctive literature, for children and young adults, for whatever's extraordinary." Averages 18-20 total titles/year.

HOW TO CONTACT Query. Please follow submission guidelines. Responds in 1 month to queries; 5 months to mss. Publishes a book 18 months after acceptance.

TERMS Picture Books: query letter and full text of pb. Novels: send query letter, first 2 chapters, and synopsis. Other: query letter, 10-page sample, and synopsis/proposal.

Ⓐ LITTLE, BROWN BOOKS FOR YOUNG READERS

Hachette Book Group USA, 1290 Avenue of the Americas, New York NY 10104. (212)364-1100. **Fax:** (212)364-0925. **Website:** littlebrown.com. "Little, Brown and Co. Children's Publishing publishes all formats including board books, picture books, middle grade fiction, and nonfiction YA titles. We are looking for strong writing and presentation, but no predetermined topics." *Only interested in solicited agented material.* **Publishes 100-150 titles/year.**

FICTION Average word length: picture books: 1,000; young readers: 6,000; middle readers: 15,000-50,000; young adults: 50,000 and up.

NONFICTION "Writers should avoid looking for the 'issue' they think publishers want to see, choosing instead topics they know best and are most enthusiastic about/inspired by."

HOW TO CONTACT Agented submissions only. Responds in 1-2 months. Publishes ms 2 years after acceptance.

ILLUSTRATION Works with 40 illustrators/year. Illustrations only: Query art director with b&w and color samples; provide résumé, promo sheet or tearsheets to be kept on file. Does not respond to art samples. Do not send originals; copies only. Accepts illustration samples by postal mail or e-mail.

PHOTOGRAPHY Works on assignment only. Model/property releases required; captions required. Publishes photo essays and photo concept books. Uses 35mm transparencies. Photographers should provide résumé, promo sheets, or tearsheets to be kept on file.

TERMS Pays authors royalties based on retail price. Pays illustrators and photographers by the project or royalty based on retail price. Sends galleys to authors; dummies to illustrators. Pays negotiable advance.

TIPS "In order to break into the field, authors and illustrators should research their competition and try to come up with something outstandingly different."

LITTLE PICKLE PRESS

3701 Sacramento St., #494, San Francisco CA 94118. (415)340-3344. **Fax:** (415)366-1520. **E-mail:** info@march4thinc.com. **Website:** www.littlepicklepress.com. Little Pickle Press is a 21st Century publisher dedicated to helping parents and educators cultivate conscious, responsible little people by stimulating explorations of the meaningful topics of their generation through a variety of media, technologies, and techniques. Submit through submission link on site. Includes YA imprint Relish Media.

TERMS Uses Author.me for submissions for Little Pickle and YA imprint Relish Media. Guidelines available on site.

TIPS "We have lots of manuscripts to consider, so it will take up to 8 weeks before we get back to you."

Ⓐ LITTLE SIMON

Imprint of Simon & Schuster, 1230 Avenue of the Americas, New York NY 10020. (212)698-1295. **Fax:** (212)698-2794. **Website:** www.simonandschuster.com/kids. "Our goal is to provide fresh material in an innovative format for preschool to age 8. Our books are often, if not exclusively, format driven." Publishes novelty and branded books only.

FICTION Novelty books include many things that do not fit in the traditional hardcover or paperback format, such as pop-up, board book, scratch and sniff, glow in the dark, lift the flap, etc. Children's/juvenile. No picture books. Large part of the list is holiday-themed.

NONFICTION "We publish very few nonfiction titles." No picture books.

HOW TO CONTACT Currently not accepting unsolicited mss.

TERMS OFFERS ADVANCE and royalties.

MAGINATION PRESS

750 First St. NE, Washington DC 20002. (202)336-5618. **Fax:** (202)336-5624. **E-mail:** magination@apa.org. **Website:** www.apa.org. Magination Press is an imprint of the American Psychological Association. "We publish books dealing with the psycho/therapeutic resolution of children's problems and psychological issues with a strong self-help component." Submit complete ms. Full guidelines available on site. Materials returned only with SASE. **Publishes 12 titles/year. 75% of books from first-time authors.**

FICTION All levels: psychological and social issues, self-help, health, parenting concerns, and special needs. Picture books, middle school readers.

NONFICTION All levels: psychological and social issues, self-help, health, multicultural, special needs.

HOW TO CONTACT Responds to queries in 1-2 months; mss in 2-6 months. Publishes a book 18-24 months after acceptance.

ILLUSTRATION Works with 10-15 illustrators/year. Reviews ms/illustration packages. Will review artwork for future assignments. Responds only if interested, or immediately if SASE or response card is included. "We keep samples on file."

MARTIN SISTERS PUBLISHING COMPANY, INC.

P.O. Box 1154, Barbourville KY 40906-1499. **Website:** www.martinsisterspublishing.com. Firm/imprint publishes trade and mass market paperback originals; electronic originals. **Publishes 12 titles/**

year. **75% of books from first-time authors. 100% from unagented writers.**
HOW TO CONTACT "Please place query letter, marketing plan, and the first 5-10 pages of your manuscript (if you are submitting fiction) directly into your e-mail." Guidelines available on site. Responds in 1 month on queries, 2 months on proposals, 3-6 months on mss. Publishes ms 9 months after acceptance.
TERMS Pays 7.5% royalty/max on print net; 35% royalty/max on e-book net. No advance offered. Catalog and guidelines online.

⊙ MASTER BOOKS

P.O. Box 726, Green Forest AR 72638. **E-mail:** submissions@newleafpress.net. **Website:** www.masterbooks.com. **Contact:** Craig Froman, acquisitions editor. Publishes 3 middle readers/year; 2 young adult nonfiction titles/year; 10 home school curriculum titles; 20 adult trade books/year. **5% of books from first-time authors. 99% from unagented writers.**
NONFICTION Picture books: activity books, animal, nature/environment, creation. Young readers, middle readers, young adults: activity books, animal, biography Christian, nature/environment, science, creation.
HOW TO CONTACT Submission guidelines on website www.nlpg.com/submissions. Receives 500 queries/year. We are no longer able to respond to every query. If you have not heard from us within 90 days, it means we are unable to partner with you on that particular project. Publishes book 1 year after acceptance.
TERMS Pays authors royalty of 3-15% based on wholesale price. Book catalog available upon request. Guidelines online.
TIPS "All of our children's books are creation-based, including topics from the Book of Genesis. We look also for home school educational material as we are expanding our home school curriculum resources."

⊙ MARGARET K. MCELDERRY BOOKS

Imprint of Simon & Schuster Children's Publishing Division, 1230 Sixth Ave., New York NY 10020. (212)698-7200. **Website:** imprints.simonandschuster.biz/margaret-k-mcelderry-books. "Margaret K. McElderry Books publishes hardcover and paperback trade books for children from pre-school age through young adult. This list includes picture books, middle grade and teen fiction, poetry, and fantasy. The style and subject matter of the books we publish is almost unlimited. We do not publish textbooks, coloring and activity books, greeting cards, magazines, pamphlets, or religious publications."
Publishes 30 titles/year. 15% of books from first-time authors. 50% from unagented writers.
FICTION *No unsolicited mss.*
NONFICTION *No unsolicited mss. Agented submissions only.*
HOW TO CONTACT *Agented submissions only.*
TERMS Pays authors royalty based on retail price. Pays illustrator royalty of by the project. Pays photographers by the project. Original artwork returned at job's completion. Offers $5,000-8,000 advance for new authors. Guidelines for #10 SASE.
TIPS "Read! The children's book field is competitive. See what's been done and what's out there before submitting. We look for high quality: an originality of ideas, clarity and felicity of expression, a well organized plot, and strong character-driven stories. We're looking for strong, original fiction, especially mysteries and middle grade humor. We are always interested in picture books for the youngest age reader. Study our titles."

ANDREWS MCMEEL

Andrews McMeel Publishing, ATTN: Book Submissions, 1130 Walnut Street, Kansas City MO 64106. **Website:** www.andrewsmcmeel.com/our-company/submissions. Andrews McMeel Publishing (AMP) is a leading publisher of cookbooks, gift books, humor books, middle-grade fiction titles, and cartoon collections, publishing as many as 250 new titles annually. AMP is also the premier calendar publisher in the country, annually publishing calendars based on many top-selling properties. **Publishes 250 titles/year.**
HOW TO CONTACT "Please allow at least 90 days to receive a response. We get many submissions a day, and we may not get to yours immediately."
TERMS Send cover letter with bio along with outline and first two chapters. "We are happy to consider submissions from both literary agents and directly from authors." Full submission guidelines listed on site.

MEDALLION PRESS

4222 Meridian Pkwy., Aurora IL 60504. (630)513-8316. **E-mail:** emily@medallionpress.com. **Website:** medallionpress.com. **Contact:** Emily Steele, editorial director. "We are an independent, innovative publisher looking for compelling, memorable stories told in distinctive voices." Publishes trade paperback, hardcover, e-book originals.

FICTION Word count: 40,000-90,000 for YA; 60,000-120,000 for all others. No short stories, anthologies, erotica, middle grade, children's fiction.

NONFICTION *Agented only.*

HOW TO CONTACT Submit first 3 consecutive chapters and a synopsis through our online submission form. Please check if submissions are currently open before submitting. Please query. Responds in 2-3 months to mss. Publishes ms 1-2 years after acceptance.

TERMS Offers advance. Guidelines online. Currently closed to submissions.

TIPS "Please visit our website for the most current guidelines prior to submitting anything to us. Please check if submissions are currently open before submitting."

MIGHTY MEDIA PRESS

1201 Currie Ave., Minneapolis MN 55403. (612)399-1969. **E-mail:** lauren@mightymedia.com. **Website:** http://mightymediapress.com/. **Contact:** Lauren Kukla, Publishing Director. Mighty Media Press delivers captivating books and media that ignite a child's curiosity, imagination, social awareness, and sense of adventure.

FICTION "We only publish books that fit all four parts of this mission. Why? Because we know the stories kids experience help shape their minds, and we want to produce books that guide kids on the path to becoming great adults. Publishes picture books and middle grade. Only publishes about 6 titles per year. We seek out stories that leap off the page. We challenge our readers to think differently, be adventurous, build forts, find shapes in the clouds, explore new perspectives, be compassionate, and grow up to be mighty adults."

TERMS Enter e-mail on the website to receive a link with submission guidelines. Doesn't accept hard copy submissions. Only accepts submissions during our reading period (October 1 to April 30). Please no phone calls regarding submissions.

MILKWEED EDITIONS

1011 Washington Ave. S., Suite 300, Minneapolis MN 55415. (612)332-3192. **Fax:** (612)215-2550. **Website:** www.milkweed.org. "Milkweed Editions publishes with the intention of making a humane impact on society, in the belief that literature is a transformative art uniquely able to convey the essential experiences of the human heart and spirit. To that end, Milkweed Editions publishes distinctive voices of literary merit in handsomely designed, visually dynamic books, exploring the ethical, cultural, and esthetic issues that free societies need continually to address." Publishes hardcover, trade paperback, and electronic originals; trade paperback and electronic reprints. **Publishes 15-20 titles/year. 25% of books from first-time authors. 75% from unagented writers.**

FICTION Novels for adults and for readers 8-13. High literary quality. For adult readers: literary fiction, nonfiction, poetry, essays. Middle readers: adventure, contemporary, fantasy, multicultural, nature/environment, suspense/mystery. Average length: middle readers: 90-200 pages. No romance, mysteries, science fiction.

HOW TO CONTACT "Please submit a query letter with three opening chapters (of a novel) or three representative stories (of a collection)." Responds in 6 months. Publishes book in 18 months.

TERMS Pays authors variable royalty based on retail price. Offers advance against royalties. Pays varied advance from $500-10,000. Book catalog online. Only accepts submissions during open submission periods. See website for guidelines.

TIPS "We are looking for excellent writing with the intent of making a humane impact on society. Please read submission guidelines before submitting and acquaint yourself with our books in terms of style and quality before submitting. Many factors influence our selection process, so don't get discouraged. Nonfiction is focused on literary writing about the natural world, including living well in urban environments."

MILKWEED FOR YOUNG READERS

Milkweed Editions, Open Book Building, 1011 Washington Ave. S., Suite 300, Minneapolis MN 55415. (612)332-3192. **Fax:** (612)215-2550. **Website:** www.milkweed.org. "We are looking first of all for high quality literary writing. We publish books with the intention of making a humane impact on soci-

ety." Publishes hardcover and trade paperback originals. **Publishes 3-4 titles/year. 25% of books from first-time authors. 50% from unagented writers.**
HOW TO CONTACT "Milkweed Editions now accepts manuscripts online through our Submission Manager. If you're a first-time submitter, you'll need to fill in a simple form and then follow the instructions for selecting and uploading your manuscript. Please make sure that your manuscript follows the submission guidelines." Responds in 6 months to queries. Publishes ms 1 year after acceptance.
TERMS Pays 7% royalty on retail price. Pays variable advance. Book catalog for $1.50. Guidelines online.

THE MILLBROOK PRESS

Lerner Publishing Group, 1251 Washington Ave N, Minneapolis MN 55401. **E-mail:** info@lernerbooks.com. **Website:** www.lernerbooks.com. **Contact:** Carol Hinz, editorial director. "Millbrook Press publishes informative picture books, illustrated nonfiction titles, and inspiring photo-driven titles for grades K–5. Our authors approach curricular topics with a fresh point of view. Our fact-filled books engage readers with fun yet accessible writing, high-quality photographs, and a wide variety of illustration styles. We cover subjects ranging from the parts of speech and other language arts skills; to history, science, and math; to art, sports, crafts, and other interests. Millbrook Press is the home of the best-selling Words Are CATegorical® series and Bob Raczka's Art Adventures. We do not accept unsolicited manuscripts from authors. Occasionally, we may put out a call for submissions, which will be announced on our website."

MITCHELL LANE PUBLISHERS, INC.

P.O. Box 196, Hockessin DE 33009. (302) 234-9426. **Fax:** (866) 834-4164. **E-mail:** barbaramitchell@mitchellane.com; customerservice@mitchelllane.com. **Website:** www.mitchelllane.com. **Contact:** Barbara Mitchell. Publishes hardcover and library bound originals. **Publishes 80 titles/year. 0% of books from first-time authors. 90% from unagented writers.**
NONFICTION Young readers, middle readers, young adults: biography, nonfiction, and curriculum-related subjects. Average word length: 4,000-50,000 words. Recently published: *My Guide to US Citizenship*, *Rivers of the World* and *Vote America*.

HOW TO CONTACT Query with SASE. *All unsolicited mss discarded.* 100 queries received/year. 5 mss received/year. Responds only if interested to queries. Publishes ms 1 year after acceptance.
ILLUSTRATION Works with 2-3 illustrators/year. Reviews ms/illustration packages from artists. Query. Illustration only: Query with samples; send résumé, portfolio, slides, tearsheets. Responds only if interested. Samples not returned; samples filed.
PHOTOGRAPHY Buys stock images. Needs photos of famous and prominent minority figures. Captions required. Uses color prints or digital images. Submit cover letter, résumé, published samples, stock photo list.
TERMS Work purchased outright from authors (range: $350-2,000). Pays illustrators by the project (range: $40-400). Book catalog available free.
TIPS "We hire writers on a 'work-for-hire' basis to complete book projects we assign. Send résumé and writing samples that do not need to be returned."

MOODY PUBLISHERS

Moody Bible Institute, 820 N. LaSalle Blvd., Chicago IL 60610. (800)678-8812. **Fax:** (312)329-4157. **Website:** www.moodypublishers.org. **Contact:** Acquisitions Coordinator. "The mission of Moody Publishers is to educate and edify the Christian and to evangelize the non-Christian by ethically publishing conservative, evangelical Christian literature and other media for all ages around the world, and to help provide resources for Moody Bible Institute in its training of future Christian leaders." Publishes hardcover, trade, and mass market paperback originals. **Publishes 60 titles/year. 1% of books from first-time authors. 80% from unagented writers.**
NONFICTION "We are no longer reviewing queries or unsolicited manuscripts unless they come to us through an agent, are from an author who has published with us, an associate from a Moody Bible Institute ministry or a personal contact at a writer's conference. Unsolicited proposals will be returned only if proper postage is included. We are not able to acknowledge the receipt of your unsolicited proposal."
HOW TO CONTACT *Agented submissions only.* Does not accept unsolicited nonfiction submissions. 1,500 queries received/year. 2,000 mss received/year.

Responds in 2-3 months to queries. Publishes book 1 year after acceptance.

TERMS Royalty varies. Book catalog for 9×12 envelope and 4 first-class stamps. Guidelines online.

TIPS "In our fiction list, we're looking for Christian storytellers rather than teachers trying to present a message. Your motivation should be to delight the reader. Using your skills to create beautiful works is glorifying to God."

MOONDANCE PRESS

Quarto Publishing, 25 Whitman Road, Morganville NJ 07751. **Website:** www.quartoknows.com/Moon-DancePress. MoonDance Press is dedicated to entertaining, educating, and inspiring children with beautifully produced, content-rich books. "Our picture books capture young imaginations with enthralling stories brought to life by award-winning illustrators. Science, nature, and activity titles inspire the inquisitive mind with fun and fascinating information. The exquisitely produced Modern Retelling series, with unique and brilliant art, captures the essence of literature's timeless classics, bringing their characters and stories to the youngest minds. The literary world's best poets and award-winning illustrators introduce poetry to young children in the Poetry for Kids series. MoonDance publishes books for dreamers, thinkers, doodlers, puzzlers … the moon watchers, the question askers, and of course, the book lovers." **Publishes 20 titles/year.**

TERMS Complete information listed on site. Asks writers to sign submission agreement.

TIPS "If you are looking for something to enthrall a young child, our picture books do just that with stories that capture young imaginations and award-winning illustrators who bring them to life. To inspire the inquisitive mind, our science, nature, and activity-filled books, filled with fun and fascinating information, will do the trick."

❷ NATIONAL GEOGRAPHIC CHILDREN'S BOOKS

1145 17th St. NW, Washington DC 20090-8199. (800)647-5463. **Website:** kids.nationalgeographic.com. National Geographic Children's Books provides quality nonfiction for children and young adults by award-winning authors. *This market does not currently accept unsolicited mss.*

NATUREGRAPH PUBLISHERS, INC.

P.O. Box 1047, 3543 Indian Creek Rd., Happy Camp CA 96039. (530)493-5353. **Fax:** (530)493-5240. **E-mail:** nature@sisqtel.net. **Website:** www.naturegraph.com. **Contact:** Barbara Brown, owner. Publishes trade paperback originals. **Publishes 2 titles/year. 80% of books from first-time authors. 90% from unagented writers.**

HOW TO CONTACT 100 queries; 6 mss received/year. Responds in 1 month to queries; 2 months to mss. Publishes ms 2 years after acceptance.

TERMS Pays royalties. Does not pay advance. Book catalog for #10 SASE.

TIPS "Please always send a SASE. Publishers get hundreds of manuscripts yearly."

TOMMY NELSON

Imprint of Thomas Nelson, Inc., P.O. Box 141000, Nashville TN 37214-1000. (615)889-9000. **Fax:** (615)902-2219. **Website:** www.tommynelson.com. "Tommy Nelson publishes children's Christian nonfiction and fiction for boys and girls up to age 14. We honor God and serve people through books, videos, software, and Bibles for children that improve the lives of our customers." Publishes hardcover and trade paperback originals. **Publishes 50-75 titles/year.**

FICTION No stereotypical characters.

HOW TO CONTACT *Does not accept unsolicited mss.*

TERMS Guidelines online.

TIPS "Know the Christian Booksellers Association market. Check out the Christian bookstores to see what sells and what is needed."

NIGHTSCAPE PRESS

P.O. Box 1948, Smyrna TN 37167. **E-mail:** info@nightscapepress.com. **Website:** www.nightscapepress.com. Nightscape Press is seeking quality book-length words of at least 50,000 words (40,000 for young adult).

FICTION "We are not interested in erotica or graphic novels."

HOW TO CONTACT Query.

TERMS Pays monthly royalties. Offers advance. Guidelines online. Currently closed to submissions. Will announce on site when they re-open to submissions.

NOMAD PRESS

2456 Christain St., White River Junction VT 05001. (802)649-1995. **E-mail:** info@nomadpress.net. **Website:** www.nomadpress.net. **Contact:** Acquisitions Editor. "We produce nonfiction children's activity books that bring a particular science or cultural topic into sharp focus. Nomad Press does not accept unsolicited manuscripts. If authors are interested in contributing to our children's series, please send a writing résumé that includes relevant experience/expertise and publishing credits."

Nomad Press does not accept picture books, fiction, or cookbooks.

NONFICTION Middle readers: activity books, history, science. Average word length: middle readers: 30,000.

HOW TO CONTACT Responds to queries in 3-4 weeks. Publishes ms 1 year after acceptance.

TERMS Pays authors royalty based on retail price or work purchased outright. Offers advance against royalties. Catalog online.

TIPS "We publish a very specific kind of nonfiction children's activity book. Please keep this in mind when querying or submitting."

NORTHSOUTH BOOKS

600 Third Ave., 2nd Floor, New York NY 10016. (917)210-5868. **E-mail:** hlennon@northsouth.com. **Website:** www.northsouth.com.

FICTION Looking for fresh, original fiction with universal themes that could appeal to children ages 3-8. "We typically do not acquire rhyming texts, since our books must also be translated into German."

HOW TO CONTACT Submit picture book mss (1,000 words or less) via e-mail.

TERMS Guidelines online.

ONSTAGE PUBLISHING

190 Lime Quarry Rd., Suite 106-J, Madison AL 35758-8962. (256)542-3213. **Fax:** (256)542-3213. **Website:** www.onstagepublishing.com. **Contact:** Dianne Hamilton, senior editor. "At this time, we only produce fiction books for ages 8-18. We have added an e-book only side of the house for mysteries for grades 6-12. See our website for more information. We will not do anthologies of any kind. Query first for nonfiction projects as nonfiction projects must spark our interest. We no longer are accepting written submissions. We want e-mail queries

and submissions. For submissions: Put the first 3 chapters in the body of the e-mail. Do not use attachments! We will delete any submission with an attachment without acknowledgment." Suggested ms lengths: chapter books: 3,000-9,000 words, middle grade novels: 10,000-40,000 words, young adult novels: 40,000-60,000 words. **Publishes 1-5 titles/year. 80% of books from first-time authors.**

FICTION Middle readers: adventure, contemporary, fantasy, history, nature/environment, science fiction, suspense/mystery. Young adults: adventure, contemporary, fantasy, history, humor, science fiction, suspense/mystery. Average word length: chapter books: 4,000-6,000 words; middle readers: 5,000 words and up; young adults: 25,000 and up. Recently published *Mission: Shanghai* by Jamie Dodson (an adventure for boys ages 12+); *Birmingham, 1933: Alice* (a chapter book for grades 3-5). "We do not produce picture books."

HOW TO CONTACT Receives 500+ ms/year. Responds in 1-3 months.

TERMS Pays authors/illustrators/photographers advance plus royalties. Guidelines online.

TIPS "Study our titles and get a sense of the kind of books we publish, so that you know whether your project is likely to be right for us."

OOLIGAN PRESS

369 Neuberger Hall, 724 SW Harrison St., Portland OR 97201. (503)725-9410. **Website:** ooligan.pdx.edu. **Contact:** Acquisitions Co-Managers. Publishes trade paperbacks, electronic originals, and reprints. **Publishes 3-4 titles/year. 90% of books from first-time authors. 90% from unagented writers.**

FICTION "We seek to publish regionally significant works of literary, historical, and social value. We define the Pacific Northwest as Northern California, Oregon, Idaho, Washington, British Columbia, and Alaska." We recognize the importance of diversity, particularly within the publishing industry, and are committed to building a literary community that includes traditionally underrepresented voices; therefore, we are interested in works originating from, or focusing on, marginalized communities of the Pacific Northwest. Does not want romance, horror, westerns, incomplete mss.

NONFICTION Cookbooks, self-help books, how-to manuals.

HOW TO CONTACT Query with SASE. "At this time we cannot accept science fiction or fantasy submissions." Submit a query through Submittable. If accepted, then submit proposal package, outline, 4 sample chapters, projected page count, audience, marketing ideas, and a list of similar titles. 250-500 queries; 50-75 mss received/year. Responds in 3 weeks for queries; 3 months for proposals. Publishes ms 12-18 months after acceptance.

TERMS Pays negotiable royalty on retail price. Catalog online. Guidelines online.

TIPS "Search the blog for tips."

Ⓐ ORCHARD BOOKS (US)

557 Broadway, New York NY 10012. **Website:** www.scholastic.com. *Orchard is not accepting unsolicited mss.* **Publishes 20 titles/year. 10% of books from first-time authors.**

FICTION Picture books, early readers, and novelty: animal, contemporary, history, humor, multicultural, poetry.

TERMS Most commonly offers an advance against list royalties.

PAGESPRING PUBLISHING

PageSpring Publishing, P.O. Box 21133, Columbus OH 43221. **Website:** www.pagespringpublishing.com. PageSpring Publishing is a small independent publisher with two imprints: Cup of Tea Books and Lucky Marble Books. Cup of Tea Books publishes women's fiction, with particular emphasis on mystery and humor. Lucky Marble Books publishes young adult and middle grade fiction. "We are looking for engaging characters and well-crafted plots that keep our readers turning the page. We accept e-mail queries only; see our website for details." Publishes trade paperback and electronic originals. **Publishes 4-5 titles/year. 75% of books from first-time authors. 100% from unagented writers.**

FICTION Lucky Marble Books publishes middle grade and young adult novels. No children's picture books.

HOW TO CONTACT Submit proposal package via e-mail only. Include synopsis and 30 sample pages. Responds in 3 months. Publishes ms 12 months after acceptance.

TERMS Pays royalty. Guidelines online.

TIPS "Lucky Marble Books is looking for funny, age-appropriate tales for middle grade and young adult readers."

PANTS ON FIRE PRESS

2062 Harbor Cove Way, Winter Garden FL 34787. (863)546-0760. **E-mail:** submission@pantsonfire-press.com. **Website:** www.pantsonfirepress.com. **Contact:** Becca Goldman, senior editor; Emily Gerety, editor. Pants On Fire Press is an award-winning book publisher of picture, middle-grade, young adult, and adult books. Publishes hardcover originals and reprints, trade paperback originals and reprints, and electronic originals and reprints. **Publishes 10-15 titles/year. 60% of books from first-time authors. 80% from unagented writers.**

FICTION Publishes big story ideas with high concepts, new worlds, and meaty characters for children, teens, and discerning adults. Always on the lookout for action, adventure, animals, comedic, dramatic, dystopian, fantasy, historical, paranormal, romance, science-fiction, supernatural, and suspense stories.

HOW TO CONTACT Submit a proposal package including a synopsis, 3 sample chapters, and a query letter via e-mail. Receives 36,300 queries and mss per year. Responds in 3 months. Publishes ms approximately 7 months after acceptance.

TERMS Pays 10-50% royalties on wholesale price. Catalog online. Guidelines online.

PARADISE CAY PUBLICATIONS

P.O. Box 29, Arcata CA 95518-0029. (800)736-4509. **Fax:** (707)822-9163. **Website:** www.paracay.com. "Paradise Cay Publications, Inc. is a small independent publisher specializing in nautical books, videos, and art prints. Our primary interest is in manuscripts that deal with the instructional and technical aspects of ocean sailing. We also publish and will consider fiction if it has a strong nautical theme." Publishes hardcover and trade paperback originals and reprints. **Publishes 5 titles/year. 10% of books from first-time authors. 100% from unagented writers.**

FICTION All fiction must have a nautical theme.

NONFICTION Must have strong nautical theme.

HOW TO CONTACT Query with SASE. Submit proposal package, clips, 2-3 sample chapters. Include a cover letter containing a story synopsis and a short bio, including any plans to promote their work. The cover letter should describe the book's subject matter, approach, distinguishing characteristics, intended audience, author's qualifications, and why the author thinks this book is appropriate for Paradise Cay. Call first. 360-480 queries received/year. 240-360 mss received/year. Responds in 1 month to queries/proposals; 2 months to mss. Publishes book 4 months after acceptance.

TERMS Pays 10-15% royalty on wholesale price. Makes outright purchase of $1,000-10,000. Does not normally pay advances to first-time or little-known authors. Book catalog and ms guidelines free on request or online.

TIPS "Audience is recreational sailors. Call Matt Morehouse (publisher)."

PAULINE BOOKS & MEDIA

50 St. Paul's Ave., Boston MA 02130. (617)522-8911. **Fax:** (617)541-9805. **E-mail:** design@paulinemedia.com; editorial@paulinemedia.com. **Website:** www.pauline.org. "Submissions are evaluated on adherence to Gospel values, harmony with the Catholic faith tradition, relevance of topic, and quality of writing." For board books and picture books, the entire manuscript should be submitted. For easy-to-read, young readers, and middle reader books and teen books, please send a cover letter accompanied by a synopsis and two sample chapters. "Electronic submissions are encouraged. We make every effort to respond to unsolicited submissions within 2 months." Publishes trade paperback originals and reprints. **Publishes 40 titles/year. 5% from unagented writers.**

FICTION Children's and teen fiction only. "We are now accepting submissions for easy-to-read and middle reader chapter, and teen well documented historical fiction. We would also consider well-written fantasy, fairy tales, myths, science fiction, mysteries, or romance if approached from a Catholic perspective and consistent with church teaching. Please see our Writer's Guidelines."

NONFICTION Picture books, young readers, middle readers, teen: religion and fiction. Average word length: picture books: 500-1,000; young readers: 8,000-10,000; middle readers: 15,000-25,000; teen: 30,000-50,000. Recently published children's titles: *Bible Stories for Little Ones* by Genny Monchapm; *I Forgive You: Love We Can Hear, Ask For and Give* by Nicole Lataif; *Shepherds To the Rescue* (first place Catholic Book Award Winner) by Maria Grace Dateno; *FSP; Jorge from Argentina; Prayers for Young Catholics.* Teen Titles: *Teens Share the Mis-*

sion by Teens; *Martyred: The Story of Saint Lorenzo Ruiz; Ten Commandmenst for Kissing Gloria Jean* by Britt Leigh; *A.K.A. Genius* (2nd Place Catholic Book Award Winner) by Marilee Haynes; *Tackling Tough Topics with Faith and Fiction* by Diana Jenkins. No memoir/autobiography, poetry, or strictly nonreligious works currently considered.

HOW TO CONTACT Submit proposal package, including outline, 1-2 sample chapters, cover letter, synopsis, intended audience and proposed length. Responds in 2 months. Publishes a book approximately 11-18 months after acceptance.

ILLUSTRATION Works with 10-15 illustrators/year. Uses color and b&w artwork. Samples and résumés will be kept on file unless return is requested and SASE provided.

TERMS Varies by project, but generally are royalties with advance. Flat fees sometimes considered for smaller works. Book catalog online. Guidelines online.

TIPS "Manuscripts may or may not be explicitly catechetical, but we seek those that reflect a positive worldview, good moral values, awareness and appreciation of diversity, and respect for all people. All material must be relevant to the lives of readers and must conform to Catholic teaching and practice."

PEACHTREE CHILDREN'S BOOKS

Peachtree Publishers, Ltd., 1700 Chattahoochee Ave., Atlanta GA 30318. (404)876-8761. **Fax:** (404)875-2578. **E-mail:** hello@peachtree-online.com. **Website:** www.peachtree-online.com. **Contact:** Helen Harriss, submissions editor. "We publish a broad range of subjects and perspectives, with emphasis on innovative plots and strong writing." Publishes hardcover and trade paperback originals. **Publishes 30 titles/year. 25% of books from first-time authors. 25% from unagented writers.**

FICTION Looking for very well-written middle grade and young adult novels. No adult fiction. No collections of poetry or short stories; no romance or science fiction. Picture books, young readers: adventure, animal, concept, history, nature/environment. Middle readers: adventure, animal, history, nature/environment, sports. Young adults: fiction, mystery, adventure.

NONFICTION Picture books: animal, history, nature/environment. Young readers, middle readers, young adults: animal, biography, nature/environ-ment. Does not want to see religion.

HOW TO CONTACT Submit complete ms with SASE, or summary and 3 sample chapters with SASE. Responds in 6 months and mss. Publishes ms 1 year after acceptance.

TERMS Pays royalty on retail price. Book catalog for 6 first-class stamps. Guidelines online.

ILLUSTRATION Works with 8-10 illustrators/year. Illustrations only: Query production manager or art director with samples, résumé, slides, color copies to keep on file. Responds only if interested. Samples returned with SASE; samples filed.

PELICAN PUBLISHING COMPANY

1000 Burmaster St., Gretna LA 70053. (504)368-1175. **Fax:** (504)368-1195. **E-mail:** editorial@pelicanpub. com. **Website:** www.pelicanpub.com. "We believe ideas have consequences. One of the consequences is that they lead to a best-selling book. We publish books to improve and uplift the reader. Currently emphasizing business and history titles." Publishes 20 young readers/year; 1 middle reader/year. "Our children's books (illustrated and otherwise) include history, biography, holiday, and regional. Pelican's mission is to publish books of quality and perma-nence that enrich the lives of those who read them." Publishes hardcover, trade paperback and mass market paperback originals and reprints.

FICTION We publish no adult fiction. Young read-ers: history, holiday, science, multicultural and re-gional. Middle readers: Louisiana History. Multi-cultural needs include stories about African-Ameri-cans, Irish-Americans, Jews, Asian-Americans, and Hispanics. Does not want animal stories, general Christmas stories, "day at school" or "accept your-self" stories. Maximum word length: young read-ers: 1,100; middle readers: 40,000. No young adult, romance, science fiction, fantasy, gothic, mystery, erotica, confession, horror, sex, or violence. Also no psychological novels.

NONFICTION "We look for authors who can pro-mote successfully. We require that a query be made first. This greatly expedites the review process and can save the writer additional postage expenses." Young readers: biography, history, holiday, multi-cultural. Middle readers: Louisiana history, holiday, regional. No multiple queries or submissions.

HOW TO CONTACT Submit outline, clips, 2 sample chapters, SASE. Full guidelines on website. Responds in 1 month to queries; 3 months to mss. Requires exclusive submission. Publishes a book 9-18 months after acceptance.

ILLUSTRATION Works with 20 illustrators/year. Reviews ms/illustration packages from artists. Query first. Illustrations only: Query with samples (no origi-nals). Responds only if interested. Samples returned with SASE; samples kept on file.

TERMS Pays authors in royalties; buys ms outright "rarely." Illustrators paid by "various arrangements." Advance considered. Book catalog and ms guide-lines online.

TIPS "We do extremely well with cookbooks, popular histories, and business. We will continue to build in these areas. The writer must have a clear sense of the market and knowledge of the competition. A query letter should describe the project briefly, give the au-thor's writing and professional credentials, and pro-motional ideas."

Ⓐ PENGUIN RANDOM HOUSE, LLC

Division of Bertelsmann Book Group, 1745 Broad-way, New York NY 10019. (212)782-9000. **Website:** www.penguinrandomhouse.com. Penguin Random House, LLC is the world's largest English-language general trade book publisher. *Agented submissions only. No unsolicited mss.*

PERSEA BOOKS

277 Broadway, Suite 708, New York NY 10007. (212)260-9256. **Fax:** (212)267-3165. **E-mail:** info@ perseabooks.com. **Website:** www.perseabooks.com. The aim of Persea is to publish works that endure by meeting high standards of literary merit and rel-evance. "We have often taken on important books other publishers have overlooked, or have made significant discoveries and rediscoveries, whether of a single work or writer's entire oeuvre. Our books cover a wide range of themes, styles, and genres. We have published poetry, fiction, essays, memoir, bi-ography, titles of Jewish and Middle Eastern interest, women's studies, American Indian folklore, and re-vived classics, as well as a notable selection of works in translation."

HOW TO CONTACT Queries should include a cover letter, author background and publication his-tory, a detailed synopsis of the proposed work, and a sample chapter. Please indicate if the work is simultaneously submitted. Responds in 8 weeks to proposals; 10 weeks to mss.

TERMS Guidelines online.

PHAIDON PRESS

65 Bleecker Street, 8th Floor, New York NY 10012. (212)652-5400. **Fax:** (212)652-5410. **Contact:** Meagan Bennet, Art Director and Cecily Kaiser, Children's Publishing Director. "Phaidon is the premier global publisher of the creative arts with over 1,500 titles in print. We work with the world's most influential artists, chefs, writers, and thinkers to produce innovative books on art, photography, design, architecture, fashion, food and travel, and illustrated books for children."

TERMS If you are interested in submitting a children's book proposal to us, please bear in mind that we currently publish for children ages 0-8 in the categories of: board book, novelty book, and picture book. Subject matter must be relevant to the target age group and quality must be commensurate with the Phaidon brand." Priority is given to submissions that have been solicited or agented, and we will not reply to those that are not. Appropriate submissions should be emailed to submissions@phaidon. com. **Please do not send hard copies.** Phaidon cannot assume responsibility for any submissions sent by mail."

Ⓐ PHILOMEL BOOKS

Imprint of Penguin Group (USA), Inc., 375 Hudson St., New York NY 10014. (212)414-3610. **Website:** www.penguin.com. **Contact:** Michael Green, president/publisher. "We look for beautifully written, engaging manuscripts for children and young adults." Publishes hardcover originals. **Publishes 8-10 titles/year. 5% of books from first-time authors. 20% from unagented writers.**

NONFICTION Picture books.

HOW TO CONTACT *No unsolicited mss. Agented submissions only.*

ILLUSTRATION Works with 8-10 illustrators/year. Reviews ms/illustration packages from artists. Query with art sample first. Illustrations only: Query with samples. Send résumé and tearsheets. Responds to art samples in 1 month. Original artwork returned at job's completion. Samples returned with SASE or kept on file.

TERMS Pays authors in royalties. Average advance payment "varies." Illustrators paid by advance and in royalties. Pays negotiable advance.

PIANO PRESS

P.O. Box 85, Del Mar CA 92014. (619)884-1401. **Fax:** (858)755-1104. **E-mail:** pianopress@pianopress.com. **Website:** www.pianopress.com. **Contact:** Elizabeth C. Axford, editor. "We publish music-related books, either fiction or nonfiction, music-related coloring books, songbooks, sheet music, CDs, and music-related poetry."

FICTION Picture books, young readers, middle readers, young adults: folktales, multicultural, poetry, music. Average word length: picture books: 1,500-2,000.

NONFICTION Picture books, young readers, middle readers, young adults: multicultural, music/dance. Average word length: picture books: 1,500-2,000.

HOW TO CONTACT Responds if interested. Publishes ms 1 year after acceptance.

ILLUSTRATION Works with 1 or 2 illustrators/year. Reviews ms/illustration packages from artists. Query. Illustrations only: Query with samples. Responds in 3 months. Samples returned with SASE; samples filed.

PHOTOGRAPHY Buys stock and assigns work. Looking for music-related, multicultural. Model/property releases required. Uses glossy or flat, color or b&w prints. Submit cover letter, résumé, client list, published samples, stock photo list.

TERMS Pays authors, illustrators, and photographers royalties based on the retail price. Book catalog online.

TIPS "We are looking for music-related material only for the juvenile market. Please do not send nonmusic-related materials. Query by e-mail first before submitting anything."

PIÑATA BOOKS

Imprint of Arte Publico Press, University of Houston, 4902 Gulf Fwy., Bldg. 19, Room 100, Houston TX 77204-2004. (713)743-2845. **Fax:** (713)743-3080. **E-mail:** submapp@uh.edu. **Website:** www.artepublicopress.com. "Piñata Books is dedicated to the publication of children's and young adult literature focusing on US Hispanic culture by US Hispanic authors. Arte Publico's mission is the publication, promotion and dissemination of Latino literature for a variety of national and regional audiences, from early childhood to adult, through the complete gamut of delivery systems, including personal performance as well as print and electronic media." Publishes hardcover and trade paperback originals. **Publishes 10-15 titles/year. 80% of books from first-time authors.**

NONFICTION Piñata Books specializes in publication of children's and young adult literature that authentically portrays themes, characters, and customs unique to US Hispanic culture.

HOW TO CONTACT Submissions made through online submission form. Responds in 2-3 months to queries; 4-6 months to mss. Publishes book 2 years after acceptance.

ILLUSTRATION Works with 6 illustrators/year. Uses color artwork only. Reviews ms/illustration packages from artists. Query or send portfolio (slides, color copies). Illustrations only: Query with samples or send résumé, promo sheet, portfolio, slides, client list, and tearsheets. Responds only if interested. Samples not returned; samples filed.

TERMS Pays 10% royalty on wholesale price. Pays $1,000-3,000 advance. Book catalog and guidelines online.

TIPS "Include cover letter with submission explaining why your manuscript is unique and important, why we should publish it, who will buy it, etc."

PINEAPPLE PRESS, INC.

P.O. Box 3889, Sarasota FL 34230. (941)706-2507. **Fax:** (800)746-3275. **Website:** www.pineapplepress. com. **Contact:** June Cussen, executive editor. "We are seeking quality nonfiction on diverse topics for the library and book trade markets. Our mission is to publish good books about Florida." Publishes hardcover and trade paperback originals. **Publishes 21 titles/year. 50% of books from first-time authors. 95% from unagented writers.**

FICTION Picture books, young readers, middle readers, young adults: animal, folktales, history, nature/environment.

NONFICTION Picture books: animal, history, nature/environmental, science. Young readers, middle readers, young adults: animal, biography, geography, history, nature/environment, science.

HOW TO CONTACT Query or submit outline/synopsis and intro and 3 sample chapters. 1,000 queries; 500 mss received/year. Responds in 2 months. Publishes a ms 1 year after acceptance.

ILLUSTRATION Works with 2 illustrators/year. Reviews ms/illustration packages from artists. Query with nonreturnable samples. Contact: June Cussen, executive editor. Illustrations only: Query with brochure, nonreturnable samples, photocopies, résumé. Responds only if interested. Samples returned with SASE, but prefers nonreturnable; samples filed.

TERMS Pays authors royalty of 10-15%. Book catalog for 9×12 SAE with $1.32 postage. Guidelines online.

TIPS "Quality first novels will be published, though we usually only do one or two novels per year and they must be set in Florida. We regard the author/editor relationship as a trusting relationship with communication open both ways. Learn all you can about the publishing process and about how to promote your book once it is published. A query on a novel without a brief sample seems useless."

THE POISONED PENCIL

Poisoned Pen Press, 6962 E. 1st Ave., Suite 103, Scottsdale AZ 85251. (480)945-3375. **Fax:** (480)949-1707. **E-mail:** info@thepoisonedpencil.com. **Website:** www.thepoisonedpencil.com. **Contact:** Ellen Larson, editor. Publishes trade paperback and electronic originals. **Publishes 4-6 titles/year.**

FICTION "We publish only young adult mystery novels, 45,000 to 90,000 words in length. For our purposes, a young adult book is a book with a protagonist between the ages of 13 and 18. We are looking for both traditional and cross-genre young adult mysteries. We encourage off-beat approaches and narrative choices that reflect the complexity and ambiguity of today's world. Submissions from teens are very welcome. Avoid serial killers, excessive gore, and vampires (and other heavy supernatural themes). We only consider authors who live in the US or Canada, due to practicalities of marketing promotion. Avoid coincidence in plotting. Avoid having your sleuth leap to conclusions rather than discover and deduce. Pay attention to the resonance between character and plot; between plot and theme; between theme and character. We are looking for clean style, fluid storytelling, and solid structure. Unrealistic dialogue is a real turn-off."

HOW TO CONTACT Submit proposal package including synopsis, complete ms, and cover letter. 150 submissions received/year. Responds in 6 weeks to mss. Publishes ms 15 months after acceptance.

TERMS Pays 9-15% for trade paperback; 25-35% for e-books. Pays advance of $1,000. Guidelines online.
TIPS "Our audience is made up of young adults and adults who love YA mysteries."

POLIS BOOKS

E-mail: info@polisbooks.com. **Website:** www.polisbooks.com. "Polis Books is an independent publishing company actively seeking new and established authors for our growing list. We are actively acquiring titles in mystery, thriller, suspense, procedural, traditional crime, science fiction, fantasy, horror, supernatural, urban fantasy, romance, erotica, commercial women's fiction, commercial literary fiction, young adult, and middle grade books." **Publishes 40 titles/year. 33% of books from first-time authors. 10% from unagented writers.**
HOW TO CONTACT Query with 3 sample chapters and bio via e-mail. Receives 500+ queries/year. Only responds to submissions if interested. For e-book originals, ms published 6-9 months after acceptance. For front list print titles, 9-15 months.
TERMS Offers advance against royalties. Guidelines online.

POMEGRANATE KIDS

19018 NE Portal Way, Portland OR 97230. (503)328-6500; (800)227-1428. **Website:** www.pomegranate.com/arsub.html. "With a focus on fine art and illustration, Pomegranate collaborates with individual artists as well as museums, galleries, and libraries across the world.We publish artful and educational items for adults and children. Popular product lines include art books, bookplates, calendars, children's books, coloring books, coloring cards, home décor, puzzles, stationery, and a myriad of other high-quality paper gift products. We continually introduce new formats and designs, with the mission to inspire through art. We delight in collaborating with many artists and writers in the creation of new products, so we're happy to review your work for possible publication."
HOW TO CONTACT Responds in 8 weeks.
ILLUSTRATION "If you are an artist looking to submit a query or proposal, visit our Art Submissions page. Email us with "Your Name: Artist Submission" in the subject line. Please provide a link to your website, or digital portfolio, and if there is a specific body of work you would like us to consider, please provide a direct link. If you do not have a website, you may include 5-8 images of your work. Image resolution should be 72 dpi and the images under 1MB each. Please attach a PDF of your resume. You may mail a CD or flash drive with images, or you may mail color printouts/photocopies. Never send originals! We are careful and attentive, but we can't assume responsibility for lost or mangled materials. Please include your résumé."

POW!

37 Main Street, Brooklyn NY 11201. (212)604-9074. POW! publishes books for children that are visually striking, imaginative, funny, and have an offbeat or edgy sensibility. If you have a book project that meets these criteria, and you would like POW! to consider your book for publication, you can send us a submission. Publishes mainly picture books.
HOW TO CONTACT "Include in your proposal a brief description of your book and why it's right for us, an analysis of the market for your book and a list of recent comparable titles, the full text (if it's reasonably short; a sample chapter otherwise), sample pages with illustrations."
TIPS "The best way to send it to us is by email: info@powkidsbooks.com. NO ATTACHMENTS, PLEASE! Submissions containing attachments will be rejected. Please send a link instead."

ⓐ PRICE STERN SLOAN, INC.

Penguin Group, 375 Hudson St., New York NY 10014. (212)366-2000. **Website:** www.penguin.com. "Price Stern Sloan publishes quirky mass market novelty series for childrens as well as licensed movie tie-in books." Price Stern Sloan only responds to submissions it's interested in publishing.
FICTION Publishes picture books and novelty/board books.
HOW TO CONTACT *Agented submissions only.*
TERMS Book catalog online.
TIPS "Price Stern Sloan publishes unique, fun titles."

ⓒ PRUFROCK PRESS, INC.

P.O. Box 8813, Waco TX 76714. (800)988-2208. **Fax:** (800)240-0333. **Website:** www.prufrock.com. "Prufrock Press offers award-winning products focused on gifted education, gifted children, advanced learning, and special needs learners, including trade nonfiction (not narrative nonfiction, however) for adults and children/teens. For more than 20 years, Prufrock has supported gifted children and their education and development. The company publishes more than 300 products that enhance the lives of gifted children and the teachers and parents who support them." Accepts simultaneous submissions, but must be notified about it. **20% of books from first-time authors. 100% from unagented writers.**

NONFICTION "We are always looking for truly original, creative materials for teachers."

HOW TO CONTACT "Prufrock Press does not consider unsolicited manuscripts." Query with SASE. Submit outline, 1-3 sample chapters. 50 queries; 40 mss received/year. Publishes ms 1-2 year after acceptance.

TERMS Book catalog available. Guidelines online.

Ⓐ PUFFIN BOOKS

Imprint of Penguin Group (USA), Inc., 375 Hudson St., New York NY 10014. (212)366-2000. **Website:** www.penguin.com. "Puffin Books publishes high-end trade paperbacks and paperback reprints for preschool children, beginning and middle readers, and young adults." Publishes trade paperback originals and reprints. **Publishes 175-200 titles/year.**

NONFICTION "Women in history books interest us."

HOW TO CONTACT *No unsolicited mss. Agented submissions only.* Publishes ms 1 year after acceptance.

ILLUSTRATION Reviews artwork. Send color copies.

PHOTOGRAPHY Reviews photos. Send color copies.

TIPS "Our audience ranges from little children 'first books' to young adult (ages 14-16). An original idea has the best luck."

Ⓐ G.P. PUTNAM'S SONS HARDCOVER

Imprint of Penguin Group (USA), Inc., 375 Hudson, New York NY 10014. (212)366-2000. **Fax:** (212)366-2664. **Website:** www.penguin.com. Publishes hardcover originals.

HOW TO CONTACT *Agented submissions only. No unsolicited mss.*

TERMS Pays variable royalties on retail price. Pays variable advance. Request book catalog through mail order department.

QUIRK BOOKS

215 Church Street, Philadelphia PA 19106. **E-mail:** blair@quirkbooks.com; jason@quirkbooks.com. "Quirk Books is headquartered on a quiet cobblestone street in the historic Old City district of Philadelphia. Quirk publishes just 25 books per year and every title is a labor of love. Some of our more popular recent titles include the bestselling YA series *Miss Peregrine's Peculiar Children*, the Edgar Award-winning mystery *The Last Policeman*, the legendary *Pride and Prejudice Zombies*, and classroom favorite *William Shakespeare's Star Wars*." **Publishes 25 titles/year.**

FICTION "We publish across a broad range of categories—always with the goal of delivering innovative books to discerning readers. Put more simply, we publish books that are smart, original, cool, and fun."

TERMS "The easiest way to submit your idea is to e-mail a query letter to one of our editors. The query letter should be a short description of your project. Try to limit your letter to a single page. If you have sample chapters, go ahead and include them. You can also mail materials directly to our office. If you would like a reply, please include a SASE. If you want your materials returned, please include adequate postage. If your project involves fiction (adult, young adult, or middle grade), humor, pop culture, history, sports, literature, sex, monsters, or "guy stuff," send it to Jason Rekulak (jason@quirkbooks.com). If your project involves fiction (adult or young adult) about falling in love, avoiding falling in love, books-within-books, unconventional narrative (epistolary, text-message-o-lary, diary novels, etc.), wordplay, smart teenagers, travel, or medievalists, send a query letter and the first chapter pasted into the body of the email (no attachments) to Blair Thornburgh (blair@quirkbooks.com)."

Ⓐ RANDOM HOUSE CHILDREN'S BOOKS

1745 Broadway, New York NY 10019. (212)782-9000. **Website:** www.penguinrandomhouse.com. "Producing books for preschool children through young adult readers, in all formats from board to activity books to picture books and novels, Random House Children's Books brings together world-famous franchise characters, multimillion-copy series and top-flight, award-winning authors, and illustrators." Submit mss through a literary agent.

FICTION "Random House publishes a select list of first chapter books and novels, with an emphasis on fantasy and historical fiction." Chapter books, middle-grade readers, young adult.

HOW TO CONTACT *Does not accept unsolicited mss.*

ILLUSTRATION The Random House publishing divisions hire their freelancers directly. To contact the appropriate person, send a cover letter and résumé to the department head at the publisher as follows: "Department Head" (e.g., Art Director, Production Director), "Publisher/Imprint" (e.g., Knopf, Doubleday, etc.), 1745 Broadway New York, NY 10019. Works with 100-150 freelancers/year. Works on assignment only. Send query letter with résumé, tearsheets and printed samples; no originals. Samples are filed. Negotiates rights purchased. Assigns 5 freelance design jobs/year. Pays by the project.

TIPS "We look for original, unique stories. Do something that hasn't been done before."

RAZORBILL

Penguin Young Readers Group, 345 Hudson St., New York NY 10014. (212)414-3427. **E-mail:** asanchez@penguinrandomhouse.com; bschrank@penguinrandomhouse.com; jharriton@penguinrandomhouse.com. **Website:** www.razorbillbooks.com. **Contact:** Jessica Almon, executive editor; Casey McIntyre, associate publisher; Deborah Kaplan, vice president and executive art director, Marissa Grossman; assistant editor, Tiffany Liao; associate editor. "This division of Penguin Young Readers is looking for the best and the most original of commercial contemporary fiction titles for middle grade and young adult readers. A select quantity of nonfiction titles will also be considered." **Publishes 30 titles/year.**

FICTION Middle Readers: adventure, contemporary, graphic novels, fantasy, humor, problem novels. Young adults/teens: adventure, contemporary, fantasy, graphic novels, humor, multicultural, suspense, paranormal, science fiction, dystopian, literary, romance. Average word length: middle readers: 40,000; young adult: 60,000.

NONFICTION Middle readers and young adults/teens: concept.

HOW TO CONTACT Submit cover letter with up to 30 sample pages. Responds in 1-3 months. Publishes book 1-2 after acceptance.

TERMS Offers advance against royalties.

TIPS "New writers will have the best chance of acceptance and publication with original, contemporary material that boasts a distinctive voice and well-articulated world. Check out website to get a better idea of what we're looking for."

REDLEAF LANE

Redleaf Press, 10 Yorkton Ct., St. Paul MN 55117. (800)423-8309. **E-mail:** info@redleafpress.org. **Website:** www.redleafpress.org. **Contact:** David Heath, director. Redleaf Lane publishes engaging, high-quality picture books for children. "Our books are unique because they take place in group-care settings and reflect developmentally appropriate practices and research-based standards."

TERMS Guidelines online.

RIPPLE GROVE PRESS

P.O. Box 86740, Portland OR 97286. **Website:** www.ripplegrovepress.com. **Contact:** Amanda Broder, Rob Broder. Ripple Grove Press is a family-owned children's picture book publishing company. "We started Ripple Grove Press because we have a passion for well-told and beautifully illustrated stories for children. Our mission is to surround ourselves with great writers and talented illustrators to make the most beautiful books possible. We hope our books that find their way to the cozy spot in your home." Publishes hardcover originals. **Publishes 3-6 titles/year.**

FICTION We are looking for something unique, that has not been done before; an interesting story that captures a moment with a timeless feel. We are looking for picture driven stories for children ages 2-6. Please do not send early readers, middle grade, or young adult mss. No religious or holiday themed stories. Please do not submit your story with page breaks or illustration notes. Do not submit a story with doodles or personal photographs. Do not send your "idea" for a story, send your story in manuscript form.

HOW TO CONTACT Submit completed mss. Accepts submissions by mail and e-mail. E-mail preferred. Please submit a cover letter including a summary of your story, the age range of the story, a brief biography of yourself, and contact information. Receives 3,000 queries/year. Given the volume of submissions we receive we are no longer able to individually respond to each. Please allow 5 months for us to review your submission. If we are interested in your story, you can expect to hear from us within that time. If you do not hear from us after that time, we are not interested in publishing your story. It's not you, it's us! We receive thousands of submissions and only publish a few books each year. Don't give up! Average length of time between acceptance of a book-length ms and publication is 12-18 months.

TERMS Authors and illustrators receive royalties on net receipts. Pays negotiable advance. Catalog online. Guidelines online.

TIPS Please read children's picture books. We create books that children and adults want to read over and over again. Our books showcase art as well as stories and tie them together in a unique and creative way.

Ⓐ ROARING BROOK PRESS

Macmillan Children's Publishing Group, 175 Fifth Ave., New York NY 10010. (646)307-5151. **Website:** us.macmillan.com. Roaring Brook Press is an imprint of MacMillan, a group of companies that includes Henry Holt and Farrar, Straus & Giroux. *Roaring Brook is not accepting unsolicited mss.*

FICTION Picture books, young readers, middle readers, young adults: adventure, animal, contemporary, fantasy, history, humor, multicultural, nature/environment, poetry, religion, science fiction, sports, suspense/mystery.

NONFICTION Picture books, young readers, middle readers, young adults: adventure, animal, contemporary, fantasy, history, humor, multicultural, nature/environment, poetry, religion, science fiction, sports, suspense/mystery.

HOW TO CONTACT *Not accepting unsolicited mss or queries.*

ILLUSTRATION Works with 25 illustrators/year. Illustrations only: Query with samples. Do not send original art; copies only through the mail. Samples returned with SASE.

TERMS Pays authors royalty based on retail price.

TIPS "You should find a reputable agent and have him/her submit your work."

Ⓒ ROSEN PUBLISHING

29 E. 21st St., New York NY 10010. (800)237-9932. **Fax:** (888)436-4643. **Website:** www.rosenpublishing.com. Artists and writers should contact customer service team through online form for information about contributing to Rosen Publishing. Rosen Publishing is an independent educational publishing house, established to serve the needs of students in grades Pre-K-12 with high interest, curriculum-correlated materials. Rosen publishes more than

700 new books each year and has a backlist of more than 7,000.

SADDLEBACK EDUCATIONAL PUBLISHING

3120-A Pullman St., Costa Mesa CA 92626. (888)735-2225. **E-mail:** contact@sdlback.com. **Website:** www.sdlback.com. Saddleback is always looking for fresh, new talent. "Please note that we primarily publish books for kids ages 12-18."

FICTION "We look for diversity for our characters and content."

HOW TO CONTACT Mail typed submission along with a query letter describing the work simply and where it fits in with other titles.

SALINA BOOKSHELF

1120 W. University Ave., Suite 102, Flagstaff AZ 86001. (877)527-0070. **Fax:** (928)526-0386. **Website:** www.salinabookshelf.com. Publishes trade paperback originals and reprints. **Publishes 4-5 titles/year. 50% of books from first-time authors. 100% from unagented writers.**

FICTION Submissions should be in English or Navajo. "All our books relate to the Navajo language and culture."

NONFICTION "We publish children's bilingual readers." Nonfiction should be appropriate to science and social studies curriculum grades 3-8.

HOW TO CONTACT Query with SASE. Query with SASE. Responds in 3 months to queries. Publishes ms 1 year after acceptance.

TERMS Pays varying royalty. Pays advance.

SASQUATCH BOOKS

1904 Third Ave., Suite 710, Seattle WA 98101. (206)467-4300. **Fax:** (206)467-4301. **E-mail:** custserv@sasquatchbooks.com. **Website:** www.sasquatchbooks.com. "Sasquatch Books publishes books for and from the Pacific Northwest, Alaska, and California is the nation's premier regional press. Sasquatch Books' publishing program is a veritable celebration of regionally written words. Undeterred by political or geographical borders, Sasquatch defines its region as the magnificent area that stretches from the Brooks Range to the Gulf of California and from the Rocky Mountains to the Pacific Ocean. Our top-selling Best Places® travel guides serve the most popular destinations and locations of the West. We also publish widely in the areas of food and wine, gardening, nature, photography, children's books, and regional history, all facets of the literature of

179

place. With more than 200 books brimming with insider information on the West, we offer an energetic eye on the lifestyle, landscape, and worldview of our region. Considers queries and proposals from authors and agents for new projects that fit into our West Coast regional publishing program. We can evaluate query letters, proposals, and complete mss." Publishes regional hardcover and trade paperback originals. **Publishes 30 titles/year. 20% of books from first-time authors. 75% from unagented writers.**

FICTION Young readers: adventure, animal, concept, contemporary, humor, nature/environment.

NONFICTION "We are seeking quality nonfiction works about the Pacific Northwest and West Coast regions (including Alaska to California). The literature of place includes how-to and where-to as well as history and narrative nonfiction." Picture books: activity books, animal, concept, nature/environment. "We publish a variety of nonfiction books, as well as children's books under our Little Bigfoot imprint."

HOW TO CONTACT Query first, then submit outline and sample chapters with SASE. Send submissions to The Editors. E-mailed submissions and queries are not recommended. Please include return postage if you want your materials back. Responds to queries in 3 months. Publishes ms 6-9 months after acceptance.

ILLUSTRATION Accepts material from international illustrators. Works with 5 illustrators/year. Uses both color and b&w. Reviews ms/illustration packages. For ms/illustration packages: Query. Submit ms/illustration packages to The Editors. Reviews work for future assignments. If interested in illustrating future titles, query with samples. Samples returned with SASE. Samples filed.

TERMS Pays royalty on cover price. Pays wide range advance. Guidelines online.

TIPS "We sell books through a range of channels in addition to the book trade. Our primary audience consists of active, literate residents of the West Coast."

SCHOLASTIC, INC.

557 Broadway, New York NY 10012. (212)343-6100. **Website:** www.scholastic.com.

"Scholastic Trade Books is an award-winning publisher of original children's books. Scholastic publishes approximately 600 new hardcover, paperback and novelty books each year. The list includes the phenomenally successful publishing properties Harry Potter®, Goosebumps®, The 39 Clues™, I Spy™, and The Hunger Games; best-selling and award-winning authors and illustrators, including Blue Balliett, Jim Benton, Suzanne Collins, Christopher Paul Curtis, Ann M. Martin, Dav Pilkey, J.K. Rowling, Pam Muñoz Ryan, Brian Selznick, David Shannon, Mark Teague, and Walter Wick, among others; as well as licensed properties such as Star Wars® and Rainbow Magic®."

Ⓐ SCHOLASTIC LIBRARY PUBLISHING

90 Old Sherman Turnpike, Danbury CT 6816. (203)797-3500. **Fax:** (203)797-3197. **E-mail:** slpservice@scholastic.com. **Website:** www.scholastic.com/librarypublishing. **Contact:** Phil Friedman, vice president/publisher; Kate Nunn, editor-in-chief; Marie O'Neil, art director. "Scholastic Library is a leading publisher of reference, educational, and children's books. We provide parents, teachers, and librarians with the tools they need to enlighten children to the pleasure of learning and prepare them for the road ahead. Publishes informational (nonfiction) for K-12; picture books for young readers, grades 1-3." Publishes hardcover and trade paperback originals.

○ *Accepts agented submissions only.*

FICTION Publishes 1 picture book series, Rookie Readers, for grades 1-2. Does not accept unsolicited mss.

NONFICTION Photo-illustrated books for all levels: animal, arts/crafts, biography, careers, concept, geography, health, history, hobbies, how-to, multicultural, nature/environment, science, social issues, special needs, sports. Average word length: young readers: 2,000; middle readers: 8,000; young adult: 15,000.

HOW TO CONTACT *Does not accept fiction proposals.* Query; submit outline/synopsis, resume, and/or list of publications, and writing sample. SASE required for response.

ILLUSTRATION Works with 15-20 illustrators/year. Uses color artwork and line drawings. Illustrations only: Query with samples or arrange personal portfolio review. Responds only if interested. Samples returned with SASE. Samples filed. Do not send originals. No phone or e-mail inquiries; contact only by mail.

TERMS Pays authors royalty based on net or work purchased outright. Pays illustrators at competitive rates.

Ⓐ SCHOLASTIC PRESS

Imprint of Scholastic, Inc., 557 Broadway, New York NY 10012. (212)343-6100. **Fax:** (212)343-4713. **Website:** www.scholastic.com. Scholastic Press publishes fresh, literary picture book fiction and nonfiction; fresh, literary nonseries or nongenre-oriented middle grade and young adult fiction. Currently emphasizing subtly handled treatments of key relationships in children's lives; unusual approaches to commonly dry subjects, such as biography, math, history, or science. De-emphasizing fairy tales (or retellings), board books, genre, or series fiction (mystery, fantasy, etc.). Publishes hardcover originals. **Publishes 60 titles/year. 1% of books from first-time authors.**

FICTION Looking for strong picture books, young chapter books, appealing middle grade novels (ages 8-11) and interesting and well-written young adult novels. Wants fresh, exciting picture books and novels—inspiring, new talent.

HOW TO CONTACT *Agented submissions only.* Agented submissions and previously published authors only 2,500 queries received/year. Responds in 3 months to queries; 6-8 months to mss. Publishes ms 2 years after acceptance.

ILLUSTRATION Works with 30 illustrators/year. Uses both b&w and color artwork. Illustrations only: Query with samples; send tearsheets. Responds only if interested. Samples returned with SASE. Original artwork returned at job's completion.

TERMS Pays royalty on retail price. Pays variable advance.

TIPS "Read *currently* published children's books. Revise, rewrite, rework and find your own voice, style and subject. We are looking for authors with a strong and unique voice who can tell a great story and have the ability to evoke genuine emotion. Children's publishers are becoming more selective, looking for irresistible talent and fairly broad appeal, yet still very willing to take risks, just to keep the game interesting."

SCHWARTZ & WADE BOOKS

1745 Broadway, 10-4, New York NY 10019. **Website:** www.penguinrandomhouse.com/.

TERMS "Schwartz & Wade accepts submissions directly from authors. Schwartz & Wade also accepts unsolicited picture book manuscripts and proposals for longer books. However, we advise that you first take a look at a selection of our books to make sure that your submission is a good fit for our small imprint."

Ⓒ SEEDLING CONTINENTAL PRESS

520 E. Bainbridge St., Elizabethtown PA 17022. (800)233-0759. **Website:** www.continentalpress.com. "Continental publishes educational materials for grades K-12, specializing in reading, mathematics, and test preparation materials. We are not currently accepting submissions for Seedling leveled readers or instructional materials."

FICTION Young readers: adventure, animal, folktales, humor, multicultural, nature/environment. Does not accept texts longer than 12 pages or over 300 words. Average word length: young readers: 100.

NONFICTION Young readers: animal, arts/crafts, biography, careers, concept, multicultural, nature/environment, science. Does not accept texts longer than 12 pages or over 300 words. Average word length: young readers—100.

HOW TO CONTACT Submit complete ms. Responds to mss in 6 months. Publishes ms 1-2 years after acceptance.

ILLUSTRATION Works with 8-10 illustrators/year. Uses color artwork only. Reviews ms/illustration packages from artists. Submit ms with dummy. Illustrations only: Color copies or line art. Responds only if interested. Samples returned with SASE only; samples filed if interested.

PHOTOGRAPHY Buys photos from freelancers. Works on assignment only. Model/property releases required. Uses color prints and 35mm transparencies. Submit cover letter and color promo piece.

TERMS Work purchased outright from authors.

TIPS "See our website. Follow writers' guidelines carefully and test your story with children and educators."

SILVER DOLPHIN BOOKS

(858)457-2500. **E-mail:** infosilverdolphin@readerlink.com. **Website:** www.silverdolphinbooks.com. Silver Dolphin Books publishes activity, novelty, and educational nonfiction books for preschoolers to 12 year olds. Highly interactive formats such as the Field Guides and Uncover series both educate and entertain older children. "We will consider submissions only from authors with previously published works."

HOW TO CONTACT Submit cover letter with full proposal and SASE.

Ⓐ SIMON & SCHUSTER BOOKS FOR YOUNG READERS

Imprint of Simon & Schuster Children's Publishing, 1230 Avenue of the Americas, New York NY 10020. (212)698-7000. **Fax:** (212)698-2796. **Website:** www.simonsayskids.com. "Simon & Schuster Books For Young Readers is the Flagship imprint of the S&S Children's Division. We are committed to publishing a wide range of contemporary, commercial, award-winning fiction and nonfiction that spans every age of children's publishing. BFYR is constantly looking to the future, supporting our foundation authors and franchises, but always with an eye for breaking new ground with every publication. We publish high-quality fiction and nonfiction for a variety of age groups and a variety of markets. Above all, we strive to publish books that we are passionate about." *No unsolicited mss.* All unsolicited mss returned unopened. Publishes hardcover originals. **Publishes 75 titles/year.**

NONFICTION Picture books: concept. All levels: narrative, current events, biography, history. "We're looking for picture books or middle grade nonfiction that have a retail potential. No photo essays."

HOW TO CONTACT *Agented submissions only.* *Agented submissions only.* Publishes ms 2-4 years after acceptance.

ILLUSTRATION Works with 70 illustrators/year. Do not submit original artwork. Does not accept unsolicited or unagented illustration submissions.

TERMS Pays variable royalty on retail price. Guidelines online.

TIPS "We're looking for picture books centered on a strong, fully-developed protagonist who grows or changes during the course of the story; young adult novels that are challenging and psychologically complex; also imaginative and humorous middle-grade fiction. And we want nonfiction that is as engaging as fiction. Our imprint's slogan is 'Reading You'll Remember.' We aim to publish books that are fresh, accessible, and family-oriented; we want them to have an impact on the reader."

SKINNER HOUSE BOOKS

The Unitarian Universalist Association, 24 Farnsworth St., Boston MA 02210. (617)742-2100, ext. 603. **Fax:** (617)948-6466. **E-mail:** bookproposals@uua.org. **Website:** www.uua.org/publications/skinnerhouse. **Contact:** Betsy Martin. "We publish titles in Unitarian Universalist faith, liberal religion, history, biography, worship, and issues of social justice. Most of our children's titles are intended for religious education or worship use. They reflect Unitarian Universalist values. We also publish inspirational titles of poetic prose and meditations. Writers should know that Unitarian Universalism is a liberal religious denomination committed to progressive ideals. Currently emphasizing social justice concerns." Publishes trade paperback originals and reprints. **Publishes 10-20 titles/year. 30% of books from first-time authors. 100% from unagented writers.**

FICTION Only publishes fiction for children's titles for religious instruction.

NONFICTION All levels: activity books, multicultural, music/dance, nature/environment, religion.

HOW TO CONTACT Query or submit proposal with cover letter, TOC, 2 sample chapters. Responds to queries in 1 month. Publishes ms 1 year after acceptance.

ILLUSTRATION Works with 2 illustrators/year. Uses both color and b&w. Reviews ms/illustration packages from artists. Query. Contact: Suzanne Morgan, design director. Responds only if interested. Samples returned with SASE.

PHOTOGRAPHY Buys stock images and assigns work. Contact: Suzanne Morgan, design director. Uses inspirational types of photo's. Model/property releases required; captions required. Uses color, b&w. Submit cover letter, resume.

TERMS Book catalog for 6×9 SAE with 3 first-class stamps. Guidelines online.

TIPS "From outside our denomination, we are interested in manuscripts that will be of help or interest to liberal churches, Sunday School classes, parents, ministers, and volunteers. Inspirational/spiritual and children's titles must reflect liberal Unitarian Universalist values."

Ⓐ LIZZIE SKURNICK BOOKS

(718)797-0676. **Website:** lizzieskurnickbooks.com. Lizzie Skurnick Books, an imprint of Ig Publishing, is devoted to reissuing the very best in young adult literature, from the classics of the 1930s and 1940s to the social novels of the 1970s and 1980s. Ig does not accept unsolicited mss, either by e-mail or regular mail. If you have a ms that you would like Ig to take a look at, send a query through online contact form. If interested, they will contact. All unsolicited mss will be discarded.

SKY PONY PRESS

307 W. 36th St., 11th Floor, New York NY 10018. (212)643-6816. **Fax:** (212)643-6819. **Website:** skyponypress.com. Sky Pony Press is the children's book imprint of Skyhorse Publishing. "Following in the footsteps of our parent company, our goal is to provide books for readers with a wide variety of interests."

FICTION "We will consider picture books, early readers, midgrade novels, novelties, and informational books for all ages."

NONFICTION "Our parent company publishes many excellent books in the fields of ecology, independent living, farm living, wilderness living, recycling, and other green topics, and this will be a theme in our children's books. We are also searching for books that have strong educational themes and that help inform children of the world in which they live."

HOW TO CONTACT Submit ms or proposal. Submit proposal via e-mail.

TERMS Guidelines online.

SLEEPING BEAR PRESS

2395 South Huron Parkway #200, Ann Arbor MI 48104. (800)487-2323. **Fax:** (734)794-0004. **E-mail:** submissions@sleepingbearpress.com. **Website:** www.sleepingbearpress.com. **Contact:** Manuscript Submissions.

FICTION Picture books: adventure, animal, concept, folktales, history, multicultural, nature/environment, religion, sports. Young readers: adventure, animal, concept, folktales, history, humor, multicultural, nature/environment, religion, sports. Average word length: picture books: 1,800.

HOW TO CONTACT Accepts unsolicited queries 3 times per year. See website for details. Query with sample of work (up to 15 pages) and SASE. Please address packages to Manuscript Submissions.

TERMS Book catalog available via e-mail.

Ⓐ SOURCEBOOKS FIRE

1935 Brookdale Rd., Suite 139, Naperville IL 60563. (630)961-3900. **Fax:** (630)961-2168. **E-mail:** submissions@sourcebooks.com. **Website:** www.sourcebooks.com. "We're actively acquiring knockout books for our YA imprint. We are particularly looking for strong writers who are excited about promoting and building their community of readers, and whose books have something fresh to offer the ever-growing young adult audience. *We are not accepting any unsolicited or unagented manuscripts at this time.* Unfortunately, our staff can no longer handle the large volume of manuscripts that we receive on a daily basis. We will continue to consider agented manuscripts." See website for details.

HOW TO CONTACT Query with the full ms attached in Word doc.

SPENCER HILL PRESS

27 W. 20th St., Suite 1102, New York NY 10011. **Website:** www.spencerhillpress.com. Spencer Hill Press is an independent publishing house specializing in science-fiction, urban fantasy, and paranormal romance for young adult readers. "Our books have that 'I couldn't put it down!' quality."

FICTION "We are interested in young adult, new adult, and middle grade science-fiction, psychological fiction, paranormal, or urban fantasy, particularly those with a strong and interesting voice."

HOW TO CONTACT Check website for open submission periods.

TERMS Guidelines online.

SPINNER BOOKS

University Games, 2030 Harrison St., San Francisco CA 94110. (415)503-1600. **Fax:** (415)503-0085. **E-mail:** info@ugames.com. **Website:** www.ugames.com. "Spinners Books publishes books of puzzles, games and trivia."

NONFICTION Picture books: games and puzzles.

HOW TO CONTACT Query. Responds to queries in 3 months; mss in 2 months only if interested. Publishes ms 6 months after acceptance.

ILLUSTRATION Only interested in agented material. Uses both color and b&w. Illustrations only: Query with samples. Responds in 3 months only if interested. Samples not returned.

SPLASHING COW BOOKS

P.O. Box 867, Manchester VT 05254. **Website:** www. splashingcowbooks.com. **Contact:** Gordon McClellan, publisher. Splashing Cow Books publishes books under three imprints: Splashing Cow (children), Blue Boot (women), and Yellow Dot (family). Publishes mass market paperback and hardcover books. We do not publish digital books. **Publishes 10 titles/year. 100% of books from first-time authors. 100% from unagented writers.**

FICTION Interested in a wide range of subject matter for children, women, and families.

NONFICTION Open to any topic that would be of interest to children, women, or families.

HOW TO CONTACT Please check our website for submission guidelines. We try to reply as soon as possible, but may take up to 3 months.

TERMS Pays royalties on retail price. Does not offer an advance. Catalog online. Guidelines online.

STANDARD PUBLISHING

Standex International Corp., 4050 Lee Vance View, Colorado Springs CO 80918. (800)323-7543. **Fax:** (800)323-0726. **Website:** www.standardpub.com. Publishes resources that meet church and family needs in the area of children's ministry.

TERMS Guidelines online.

STAR BRIGHT BOOKS

13 Landsdowne St., Cambridge MA 02139. (617)354-1300. **Fax:** (617)354-1399. **E-mail:** info@starbrightbooks.com. **Website:** www.starbrightbooks.com. Star Bright Books does accept unsolicited mss and art submissions. "We welcome submissions for picture books and longer works, both fiction and nonfiction." Also beginner readers and chapter books. Query first. **Publishes 18 titles/year. 75% of books from first-time authors. 99% from unagented writers.**

NONFICTION Almost anything of interest to children. Very keen on biographies and any thing of interest to children.

HOW TO CONTACT Responds in several months. Publishes ms 1-2 years after acceptance.

TERMS Pays advance. Catalog available.

STERLING PUBLISHING CO., INC.

1166 Avenue of the Americas, 17th Floor, New York NY 10036. (212)532-7160. **Website:** www.sterlingpublishing.com. "Sterling publishes highly illustrat-ed, accessible, hands-on, practical books for adults and children. Our mission is to publish high-quality books that educate, entertain, and enrich the lives of our readers." Publishes hardcover and paperback originals and reprints. **15% of books from first-time authors.**

FICTION Publishes fiction for children.

NONFICTION Proposals on subjects such as crafting, decorating, outdoor living, and photography should be sent directly to Lark Books at their Asheville, North Carolina offices. Complete guidelines can be found on the Lark site: www.larkbooks.com/submissions. Publishes nonfiction only.

HOW TO CONTACT Submit to attention of "Children's Book Editor." Submit outline, publishing history, 1 sample chapter (typed and double-spaced), SASE. "Explain your idea. Send sample illustrations where applicable. For children's books, please submit full mss. We do not accept electronic (e-mail) submissions. Be sure to include information about yourself with particular regard to your skills and qualifications in the subject area of your submission. It is helpful for us to know your publishing history—whether or not you've written other books and, if so, the name of the publisher and whether those books are currently in print."

ILLUSTRATION Works with 50 illustrators/year. Reviews ms/illustration packages from artists. Illustrations only: Send promo sheet. Contact: Karen Nelson, creative director. Responds in 6 weeks. Samples returned with SASE; samples filed.

PHOTOGRAPHY Buys stock and assigns work. Contact: Karen Nelson.

TERMS Pays royalty or work purchased outright. Offers advances (average amount: $2,000). Catalog online. Guidelines online.

TIPS "We are primarily a nonfiction activities-based publisher. We have a picture book list, but we do not publish chapter books or novels. Our list is not trend-driven. We focus on titles that will backlist well. "

STONE ARCH BOOKS

1710 Roe Crest Rd., North Mankato MN 56003. **Website:** www.stonearchbooks.com.

FICTION Imprint of Capstone Publishers. Young readers, middle readers, young adults: adventure, contemporary, fantasy, humor, light humor, mystery, science fiction, sports, suspense. Average word length: young readers: 1,000-3,000; middle readers and early young adults: 5,000-10,000.

HOW TO CONTACT Submit outline/synopsis and 3 sample chapters. Electronic submissions preferred. Full guidelines available on website.

ILLUSTRATION Works with 35 illustrators/year. Uses both color and b&w.

TERMS Work purchased outright from authors. Catalog online.

TIPS "A high-interest topic or activity is one that a young person would spend their free time on without adult direction or suggestion."

STRAWBERRIES PRESS

750 Pinehurst Dr., Rio Vista CA 94571. (707)398-6430. **E-mail:** books@strawberriespress.com. **Website:** www.strawberriespress.com. **Contact:** Susan Zhang, Executive Editor. Strawberries books are beautifully illustrated and designed to be high-quality publications that children will love and treasure. For example, our interactive picture book for train enthusiasts entitled *Choo-Choo Charlie Presents Steam Locomotives* provides a fun story by Charlie the Locomotive while teaching kids about steam engines and how they work, the definition of a train, the history of steam locomotives, and how to determine a locomotive's wheel configuration number. Children even get to watch a singing cartoon video of Choo-Choo Charlie the Engineer and how he uses candy to make his train run. A fun test is included at the end of each book. Just send Strawberries the completed test and your child will receive a beautifully printed Reading Certificate that he or she can proudly frame and display for all his or her friends to see. Reading traditional picture books, watching videos, visiting websites that contain associated subjects, taking fun tests, and earning Reading Certificates represent the interactive parts of the Strawberries reading and learning concept. Publishes interactive picture books in the 8-1/2" x 11" softcover format. **Publishes 6 titles/year. 50% of books from first-time authors. 100% from unagented writers.**

NONFICTION Interested in topics that explore exciting subjects that stimulate young minds in both the fiction and nonfiction genres. For examples of subject matter and format requirements, see online catalog of picture book titles. "We only publish wholesome learning resources and educationally constructive subject matter that retains, promotes, and enhances the innocence of children. Political, immoral, antisocial, propagandist, and other age-inappropriate themes are strictly prohibited at Strawberries Press. We do not use our publications as social engineering and brainwashing tools."

HOW TO CONTACT Submit completed ms. Receives 12-20 queries/year; 12 mss/year. Responds in 1 month. Publishes mss in 3-4 months upon acceptance.

TERMS Pays for outright purchase between $250-500. Catalog available online. Guidelines available by e-mail.

TIPS "Although there are no restrictions on the number of sentences on a single page, all picture books are limited to 40 pages. For text, illustrating, and formatting examples, view our sample online picture book."

SUNSTONE PRESS

Box 2321, Santa Fe NM 87504. (800)243-5644. **Website:** www.sunstonepress.com. **Contact:** Submissions Editor. Sunstone's original focus was on nonfiction subjects that preserved and highlighted the richness of the American Southwest but it has expanded its view over the years to include mainstream themes and categories—both nonfiction and fiction—that have a more general appeal.

HOW TO CONTACT Query with 1 sample chapter. Query with 1 sample chapter.

TERMS Guidelines online.

Ⓐ KATHERINE TEGEN BOOKS

HarperCollins, 10 E. 53rd St., New York NY 10022. **Website:** www.harpercollins.com. Katherine Tegen Books publishes high-quality, commercial literature for children of all ages, including teens. Talented authors and illustrators who offer powerful narratives that are thought-provoking, well-written, and entertaining are the core of the Katherine Tegen Books imprint. *Katherine Tegen Books accepts agented work only.*

Ⓒ THUNDERSTONE BOOKS

6575 Horse Dr., Las Vegas NV 89131. **E-mail:** info@thunderstonebooks.com. **Website:** www.thunderstonebooks.com. **Contact:** Rachel Noorda, editorial director. "At ThunderStone Books, we aim to publish children's books that have an educational aspect. We are not looking for curriculum for learning certain subjects, but rather stories that encourage learning for children, whether that be learning about a new language/culture or learning more about science and math in a fun, fictional format. We want to help children to gain a love for other languages and subjects so that they are curious about the world around them. We are currently accepting fiction and nonfiction submissions. Picture books without accompanying illustration will not be accepted." Publishes hardcover, trade paperback, mass market paperback, and electronic originals. **Publishes 2-5 titles/year. 100% of books from first-time authors. 100% from unagented writers.**

FICTION Interested in multicultural stories with an emphasis on authentic culture and language (these may include mythology).

NONFICTION Looking for engaging educational materials, not a set curriculum, but books that teach as well as have some fun. Open to a variety of educational subjects, but specialty and main interest lies in language exposure/learning, science, math, and history.

HOW TO CONTACT "If you think your book is right for us, send a query letter with a word attachment of the first 50 pages to info@thunderstonebooks.com. If it is a picture book or chapter book for young readers that is shorter than 50 pages send the entire manuscript." Receives 30 queries and mss/year. Responds in 3 months. Publishes ms 6 months after acceptance.

TERMS Pays 5-15% royalties on retail price. Pays $300-1,000 advance. Catalog available for SASE. Guidelines available.

TILBURY HOUSE PUBLISHERS

WordSplice Studio, Inc., 12 Starr St., Thomaston ME 04861. (800)582-1899. **Fax:** (207)582-8772. **E-mail:** info@tilburyhouse.com. **Website:** www.tilburyhouse.com. **Publishes 10 titles/year.**

FICTION Picture books: multicultural, nature/environment. Special needs include books that teach children about tolerance and honoring diversity.

NONFICTION Regional adult biography/history/maritime/nature, and children's picture books that deal with issues, such as bullying, multiculturalism, etc., science/nature.

HOW TO CONTACT Send art/photography samples and/or complete ms to Audrey Maynard, children's book editor. Submit complete ms for picture books or outline/synopsis for longer works. Now

uses online submission form. Responds to mss in 3 months. Publishes ms 1 year after acceptance.

ILLUSTRATION Works with 2-3 illustrators/year. Illustrations only: Query with samples. Responds in 1 month. Samples returned with SASE. Original artwork returned at job's completion.

PHOTOGRAPHY Buys photos from freelancers. Works on assignment only.

TERMS Pays royalty based on wholesale price. Guidelines and catalog online.

TIPS "We are always interested in stories that will encourage children to understand the natural world and the environment, as well as stories with social justice themes. We really like stories that engage children to become problem solvers as well as those that promote respect, tolerance, and compassion. We do not publish books with personified animal characters; historical fiction; young adult or middle-grade fiction or chapter books; fantasy."

TIMBER PRESS

Website: www.timberpress.com/books/tag/bestsellers/. "Our mission is to share the wonders of the natural world by publishing books from experts in the fields of gardening, horticulture, and natural history. Grow with us."

TOR BOOKS

Tom Doherty Associates, 175 Fifth Ave., New York NY 10010. **Website:** www.tor-forge.com. Tor Books is the "world's largest publisher of science fiction and fantasy, with strong category publishing in historical fiction, mystery, western/Americana, thriller, YA." **Publishes 10-20 titles/year.**

HOW TO CONTACT Submit first 3 chapters, 3-10 page synopsis, dated cover letter, SASE.

TERMS Pays author royalty. Pays illustrators by the project. Book catalog available. Guidelines online.

TRIANGLE SQUARE

Seven Stories Press, 140 Watts St., New York NY 10013. (212)226-8760. **Fax:** (212)226-1411. **E-mail:** info@sevenstories.com. **Website:** www.sevenstories.com/imprints/triangle-square. Triangle Square is a children's and young adult imprint of Seven Story Press.

HOW TO CONTACT Send a cover letter with 2 sample chapters and SASE. Send c/o Acquisitions.

TU BOOKS

Lee & Low Books, 95 Madison Ave., Suite #1205, New York NY 10016. **Website:** www.leeandlow.com/imprints/3. **Contact:** Stacy Whitman, Publisher. The Tu imprint spans many genres: science fiction, fantasy, mystery, contemporary, and more. We don't believe in labels or limits, just great stories. Join us at the crossroads where fantasy and real life collide. You'll be glad you did. Young adult and middle grade novels and graphic novels: science fiction, fantasy, contemporary realism, mystery, historical fiction, and more, with particular interest in books with strong literary hooks. **Publishes 3-6 titles/year. 25% of books from first-time authors.**

For new writers of color, please be aware of the New Visions Award writing contest, which runs every year from June-October. Previously unpublished writers of color and Native American writers may submit their middle grade and young adult novels. See submission guidelines for the contest at www.leeandlow.com/writers-illustrators/new-visions-award.

FICTION At Tu Books, an imprint of Lee & Low Books, our focus is on well-told, exciting, adventurous fantasy, science fiction, and mystery novels and graphic novels starring people of color. We also selectively publish realism that explores the contemporary and historical experiences of people of color. We look for fantasy set in worlds inspired by nonWestern folklore or culture, contemporary mysteries and fantasy set all over the world starring POC, and science fiction that centers the possibilities for people of color in the future. We welcome intersectional narratives that feature LGBTQIA and disabled POC as heroes in their own stories. We are looking specifically for stories for both middle grade (ages 8-12) and young adult (ages 12-18) readers. Occasionally a manuscript might fall between those two categories; if your manuscript does, let us know. (We are not looking for picture books, chapter books, or short stories at this time. Please do not send submissions in these categories.) Manuscript Submissions: Please include a synopsis and first three chapters of the novel. Do not send the complete manuscript. Manuscripts should be doubled-spaced. Manuscripts should be accompanied by a cover letter that includes a brief biography of the author, including publishing history. The letter should also state if the manuscript is a simultaneous or an exclusive submission. Be sure to include full contact information on the first page of the manuscript. Page numbers and your last name/title of the book should appear on subsequent pages. Unsolicited manuscripts should be submitted online at https://tubooks.submittable.com/submit. (See the Lee & Low Books guidelines for books for younger young readers.) Not seeking picture books or chapter books.

NONFICTION Not seeking nonfiction.

ILLUSTRATION "Tu Books, an imprint of Lee & Low Books, is not interested in illustrations for picture books, but will consider artwork for graphic novels and for book covers and spot illustrations for novels aimed at older readers (ages 8-18). Artists are welcome to submit a sample with the address of their website portfolio following the guidelines below. Our books feature children and teens of color and include a variety of fantasy, science fiction, and mystery. We are particularly interested in hearing from illustrators whose cultural, ethnic, or racial backgrounds and experiences support their knowledge of diverse cultures. We are open to seeing work from professional illustrators and artists at all levels of experience. Illustrators who have worked in other fields and are interested in creating cover and spot art for novels are also welcome."

TERMS Advance against royalties. Pays advance.

TUMBLEHOME LEARNING

P.O. Box 71386, Boston MA 02117. **E-mail:** info@tumblehomelearning.com. **Website:** www.tumblehomelearning.com. **Contact:** Pendred Noyce, editor. Tumblehome Learning helps kids imagine themselves as young scientists or engineeers and encourages them to experience science through adventure and discovery. "We do this with exciting mystery and adventure tales as well as experiments carefully designed to engage students from ages 8 and up." Publishes hardcover, trade paperback, and electronic originals. **Publishes 8-10 titles/year. 50% of books from first-time authors. 100% from unagented writers.**

FICTION "All our fiction has science at its heart. This can include using science to solve a mystery (see *The Walking Fish* by Rachelle Burk or *Something Stinks!* by Gail Hedrick), realistic science fiction, books in our Galactic Academy of Science series, science-based adventure tales, and the occasional picture book with a science theme, such as appreciation of the stars and constellations in *Elizabeth's Constellation Quilt* by Olivia Fu. A graphic novel about science would also be welcome."

NONFICTION Rarely publishes nonfiction. Book would need to be sold to trade, not just the school market.

HOW TO CONTACT Submit completed ms electronically. Receives 20 queries and 20 mss/year. Responds in 1 month to queries and proposals, and 2 months to mss. Publishes ms 8 months after acceptance.

TERMS Pays authors 8-12% royalties on retail price. Pays $500 advance. Catalog available online. Guideliens available on request for SASE.

TIPS "Please don't submit to us if your book is not about science. We don't accept generic books about animals or books with glaring scientific errors in the first chapter. That said, the book should be fun to read and the science content can be subtle. We work closely with authors, including first-time authors, to edit and improve their books. As a small publisher, the greatest benefit we can offer is this friendly and respectful partnership with authors."

TUTTLE PUBLISHING

364 Innovation Drive, Editorial Acquisitions, North Clarendon VT 05759. (800)526-2778. **Fax:** (800)329-8885. **Website:** www.tuttlepublishing.com. **Contact:** Editorial Acquisitions. "Since 1948, Tuttle has been a leader in the field of Asian cultures, Language, and Martial Arts. Genres include children's. Today, we currently have a backlist of over 6,000 titles and publish 150 new titles per year." **Publishes 150 titles/year.**

FICTION Publishes children's craft, origami and activity kits, folktales, celebrations, customs and traditions, and young adult.

HOW TO CONTACT Responds to queries in 3 months.

TERMS If you wish to submit a project for consideration for publication, please send a complete book proposal consisting of: A cover letter, annotated table of contents and 1 to 2 sample chapters. Include a description of your target audience and comparison titles.

ⒶTYNDALE HOUSE PUBLISHERS, INC.

351 Executive Dr., Carol Stream IL 60188. (800)323-9400. **Fax:** (800)684-0247. **Website:** www.tyndale.com. "Tyndale House publishes practical, user-friendly Christian books for the home and family." Publishes hardcover and trade paperback originals and mass paperback reprints. **Publishes 15 titles/year.**

FICTION "Christian truths must be woven into the story organically. No short story collections. Youth books: character building stories with Christian perspective. Especially interested in ages 10-14. We primarily publish Christian historical romances, with occasional contemporary, suspense, or stand-alones."

HOW TO CONTACT *Agented submissions only. No unsolicited mss.*

ILLUSTRATION Uses full-color for book covers, b&w or color spot illustrations for some nonfiction. Illustrations only: Query with photocopies (color or b&w) of samples, résumé.

PHOTOGRAPHY Buys photos from freelancers. Works on assignment only.

TERMS Pays negotiable royalty. Pays negotiable advance. Guidelines online.

TIPS "All accepted manuscripts will appeal to Evangelical Christian children and parents."

ⒶVIKING CHILDREN'S BOOKS

375 Hudson St., New York NY 10014. **Website:** www.penguin.com. "Viking Children's Books is known for humorous, quirky picture books, in addition to more traditional fiction. We publish the highest quality fiction, nonfiction, and picture books for preschoolers through young adults." *Does not accept unsolicited submissions.* Publishes hardcover originals. **Publishes 70 titles/year.**

FICTION All levels: adventure, animal, contemporary, fantasy, history, humor, multicultural, nature/environment, poetry, problem novels, romance, science fiction, sports, suspense/mystery.

NONFICTION All levels: biography, concept, history, multicultural, music/dance, nature/environment, science, and sports.

HOW TO CONTACT *Accepts agented mss only.* Responds in 6 months. Publishes ms 1-2 years after acceptance.

ILLUSTRATION Works with 30 illustrators/year. Responds to artist's queries/submissions only if interested. Samples returned with SASE only or samples filed. Originals returned at job's completion.

TERMS Pays 2-10% royalty on retail price or flat fee. Pays negotiable advance.

TIPS "No 'cartoony' or mass-market submissions for picture books."

WESTERN PSYCHOLOGICAL SERVICES

625 Alaska Ave., Torrance CA 90503. (424)201-8800 or (800)648-8857. **Fax:** (424)201-6950. **Website:** www.wpspublish.com. "Western Psychological Services publishes psychological and educational assessments that practitioners trust. Our products allow helping professionals to accurately screen, diagnose, and treat people in need. WPS publishes practical books and games used by therapists, counselors, social workers, and others in the helping professionals who work with children and adults." Publishes psychological and educational assessments and some trade paperback originals. **Publishes 2 titles/year. 90% of books from first-time authors. 95% from unagented writers.**

NONFICTION "We publish children's books dealing with feelings, anger, social skills, autism, family problems."

HOW TO CONTACT Submit complete ms. 60 queries received/year. 30 mss received/year. Responds in 2 months to queries. Publishes ms 1 year after acceptance.

TERMS Pays 5-10% royalty on wholesale price. Book catalog available free. Guidelines online.

WHITE MANE KIDS

73 W. Burd St., Shippensburg PA 17257. (717)532-2237. **Fax:** (717)532-6110. **E-mail:** marketing@whitemane.com. **Website:** www.whitemane.com. **Contact:** Harold Collier, acquisitions editor.

FICTION Middle readers, young adults: history (primarily American Civil War). Average word length: middle readers: 30,000. Does not publish picture books.

NONFICTION Middle readers, young adults: history. Average word length: middle readers: 30,000. Does not publish picture books.

HOW TO CONTACT Query. Submit outline/synopsis and 2-3 sample chapters. Book proposal form on website. Responds to queries in 1 month, mss in 6-9 months. Publishes book 18 months after acceptance.

ILLUSTRATION Works with 4 illustrators/year. Illustrations used for cover art only. Responds only if interested. Samples returned with SASE.

PHOTOGRAPHY Buys stock and assigns work. Submit cover letter and portfolio.

TERMS Pays authors royalty of 7-10%. Pays illustrators and photographers by the project. Book catalog and writer's guidelines available for SASE.

TIPS "Make your work historically accurate. We are interested in historically accurate fiction for middle and young adult readers. We do *not* publish picture books. Our primary focus is the American Civil War and some America Revolution topics."

ALBERT WHITMAN & COMPANY

250 S. Northwest Hwy., Suite 320, Park Ridge IL 60068. (800)255-7675. **Fax:** (847)581-0039. **E-mail:** submissions@albertwhitman.com. **Website:** www.albertwhitman.com. Albert Whitman & Company publishes books for the trade, library, and school library market. Interested in reviewing the following types of projects: Picture book manuscripts for ages 2-8; novels and chapter books for ages 8-12; young adult novels; nonfiction for ages 3-12 and young adult; art samples showing pictures of children. Best known for the classic series The Boxcar Children® Mysteries. "We are no longer reading unsolicited queries and manuscripts sent through the US mail. We now require these submissions to be sent by e-mail. You must visit our website for our guidelines, which include instructions for formatting your e-mail. E-mails that do not follow this format may not be read. We read every submission within 4 months of receipt, but we can no longer respond to every one. If you do not receive a response from us after 4 months, we have declined to publish your submission." Publishes in original hardcover, paperback, boardbooks. **Publishes 60 titles/year. 10% of books from first-time authors. 50% from unagented writers.**

FICTION Picture books (up to 1,000 words); middle grade (up to 35,000 words); young adult (up to 70,000 words).

NONFICTION Picture books up to 1,000 words.

HOW TO CONTACT For picture books, submit cover letter and brief description. For middle grade and young adult, send query, synopsis, and first 3 chapters. Submit cover letter, brief description.

TERMS Guidelines online.

WINDWARD PUBLISHING

Finney Company, 5995 149th St. W., Suite 105, Apple Valley MN 55124. **E-mail:** info@finneyco.com. **Website:** www.finneyco.com. **Contact:** Alan E. Krysan, President. Windward publishes illustrated natural history, recreation books, and children's books. "Covers topics of natural history and science, outdoor recreation, and children's literature. Its principal markets are book, retail, and specialty stores. While primarily a nonfiction publisher, we will occasionally accept fiction books with educational value." Publishes trade paperback originals. **Publishes 6-10 titles/year. 50% of books from first-time authors. 100% from unagented writers.**
NONFICTION Young readers, middle readers, young adults: activity books, animal, careers, nature/environment, science. Young adults: textbooks.
HOW TO CONTACT Query with SASE. Does not accept e-mail or fax submissions. 120 queries; 50 mss received/year. Responds in 8-10 weeks to queries. Publishes book 1 year after acceptance.
ILLUSTRATION Reviews ms/illustration packages from artists. Send ms with dummy. Query with samples. Responds in 2 months. Samples returned with SASE; samples filed.
TERMS Pays 10% royalty on wholesale price. No advance.

PAULA WISEMAN BOOKS

1230 Sixth Ave., New York NY 10020. (212)698-7000. **Fax:** (212)698-2796. **Website:** kids.simonandschuster.com. Paula Wiseman Books is an imprint of Simon & Schuster Children's Publishing that launched in 2003. It has since gone on to publish over 70 award-winning and bestselling books, including picture books, novelty books, and novels. The imprint focuses on stories and art that are childlike, timeless, innovative, and centered in emotion. "We strive to publish books that entertain while expanding the experience of the children who read them, as well as stories that will endure, including those based in other cultures. We are committed to publishing new talent in both picture books and novels. We are actively seeking submissions from new and published authors and artists through agents and from SCBWI conferences." **Publishes 30 titles/year. 15% of books from first-time authors.**
FICTION Considers all categories. Average word length: picture books: 500; others standard length.

NONFICTION Picture books: animal, biography, concept, history, nature/environment. Young readers: animal, biography, history, multicultural, nature/environment, sports. Average word length: picture books: 500; others standard length.
HOW TO CONTACT *Does not accept unsolicited or unagented mss.*
ILLUSTRATION Works with 15 illustrators/year. *Does not accept unsolicited or unagented illustrations or submissions.*

WOODBINE HOUSE

6510 Bells Mill Rd., Bethesda MD 20817. (301)897-3570. **Fax:** (301)897-5838. **E-mail:** info@woodbinehouse.com. **Website:** www.woodbinehouse.com. **Contact:** Acquisitions Editor. Woodbine House publishes books for or about individuals with disabilities to help those individuals and their families live fulfilling and satisfying lives in their homes, schools, and communities. Publishes trade paperback originals. **Publishes 10 titles/year. 15% of books from first-time authors. 90% from unagented writers.**
FICTION Receptive to stories re: developmental and intellectual disabilities, e.g., autism and cerebral palsy.
NONFICTION Publishes books for and about children with disabilities. No personal accounts or general parenting guides.
HOW TO CONTACT Submit complete ms with SASE. Submit outline, and at least 3 sample chapters. Responds in 3 months to queries. Publishes ms 18 months after acceptance.
TERMS Pays 10-12% royalty. Guidelines online.
TIPS "Do not send us a proposal on the basis of this description. Examine our catalog or website and a couple of our books to make sure you are on the right track. Put some thought into how your book could be marketed (aside from in bookstores). Keep cover letters concise and to the point; if it's a subject that interests us, we'll ask to see more."

WORDSONG

815 Church St., Honesdale PA 18431. **Fax:** (570)253-0179. **Website:** www.wordsongpoetry.com. "We publish fresh voices in contemporary poetry."
HOW TO CONTACT Responds to mss in 3 months.
ILLUSTRATION Works with 7 illustrators/year. Reviews ms/illustration packages from artists. Sub-

mit complete ms with 1 or 2 pieces of art. Illustrations only: Query with samples best suited to the art (postcard, 8½ × 11, etc.). Label package "Art Sample Submission." Responds only if interested. Samples returned with SASE.

PHOTOGRAPHY Assigns work.

TERMS Pays authors royalty or work purchased outright.

TIPS "Collections of original poetry, not anthologies, are our biggest need at this time. Keep in mind that the strongest collections demonstrate a facility with multiple poetic forms and offer fresh images and insights. Check to see what's already on the market and on our website before submitting."

WORKMAN BOOKS

225 Varick Street, New York NY 10014. **Website:** www.workman.com/resources/submission_guidelines//#1.

TERMS "When submitting work to us, please send as much of the proposed book or calendar as possible. If the project contains or consists primarily of artwork, please send photocopies or another type of reproduction. We will contact you if we need to see the originals. We prefer electronic submissions, which may be sent to submissions@workman.com in the form of a Word document or a PDF. You may also send hard-copy submissions to the attention of the Editorial Department. For children's book submissions, please note that we do not publish picture books or middle grade and young adult fiction. Send your submissions to the attention of the Children's Department."

WORLD BOOK, INC.

180 N. LaSalle St., Suite 900, Chicago IL 60601. (312)729-5800. **Fax:** (312)729-5600. **E-mail:** service@worldbook.com. **Website:** www.worldbook.com. World Book, Inc. (publisher of The World Book Encyclopedia), publishes reference sources and nonfiction series for children and young adults in the areas of science, mathematics, English-language skills, basic academic and social skills, social studies, history, and health and fitness. "We publish print and nonprint material appropriate for children ages 3-14. WB does not publish fiction, poetry, or wordless picture books."

NONFICTION Young readers: animal, arts/crafts, careers, concept, geography, health, reference. Middle readers: animal, arts/crafts, careers, geography, health, history, hobbies, how-to, nature/environment, reference, science. Young adult: arts/crafts, careers, geography, health, history, hobbies, how-to, nature/environment, reference, science.

HOW TO CONTACT Query. Responds to queries in 2 months. Publishes ms 18 months after acceptance.

ILLUSTRATION Works with 10-30 illustrators/year. Illustrations only: Query with samples. Responds only if interested. Samples returned with SASE; samples filed "if extra copies and if interested."

PHOTOGRAPHY Buys stock and assigns work. Needs broad spectrum; editorial concept, specific natural, physical and social science spectrum. Model/property releases required; captions required. Submit cover letter, résumé, promo piece (color and b&w).

TERMS Payment negotiated on project-by-project basis.

WORLD WEAVER PRESS

E-mail: submissions@worldweaverpress.com. **Website:** www.worldweaverpress.com. **Contact:** WWP Editors. World Weaver Press publishes digital and print editions of speculative fiction at various lengths for adult, young adult, and new adult audiences. "We believe in great storytelling." **Publishes 10-12 titles/year. 85% from unagented writers.**

FICTION "We believe that publishing speculative fiction isn't just printing words on the page — it's the act of weaving brand new worlds. Seeking speculative fiction in many varieties: protagonists who have strength, not fainting spells; intriguing worlds with well-developed settings; characters that are to die for (we'd rather find ourselves in love than just in lust)." Full list of interests on website. Does not want giant bugs, ghosts, post-apocalyptic and/or dystopia, angels, zombies, magical realism, surrealism, middle grade (MG) or younger.

HOW TO CONTACT Queries accepted only during February unless otherwise stated on website. Full guidelines will be updated approximately one month before submissions open. Responds to query letters within 3 weeks. Responses to mss requests take longer. Publishes ms 6-24 months after acceptance.

TERMS Average royalty rate of 39% net on all editions. No advance. Catalog online. Guidelines on website.

TIPS "Use your letter to pitch us the story, not talk about its themes or inception."

WORTHYKIDS/IDEALS

Worthy Publishing Group, 6100 Tower Circle, Suite 210, Franklin TN 37067. (615)932-7600. **E-mail:** idealsinfo@worthypublishing.com. **Website:** www.idealsbooks.com. "WorthyKids/Ideals is a division of Worthy Publishing Group and publishes 25-30 new children's titles a year, primarily for 2-8 year-olds. Our backlist includes more than 400 titles, including The Berenstain Bears, VeggieTales, and Frosty the Snowman. We publish picture books, activity books, board books, and novelty/sound books covering a wide array of topics, such as Bible stories, holidays, early learning, history, family relationships, and values. Our best-selling titles include *The Story of Christmas, The Story of Easter, Seaman's Journal, How Do I Love You?, God Made You Special, The Berenstain Bears' Please and Thank You Book*, and *My Daddy and I*. Through our dedication to publishing high-quality and engaging books, we never forget our obligation to our littlest readers to help create those special moments with books."

FICTION WorthyKids/Ideals publishes fiction and nonfiction picture books for children ages 2 to 8. Subjects include holiday, faith/inspirational, family values, and patriotic themes; relationships and values; and general fiction. Picture book mss should be no longer than 800 words. Board book mss should be no longer than 250 words.

HOW TO CONTACT Editors will review complete mss only; please do not send query letters or proposals. Previous publications, relevant qualifications or background, and a brief synopsis of your manuscript may be included in a cover letter. Please send copies only—we cannot be responsible for an original ms. Include your name, address, and phone number or e-mail address on every page. Do not include original art or photographs. We do not accept digital submissions via e-mail or other electronic means. Send complete mss to: WorthyKids/Ideals, Attn: SUBMISSIONS, 6100 Tower Circle, Suite 210, Franklin TN 37067. Due to the high volume of submissions, we respond only to manuscripts of interest to our publishing program. Due to the number of submissions we receive, we cannot discuss submissions by telephone or in person, and we cannot provide detailed editorial feedback.

ZEST BOOKS

2443 Fillmore St., Suite 340, San Francisco CA 94115. (415)777-8654. **Fax:** (415)777-8653. **Website:** zestbooks.net. **Contact:** Dan Harmon, publishing director. Zest Books is a leader in young adult non-fiction, publishing books on entertainment, history, science, health, fashion, and lifestyle advice since 2006. Zest Books is distributed by Houghton Mifflin Harcourt.

HOW TO CONTACT Submit proposal.

ILLUSTRATION "If you are interested in becoming part of our team of illustrators, please send examples of printed work to adam@zestbooks.net."

TERMS Guidelines online.

TIPS "If you're interested in becoming a member of our author pool, send a cover letter stating why you are interested in young adult nonfiction, plus your specific areas of interest and specialties, your résumé, 3-5 writing samples."

ZUMAYA PUBLICATIONS, LLC

3209 S. Interstate 35, Austin TX 78741. (512)537-3145. **Fax:** (512)276-6745. **E-mail:** business@zumayapublishing.com. **Website:** www.zumayapublications.com. **Contact:** Rie Sheridan Rose, acquisitions editor. Zumaya Publications is a digitally-based micro-press publishing mainly in on-demand trade paperback and e-book formats. "We currently offer approximately 190 fiction titles in the mystery, science-fiction/fantasy, historical, romance, LGBTQ, horror, and occult genres in adult, young adult, and middle reader categories. We publish approximately 10-15 new titles annually, at least five of which are from new authors. We do not publish erotica or graphic erotic romance at this time. We accept only electronic queries; all others will be discarded unread. A working knowledge of computers and relevant software is a necessity, as our production process is completely digital." Publishes trade paperback and electronic originals and reprints. **Publishes 10-15 titles/year. 5% of books from first-time authors. 98% from unagented writers.**

FICTION "We are open to all genres, particularly LGBT and young adult/middle grade, historical and western, New Age/inspirational (no overtly Christian materials, please), noncategory romance, thrillers. We encourage people to review what we've already published so as to avoid sending us more of the same, at least, insofar as the plot is concerned.

While we're always looking for good mysteries, especially cozies, mysteries with historical settings, and police procedurals, we want original concepts rather than slightly altered versions of what we've already published." Does not want erotica, graphically erotic romance, experimental, literary (unless it fits into one of our established imprints).

NONFICTION "The easiest way to figure out what we're looking for is to look at what we've already done. Our main nonfiction interests are in collections of true ghost stories, ones that have been investigated or thoroughly documented, memoirs that address specific regions and eras from a 'normal person' viewpoint, and books on the craft of writing. That doesn't mean we won't consider something else."

HOW TO CONTACT A copy of our rules of submission is posted on our website and can be downloaded. They are rules rather than guidelines and should be read carefully before submitting. It will save everyone time and frustration. Electronic query only. 1,000 queries; 50 mss requested/year. Responds in 3 months to queries and proposals; 6 months to mss. Publishes ms 2 years after acceptance.

TERMS Pay 20% of net on paperbacks, net defined as cover price less printing and other associated costs; 50% of net on all e-books. Does not pay advance. Guidelines online.

TIPS "We're catering to readers who may have loved last year's bestseller but not enough to want to read 10 more just like it. Have something different. If it does not fit standard pigeonholes, that's a plus. On the other hand, it has to have an audience. And if you're not prepared to work with us on promotion and marketing, particularly via social media, it would be better to look elsewhere."

CANADIAN & INTERNATIONAL BOOK PUBLISHERS

While the United States is considered the largest market in children's publishing, the children's publishing world is by no means strictly dominated by the United States. After all, the most prestigious children's book extravaganza in the world occurs each year in Bologna, Italy, at the Bologna Children's Book Fair and some of the world's most beloved characters were born in the United Kingdom (i.e., Winnie-the-Pooh and Mr. Potter).

In this section you'll find book publishers from English-speaking countries around the world from Canada, Australia, New Zealand, and the United Kingdom. The listings in this section look just like the United States Book Publishers section; and the publishers listed are dedicated to the same goal—publishing great books for children.

Like always, be sure to study each listing and research each publisher carefully before submitting material. Determine whether a publisher is open to United States or international submissions, as many publishers accept submissions only from residents of their own country. Some publishers accept illustration samples from foreign artists, but do not accept manuscripts from foreign writers. Illustrators do have a slight edge in this category as many illustrators generate commissions from all around the globe. Visit publishers' websites to be certain they publish the sort of work you do. Visit online bookstores to see if publishers' books are available there. Write or e-mail to request catalogs and submission guidelines.

When mailing requests or submissions out of the United States, remember that United States postal stamps are useless on your SASE. Always include International Reply Coupons (IRCs) with your SAE. Each IRC is good for postage for one letter. So if you want the publisher to return your manuscript or send a catalog, be sure to enclose enough IRCs to pay the postage. For more help visit the United State Postal Service website at www.usps.com/global. Visit www.timeanddate.com/worldclock and American Computer Resources, Inc.'s International Calling Code Directory at www.the-acr.com/codes/ cntrycd.htm before calling or faxing internationally to make sure you're calling at a reasonable time and using the correct numbers.

As in the rest of *Children's Writer's & Illustrator's Market*, the maple leaf ☉ symbol identifies Canadian markets. Look for International ☮ symbol throughout *Children's Writer's & Illustrator's Market* as well. Several of the Society of Children's Book Writers and Illustrator's (SCBWI) international conferences are listed in the Conferences & Workshops section along with other events in locations around the globe. Look for more information about SCBWI's international chapters on the organization's website, www. scbwi.org.

⬤ ALLEN & UNWIN

406 Albert St., East Melbourne VIC 3002, Australia. (61)(3)9665-5000. **E-mail:** fridaypitch@allenandunwin.com. **Website:** www.allenandunwin.com. Allen & Unwin publish over 80 new books for children and young adults each year, many of these from established authors and illustrators. "However, we know how difficult it can be for new writers to get their work in front of publishers, which is why we've decided to extend our innovative and pioneering Friday Pitch service to emerging writers for children and young adults.

TERMS Guidelines online.

⬤ ANDERSEN PRESS

20 Vauxhall Bridge Rd., London SW1V 2SA, United Kingdom. **E-mail:** andersoneditorial@penguinrandomhouse.co.uk. **Website:** www.andersenpress.co.uk. Andersen Press is a specialist children's publisher. "We publish picture books, for which the required text would be approximately 500 words (maximum 1,000), juvenile fiction for which the text would be approximately 3,000-5,000 words and older fiction up to 75,000 words. We do not publish adult fiction, nonfiction, poetry, or short story anthologies."

HOW TO CONTACT Send all submissions by post: Query and full ms for picture books; synopsis and 3 chapters for longer fiction.

TERMS Guidelines online.

⬤ ANNICK PRESS, LTD.

15 Patricia Ave., Toronto, Ontario M2M 1H9, Canada. (416)221-4802. **Fax:** (416)221-8400. **Website:** www.annickpress.com. **Contact:** The Editors. Annick Press maintains a commitment to high quality books that entertain and challenge. Our publications share fantasy and stimulate imagination, while encouraging children to trust their judgment and abilities. *Does not accept unsolicited mss.* Publishes picture books, juvenile and young adult fiction and nonfiction; specializes in trade books. **Publishes 25 titles/year. 20% of books from first-time authors. 80-85% from unagented writers.**

FICTION Publisher of children's books. Not accepting picture books at this time.

HOW TO CONTACT 5,000 queries received/year. 3,000 mss received/year. Publishes a book 2 years after acceptance.

TERMS Pays authors royalty of 5-12% based on retail price. Offers advances (average amount: $3,000). Pays illustrators royalty of 5% minimum. Book catalog and guidelines online.

⬤ THE BRUCEDALE PRESS

P.O. Box 2259, Port Elgin, Ontario N0H 2C0, Canada. (519)832-6025. **E-mail:** info@brucedalepress.ca. **Website:** brucedalepress.ca. The Brucedale Press publishes books and other materials of regional interest and merit, as well as literary, historical, and/or pictorial works. Publishes hardcover and trade paperback originals. **Publishes 3 titles/year. 75% of books from first-time authors. 100% from unagented writers.**

⬤ Accepts works by Canadian authors only. Book submissions reviewed November to January. Submissions to *The Leaf Journal* accepted in September and March only. Manuscripts must be in English and thoroughly proofread before being sent. Use Canadian spellings and style.

HOW TO CONTACT 50 queries; 30 mss received/year. Publishes ms 1 year after acceptance.

TERMS Pays royalty. Book catalog online. "Unless responding to an invitation to submit, query first by Canada Post with outline and sample chapter to book-length manuscripts. Send full manuscripts for work intended for children." Guidelines online.

TIPS "Our focus is very regional. In reading submissions, I look for quality writing with a strong connection to the Queen's Bush area of Ontario. All authors should visit our website, get a catalog, and read our books before submitting."

⬤ BUSTER BOOKS

16 Lion Yard, Tremadoc Rd., London WA SW4 7NQ, United Kingdom. (020)7720-8643. **Fax:** (022)7720-8953. **E-mail:** enquiries@mombooks.com. **Website:** www.busterbooks.co.uk. **Contact:** Buster Submissions. "We are dedicated to providing irresistible and fun books for children of all ages. We typically publish b&w nonfiction for children aged 8-12 novelty titles-including doodle books."

HOW TO CONTACT Prefers synopsis and sample text over complete ms.

TIPS "We do not accept picture book or poetry submissions. Please do not send original artwork as we cannot guarantee its safety." Visit website before submitting.

CHILD'S PLAY (INTERNATIONAL), LTD.

Child's Play, Ashworth Rd. Bridgemead, Swindon, Wiltshire SN5 7YD, United Kingdom. 01793 616286. **E-mail:** neil@childs-play.com; office@childs-play. com. **Website:** www.childs-play.com. **Contact:** Sue Baker, Neil Burden, manuscript acquisitions. Specializes in nonfiction, fiction, educational material, multicultural material. Produces 30 picture books/ year; 10 young readers/year. "A child's early years are more important than any other. This is when children learn most about the world around them and the language they need to survive and grow. Child's Play aims to create exactly the right material for this all-important time." **Publishes 40 titles/ year.**

○ "Due to a backlog of submissions, Child's Play is currently no longer able to accept anymore mss."

FICTION Picture books: adventure, animal, concept, contemporary, folktales, multicultural, nature/ environment. Young readers: adventure, animal, anthology, concept, contemporary, folktales, humor, multicultural, nature/environment, poetry. Average word length: picture books: 1,500; young readers: 2,000.

NONFICTION Picture books: activity books, animal, concept, multicultural, music/dance, nature/ environment, science. Young readers: activity books, animal, concept, multicultural, music/dance, nature/environment, science. Average word length: picture books: 2,000; young readers: 3,000.

HOW TO CONTACT Publishes ms 2 years after acceptance.

ILLUSTRATION Accepts material from international illustrators. Works with 10 illustrators/year. Uses color artwork only. Reviews ms/illustration packages. For ms/illustration packages: Query or submit ms/ illustration packages to Sue Baker, editor. Reviews work for future assignments. If interested in illustrating future titles, query with samples, CD, website address. Submit samples to Annie Kubler, art director. Responds in 10 weeks. Samples not returned. Samples filed.

TIPS "Look at our website to see the kind of work we do before sending. Do not send cartoons. We do not publish novels. We do publish lots of books with pictures of babies/toddlers."

CHRISTIAN FOCUS PUBLICATIONS

Geanies House, Fearn, Tain Ross-shire Scotland IV20 1TW, United Kingdom. (44)1862-871-011. **Fax:** (44)1862-871-699. **E-mail:** submissions@christian-focus.com. **Website:** www.christianfocus.com. **Contact:** Director of Publishing. Specializes in Christian material, nonfiction, fiction, educational material. **Publishes 22-32 titles/year. 2% of books from first-time authors.**

FICTION Picture books, young readers, adventure, history, religion. Middle readers: adventure, problem novels, religion. Young adult/teens: adventure, history, problem novels, religion. Average word length: young readers: 5,000; middle readers: max 10,000; young adult/teen: max 20,000.

NONFICTION All levels: activity books, biography, history, religion, science. Average word length: picture books: 5,000; young readers: 5,000; middle readers: 5,000-10,000; young adult/teens: 10,000-20,000.

HOW TO CONTACT Query or submit outline/ synopsis and 3 sample chapters. Include Author Information Form from site with submission. Will consider electronic submissions and previously published work. Responds to queries in 2 weeks; mss in 3-6 months. Publishes ms 1 year after acceptance.

ILLUSTRATION Works on 15-20 potential projects. "Some artists are chosen to do more than one. Some projects just require a cover illustration, some require full color spreads, others b&w line art." Contact: Catherine Mackenzie, children's editor. Responds in 2 weeks only if interested. Samples are not returned.

PHOTOGRAPHY "We only purchase royalty free photos from particular photographic associations. However portfolios can be presented to our designer." Contact: Daniel van Straaten. Photographers should send cover letter, résumé, published samples, client list, portfolio.

TIPS "Be aware of the international market as regards writing style/topics as well as illustration styles. Our company sells rights to European as well as Asian countries. Fiction sales are not as good as they were. Christian fiction for youngsters is not a product that is performing well in comparison to nonfiction such as Christian biography/Bible stories/church history, etc."

☼ COTEAU BOOKS

Thunder Creek Publishing Co-operative Ltd., 2517 Victoria Ave., Regina, Saskatchewan S4P 0T2, Canada. (306)777-0170. **Fax:** (306)522-5152. **E-mail:** coteau@coteaubooks.com. **Website:** www.coteaubooks.com. **Contact:** Geoffrey Ursell, publisher. "Our mission is to publish the finest in Canadian fiction, nonfiction, poetry, drama, and children's literature, with an emphasis on Saskatchewan and prairie writers. De-emphasizing science fiction, picture books." Publishes chapter books for young readers aged 9-12 and novels for older kids ages 13-15 and for ages 15 and up. Publishes trade paperback originals and reprints. **Publishes 12 titles/year. 25% of books from first-time authors. 90% from unagented writers.**

FICTION No science fiction. No children's picture books. *Canadian authors only.*

NONFICTION *Canadian authors only.*

HOW TO CONTACT Query. Submit hard copy query, bio, 3-4 sample chapters, SASE. 200 queries; 40 mss received/year. Responds in 3 months. Publishes book 1 year after acceptance.

TERMS Pays 10% royalty on retail price. Book catalog available free. Guidelines online.

TIPS "Look at past publications to get an idea of our editorial program. We do not publish romance, horror, or picture books but are interested in juvenile and teen fiction from Canadian authors. Submissions, even queries, must be made in hard copy only. We do not accept simultaneous/multiple submissions. Check our website for new submission timing guidelines."

☼ CURIOUS FOX

Brunel Rd., Houndmills, Basingstoke Hants RG21 6XS, United Kingdom. **E-mail:** submissions@curious-fox.com. **Website:** www.curious-fox.com. "Do you love telling good stories? If so, we'd like to hear from you. Curious Fox is on the lookout for UK-based authors, whether new talent or established authors with exciting ideas. We take submissions for books aimed at ages 3-young adult. If you have story ideas that are bold, fun, and imaginative, then please do get in touch!"

HOW TO CONTACT "Send your submission via e-mail to submissions@curious-fox.com. Include the following in the body of the email, not as attachments: sample chapters, résumé, list of previous publishing credits, if applicable. We will respond only if your writing samples fit our needs."

ILLUSTRATION Please submit any illustrations/artwork by e-mail.

TERMS Guidelines online.

☼ FAT FOX BOOKS

The Den, P.O. Box 579, Tonbridge TN9 9NG, United Kingdom. (44)(0)1580-857249. **E-mail:** hello@fatfoxbooks.com. **Website:** fatfoxbooks.com. "Can you write engaging, funny, original and brilliant stories? We are looking for fresh new talent as well as exciting new ideas from established writers and illustrators. We publish books for children from 3-14, and if we think the story is brilliant and fits our list, then as one of the few publishers who accepts unsolicited material, we will take it seriously. We will consider books of all genres."

HOW TO CONTACT For picture books, send complete ms; for longer works, send first 3 chapters and estimate of final word count.

ILLUSTRATION "We are looking for beautiful, original, distinctive illustration that stands out."

TERMS Guidelines online. *Currently closed to submissions.*

☼ DAVID FICKLING BOOKS

31 Beamont St., Oxford OX1 2NP, United Kingdom. (018)65-339000. **Fax:** (018)65-339009. **Website:** www.davidficklingbooks.co.uk. **Contact:** Simon Mason, managing director. David Fickling Books is a story house." For nearly twelve years DFB has been run as an imprint—first as part of Scholastic, then of Random House. Now we've set up as an independent business." **Publishes 12-20 titles/year.**

FICTION Considers all categories.

HOW TO CONTACT Submit cover letter and 3 sample chapters as PDF attachment saved in format "Author Name_Full Title." Responds to mss in 3 months, if interested.

ILLUSTRATION Reviews ms/illustration packages from artists. Illustrations only: query with samples.

PHOTOGRAPHY Submit cover letter, résumé, promo pieces.

TERMS Guidelines online. *Closed to submissions.* Check website for when they open to submissions and for details on the Inkpot competition.

TIPS "We adore stories for all ages, in both text and pictures. Quality is our watch word."

✪ FITZHENRY & WHITESIDE LTD.

195 Allstate Pkwy., Markham, Ontario L3R 4T8, Canada. (905)477-9700. **Fax:** (905)477-2834. **E-mail:** godwit@fitzhenry.ca. **Website:** www.fitzhenry.ca/. Emphasis on Canadian authors and illustrators, subject or perspective. *"Until further notice, we will not be accepting unsolicited submissions."* **Publishes 15 titles/year. 10% of books from first-time authors.**

HOW TO CONTACT Publishes ms 1-2 years after acceptance.

ILLUSTRATION Works with approximately 10 illustrators/year. Reviews ms/illustration packages from artists. Submit outline and sample illustration (copy). Illustrations only: Query with samples and promo sheet. Samples not returned unless requested.

PHOTOGRAPHY Buys photos from freelancers. Buys stock and assigns work. Captions required. Uses b&w 8"×10" prints; 35mm and 4"×5" transparencies, 300+ dpi digital images. Submit stock photo list and promo piece.

TERMS Pays authors 8-10% royalty with escalations. Offers "respectable" advances for picture books, split 50/50 between author and illustrator. Pays illustrators by project and royalty. Pays photographers per photo.

TIPS "We respond to quality."

✪ FLYING EYE BOOKS

62 Great Eastern St., London EC2A 3QR, United Kingdom. (44)(0)207-033-4430. **E-mail:** picturbksubs@nobrow.net. **Website:** www.flyingeyebooks.com. Flying Eye Books is the children's imprint of award-winning visual publishing house Nobrow. FEB seeks to retain the same attention to detail and excellence in illustrated content as its parent publisher, but with a focus on the craft of children's storytelling and nonfiction.

TERMS Guidelines online.

✪ FRANCES LINCOLN CHILDREN'S BOOKS

Frances Lincoln, 74-77 White Lion St., London N1 9PF, United Kingdom. (44)(20)7284-4009. **Website:** www.franceslincoln.com. "Our company was founded by Frances Lincoln in 1977. We published our first books two years later, and we have been creating illustrated books of the highest quality ever since, with special emphasis on gardening, walking and the outdoors, art, architecture, design and landscape. In 1983, we started to publish illustrated books for children. Since then we have won many awards and prizes with both fiction and nonfiction children's books." **Publishes 100 titles/year. 6% of books from first-time authors.**

FICTION Average word length: picture books: 1,000; young readers: 9,500; middle readers: 20,500; young adults: 35,000.

NONFICTION Average word length: picture books: 1,000; middle readers: 30,000.

HOW TO CONTACT Query by e-mail. Responds in 6 weeks to mss. Publishes ms 18 months after acceptance.

ILLUSTRATION Works with approx 56 illustrators/year. Uses both color and b&w. Reviews ms/illustration packages from artist. Sample illustrations. Illustrations only: Query with samples. Responds only if interested. Samples are returned with SASE. Samples are kept on file only if interested.

PHOTOGRAPHY Buys stock images and assigns work. Uses children, multicultural photos. Submit cover letter, published samples, or portfolio.

✪✪ FRANKLIN WATTS

Hachette Children's Books, Carmelite House, 50 Victoria Embankment, London EC4Y 0DZ, United Kingdom. (44)(20)7873-6000. **Fax:** (44)(20)7873-6024. **Website:** www.franklinwatts.co.uk. Franklin Watts is well known for its high quality and attractive information books, which support the National Curriculum and stimulate children's enquiring minds. *Generally does not accept unsolicited mss.*

✪ KIDS CAN PRESS

25 Dockside Dr., Toronto, Ontario M5A 0B5, Canada. (416)479-7000. **Fax:** (416)960-5437. **Website:** www.kidscanpress.com. **Contact:** Corus Quay, acquisitions.

✪ Kids Can Press is currently accepting unsolicited mss from Canadian adult authors only.

FICTION Picture books, young readers: concepts. "We do not accept young adult fiction or fantasy novels for any age." Adventure, animal, contemporary, folktales, history, humor, multicultural, nature/environment, special needs, sports, suspense/mystery. Average word length: picture books: 1,000-2,000; young readers: 750-1,500; middle readers: 10,000-15,000; young adults: 15,000+.

NONFICTION Picture books: activity books, animal, arts/crafts, biography, careers, concept, health, history, hobbies, how-to, multicultural, nature/environment, science, social issues, special needs, sports. Young readers: activity books, animal, arts/crafts, biography, careers, concept, history, hobbies, how-to, multicultural. Middle readers: cooking, music/dance. Average word length: picture books: 500-1,250; young readers: 750-2,000; middle readers: 5,000-15,000.

HOW TO CONTACT Submit outline/synopsis and 2-3 sample chapters. For picture books submit complete ms. Responds in 6 months only if interested. Publishes ms 18-24 months after acceptance.

ILLUSTRATION Works with 40 illustrators/year. Reviews ms/illustration packages from artists. Send color copies of illustration portfolio, cover letter outlining other experience. Contact: Art Director. Illustrations only: Send tearsheets, color photocopies. Responds only if interested.

⚫ LITTLE TIGER PRESS

1 The Coda Centre, 189 Munster Rd., London SW6 6AW, United Kingdom. (44)(20)7385-6333. **Website:** www.littletigerpress.com. Little Tiger Press is a dynamic and busy independent publisher. Also includes imprints: Caterpillar Books and Stripes Publishing.

FICTION Picture books: animal, concept, contemporary, humor. Average word length: picture books: 750 words or less.

HOW TO CONTACT *"We are no longer accepting unsolicited manuscripts.* We will however, continue to accept illustration submissions and samples."

ILLUSTRATION Digital submissions preferred. Please send in digital samples as pdf or jpeg attachments to artsubmissions@littletiger.co.uk. Files should be flattened and no bigger than 1 mb per attachment. Include name and contact details on any attachments. Printed submissions please send in printed color samples as A4 printouts. Do not send in original artwork as we cannot be held responsible for unsolicited original artwork being lost or damaged in the post. We aim to acknowledge unsolicited material and to return material if so requested within 3 months. Please include SAE if return of material is requested.

⚫ MANOR HOUSE PUBLISHING, INC.

452 Cottingham Crescent, Ancaster, Ontario L9G 3V6, Canada. (905)648-2193. **E-mail:** mbdavie@manor-house.biz. **Website:** www.manor-house.biz.

Contact: Mike Davie, president (novels and nonfiction). Publishes hardcover, trade paperback, and mass market paperback originals (and reprints if they meet specific criteria—best to inquire with publisher). **Publishes 5-6 titles/year. 90% of books from first-time authors. 90% from unagented writers.**

FICTION Stories should mainly be by Canadian authors residing in Canada, have Canadian settings, and characters should be Canadian, but content should have universal appeal to wide audience. In some cases, we will consider publishing nonCanadian fiction authors provided they demonstrate publishing their book will be profitable for author and publisher.

NONFICTION Of primary interest are business and self-help titles along with other nonfiction, including new age. We are also open to publishing nonCanadian authors (nonfiction works only) provided nonCanadian authors can further provide us with a very good indication of demand for their book (Eg: actual or expected advance book orders from speaker venues, corporations, agencies or authors on a nonreturnable basis) so we are assured the title will likely be a profitable venture for both author and publisher.

HOW TO CONTACT Query via e-mail. Submit proposal package, clips, bio, 3 sample chapters. Submit complete ms. Query via e-mail. Submit proposal package, outline, bio, 3 sample chapters. Submit complete ms. 30 queries; 20 mss received/year. Queries and mss to be sent by e-mail only. "We will respond in 30 days if interested; if not, there is no response. Do not follow up unless asked to do so." Publishes book 6-12 months after acceptance.

TERMS Pays 10% royalty on retail price. Book catalog online. Guidelines available.

TIPS "Our audience includes everyone—the general public/mass audience. Self-edit your work first, make sure it is well written and well edited with strong Canadian content and/or content of universal appeal (preferably with a Canadian connection of some kind)."

⚫⚫ ON THE MARK PRESS

15 Dairy Ave., Napanee, Ontario K7R 1M4, Canada. (800)463-6367. **Fax:** (800)290-3631. **Website:** www.onthemarkpress.com. Publishes books for the Ca-

nadian curriculum. **15% of books from first-time authors.**

PHOTOGRAPHY Buys stock images.

ORCA BOOK PUBLISHERS

1016 Balmoral Rd., Victoria, British Columbia V8T 1A8, Canada. (800)210-5277. **Fax:** (877)408-1551. **E-mail:** orca@orcabook.com. **Website:** www.orcabook.com. **Contact:** Amy Collins, editor (picture books); Sarah Harvey, editor (young readers); Andrew Wooldridge, editor (juvenile and teen fiction); Bob Tyrrell, publisher (young adult, teen); Ruth Linka, associate editor (rapid reads). *Only publishes Canadian authors.* Publishes hardcover and trade paperback originals, and mass market paperback originals and reprints. **Publishes 30-50 titles/year. 20% of books from first-time authors. 75% from unagented writers.**

FICTION Picture books: animals, contemporary, history, nature/environment. Middle readers: contemporary, history, fantasy, nature/environment, problem novels, graphic novels. Young adults: adventure, contemporary, hi-lo (Orca Soundings), history, multicultural, nature/environment, problem novels, suspense/mystery, graphic novels. Average word length: picture books: 500-1,500; middle readers: 20,000-35,000; young adult: 25,000-45,000; Orca Soundings: 13,000-15,000; Orca Currents: 13,000-15,000. No romance, science fiction.

HOW TO CONTACT Query with SASE. Submit proposal package, outline, clips, 2-5 sample chapters, SASE. Query with a SASE. 2,500 queries; 1,000 mss received/year. Responds in 1 month to queries; 2 months to proposals and mss. Publishes ms 12-18 months after acceptance.

ILLUSTRATION Works with 8-10 illustrators/year. Reviews ms/illustration packages from artists. Submit ms with 3-4 pieces of final art. "Reproductions only, no original art please." Illustrations only: Query with samples; provide résumé, online portfolio. Responds in 2 months. Samples returned with SASE; samples filed. 4 to 8 copies, digital proofs, tear sheets, press sheets.

TERMS Pays 10% royalty. Book catalog for 8½"x11" SASE. Guidelines online.

TIPS "Our audience is students in grades K-12. Know our books, and know the market."

PAJAMA PRESS

181 Carlaw Ave., Suite 207, Toronto, Ontario M4M 2S1, Canada. 4164662222. **E-mail:** annfeatherstone@pajamapress.ca. **Website:** pajamapress.ca. **Contact:** Ann Featherstone, senior editor. "We publish picture books—both for the very young and for school-aged readers, as well as novels for middle grade readers and contemporary or historical fiction for young adults aged 12+. Our nonfiction titles typically contain a strong narrative element. Pajama Press is also looking for mss from authors of diverse backgrounds. Stories about immigrants are of special interest." **Publishes 15-20 titles/year. 20% of books from first-time authors. 80% from unagented writers.**

FICTION Vampire novels; romance (except as part of a literary novel); fiction with overt political or religious messages

NONFICTION "Our nonfiction titles typically contain a strong narrative element; for example, juvenile biographies and narratives about wildlife rescue." Does not want how-to books, activity books, books for adults, psychology books, educational resources.

HOW TO CONTACT Pajama Press considers digital queries accompanied by picture books texts or the first 3 chapters of novel length projects. Your query should include an overview of your submission and some information about your writing background. Pajama Press prefers not to look at simultaneous submissions. Please notify us if you are submitting your project to another publisher. Please e-mail your queries and submissions to annfeatherstone@pajamapress.ca. In the interest of saving trees, Pajama Press does not accept physical mss. Any mss mailed to our office will be recycled unopened. 1,000 Responds in 6 weeks. Publishes ms 1-3 years after acceptance.

TERMS Pays advance. Guidelines online.

REBELIGHT PUBLISHING, INC.

23-845 Dakota St., Suite 314, Winnipeg Manitoba R2M 5M3, Canada. **Website:** www.rebelight.com. **Contact:** Editor. Rebelight Publishing is interested in "crack the spine, blow your mind" manuscripts for middle grade, young adult, and new adult novels. *Only considers submissions from Canadian writers.* Publishes paperback and electronic originals. **Pub-**

lishes 6-10 titles/year. **25-50% of books from first-time authors. 100% from unagented writers.**

FICTION All genres are considered, provided they are for a middle grade, young adult, or new adult audience. "Become familiar with our books. Study our website. Stick within the guidelines. Our tag line is 'crack the spine, blow your mind'—we are looking for well-written, powerful, fresh, fast-paced fiction. Keep us turning the pages. Give us something we just have to spread the word about."

HOW TO CONTACT Submit proposal package, including a synopsis and 3 sample chapters. Read guidelines carefully. Receive about 500 submissions/year. Responds in 3 months to queries and mss. Submissions accepted via email only. Publishes ms 12-18 months after acceptance.

TERMS Pays 12-22% royalties on retail price. Does not offer an advance. Catalog online or PDF available via e-mail request. Guidelines online.

TIPS "Review your manuscript for passive voice prior to submitting! (And that means get rid of it.)"

RONSDALE PRESS

3350 W. 21st Ave., Vancouver, British Columbia V6S 1G7, Canada. (604)738-4688. **Fax:** (604)731-4548. **Website:** ronsdalepress.com. **Contact:** Ronald B. Hatch (fiction, poetry, nonfiction, social commentary); Veronica Hatch (YA novels and short stories). "Ronsdale Press is a Canadian literary publishing house that publishes 12 books each year, 4 of which are young adult titles. Of particular interest are books involving children exploring and discovering new aspects of Canadian history." Publishes trade paperback originals. **Publishes 12 titles/year. 40% of books from first-time authors. 95% from unagented writers.**

FICTION Young adults: Canadian novels. Average word length: middle readers and young adults: 50,000.

NONFICTION Middle readers, young adults: animal, biography, history, multicultural, social issues. "We publish a number of books for children and young adults in the age 10 to 15 range. We are especially interested in young adult historical novels. We regret that we can no longer publish picture books."

HOW TO CONTACT Submit complete ms. 40 queries; 800 mss received/year. Responds to queries in 2 weeks; mss in 2 months. Publishes ms 1 year after acceptance.

ILLUSTRATION Works with 2 illustrators/year. Reviews ms/illustration packages from artists. Requires only cover art. Responds in 2 weeks. Samples returned with SASE. Originals returned to artist at job's completion.

TERMS Pays 10% royalty on retail price. Book catalog for #10 SASE. Guidelines online.

TIPS "Ronsdale Press is a literary publishing house, based in Vancouver, and dedicated to publishing books from across Canada, books that give Canadians new insights into themselves and their country. We aim to publish the best Canadian writers."

SECOND STORY PRESS

20 Maud St., Suite 401, Toronto, Ontario M5V 2M5, Canada. (416)537-7850. **Fax:** (416)537-0588. **E-mail:** info@secondstorypress.ca. **Website:** www.secondstorypress.ca. "Please keep in mind that as a feminist press, we are looking for nonsexist, nonracist, and nonviolent stories, as well as historical fiction, chapter books, novels, and biography."

FICTION Considers nonsexist, nonracist, and nonviolent stories, as well as historical fiction, chapter books, picture books.

NONFICTION Picture books: biography.

HOW TO CONTACT *Accepts appropriate material from residents of Canada only.* "Send a synopsis and up to 3 sample chapters. If you are submitting a picture book you can send the entire manuscript. Illustrations are not necessary." No electronic submissions or queries. Guidelines on site.

SIMPLY READ BOOKS

501-5525 W. Blvd., Vancouver, British Columbia V6M 3W6, Canada. **E-mail:** go@simplyreadbooks.com. **Website:** www.simplyreadbooks.com. Simply Read Books is current seeking mss in picture books, early readers, early chapter books, middle grade fiction, and graphic novels.

HOW TO CONTACT Query or submit complete ms.

SWEET CHERRY PUBLISHING

Unit 36, Vulcan Business Complex, Vulcan Rd., Leicester Leicestershire LE5 3EF, United Kingdom. **E-mail:** info@sweetcherrypublishing.com. **Website:** www.sweetcherrypublishing.com. Sweet Cherry Publishing is an independent publishing company based in Leicester. Our aim is to provide children with compelling worlds and engaging characters that they will want to revisit time and time again.

FICTION No erotica.

HOW TO CONTACT Submit a cover letter and a synopsis with 3 sample chapters via post or e-mail. Please note that we strongly prefer e-mail submissions.

ILLUSTRATION Submissions may include illustrations, but Sweet Cherry employs in-house illustrators and would therefore by unlikely to use them in the event of publication.

TERMS Offers one-time fee for work that is accepted. Guidelines online.

TIPS "We strongly prefer e-mail submissions over postal submissions. If your work is accepted, Sweet Cherry may consider commissioning you for future series."

TAFELBERG PUBLISHERS

Imprint of NB Publishers, P.O. Box 879, Cape Town 8000, South Africa. (27)(21)406-3033. **Fax:** (27)(21)406-3812. **E-mail:** engela.reinke@nb.co.za. **Website:** www.tafelberg.com. **Contact:** Engela Reinke. General publisher best known for Afrikaans fiction, authoritative political works, children's/youth literature, and a variety of illustrated and nonillustrated nonfiction. **Publishes 10 titles/year.**

FICTION Picture books, young readers: animal, anthology, contemporary, fantasy, folktales, hi-lo, humor, multicultural, nature/environment, science fiction, special needs. Middle readers, young adults: animal (middle reader only), contemporary, fantasy, hi-lo, humor, multicultural, nature/environment, problem novels, science fiction, special needs, sports, suspense/mystery. Average word length: picture books: 1,500-7,500; young readers: 25,000; middle readers: 15,000; young adults: 40,000.

HOW TO CONTACT Submit complete ms. Submit outline, information on intended market, bio, and 1-2 sample chapters. Responds to queries in 2 weeks; mss in 6 months. Publishes ms 1 year after acceptance.

ILLUSTRATION Works with 2-3 illustrators/year. Reviews ms/illustration packages from artists. Send ms with dummy or e-mail and jpegs. Contact: Louise Steyn, publisher. Illustrations only: Query with brochure, photocopies, résumé, URL, JPEGs. Responds only if interested. Samples not returned.

TERMS Pays authors royalty of 15-18% based on wholesale price.

TIPS "Writers: Story needs to have a South African or African style. Illustrators: I'd like to look, but the chances of getting commissioned are slim. The market is small and difficult. Do not expect huge advances. Editorial staff attended or plans to attend the following conferences: IBBY, Frankfurt, SCBWI Bologna."

THISTLEDOWN PRESS LTD.

410 2nd Ave., Saskatoon, Sasketchewan S7K 2C3, Canada. (306)244-1722. **Fax:** (306)244-1762. **E-mail:** editorial@thistledownpress.com. **Website:** www.thistledownpress.com. **Contact:** Allan Forrie, publisher. "Thistledown originates books by Canadian authors only, although we have co-published titles by authors outside Canada. We do not publish children's picture books." **40% of books from first-time authors. 40% from unagented writers.**

FICTION Young adults: adventure, anthology, contemporary, fantasy, humor, poetry, romance, science fiction, suspense/mystery, short stories. Average word length: young adults: 40,000.

HOW TO CONTACT Submit outline/synopsis and sample chapters. *Does not accept mss.* Do not query by e-mail. "Please note: we are not accepting middle years (ages 8-12) nor children's manuscripts at this time." See Submission Guidelines on Website. Receives 150-250 submissions/year. Responds to queries in 6 months. Publishes ms 1 year after acceptance.

ILLUSTRATION Prefers agented illustrators but "not mandatory." Works with few illustrators. Illustrations only: Query with samples, promo sheet, slides, tearsheets. Responds only if interested. Samples returned with SASE; samples filed.

TERMS Pays authors royalty of 10-12% based on net dollar sales. Pays illustrators and photographers by the project (range: $250-750). Rarely pays advance. Book catalog on website. Guidelines online.

TIPS "Send cover letter including publishing history and SASE."

TRADEWIND BOOKS

202-1807 Maritime Mews, Granville Island, Vancouver, British Columbia V6H 3W7, Canada. (604)662-4405. **Website:** www.tradewindbooks.com. "Tradewind Books publishes juvenile picture books and young adult novels. Requires that submissions include evidence that author has read at

least 3 titles published by Tradewind Books." Publishes hardcover and trade paperback originals. **Publishes 5 titles/year. 15% of books from first-time authors. 50% from unagented writers.**
FICTION Average word length: 900 words.
HOW TO CONTACT Send complete ms for picture books. *Young adult novels by Canadian authors only. Chapter books by US authors considered.* For chapter books/middle grade fiction, submit the first 3 chapters, a chapter outline and plot summary. Responds to mss in 2 months. Publishes ms 3 years after acceptance.
ILLUSTRATION Works with 3-4 illustrators/year. Reviews ms/illustration packages from artists. Send illustrated ms as dummy. Illustrations only: Query with samples. Responds only if interested. Samples returned with SASE; samples filed.
TERMS Pays 7% royalty on retail price. Pays variable advance. Book catalog and ms guidelines online.

🅰🗨 USBORNE PUBLISHING

83-85 Saffron Hill, London EC1N 8RT, United Kingdom. (44)207430-2800. **Fax:** (44)207430-1562. **E-mail:** mail@usborne.co.uk. **Website:** www.usborne.com. "Usborne Publishing is a multiple-award-winning, worldwide children's publishing company publishing almost every type of children's book for every age from baby to young adult."
FICTION Young readers, middle readers: adventure, contemporary, fantasy, history, humor, multicultural, nature/environment, science fiction, suspense/mystery, strong concept-based or character-led series. Average word length: young readers: 5,000-10,000; middle readers: 25,000-50,000; young adult: 50,000-100,000.
HOW TO CONTACT *Agented submissions only.*
ILLUSTRATION Works with 100 illustrators per year. Illustrations only: Query with samples. Samples not returned; samples filed.
PHOTOGRAPHY Contact: Usborne Art Department. Submit samples.
TERMS Pays authors royalty.
TIPS "Do not send any original work and, sorry, but we cannot guarantee a reply."

⬤ WHITECAP BOOKS, LTD.

210 - 314 W. Cordova St., Vancouver, British Columbia V6B 1 E8, Canada. (604)681-6181. **Fax:** (905)477-9179. **Website:** www.whitecap.ca. "Whitecap Books

is a general trade publisher with a focus on food and wine titles. Although we are interested in reviewing unsolicited ms submissions, please note that we only accept submissions that meet the needs of our current publishing program. Please see some of most recent releases to get an idea of the kinds of titles we are interested in." Publishes hardcover and trade paperback originals. **Publishes 30 titles/year. 20% of books from first-time authors. 90% from unagented writers.**
FICTION No children's picture books or adult fiction.
NONFICTION Young children's and middle reader's nonfiction focusing mainly on nature, wildlife and animals. "Writers should take the time to research our list and read the submission guidelines on our website. This is especially important for children's writers and cookbook authors. We will only consider submissions that fall into these categories: cookbooks, wine and spirits, regional travel, home and garden, Canadian history, North American natural history, juvenile series-based fiction. At this time, we are not accepting the following categories: self-help or inspirational books, political, social commentary, or issue books, general how-to books, biographies or memoirs, business and finance, art and architecture, religion and spirituality."
HOW TO CONTACT See guidelines. Submit cover letter, synopsis, SASE via ground mail. See guidelines online. 500 queries received/year; 1,000 mss received/year. Responds in 2-3 months to proposals. Publishes ms 1 year after acceptance.
ILLUSTRATION Works with 1-2 illustrators/year. Uses color artwork only. Reviews ms/illustration packages from artists. Query. Contact: Rights and Acquisitions. Illustrations only: Send postcard sample with tearsheets. Contact: Michelle Furbacher, art director. Responds only if interested.
PHOTOGRAPHY Only accepts digital photography. Submit stock photo list. Buys stock and assigns work. Model/property releases required.
TERMS Pays royalty. Pays negotiated advance. Catalog and guidelines online.
TIPS "We want well-written, well-researched material that presents a fresh approach to a particular topic."

MAGAZINES

///

Children's magazines are a great place for unpublished writers and illustrators to break into the market. Writers, illustrators, and photographers alike may find it easier to get book assignments if they have tearsheets from magazines. Having magazine work under your belt shows you're professional and have experience working with editors and art directors and meeting deadlines.

But magazines aren't merely a breaking-in point. Writing, illustration and photo assignments for magazines let you see your work in print quickly, and the magazine market can offer steady work and regular paychecks (a number of them pay on acceptance). Book authors and illustrators may have to wait a year or two before receiving royalties from a project. The magazine market is also a good place to use research material that didn't make it into a book project you're working on. You may even work on a magazine idea that blossoms into a book project.

TARGETING YOUR SUBMISSIONS

It's important to know the topics typically covered by different children's magazines. To help you match your work with the right publications, we've included several indexes in the back of this book. The **Subject Index** lists both book and magazine publishers by the fiction and nonfiction subjects they're seeking.

If you're a writer, use the Subject Index in conjunction with the **Age-Level Index** to narrow your list of markets. Targeting the correct age group with your submission is an important consideration. Many rejection slips are sent because a writer has not targeted a manuscript to the correct age. Few magazines are aimed at children of all ages, so you must be certain your manuscript is written for the audience level of the particular magazine you're submitting to. Magazines for children (just as magazines for adults) may also target a specific gender.

If you're a poet, refer to the **Poetry Index** to find which magazines publish poems.

Each magazine has a different editorial philosophy. Language usage also varies between periodicals, as does the length of feature articles and the use of artwork and photographs. Reading magazines *before* submitting is the best way to determine if your material is appropriate. Also, because magazines targeted to specific age groups have a natural turnover in readership every few years, old topics (with a new slant) can be recycled.

If you're a photographer, the **Photography Index** lists children's magazines that use photos from freelancers. Using it in combination with the subject index can narrow your search. For instance, if you photograph sports, compare the Magazine list in the Photography Index with the list under Sports in the Subject Index. Highlight the markets that appear on both lists, then read those listings to decide which magazines might be best for your work.

Because many kids' magazines sell subscriptions through direct mail or schools, you may not be able to find a particular publication at bookstores or newsstands. Check your local library, or send for copies of the magazines you're interested in. Most magazines in this section have sample copies available and will send them for a SASE or small fee.

Also, many magazines have submission guidelines and theme lists available for a SASE. Check magazines' websites, too. Many offer excerpts of articles, submission guidelines, and theme lists and will give you a feel for the editorial focus of the publication.

Watch for the Canadian ✪ and International ➒ symbols. These publications' needs and requirements may differ from their United States counterparts.

ADVOCATE, PKA'S PUBLICATION

PKA Publications, 1881 Little Westkill Rd., Prattsville NY 12468, USA. (518)299-3103. **Website:** advocatepka.weebly.com; www.facebook.com/Advocate/PKAPublications. **Contact:** Patricia Keller, publisher. *Advocate, PKA's Publication*, published bimonthly, is an advertiser-supported tabloid using "original, previously unpublished works, such as feature stories, essays, 'think' pieces, letters to the editor, profiles, humor, fiction, poetry, puzzles, cartoons, or line drawings. Advocates for good writers and quality writings. We publish art, fiction, photos, and poetry. *Advocate*'s submiters are talented people of all ages who do not earn their livings as writers. We wish to promote the arts and to give those we publish the opportunity to be published." Estab. 1987. Circ. 5,000.

○ This publication has a strong horse orientation: horse-oriented stories, poetry, art, and photos are currently needed.

FICTION Looks for "well-written, entertaining work, whether fiction or nonfiction." Wants to see more humorous material, nature/environment, and romantic comedy. Needs adventure, ethnic, fantasy, historical, humorous, mainstream, mystery, romance, science fiction, short stories, slice-of-life vignettes, suspense, western, middle readers, young adults/teens, adults: adventure, animal, contemporary, fantasy, folktales, health, humorous, nature/environment, problem-solving, romance, science fiction, sports, suspense/mystery. "Nothing religious, pornographic, violent, erotic, pro-drug, or anti-enviroment." Send complete ms. Length: up to 1,500 words. Pays contributor copies.

NONFICTION Needs essays, general interest, humor, inspirational, memoir, nostalgic, personal experience, photo feature. Send complete ms with SASE. Length: up to 1,500 words. Pays contributor copies.

POETRY "Poetry ought to speak to people and not be so oblique as to have meaning only to the poet. If I had to be there to understand the poem, don't send it. Also looking for horse-related poems, stories, drawings, and photos." Considers poetry by children and teens (when included with release form signed by adult). Accepts about 25% of poems received. Wants "nearly any kind of poetry, any length." Occasionally comments on rejected poems.

Submit any number of poems at a time. No religious or pornographic poetry. Pays contributor copies.

HOW TO CONTACT Responds to queries in 6 weeks; mss in 2 months. Publishes ms 2-18 months after acceptance. Accepts queries by mail.

ILLUSTRATION Uses b&w artwork only. Uses cartoons. Reviews ms/illustration packages from artists. Submit a photo print (b&w or color), an excellent copy of work (no larger than 8"×10") or original. Prints in b&w but accepts color work that converts well to gray scale. Illustrations only: "Send previous unpublished art with SASE, please." Responds in 2 months. Samples returned with SASE; samples not filed. Credit line given.

PHOTOS Buys photos from freelancers. Model/property releases required. Uses color and b&w prints (no slides). Send unsolicited photos by mail with SASE. Wants nature, artistic, and humorous photos. Send images 300 dpi about 4 inches in size. Pays in contributor copies.

TERMS Acquires first rights for mss, artwork, and photographs. Byline given. Pays on publication with contributor's copies. 100% freelance written. Sample copy: $5 (includes guidelines). Subscription: $20.00 (6 issues). Previous 6 issues are on our website. *Advocate* publishes only original, previously unpublished works by writers who do not yet earn their living by writing. It is published six times per year. All submissions must be typed or legibly handwritten and accompanied by a SASE. Please, no simultaneous submissions, work that has appeared on the Internet, pornography, overt religiosity, anti-environmentalism, nor gratuitous violence. "We have a backlog of short stories. If your story is accepted it will be several months before it is published." Queries are welcome if editorial input is desired, but they are not required. *Advocate* is primarily seeking works that will hold the reader's interest as much by quality of the writing as by the subject matter. Advocate pays in contributor copies upon publication. Sample copy available for $5.00 or $18.50 for a year (6 issues).

TIPS "Please, no simultaneous submissions, work that has appeared on the Internet, pornography, overt religiousity, anti-environmentalism, or gratuitous violence. Artists and photographers should keep in mind that we are a b&w paper. Please do not send postcards. Use envelope with SASE."

AQUILA

Studio 2 Willowfield Studios, 67a Willowfield Rd., Eastbourne BN22 8AP, England. (44)(132)343-1313. **E-mail:** editor@aquila.co.uk. **Website:** www.aquila.co.uk. *"Aquila* is an educational magazine for readers ages 8-13 including factual articles (no pop/celebrity material), arts/crafts, and puzzles." Entire publication aimed at juvenile market. Estab. 1993. Circ. 40,000.

FICTION Young Readers: animal, contemporary, fantasy, folktales, health, history, humorous, multicultural, nature/environment, problem solving, religious, science fiction, sports, suspense/mystery. Middle Readers: animal, contemporary, fantasy, folktales, health, history, humorous, multicultural, nature/environment, problem solving, religious, romance, science fiction, sports, suspense/mystery. Length: 1,000-1,150 words. Pays £90.

NONFICTION Young Readers: animal, arts/crafts, concept, cooking, games/puzzles, health, history, how-to, interview/profile, math, nature/environment, science, sports. Middle Readers: animal, arts/crafts, concept, cooking, games/puzzles, health, history, interview/profile, math, nature/environment, science, sports. Query. Length: 600-800 words. Pays £90.

HOW TO CONTACT Accepts queries by mail, e-mail.

TERMS Pays on publication. Sample copy: £5. Guidelines online.

TIPS "We only accept a high level of educational material for children ages 8-13 with a good standard of literacy and ability."

ASCENT ASPIRATIONS

Friday's Poems, 1560 Arbutus Dr., Nanoose Bay, British Columbia C9P 9C8, Canada. **E-mail:** ascentaspirations@shaw.ca. **Website:** www.ascentaspirations.ca. **Contact:** David Fraser, editor. E-zine specializing in poetry and visual art. *"Ascent Aspirations* magazine publishes weekly online and in print annually. The print issues are operated as contests or as anthologies of a year's accepted submissions. Please refer to current guidelines before submitting. *Ascent Aspirations* is a quality electronic publication dedicated to the promotion and encouragement of aspiring writers of poetry. For Friday's Poems we accept submissions all the time, publish 3 poems per week, and archive then after that week is over. Estab.

1997. Magazine: 3 electronic pages; photos. Receives 100-200 unsolicited mss/month. Accepts 3 mss/issue; 156 mss/year. Publishes 10-50 new writers/year. Has published work by Taylor Graham, Janet Buck, Jim Manton, Steve Cartwright, Don Stockard, Penn Kemp, Sam Vargo, Vernon Waring, Margaret Karmazin, Bill Hughes, and spoken-word artists Sheri-D Wilson, Missy Peters, Ian Ferrier, Cathy Petch, and Bob Holdman.

NONFICTION Query by e-mail with Word attachment. Include a brief bio. "If you have to submit by mail because it is your only avenue, provide a SASE with either International Coupons or Canadian stamps only, but provide an e-mail address for notification of publication.

POETRY Submit 1-5 poems at a time. Prefers e-mail submissions (pasted into body of message or as attachment in Word); no disk submissions. "If you must submit by postal mail because it is your only avenue, provide a SASE with IRCs or Canadian stamps." Reads submissions on a regular basis year round. "We accept all forms of poetry on any theme. Poetry needs to be unique and touch the reader emotionally with relevant human, social, and philosophical imagery." Considers poetry by children and teens. Does not want poetry "that focuses on mainstream, overtly religious verse." "No payment offered at this time."

HOW TO CONTACT Responds in 1 to week to queries; 3 months to mss. Sometimes comments on rejected mss. Publishes ms 3 months or less after acceptance.

TERMS Rights remain with author. Guidelines by e-mail or on website.

TIPS Poetry should use language lyrically and effectively, be experimental in either form or content, and take the reader into realms where they can analyze and think about the human condition. Write with passion for your material, be concise and economical, and let the reader work to unravel your story. In terms of editing, always proofread to the point where what you submit is the best it possibly can be. Never be discouraged if your work is not accepted; it may just not be the right fit for a current publication."

BOYS' LIFE

Boy Scouts of America, P.O. Box 152079, 1325 W. Walnut Hill Ln., Irving TX 75015. **Website:** www.boyslife.org. **Contact:** Paula Murphey, senior editor;

Clay Swartz, associate editor. *Boys' Life* is a monthly 4-color general interest magazine for boys 7-18, most of whom are Cub Scouts, Boy Scouts, or Venturers. Estab. 1911. Circ. 1.1 million.

NONFICTION Scouting activities and general interests. Query senior editor with SASE. No phone or e-mail queries. Length: 500-1,500 words. Pay ranges from $400-1,500.

HOW TO CONTACT Responds to queries/mss in 2 months. Publishes ms approximately 1 year after acceptance. Accepts queries by mail.

ILLUSTRATION Buys 10-12 illustrations/issue; 100-125 illustrations/year. Works on assignment only. Reviews ms/illustration packages from artists. "Query first." Illustrations only: Send tearsheets. Responds to art samples only if interested. Samples returned with SASE. Original artwork returned at job's completion. Works on assignment only.

PHOTOS Photo guidelines free with SASE. Pays $500 base editorial day rate against placement fees, plus expenses. Pays on acceptance. Buys one-time rights.

TERMS Buys one-time rights. Byline given. Pays on acceptance. 75% freelance written. Prefers to work with published/established writers; works with small number of new/unpublished writers each year. Sample copy: $3.95 plus 9x12 SASE. Guidelines online.

TIPS "We strongly recommend reading at least 12 issues of the magazine before submitting queries. We are a good market for any writer willing to do the necessary homework. Write for a boy you know who is 12. Our readers demand punchy writing in relatively short, straightforward sentences. The editors demand well-reported articles that demonstrate high standards of journalism. We follow the *Associated Press* manual of style and usage. Learn and read our publications before submitting anything."

BREAD FOR GOD'S CHILDREN

Bread Ministries, INC., P.O. Box 1017, Arcadia FL 34265. (863)494-6214. **E-mail:** bread@breadministries.org. **Website:** www.breadministries.org. **Contact:** Judith M. Gibbs, editor. An interdenominational Christian teaching publication published 4-6 times/year written to aid children and youth in leading a Christian life. Estab. 1972. Circ. 10,000 (US and Canada).

FICTION "We are looking for writers who have a solid knowledge of Biblical principles and are concerned for the youth of today living by those principles. Stories must be well written, with the story itself getting the message across—no preaching, moralizing, or tag endings." Needs historical, religious. Young readers, middle readers, young adult/teen: adventure, religious, problem-solving, sports. Looks for "teaching stories that portray Christian lifestyles without preaching." Send complete ms. Length: 600-800 words for young children; 900-1,500 words for older children. Pays $40-50.

NONFICTION Needs inspirational. , All levels: how-to. "We do not want anything detrimental to solid family values. Most topics will fit if they are slanted to our basic needs." Send complete ms. Length: 500-800 words. Pays on publication

HOW TO CONTACT Responds in 6 months to mss. Publishes ms an average of 6 months after acceptance. Accepts queries by mail.

ILLUSTRATION "The only illustrations we purchase are those occasional good ones accompanying an accepted story."

TERMS Pays on publication. Pays $30-50 for stories; $30 for articles. Sample copies free for 9"x12" SAE and 5 first-class stamps (for 2 copies). Buys first rights. Byline given. No kill fee. 10% freelance written. Sample copy for 9x12 SAE and 5 first-class stamps. Guidelines for #10 SASE.

TIPS "We want stories or articles that illustrate overcoming obstacles by faith and living solid, Christian lives. Know our publication and what we have used in the past. Know the readership and publisher's guidelines. Stories should teach the value of morality and honesty without preaching. Edit carefully for content and grammar."

☻ BRILLIANT STAR

1233 Central St., Evanston IL 60201. (847)853-2354. **E-mail:** brilliant@usbnc.org; arenshaw@usbnc.org. **Website:** www.brilliantstarmagazine.org. **Contact:** Amy Renshaw, senior editor. *Brilliant Star* empowers kids to explore their roles as world citizens. Inspired by the principles of peace and unity in the Baha'i Faith, the magazine and website encourage readers to use their virtues to make the world a better place. Universal values of good character, such as kindness, courage, creativity, and helpfulness, are presented through fiction, nonfiction, activities, interviews, puzzles, cartoons, games, music, and art. " Estab. 1969.

FICTION "We print fiction with kids ages 10-12 as the protagonists who resolve their problems themselves." Submit complete ms. Length: 700-1,400 words. Pays 3 contributor's copies.

NONFICTION Middle readers: arts/crafts, games/ puzzles, geography, how-to, humorous, multicultural, nature/environment, religion, social issues. Query. Length: 300-700 words. Pays 3 contributor's copies.

POETRY "We only publish poetry written by children at the moment."

HOW TO CONTACT Accepts queries by e-mail.

ILLUSTRATION Reviews ms/illustration packages from artists. Illustrations only; query with samples. Contact: Aaron Kreader, graphic designer, at brilliant@usbnc.org. Responds only if interested. Samples kept on file. Credit line given.

PHOTOS Buys photos with accompanying ms only. Model/property release required; captions required. Responds only if interested.

TERMS Buys first rights and reprint rights for mss, artwork, and photos. Byline given. Guidelines available for SASE or via e-mail.

TIPS "*Brilliant Star*'s content is developed with a focus on children in their 'tween' years, ages 8-12. This is a period of intense emotional, physical, and psychological development. Familiarize yourself with the interests and challenges of children in this age range. Protagonists in our fiction are usually in the upper part of our age range: 10-12 years old. They solve their problems without adult intervention. We appreciate seeing a sense of humor but not related to bodily functions or put-downs. Keep your language and concepts age-appropriate. Use short words, sentences, and paragraphs. Activities and games may be submitted in rough or final form. Send us a description of your activity along with short, simple instructions. We avoid long, complicated activities that require adult supervision. If you think they will be helpful, please provide step-by-step rough sketches of the instructions. You may also submit photographs to illustrate the activity."

CADET QUEST MAGAZINE

Calvinist Cadet Corps, 1333 Alger St. SE, Grand Rapids MI 49507. (616)241-5616. **Fax:** (616)241-5558. **E-mail:** submissions@calvinistcadets.org. **Website:** www.calvinistcadets.org. **Contact:** Steve Bootsma, editor. Magazine published 7 times/year. *Cadet Quest Magazine* shows boys 9-14 how God is at work in their lives and in the world around them. Estab. 1958. Circ. 6,000.

FICTION "Fast-moving, entertaining stories that appeal to a boy's sense of adventure or to his sense of humor are welcomed. Stories must present Christian life realistically and help boys relate Christian values to their own lives. Stories must have action without long dialogues. Favorite topics for boys include sports and athletes, humor, adventure, mystery, friends, etc. They must also fit the theme of that issue of *Cadet Quest*. Stories with preachiness and/ or clichés are not of interest to us." No fantasy, science fiction, fashion, horror, or erotica. Send complete ms by mail or e-mail (in body of e-mail; no attachments). Length: 1,000-1,300 words. Pays 5¢/ word and 1 contributor's copy.

NONFICTION Informational. Send complete ms via postal mail or e-mail (in body of e-mail; no attachments). Length: up to 1,500 words. Pays 5¢/ word and 1 contributor's copy.

HOW TO CONTACT Responds in 2 months to mss. Publishes ms 4-11 months after acceptance.

ILLUSTRATION Works on assignment only. Reviews ms/illustration packages from artists.

PHOTOS Pays $5 each for photos purchased with ms.

TERMS Buys all rights, first rights, and second rights. Rights purchased vary with author and material. Byline given. Pays on acceptance. No kill fee. Sample copy for 9"x12" SASE and $1.45 postage. Guidelines online.

TIPS "The best time to submit stories/articles is early in the year (January-April). Also remember readers are boys ages 9-14. Stories must reflect or add to the theme of the issue and be from a Christian perspective."

CLICK

E-mail: click@cricketmedia.com. **Website:** www. cricketmag.com. Magazine covering areas of interest for children ages 3-7. "*Click* is a science and exploration magazine for children ages 3-7. Designed and written with the idea that it's never too early to encourage a child's natural curiosity about the world, *Click*'s 40 full-color pages are filled with amazing photographs, beautiful illustrations, and stories and articles that are both entertaining and thought-provoking." *Does not accept unsolicited mss.*

NONFICTION Query by e-mail with résumé and published clips. Length: 200-500 words.

HOW TO CONTACT Send submissions to: Art Submissions Coordinator, Cricket Media, 70 E. Lake St., Suite 800, Chicago IL 60601. Buys print, digital, promotional rights. Accepts queries by e-mail.

ILLUSTRATION Illustrations are by assignment only. Do not send original artwork. Send postcards, promotional brochures, or color photocopies. Be sure that each sample is marked with your name, address, phone number, and website or blog. Art submissions will not be returned.

TERMS Rights vary. Sample copy available online. Guidelines available online.

TIPS "The best way for writers to understand what *Click* is looking for is to read the magazine. Writers are encouraged to examine several past copies before submitting a query."

COLLEGEXPRESS MAGAZINE

Carnegie Communications, LLC, 2 LAN Dr., Suite 100, Westford MA 01886. **E-mail:** info@carnegiecomm.com. **Website:** www.collegexpress.com. *CollegeXpress Magazine,* formerly *Careers and Colleges,* provides juniors and seniors in high school with editorial, tips, trends, and websites to assist them in the transition to college, career, young adulthood, and independence.

○ Distributed to 10,000 high schools and reaches 1.5 million students.

TIPS "Articles with great quotes, good reporting, good writing. Rich with examples and anecdotes. Must tie in with the objective to help teenaged readers plan for their futures. Current trends, policy changes, and information regarding college admissions, financial aid, and career opportunities."

DIG INTO HISTORY

Cricket Media, Inc., 70 E. Lake Street, #800m, Chicago IL 60601. **E-mail:** dig@cricketmedia.com. **Website:** www.cricketmedia.com. **Contact:** Rosalie F. Baker. *Dig into History* is a magazine on world history and archaeology for kids ages 10-14. Publishes engaging, accurate, educational stories about historical events and people. Its Let's Go Digging section includes articles on archaeological discoveries, as well as the people who discovered them and those who help to preserve them. Estab. 1999.

○ Kids who love DIG are seriously curious and want to immerse themselves in the world of the past. They love the thrill of being transported to ancient times and want to know more about what people did then and why they did it. They are particularly fascinated by traces of long-ago peoples and cultures that have been digging in the dirt and in historical records—and how these traces offer insights into how people live and act today.

FICTION Authentic historical and biographical fiction, adventure, and retold legends relating to the theme. Query by e-mail with brief cover letter, one-page outline, bibliography. Length: 750-1,000 words.

NONFICTION Query by e-mail with brief cover letter, one-page outline, bibliography. Length: 750-1000 words for feature articles; 250-500 words for supplemental nonfiction; up to 700 words for activities.

HOW TO CONTACT Send submissions to: Art Submissions Coordinator, Cricket Media, 70 E. Lake St., Suite 800, Chicago IL 60601. Buys print, digital, promotional rights. Responds to queries in 3-6 months. Accepts queries by mail, e-mail.

ILLUSTRATION Illustrations are by assignment only. Do not send original artwork. Send postcards, promotional brochures, or color photocopies. Be sure that each sample is marked with your name, address, phone number, and website or blog. Art submissions will not be returned.

TERMS Pays after publication. Sample copy available online. Guidelines available online.

TIPS "We are looking for writers who can communicate world history and archaeological concepts in a conversational, interesting, informative, and accurate style for kids. Always welcome if authors can suggest where photography can be located to support their articles."

DRAMATICS MAGAZINE

Educational Theatre Association, 2343 Auburn Ave., Cincinnati OH 45219. (513)421-3900. **E-mail:** gbossler@schooltheatre.org. **Website:** schooltheatre.org. **Contact:** Gregory Bossler, editor-in-chief. *Dramatics* is for students (mainly high school age) and teachers of theater. The magazine wants student readers to grow as theater artists and become a more discerning and appreciative audience. Material is directed to both theater students and their teachers, with strong student slant. Tries to portray the theater community in all its diversity. Estab. 1929. Circ. 45,000.

FICTION Young adults: drama (one-act and full-length plays). "We prefer unpublished scripts that have been produced at least once." Does not want to see plays that show no understanding of the conventions of the theater. No plays for children, no Christmas or didactic "message" plays. Submit complete ms. Buys 5-9 plays/year. Emerging playwrights have better chances with résumé of credits. Length: 10 minutes to full length. Pays $100-500 for plays.

NONFICTION Needs how-to, profile, practical articles on acting, directing, design, production, and other facets of theater; career-oriented profiles of working theater professionals. Submit complete ms. Length: 750-3,000 words. Pays $50-500 for articles.

HOW TO CONTACT Publishes ms 3 months after acceptance. Accepts queries by mail, e-mail.

ILLUSTRATION Buys 3-8 illustrations/year. Works on assignment only. Arrange portfolio review; send résumé, promo sheets, and tearsheets. Responds only if interested. Samples returned with SASE; sample not filed. Credit line given. Pays up to $300 for illustrations.

PHOTOS Buys photos with accompanying ms only. Looking for "good-quality production or candid photography to accompany article. We very occasionally publish photo essays." Model/property release and captions required. Prefers hi-res JPG files. Will consider prints or transparencies. Query with résumé of credits. Responds only if interested.

TERMS Byline given. Pays on acceptance. Sample copy available for 9"x12" SAE with 4-ounce first-class postage. Guidelines available for SASE.

TIPS "Obtain our writer's guidelines and look at recent back issues. The best way to break in is to know our audience—drama students, teachers, and others interested in theater—and write for them. Writers who have some practical experience in theater, especially in technical areas, have an advantage, but we'll work with anybody who has a good idea. Some freelancers have become regular contributors."

FACES

E-mail: faces@cricketmedia.com. **Website:** www.cricketmedia.com. "Published 9 times/year, *Faces*

covers world culture for ages 9-14. It stands apart from other children's magazines by offering a solid look at 1 subject and stressing strong editorial content, color photographs throughout, and original illustrations. *Faces* offers an equal balance of feature articles and activities, as well as folktales and legends." Estab. 1984. Circ. 15,000.

FICTION Fiction accepted: retold legends, folktales, stories, and original plays from around the world, etc., relating to the theme. Needs ethnic. Query with cover letter, one-page outline, bibliography. Pays 20-25¢/word.

NONFICTION Needs historical, interview, personal experience, photo feature, feature articles (in-depth nonfiction highlighting an aspect of the featured culture, interviews, and personal accounts), 700-800 words; supplemental nonfiction (subjects directly and indirectly related to the theme), 300-600 words. Query by e-mail with cover letter, one-page outline, bibliography. Pays 20-25¢/word.

HOW TO CONTACT Send submissions to: Art Submissions Coordinator, Cricket Media, 70 E. Lake St., Suite 800, Chicago IL 60601.

ILLUSTRATION Illustrations are by assignment only. Do not send original artwork. Send postcards, promotional brochures, or color photocopies. Be sure that each sample is marked with your name, address, phone number, and website or blog. Art submissions will not be returned.

TERMS Buys print, digital, promotional rights. Buys all rights. Byline given. Pays on publication. Offers 50% kill fee. 90-100% freelance written. Sample copy available online. Guidelines available online.

TIPS "Writers are encouraged to study past issues of the magazine to become familiar with our style and content. Writers with anthropological and/or travel experience are particularly encouraged; *Faces* is about world cultures. All feature articles, recipes, and activities are freelance contributions."

FCA MAGAZINE

Fellowship of Christian Athletes, 8701 Leeds Rd., Kansas City MO 64129. (816)921-0909; (800)289-0909. **Fax:** (816)921-8755. **E-mail:** mag@fca.org. **Website:** www.fca.org/mag. **Contact:** Clay Meyer, editor; Matheau Casner, creative director. Published 6 times/year. *FCA Magazine*'s mission is to serve as a ministry tool of the Fellowship of Christian Athletes by informing, inspiring, and involving coaches, athletes and all whom they influence, that they may make an impact for Jesus Christ. Estab. 1959. Circ. 75,000.

NONFICTION Needs inspirational, personal experience, photo feature. Articles should be accompanied by at least 3 quality photos. Query and submit via e-mail. Length: 1,000-2,000 words. Pays $150-400 for assigned and unsolicited articles.

HOW TO CONTACT Responds to queries/mss in 3 months. Publishes ms an average of 4 months after acceptance.

PHOTOS Purchases photos separately. Looking for photos of sports action. Uses color prints and high resolution electronic files of 300 dpi or higher. State availability. Reviews contact sheets. Payment based on size of photo.

TERMS Buys first rights and second serial (reprint) rights. Byline given. Pays on publication. No kill fee. 50% freelance written. Prefers to work with published/established writers, but works with a growing number of new/unpublished writers each year. Sample copy for $2 and 9"x12" SASE with 3 first-class stamps. Guidelines available at www.fca.org/mag/media-kit.

TIPS "Profiles and interviews of particular interest to coed athlete, primarily high school and college age. Our graphics and editorial content appeal to youth. The area most open to freelancers is profiles on or interviews with well-known athletes or coaches (male, female, minorities) who have been or are involved in some capacity with FCA."

THE FRIEND MAGAZINE

The Church of Jesus Christ of Latter-day Saints, 50 E. North Temple St., Salt Lake City UT 84150. (801)240-2210. **Fax:** (801)240-2270. **E-mail:** friend@ldschurch.org. **Website:** www.lds.org/friend. **Contact:** Paul B. Pieper, editor; Mark W. Robison, art director. Monthly magazine for 3-12 year olds. "*The Friend* is published by The Church of Jesus Christ of Latter-day Saints for boys and girls up to 3-12 years of age." Estab. 1971.

FICTION Wants illustrated stories and "For Little Friends" stories. See guidelines online.

NONFICTION Needs historical, humor, inspirational.

POETRY Pays $30 for poems.

ILLUSTRATION Illustrations only: Query with samples; arrange personal interview to show portfolio; provide résumé and tearsheets for files.

TERMS Available online.

FUN FOR KIDZ

P.O. Box 227, Bluffton OH 45817. 419-358-4610. **Website:** funforkidz.com. **Contact:** Marilyn Edwards, articles editor. "*Fun For Kidz* is an activity magazine that maintains the wholesome values. Each issue is also created around a theme. There is nothing in the magazine to make it out dated. *Fun For Kidz* offers creative activities for children with extra time on their hands." Estab. 2002.

NONFICTION Picture-oriented material. Young readers, middle readers: animal, arts/crafts, cooking, games/puzzles, history, hobbies, how-to, humorous, problem-solving, sports, carpentry projects. Submit complete ms with SASE, contact info, and notation of which upcoming theme your content should be considered for. Length: 300-750 words. Pays minimum 5¢/word for articles; variable rate for games and projects, etc.

HOW TO CONTACT Accepts queries by mail.

ILLUSTRATION Works on assignment mostly. "We are anxious to find artists capable of illustrating stories and features. Our inside art is pen and ink." Query with samples. Samples kept on file. Pays $35 for full page and $25 for partial page.

PHOTOS "We use a number of b&w photos inside the magazine; most support the articles used." Photos should be in color. Pays $5 per photo.

TERMS Buys first North American serial rights. Byline given. Pays on acceptance. Sample copy: $6 in US, $9 in Canada, and $12.25 internationally. Guidelines online.

TIPS "Our point of view is that every child deserves the right to be a child for a number of years before he or she becomes a young adult. As a result, *Fun for Kidz* looks for activities that deal with timeless topics, such as pets, nature, hobbies, science, games, sports, careers, simple cooking, and anything else likely to interest a child."

GIRLS' LIFE

3 S. Frederick St., Suite 806, Baltimore MD 21202. (410)426-9600. **Fax:** (866)793-1531. **Website:** www.girlslife.com. **Contact:** Karen Bokram, founding editor and publisher; Kelsey Haywood, senior editor;

Chun Kim, art director. Bimonthly magazine covering girls ages 9-15. Estab. 1994. Circ. 2.16 million.

FICTION "We accept short fiction. They should be stand-alone stories and are generally 2,500-3,500 words." Needs short stories.

NONFICTION Needs book excerpts, essays, general interest, how-to, humor, inspirational, interview, new product, travel. Query by mail with published clips. Submit complete ms on spec only. "Features and articles should speak to young women ages 10-15 looking for new ideas about relationships, family, friends, school, etc., with fresh, savvy advice. Front-of-the-book columns and quizzes are a good place to start." Length: 700-2,000 words. Pays $350/regular column; $500/feature.

HOW TO CONTACT Editorial lead time 4 months. Responds in 1 month to queries. Publishes an average of 3 months after acceptance. Accepts queries by mail, e-mail.

PHOTOS State availability with submission if applicable. Reviews contact sheets, negatives, transparencies. Negotiates payment individually. Captions, identification of subjects, model releases required. State availability. Captions, identification of subjects, model releases required. Reviews contact sheets, negatives, transparencies. Negotiates payment individually.

TERMS Buys all rights. Byline given. Pays on publication. Sample copy for $5 or online. Guidelines available online.

TIPS "Send thought-out queries with published writing samples and detailed résumé. Have fresh ideas and a voice that speaks to our audience—not down to them. And check out a copy of the magazine or visit girlslife.com before submitting."

GREEN TEACHER

Green Teacher, 95 Robert St., Toronto, Ontario M5S 2K5, Canada. (416)960-1244. **Fax:** (416)925-3474. **E-mail:** tim@greenteacher.com; info@greenteacher.com. **Website:** www.greenteacher.com. **Contact:** Tim Grant, co-editor; Amy Stubbs, editorial assistant. "We're a nonprofit organization dedicated to helping educators, both inside and outside of schools, promote environmental awareness among young people aged 6-19." Estab. 1991. Circ. 15,000.

NONFICTION Multicultural, nature, environment. Query. Submit one-page summary or outline. Length: 1,500-3,500 words.

HOW TO CONTACT Responds to queries in 1 week. Publishes ms 8 months after acceptance. Accepts queries by mail, e-mail.

ILLUSTRATION Buys 3 illustrations/issue from freelancers; 10 illustrations/year from freelancers. B&w artwork only. Works on assignment only. Reviews ms/illustration packages from artists. Query with samples; tearsheets. Responds only if interested. Samples not returned. Samples filed. Credit line given.

PHOTOS Purchases photos both separately and with accompanying mss. "Activity photos, environmental photos." Query with samples. Responds only of interested.

HIGHLIGHTS FOR CHILDREN

803 Church St., Honesdale PA 18431. (570)253-1080. **Fax:** (570)251-7847. **Website:** www.highlights.com. **Contact:** Christine French Cully, editor-in-chief. Monthly magazine for children up to ages 6-12. "This book of wholesome fun is dedicated to helping children grow in basic skills and knowledge, in creativeness, in ability to think and reason, in sensitivity to others, in high ideals, and worthy ways of living—for children are the world's most important people. We publish stories for beginning and advanced readers. Up to 500 words for beginning readers, up to 800 words for advanced readers." Estab. 1946. Circ. approximately 1.5 million.

FICTION Meaningful stories appealing to both girls and boys, up to age 12. Vivid, full of action. Engaging plot, strong characterization, lively language. Prefers stories in which a child protagonist solves a dilemma through his or her own resources. Seeks stories that the child ages 8-12 will eagerly read, and the younger child will like to hear when read aloud (500-800 words). Stories require interesting plots and a number of illustration possiblities. Also need rebuses (picture stories 100 words), stories with urban settings, stories for beginning readers (100-500 words), sports and humorous stories, adventures, holiday stories, and mysteries. We also would like to see more material of 1-page length (300 words), both fiction and factual. Needs adventure, fantasy, historical, humorous, animal, contemporary, folktales, multicultural, problem-solving, sports. No stories glorifying war, crime, or violence. Send complete ms. Pays $150 minimum plus 2 contributor's copies.

NONFICTION "Generally we prefer to see a manuscript rather than a query. However, we will review queries regarding nonfiction." Length: 800 words maximum. Pays $25 for craft ideas and puzzles; $25 for fingerplays; $150 and up for articles.

POETRY Lines/poem: 16 maximum ("most poems are shorter"). Considers simultaneous submissions ("please indicate"); no previously published poetry. No e-mail submissions. "Submit typed manuscript with very brief cover letter." Occasionally comments on submissions "if manuscript has merit or author seems to have potential for our market." Guidelines available for SASE. Responds "generally within 2 months." Always sends prepublication galleys. Pays 2 contributor's copies; "money varies." Acquires all rights.

HOW TO CONTACT Responds in 2 months to queries. Accepts queries by mail.

PHOTOS Reviews electronic files, color 35mm slides, photos.

TERMS Buys all rights. Pays on acceptance. 80% freelance written. Sample copy free. Guidelines on website in "Company" area.

TIPS "Know the magazine's style before submitting. Send for guidelines and sample issue if necessary." Writers: "At *Highlights* we're paying closer attention to acquiring more nonfiction for young readers than we have in the past." Illustrators: "Fresh, imaginative work encouraged. Flexibility in working relationships a plus. Illustrators presenting their work need not confine themselves to just children's illustrations as long as work can translate to our needs. We also use animal illustrations, real and imaginary. We need crafts, puzzles, and any activity that will stimulate children mentally and creatively. Know our publication's standards and content by reading sample issues, not just the guidelines. Avoid tired themes, or put a fresh twist on an old theme so that its style is fun and lively. Write what inspires you, not what you think the market needs. We are pleased that many authors of children's literature report that their first published work was in the pages of *Highlights*. It is not our policy to consider fiction on the strength of the reputation of the author. We judge each submission on its own merits. Query with simple letter to establish whether the nonfiction subject is likely to be of interest. Expert reviews and complete bibliography required for nonfiction. A beginning writer should first become familiar with the type of material that *Highlights* publishes. Include special qualifications, if any, of author.

Write for the child, not the editor. Write in a voice that children understand and relate to. Speak to today's kids, avoiding didactic, overt messages. Even though our general principles haven't changed over the years, we are contemporary in our approach to issues. Avoid worn themes."

HUNGER MOUNTAIN

Vermont College of Fine Arts, 36 College St., Montpelier VT 05602. (802)828-8517. **E-mail:** hunger-mtn@vcfa.edu. **Website:** www.hungermtn.org. "We accept picture book, middle grade, young adult, and young adult crossover work (text only—for now). We're looking for polished pieces that entertain, that show the range of adolescent experience, and that are compelling, creative, and will appeal to the devoted followers of the kid-lit craft, as well as the child inside us all." Miciah Gault, Editor. **Contact:** Katie Stromme, Assistant Editor. Annual perfect-bound journal covering high-quality fiction, poetry, creative nonfiction, craft essays, writing for children, and artwork. Four contests held annually, one in each genre. Accepts high-quality work from unknown, emerging, or successful writers. Publishing fiction, creative nonfiction, poetry, and young adult & children's writing. Four writing contests annually. Estab. 2002. Circ. 1,000.

Hunger Mountain is a print and online journal of the arts. The print journal is about 200 pages, 7"x9", professionally printed, perfect-bound, with full-bleed color artwork on cover. Press run is 1,000. Over 10,000 visits online monthly. Uses online submissions manager (Submittable). Member: CLMP.

FICTION "We look for work that is beautifully crafted and tells a good story, with characters that are alive and kicking, storylines that stay with us long after we've finished reading, and sentences that slay us with their precision." Needs experimental, humorous, novel excerpts, short stories, slice-of-life vignettes. No genre fiction, meaning science fiction, fantasy, horror, detective, erotic, etc. Submit ms using online submissions manager: https://hunger-mtn.submittable.com/submit. Length: up to 10,000 words. $50 for general fiction.

NONFICTION "We welcome an array of traditional and experimental work, including, but not limited to, personal, lyrical, and meditative essays, memoirs, collages, rants, and humor. The only requirements are recognition of truth, a unique voice with a firm command of language, and an engaging story with multiple pressure points.". Submit complete ms using online submissions manager at Submittable: https://hungermtn.submittable.com/submit. Length: up to 10,000 words. $50 for general fiction or creative nonfiction, for both children's lit and general adult lit.

POETRY Submit 1-5 poems at a time. "We are looking for truly original poems that run the aesthetic gamut: lively engagement with language in the act of pursuit. Some poems remind us in a fresh way of our own best thoughts; some poems bring us to a place beyond language for which there aren't quite words; some poems take us on a complicated language ride that is, itself, its own aim. Complex poem-architectures thrill us and still-points in the turning world do, too. Send us the best of what you have." Submit using online submissions manager. No light verse, humor/quirky/catchy verse, greeting card verse. $25 for poetry up to two poems (plus $5 per poem for additional poems); $25 for poetry, up to two poems (plus $5 per poem for additional poems).

HOW TO CONTACT Responds in 4 months to mss. Publishes ms an average of 1 year after acceptance. Accepts queries by online submission form.

PHOTOS Send photos. Reviews contact sheets, transparencies, prints, GIF/JPEG files. Slides preferred. Negotiates payment individually.

TERMS Buys first worldwide serial rights. Byline given. Pays on publication. No kill fee. Single issue: $12; subscription: $18 for 2 issues/2 years; back issue: $8. Checks payable to Vermont College of Fine Arts, or purchase online http://hungermtn.org/subscribe. Guidelines online at http://hungermtn.org/submit.

TIPS "Mss must be typed, prose double-spaced. Poets submit poems as one document. No multiple genre submissions. Fresh viewpoints and human interest are very important, as is originality and diversity. We are committed to publishing an outstanding journal of the arts. Do not send entire novels, mss, or short story collections. Do not send previously published work."

IMAGINATION CAFÉ

Imagination Café, P.O. Box 1536, Valparaiso IN 46384. (219)510-4467. **E-mail:** editor@imagination-cafe.com. **Website:** www.imagination-cafe.com. **Contact:** Rosanne Tolin, contact. "*Imagination Café* is dedicated to empowering kids and tweens by encouraging curiosity in the world around them, as well as exploration of their talents and aspirations. *Imagination Café*'s mission is to offer children tools to discover their passions by providing them with reliable information, resources and safe opportunities for self-expression." Estab. 2006.

NONFICTION Manuscripts are preferred over queries. Varies. Under 1,000 words.

HOW TO CONTACT Accepts queries by e-mail.

KEYS FOR KIDS DEVOTIONAL

Keys for Kids Ministries, 2060 43rd St. SE, Grand Rapids MI 49508. **E-mail:** editorial@keysforkids.org. **Website:** www.keysforkids.org. **Contact:** Courtney Lasater, editor. Quarterly devotional featuring daily stories and Scripture verses for children ages 6-12 that ignite a passion for Christ in kids and their families. Estab. 1982. Circ. 60,000 print (not including digital circulation).

○ Please put your name and contact information on the first page of your submission. We strongly prefer receiving submissions via our website. Story length is typically 340-375 words. Devotional submissions for teens ages 13-17 also welcome. To see full guidelines or submit a story, please go to www.keysforkids.org/writersguidelines.

FICTION Needs short contemporary stories with spiritual applications for kids. Please suggest a key verse and an appropriate Scripture passage, generally 3-10 verses, to reinforce the theme of your story. Up to 375 words. Pays $30.

HOW TO CONTACT Editorial lead time 6-8 months. Responds in 2-4 months. Typically publishes stories 6-9 months after acceptance. Accepts queries by e-mail.

TERMS Buys all rights. Byline given. Pays on acceptance. 95% freelance. Sample copy online. Guidelines online: www.keysforkids.org/writersguidelines.

TIPS "Please follow writer's guidelines at www.keysforkids.org/writersguidelines."

LEADING EDGE MAGAZINE

4087 JKB, Provo UT 84602. **E-mail:** editor@leadingedgemagazine.com; fiction@leadingedgemagazine.com; art@leadingedgemagazine.com; poetry@

leadingedgemagazine.com; nonfiction@lead-ingedgemagazine.com. **Website:** www.leading-edgemagazine.com. **Contact:** Hayley Brooks, editor in chief. Semiannual magazine covering science fiction and fantasy. "*Leading Edge* is a magazine dedicated to new and upcoming talent in the fields of science fiction and fantasy. We strive to encourage developing and established talent and provide high-quality speculative fiction to our readers." Does not accept mss with sex, excessive violence, or profanity. Estab. 1981. Circ. 200.

Accepts unsolicited submissions.

FICTION Needs fantasy, science fiction. Send complete ms with cover letter and SASE. Include estimated word count. Length: up to 15,000 words. Pays 1¢/word; $50 maximum.

NONFICTION Needs essays, expose, interview, reviews. Send complete ms with cover letter and SASE. Include estimated word count. Length: up to 15,000 words. Pays 1¢/word; $50 maximum.

POETRY Publishes 2-4 poems per issue. Poetry should reflect both literary value and popular appeal and should deal with science fiction- or fantasy-related themes. No e-mail submissions. Cover letter is preferred. Include name, address, phone number, length of poem, title, and type of poem at the top of each page. Please include SASE with every submission. Pays $10 for first 4 pages; $1.50/each subsequent page.

HOW TO CONTACT Responds within 12 months to mss. Publishes ms an average of 2-4 months after acceptance. Accepts queries by mail, e-mail.

ILLUSTRATION Buys 24 illustrations/issue; 48 illustrations/year. Uses b&w artwork only. Works on assignment only. Contact: Art Director. Illustrations only: Send postcard sample with portfolio, samples, URL. Responds only if interested. Samples filed. Credit line given.

TERMS Buys first North American serial rights. Byline given. Pays on publication. No kill fee. 90% freelance written. Single copy: $5.95. "We no longer provide subscriptions, but *Leading Edge* is now available on Amazon Kindle, as well as print-on-demand." Guidelines available online.

TIPS "Buy a sample issue to know what is currently selling in our magazine. Also, make sure to follow the writer's guidelines when submitting."

THE LOUISVILLE REVIEW

Spalding University, 851 S. Fourth St., Louisville KY 40203. (502)873-4398. **Fax:** (502)992-2409. **E-mail:** louisvillereview@spalding.edu. **Website:** www.louisvillereview.org. **Contact:** Ellyn Lichvar, managing editor. *The Louisville Review*, published twice/year, prints poetry, fiction, nonfiction, and drama. Has a section devoted to poetry by writers under age 18 (grades K-12) called "The Children's Corner." Estab. 1976.

The Louisville Review is 150 pages, digest-sized, flat-spined. Receives about 700 submissions/year, accepts about 10% of submissions.

FICTION Needs short stories. Submit complete ms by mail or online submissions manager. Also publishes plays. No word limit, but prefers shorter pieces. Pays contributor's copies.

NONFICTION Needs essays. Submit complete ms by mail or online submissions manager. No word limit, but prefers shorter pieces. Pays contributor's copies.

POETRY Accepts submissions via mail and online manager; please see website for more information. "Poetry by children must include permission of parent to publish if accepted. Address those submissions to 'The Children's Corner.'" Reads submissions year round. Has published poetry by Wendy Bishop, Gary Fincke, Michael Burkard, and Sandra Kohler. Pays contributor's copies.

HOW TO CONTACT Responds in 3-6 months to mss. Accepts queries by mail, online submission form.

TERMS Sample copy: $5. Single copy: $8. Subscription: $14/year, $27/2 years, $40/3 years (foreign subscribers add $6/year for s&h). Guidelines online.

MAGIC DRAGON

Association for Encouragement of Children's Creativity, P.O. Box 687, Webster NY 14580. **E-mail:** magicdragonmagazine@gmail.com; info.@magicdragonmagazine.com. **Website:** www.magicdragonmagazine.com. **Contact:** Patricia A. Roesch. Quarterly magazine publishes children's writing and art (no photography). "All work is created by children age 12 and younger (elementary school grades). We consider stories, poems, and artwork. Queries, writing, and art accepted by USPS mail and by e-mail." Nonprofit, educational magazine. Estab. 2005. Circ. 3,500.

O   Magic Dragon exists solely to encourage creative expression in young children and to support the arts in education.

FICTION Needs adventure, fantasy, historical, humorous. Submit complete ms. Pays 1 contributor's copy.

NONFICTION Needs essays, humor, inspirational, personal experience. Send complete ms. Length: up to 250 words. Pays 1 contributor's copy.

POETRY Length: up to 30 lines/poem. Pays 1 contributor's copy.

HOW TO CONTACT Editorial lead time 3-6 months. Time between acceptance and publication varies. Accepts queries by mail, e-mail.

TERMS No rights purchased. Byline given. Pays contributor's copy on publication. No kill fee. No freelance. Sample: $4. Guidelines available online. Submit writing as Word document or Word document attachment, 12 point New Times Roman or carefully printed; art as jpeg or original. Include SASE for return of art. Be sure postage is adequate.

TIPS "Artists: Include a SASE with adequate postage with all original artwork. If it's a copy, make sure the colors and copy are the same and the lines are clear. Include an explanation of how you created the art (crayon, watercolor, paper sculpture, etc.)."

NATIONAL GEOGRAPHIC KIDS

National Geographic Society, 1145 17th St. NW, Washington DC 20036. **E-mail:** ashaw@ngs.org. **Website:** www.kids.nationalgeographic.com. **Contact:** Michelle Tyler, editorial assistant. Magazine published 10 times/year. "It's our mission to find fresh ways to entertain children while educating and exciting them about their world." Estab. 1975. Circ. 1.3 million.

O   "We do not want poetry, sports, fiction, or story ideas that are too young—our audience is between ages 6-14."

NONFICTION Needs general interest, humor, interview, technical. Query with published clips and résumé. Length: 100-1,000 words. Pays $1/word for assigned articles.

HOW TO CONTACT Editorial lead time 6+ months. Publishes ms an average of 6 months after acceptance. Accepts queries by mail.

PHOTOS State availability. Captions, identification of subjects, model releases required. Reviews

contact sheets, negatives, transparencies, prints. Negotiates payment individually.

TERMS Buys all rights. Makes work-for-hire assignments. Byline given. Pays on acceptance. Offers 10% kill fee. 70% freelance written. Sample copy for #10 SASE. Guidelines online.

TIPS "Submit relevant clips. Writers must have demonstrated experience writing for kids. Read the magazine before submitting."

NATURE FRIEND MAGAZINE

4253 Woodcock Lane, Dayton VA 22821. (540)867-0764. **E-mail:** info@naturefriendmagazine.com; editor@naturefriendmagazine.com; photos@naturefriendmagazine.com. **Website:** www.naturefriendmagazine.com. **Contact:** Kevin Shank, editor. Monthly children's magazine covering creation-based nature. *Nature Friend* includes stories, puzzles, science experiments, and nature experiments. All submissions need to honor God as creator. Estab. 1983. Circ. 8,000.

O   Picture-oriented material and conversational material needed.

NONFICTION Needs how-to. Send complete ms. Length: 250-900 words. Pays 5¢/word.

HOW TO CONTACT Editorial lead time 4 months. Responds in 6 months to mss.

PHOTOS Send photos. Captions, identification of subjects required. Reviews prints. Offers $20-75/photo.

TERMS Buys first rights, buys one-time rights. Byline given. Pays on publication. No kill fee. 80% freelance written. Sample copy: $5, postage paid. Guidelines available on website.

TIPS "We want to bring joy and knowledge to children by opening the world of God's creation to them. We endeavor to create a sense of awe about nature's Creator and a respect for His creation. We'd like to see more submissions on hands-on things to do with a nature theme (not collecting rocks or leaves—real stuff). Also looking for good stories that are accompanied by good photography."

NEW MOON GIRLS

New Moon Girl Media, P.O. Box 161287, Duluth MN 55816. (218)728-5507. **Fax:** (218)728-0314. **Website:** www.newmoon.com. Bimonthly magazine covering girls ages 8-14, edited by girls ages 8-14. *"New Moon Girls* is for every girl who wants her voice heard and her dreams taken seriously. *New Moon* celebrates girls, explores the passage from girl to woman, and builds healthy resistance to gender inequities. The *New Moon* girl is true to herself, and *New Moon Girls* helps her as she pursues her unique path in life, moving confidently into the world." Estab. 1992. Circ. 30,000.

○ In general, all material should be pro-girl and feature girls and women as the primary focus.

FICTION Prefers girl-written material. All girl-centered. Needs adventure, fantasy, historical, humorous, slice-of-life vignettes. Send complete ms by e-mail. Length: 900-1,600 words. Pays 6-12¢/word.

NONFICTION Needs essays, general interest, humor, inspirational, interview, opinion, personal experience, photo feature, religious. Send complete ms by e-mail. Publishes nonfiction by adults in Herstory and Women's Work departments only. Length: 600 words. Pays 6-12¢/word.

POETRY No poetry by adults.

HOW TO CONTACT Editorial lead time 6 months. Responds in 2 months to mss. Publishes ms an average of 6 months after acceptance. Accepts queries by mail, e-mail, fax.

ILLUSTRATION Buys 6-12 illustrations/year from freelancers. *New Moon* seeks 4-color cover illustrations. Reviews ms/illustrations packages from artists. Query. Submit ms with rough sketches. Illustration only: Query; send portfolio and tearsheets. Samples not returned; samples filed. Responds in 6 months only if interested. Credit line given.

PHOTOS State availability. Captions, identification of subjects required. Negotiates payment individually.

TERMS Buys all rights. Byline given. Pays on publication. 25% freelance written. Sample copy: $7.50 or online. Guidelines available at website.

TIPS "We'd like to see more girl-written feature articles that relate to a theme. These can be about anything the girl has done personally, or she can write about something she's studied. Please read *New Moon Girls* before submitting to get a sense of our style. Writers and artists who comprehend our goals have the best chance of publication. We love creative articles—both nonfiction and fiction—that are not condescending to our readers. Keep articles to suggested word lengths; avoid stereotypes. Refer to our guidelines and upcoming themes online."

ON COURSE

The General Council of the Assemblies of God, 1445 Boonville Ave., Springfield MO 65802-1894. (417)862-2781. **Fax:** (417)862-1693. **E-mail:** oncourse@ag.org. **Website:** www.oncourse.ag.org. **Contact:** Amber Weigand-Buckley, editor; Josh Carter, art director. *ONCOURSE* is a magazine to empower students to grow in a real-life relationship with Christ. Estab. 1991.

○ *ONCOURSE* no longer uses illustrations, only photos. Works on assignment basis only. Résumés and writing samples will be considered for inclusion in Writer's File to receive story assignments.

FICTION Length: 800 words.

NONFICTION "Submit an audition manuscript of less than 1,200 words. *ONCOURSE* evaluates manuscripts to determine if you, as a writer, fit our magazine. We will not print them—we do not purchase unsolicited articles. Article assignments go to writers listed in our Writer's File and focus on scheduled topics. If we approve you for our Writers File, we will also issue you a password for Writers Only, where we post these themes." Pays $40 for columns, $80 for two-page features, $15 for sidebars/reviews, and $30 for Web-only features.

PHOTOS Buys photos from freelancers. "Teen life, church life, college life; unposed; often used for illustrative purposes." Model/property releases required. Uses color glossy prints and 35mm or 2½"×2¼" transparencies. Query with samples; send business card, promotional literature, tearsheets or catalog. Responds only if interested.

TERMS Buys first or reprint rights for mss. Byline given. Pays on acceptance. Sample copy free for 9"x11" SASE. Guidelines on website.

POCKETS

The Upper Room, P.O. Box 340004, Nashville TN 37203. (615)340-7333. **E-mail:** pockets@upperroom.org. **Website:** pockets.upperroom.org. **Contact:** Lynn W. Gilliam, editor. Magazine published 11 times/year. "*Pockets* is a Christian devotional magazine for children ages 6-12. All submissions should address the broad theme of the magazine. Each issue is built around a theme with material which can be used by children in a variety of ways. Scripture stories, fiction, poetry, prayers, art, graphics, puzzles and activities are included. Submissions do not need to be overtly religious. They should help children experience a Christian lifestyle that is not always a neatly wrapped moral package but is open to the continuing revelation of God's will. Seasonal material, both secular and liturgical, is desired." Estab. 1981.

🔾 Does not accept e-mail or fax submissions.

FICTION "Stories should contain lots of action, use believable dialogue, be simply written, and be relevant to the problems faced by this age group in everyday life." Submit complete ms by mail. No e-mail submissions. Length: 600-1,000 words.

NONFICTION , Picture-oriented, young readers, middle readers: cooking, games/puzzles. Submit complete ms by mail. No e-mail submissions. Length: 400-1,000 words. Pays 14¢/word.

POETRY Both seasonal and theme poems needed. Considers poetry by children. Length: up to 20 lines. Pays $25 minimum.

HOW TO CONTACT Responds in 8 weeks to mss. Publishes ms an average of 1 year after acceptance.

PHOTOS Send 4-6 close-up photos of children actively involved in peacemakers at work activities. Send photos, contact sheets, prints, or digital images. Must be 300 dpi. Pays $25/photo.

TERMS Buys first North American serial rights. Byline given. Pays on acceptance. No kill fee. 60% freelance written. Each issue reflects a specific theme. Guidelines online.

TIPS "Theme stories, role models, and retold scripture stories are most open to freelancers. Poetry is also open. It is very helpful if writers read our writers' guidelines and themes on our website."

Ⓐ SEVENTEEN MAGAZINE

300 W. 57th St., 17th Floor, New York NY 10019. (917)934-6500. **Fax:** (917)934-6574. **E-mail:** mail@seventeen.com. **Website:** www.seventeen.com. **Contact:** Consult masthead to contact appropriate editor. Monthly magazine covering topics geared toward young adult American women. "We reach 14.5 million girls each month. Over the past 6 decades, *Seventeen* has helped shape teenage life in America. We represent an important rite of passage, helping to define, socialize, and empower young women. We create notions of beauty and style, proclaim what's hot in popular culture, and identify social issues." Estab. 1944. Circ. 2,000,000.

🔾 *Seventeen* no longer accepts fiction submissions.

NONFICTION Query by mail. Consult masthead to pitch appropriate editor. Length: 200-2,000 words.

HOW TO CONTACT Accepts queries by mail.

ILLUSTRATION *Only interested in agented material.* Buys 10 illustrations/issue; 120 illustrations/year. Works on assignment only. Reviews ms/illustration packages. Illustrations only: Query with samples. Responds only if interested. Samples not returned; samples filed. Credit line given.

PHOTOS Looking for photos to match current stories. Model/property releases required; captions required. Uses color, 8×10 prints; 35mm, 2¼×2¼, 4×5, or 8×10 transparencies. Query with samples or résumé of credits, or submit portfolio for review. Responds only if interested.

TERMS Buys first North American serial rights, first rights, or all rights. Buys exclusive rights for 3 months. Byline sometimes given. Pays on publication. Writer's guidelines for SASE.

TIPS "Send for guidelines before submitting."

SHINE BRIGHTLY

GEMS Girls' Clubs, 1333 Alger St., SE, Grand Rapids MI 49507. (616)241-5616. **Fax:** (616)241-5558. **E-mail:** shinebrightly@gemsgc.org. **Website:** www.gemsgc.org. **Contact:** Kelli Gilmore, managing editor. Monthly magazine (with combined May/June/July/August summer issue). "Our purpose is to lead girls into a living relationship with Jesus Christ and to help them see how God is at work in their lives and the world around them. Puzzles, crafts, stories, and articles for girls ages 9-14." Estab. 1970. Circ. 14,000.

FICTION Does not want "unrealistic stories and those with trite, easy endings. We are interested in manuscripts that show how real girls can change the world." Needs ethnic, historical, humorous, mystery, religious, slice-of-life vignettes. Believable only. Nothing too preachy. Submit complete ms in body of e-mail. No attachments. Length: 700-900 words. Pays up to $35, plus 2 copies.

NONFICTION Needs humor, inspirational, interview, personal experience, photo feature, religious, travel. Submit complete ms in body of e-mail. No attachments. Length: 100-800 words. Pays up to $35, plus 2 copies.

POETRY Limited need for poetry. Pays $5-15.

HOW TO CONTACT Responds in 2 months to mss. Publishes ms an average of 4 months after acceptance.

ILLUSTRATION Samples returned with SASE. Credit line given.

PHOTOS Purchased with or without ms. Appreciate multicultural subjects. Reviews 5"x7" or 8"x10" clear color glossy prints. Pays $25-50 on publication.

TERMS Buys first North American serial rights, buys second serial (reprint) rights, buys simultaneous rights. Byline given. Pays on publication. No kill fee. 60% freelance written. Works with new and published/established writers. Sample copy with 9"x12" SASE with 3 first class stamps and $1. Guidelines available online.

TIPS Writers: "Please check our website before submitting. We have a specific style and theme that deals with how girls can impact the world. The stories should be current, deal with pre-adolescent problems and joys, and help girls see God at work in their lives through humor as well as problem-solving." Prefers not to see anything on the adult level, secular material, or violence. Writers frequently oversimplify the articles and often write with a Pollyanna attitude. An author should be able to see his/her writing style as exciting and appealing to girls ages 9-14. The style can be fun, but also teach a truth. Subjects should be current and important to *SHINE brightly* readers. Use our theme update as a guide. We would like to receive material with a multicultural slant."

SKIPPING STONES: A MULTICULTURAL LITERARY MAGAZINE

P.O. Box 3939, Eugene OR 97403-0939. (541)342-4956. **E-mail:** editor@skippingstones.org. **Website:** www.skippingstones.org. **Contact:** Arun Toké, editor. "*Skipping Stones* is an award-winning multicultural, nonprofit magazine designed to promote cooperation, creativity, and celebration of cultural and ecological richness. We encourage submissions by children of color, minorities, and under-represented populations. We want material meant for children and young adults/teenagers with multicultural or ecological awareness themes. Think, live, and write as if you were a child, tween, or teen. We want material that gives insight to cultural celebrations, lifestyle, customs and traditions, glimpse of daily life in other countries and cultures. Photos, songs, artwork are most welcome if they illustrate/highlight the points. Translations are invited if your submission is in a language other than English." Themes may include cultural celebrations, living abroad, challenging disability, hospitality customs of various cultures, cross-cultural understanding, African, Asian, and Latin American cultures, humor, international understanding, turning points, and magical moments in life, caring for the earth, spirituality, and multicultural awareness. *Skipping Stones* is magazine-sized, saddle-stapled, printed on recycled paper. Published quarterly during the school year (4 issues). Estab. 1988. Circ. 1,600 print, plus Web.

FICTION Middle readers, young adult/teens: contemporary, meaningful, humorous. All levels: folktales, multicultural, nature/environment. Multicultural needs include: bilingual or multilingual pieces; use of words from other languages; settings in other countries, cultures, or multiethnic communities. Needs adventure, ethnic, historical, humorous, multicultural, international, social issues. No suspense or romance stories. Send complete ms. Length: 1,000 words maximum. Pays 6 contributor's copies.

NONFICTION Needs essays, general interest, humor, inspirational, interview, opinion, personal experience, photo feature, travel. All levels: animal, biography, cooking, games/puzzles, history, humorous, interview/profile, multicultural, nature/environment, creative problem-solving, religion and cultural celebrations, sports, travel, social and international awareness. Does not want to see preaching, violence, or abusive language. Send complete ms. Length: 1,000 words maximum. Pays 6 contributor's copies.

POETRY Submit up to 5 poems at a time. Considers simultaneous submissions; no previously published poems. Accepts e-mail submissions. Cover letter is preferred. "Include your cultural background, experiences, and the inspiration behind your creation." Time between acceptance and publication is 6-9 months. "A piece is chosen for publication when most of the editorial staff feel good about it." Seldom comments on rejected poems. Publishes multi-theme issues. Responds in up to 4 months. Length: 30 lines maximum. Pays 2 contributor's copies, offers 40% discount for more copies and subscription, if desired.

HOW TO CONTACT Editorial lead time 3-4 months. Responds only if interested. Send nonreturnable samples. Publishes ms an average of 4-8 months after acceptance. Accepts queries by mail, e-mail.

ILLUSTRATION Prefers illustrations by teenagers and young adults. Will consider all illustration packages. Manuscript/illustration packages: Query; submit complete ms with final art; submit tearsheets. Responds in 4 months. Credit line given.

PHOTOS Black & white photos preferred, but color photos with good contrast are welcome. Needs: youth 7-17, international, nature, celebrations. Send photos. Captions required. Reviews 4"x6" prints, low-res JPEG files. Offers no additional payment for photos.

TERMS Buys first North American serial rights, nonexclusive reprint, and electronic rights. Byline given. Sends contributor copies upon publication. No kill fee. 80% freelance written. Sample: $7. Subscription: $25. Guidelines available online or for SASE.

TIPS "Be original and innovative. Use multicultural, nature, or cross-cultural themes. Multilingual submissions are welcome."

SPARKLE

GEMS Girls' Clubs, 1333 Alger St. SE, Grand Rapids MI 49507. (616)241-5616. **Fax:** (616)241-5558. **E-mail:** sparkle@gemsgc.org. **Website:** www.gemsgc. org. **Contact:** Kelli Gilmore, managing editor; Lisa Hunter, art director/photo editor. Monthly magazine for girls ages 6-9 from October to March. Mission is to prepare young girls to live out their faith and become world-changers. Strives to help girls make a difference in the world. Looks at the application of scripture to everyday life. Also strives to delight the reader and cause the reader to evalute her own life in light of the truth presented. Finally, attempts to teach practical life skills. Estab. 2002. Circ. 9,000.

FICTION Young readers: adventure, animal, contemporary, ethnic/multicultural, fantasy, folktale, health, history, humorous, music and musicians, mystery, nature/environment, problem-solving, religious, recipes, service projects, slice-of-life, sports, suspense/mystery, vignettes, interacting with family and friends. Send complete ms. Length: 100-400 words. Pays $35 maximum.

NONFICTION Young readers: animal, arts/crafts, biography, careers, cooking, concept, games/puzzles, geography, health, history, hobbies, how-to, humor, inspirational, interview/profile, math, multicultural, music/drama/art, nature/environment, personal experience, photo feature, problem-solving, quizzes, recipes, religious, science, social issues, sports, travel. Looking for inspirational biographies, stories from Zambia, and ideas on how to live a green lifestyle. Send complete ms. Length: 100-400 words. Pays $35 maximum.

POETRY Prefers rhyming. "We do not wish to see anything that is too difficult for a first grader to read. We wish it to remain light. The style can be fun but should also teach a truth." No violence or secular material.

HOW TO CONTACT Editorial lead time 3 months. Responds 3 months to mss. Accepts queries by e-mail.

ILLUSTRATION Buys 1-2 illustrations/issue; 8-10 illustrations/year. Uses color artwork only. Works on assignment only. Reviews ms/illustration packages from artists. Send ms with dummy. Illustrations only: send promo sheet. Contact: Sara DeRidder. Responds in 3 weeks only if interested. Samples returned with SASE; samples filed. Credit line given.

PHOTOS Send photos. Identification of subjects required. Reviews at least 5"x7" clear color glossy prints, GIF/JPEG files on CD. Offers $25-50/photo.

TERMS Buys first North American serial rights, first rights, one-time rights, second serial (reprint), first rights, second rights. Byline given. Pays on publication. 40% freelance written. Sample copy for 9"x13" SASE, 3 first-class stamps, and $1 for coverage/publication cost. Guidelines available for #10 SASE or online.

TIPS "Keep it simple. We are writing to first to third graders. It must be simple yet interesting. Mss should build girls up in Christian character but not be preachy. They are just learning about God and how He wants them to live. Mss should be delightful as well as educational and inspirational. Writers should keep stories simple but not write with a 'Pollyanna' attitude. Authors should see their writing style as exciting and appealing to girls ages 6-9. Subjects should be current and important to *Sparkle* readers. Use our theme as a guide. We would like to receive material with a multicultural slant."

STONE SOUP

The Magazine by Young Writers & Artists, Children's Art Foundation, P.O. Box 83, Santa Cruz CA 95063-0083. (831)426-5557. **E-mail:** editor@stonesoup.com. **Website:** https://stonesoup.com/. **Contact:** Ms. Gerry Mandel, editor. Bimonthly magazine of writing and art by children age 13 and under, including fiction, poetry, book reviews, and art. *Stone Soup,* available in print and digital formats, is the national magazine of writing and art by kids, founded in 1973. The print edition is 48 pages, 7x10, professionally printed in color on heavy stock, saddle-stapled, with coated cover with full-color illustration. Receives 5,000 poetry submissions/year, accepts about 12. Press run is 12,000. Subscription: $38/year (U.S.). "We have a preference for writing and art based on real-life experiences; no formula stories or poems. We only publish writing by children ages 8 to 13. We do not publish writing by adults." Estab. 1973.

○ Print subscriptions include digital access, including more than 10 years of back issues at stonesoup.com.

FICTION Needs adventure, ethnic, experimental, fantasy, historical, humorous, mystery, science fiction, slice-of-life vignettes, suspense. "We do not like assignments or formula stories of any kind." Send complete ms; no SASE. Length: 150-2,500 words. Pays $25 for stories, a certificate and 2 contributor's copies, plus discounts.

NONFICTION Needs historical, humor, memoir, personal experience, reviews. Submit complete ms; no SASE. Pays $25, a certificate and 2 contributor's copies, plus discounts.

POETRY Wants free verse poetry. Does not want rhyming poetry, haiku, or cinquain. Pays $25/poem, a certificate, and 2 contributor's copies, plus discounts.

HOW TO CONTACT Publishes ms an average of 4 months after acceptance.

TERMS Buys all rights. Pays on publication. 100% freelance written. View a PDF sample copy at www.stonesoup.com. Purchase a single copy at www.stonesoupstore.com. Guidelines available at https://stonesoup.com/how-to-submit-writing-and-art-to-stone-soup/.

TIPS "All writing we publish is by young people ages 13 and under. We do not publish any writing by adults. We can't emphasize enough how important it is to read a couple of issues of the magazine. You can read stories and poems from past issues online. We have a strong preference for writing on subjects that mean a lot to the author. If you feel strongly about something that happened to you or something you observed, use that feeling as the basis for your story or poem. Stories should have good descriptions, realistic dialogue, and a point to make. In a poem, each word must be chosen carefully. Your poem should present a view of your subject, and a way of using words that are special and all your own."

YOUNG RIDER

2030 Main Street, Irvine CA 92614. (949) 855-8822. **Fax:** (949) 855-3045. **E-mail:** yreditor@i5publishing.com. **Website:** www.youngrider.com. "*Young Rider* magazine teaches young people, in an easy-to-read and entertaining way, how to look after their horses properly, and how to improve their riding skills safely."

FICTION Young adults: adventure, animal, horses. "We would prefer funny stories, with a bit of conflict, which will appeal to the 13-year-old age group. They should be written in the third person, and about kids." Query. Length: 800-1,000 words. Pays $150.

NONFICTION Young adults: animal, careers, famous equestrians, health (horse), horse celebrities, riding. Query with published clips. Length: 800-1,000 words. Pays $200/story.

PHOTOS Buys photos with accompanying ms only. Uses high-res digital images only—in focus, good light. Model/property release required; captions required.

TERMS Byline given. Guidelines available online.

TIPS "Fiction must be in third person. Read magazine before sending in a query. No 'true story from when I was a youngster.' No moralistic stories. Fiction must be up-to-date and humorous, teen-oriented."

AGENTS & ART REPS

///

This section features listings of literary agents and art reps who either specialize in, or represent a good percentage of, children's writers and/or illustrators. While there are a number of children's publishers who are open to nonagented material, using the services of an agent or rep can be beneficial to a writer or artist. Agents and reps can get your work seen by editors and art directors more quickly. They are familiar with the market and have insights into which editors and art directors would be most interested in your work. Also, they negotiate contracts and will likely be able to get you a better deal than you could get on your own.

Agents and reps make their income by taking a percentage of what writers and illustrators receive from publishers. The standard percentage for agents is 10 to 15 percent; art reps generally take 25 to 30 percent. We have not included any agencies in this section that charge reading fees.

WHAT TO SEND

When putting together a package for an agent or rep, follow the guidelines given in their listings. Most agents open to submissions prefer initially to receive a query letter describing your work. For novels and longer works, some agents ask for an outline and a number of sample chapters, but you should send these only if you're asked to do so. Never fax or e-mail query letters or sample chapters to agents without their permission. Just as with publishers, agents receive a large volume of submissions. It may take them a long time to reply, so you may want to query several agents at one time. It's best, however, to have a complete manuscript considered by only one agent at a time. Always include a self-addressed, stamped envelope (SASE).

For initial contact with art reps, send a brief query letter and self-promo pieces, following the guidelines given in the listings. If you don't have a flier or brochure, send photocopies. Always include a SASE.

For those who both write and illustrate, some agents listed will consider the work of author/illustrators. Read through the listings for details.

As you consider approaching agents and reps with your work, keep in mind that they are very choosy about whom represent. Your work must be high quality and presented professionally to make an impression on them. For more information on approaching agents and additional listings, see *Guide to Literary Agents* (Writer's Digest Books). For additional listings of art reps see *Artist's Market* (North Light Books).

AN ORGANIZATION FOR AGENTS

In some listings of agents you'll see references to AAR (The Association of Authors' Representatives). This organization requires its members to meet an established list of professional standards and code of ethics.

The objectives of AAR include keeping agents informed about conditions in publishing and related fields; encouraging cooperation among literary organizations; and assisting agents in representing their author-clients' interests. Officially, members are prohibited from directly or indirectly charging reading fees. They offer writers a list of member agents on their website. They also offer a list of recommended questions an author should ask an agent and other FAQs, all found on their website. They can be contacted at AAR, 676A 9th Ave. #312, New York NY 10036. (212)840-5777. E-mail: aarinc@mindspring.com. Website: www.aar-online.org.

A+B WORKS

Website: http://aplusbworks.com. **Contact:** Amy Jameson, Brandon Jameson. Estab. 2004.

◌   Ms. Jameson began her career in New York with esteemed literary agency Janklow & Nesbit Associates, where she launched Shannon Hale's career.

MEMBER AGENTS Amy Jameson (middle-grade, young adult).
REPRESENTS novels. **Considers these fiction areas:** middle-grade, young adult.
HOW TO CONTACT Query via online submission form. "Due to the high volume of queries we receive, we can't guarantee a response." Accepts simultaneous submissions.

ADAMS LITERARY

7845 Colony Rd., C4 #215, Charlotte NC 28226. (704)542-1440. **Fax:** (704)542-1450. **E-mail:** info@adamsliterary.com. **Website:** www.adamsliterary.com. **Contact:** Tracey Adams, Josh Adams. Adams Literary is a full-service literary agency exclusively representing children's and young adult authors and artists. Estab. 2004. Member of AAR, SCBWI, WNBA.

MEMBER AGENTS Tracey Adams, Josh Adams, Lorin Oberweger.
REPRESENTS Considers these fiction areas: middle-grade, picture books, young adult.

☞   Represents "the finest children's book and young adult authors and artists."

HOW TO CONTACT Submit through online form on website only. Send e-mail if that is not operating correctly. All submissions and queries should first be made through the online form on website. Will not review—and will promptly recycle—any unsolicited submissions or queries received by mail. Before submitting work for consideration, review complete guidelines online, as the agency sometimes shuts off to new submissions. Accepts simultaneous submissions. Responds in 6 weeks if interested. "While we have an established client list, we do seek new talent—and we accept submissions from both published and aspiring authors and artists."
TERMS Agent receives 15% commission on domestic sales; 20% on foreign sales. Offers written contract.

RECENT SALES *The Cruelty*, by Scott Bergstrom (Feiwel & Friends); *The Little Fire Truck*, by Margery Cuyler (Christy Ottaviano); *Unearthed*, by Amie Kaufman and Meagan Spooner (Disney-Hyperion); *A Handful of Stars*, by Cynthia Lord (Scholastic); *Under Their Skin*, by Margaret Peterson Haddix (Simon & Schuster); *The Secret Horses of Briar Hill*, by Megan Shepherd (Delacorte); *The Secret Subway*, by Shana Corey (Schwartz & Wade); *Impyrium*, by Henry Neff (HarperCollins).
TIPS "Guidelines are posted (and frequently updated) on our website."

AZANTIAN LITERARY AGENCY

Website: www.azantianlitagency.com. **Contact:** Jennifer Azantian. Estab. 2014.

◌   Prior to her current position, Ms. Azantian was with Sandra Dijkstra Literary Agency.

REPRESENTS novels. **Considers these fiction areas:** fantasy, horror, middle-grade, science fiction, urban fantasy, young adult.

☞   Actively seeking fantasy, science fiction, and psychological horror for adult, young adult, and middle-grade readers.

HOW TO CONTACT To submit, send your query letter, 1-2 page synopsis, and first 10-15 pages all pasted in an e-mail (no attachments). Please note in the e-mail subject line if your work was requested at a conference, is an exclusive submission, or was referred by a current client. Accepts simultaneous submissions. Responds within 6 weeks. Check the website before submitting to make sure Ms. Azantian is currently open to queries.

THE BENT AGENCY

E-mail: info@thebentagency.com. **Website:** www.thebentagency.com. **Contact:** Jenny Bent, Molly Ker Hawn, Gemma Cooper, Louise Fury, Beth Phelan, Victoria Lowes, Heather Flaherty. Estab. 2009. Member of AAR.

◌   Prior to forming her own agency, Ms. Bent was an agent and vice president at Trident Media Group.

MEMBER AGENTS Jenny Bent (adult fiction, including women's fiction, romance, crime/suspense; particularly likes novels with magical or fantasy elements that fall outside genre fiction; young adult and middle-grade fiction; memoir; humor); **Molly Ker Hawn** (young adult and middle-grade books, including contemporary, historical, fantasy, science fiction, thriller, mystery); **Gemma Cooper** (all ages of children's and young adult books, including picture books; likes historical, contemporary, thriller, mystery, humor, science fiction); **Louise Fury** (children's fiction: picture books, literary middle-grade, all young adult; adult fiction: speculative fiction, suspense/thriller, commercial fiction, all subgenres of romance including erotic; nonfiction: cookbooks, pop culture); **Beth Phelan** (young adult, thriller, suspense and mystery, romance and women's fiction, literary and general fiction, cookbooks, lifestyle, pets/animals); **Victoria Lowes** (romance and women's fiction, thriller and mystery, young adult); **Heather Flaherty** (young adult, middle-grade fiction: all genres; select adult fiction: upmarket fiction, women's fiction, female-centric thriller; select nonfiction: pop culture, humorous, social media-based projects, teen memoir).

REPRESENTS nonfiction, novels, short story collections, juvenile books. **Considers these nonfiction areas:** animals, cooking, creative nonfiction, foods, juvenile nonfiction, popular culture, women's issues, young adult. **Considers these fiction areas:** adventure, commercial, crime, erotica, fantasy, feminist, historical, horror, humor, juvenile, literary, mainstream, middle-grade, multicultural, mystery, New Adult, picture books, romance, short story collections, suspense, thriller, women's, young adult.

HOW TO CONTACT For Jenny Bent, e-mail queries@thebentagency.com; for Molly Ker Hawn, e-mail hawnqueries@thebentagency.com; for Gemma Cooper, e-mail cooperqueries@thebentagency.com; for Louise Fury, e-mail furyqueries@thebentagency.com; for Beth Phelan, e-mail phelanagencies@thebentagency.com; for Victoria Lowes, e-mail lowesqueries@thebentagency.com; for Heather Flaherty, e-mail flahertyqueries@thebentagency.com. "Tell us briefly who you are, what your book is, and why you're the one to write it. Then include the first 10 pages of your material in the body of your e-mail. We respond to all queries, please resend your query if you haven't had a response within 4 weeks." Accepts simultaneous submissions.

RECENT SALES *Caraval* by Stephanie Garber (Flatiron); *Rebel of the Sands* by Alwyn Hamilton (Viking Children's/Penguin BFYR); *My Perfect Me* by J.M.M. Nuanez (Kathy Dawson Books/Penguin BFYR); *The Square Root of Summer* by Harriet Re-

uter Hapgood (Roaring Brook/Macmillan); *Dirty Money* by Lisa Renee Jones (Simon & Schuster); *True North* by Liora Blake (Pocket Star).

DAVID BLACK LITERARY AGENCY

335 Adams St., Suite 2707, Brooklyn NY 11201. (718)852-5500. **Fax:** (718)852-5539. **Website:** www.davidblackagency.com. **Contact:** David Black, owner. Estab. 1989 Member of AAR. Represents 150 clients.

MEMBER AGENTS David Black; Jenny Herrera; Gary Morris; Joy E. Tutela (narrative nonfiction, memoir, history, politics, self-help, investment, business, science, women's issues, LGBTQ issues, parenting, health and fitness, humor, craft, cooking and wine, lifestyle and entertainment, commercial fiction, literary fiction, Middle-grade, young adult); **Susan Raihofer** (commercial fiction and nonfiction, memoir, pop culture, music, inspirational, thriller, literary fiction); **Sarah Smith** (memoir, biography, food, music, narrative history, social studies, literary fiction).

REPRESENTS nonfiction, novels. **Considers these nonfiction areas:** biography, business, cooking, crafts, gay/lesbian, health, history, humor, inspirational, memoirs, music, parenting, popular culture, politics, science, self-help, sociology, sports, women's issues. **Considers these fiction areas:** commercial, literary, middle-grade, thriller, young adult.

HOW TO CONTACT "To query an individual agent, please follow the specific query guidelines outlined in the agent's profile on our website. Not all agents are currently accepting unsolicited queries. To query the agency, please send a 1-2 page query letter describing your book, and include information about any previously published works, your audience, and your platform." Do not e-mail your query unless an agent specifically asks for an e-mail. Accepts simultaneous submissions. Responds in 2 months to queries.

RECENT SALES Some of the agency's best-selling authors include: Erik Larson, Stuart Scott, Jeff Hobbs, Mitch Albom, Gregg Olsen, Jim Abbott, John Bacon.

THE BOOK GROUP

20 W. 20th St., Suite 601, New York NY 10011. (212)803-3360. **E-mail:** submissions@thebookgroup.com. **Website:** www.thebookgroup.com. Estab. 2015. Member of AAR. Signatory of WGA.

MEMBER AGENTS Julie Barer; Faye Bender; **Brettne Bloom** (fiction: literary and commercial fiction, select young adult; nonfiction, including cookbooks, lifestyle, investigative journalism, history, biography, memoir, psychology); **Elisabeth Weed** (upmarket fiction, especially plot-driven novels with a sense of place); **Rebecca Stead** (innovative forms, diverse voices, open-hearted fiction for children, young adults, adults); **Dana Murphy** (story-driven fiction with a strong sense of place, narrative nonfiction/essays with a pop-culture lean, young adult with an honest voice).

REPRESENTS Considers these nonfiction areas: biography, cooking, history, investigative, memoirs, psychology. **Considers these fiction areas:** commercial, literary, mainstream, women's, young adult.

☛ Please do not send poetry or screenplays.

HOW TO CONTACT Send a query letter and 10 sample pages to submissions@thebookgroup.com, with the first and last name of the agent you are querying in the subject line. All material must be in the body of the e-mail, as the agents do not open attachments. "If we are interested in reading more, we will get in touch with you as soon as possible." Accepts simultaneous submissions.

RECENT SALES *This Is Not Over*, by Holly Brown; *Perfect Little World*, by Kevin Wilson; *City of Saints & Thieves*, by Natalie C. Anderson; *The Runaway Midwife*, by Patricia Harman; *Always*, by Sarah Jio; *The Young Widower's Handbook*, by Tom McAllister.

BOOKSTOP LITERARY AGENCY

67 Meadow View Rd., Orinda CA 94563. (925)254-2664. **E-mail:** info@bookstopliterary.com. **Website:** www.bookstopliterary.com. Represents authors and illustrators of books for children and young adults. Estab. 1984.

REPRESENTS nonfiction, fiction, novels, short story collections, juvenile books, poetry books. **Considers these nonfiction areas:** juvenile nonfiction, young adult. **Considers these fiction areas:** hi-lo, middle-grade, picture books, plays, poetry, young adult.

☛ "Special interest in Hispanic, Asian-American, African-American, and multicultural writers. Also seeking quirky picture books, clever adventure/mystery novels, eye-opening nonfiction, heartfelt middle-grade, unusual teen romance."

HOW TO CONTACT Send:cover letter, entire ms for picture books, first 10 pages of novels; proposal and sample chapters OK for nonfiction. E-mail submissions: Paste cover letter and first 10 pages of ms into body of e-mail and send to info@bookstopliterary.com. Send sample illustrations only if you are an illustrator. Illustrators: send postcard or link to online portfolio. Do not send original artwork. Accepts simultaneous submissions.

TERMS Agent receives 15% commission on domestic sales. Offers written contract, binding for 1 year.

BRADFORD LITERARY AGENCY

5694 Mission Center Rd., #347, San Diego CA 92108. (619)521-1201. **E-mail:** queries@bradfordlit.com. **Website:** www.bradfordlit.com. **Contact:** Laura Bradford, Natalie Lakosil, Sarah LaPolla, Monica Odom. Estab. 2001. Member of AAR, RWA, SCBWI, ALA. Represents 130 clients.

MEMBER AGENTS **Laura Bradford** (romance: historical, romantic suspense, paranormal, category, contemporary, erotic; mystery, women's fiction, thriller/suspense, middle-grade, young adult); **Natalie Lakosil** (children's literature from picture book through teen and New Adult, contemporary and historical romance, cozy mystery/crime, upmarket women's/general fiction, select children's nonfiction); **Sarah LaPolla** (YA, middle-grade, literary fiction, science fiction, magical realism, dark/psychological mystery, literary horror, upmarket contemporary fiction); **Monica Odom** (nonfiction by authors with demonstrable platforms in the areas of pop culture, illustrated/graphic design, food and cooking, humor, history and social issues; narrative nonfiction, memoir, literary fiction, upmarket commercial fiction, compelling speculative fiction and magic realism, historical fiction, alternative histories, dark and edgy fiction, literary psychological thriller, illustrated/picture books).

REPRESENTS nonfiction, fiction, novels, juvenile books. **Considers these nonfiction areas:** biography, cooking, creative nonfiction, cultural interests, foods, history, humor, juvenile nonfiction, memoirs, parenting, popular culture, politics, self-help, women's issues, women's studies, young adult. **Considers these fiction areas:** commercial, crime, ethnic, gay, historical, juvenile, lesbian, literary, mainstream, middle-grade, multicultural, mystery, New Adult, paranormal, picture books, romance, science fiction, thriller, women's, young adult.

- Laura Bradford does not want to receive poetry, screenplays, short stories, westerns, horror, new age, religion, crafts, cookbooks, or gift books. Natalie Lakosil does not want to receive inspirational novels, memoir, romantic suspense, adult thriller, poetry, or screenplays. Sarah LaPolla does not want to receive nonfiction, picture books, inspirational/spiritual novels, romance, or erotica. Monica Odom does not want to receive genre romance, erotica, military, poetry, or inspirational/spiritual works.

HOW TO CONTACT Accepts e-mail queries only. For submissions to Laura Bradford or Natalie Lakosil, send to queries@bradfordlit.com. For submissions to Sarah LaPolla, send to sarah@bradfordlit.com. For submissions to Monica Odom, send to monica@bradfordlit.com. The entire submission must appear in the body of the e-mail and not as an attachment. The subject line should begin as follows: "QUERY: (the title of the ms or any short message that is important)." For fiction: e-mail a query letter along with the first chapter of ms and a synopsis. Include the genre and word count in your query letter. Nonfiction: e-mail full nonfiction proposal, including a query letter and a sample chapter. Accepts simultaneous submissions. Responds in 4 weeks to queries, 10 weeks to mss. Obtains most new clients through queries.

TERMS Agent receives 15% commission on domestic sales; 25% commission on foreign sales. Offers written contract. Charges for extra copies of books for foreign submissions.

RECENT SALES Sold 115 titles in the last year, including *Snowed in with Murder*, by Auralee Wallace (St. Martin's); *All the Secrets We Keep*, by Megan Hart (Montlake); *The Notorious Bargain*, by Joanna Shupe (Avon); *Allegedly*, by Tiffany Jackson (Katherine Tegen Books); *Wives of War*, by Soraya Lane (Amazon).

WRITERS CONFERENCES RWA National Conference, Romantic Times Booklovers Convention.

BRANDT & HOCHMAN LITERARY AGENTS, INC.

1501 Broadway, Suite 2310, New York NY 10036. (212)840-5760. **Fax:** (212)840-5776. **Website:** brandthochman.com. **Contact:** Gail Hochman. Member of AAR. Represents 200 clients.

MEMBER AGENTS Gail Hochman (literary fiction, idea-driven nonfiction, literary memoir, children's books); **Marianne Merola** (fiction, nonfiction and children's books with strong and unique narrative voices); **Bill Contardi** (voice-driven young adult and middle-grade fiction, commercial thriller, psychological suspense, quirky mystery, high fantasy, commercial fiction, memoir); **Emily Forland** (voice-driven literary fiction and nonfiction, memoir, narrative nonfiction, history, biography, food writing, cultural criticism, graphic novels, young adult fiction); **Emma Patterson** (fiction from dark literary novels to upmarket women's and historical fiction; narrative nonfiction, including memoir, investigative journalism, popular history; young adult fiction); **Jody Kahn** (literary and upmarket fiction; narrative nonfiction, particularly books related to sports, food, history, science, pop culture—including cookbooks; literary memoir, journalism); **Henry Thayer** (nonfiction on a wide variety of subjects; fiction that inclines toward the literary). The e-mail addresses and specific likes of each of these agents is listed on the agency website.

REPRESENTS nonfiction, novels. **Considers these nonfiction areas:** biography, cooking, current affairs, foods, health, history, memoirs, music, popular culture, science, sports, narrative nonfiction, journalism. **Considers these fiction areas:** fantasy, historical, literary, middle-grade, mystery, suspense, thriller, women's, young adult.

- No screenplays or textbooks.

HOW TO CONTACT "We accept queries by e-mail and regular mail; however, we cannot guarantee a response to e-mailed queries. For queries via regular mail, be sure to include a SASE for our reply. Query letters should be no more than 2 pages and should include a convincing overview of the book project and information about the author and his or her writing credits. Address queries to the specific Brandt & Hochman agent whom you would like to consider your work. Agent e-mail addresses and query preferences may be found at the end of each agent profile on the Agents page of our website." Accepts simultaneous submissions. Obtains most new clients through recommendations from others.

TERMS Agent receives 15% commission on domestic sales; 20% commission on foreign sales.

RECENT SALES This agency sells 40-60 new titles each year. A full list of their hundreds of clients is on the agency website.

TIPS "Write a letter that will give the agent a sense of you as a professional writer—your long-term interests as well as a short description of the work at hand."

ANDREA BROWN LITERARY AGENCY, INC.

E-mail: andrea@andreabrownlit.com, caryn@andreabrownlit.com, lauraqueries@gmail.com, jennifer@andreabrownlit.com, kelly@andreabrownlit.com, jennl@andreabrownlit.com, jamie@andreabrownlit.com, jmatt@andreabrownlit.com, kathleen@andreabrownlit.com, lara@andreabrownlit.com, soloway@andreabrownlit.com. **Website:** www.andreabrownlit.com. Member of AAR.

- Prior to opening her agency, Ms. Brown served as an editorial assistant at Random House and Dell Publishing and as an editor with Knopf.

MEMBER AGENTS Andrea Brown, president; **Laura Rennert**, executive agent; **Caryn Wiseman**, senior agent; **Jennifer Laughran**, senior agent; **Jennifer Rofé**, senior agent; **Kelly Sonnack**, agent; **Jamie Weiss Chilton**, agent; **Jennifer Mattson**, agent; **Kathleen Rushall**, agent; **Lara Perkins**, associate agent, digital manager; **Jennifer March Soloway**, assistant agent.

REPRESENTS nonfiction, fiction, juvenile books. **Considers these nonfiction areas:** juvenile nonfiction, young adult, narrative. **Considers these fiction areas:** juvenile, picture books, young adult, middlegrade, all juvenile genres.

- Specializes in all kinds of children's books—illustrators and authors. 98% juvenile books. Considers nonfiction, fiction, picture books, young adult.

HOW TO CONTACT For picture books, submit a query letter and complete ms in the body of the e-mail. For fiction, submit a query letter and the first 10 pages in the body of the e-mail. For nonfiction, submit proposal, first 10 pages in the body of the e-mail. Illustrators: submit a query letter and 2-3 illustration samples (in JPEG format), link to online portfolio, and text of picture book, if applicable. "We only accept queries via e-mail. No attachments, with the exception of JPEG illustrations from illustrators." Visit the agents' bios on our website and choose only *one* agent to whom you will submit your

e-query. Send a short e-mail query letter to that agent with "QUERY" in the subject field. Accepts simultaneous submissions. "If we are interested in your work, we will certainly follow up by e-mail or by phone. However, if you haven't heard from us within 6 to 8 weeks, please assume that we are passing on your project." Obtains most new clients through referrals from editors, clients and agents. Check website for guidelines and information.

TERMS Agent receives 15% commission on domestic sales; 25% commission on foreign sales. Offers written contract.

RECENT SALES *The Scorpio Races*, by Maggie Stiefvater (Scholastic); *The Future of Us*, by Jay Asher; *Triangles*, by Ellen Hopkins (Atria); *Crank*, by Ellen Hopkins (McElderry/S&S); *Burned*, by Ellen Hopkins (McElderry/S&S); *Impulse*, by Ellen Hopkins (McElderry/S&S); *Glass*, by Ellen Hopkins (McElderry/S&S); *Tricks*, by Ellen Hopkins (McElderry/S&S); *Fallout*, by Ellen Hopkins (McElderry/S&S).

CURTIS BROWN, LTD.

10 Astor Place, New York NY 10003. (212)473-5400. **Fax:** (212)598-0917. **Website:** www.curtisbrown.com. **Contact:** Ginger Knowlton. Represents authors and illustrators of fiction, nonfiction, picture books, middle-grade, young adult. Member of AAR. Signatory of WGA.

MEMBER AGENTS Noah Ballard (literary debuts, upmarket thriller and narrative nonfiction, and always on the lookout for honest and provocative new writers); **Ginger Clark** (science fiction, fantasy, paranormal romance, literary horror, young adult and middle-grade fiction); **Kerry D'Agostino** (a wide range of literary and commercial fiction; narrative nonfiction, memoir); **Katherine Fausset** (literary fiction, upmarket commercial fiction, journalism, memoir, popular science, narrative nonfiction); **Holly Frederick**; **Peter Ginsberg**, president; **Elizabeth Harding**, vice president (represents authors and illustrators of juvenile, middle-grade, young adult fiction); **Steve Kasdin** (commercial fiction, including mystery/thriller, romantic suspense—emphasis on the suspense—and historical fiction; narrative nonfiction, including biography, history, and current affairs; young adult fiction, particularly if it has adult crossover appeal; not interested in science fiction/fantasy, memoirs, vampires, writers trying to capitalize on trends); **Ginger Knowlton**, executive vice president (authors and illustrators of children's books in all genres); **Timothy Knowlton**, CEO; **Jonathan Lyons** (biography, history, science, pop culture, sports, general narrative nonfiction, mystery, thriller, science fiction and fantasy, young adult fiction); **Laura Blake Peterson**, vice president (memoir and biography, natural history, literary fiction, mystery, suspense, women's fiction, health and fitness, children's and young adult, faith issues, popular culture); **Maureen Walters**, senior vice president (primarily women's fiction and nonfiction, parenting and child care, popular psychology, inspirational/motivational volumes, a few medical/nutrition books); **Mitchell Waters** (literary and commercial fiction and nonfiction, including mystery, history, biography, memoir, young adult, cookbooks, self-help, popular culture); **Monika Woods**.

REPRESENTS NONFICTION, novels. **Considers these nonfiction areas:** biography, computers, cooking, current affairs, ethnic, health, history, humor, memoirs, popular culture, psychology, science, self-help, spirituality, sports. **Considers these fiction areas:** fantasy, horror, humor, juvenile, literary, mainstream, middle-grade, mystery, paranormal, picture books, religious, romance, spiritual, sports, suspense, thriller, women's, young adult.

HOW TO CONTACT Please refer to the Agents page on the website for each agent's submission guidelines. Accepts simultaneous submissions. Responds in 3 weeks to queries, 5 weeks to mss. Obtains most new clients through recommendations from others, solicitations, conferences.

TERMS Agent receives 15% commission on domestic sales; 20% on foreign sales. Offers written contract; 75-day notice must be given to terminate contract. Charges for some postage (overseas, etc.).

RECENT SALES This agency prefers not to share information on specific sales.

MARIE BROWN ASSOCIATES, INC.

412 W. 154th St., New York NY 10032. (212)939-9725 for Marie Brown, (678)515-7907 for Janell Walden Agyeman. **Fax:** (212)939-9728. **E-mail:** info@janellwaldenagyeman.com. **Website:** www.janellwaldenagyeman.com. **Contact:** Marie Brown, Janell Walden Agyeman. Estab. 1984. Authors Guild, Independent Book Publishers Association, SCBWI.

MEMBER AGENTS Marie Brown, Janell Walden Agyeman (middle-grade, young adult, and New Adult fiction featuring multicultural protagonists in contemporary or historical settings; narrative nonfiction that illuminates the experiences of people of color or enlightened responses to the human journey).

REPRESENTS nonfiction, novels, juvenile books. **Considers these nonfiction areas:** creative nonfiction, cultural interests, education, ethnic, history, inspirational, juvenile nonfiction, memoirs, multicultural, popular culture, spirituality, sports, women's studies, young adult. **Considers these fiction areas:** contemporary issues, ethnic, hi-lo, historical, juvenile, literary, mainstream, middle-grade, multicultural, New Adult, paranormal, picture books, supernatural, urban fantasy, women's, young adult.

Ms. Brown's special interests include sports and performing arts. Ms. Agyeman's special interests include spirituality and cultural issues. Actively seeking debut fiction for adults (literary and popular) and for young readers. Ms. Brown does not want to receive genre fiction or poetry. Ms. Agyeman does not want to receive true crime, high fantasy, thriller, or poetry.

HOW TO CONTACT "We are closed to unsolicited submissions from time to time; check the website to confirm our review status before querying. Marie Brown will consider hard-copy materials submitted according to her guidelines (on website). Janell Agyeman welcomes e-mailed queries when she is open to unsolicited submissions. Check the website for her current submissions review policy before sending queries." Responds within 3 months. Primarily obtains new clients through recommendations and conferences.

TERMS Agent receives 15% commission on domestic sales; 20% commission on foreign sales. Offers written contract.

RECENT SALES *The Man in 3B*, by Carl Weber; *Pushout*, by Monique Morris; *Born Bright*, by C. Nicole Mason; *Degree Zombie Zone*, by Patrik Henry Bass; *Harlem Renaissance Party*, by Faith Ringgold; *Stella by Starlight*, by Sharon M. Draper.

TIPS "Have your project professionally edited and/or critiqued before submitting; show us your very best work."

KIMBERLEY CAMERON & ASSOCIATES

1550 Tiburon Blvd., #704, Tiburon CA 94920. (415)789-9191. **Website:** www.kimberleycameron. com. **Contact:** Kimberley Cameron. Member of AAR. Signatory of WGA.

○ Kimberley Cameron & Associates (formerly The Reece Halsey Agency) has had an illustrious client list of established writers, including Aldous Huxley, Upton Sinclair, William Faulkner, and Henry Miller.

MEMBER AGENTS Kimberley Cameron; Elizabeth Kracht (temporarily closed to submissions); Amy Cloughley (literary and upmarket fiction, women's, historical, narrative nonfiction, travel or adventure memoirs); Mary C. Moore (fantasy, science fiction, upmarket "book club," genre romance, thriller with female protagonists, stories from marginalized voices); Lisa Abellera (currently closed to unsolicited submissions); Douglas Lee (only accepting submissions via conference and in-person meetings in the Bay Area).

REPRESENTS Considers these nonfiction areas: animals, environment, health, memoirs, science, spirituality, travel, true crime, narrative nonfiction. **Considers these fiction areas:** commercial, fantasy, historical, literary, mystery, romance, science fiction, thriller, women's, young adult, LGBTQ.

○— "We are looking for a unique and heartfelt voice that conveys a universal truth."

HOW TO CONTACT Prefers queries via site. Only query one agent at a time. For fiction, fill out the correct submissions form for the individual agent and attach the first 50 pages and a synopsis (if requested) as a Word doc or PDF. For nonfiction, fill out the correct submission form of the individual agent and attach a full book proposal and sample chapters (includes the first chapter and no more than 50 pages) as a Word doc or PDF. Accepts simultaneous submissions. Obtains new clients through recommendations from others, solicitations.

MARIA CARVAINIS AGENCY, INC.

Rockefeller Center, 1270 Avenue of the Americas, Suite 2915, New York NY 10020. (212)245-6365. **Fax:** (212)245-7196. **E-mail:** mca@mariacarvainisagency.com. **E-mail:** mca@mariacarvainisagency.com. **Website:** www.mariacarvainisagency.com. Estab. 1977. Member of AAR, Authors Guild, Women's Media Group, ABA, MWA, RWA. Represents 75 clients.

○ Prior to opening her agency, Ms. Carvainis spent more than 10 years in the publishing industry as a senior editor with Macmillan, Basic Books, Avon Books, and Crown Publishers. Ms. Carvainis has served as a member of the AAR Board of Directors and as the AAR treasurer, as well as serving as chair of the AAR Contracts Committee. She presently serves on the AAR Royalty Committee.

MEMBER AGENTS Maria Carvainis, president/literary agent; Elizabeth Copps, associate agent.

REPRESENTS nonfiction, novels. **Considers these nonfiction areas:** biography, business, history, memoirs, popular culture, psychology, science. **Considers these fiction areas:** action, adventure, commercial, contemporary issues, crime, family saga, historical, horror, humor, juvenile, literary, mainstream, middle-grade, multicultural, mystery, romance, suspense, thriller, women's, young adult.

○— The agency does not represent screenplays, children's picture books, science fiction, or poetry.

HOW TO CONTACT If you would like to query the agency, please send a query letter, a synopsis of the work, first 5-10 pages, and note of any writing credentials. Please e-mail queries to mca@mariacarvainisagency.com. All attachments must be either Word documents or PDF files. The agency also accepts queries by mail to Maria Carvainis Agency, Inc., Attention: Query Department. If you want the materials returned to you, please enclose a SASE; otherwise, please be sure to include your e-mail address. There is no reading fee. Accepts simultaneous submissions. Responds to queries within 1 month. Obtains most new clients through recommendations from others, conferences, query letters.

TERMS Agent receives 15% commission on domestic sales; 20% commission on foreign sales. Offers written contract. Charges clients for foreign postage.

RECENT SALES *Someone To Love*, by Mary Balogh (Signet); *Sting*, by Sandra Brown (Grand Central); *Enraptured*, by Candace Camp (Pocket Books); *If You Only Knew*, by Kristan Higgins (HQN Books); *Palindrome*, by E.Z. Rinsky (Witness Impulse); *Almost Paradise*, by Corabel Shofner (Farrar Straus & Giroux Books for Young Readers).

CHALBERG & SUSSMAN

115 W. 29th St., Third Floor, New York NY 10001. (917)261-7550. **Website:** www.chalbergsussman. com. Member of AAR. Signatory of WGA.

○ Prior to her current position, Ms. Chalberg held a variety of editorial positions and was an agent with The Susan Golomb Literary Agency. Ms. Sussman was an agent with Zachary Shuster Harmsworth. Ms. James was with The Aaron Priest Literary Agency.

MEMBER AGENTS Terra Chalberg; Rachel Sussman (narrative journalism, memoir, psychology, history, humor, pop culture, literary fiction); **Nicole James** (plot-driven fiction, psychological suspense, uplifting female-driven memoirs, upmarket self-help, lifestyle books); **Lana Popovic** (young adult, middle-grade, contemporary realism, speculative fiction, fantasy, horror, sophisticated erotica, romance, select nonfiction, international stories).

REPRESENTS nonfiction, fiction, novels. **Considers these nonfiction areas:** history, humor, memoirs, popular culture, psychology, self-help, narrative journalism. **Considers these fiction areas:** erotica, fantasy, horror, literary, middle-grade, romance, science fiction, suspense, young adult, contemporary realism, speculative fiction.

HOW TO CONTACT To query by e-mail, please contact one of the following: terra@chalbergsussman. com, rachel@chalbergsussman.com, nicole@chalbergsussman.com, lana@chalbergsussman.com. To query by regular mail, please address your letter to one agent and include SASE. Accepts simultaneous submissions.

RECENT SALES The agents' sales and clients are listed on the website.

THE CHUDNEY AGENCY

72 N. State Rd., Suite 501, Briarcliff Manor NY 10510. (914)465-5560. **E-mail:** steven@thechudney-agency.com. **Website:** www.thechudneyagency.com. **Contact:** Steven Chudney. Estab. 2001.

○ Prior to becoming an agent, Mr. Chudney held various sales positions with major publishers.

REPRESENTS novels. **Considers these fiction areas:** historical, juvenile, literary, middle-grade, picture books, young adult.

○— "At this time, the agency is only looking for author/illustrators (one individual) who can both write and illustrate wonderful picture books. The author/illustrator must really know and understand the needs and wants of the child reader! Storylines should be engaging and fun, with a hint of a life lesson and cannot be longer than 800 words. With chapter books, middle-grade, and teen novels, I'm primarily looking for quality contemporary literary fiction: novels that are exceedingly well-written, with wonderful settings and developed, unforgettable characters. I'm looking for historical fiction that will excite me, young readers, editors, and reviewers, and that will introduce us to unique characters in settings and situations, countries, and eras we haven't encountered too often yet in children's and teen literature."

HOW TO CONTACT No snail mail submissions. Queries only. Submit proposal package, 4-6 sample chapters. For children's, submit full text and 3-5 illustrations. Accepts simultaneous submissions. Responds if interested in 2-3 weeks to queries.

DON CONGDON ASSOCIATES INC.

110 William St., Suite 2202, New York NY 10038. (212)645-1229. **Fax:** (212)727-2688. **E-mail:** dca@doncongdon.com. **Website:** doncongdon.com. Estab. 1983. Member of AAR.

MEMBER AGENTS Cristina Concepcion (crime fiction, narrative nonfiction, political science, journalism, history, books on cities, classical music, biography, science for a popular audience, philosophy, food and wine, iconoclastic books on health and human relationships, essays, arts criticism); **Michael Congdon** (commercial and literary fiction, suspense, mystery, thriller, history, military history, biography, memoir, current affairs, narrative nonfiction [adventure, medicine, science, nature]); **Katie Grimm** (literary fiction, historical, women's fiction, short story collections, graphic novels, mystery, young adult, middle-grade, memoir, science, academic); **Katie Kotchman** (business [all areas], narrative nonfiction [particularly popular science and social/cultural issues], self-help, success, motivation, psychology, pop culture, women's fiction, realistic young adult, literary fiction, psychological thriller); **Maura Kye-Casella** (narrative nonfiction, cookbooks, women's fiction, young adult, self-help, parenting); **Susan Ramer** (literary fiction, upmarket commercial fiction [contemporary and historical], narrative nonfiction, social history, cultural history, smart pop culture [music, film, food, art], women's issues, psychology and mental health, memoir). **REPRESENTS** nonfiction, novels, short story collections. **Considers these nonfiction areas:** art, biography, business, cooking, creative nonfiction, cultural interests, current affairs, film, foods, history, humor, literature, medicine, memoirs, military, multicultural, music, parenting, philosophy, popular culture, politics, psychology, science, self-help, sociology, sports, women's issues, young adult. **Considers these fiction areas:** crime, hi-lo, historical, literary, middle-grade, mystery, short story collections, suspense, thriller, women's, young adult.

⚯ Susan Ramer: "Not looking for romance, science fiction, fantasy, espionage, mystery, politics, health/diet/fitness, self-help, or sports." Katie Kotchman: "Please do not send screenplays or poetry."

HOW TO CONTACT "For queries via e-mail, you must include the word 'query' and the agent's full name in your subject heading. Please also include your query and sample chapter in the body of the e-mail, as we do not open attachments for security reasons. Please query only one agent within the agency at a time. If you are sending your query via regular mail, please enclose a SASE for our reply. If you would like us to return your materials, please make sure your postage will cover their return." Accepts simultaneous submissions.

RECENT SALES THIS agency represents many best-selling clients, such as David Sedaris and Kathryn Stockett.

CORVISIERO LITERARY AGENCY

275 Madison Ave., at 40th, 14th Floor, New York NY 10016. **E-mail:** query@corvisieroagency.com. **Website:** www.corvisieroagency.com. **Contact:** Marisa A. Corvisiero, senior agent and literary attorney. "We are a boutique literary agency founded by Marisa A. Corvisiero, Esq. This agency is a place where authors can find professional and experienced representation." *Does not accept unsolicited mss.* Member of AAR. Signatory of WGA.

MEMBER AGENTS Marisa A. Corvisiero, senior agent and literary attorney (contemporary romance, thriller, adventure, paranormal, urban fantasy, science fiction, Middle-grade, young adult, picture books, Christmas themes, time travel, space sci-

ence fiction, nonfiction, self-help, science business); **Saritza Hernandez,** senior agent (all kinds of romance, GLBT, young adult, erotica); **Doreen Thistle** (do not query); **Cate Hart** (YA, fantasy, magical realism, Middle-grade, mystery, fantasy, adventure, historical romance, LGBTQ, erotic, history, biography); **Veronica Park** (dark or edgy young adult/NA, commercial adult, adult romance and romantic suspense, funny and/or current/controversial nonfiction); **Vanessa Robins** (New Adult, human, young adult, thriller, romance, science fiction, sports-centric plots, memoirs, cultural/ethnic/sexuality, humor, medical narratives); **Kelly Peterson** (Middle-grade, fantasy, paranormal, science fiction, young adult, steampunk, historical, dystopian, sword and sorcery, romance, historical romance, adult, fantasy, romance); **Justin Wells; Kaitlyn Johnson.** **REPRESENTS** nonfiction, fiction, novels. **Considers these nonfiction areas:** biography, business, history, medicine, memoirs, science, self-help, spirituality. **Considers these fiction areas:** adventure, erotica, fantasy, gay, historical, lesbian, middle-grade, mystery, paranormal, picture books, romance, science fiction, suspense, thriller, urban fantasy, young adult, magical realism, steampunk, dystopian, sword and sorcery.

HOW TO CONTACT Accepts submissions via e-mail only. Include 5 pages of complete and polished ms pasted into the body of an e-mail and a 1-2 page synopsis. For nonfiction, include a proposal instead of the synopsis. Put "Query for [Agent]" in the e-mail subject line. Accepts simultaneous submissions.

D4EO LITERARY AGENCY

7 Indian Valley Rd., Weston CT 06883. (203)544-7180. **Fax:** (203)544-7160. **Website:** www.d4eoliteraryagency.com. **Contact:** Bob Diforio. Estab. 1990.

◐ Prior to opening his agency, Mr. Diforio was a publisher.

MEMBER AGENTS Bob Diforio, Joyce Holland, Pam Howell, Quressa Robinson, Kelly Van Sant. **REPRESENTS** nonfiction, novels. **Considers these nonfiction areas:** biography, business, health, history, humor, money, psychology, science, sports. **Considers these fiction areas:** adventure, detective, erotica, juvenile, literary, mainstream, middle-grade, mystery, New Adult, romance, sports, thriller, young adult.

HOW TO CONTACT Each of these agents has a different submission e-mail and different tastes regarding how they review material. See all on their individual agent pages on the agency website. Responds in 1 week to queries if interested. Obtains most new clients through recommendations from others.

TERMS Offers written contract, binding for 2 years; automatic renewal unless 60 days notice given prior to renewal date. Charges for photocopying and submission postage.

LAURA DAIL LITERARY AGENCY, INC.

350 Seventh Ave., Suite 2003, New York NY 10001. (212)239-7477. **E-mail:** ldail@ldlainc.com. **E-mail:** queries@ldlainc.com. **Website:** www.ldlainc.com. Member of AAR.

MEMBER AGENTS Laura Dail, Tamar Rydzinski, Elana Roth Parker.

REPRESENTS nonfiction, fiction, novels, juvenile books. **Considers these nonfiction areas:** biography, cooking, creative nonfiction, current affairs, government, history, investigative, juvenile nonfiction, memoirs, multicultural, popular culture, politics, psychology, sociology, true crime, war, women's studies, young adult. **Considers these fiction areas:** commercial, crime, detective, fantasy, feminist, historical, juvenile, mainstream, middle-grade, multicultural, mystery, thriller, women's, young adult.

⊷ Specializes in women's fiction, literary fiction, young adult fiction, and both practical and idea-driven nonfiction. "Tamar is not interested in prescriptive or practical nonfiction, humor, coffee table books, or children's books (meaning anything younger than middle-grade). She is interested in everything else that is well written and has great characters, including graphic novels." "Due to the volume of queries and mss received, we apologize for not answering every e-mail and letter. None of us handles children's picture books or chapter books. No New Age. We do not handle screenplays or poetry."

HOW TO CONTACT "If you would like, you may include a synopsis and no more than 10 pages. If you are mailing your query, please be sure to include a self-addressed, stamped envelope; without it, you may not hear back from us. To save money, time, and trees, we prefer queries by e-mail to queries@

ldlainc.com. We get a lot of spam and are wary of computer viruses, so please use the word 'Query' in the subject line and include your detailed materials in the body of your message, not as an attachment." Accepts simultaneous submissions. Responds in 2-4 weeks.

LIZA DAWSON ASSOCIATES

350 Seventh Ave., Suite 2003, New York NY 10001. (212)465-9071. **E-mail:** querycaitie@lizadawsonassociates.com. **Website:** www.lizadawsonassociates.com. **Contact:** Caitie Flum. Member of AAR, MWA, Women's Media Group. Represents 50+ clients.

○ Prior to becoming an agent, Ms. Dawson was an editor for 20 years, spending 11 years at William Morrow as vice president and 2 years at Putnam as executive editor. Ms. Blasdell was a senior editor at HarperCollins and Avon. Ms. Johnson-Blalock was an assistant at Trident Media Group. Ms. Flum was the coordinator for the Children's Book of the Month club.

MEMBER AGENTS Liza Dawson, queryliza@lizadawsonassociates.com (plot-driven literary and popular fiction, historical, thriller, suspense, history, psychology [both popular and clinical], politics, narrative nonfiction, memoirs); **Caitlin Blasdell**, querycaitlin@lizadawsonassociates.com (science fiction, fantasy [both adult and young adult], parenting, business, thriller, women's fiction; **Hannah Bowman**, queryhannah@lizadawsonassociates.com (commercial fiction [especially science fiction and fantasy, young adult] nonfiction [mathematics, science, and spirituality]); **Jennifer Johnson-Blalock**, queryjennifer@lizadawsonassociates.com (nonfiction, particularly current events, social sciences, women's issues, law, business, history, the arts and pop culture, lifestyle, sports, food; commercial and upmarket fiction, especially thriller/mystery, women's fiction, contemporary romance, young adult, middle-grade); **Caitie Flum**, querycaitie@lizadawsonassociates.com (commercial fiction, especially historical, women's fiction, mystery, crossover fantasy, young adult, middle-grade; nonfiction [theater, current affairs, pop culture].

REPRESENTS nonfiction, novels. **Considers these nonfiction areas:** agriculture, Americana, animals, anthropology, archeology, architecture, art, autobiography, biography, business, computers, cooking, creative nonfiction, cultural interests, current affairs, environment, ethnic, film, gardening, gay/lesbian, history, humor, investigative, juvenile nonfiction, memoirs, multicultural, parenting, popular culture, politics, psychology, religious, science, sex, sociology, spirituality, theater, travel, true crime, women's issues, women's studies, young adult. **Considers these fiction areas:** action, adventure, commercial, contemporary issues, crime, detective, ethnic, family saga, fantasy, feminist, gay, historical, horror, humor, juvenile, lesbian, mainstream, middle-grade, multicultural, mystery, New Adult, police, romance, science fiction, supernatural, suspense, thriller, urban fantasy, women's, young adult.

This agency specializes in readable literary fiction, thriller, mainstream historicals, women's fiction, young adult, middle-grade, academics, historians, journalists, and psychology.

HOW TO CONTACT Query by e-mail only. No phone calls. Each of these agents has specific submission requirements, which you can find online at the agency's website. Obtains most new clients through recommendations from others, conferences, queries.

TERMS Agent receives 15% commission on domestic sales; 20% commission on foreign sales. Offers written contract.

THE JENNIFER DE CHIARA LITERARY AGENCY

299 Park Ave., Sixth Floor, New York NY 10171. (212)739-0803. **E-mail:** jenndec@aol.com. **Website:** www.jdlit.com. **Contact:** Jennifer De Chiara. Estab. 2001.

MEMBER AGENTS Jennifer De Chiara, jenndec@aol.com (fiction: literary, commercial, women's fiction [no bodice-rippers, please], chick lit, mystery, suspense, thriller, funny/quirky picture books, middle-grade, young adult; nonfiction: celebrity memoirs and biography, LGBTQ, memoirs, arts and performing arts, behind-the-scenes-type books, popular culture); **Stephen Fraser**, fraserstephena@gmail.com (one-of-a-kind picture books, strong chapter book series, whimsical, dramatic, or humorous middle-grade, dramatic or high-concept young adult, powerful and unusual nonfiction on a broad range of topics); **Marie Lamba**, marie.jdlit@gmail.com (young adult and middle-grade fiction, general and women's fiction, some memoir; interested in established illustrators and picture book authors);

Roseanne Wells, queryroseanne@gmail.com (literary fiction, young adult, middle-grade, narrative nonfiction, select memoir, science (popular or trade, not academic), history, religion (not inspirational), travel, humor, food/cooking, and similar subjects); **Victoria Selvaggio**, vselvaggio@windstream.net (board books, picture books, chapter books, middle-grade, young adult, New Adult, adult; nonfiction and fiction in all genres); **Damian McNicholl**, damianmcnichollvarney@gmail.com (accessible literary, historical [except naval, World War II, romance], legal thriller, offbeat/quirky, memoir, narrative nonfiction [especially biography, investigative journalism, cultural, legal, LGBTQ]); **Alexandra Weiss**, alexweiss.jdlit@gmail.com (voice-driven young adult stories, especially contemporary, science fiction, paranormal; quirky and fun middle-grade and children's books, magical realism, literary fiction).

REPRESENTS nonfiction, novels, juvenile books. **Considers these nonfiction areas:** art, autobiography, biography, child guidance, cooking, creative nonfiction, cultural interests, current affairs, dance, film, foods, gay/lesbian, health, history, humor, investigative, juvenile nonfiction, literature, memoirs, multicultural, parenting, philosophy, popular culture, politics, psychology, religious, science, self-help, sex, spirituality, technology, theater, travel, true crime, war, women's issues, women's studies, young adult. **Considers these fiction areas:** commercial, contemporary issues, crime, detective, ethnic, family saga, fantasy, feminist, gay, historical, horror, humor, inspirational, juvenile, lesbian, literary, mainstream, middle-grade, multicultural, mystery, New Adult, New Age, paranormal, picture books, science fiction, suspense, thriller, urban fantasy, women's, young adult.

HOW TO CONTACT Each agent has specific e-mail submission instructions; check the website for updates, as policies do change. Accepts simultaneous submissions. Obtains most new clients through recommendations from others, conferences, query letters.

TERMS Agent receives 15% commission on domestic sales. Offers written contract.

DEFIORE & COMPANY

47 E. 19th St., Third Floor, New York NY 10003. (212)925-7744. **Fax:** (212)925-9803. **E-mail:** info@

defliterary.com, submissions@defliterary.com.
Website: www.defliterary.com. Member of AAR.
Signatory of WGA.

○ Prior to becoming an agent, Mr. DeFiore was
publisher of Villard Books (1997-1998), editor-in-chief of Hyperion (1992-1997), editorial director of Delacorte Press (1988-1992),
and an editor at St. Martin's Press (1984-
1988).

MEMBER AGENTS Brian DeFiore (popular nonfiction, business, pop culture, parenting, commercial fiction); Laurie Abkemeier (memoir, parenting,
business, how-to/self-help, popular science); **Matthew Elblonk** (young adult, popular culture, narrative nonfiction); **Caryn Karmatz-Rudy** (popular fiction, self-help, narrative nonfiction); **Adam Schear**
(commercial fiction, humor, young adult, smart
thriller, historical fiction, quirky debut literary
novels, popular science, politics, popular culture,
current events); **Meredith Kaffel Simonoff** (smart
upmarket women's fiction, literary fiction [espe-
cially debut], literary thriller, narrative nonfiction,
nonfiction about science and tech, sophisticated
pop culture/humor books); **Rebecca Strauss** (literary and commercial fiction, women's fiction, urban
fantasy, romance, mystery, young adult, memoir,
pop culture, select nonfiction); **Lisa Gallagher** (fiction, nonfiction); **Nicole Tourtelot** (narrative and
prescriptive nonfiction, food, lifestyle, wellness, pop
culture, history, humor, memoir, select young adult
adult fiction); **Ashely Collom** (women's fiction, children's and young adult, psychological thriller, memoir, politics, photography, cooking, narrative nonfiction, LGBTQ issues, feminism, occult); **Miriam
Altshuler** (adult literary and commercial fiction,
narrative nonfiction, middle-grade, young adult,
memoir, narrative nonfiction, self-help, family sagas, historical novels); **Reiko Davis** (adult literary
and upmarket fiction, narrative nonfiction, young
adult, middle-grade, memoir).

REPRESENTS nonfiction, novels, short story collections, juvenile books, poetry books. **Considers
these nonfiction areas:** autobiography, biography, business, child guidance, cooking, economics,
foods, gay/lesbian, how-to, inspirational, money,
multicultural, parenting, photography, popular
culture, politics, psychology, religious, science, self-
help, sex, sports, technology, travel, women's issues,

young adult. **Considers these fiction areas:** comic
books, commercial, ethnic, feminist, gay, lesbian,
literary, mainstream, middle-grade, mystery, paranormal, picture books, poetry, romance, short story
collections, suspense, thriller, urban fantasy, wom-
en's, young adult.

☞ "Please be advised that we are not considering dramatic projects at this time."

HOW TO CONTACT Query with SASE or e-mail
to submissions@defliterary.com. "Please include the
word 'query' in the subject line. All attachments will
be deleted; please insert all text in the body of the e-
mail. For more information about our agents, their
individual interests, and their query guidelines,
please visit our About Us page on our website." Accepts simultaneous submissions. Obtains most new
clients through recommendations from others.

TERMS Agent receives 15% commission on domestic sales; 20% commission on foreign sales. Offers
written contract; 10-day notice must be given to
terminate contract. Charges clients for photocopying and overnight delivery (deducted only after a
sale is made).

SANDRA DIJKSTRA LITERARY AGENCY

1155 Camino del Mar, PMB 515, Del Mar CA 92014.
E-mail: elise@dijkstraagency.com. **E-mail:** que-
ries@dijkstraagency.com. **Website:** www.dijkstraa-
gency.com. The Dijkstra Agency was established
over 30 years ago and is known for guiding the
careers of many best-selling fiction and nonfiction authors, including Amy Tan, Lisa See, Maxine
Hong Kingston, Chitra Divakaruni, Eric Foner, and
Marcus Rediker. "We handle nearly all genres, except for poetry." Please see www.dijkstraagency.com
for each agent's interests. Member of AAR, Authors
Guild, Organization of American Historians, RWA.
Represents 100+ clients.

MEMBER AGENTS Sandra Dijkstra, president
(adult), **Elise Capron** (adult), **Jill Marr** (adult), **Thao
Le** (adult, young adult), **Roz Foster** (adult, young
adult), **Jessica Watterson** (subgenres of adult and
New Adult romance, women's fiction), **Suzy Evans**
(adult, young adult), and **Jennifer Kim** (adult and
young adult).

REPRESENTS nonfiction, fiction, novels, short
story collections, juvenile books, scholarly books.
Considers these nonfiction areas: Americana, animals, anthropology, art, biography, business, cre-

ative nonfiction, cultural interests, current affairs, design, economics, environment, ethnic, gardening, government, health, history, juvenile nonfiction, literature, memoirs, multicultural, parenting, popular culture, politics, psychology, science, self-help, sports, true crime, women's issues, women's studies, young adult, narrative. **Considers these fiction areas:** commercial, contemporary issues, detective, family saga, fantasy, feminist, historical, horror, juvenile, literary, mainstream, middle-grade, multicultural, mystery, New Adult, romance, science fiction, short story collections, sports, suspense, thriller, urban fantasy, women's, young adult.

HOW TO CONTACT "Please see guidelines on our website, www.dijkstraagency.com. Please note that we only accept e-mail submissions. Due to the large number of unsolicited submissions we receive, we are only able to respond those submissions in which we are interested." Accepts simultaneous submissions. Responds to queries of interest within 6 weeks.

TERMS Works in conjunction with foreign and film agents. Agent receives 15% commission on domestic sales; 20% commission on foreign sales. Offers written contract. No reading fee.

TIPS "Remember that publishing is a business. Do your research and present your project in as professional a way as possible. Only submit your work when you are confident that it is polished and ready for primetime. Make yourself a part of the active writing community by getting stories and articles published, networking with other writers, and getting a good sense of where your work fits in the market."

◎ DONADIO & OLSON, INC.

40 W. 27th St., Fifth Floor, New York NY 10001. (212)691-8077. **Fax:** (212)633-2837. **E-mail:** neil@donadio.com. **E-mail:** mail@donadio.com. **Website:** http://donadio.com. **Contact:** Neil Olson. Member of AAR. **MEMBER AGENTS** Neil Olson (no queries); Edward Hibbert (no queries); Carrie Howland, carrie@donadio.com (adult literary fiction, narrative nonfiction, young adult, middle-grade, picture books).

REPRESENTS nonfiction, novels. **Considers these nonfiction areas:** creative nonfiction. **Considers these fiction areas:** literary, middle-grade, picture books, young adult.

This agency represents mostly fiction and is very selective.

HOW TO CONTACT "Please send a query letter and the first three chapters/first 25 pages of the manuscript to mail@donadio.com. Please allow a minimum of 1 month for a reply. Accepts simultaneous submissions.

DONAGHY LITERARY GROUP

(647)527-4353. **E-mail:** stacey@donaghyliterary.com. **E-mail:** query@donaghyliterary.com. **Website:** www.donaghyliterary.com. **Contact:** Stacey Donaghy. "Donaghy Literary Group provides full-service literary representation to our clients at every stage of their writing careers. Specializing in commercial fiction, we seek middle-grade, young adult, New Adult, and adult novels."

Prior to opening her agency, Ms. Donaghy served as an agent at the Corvisiero Literary Agency. Before this, she worked in training and education, acquiring and editing academic materials for publication and training. Ms. Noble interned for Jessica Sinsheimer of Sarah Jane Freymann Literary Agency. Ms. Miller previously worked in children's publishing with Scholastic Canada and also interned with Bree Ogden during her time at the D4EO Agency. Ms. Ayers-Barnett is a former associate editor for Pocket Books, acquisitions editor for Re.ad Publishing, and a freelance book editor for New York Book Editors. Mr. Franks is a former bookseller and book club organizer for The Mysterious Bookshop in New York City, freelance editor for mysteriouspress.com, and proofreader for Europa Editions.

MEMBER AGENTS Stacey Donaghy (romantic suspense, LGBTQ, thriller, mystery, contemporary romance, erotic romance, young adult); **Valerie Noble** (historical, science fiction, fantasy [think Kristin Cashore and Suzanne Collins] for young adults and adults); **Sue Miller** (YA, urban fantasy, contemporary romance); **Amanda Ayers Barnett** (mystery/thriller, middle-grade, young adult, New Adult, women's fiction); **Alex Franks** (contemporary fiction, literary fiction, science fiction, espionage, thriller, mystery).

REPRESENTS fiction. **Considers these fiction areas:** commercial, crime, detective, erotica, ethnic, family saga, fantasy, feminist, gay, historical, horror, juvenile, lesbian, literary, mainstream, middle-grade, multicultural, mystery, New Adult, paranormal, police, psychic, romance, science fiction, sports, supernatural, suspense, thriller, urban fantasy, women's, young adult.

HOW TO CONTACT Query via e-mail, no attachments. Visit agency website for submission guidelines and for team to view agent bios. Do not e-mail agents directly. Accepts simultaneous submissions. Responds in 6-8 weeks to queries. Responds in 8-12 weeks to mss. Time may vary during holidays and closures.

TERMS Agent receives 15% commission on domestic sales; 20% commission on foreign sales. Offers written contract; 30-day notice must be given to terminate contract.

WRITERS CONFERENCES Romantic Times Booklovers Convention, Windsor International Writers Conference, OWC Ontario Writers Conference, SoCal Writers Conference, WD Toronto Writer's Workshop.

TIPS "Only submit to one DLG agent at a time; we work collaboratively and often share projects that may be better suited to another agent at the agency."

DUNHAM LITERARY, INC.

110 William St., Suite 2202, New York NY 10038. (212)929-0994. **E-mail:** query@dunhamlit.com. **Website:** www.dunhamlit.com. **Contact:** Jennie Dunham. Estab. 2000. Member of AAR, SCBWI. Represents 50 clients.

O   Prior to opening her agency, Ms. Dunham worked as a literary agent for Russell & Volkening. The Rhoda Weyr Agency is now a division of Dunham Literary, Inc.

MEMBER AGENTS Jennie Dunham, **Bridget Smith**.

REPRESENTS nonfiction, fiction, novels, short story collections, juvenile books. **Considers these nonfiction areas:** anthropology, archeology, art, biography, creative nonfiction, cultural interests, environment, health, history, language, literature, medicine, memoirs, multicultural, parenting, popular culture, politics, psychology, science, sociology, technology, women's issues, women's studies, young adult. **Considers these fiction areas:** family saga, fantasy, gay, historical, humor, juvenile, literary, mainstream, middle-grade, multicultural, mystery, New Adult, picture books, science fiction, short story collections,

sports, urban fantasy, women's, young adult, Westerns, horror, genre romance, poetry.

HOW TO CONTACT E-mail queries preferred, with all materials pasted in the body of the e-mail. Attachments will not be opened. Paper queries are also accepted. Please include a SASE for response and return of materials. If submitting to Bridget Smith, please include the first 5 pages with the query. Accepts simultaneous submissions. Responds in 4 weeks to queries, 2 months to mss. Obtains most new clients through recommendations from others, solicitations.

TERMS Agent receives 15% commission on domestic sales; 20% commission on foreign sales.

RECENT SALES Sales include *The Bad Kitty Series*, by Nick Bruel (Macmillan); *The Christmas Story*, by Robert Sabuda (Simon & Schuster); *The Gollywhopper Games* and sequels, by Jody Feldman (HarperCollins); *First & Then*, by Emma Mills (Macmillan); *Learning Not To Drown*, by Anna Shinoda (Simon & Schuster); *Gangsterland*, by Tod Goldberg (Counterpoint); *A Shadow All of Light*, by Fred Chappell (Tor); *Forward from Here*, by Reeve Lindbergh (Simon & Schuster).

DUNOW, CARLSON, & LERNER AGENCY

27 W. 20th St., Suite 1107, New York NY 10011. (212)645-7606. **E-mail:** mail@dclagency.com. **Website:** www.dclagency.com. Member of AAR.

MEMBER AGENTS Jennifer Carlson (narrative nonfiction writing and journalism: current events and ideas, cultural history; literary and upmarket commercial fiction); **Henry Dunow** (literary, historical, strongly written commercial fiction and voice-driven nonfiction across a range of area:–narrative history, biography, memoir, current affairs, cultural trends and criticism, science, sports); **Erin Hosier** (nonfiction: popular culture, music, sociology, memoir); **Betsy Lerner** (nonfiction: psychology, history, cultural studies, biography, current events, business; fiction: literary, dark, funny, voice driven); **Yishai Seidman** (fiction: literary, postmodern, thriller; nonfiction: sports, music, pop culture); **Amy Hughes** (nonfiction: history, cultural studies, memoir, current events, wellness, health, food, pop culture, biography; literary fiction); **Eleanor Jackson** (literary, commercial, memoir, art, food, science, history); **Julia Kenny** (adult, middle-grade, young adult, especially interested in dark, literary thriller and suspense); **Edward Necarsulmer IV** (strong new voices in teen & middle-grade, picture books); **Stacia Decker; Ari-**

elle Datz (adult, young adult, middle-grade, literary and commercial; nonfiction: essays, unconventional memoir, pop culture, sociology).

REPRESENTS nonfiction, fiction, novels, short story collections. **Considers these nonfiction areas:** art, biography, creative nonfiction, cultural interests, current affairs, foods, health, history, memoirs, music, popular culture, psychology, science, sociology, sports. **Considers these fiction areas:** commercial, literary, mainstream, middle-grade, mystery, picture books, thriller, young adult.

HOW TO CONTACT Query via snail mail with SASE or by e-mail; e-mail preferred. Paste 10 sample pages below query letter. No attachments. Will respond only if interested. Accepts simultaneous submissions. Responds in 4-6 weeks if interested.

RECENT SALES A full list of agency clients is on the website.

DYSTEL, GODERICH & BOURRET LLC

1 Union Square W., Suite 904, New York NY 10003. (212)627-9100. **Fax:** (212)627-9313. **Website:** www.dystel.com. Estab. 1994. Member of AAR, SCBWI. Represents 600+ clients.

MEMBER AGENTS Jane Dystel; **Miriam Goderich**, miriam@dystel.com (literary and commercial fiction, genre fiction, narrative nonfiction, pop culture, psychology, history, science, art, business books, biography/memoir); **Stacey Glick**, sglick@dystel.com (adult narrative nonfiction: memoir, parenting, cooking and food, psychology, science, health and wellness, lifestyle, current events, pop culture; young adult, middle-grade, children's nonfiction, select adult contemporary fiction); **Michael Bourret**, mbourret@dystel.com (middle-grade and young adult fiction, commercial adult fiction, and all sorts of nonfiction, from practical to narrative; especially interested in food and cocktail related books, memoir, popular history, politics, religion [though not spirituality], popular science, current events); **Jim McCarthy**, jmccarthy@dystel.com (literary women's fiction, underrepresented voices, mystery, romance, paranormal fiction, narrative nonfiction, memoir, paranormal nonfiction); **Jessica Papin**, jpapin@dystel.com (plot-driven literary and smart commercial fiction, narrative nonfiction: history, medicine, science, economics, women's issues); **Lauren Abramo**, labramo@dystel.com (humorous middle-grade and contemporary young adult, upmarket commercial adult fiction and well-paced literary fiction; adult narrative nonfiction: pop culture, psychology, pop science, reportage, media, contemporary culture; in nonfiction, has a strong preference for interdisciplinary approaches, and in all categories especially interested in underrepresented voices); **John Rudolph**, jrudolph@dystel.com (picture book author/illustrators, middle-grade, young adult, select commercial fiction, and narrative nonfiction—especially in music, sports, history, popular science, "big think," performing arts, health, business, memoir, military history, humor); **Sharon Pelletier**, spelletier@dystel.com (smart commercial fiction: upmarket women's fiction, domestic suspense, literary thriller; strong contemporary romance novels, compelling nonfiction projects, especially feminism and religion); **Michael Hoogland**, mhoogland@dystel.com (thriller, science fiction and fantasy, young adult, upmarket women's fiction, narrative nonfiction); **Erin Young**, eyoung@dystel.com (YA/Middle-grade, literary and intellectual commercial thriller, memoirs, biography, sport and science narratives); **Amy Bishop**, abishop@dystel.com (commercial and literary women's fiction, fiction from diverse authors, historical fiction, young adult, personal narratives, biography); **Kemi Faderin**, kfaderin@dystel.com (smart, plot-driven young adult, historical fiction/nonfiction, contemporary women's fiction, and literary fiction).

REPRESENTS Considers these nonfiction areas: animals, art, autobiography, biography, business, cooking, cultural interests, current affairs, ethnic, foods, gay/lesbian, health, history, humor, inspirational, investigative, medicine, memoirs, metaphysics, military, New Age, parenting, popular culture, politics, psychology, religious, science, sports, women's issues, women's studies. **Considers these fiction areas:** commercial, ethnic, gay, lesbian, literary, mainstream, middle-grade, mystery, paranormal, romance, suspense, thriller, women's, young adult.

☞ "We are actively seeking fiction for all ages, in all genres." No plays, screenplays, or poetry.

HOW TO CONTACT Query via e-mail and put "Query" in the subject line. "Synopses, outlines, or sample chapters (say, 1 chapter or the first 25 pages of your manuscript) should either be included below the cover letter or attached as a separate document. We won't open attachments if they come with a blank e-mail." Accepts simultaneous submissions. Responds in 6 to 8 weeks to queries, in 8 weeks to mss. Obtains most new clients through recommendations from others, solicitations, conferences.

TERMS Agent receives 15% commission on domestic sales; 19% commission on foreign sales. Offers written contract.

TIPS "DGLM prides itself on being a full-service agency. We're involved in every stage of the publishing process, from offering substantial editing on mss and proposals to coming up with book ideas for authors looking for their next project, negotiating contracts, and collecting monies for our clients. We follow a book from its inception through its sale to a publisher, its publication, and beyond. Our commitment to our writers does not, by any means, end when we have collected our commission. This is one of the many things that makes us unique in a very competitive business."

EDEN STREET LITERARY

P.O. Box 30, Billings NY 12510. **E-mail:** info@edenstreetlit.com. **E-mail:** submissions@edenstreetlit.com. **Website:** www.edenstreetlit.com. **Contact:** Liza Voges. Eden Street represents over 40 authors and author-illustrators of books for young readers from preschool through young adult. Its books have won numerous awards over the past 30 years. Eden Street prides itself on tailoring services to each client's goals, working in tandem with them to achieve literary, critical, and commercial success. Welcomes the opportunity to work with additional authors and illustrators. This agency gives priority to members of SCBWI. Member of AAR. Signatory of WGA. Represents over 40 clients.

REPRESENTS nonfiction, fiction, novels, juvenile books. **Considers these fiction areas:** juvenile, middle-grade, picture books, young adult.

HOW TO CONTACT E-mail a picture book ms or dummy, a synopsis and 3 chapters of a Middle-grade or young adult novel, or a proposal and 3 sample chapters for nonfiction. Accepts simultaneous submissions. Responds only to submissions of interest.

RECENT SALES *Dream Dog*, by Lou Berger; *Biscuit Loves the Library*, by Alyssa Capucilli; *The Scraps Book*, by Lois Ehlert; *Two Bunny Buddies*, by Kathryn O. Galbraith; *Between Two Worlds*, by Katherine Kirkpatrick.

JUDITH EHRLICH LITERARY MANAGEMENT, LLC

146 Central Park W., 20E, New York NY 10023. (646)505-1570. **Fax:** (646)505-1570. **E-mail:** jehrlich@judithehrlichliterary.com. **Website:** www.judithehrlichliterary.com. Judith Ehrlich Literary Management LLC, established in 2002 and based in New York City, is a full-service agency. "We represent nonfiction and fiction, both literary and commercial, for the mainstream trade market. Our approach is very hands-on, editorial, and constructive with the primary goal of helping authors build successful writing careers. Special areas of interest include compelling narrative nonfiction, outstanding biography and memoirs, lifestyle books, works that reflect our changing culture, women's issues, psychology, science, social issues, current events, parenting, health, history, business, and prescriptive books offering fresh information and advice. We also seek and represent stellar commercial and literary fiction, including romance and other women's fiction, historical fiction, literary mystery, and select thriller. Our agency deals closely with all major and independent publishers. When appropriate, we place our properties with foreign agents and co-agents at leading film agencies in New York and Los Angeles." Estab. 2002. Member of the Authors' Guild, American Society of Journalists and Authors.

Prior to her current position, Ms. Ehrlich was a senior associate at the Linda Chester Agency and is an award-winning journalist. She is the co-author of *The New Crowd: The Changing of the Jewish Guard on Wall Street* (Little, Brown).

MEMBER AGENTS Judith Ehrlich, jehrlich@judithehrlichliterary.com (upmarket, literary, and quality commercial fiction, nonfiction: narrative, women's, business, prescriptive, medical and health-related topics, history, current events).

REPRESENTS nonfiction, fiction, novels, short story collections, juvenile books. **Considers these nonfiction areas:** animals, art, autobiography, biography, business, creative nonfiction, cultural interests, current affairs, diet/nutrition, health, history, how-to, humor, inspirational, investigative, juvenile nonfiction, memoirs, parenting, photography, popular culture, politics, psychology, science, self-help, sociology, true crime, women's issues, young adult. **Considers these fiction areas:** adventure, commercial, contemporary issues, crime, detective, family saga, historical, humor, juvenile, literary, middle-grade, mystery, picture books, short story collections, suspense, thriller, women's, young adult.

Does not want to receive novellas, poetry, textbooks, plays, or screenplays.

HOW TO CONTACT E-query, with a synopsis and some sample pages. The agency will respond only if interested. Accepts simultaneous submissions.

RECENT SALES *The Bicycle Spy*, by Yona Zeldis McDonough (Scholastic); *The House on Primrose Pond*, by Yona McDonough (NAL/Penguin); *You Were Meant for Me*, by Yona McDonough (NAL/Penguin); *Echoes of Us: The Hybrid Chronicles*, Book 3 by Kat Zhang (HarperCollins); *Once We Were: The Hybrid Chronicles* Book 2, by Kat Zhang (HarperCollins).

EINSTEIN LITERARY MANAGEMENT

27 W. 20th St., #1003, New York NY 10011. (212)221-8797. **E-mail:** info@einsteinliterary.com. **E-mail:** submissions@einsteinliterary.com. **Website:** http://einsteinliterary.com. **Contact:** Susanna Einstein. Estab. 2015. Member of AAR. Signatory of WGA.

○ Prior to her current position, Ms. Einstein was with LJK Literary Management and the Einstein Thompson Agency.

MEMBER AGENTS Susanna Einstein, Susan Graham, Shana Kelly.

REPRESENTS nonfiction, fiction, novels, short story collections, juvenile books. **Considers these nonfiction areas:** cooking, creative nonfiction, memoirs, blog-to-book projects. **Considers these fiction areas:** comic books, commercial, crime, fantasy, historical, juvenile, literary, middle-grade, mystery, picture books, romance, science fiction, suspense, thriller, women's, young adult.

⌐ "As an agency we represent a broad range of literary and commercial fiction, including upmarket women's fiction, crime fiction, historical fiction, romance, and books for middle-grade children and young adults, including picture books and graphic novels. We also handle nonfiction, including cookbooks, memoir, and narrative, and blog-to-book projects. Please see agent bios on the website for specific information about what each of ELM's agents represents." Does not want poetry, textbooks, or screenplays.

HOW TO CONTACT Please submit a query letter and the first 10 double-spaced pages of your manuscript in the body of the e-mail (no attachments). Does not respond to mail queries, telephone queries, or queries that are not specifically addressed to agency. Accepts simultaneous submissions. Responds in 6 weeks if interested.

ETHAN ELLENBERG LITERARY AGENCY

155 Suffolk St., #2R, New York NY 10002. (212)431-4554. **E-mail:** agent@ethanellenberg.com. **Website:** http://ethanellenberg.com. **Contact:** Ethan Ellenberg. This agency specializes in commercial fiction and nonfiction. Estab. 1984. Member of AAR, Science Fiction and Fantasy Writer's of America, SCBWI, RWA, MWA.

MEMBER AGENTS Ethan Ellenberg, president; Evan Gregory, senior agent; Bibi Lewis, associate agent (YA, women's fiction).

REPRESENTS nonfiction, fiction. **Considers these nonfiction areas:** biography, cooking, current affairs, health, history, memoirs, New Age, popular culture, psychology, science, spirituality, true crime, adventure. **Considers these fiction areas:** commercial, ethnic, fantasy, literary, middle-grade, mystery, picture books, romance, science fiction, thriller, women's, young adult, general.

⌐ "We specialize in commercial fiction and children's books. In commercial fiction, we want to see science fiction, fantasy, romance, mystery, thriller, women's fiction; all genres welcome. In children's books, we want to see everything: picture books, early reader, middle-grade, and young adult. We do some nonfiction: history, biography, military, popular science, and cutting-edge books about any subject." Does not want to receive poetry, short stories, or screenplays.

HOW TO CONTACT Query by e-mail. Paste all of the material in the order listed. Fiction: query letter, synopsis, first 50 pages. Nonfiction: query letter, book proposal. Picture books: query letter, complete ms, 4-5 sample illustrations. Illustrators: query letter, 4-5 sample illustrations, link to online portfolio. Will not respond unless interested. Accepts simultaneous submissions. Responds in 2 weeks.

EMERALD CITY LITERARY AGENCY

2522 North Proctor St., Suite 359, Tacoma WA 98406. **E-mail:** Mandy@EmeraldCityLiterary.com, QueryLinda@EmeraldCityLiterary.com, querylindsay@emeraldcityliterary.com. **Website:** https://emeraldcityliterary.com. "Emerald City Literary Agency is a boutique literary agency located just outside of Seattle, Washington—otherwise known as the

Emerald City; hence, the agency's name. But our location isn't the only reason we chose this moniker. The desire to be published might just be the biggest dream you can imagine. And if you found this website, then you must have something in common with Dorothy and her trio of new friends—you're on a journey to find someone who can grant your greatest wish." Estab. 2015.

MEMBER AGENTS Mandy Hubbard (closed to submissions); **Linda Epstein** (picture books, middle-grade and young adult fiction, children's nonfiction); **Lindsay Mealing** (science fiction, fantasy, young adult); **Kirsten Wolf** (contracts manager). **REPRESENTS** nonfiction, fiction, novels, juvenile books. **Considers these nonfiction areas:** juvenile nonfiction. **Considers these fiction areas:** fantasy, middle-grade, picture books, science fiction, young adult.

⚷ Linda Epstein: no adult literature. Lindsay Mealing: no middle-grade, nonfiction, short fiction, or adult fiction outside the science fiction and fantasy genres.

HOW TO CONTACT To query Linda Epstein: include a one-page query letter and the first 20 pages of your manuscript in the body of the e-mail. If you're sending a picture book, include the full text of the manuscript in the body of the e-mail. To query Lindsay Mealing: paste the first 5 pages of your manuscript below your query; attachments will not be opened. Accepts simultaneous submissions.

EVATOPIA, INC.

8447 Wilshire Blvd., Suite 401, Beverly Hills CA 90211. **E-mail:** submissions@evatopia.com. **Website:** www.evatopia.com. **Contact:** Margery Walshaw. Evatopia supports writers through consulting, literary management, and publishing services. Estab. 2004. Member of BAFTA, IBPA, NetGalley. Represents 15 clients.

◖ Prior to becoming an agent, Ms. Walshaw was a writer and publicist for the entertainment industry.

MEMBER AGENTS Mary Kay, story development; **Jamie Davis**, story editor; **Jill Jones**, story editor. **REPRESENTS** nonfiction, fiction, novels, juvenile books, movie scripts, feature film, TV movie of the week. **Considers these fiction areas:** crime, detective, fantasy, juvenile, New Adult, paranormal, romance, supernatural, thriller, women's, young adult, proj-

ects aimed at women, teens, and children. **Considers these script areas:** action, contemporary issues, detective, movie scripts, romantic drama, supernatural, TV movie of the week, projects aimed at women, teens, and children. Represents screenplays and novels. Provides self-publishing support to novelists.

⚷ "All of our staff members have strong writing and entertainment backgrounds, making us sympathetic to the needs of our clients."

HOW TO CONTACT Submit via online submission form at www.evatopiaentertainment.com. Accepts simultaneous submissions. Obtains most new clients through recommendations.

TERMS Agent receives 15% commission on domestic sales; 15% commission on foreign sales. Offers written contract; 30-day notice must be given to terminate contract.

TIPS "Remember that you only have one chance to make that important first impression. Make your loglines original and your synopses concise. The secret to a screenwriter's success is creating an original story and telling it in a manner that we haven't heard before."

DIANA FINCH LITERARY AGENCY

116 W. 23rd St., Suite 500, New York NY 10011. (917)544-4470. **E-mail:** diana.finch@verizon.net. **E-mail:** diana.finch@verizon.net or via link at the website (preferred). **Website:** http://dianafinchliteraryagency.blogspot.com; www.facebook.com/DianaFinchLitAg. **Contact:** Diana Finch. A boutique agency in Manhattan's Chelsea neighborhood. "Many of the agency's clients are journalists, and I handle book-related magazine assignments as well as book deals. I am the chair of the AAR's International Committee, attend overseas book fairs, and actively handle foreign rights to my clients' work." Estab. 2003. Member of AAR. Represents 40 clients.

◖ Seeking to represent books that change lives. Prior to opening her agency in 2003, Ms. Finch worked at Ellen Levine Literary Agency for 18 years and started her publishing career in the editorial department at St. Martin's Press.

REPRESENTS nonfiction, fiction, novels, scholarly books. **Considers these nonfiction areas:** autobiography, biography, business, child guidance, computers, cultural interests, current affairs, dance, diet/nutrition, economics, environment, ethnic, film, government, health, history, how-to, humor, investigative, juvenile nonfiction, law, medicine, memoirs, military, money, music, parenting, photography, popular culture, politics, psychology, satire, science, self-help, sex, sports, technology, theater, translation, true crime, war, women's issues, women's studies, young adult. **Considers these fiction areas:** action, adventure, contemporary issues, crime, detective, ethnic, historical, literary, mainstream, New Adult, police, sports, thriller, young adult.

> Does not want romance, mystery, or children's picture books.

HOW TO CONTACT This agency prefers submissions via its online form. Accepts simultaneous submissions. Obtains most new clients through recommendations from others.

TERMS Agent receives 15% commission on domestic sales; 20% commission on foreign sales. Offers written contract. "I charge for overseas postage, galleys, and books purchased, and try to recoup these costs from earnings received for a client, rather than charging outright."

RECENT SALES *Stealing Schooling*, by Professor Noliwe Rooks (The New Press); *Merchants of Men*, by Loretta Napoleoni (Seven Stories Press); *Beyond $15*, by Jonathan Rosenblum (Beacon Press); *The Age of Inequality*, by the Editors of In These Times (Verso Books); *Seeds of Rebellion*, by Mark Schapiro (Hot Books/Skyhorse).

WRITERS CONFERENCES Florida Writers Conference; Washington Writers Conference; Writers Digest NYC Conference; CLMP/New School conference, and more.

TIPS "Do as much research as you can on agents before you query. Have someone critique your query letter before you send it. It should be only 1 page and describe your book clearly—and why you are writing it—but also demonstrate creativity and a sense of your writing style."

FINEPRINT LITERARY MANAGEMENT

207 W. 106th St., Suite 1D, New York NY 10025. (212)279-1282. **Website:** www.fineprintlit.com. Estab. 2007. Member of AAR.

MEMBER AGENTS Peter Rubie, CEO, peter@ fineprintlit.com (nonfiction: narrative nonfiction, popular science, spirituality, history, biography, pop culture, business, technology, parenting, health, self-help, music, food; fiction: literary thriller, crime fiction, science fiction and fantasy, military fiction and literary fiction, middle-grade, boy-oriented young adult fiction); Stephany Evans, stephany@fineprintlit.com (nonfiction: health and wellness, spirituality, lifestyle, food and drink, sustainability, running and fitness, memoir, narrative nonfiction; fiction: mystery/crime, women's fiction, from literary to commercial to romance); Laura Wood, laura@fineprintlit.com (serious nonfiction:, science and nature, business, history, religion, and other areas by academics, experienced professionals, journalists; select genre fiction only: science fiction and fantasy and mystery); June Clark, june@fineprintlit.com (nonfiction: entertainment, self-help, parenting, reference/how-to books, food and wine, style/beauty, prescriptive business titles); Jacqueline Murphy, jacqueline@fineprintlit.com.

REPRESENTS nonfiction, fiction, novels, short story collections. **Considers these nonfiction areas:** biography, business, cooking, cultural interests, current affairs, diet/nutrition, environment, foods, health, history, how-to, humor, investigative, medicine, memoirs, music, parenting, popular culture, psychology, science, self-help, spirituality, technology, travel, women's issues, fitness, lifestyle. **Considers these fiction areas:** commercial, crime, fantasy, historical, literary, mainstream, middle-grade, mystery, romance, science fiction, suspense, thriller, women's, young adult.

HOW TO CONTACT E-query. For fiction, send a query, synopsis, bio, and 30 pages pasted into the e-mail. No attachments. For nonfiction, send a query only; proposal requested later if the agent is interested. Accepts simultaneous submissions. Obtains most new clients through recommendations from others, solicitations.

TERMS Agent receives 15% commission on domestic sales; 20% commission on foreign sales.

FLANNERY LITERARY

1140 Wickfield Ct., Naperville IL 60563. **E-mail:** jennifer@flanneryliterary.com. **Website:** flanneryliterary.com. **Contact:** Jennifer Flannery. "Flannery Literary is a Chicago-area literary agency representing writers of books for children and young adults, because the most interesting, well-written, and time-honored books are written with young people in mind." Estab. 1992. Represents 40 clients.

REPRESENTS nonfiction, fiction, novels, juvenile books. **Considers these nonfiction areas:** young adult. **Considers these fiction areas:** juvenile, middle-grade, New Adult, picture books, young adult.

- ☞ This agency specializes in children's and young adult fiction and nonfiction. It also accepts picture books. 100% juvenile books.

HOW TO CONTACT Query by e-mail only. "Multiple queries are fine, but please inform us. Please, no attachments. If you're sending a query about a novel, please include in the e-mail the first 5-10 pages; if it's a picture book, please include the entire text." Accepts simultaneous submissions. Responds in 2 weeks to queries, 1 month to mss. Obtains new clients through referrals, queries.

TERMS Agent receives 15% commission on domestic sales; 20% commission on foreign sales. Offers written contract, binding for life of book in print.

TIPS "Write an engrossing, succinct query describing your work. We are always looking for a fresh new voice."

FLETCHER & CO.

78 Fifth Ave., Third Floor, New York NY 10011. **E-mail:** info@fletcherandco.com. **Website:** www.fletcherandco.com. **Contact:** Christy Fletcher. Today, Fletcher & Co. is a full-service literary management and production company dedicated to writers of upmarket nonfiction as well as commercial and literary fiction. Estab. 2003. Member of AAR.

MEMBER AGENTS Christy Fletcher (referrals only); Melissa Chinchillo (select list of her own authors); Rebecca Gradinger (literary fiction, up-market commercial fiction, narrative nonfiction, self-help, memoir, women's studies, humor, pop culture); Gráinne Fox (literary fiction, quality commercial authors, award-winning journalists and food writers, American voices, international, literary crime, upmarket fiction, narrative nonfiction); Lisa Grubka (fiction: literary, upmarket women's, young adult; and nonfiction: narrative, food, science, and more); Sylvie Greenberg (literary fiction, business, sports, science, memoir, history); Donald Lamm (history, biography, investigative journalism, politics, current affairs, business); Todd Sattersten (business); Eric Lupfer; Sarah Fuentes; Veronica Goldstein; Mink Choi; Erin McFadden.

REPRESENTS nonfiction, novels. **Considers these nonfiction areas:** biography, business, creative nonfiction, current affairs, foods, history, humor, investigative, memoirs, popular culture, politics, science, self-help, sports, women's studies. **Considers these**

fiction areas: commercial, crime, literary, women's, young adult.

HOW TO CONTACT Send queries to info@fletcherandco.com. Please do not include e-mail attachments with your initial query, as they will be deleted. Address your query to a specific agent. No snail mail queries. Accepts simultaneous submissions.

RECENT SALES *The Profiteers*, by Sally Denton; *The Longest Night*, by Andrea Williams; *Disrupted: My Misadventure in the Start-Up Bubble*, by Dan Lyons; *Free Re-Fills: A Doctor Confronts His Addiction*, by Peter Grinspoon, M.D.; *Black Man in a White Coat: A Doctor's Reflections on Race and Medicine*, by Damon Tweedy, M.D.

FOLIO LITERARY MANAGEMENT, LLC

The Film Center Building, 630 Ninth Ave., Suite 1101, New York NY 10036. (212)400-1494. **Fax:** (212)967-0977. **Website:** www.foliolit.com. Member of AAR. Represents 100+ clients.

- ○ Prior to creating Folio Literary Management, Mr. Hoffman worked for several years at another agency. Mr. Kleinman was an agent at Graybill & English.

MEMBER AGENTS Claudia Cross (romance novels, commercial women's fiction, cooking and food, serious nonfiction on religious and spiritual topics); Scott Hoffman (literary and commercial fiction, journalistic or academic nonfiction, narrative nonfiction, pop culture books, business, history, politics, spiritual or religious-themed fiction and nonfiction, science fiction/fantasy literary fiction, heartbreaking memoirs, humorous nonfiction); Jeff Kleinman (bookclub fiction [not genre commercial like mystery or romances], literary fiction, thriller and suspense novels, narrative nonfiction, memoir); Dado Derviskadic (nonfiction: cultural history, biography, memoir, pop science, motivational self-help, health/nutrition, pop culture, cookbooks; fiction that's gritty, introspective, or serious); Frank Weimann (biography, business/investing/finance, history, religious, mind/body/spirit, health, lifestyle, cookbooks, sports, African-American, science, memoir, special forces/CIA/FBI/Mafia, military, prescriptive nonfiction, humor, celebrity, adult and children's fiction); Michael Harriot (commercial nonfiction (both narrative and prescriptive) and fantasy/science fiction); Erin Harris (book club, historical fiction, literary, narrative nonfiction, psychological suspense, young adult); **Katherine Latshaw** (blogs-to-books, food/cooking, middle-grade, narrative and prescriptive nonfiction); **Annie Hwang** (literary and upmarket fiction with commercial appeal; select nonfiction: popular science, diet/health/fitness, lifestyle, narrative nonfiction, pop culture, humor); **Erin Niumata** (fiction: commercial women's fiction, romance, historical fiction, mystery, psychological thriller, suspense, humor; nonfiction: self-help, women's issues, pop culture and humor, pet care/pets, memoirs, anything blogger); **Ruth Pomerance** (narrative nonfiction and commercial fiction); **Marcy Posner** (adult: commercial women's fiction, historical fiction, mystery, biography, history, health, lifestyle, commercial novels, thriller, narrative nonfiction; children's: contemporary young adult and Middle-grade, mystery series for boys, select historical fiction, fantasy); **Jeff Silberman** (narrative nonfiction, biography, history, politics, current affairs, health, lifestyle, humor, food/cookbook, memoir, pop culture, sports, science, technology; commercial, literary, book club fiction); **Steve Troha**; **Emily van Beek** (YA, Middle-grade, picture books), **Melissa White** (general nonfiction, literary and commercial fiction, Middle-grade, young adult); **John Cusick** (middle-grade, picture books, young adult); **Jamie Chambliss**.

REPRESENTS nonfiction, novels. **Considers these nonfiction areas:** animals, art, biography, business, cooking, creative nonfiction, economics, environment, foods, health, history, how-to, humor, inspirational, memoirs, military, parenting, popular culture, politics, psychology, religious, satire, science, self-help, technology, war, women's issues, women's studies. **Considers these fiction areas:** commercial, fantasy, horror, literary, middle-grade, mystery, picture books, religious, romance, thriller, women's, young adult.

☛ No poetry, stage plays, or screenplays.

HOW TO CONTACT Query via e-mail only (no attachments). Read agent bios online for specific submission guidelines and e-mail addresses, and to check if someone is closed to queries. "All agents respond to queries as soon as possible, whether interested or not. If you haven't heard back from the individual agent within the time period specified on his or her bio page, it's possible that something has gone wrong and your query has been lost—in that case, please e-mail a follow-up."

TIPS "Please do not submit simultaneously to more than one agent at Folio. If you're not sure which of us is exactly right for your book, don't worry; we work closely as a team, and if one of our agents gets a query that might be more appropriate for someone else, we'll always pass it along. It's important that you check each agent's bio page for clear directions as to how to submit, as well as when to expect feedback."

FOUNDRY LITERARY + MEDIA

33 W. 17th St., PH, New York NY 10011. (212)929-5064. **Fax:** (212)929-5471. **Website:** www.foundry-media.com.

MEMBER AGENTS Peter McGuigan, pmsubmissions@foundrymedia.com (smart, offbeat voices in all genres of fiction and nonfiction); **Yfat Reiss Gendell**, yrgsubmissions@foundrymedia.com (practical nonfiction: health and wellness, diet, lifestyle, how-to, parenting; narrative nonfiction: humor, memoir, history, science, pop culture, psychology, adventure/travel stories; unique commercial fiction, including young adult fiction, that touch on her nonfiction interests, including speculative fiction, thriller, historical fiction); **Chris Park**, cpsubmissions@foundrymedia.com (memoirs, narrative nonfiction, sports books, Christian nonfiction, character-driven fiction); **Hannah Brown Gordon**, hbgsubmissions@foundrymedia.com (stories and narratives that blend genres, including thriller, suspense, historical, literary, speculative, memoir, pop-science, psychology, humor, pop culture); **Brandi Bowles,** bbsubmissions@foundrymedia.com (nonfiction: cookbooks to prescriptive books, science, pop culture, real-life inspirational stories; high-concept novels that feature strong female bonds and psychological or scientific themes); **Kirsten Neuhaus**, knsubmissions@foundrymedia.com (platform-driven narrative nonfiction: memoir, business, lifestyle [beauty/fashion/relationships], current events, history, stories with strong female voices; smart fiction that appeals to a wide market); **Jessica Regel**, jrsubmissions@foundrymedia.com (young adult and middle-grade books, as well as a select list of adult general fiction, women's fiction, adult nonfiction); **Anthony Mattero**, amsubmissions@foundrymedia.com (smart, platform-driven nonfiction: pop culture, humor, music, sports, pop-business); **Peter Steinberg**, pssubmissions@foundrymedia.com (narrative nonfiction, commercial and literary fiction, memoir, health, history, lifestyle, humor, sports, young adult); **Roger Freet**, rfsubmissions@foundrymedia.com (narrative and idea-driven nonfictio:n religion, spirituality, memoir, cultural issues by leading scholars, pastors, historians, activists and musicians); **Adriann Ranta**, arsubmissions@foundrymedia.com (accepts all genres and age groups; loves gritty, realistic, true-to-life narratives; women's fiction and nonfiction; accessible, pop nonfiction in science, history, craft; smart, fresh, genre-bending works for children).

REPRESENTS Considers these nonfiction areas: creative nonfiction, current affairs, diet/nutrition, health, history, how-to, humor, medicine, memoirs, music, parenting, popular culture, psychology, science, sports, travel. **Considers these fiction areas:** commercial, historical, humor, literary, middle-grade, suspense, thriller, women's, young adult.

HOW TO CONTACT Target one agent only. Send queries to the specific submission e-mail of the agent. For fiction, send query, synopsis, author bio, first 3 chapters—all pasted in the e-mail. For nonfiction, send query, sample chapters, TOC, author bio (all pasted). "We regret that we cannot guarantee a response to every submission we receive. If you do not receive a response within 8 weeks, your submission is not right for our lists at this time." Accepts simultaneous submissions.

TIPS "Consult website for each agent's submission instructions."

FOX LITERARY

110 W. 40th St., Suite 2305, New York NY 10018. **E-mail:** submissions@foxliterary.com. **Website:** foxliterary.com. Fox Literary is a boutique agency that represents commercial fiction, along with select works of literary fiction and nonfiction that have broad commercial appeal.

MEMBER AGENTS Diana Fox.

REPRESENTS nonfiction, fiction, graphic novels. **Considers these nonfiction areas:** biography, creative nonfiction, history, popular culture, mind/body/spirit. **Considers these fiction areas:** fantasy, historical, romance, science fiction, thriller, young adult, general.

HOW TO CONTACT E-mail query and first 5 pages in body of e-mail; e-mail queries preferred. No e-mail attachments. For snail mail queries, must include an e-mail address for response and no response means "No." Do not send SASE. Accepts simultaneous submissions.

FRASER-BUB LITERARY, LLC

401 Park Avenue South, 10th Floor, New York NY 10016. (917)524-6982. **E-mail:** mackenzie@fraserbubliterary.com. **E-mail:** submissions@fraserbubliterary.com. **Website:** http://www.fraserbubliterary.com/. "Fraser-Bub Literary enthusiastically capitalizes on all subsidiary rights platforms, including eBook, audio, serial, performance, and translation rights. MacKenzie Fraser-Bub has a solid network of media professionals that can be called upon to assist her in implementing her clients' goals; these include eBook experts, film and TV agents, scouts, and publicity and marketing gurus. " Estab. 2016.

○ MacKenzie Fraser-Bub began her career in publishing as a teenager reading manuscripts and writing readers reports at the Crown Publishing Group, a division of Penguin Random House. She is a veteran of the Columbia Publishing Course, having taught and worked there. She also spent several years at Simon and Schuster (Touchstone Books), in one of the industry's finest marketing departments, before becoming an agent at the venerable Trident Media Group.

MEMBER AGENTS MacKenzie Fraser-Bub; **Linda Kaplan** (subrights director); **Kasey Poserina** (contracts director).

REPRESENTS nonfiction, fiction, novels. **Considers these nonfiction areas:** cooking, diet/nutrition, design, foods, psychology, self-help, true crime, fashion, exercise, relationships. **Considers these fiction areas:** crime, historical, mystery, New Adult, romance, thriller, women's, young adult.

⌐ "99.9% of the time I am not interested in science, fantasy, westerns, philosophy, sports. I am never interested in children's/picture books, middle-grade, screenplays, poetry, graphic novels/comics."

HOW TO CONTACT E-mail your query to submissions@fraserbubliterary.com. Include the word "Query" in your subject line. For fiction submissions, your query may include the first chapter in the body of the e-mail. For nonfiction submissions, your query may include the first 10 pages in the body of the e-mail. No attachments. Accepts simultaneous submissions. Responds in 1 week for queries, 6 weeks for mss.

SARAH JANE FREYMANN LITERARY AGENCY

(212)362-9277. **E-mail:** sarah@sarahjanefreymann.com, submissions@sarahjanefreymann.com. **Website:** www.sarahjanefreymann.com. **Contact:** Sarah Jane Freymann, Steve Schwartz.

MEMBER AGENTS Sarah Jane Freymann (nonfiction: spiritual, psychology, self-help, women/men's issues, books by health experts [conventional and alternative], cookbooks, narrative nonfiction, natural science, nature, memoirs, cutting-edge journalism, travel, multicultural issues, parenting, lifestyle, fiction: literary, mainstream young adult); **Jessica Sinsheimer**, jessica@sarahjanefreymann.com; **Steven Schwartz**, steve@sarahjanefreymann.com (popular fiction [crime, thriller, historical novels], world and national affairs, business books, self-help, psychology, humor, sports, travel).

REPRESENTS nonfiction, fiction, novels. **Considers these nonfiction areas:** business, cooking, creative nonfiction, current affairs, health, humor, memoirs, multicultural, parenting, psychology, science, self-help, spirituality, sports, travel, women's issues, men's issues, nature, journalism, lifestyle. **Considers these fiction areas:** crime, historical, literary, mainstream, thriller, young adult, popular fiction.

HOW TO CONTACT Query via e-mail. No attachments. Below the query, please paste the first 10 pages of your work. Accepts simultaneous submissions.

TERMS Charges clients for long distance, overseas postage, photocopying. 100% of business is derived from commissions on ms sales.

REBECCA FRIEDMAN LITERARY AGENCY

E-mail: brandie@rfliterary.com. **Website:** www.rfliterary.com. Estab. 2013. Member of AAR. Signatory of WGA.

○ Prior to opening her own agency in 2013, Ms. Friedman was with Sterling Lord Literistic from 2006 to 2011, then with Hill Nadell Agency.

MEMBER AGENTS Rebecca Friedman (commercial and literary fiction, with a focus on literary novels of suspense, women's fiction, contemporary romance, young adult; journalistic nonfiction and memoir); **Susan Finesman**, susan@rfliterary.com (fiction, cookbooks, lifestyle); **Abby Schulman**, abby@rfliterary.com (YA and nonfiction: health,

wellness, personal development); **Brandie Coonis**, brandie@rfliterary.com (writers that defy genre).

REPRESENTS nonfiction, fiction. **Considers these nonfiction areas:** cooking, health, memoirs, journalistic nonfiction. **Considers these fiction areas:** commercial, fantasy, literary, mystery, New Adult, romance, science fiction, suspense, women's, young adult.

HOW TO CONTACT Please submit your query letter and first chapter (no more than 15 pages, double-spaced). If querying Kimberly, paste a full synopsis into the e-mail submission; no attachments. Accepts simultaneous submissions. Tries to respond in 6-8 weeks.

RECENT SALES A complete list of agency authors is available online.

THE FRIEDRICH AGENCY

19 W. 21st St., Suite 201, New York NY 10010. (212)317-8810. **E-mail:** mfriedrich@friedrichagency.com; lcarson@friedrichagency.com; kwolf@friedrichagency.com. **Website:** www.friedrichagency.com. **Contact:** Molly Friedrich; Lucy Carson; Kent D. Wolf. Estab. 2006. Member of AAR. Signatory of WGA. Represents 50+ clients.

○ Prior to her current position, Ms. Friedrich was an agent at the Aaron Priest Literary Agency.

MEMBER AGENTS Molly Friedrich, founder and agent; **Lucy Carson**, TV/film rights director and agent; **Kent D. Wolf**, foreign rights director and agent.

REPRESENTS nonfiction, fiction, novels, short story collections. **Considers these nonfiction areas:** creative nonfiction, memoirs. **Considers these fiction areas:** commercial, literary, multicultural, suspense, women's, young adult.

HOW TO CONTACT Query by e-mail only. Please query only one agent at this agency. Accepts simultaneous submissions.

RECENT SALES *W is for Wasted*, by Sue Grafton; *Olive Kitteridge*, by Elizabeth Strout. Other clients include Frank McCourt, Jane Smiley, Esmeralda Santiago, Terry McMillan, Cathy Schine, Ruth Ozeki, Karen Joy Fowler.

FULL CIRCLE LITERARY, LLC

3268 Governor Dr. #323, San Diego CA 92122. **E-mail:** info@fullcircleliterary.com. **Website:** www.fullcircleliterary.com. **Contact:** Stefanie Von Borstel. "Full Circle Literary is a full-service literary agency, offering a full-circle approach to literary representation. Our team has diverse experience in book publishing, including editorial, marketing, publicity, legal, and rights, which we use collectively to build careers book by book. We work with both award-winning veteran and debut writers and artists, and our team has a knack for finding and developing new and diverse talent. Learn more about our agency and submission guidelines by visiting our website." This agency goes into depth about what they are seeking and submission guidelines on its website. Estab. 2005. Member of AAR, SCBWI, Authors Guild. Represents 100+ clients.

MEMBER AGENTS Stefanie Von Borstel; Adriana Dominguez; **Taylor Martindale Kean** (multicultural voices); **Lilly Ghahremani**.

REPRESENTS Considers these nonfiction areas: creative nonfiction, how-to, interior design, multicultural, women's issues, young adult. **Considers these fiction areas:** literary, middle-grade, multicultural, picture books, women's, young adult.

⌖ Actively seeking nonfiction by authors with a unique voice and strong platform, projects that offer new and diverse viewpoints, and literature with a global or multicultural perspective. "We are particularly interested in books with a Latino or Middle Eastern angle."

HOW TO CONTACT Online submissions only via submissions form online. Please complete the form and submit cover letter, author information and sample writing. For fiction, include the first 10 ms pages. For nonfiction, include a proposal with 1 sample chapter. Accepts simultaneous submissions. "Due to the high volume of submissions, please keep in mind that we are no longer able to personally respond to every submission. If you have not heard from us in 6-8 weeks, your project is not right for our agency at the current time and we wish you all the best with your writing."

TERMS Agent receives 15% commission on domestic sales; 25% commission on foreign sales. Offers written contract that outlines responsibilities of the author and the agent.

FUSE LITERARY

Foreword Literary, Inc. dba Fuse Literary, P.O. Box 258, La Honda CA 94020. **E-mail:** info@fuseliterary.com. **E-mail:** query[firstnameofagent]@fuseliterary.com. **Website:** www.fuseliterary.com. **Contact:** Con-

tact one agent directly via e-mail. Estab. 2013. Member of RWA, SCBWI. Represents 100+ clients.

MEMBER AGENTS Laurie McLean (only accepting referral inquiries and submissions requested at conferences or online events, with the exception of unsolicited adult and children's science fiction); **Gordon Warnock**, querygordon@fuseliterary.com (fiction: high-concept commercial fiction, literary fiction [adults through young adult], graphic novels [adults through Middle-grade]; nonfiction: memoir [adult, young adult, NA, graphic], cookbooks/food narrative/food studies, illustrated/art/photography [especially graphic nonfiction], political and current events, pop science, pop culture [especially punk culture and geek culture], self-help, how-to, humor, pets, business and career); **Connor Goldsmith**, queryconnor@fuseliterary.com (fiction: science fiction/fantasy/horror, thriller, upmarket commercial fiction with a unique and memorable hook; books by and about people from marginalized perspectives, such as LGBTQ people and/or racial minorities; nonfiction [from recognized experts with established platforms]: history [particularly of the ancient world], theater, cinema, music, television, mass media, popular culture, feminism and gender studies, LGBTQ issues, race relations, the sex industry); **Michelle Richter**, querymichelle@fuseliterary.com (primarily seeking fiction, specifically book club reads, literary fiction, mystery/suspense/thriller; for nonfiction: fashion, pop culture, science/medicine, sociology/social trends, economics); **Emily S. Keyes**, queryemily@fuseliterary.com (young adult, middle-grade, select commercial fiction, including fantasy & science fiction, women's fiction, New Adult fiction, pop culture, humor); **Tricia Skinner**, querytricia@fuseliterary.com (Romance: science fiction, futuristic, fantasy, military/special ops, medieval historical; brand new relationships; diversity); **Jennifer Chen Tran**, queryjennifer@fuseliterary.com (literary fiction, commercial fiction, women's fiction, upmarket fiction, contemporary romance, mature young adult, New Adult, suspense/thriller, select graphic novels [adult, young adult, Middle-grade]; memoir, narrative nonfiction in the areas of adventure, biography, business, current affairs, medical, history, how-to, pop-culture, psychology, social entrepreneurism, social justice, travel, lifestyle books [home, design, fashion, food].

HOW TO CONTACT E-query an individual agent. Check the website to see if any individual agent is closed to submissions, as well as each agent's individual submission preferences. (You can find these details by clicking on 'Team Fuse' and then clicking on each agent's photo.) Usually responds in 4-6 weeks, but sometimes more if an agent is exceptionally busy. Check each agent's bio/submissions page on the website. Only accepts e-mailed queries that follow online guidelines.

TERMS "We earn 15% on negotiated deals for books and with our co-agents earn between 20-30% on foreign translation deals depending on the territory; 20% on TV/movies/plays. Other multimedia deals are so new there is no established commission rate. The author has the last say, approving or not approving all deals." After the initial 90-day period, there is a 30-day termination of the agency agreement clause. No fees.

RECENT SALES Seven-figure deal for *NYT* bestseller Julie Kagawa (YA); mid-six-figure deal for Michael J. Sullivan (fantasy); quarter-million-dollar deal for Melissa D. Savage (Middle-grade); *First Watch*, by Dale Lucas (fantasy); *Elektra's Adventures in Tragedy*, by Douglas Rees (YA); Runebinder Trilogy, by Alex Kahler (YA); *Perceptual Intelligence*, by Dr. Brian Boxler Wachler (science); *Game Programming for Artists*, by Huntley & Brady (how-to); *Pay Day*, by Kellye Garrett (mystery); *Reality Star*, by Laura Heffernan (women's fiction); *Everything We Keep, Things We Leave Behind*, by Kerry Lonsdale (women's fiction); *Maggie and Abby's Neverending Pillow Fort*, by Will Taylor (Middle-grade); *The Sky Between You and Me*, by Catherine Alene (YA).

GALLT AND ZACKER LITERARY AGENCY

273 Charlton Ave., South Orange NJ 07079. (973)761-6358. **Website:** www.galltzacker.com. **Contact:** Nancy Gallt, Marietta Zacker. "At the Gallt and Zacker Literary Agency, we represent people, not projects, and we focus solely on writers and illustrators of children's books." Estab. 2000. Represents 60 clients.

Ms. Gallt was subsidiary rights director of the children's book division at Morrow, Harper and Viking. Ms. Zacker started her career as a teacher, championing children's and young adult books, then worked in the children's book world, bookselling, marketing, and editing.

MEMBER AGENTS Nancy Gallt, Marietta Zacker.

REPRESENTS **Considers these fiction areas:** juvenile, middle-grade, picture books, young adult.

➤ Actively seeking author/illustrators who create books for young adults and younger readers.

HOW TO CONTACT Submit through online submission form on agency website. No e-mail queries, please. Accepts simultaneous submissions. Obtains new clients through submissions, conferences and recommendations from others.

TERMS Agent receives 15% commission on domestic sales; commission on foreign sales. Offers written contract; 30-day notice must be given to terminate contract.

RECENT SALES Rick Riordan's books (Hyperion); *This Is It*, by Daria Peoples (Harper); *Playing Possum*, by Jennifer Black Reinhardt (Clarion/HMH); *Brave Molly*, by Brooke Boynton Hughes (Chronicle); *Brown Baby Lullaby*, by Tameka Fryer Brown (Macmillan); *Fenway and Hattie Up to New Tricks*, by Victoria J. Coe (Putnam/Penguin); *Caterpillar Summer*, by Gillian McDunn (Bloomsbury); *The Kids Are Alright*, by Dana Alison Levy (Delacorte/Random House); *Namesake*, by Paige Britt (Scholastic); *The Turning*, by Emily Whitman (Harper); *Rot*, by Ben Clanton (Simon & Schuster).

TIPS "Writing and illustrations stand on their own, so submissions should tell the most compelling stories possible—whether visually, in narrative, or both."

GELFMAN SCHNEIDER/ICM PARTNERS

850 Seventh Ave., Suite 903, New York NY 10019. **E-mail:** mail@gelfmanschneider.com. **Website:** www.gelfmanschneider.com. **Contact:** Jane Gelfman, Deborah Schneider. Member of AAR. Represents 300+ clients.

MEMBER AGENTS Deborah Schneider (all categories of literary and commercial fiction and nonfiction); **Jane Gelfman**; **Heather Mitchell** (particularly interested in narrative nonfiction, historical fiction, young debut authors with strong voices); **Penelope Burns**, penelope.gsliterary@gmail.com (literary and commercial fiction and nonfiction, a variety of young adult and middle-grade).

REPRESENTS nonfiction, fiction, juvenile books. **Considers these nonfiction areas:** creative nonfiction, popular culture. **Considers these fiction areas:** commercial, fantasy, historical, literary, mainstream, middle-grade, mystery, science fiction, suspense, women's, young adult.

- "Among our diverse list of clients are novelists, journalists, playwrights, scientists, activists and humorists writing narrative nonfiction, memoir, political and current affairs, popular science and popular culture nonfiction, as well as literary and commercial fiction, women's fiction, and historical fiction." Does not currently accept screenplays or scripts, poetry, or picture book queries.

HOW TO CONTACT Query. Check Submissions page of website to see which agents are open to queries and further instructions. Accepts simultaneous submissions.

TERMS Agent receives 15% commission on domestic sales; 20% commission on foreign sales; 15% commission on film sales. Offers written contract. Charges clients for photocopying and messengers/couriers.

THE GERNERT COMPANY

136 E. 57th St., New York NY 10022. (212)838-7777. **E-mail:** info@thegernertco.com. **Website:** www. thegernertco.com. **Contact:** Sarah Burnes. "Our client list is as broad as the market; we represent equal parts fiction and nonfiction." Estab. 1996.

- Prior to her current position, Ms. Burnes was with Burnes & Clegg, Inc.

MEMBER AGENTS Sarah Burnes (literary fiction and nonfiction; children's fiction); **Stephanie Cabot** (represents a variety of genres, including crime/thriller, commercial and literary fiction, latte lit, nonfiction); **Chris Parris-Lamb** (nonfiction, literary fiction); **Seth Fishman** (looking for the new voice, the original idea, the entirely breathtaking creative angle in both fiction and nonfiction); **Logan Garrison Savits** (young adult fiction); **Will Roberts** (smart, original thriller with distinctive voices, compelling backgrounds, and fast-paced narratives); **Erika Storella** (nonfiction projects that make an argument, narrate a history, and/or provide a new perspective); **Anna Worrall** (smart women's literary and commercial fiction, psychological thriller, narrative nonfiction); **Ellen Coughtrey** (women's literary and commercial fiction, historical fiction, narrative nonfiction and smart, original thriller, well-written Southern Gothic anything); **Jack Gernert** (stories about heroes—both real and imagined); **Libby McGuire**

(distinctive storytelling in both fiction and nonfiction, across a wide range of genres). At this time, **Courtney Gatewood** and **Rebecca Gardner** are closed to queries. See the website to find out the tastes of each agent.

REPRESENTS nonfiction, novels. **Considers these fiction areas:** commercial, crime, fantasy, historical, literary, middle-grade, science fiction, thriller, women's, young adult.

HOW TO CONTACT "Please send us a query letter by e-mail to info@thegernertco.com describing the work you'd like to submit, along with some information about yourself and a sample chapter, if appropriate. Please indicate in your letter which agent you are querying. Please do not send e-mails directly to individual agents. It's our policy to respond to your query only if we are interested in seeing more material, usually within 4-6 weeks." See company website for more instructions. Accepts simultaneous submissions. Obtains most new clients through recommendations from others, solicitations.

RECENT SALES *Partners*, by John Grisham; *The River Why*, by David James Duncan; *The Thin Green Line*, by Paul Sullivan; *A Fireproof Home for the Bride*, by Amy Scheibe; *The Only Girl in School*, by Natalie Standiford.

BARRY GOLDBLATT LITERARY LLC

320 Seventh Ave. #266, Brooklyn NY 11215. **E-mail:** query@bgliterary.com. **Website:** www.bgliterary. com. **Contact:** Barry Goldblatt. Estab. 2000. Member of AAR. Signatory of WGA.

MEMBER AGENTS Barry Goldblatt; **Jennifer Udden**, query.judden@gmail.com (speculative fiction of all stripes, especially innovative science fiction or fantasy, contemporary/erotic/LGBTQ/paranormal/historical romance, contemporary or speculative young adult. select mystery, thriller, urban fantasies).

REPRESENTS fiction. **Considers these fiction areas:** fantasy, middle-grade, mystery, romance, science fiction, thriller, young adult.

- "Please see our website for specific submission guidelines and information on our particular tastes."

HOW TO CONTACT "E-mail queries can be sent to query@bgliterary.com and should include the word 'query' in the subject line. To query Jen Udden specifically, e-mail queries can be sent to query.judden@gmail.com. Please know that we will read and respond to every e-query that we receive, provided it is properly addressed and follows the submission guidelines below. We will not respond to e-queries that are addressed to no one, or to multiple recipients. While we do not require exclusivity, exclusive submissions will receive priority review. If your submission is exclusive to Barry Goldblatt Literary, please indicate so by including the word 'Exclusive' in the subject line of your e-mail. Your e-query should include the following within the body of the e-mail: your query letter, a synopsis of the book, and the first 5 pages of your manuscript. We will not open or respond to any e-mails that have attachments. Our response time is 4 weeks on queries, 6-8 weeks on full manuscripts. If you haven't heard from us within that time, feel free to check in via e-mail." Accepts simultaneous submissions. Obtains clients through referrals, queries, conferences.

TERMS Agent receives 15% commission on domestic sales; 20% on foreign and dramatic sales. Offers written contract; 60-day notice must be given to terminate contract.

RECENT SALES *Other Broken Things*, by C. Desir; *Masks and Shadows*, by Stephanie Burgis; *Wishing Day*, by Lauren Myracle; *Mother-Daughter Book Camp*, by Heather Vogel Frederick.

TIPS "We're a hands-on agency, focused on building an author's career, not just making an initial sale. We don't care about trends or what's hot; we just want to sign great writers."

IRENE GOODMAN LITERARY AGENCY

27 W. 24th St., Suite 700B, New York NY 10010. **E-mail:** miriam.queries@irenegoodman.com, barbara.queries@irenegoodman.com, rachel.queries@irenegoodman.com, kim.queries@irenegoodman.com, victoria.queries@irenegoodman.com, irene.queries@irenegoodman.com, submissions@irenegoodman.com. **Website:** www.irenegoodman.com. Estab. 1978. Member of AAR. Represents 150 clients.

MEMBER AGENTS Irene Goodman, Miriam Kriss, Barbara Poelle, Rachel Ekstrom, Kim Perel, Victoria Marini.

REPRESENTS nonfiction, fiction, novels, juvenile books. **Considers these nonfiction areas:** animals, autobiography, cooking, creative nonfiction, cultural interests, current affairs, decorating, diet/nutrition, design, foods, health, history, how-to, humor, interior design, juvenile nonfiction, memoirs, parenting, politics, science, self-help, women's issues, young adult, parenting, social issues, francophilia, anglophilia, Judaica, lifestyles, cooking, memoir. **Considers these fiction areas:** action, crime, detective, family saga, historical, horror, middle-grade, mystery, romance, science fiction, suspense, thriller, urban fantasy, women's, young adult.

⌐ Commercial and literary fiction and nonfiction. No screenplays, poetry, or inspirational fiction.

HOW TO CONTACT Query. Submit synopsis, first 10 pages pasted into the body of the e-mail. E-mail queries only! See the website submission page. No e-mail attachments. Query one agent only. Accepts simultaneous submissions. Responds in 2 months to queries. Consult website for each agent's submission guidelines.

TERMS Agent receives 15% commission.

TIPS "We are receiving an unprecedented amount of e-mail queries. If you find that the mailbox is full, please try again in 2 weeks. E-mail queries to our personal addresses will not be answered. E-mails to our personal inboxes will be deleted."

KATHRYN GREEN LITERARY AGENCY, LLC

157 Columbus Ave., Suite 510, New York NY 10023. (212)245-4225. **E-mail:** query@kgreenagency.com. **Website:** www.kathryngreenliteraryagency.com. **Contact:** Kathy Green. Estab. 2004. Member of Women's Media Group. Represents approximately 20 clients.

○ Prior to becoming an agent, Ms. Green was a book and magazine editor.

REPRESENTS nonfiction, fiction, novels, short story collections, juvenile books. **Considers these nonfiction areas:** autobiography, biography, business, cooking, cultural interests, current affairs, diet/nutrition, foods, history, how-to, humor, inspirational, memoirs, parenting, popular culture, psychology, satire, science, spirituality, sports, true crime, women's issues, young adult. **Considers these fiction areas:** commercial, crime, detective, family saga, historical, humor, juvenile, literary, mainstream, middle-grade, multicultural, mystery, police, romance, satire, suspense, thriller, women's, young adult.

⌐ "Considers all types of fiction but particularly like historical fiction, cozy mystery, young adult and middle-grade. For nonfiction, I am interested in memoir, parenting, humor with a pop culture bent, and history. Quirky nonfiction is also a particular favorite." Does not want to receive science fiction, fantasy, children's picture books, screenplays, or poetry.

HOW TO CONTACT Query by e-mail. Send no attachments unless requested. Do not send queries via regular mail. Responds in 4 weeks. "Queries do not have to be exclusive; however, if further material is requested, please be in touch before accepting other representation." Accepts simultaneous submissions. Obtains most new clients through recommendations from others, solicitations, conferences.

TERMS Agent receives 15% commission on domestic sales; 20% commission on foreign sales.

RECENT SALES *Sit Stay Heal*, by Mel C. Miskimen; *Unholy City*, by Carrie Smith.

SANFORD J. GREENBURGER ASSOCIATES, INC.

55 Fifth Ave., New York NY 10003. (212)206-5600. **Fax:** (212)463-8718. **Website:** www.greenburger.com. Member of AAR. Represents 500 clients.

MEMBER AGENTS Matt Bialer, lribar@sjga. com (fantasy, science fiction, thriller, mystery, select group of literary writers; loves smart narrative nonfiction: current events, popular culture, biography, history, music, race, sports); **Brenda Bowen**, querybb@sjga.com (literary fiction, writers and illustrators of picture books, chapter books, middle-grade and teen fiction); **Faith Hamlin**, fhamlin@sjga.com (receives submissions by referral); **Heide Lange**, queryhl@sjga.com (receives submissions by referral); **Daniel Mandel**, querydm@sjga.com (literary and commercial fiction, memoirs and nonfiction about business, art, history, politics, sports, popular culture); **Courtney Miller-Callihan**, cmiller@ sjga.com (YA, middle-grade, women's fiction, romance, and historical novels, nonfiction projects on unusual topics, humor, pop culture, lifestyle books); **Nicholas Ellison**, nellison@sjga.com; **Chelsea Lindman**, clindman@sjga.com (playful literary fiction, upmarket crime fiction, forward thinking or boundary-pushing nonfiction); **Rachael Dillon Fried**, rfried@sjga.com (both fiction and nonfiction authors, with a keen interest in unique literary voices, women's fiction, narrative nonfiction, memoir, comedy); **Lindsay Ribar**, co-agents with Matt Bialer (young adult and middle-grade fiction); **Bethany Buck** querybbuck@sjga.com (middle-grade

and chapter books, teen fiction, select list of picture book authors and illustrators); **Stephanie Delman** sdelman@sjga.com (literary/upmarket contemporary fiction, psychological thriller/suspense, atmospheric, near-historical fiction); **Ed Maxwell** emaxwell@sjga.com (expert and narrative nonfiction authors, novelists and graphic novelists, children's book authors and illustrators).

REPRESENTS nonfiction, fiction, novels, juvenile books. **Considers these nonfiction areas:** art, biography, business, creative nonfiction, current affairs, ethnic, history, humor, memoirs, music, popular culture, politics, sports. **Considers these fiction areas:** commercial, crime, family saga, fantasy, feminist, historical, literary, middle-grade, multicultural, mystery, picture books, romance, science fiction, thriller, women's, young adult.

HOW TO CONTACT E-query. "Please look at each agent's profile page for current information about what each agent is looking for and for the correct e-mail address to use for queries to that agent. Please be sure to use the correct query e-mail address for each agent." Agents may not respond to all queries, will respond within 6-8 weeks if interested. Obtains most new clients through recommendations from others.

TERMS Agent receives 15% commission on domestic sales; 20% commission on foreign sales. Charges for photocopying and books for foreign and subsidiary rights submissions.

RECENT SALES *Inferno* by Dan Brown, *Sweet Pea and Friends: A Sheepover* by John Churchman and Jennifer Churchman, *Code of Conduct* by Brad Thor.

THE GREENHOUSE LITERARY AGENCY

E-mail: submissions@greenhouseliterary.com. **Website:** www.greenhouseliterary.com. **Contact:** Sarah Davies. Estab. 2008. Member of AAR. Other memberships include SCBWI. Represents 50 clients.

Before launching Greenhouse, Sarah Davies had an editorial and management career in children's publishing spanning 25 years; for 5 years prior to launching the Greenhouse she was publishing director of Macmillan Children's Books in London, and published leading authors from both sides of the Atlantic.

MEMBER AGENTS Sarah Davies, vice president (fiction and nonfiction by North American authors, chapter books through to middle-grade, young adult); **Polly Nolan**, agent (fiction by UK, Irish, Commonwealth—including Australia, New Zealand and India—authors, plus European authors writing in English, author/illustrators (texts under 1,000 words) to young fiction series, through middle-grade, young adult).

REPRESENTS juvenile books. **Considers these nonfiction areas:** juvenile nonfiction, young adult. **Considers these fiction areas:** juvenile, young adult.

⚷ "We represent authors writing fiction and nonfiction for children and teens. The agency has offices in both the US and UK, and the agency's commission structure reflects this—taking 15% for sales to both US and UK, thus treating both as 'domestic' market." All genres of children's and young adult fiction. Very occasionally, a nonfiction proposal will be considered. Does not want to receive picture book texts (i.e., written by writers who aren't also illustrators) or short stories, educational or religious/inspirational work, pre-school/novelty material, screenplays, or writing aimed at adults. Represents novels and some nonfiction. Considers these fiction areas: juvenile, chapter book series, middle-grade, young adult.

HOW TO CONTACT Query one agent only. Put the target agent's name in the subject line. Paste the first 5 pages of your story (or your complete picture book) after the query. Accepts simultaneous submissions.

TERMS Agent receives 15% commission on domestic sales; 25% commission on foreign sales. Offers written contract. This agency occasionally charges for submission copies to film agents or foreign publishers.

RECENT SALES *Places No One Knows*, by Brenna Yovanoff (Delacorte); *Race to the Bottom of the Sea*, by Lindsay Eagar (Candlewick); *Cheerful Chick*, by Martha Brockenbrough (Scholastic); *Olive and the Backstage Ghost*, by Michelle Schusterman (Random House); *Wanted: Women Mathematicians*, by Tami Lewis Brown & Debbie Loren Dunn (Disney-Hyperion).

WRITERS CONFERENCES Bologna Children's Book Fair, ALA, SCBWI, BookExpo America.

TIPS "Before submitting material, authors should visit the Greenhouse Literary Agency website and carefully read all submission guidelines."

JILL GRINBERG LITERARY MANAGEMENT

392 Vanderbilt Ave., Brooklyn NY 11238. (212)620-5883. **E-mail:** info@jillgrinbergliterary.com. **Website:** www.jillgrinbergliterary.com. Estab. 1999. Member of AAR.

💭 Prior to her current position, Ms. Grinberg was at Anderson Grinberg Literary Management.

MEMBER AGENTS Jill Grinberg, Cheryl Pientka, Katelyn Detweiler, Sophia Seidner.

REPRESENTS nonfiction, fiction, novels. **Considers these nonfiction areas:** biography, creative nonfiction, current affairs, ethnic, history, language, literature, memoirs, parenting, popular culture, politics, science, sociology, spirituality, sports, travel, women's issues, young adult. **Considers these fiction areas:** fantasy, historical, juvenile, literary, mainstream, middle-grade, picture books, romance, science fiction, women's, young adult.

HOW TO CONTACT "Please send queries via e-mail to info@jillgrinbergliterary.com—include your query letter, addressed to the agent of your choice, along with the first 50 pages of your ms pasted into the body of the e-mail or attached as a .doc. or .docx file. We also accept queries via mail, though e-mail is preferred. Please send your query letter and the first 50 pages of your ms by mail, along with a SASE, to the attention of your agent of choice. Please note that unless a SASE with sufficient postage is provided, your materials will not be returned. As submissions are shared within the office, please only query one agent with your project." Accepts simultaneous submissions.

TIPS "We prefer submissions by electronic mail."

HARTLINE LITERARY AGENCY

123 Queenston Dr., Pittsburgh PA 15235-5429. (412)829-2483. **E-mail:** joyce@hartlineliterary.com. **Website:** www.hartlineliterary.com. **Contact:** Joyce A. Hart. Many of the agents at this agency are generalists. This agency also handles inspirational and Christian works. Estab. 1992. Member of ACFW. Represents 200 clients.

💭 Joyce Hart was the vice president of marketing at Whitaker House Publishing. Jim Hart was a production journalist for 20 years.

MEMBER AGENTS Joyce A. Hart, principal agent (no unsolicited queries); **Jim Hart**, jim@hartlineliterary.com; **Diana Flegal**, diana@hartlineliterary.com; **Linda Glaz**, linda@hartlineliterary.com; **Andy Scheer**, andy@hartlineliterary.com; **Cyle Young**, cyle@hartlineliterary.com.

REPRESENTS nonfiction, fiction, novels, novellas, juvenile books, scholarly books. **Considers these nonfiction areas:** diet/nutrition, health, history, inspirational, parenting, philosophy, popular culture, politics, psychology, recreation, religious, spirituality, women's issues. **Considers these fiction areas:** contemporary issues, family saga, humor, inspirational, New Adult, religious, romance, suspense, women's, young adult.

> ☞ "This agency specializes in the Christian bookseller market." Actively seeking adult fiction, self-help, nutritional books, Christian living, devotional, and business. Does not want to receive erotica, gay/lesbian, fantasy, horror.

HOW TO CONTACT E-query preferred, USPS to the Pittsburgh office. Target one agent only. "All e-mail submissions sent to Hartline Agents should be sent as a Word document (or in rich text file format from another word processing program) attached to an e-mail with 'submission: title, author's name, and word count' in the subject line. A proposal is a single document, not a collection of files. Place the query letter in the e-mail itself. Do not send the entire proposal in the body of the e-mail or send PDF files." Further guidelines online. Accepts simultaneous submissions. Responds in 2 months to queries, 3 months to mss. Obtains most new clients through recommendations from others, conferences.

TERMS Agent receives 15% commission on domestic sales. Offers written contract.

☉ HELEN HELLER AGENCY INC.

4-216 Heath St. W., Toronto ON M5P 1N7 Canada. (416)489-0396. **E-mail:** info@helenhelleragency.com. **Website:** www.helenhelleragency.com. **Contact:** Helen Heller. Represents 30+ clients.

> ☉ Prior to her current position, Ms. Heller worked for Cassell & Co. (England), was an editor for Harlequin Books, a senior editor for Avon Books, and editor-in-chief for Fitzhenry & Whiteside.

MEMBER AGENTS Helen Heller, helen@helenhelleragency.com (thriller and front-list general fiction); Sarah Heller, sarah@helenhelleragency.com (front list commercial young adult and adult fiction, with a particular interest in high concept historical fiction); **Barbara Berson**, barbara@helenhelleragency.com (literary fiction, nonfiction, and young adult).

REPRESENTS nonfiction, novels. **Considers these fiction areas:** commercial, crime, historical, literary, mainstream, thriller, young adult.

HOW TO CONTACT E-mail info@helenhelleragency.com. Submit a brief synopsis, publishing history, author bio, and writing sample, pasted in the body of the e-mail. No attachments with e-queries. Accepts simultaneous submissions. Responds within 3 months if interested. Accepts simultaneous submissions. Obtains most new clients through recommendations from others, solicitations.

TIPS "Whether you are an author searching for an agent, or whether an agent has approached you, it is in your best interest to first find out who the agent represents, what publishing houses has that agent sold to recently and what foreign sales have been made. You should be able to go to the bookstore, or search online and find the books the agent refers to. Many authors acknowledge their agents in the front or back or their books."

RONNIE ANN HERMAN

350 Central Park W., Apt. 41, New York NY 10025. (212)749-4907. **E-mail:** ronnie@hermanagencyinc.com, katia.hermanagency@gmail.com. **Website:** www.hermanagencyinc.com. **Contact:** Ronnie Ann Herman. "We are a small boutique literary agency that represents authors and artists for the children's book market. We are only accepting submissions for middle-grade and young adult books at this time." Estab. 1999. Member of SCBWI. Represents 19 clients.

MEMBER AGENTS Ronnie Ann Herman, Katia Herman.

REPRESENTS novels, juvenile books. **Considers these nonfiction areas:** juvenile nonfiction. **Considers these fiction areas:** juvenile, middle-grade, picture books, young adult.

> ☞ Childrens' books of all genres. Actively seeking middle-grade and young adult.

HOW TO CONTACT Submit via e-mail. Accepts simultaneous submissions.

TERMS Agent receives 15% commission.

TIPS "Check our website to see if you belong with our agency."

HILL NADELL LITERARY AGENCY

6442 Santa Monica Blvd., Suite 201, Los Angeles CA 90038. (310)860-9605. **E-mail:** queries@hillnadell.com. **Website:** www.hillnadell.com. Represents 100 clients. **MEMBER AGENTS** Bonnie Nadell (nonfiction: current affairs, food, memoirs, narrative nonfiction; fiction: thriller, upmarket women's and literary fiction); **Dara Hyde** (literary and genre fiction, narrative nonfiction, graphic novels, memoir, the occasional young adult novel).

REPRESENTS nonfiction, novels. **Considers these nonfiction areas:** biography, current affairs, environment, government, health, history, language, literature, medicine, popular culture, politics, science, technology, biography, narrative nonfiction. **Considers these fiction areas:** literary, mainstream, thriller, women's, young adult.

HOW TO CONTACT Send a query and SASE. If you would like your materials returned, please include adequate postage. To submit electronically, send your query letter and the first 5-10 pages to queries@hillnadell.com. No attachments. Due to the high volume of submissions the agency receives, it cannot guarantee a response to all e-mailed queries. Accepts simultaneous submissions.

TERMS Agent receives 15% commission on domestic and film sales; 20% commission on foreign sales. Charges clients for photocopying and foreign mailings.

HOLLOWAY LITERARY

P.O. Box 771, Cary NC 27512. **E-mail:** submissions@hollowayliteraryagency.com. **Website:** hollowayliteraryagency.com. **Contact:** Nikki Terpilowski. A full-service boutique literary agency located in Raleigh, NC. Estab. 2011. Member of AAR, signatory of WGA, International Thriller Writers, Romance Writers of America. Represents 26 clients. **MEMBER AGENTS** Nikki Terpilowski (romance, women's fiction, Southern fiction, historical fiction, cozy mystery, military/political thriller, commercial, upmarket/book club fiction, African-American fiction of all types); **Rachel Burkot** (young adult contemporary, women's fiction, upmarket/book club fiction, contemporary romance, Southern fiction, literary fiction); **Michael Caligaris** (literary fiction, autobiographical fiction, short story collections or connected stories as a novel, Americana, crime fiction, mystery/noir, dystopian fiction, civil unrest/political uprising/

war novels, memoir, new journalism and/or long-form journalism, essay collections, satirical/humor writing, environmental writing).

REPRESENTS nonfiction, fiction, movie scripts, feature film. **Considers these nonfiction areas:** Americana, environment, humor, narrative nonfiction, New Journalism, essays. **Considers these fiction areas:** action, adventure, commercial, contemporary issues, crime, detective, ethnic, family saga, fantasy, glitz, historical, inspirational, literary, mainstream, metaphysical, middle-grade, military, multicultural, mystery, New Adult, New Age, regional, romance, short story collections, spiritual, suspense, thriller, urban fantasy, war, women's, young adult. **Considers these script areas:** action, adventure, biography, contemporary issues, ethnic, romantic comedy, romantic drama, teen, thriller, TV movie of the week.

☛ "Note to self-published authors: While we are happy to receive submissions from authors who have previously self-published novels, we do not represent self-published works. Send us your unpublished manuscripts only." Nikki is open to submissions and is selectively reviewing queries for cozy mystery with culinary, historical, or book/publishing industry themes written in the vein of Jaclyn Brady, Laura Childs, Julie Hyzy, and Lucy Arlington; women's fiction with strong magical realism similar to Meena van Praag's *The Dress Shop of Dreams*, Sarah Addison Allen's *Garden Spells*, Sarah Creech's *Season of the Dragonflies*, and Mary Robinette Kowal's Glamourist series. She would love to find a wine-themed mystery series similar to Nadia Gordon's Sunny McCoskey series or Ellen Crosby's Wine County Mystery that combine culinary themes with a lot of great Southern history. Nikki is also interested in seeing contemporary romance set in the southern US or any wine county, or featuring a culinary theme, dark, edgy historical romance, gritty military romance, or romantic suspense with sexy Alpha heroes and lots of technical detail. She is also interested in acquiring historical fiction written in the vein of Alice Hoffman, Lalita Tademy and Isabel Allende. Nikki is also interested in espionage, military, political, and artificial intelligence thriller similar to Tom Clancy, Robert Ludlum, Steve Berry,

Vince Flynn, Brad Thor, and Daniel Silva. Nikki has a special interest in nonfiction subjects related to governance, politics, military strategy, and foreign relations. Does not want horror, true crime, or novellas.

HOW TO CONTACT Send query and first 15 pages of ms pasted into the body of e-mail to submissions@hollowayliteraryagency.com. In the subject header write 'Agent's Name/Title/Genre.' Holloway Literary does accept submissions via mail (query letter and first 50 pages). Expect a response time of at least 3 months. Include e-mail address, phone number, social media accounts, and mailing address on your query letter. Accepts simultaneous submissions. Responds in 4-6 weeks. If the agent is interested, he or she will respond with a request for more material.

RECENT SALES A list of recent sales is available on the website's client news page.

HSG AGENCY

37 W. 28th St., Eighth Floor, New York NY 10001. **E-mail:** channigan@hsgagency.com, jsalky@hsgagency.com, jgetzler@hsgagency.com, tprasanna@hsgagency.com, leigh@hsgagency.com. **Website:** hsgagency.com. **Contact:** Carrie Hannigan, Jesseca Salky, Josh Getzler,Tanusri Prasanna, Leigh Eisenman. Estab. 2011. Member of AAR. Signatory of WGA.

○   Prior to opening HSG Agency, Ms. Hannigan, Ms. Salky. and Mr. Getzler were agents at Russell & Volkening.

MEMBER AGENTS Carrie Hannigan; **Jesseca Salky** (literary and mainstream fiction); **Josh Getzler** (foreign and historical fiction; women's fiction, straight-ahead historical fiction, thriller, mystery); **Tanusri Prasanna** (picture books, children's, Middle-grade, young adult, select nonfiction); **Leigh Eisenman** (literary and upmarket fiction, foodie/cookbooks, health and fitness, lifestyle, select narrative nonfiction).

REPRESENTS nonfiction, fiction, novels, juvenile books. **Considers these nonfiction areas:** business, cooking, creative nonfiction, current affairs, diet/nutrition, education, environment, foods, health, history, humor, literature, memoirs, multicultural, music, parenting, photography, politics, psychology, science, self-help, sports, women's issues, women's studies, young adult. **Considers these fiction areas:** adventure, commercial, contemporary issues, crime, detective, ethnic, family saga, historical, juvenile, literary, mainstream, middle-grade, multicultural, mystery, picture books, thriller, translation, women's, young adult.

HOW TO CONTACT Electronic submissions only. Send query letter, first 5 pages of ms within e-mail to appropriate agent. Avoid submitting to multiple agents within the agency. For picture books, include entire ms. Responds in 4-6 weeks if interested.

RECENT SALES A Spool of Blue Thread, by Anne Tyler (Knopf); Blue Sea Burning, by Geoff Rodkey (Putnam); The Partner Track, by Helen Wan (St. Martin's Press); The Thrill of the Haunt, by E.J. Copperman (Berkley); Aces Wild, by Erica Perl (Knopf Books for Young Readers); Steve & Wessley: The Sea Monster, by Jennifer Morris (Scholastic); Infinite Worlds, by Michael Soluri (Simon & Schuster).

✆ ICM PARTNERS

65 E. 55th St., New York NY 10022. (212)556-5600. **Website:** www.icmtalent.com. **Contact:** Literary Department. Member of AAR. Signatory of WGA.

REPRESENTS nonfiction, fiction, novels.

HOW TO CONTACT Accepts simultaneous submissions.

INKLINGS LITERARY AGENCY

3419 Virginia Beach Blvd., #183, Virginia Beach VA 23452. (757)340-1070. **Fax:** (904)758-5440. **E-mail:** michelle@inklingsliterary.com. **E-mail:** query@inklingsliterary.com. **Website:** www.inklingsliterary.com. Inklings Literary Agency is a full-service, hands-on literary agency seeking submissions from established authors as well as talented new authors. "We represent a broad range of commercial and literary fiction, as well as memoirs and true crime. We are not seeking short stories, poetry, screenplays, or children's picture books." Estab. 2013. Memberships include RWA, SinC, HRW.

○   "We offer our clients interactive representation for their work, as well as developmental guidance for their author platforms, working with them as they grow. "

MEMBER AGENTS Michelle Johnson, michelle@inklingsliterary.com (adult and young adult fiction, contemporary, suspense, thriller, mystery, horror, fantasy [including paranormal and supernatural elements within those genres], romance of every level, nonfiction in the areas of memoir and true crime); **Dr. Jamie Bodnar Drowley**, jamie@inklingsliterary.com (New Adult fiction in the areas of romance [all subgenres], fantasy [urban fantasy, light science fiction, steampunk], mystery and thriller, young adult [all subgenres], middle-grade stories); **Margaret Bail**, margaret@inklingsliterary.com (romance, science fiction, mystery, thriller, action adventure, historical fiction, Western, some fantasy, memoir, cookbooks, true crime); **Naomi Davis**, naomi@inklingsliterary.com (romance of any variety including paranormal, fresh urban fantasy, general fantasy, New Adult, light science fiction, young adult in any of those same genres, memoirs about living with disabilities, facing criticism, mental illness); **Whitley Abell**, whitley@inklingsliterary.com (young adult, middle-grade, select upmarket women's fiction); **Alex Barba**, alex@inklingsliterary.com (YA fiction).

REPRESENTS nonfiction, fiction, novels, juvenile books. **Considers these nonfiction areas:** cooking, creative nonfiction, diet/nutrition, gay/lesbian, memoirs, true crime, women's issues. **Considers these fiction areas:** action, adventure, commercial, contemporary issues, crime, detective, erotica, ethnic, fantasy, feminist, gay, historical, horror, juvenile, lesbian, mainstream, metaphysical, middle-grade, military, multicultural, multimedia, mystery, New Adult, New Age, occult, paranormal, police, psychic, regional, romance, science fiction, spiritual, sports, supernatural, suspense, thriller, urban fantasy, war, women's, young adult.

HOW TO CONTACT E-queries only. To query, type "Query (Agent Name)" plus the title of your novel in the subject line, then please send your query letter, short synopsis, and first 10 pages pasted into the body of the e-mail to query@inklingsliterary.com. Check the agency website to make sure that your targeted agent is currently open to submissions. Accepts simultaneous submissions. For queries, no response in 3 months is considered a rejection. Yes

TERMS AGENT RECEIVES 15% commission on domestic sales, 20% commission on subsidiary rights. Charges no fees.

INKWELL MANAGEMENT, LLC

521 Fifth Ave., Suite 2600, New York NY 10175. (212)922-3500. **Fax:** (212)922-0535. **E-mail:** info@inkwellmanagement.com. **E-mail:** submissions@inkwellmanagement.com. **Website:** www.inkwell-managment.com. Represents 500 clients.

MEMBER AGENTS Stephen Barbara (select adult fiction and nonfiction); **William Callahan** (nonfiction of all stripes, especially American history and memoir, pop culture and illustrated books; voice-driven fiction that stands out from the crowd); **Michael V. Carlisle; Catherine Drayton** (best-selling authors of books for children, young adults and women readers); **David Forrer** (literary, commercial, historical, and crime fiction to suspense/thriller, humorous nonfiction, and popular history); **Alexis Hurley** (literary and commercial fiction, memoir, narrative nonfiction, and more); **Nathaniel Jacks** (memoir, narrative nonfiction, social sciences, health, current affairs, business,religion, popular history, as well as fiction—literary and commercial, women's, young adult, historical, short story, among others); **Jacqueline Murphy**; (fiction, children's books, graphic novels and illustrated works, compelling narrative nonfiction); **Richard Pine; Eliza Rothstein** (literary and commercial fiction, narrative nonfiction, memoir, popular science, food writing); **David Hale Smith**; **Kimberly Witherspoon; Jenny Witherell; Charlie Olson; Liz Parker** (commercial and upmarket women's fiction; narrative, practical, and platform-driven nonfiction); **George Lucas; Lyndsey Blessing; Claire Draper; Kate Falkoff; Claire Friedman; Michael Mungiello; Jessica Mileo; Corinne Sullivan; Maria Whelan**.

REPRESENTS novels. **Considers these nonfiction areas:** biography, business, cooking, creative nonfiction, current affairs, foods, health, history, humor, memoirs, popular culture, religious, science. **Considers these fiction areas:** commercial, crime, historical, literary, middle-grade, picture books, romance, short story collections, suspense, thriller, women's, young adult.

HOW TO CONTACT "In the body of your e-mail, please include a query letter and a short writing sample (1-2 chapters). We currently accept submissions in all genres, except screenplays. Due to the volume of queries we receive, our response may take up to 2 months. Feel free to put 'Query for [Agent Name]: [Your Book Title]' in the e-mail subject line." Accepts simultaneous submissions. Obtains most new clients through recommendations from others.

TERMS Agent receives 15% commission on domestic sales; 20% commission on foreign sales. Offers written contract.

TIPS "We will not read mss before receiving a letter of inquiry."

INTERNATIONAL TRANSACTIONS, INC.

P.O. Box 97, Gila NM 88038. (845)373-9696. **Fax:** (480)393-5162. **E-mail:** submission-nonfiction@ intltrans.com, submission-fiction@intltrans.com. **Website:** www.intltrans.com. **Contact:** Peter Riva. Estab. 1975.

MEMBER AGENTS Peter Riva (nonfiction, fiction, illustrated; television and movie rights placement); **Sandra Riva** (fiction, juvenile, biography); **JoAnn Collins** (fiction, women's fiction, medical fiction).

REPRESENTS nonfiction, fiction, novels, short story collections, juvenile books, scholarly books, illustrated books, anthologies. **Considers these nonfiction areas:** Americana, anthropology, archeology, architecture, art, autobiography, biography, business, computers, cooking, cultural interests, current affairs, diet/nutrition, design, environment, ethnic, film, foods, gay/lesbian, government, health, history, humor, inspirational, investigative, language, law, literature, medicine, memoirs, military, multicultural, music, photography, popular culture, politics, religious, satire, science, self-help, sports, technology, translation, true crime, war, women's issues, women's studies, young adult. **Considers these fiction areas:** action, adventure, commercial, crime, detective, erotica, experimental, family saga, feminist, gay, historical, humor, inspirational, lesbian, literary, mainstream, middle-grade, military, multicultural, mystery, New Adult, police, satire, science fiction, spiritual, sports, suspense, thriller, translation, war, westerns, women's, young adult, chick lit.

HOW TO CONTACT First, e-query with an outline or synopsis. E-queries only. Put "Query: [Title]" in the e-mail subject line. Responds in 3 weeks to queries, 5 weeks to mss after request. Obtains most new clients through recommendations from others, solicitations.

TERMS Agent receives 15% (25% on illustrated books) commission on domestic sales; 20% commission on foreign sales and media rights. Offers written contract; 100-day notice must be given to terminate contract. No additional fees, ever.

RECENT SALES Averaging 20+ book placements per year.

JABBERWOCKY LITERARY AGENCY

49 W. 45th St., New York NY 10036. (917)388-3010. **Website:** www.awfulagent.com. **Contact:** Joshua Bilmes. Estab. 1990. Member of SFWA. Represents 40 clients.

MEMBER AGENTS Joshua Bilmes, Eddie Schneider, Lisa Rodgers, Sam Morgan, Brady McReynolds.

REPRESENTS nonfiction, fiction, novels, novellas, juvenile books. **Considers these nonfiction areas:** autobiography, biography, business, cooking, current affairs, economics, film, foods, gay/lesbian, government, health, history, humor, language, law, literature, medicine, money, music, popular culture, politics, satire, science, sociology, sports, technology, theater, war, women's issues, women's studies, young adult. **Considers these fiction areas:** action, adventure, contemporary issues, crime, detective, ethnic, family saga, fantasy, feminist, gay, glitz, historical, horror, humor, juvenile, lesbian, literary, mainstream, middle-grade, mystery, New Adult, paranormal, police, psychic, regional, romance, satire, science fiction, sports, supernatural, thriller, women's, young adult.

> This agency represents quite a lot of genre fiction, romance, and mystery, and is actively seeking to increase the amount of nonfiction projects. It does not handle children's or picture books. Book-length material only—no poetry, articles, or short fiction.

HOW TO CONTACT "We are currently open to unsolicited queries. No e-mail, phone, or fax queries, please. Query with SASE. Please check our website, as there may be times during the year when we are not accepting queries. Query letter only; no manuscript material unless requested." Accepts simultaneous submissions. Responds in 3 weeks to queries. Obtains most new clients through solicitations, recommendation by current clients.

TERMS Agent receives 15% commission on domestic sales; 20% commission on foreign sales. Offers written contract, binding for 1 year. Charges clients for book purchases, photocopying, international book/ms mailing.

RECENT SALES 188 individual deals done in 2014: 60 domestic and 128 foreign. *Alcatraz #5*, by Brandon Sanderson; *Aurora Teagarden*, by Charlaine Harris; *The Unnoticeables*, by Robert Brockway; *Messenger's Legacy*, by Peter V. Brett; *Slotter Key*, by Elizabeth Moon. Other clients include Tanya Huff, Simon Green, Jack Campbell, Myke Cole, Marie Brennan, Daniel Jose Older, Jim Hines, Mark Hodder, Toni Kelner, Ari Marmell, Ellery Queen, Erin Tettensor, Walter Jon Williams.

JANKLOW & NESBIT ASSOCIATES

285 Madison Ave., 21st Floor, New York NY 10017. (212)421-1700. **Fax:** (212)355-1403. **E-mail:** info@janklow.com. **E-mail:** submissions@janklow.com. **Website:** www.janklowandnesbit.com. Estab. 1989. **MEMBER AGENTS** Morton L. Janklow, Anne Sibbald, Lynn Nesbit, Luke Janklow, PJ Mark (interests are eclectic, including short stories and literary novels; nonfiction: journalism, popular culture, memoir/narrative, essays, cultural criticism); **Paul Lucas** (literary and commercial fiction, focusing on literary thriller, science fiction and fantasy; also seeks narrative histories of ideas and objects, as well as biography and popular science); **Emma Parry** (nonfiction by experts, but will consider outstanding literary fiction and upmarket commercial fiction); **Kirby Kim**; **Marya Spence**; **Allison Hunter**; **Melissa Flashman**; **Stefanie Lieberman**.
REPRESENTS nonfiction, fiction.
HOW TO CONTACT Query via snail mail or e-mail. Include a cover letter, synopsis, and the first 10 pages if sending fiction (no attachments). For nonfiction, send a query and full outline. Address your submission to an individual agent. Accepts simultaneous submissions. Responds in 8 weeks to queries/mss. Obtains most new clients through recommendations from others.

THE CAROLYN JENKS AGENCY

30 Cambridge Park Dr., Cambridge MA 02140. (617)354-5099. **E-mail:** queries@carolynjenksagency.com. **Website:** www.carolynjenksagency.com. **Contact:** Carolyn Jenks. "This is a boutique agency, which means we give special attention to all of our clients. We act as a mentor to young professionals and students who are entering the profession, in addition to representing established writers." Estab. 1987. Signatory of WGA.
MEMBER AGENTS Carolyn Jenks; see agency website for a list of junior agents.
REPRESENTS nonfiction, fiction, novels, juvenile books. **Considers these nonfiction areas:** animals, autobiography, biography, gay/lesbian, history, juvenile nonfiction, literature, memoirs, theater, true crime, women's issues, women's studies, young adult. **Considers these fiction areas:** action, adventure, contemporary issues, crime, ethnic, experimental, family saga, feminist, gay, historical, horror, juvenile, lesbian, literary, mainstream, mystery,

New Adult, science fiction, thriller, women's, young adult. **Considers these script areas:** biography, contemporary issues, ethnic, experimental, family saga, feminist, frontier, historical, inspirational, mainstream, mystery, romantic drama, science fiction, supernatural, suspense, thriller.
HOW TO CONTACT Please submit a 1-page query including a brief bio via the form on the agency website. "Due to the high volume of queries we receive, we are unable to respond to everyone. Queries are reviewed on a rolling basis, and we will follow up directly with the author if there is interest in a full manuscript. Queries should not be addressed to specific agents. All queries go directly to the director for distribution." Obtains new clients by recommendations from others, queries/submissions, agency outreach.
TERMS Offers written contract, binding for 1-3 years, depending on the project; 60-day notice msut be given before terminating contract. No fees.
RECENT SALES *Snafu*, by Miryam Sivan (Cuidano Press); *The Land of Forgotten Girls*, by Erin Kelly (Harper Collins); *The Christos Mosaic*, by Vincent Czyz (Blank Slate Press); *A Tale of Two Maidens*, by Anne Echols (Bagwyn Books); *Esther*, by Rebecca Kanner (Simon and Schuster); *Magnolia City*, by Duncan Alderson (Kensington Books).
TIPS "Do not make cold calls to the agency. E-mail contact only. Do not query for more than one property at a time. If possible, have a professional photograph of yourself ready to submit with your query, as it is important to be media-genic in today's marketplace. Be ready to discuss platform."

HARVEY KLINGER, INC.

300 W. 55th St., Suite 11V, New York NY 10019. (212)581-7068. **E-mail:** queries@harveyklinger.com. **Website:** www.harveyklinger.com. **Contact:** Harvey Klinger. Always interested in considering new clients, both published and unpublished. Estab. 1977. Member of AAR, PEN. Represents 100 clients.
MEMBER AGENTS Harvey Klinger; David Dunton (popular culture, music-related books, literary fiction, young adult, fiction, memoirs); **Andrea Somberg** (literary fiction, commercial fiction, romance, science fiction/fantasy, mystery/thriller, young adult, middle-grade, quality narrative nonfiction, popular culture, how-to, self-help, humor, interior design, cookbooks, health/fitness); **Wendy**

Levinson (literary and commercial fiction, occasional children's young adult or Middle-grade, wide variety of nonfiction); **Rachel Ridout** (Middle-grade and young adult).

REPRESENTS nonfiction, fiction, novels, juvenile books. **Considers these nonfiction areas:** autobiography, biography, business, child guidance, cooking, crafts, creative nonfiction, cultural interests, current affairs, diet/nutrition, foods, gay/lesbian, health, history, how-to, investigative, literature, medicine, memoirs, money, music, popular culture, psychology, science, self-help, sociology, spirituality, sports, technology, true crime, women's issues, women's studies, young adult. **Considers these fiction areas:** action, adventure, commercial, contemporary issues, crime, detective, erotica, family saga, fantasy, gay, glitz, historical, horror, juvenile, lesbian, literary, mainstream, middle-grade, mystery, New Adult, police, romance, suspense, thriller, women's, young adult.

☛ This agency specializes in big, mainstream, contemporary fiction and nonfiction.

HOW TO CONTACT Use online e-mail submission form on the website, or query with SASE via snail mail. No phone or fax queries. Don't send unsolicited mss or e-mail attachments. Make submission letter to the point and as brief as possible. Accepts simultaneous submissions. Responds in 2-4 weeks to queries, if interested. Obtains most new clients through recommendations from others.

TERMS Agent receives 15% commission on domestic sales; 25% commission on foreign sales. Offers written contract. Charges for photocopying mss and overseas postage for mss.

RECENT SALES *Land of the Afternoon Sun*, by Barbara Wood; *I Am Not a Serial Killer*, by Dan Wells; *Me, Myself and Us*, by Brian Little; *The Secret of Magic*, by Deborah Johnson; *Children of the Mist*, by Paula Quinn.

THE KNIGHT AGENCY

232 W. Washington St., Madison GA 30650. **E-mail:** deidre.knight@knightagency.net, submissions@knightagency.net. **Website:** http://knightagency.net/. **Contact:** Deidre Knight. Estab. 1996. Member of AAR, SCWBI, WFA, SFWA, RWA. Represents 200+ clients.
MEMBER AGENTS Deidre Knight (romance, women's fiction, erotica, commercial fiction, inspirational, fiction, memoir, nonfiction narrative, personal finance, true crime, business, popular culture, self-help, religion, health); **Pamela Harty** (romance, women's fiction, young adult, business, motivational, diet and health, memoir, parenting, pop culture, true crime); **Elaine Spencer** (romance [single title and category], women's fiction, commercial "book-club" fiction, cozy mystery, young adult and middle-grade material); **Lucienne Diver** (fantasy, science fiction, romance, suspense, young adult); **Nephele Tempest** (literary/commercial fiction, women's fiction, fantasy, science fiction, romantic suspense, paranormal romance, contemporary romance, historical fiction, young adult, middle-grade fiction); **Melissa Jeglinski** (romance [contemporary, category, historical, inspirational], young adult, middle-grade, women's fiction, mystery); **Kristy Hunter** (romance, women's fiction, commercial fiction, young adult, middle-grade material), **Travis Pennington** (young adult, middle-grade, mystery, thriller, commercial fiction, romance [nothing paranormal/fantasy in any genre for now]).

REPRESENTS nonfiction, fiction, novels. **Considers these nonfiction areas:** autobiography, business, creative nonfiction, cultural interests, current affairs, diet/nutrition, design, economics, ethnic, film, foods, gay/lesbian, health, history, how-to, inspirational, interior design, investigative, juvenile nonfiction, literature, memoirs, military, money, multicultural, parenting, popular culture, politics, psychology, self-help, sociology, technology, travel, true crime, women's issues, young adult. **Considers these fiction areas:** commercial, crime, erotica, fantasy, gay, historical, juvenile, lesbian, literary, mainstream, middle-grade, multicultural, mystery, New Adult, paranormal, psychic, romance, science fiction, thriller, urban fantasy, women's, young adult.

☛ Actively seeking romance in all subgenres, including romantic suspense, paranormal romance, historical romance (a particular love of mine), LGBTQ, contemporary, and also category romance. Does not want to receive screenplays, short stories, poetry, essays, or children's picture books.

HOW TO CONTACT E-queries only. "Your submission should include a 1-page query letter and the first 5 pages of your manuscript. All text must be contained in the body of your e-mail. Attachments will not be opened nor included in the consideration of your work. Queries must be addressed to a specific agent. Please do not query multiple agents." Accepts simultaneous submissions. Responds in 1-2 weeks on queries, 6-8 weeks on submissions.

TERMS 15% SIMPLE agency agreement with open-ended commitment. Agent receives 15% commission on all domestic sales; 20% on foreign and film sales.

KT LITERARY, LLC

9249 S. Broadway, #200-543, Highlands Ranch CO 80129. **E-mail:** contact@ktliterary.com. **E-mail:** katequery@ktliterary.com, saraquery@ktliterary.com, reneequery@ktliterary.com, hannahquery@ktliterary.com. **Website:** www.ktliterary.com. **Contact:** Kate Schafer Testerman, Sara Megibow, Renee Nyen, Hannah Fergesen, Hilary Harwell. Estab. 2008. Member of AAR, SCBWI, young adultLSA, ALA, SFWA, RWA. Represents 75 clients.

MEMBER AGENTS Kate Testerman (middlegrade, young adult), **Renee Nyen** (middle-grade, young adult), **Sara Megibow** (middle-grade, young adult, romance, erotica, science fiction, fantasy), **Hannah Fergesen** (middle-grade, young adult, speculative fiction). Always LGBTQ and diversity friendly.

REPRESENTS fiction. **Considers these fiction areas:** erotica, fantasy, middle-grade, romance, science fiction, young adult.

> Kate is looking only at young adult and middle-grade fiction and selective nonfiction. Sara seeks authors in middle-grade, young adult, and adult romance, erotica, science fiction, and fantasy. Renee is looking for young adult and middle-grade fiction only. Hannah is interested in speculative fiction in young adult, middle-grade, and adult. "We're thrilled to be actively seeking new clients with great writing, unique stories, and complex characters, for middle-grade, young adult, and adult fiction. We are especially interested in diverse voices." Does not want adult mystery, thriller, or adult literary fiction.

HOW TO CONTACT "To query us, please select one of the agents at KT Literary at a time. If we pass, you can feel free to submit to another. Please e-mail your query letter and the first 3 pages of your manuscript in the body of the e-mail. The subject line of your e-mail should include the word 'Query' along with the title of your manuscript. Queries should not contain attachments. Attachments will not be read, and queries containing attachments will be deleted unread. We aim to reply to all queries within 2 weeks of receipt." Accepts simultaneous submissions. Responds in 2-4 weeks to queries, 2 months to mss. Obtains most new clients through query slush pile.

TERMS Agent receives 15% commission on domestic sales; 20% commission on foreign sales. Offers written contract; 30-day notice must be given to terminate contract.

RECENT SALES *On the Wall*, by Carrie Harris; *A Red Peace*, by Spencer Ellsworth; *The Odds of Loving Grover Cleveland*, by Rebekah Crane; *Trail of Lightning*, by Rebecca Roanhorse; *Future Lost*, by Elizabeth Briggs; *Full Court Press*, by Maggie Wells; *An Enchantment of Ravens*, by Margaret Rogerson; *The Summer of Jordi Perez*, by Amy Spalding; *What Goes Up*, by Wen Baragrey.

THE LESHNE AGENCY

New York NY **E-mail:** info@leshneagency.com. **E-mail:** submissions@leshneagency.com. **Website:** www.leshneagency.com. **Contact:** Lisa Leshne, agent and owner. "We are a full-service literary and talent management agency committed to the success of our clients over the course of their careers. We represent a select and growing number of writers, artists, and entertainers interested in building their brands, audience platforms, and developing long-term relationships via all forms of traditional and social media. We take a deeply personal approach by working closely with our clients to develop their best ideas for maximum impact and reach across print, digital, and other formats, providing hands-on guidance and networking for lasting success." Estab. 2011. Member of AAR, Women's Media Group.

MEMBER AGENTS Lisa Leshne, agent and owner; **Sandy Hodgman**, director of foreign rights.

REPRESENTS nonfiction, fiction, novels. **Considers these nonfiction areas:** business, creative nonfiction, cultural interests, health, how-to, humor, inspirational, memoirs, parenting, politics, science, self-help, sports, women's issues. **Considers these fiction areas:** commercial, middle-grade, young adult.

HOW TO CONTACT The Leshne Agency is seeking new and existing authors across all genres. "We are especially interested in narrative, memoir, prescriptive nonfiction, with a particular interest in sports, health, wellness, business, political, and parenting topics, and truly terrific commercial fiction, young adult, and middle-grade books. We are not interested in screenplays, scripts, poetry, and picture books. If your submission is in a genre not specifically listed here, we are still open to considering it, but if your submission is for a genre we've mentioned as not being interested in, please don't bother sending it to us. All submissions should be made through the Authors.me portal by clicking on the link at: https://app.authors.me/#submit/the-leshne-agency." Accepts simultaneous submissions.

LEVINE GREENBERG ROSTAN LITERARY AGENCY, INC.

307 Seventh Ave., Suite 2407, New York NY 10001. (212)337-0934. **Fax:** (212)337-0948. **E-mail:** submit@lgrliterary.com. **Website:** www.lgrliterary.com. Member of AAR. Represents 250 clients.

○ Prior to opening his agency, Mr. Levine served as vice president of the Bank Street College of Education.

MEMBER AGENTS Jim Levine (nonfiction, including business, science, narrative nonfiction, social and political issues, psychology, health, spirituality, parenting); Stephanie Rostan (adult and young adult fiction; nonfiction, including parenting, health and wellness, sports, memoir); Melissa Rowland; Daniel Greenberg (nonfiction: popular culture, narrative nonfiction, memoir, humor; literary fiction); Victoria Skurnick; Danielle Svetcov (nonfiction); Lindsay Edgecombe (narrative nonfiction, memoir, lifestyle and health, illustrated books, as well as literary fiction); Monika Verma (nonfiction: humor, pop culture, memoir, narrative nonfiction, style and fashion; some young adult fiction [paranormal, historical, contemporary]); Kerry Sparks (young adult and middle-grade; select adult fiction, occasional nonfiction); Tim Wojcik (nonfiction, including food narratives, humor, pop culture, popular history, science; literary fiction); Arielle Eckstut (no queries); Sarah Bedingfield (literary and upmarket commercial fiction, epic family dramas, literary novels with notes of magical realism, darkly gothic stories, psychological suspense).
REPRESENTS nonfiction, novels. **Considers these nonfiction areas:** business, creative nonfiction, health, history, humor, memoirs, parenting, popular culture, science, spirituality, sports. **Considers these fiction areas:** commercial, literary, mainstream, middle-grade, suspense, young adult.
HOW TO CONTACT E-query to submit@lgrliterary.com, or online submission form. "If you would like to direct your query to one of our agents specifically, please feel free to name the agent in the online form or in the e-mail you send." Cannot respond to submissions by mail. Do not attach more than 50 pages. "Due to the volume of submissions we receive, we are unable to respond to each individually. If we would like more information about your project, we'll contact you within 3 weeks (though we do get backed up on occasion!)." Accepts simultaneous submissions. Obtains most new clients through recommendations from others.
TERMS Agent receives 15% commission on domestic sales; 20% commission on foreign sales. Offers written contract. Charges clients for out-of-pocket expenses—telephone, fax, postage, photocopying—directly connected to the project.
RECENT SALES *Notorious RBG*, by Irin Carmon and Shana Knizhnik; *Pogue's Basics: Life*, by David Pogue; *Invisible City*, by Julia Dahl; *Gumption*, by Nick Offerman; *All the Bright Places*, by Jennifer Niven.
TIPS "We focus on editorial development, business representation, and publicity and marketing strategy."

PAUL S. LEVINE LITERARY AGENCY

1054 Superba Ave., Venice CA 90291. (310)450-6711. **Fax:** (310)450-0181. **E-mail:** paul@paulslevinelit.com. **Website:** www.paulslevinelit.com. **Contact:** Paul S. Levine. Estab. 1992. Member of the State Bar of California. Represents over 100 clients.
MEMBER AGENTS Paul S. Levine (children's and young adult fiction and nonfiction, adult fiction and nonfiction except science fiction, fantasy, and horror); Loren R. Grossman (archeology, art/photography, architecture, child guidance/parenting, coffee table books, gardening, education/academics, health/medicine/science/technology, law, religion, memoirs, sociology).
REPRESENTS nonfiction, fiction, novels, TV movie of the week, episodic drama, sitcom, animation, documentary, miniseries, syndicated material, variety show, comic books, graphic novels. **Considers these nonfiction areas:** architecture, art, autobiography, biography, business, child guidance, cooking, crafts, creative nonfiction, current affairs, deco-

rating, diet/nutrition, design, education, foods, gardening, gay/lesbian, health, history, how-to, humor, inspirational, interior design, investigative, juvenile nonfiction, law, medicine, memoirs, money, music, New Age, parenting, philosophy, photography, popular culture, politics, psychology, recreation, religious, satire, science, self-help, sex, sociology, spirituality, sports, technology, travel, true crime, women's issues, women's studies, young adult. **Considers these fiction areas:** adventure, ethnic, mainstream, mystery, romance, thriller, young adult.

HOW TO CONTACT E-mail preferred; snail mail with SASE is also acceptable. Send a 1-page, single-spaced query letter. In your query letter, note your target market, with a summary of specifics on how your work differs from other authors' previously published work. Accepts simultaneous submissions. Responds in 1 day to queries, 6-8 weeks to mss. Obtains most new clients through conferences, referrals, listings on various websites, directories.

TERMS Agent receives 15% commission on domestic sales. Offers written contract. Charges for postage and actual, out-of-pocket costs only.

TIPS "Write good, sellable books."

LIPPINCOTT MASSIE MCQUILKIN

27 West 20th Street, Suite 305, New York NY 10011. **E-mail:** info@lmqlit.com. **Website:** www.lmqlit.com. **MEMBER AGENTS Laney Katz Becker**, laney@lmqlit.com (book club fiction, upmarket women's fiction, suspense, thriller, memoir); **Ethan Bassoff**, ethan@lmqlit.com (literary fiction, crime fiction, and narrative nonfiction: history, sports writing, journalism, science writing, pop culture, humor, food writing); **Jason Anthony**, jason@lmqlit.com (commercial fiction of all types, including young adult, and nonfiction: memoir, pop culture, true crime, general psychology and sociology); **Will Lippincott**, will@lmqlit.com (narrative nonfiction and nonfiction: politics, history, biography, foreign affairs, health); **Rob McQuilkin**, rob@lmqlit.com (literary fiction; narrative nonfiction and nonfiction: memoir, history, biography, art history, cultural criticism, popular sociology and psychology; **Rayhane Sanders**, rayhane@lmqlit.com (literary fiction, historical fiction, upmarket commercial fiction [including select young adult], narrative nonfiction [including essays], select memoir); **Stephanie Abou** (literary and upmarket commercial fiction [includ-

ing select young adult and middle-grade], crime fiction, memoir, narrative nonfiction); **Julie Stevenson** (literary and upmarket fiction, narrative nonfiction, young adult, children's books).

REPRESENTS nonfiction, novels. **Considers these nonfiction areas:** art, biography, cultural interests, foods, health, history, humor, memoirs, popular culture, politics, psychology, science, sociology, sports, true crime, narrative nonfiction. **Considers these fiction areas:** commercial, contemporary issues, crime, literary, mainstream, middle-grade, suspense, thriller, women's, young adult.

☞ "Lippincott Massie McQuilkin is a full-service literary agency that focuses on bringing fiction and nonfiction of quality to the largest possible audience."

HOW TO CONTACT E-query preferred. Include the word "Query" in the subject line of your e-mail. Review the agency's online page of agent bios (lmqlit.com/contact.html), as some agents want sample pages with their submissions and some do not. If you have not heard back from the agency in 4 weeks, assume they are not interested in seeing more. Accepts simultaneous submissions. Obtains most new clients through recommendations from others, solicitations, conferences.

TERMS Agent receives 15% commission on domestic sales; 20% commission on foreign sales. Offers written contract; 30-day notice must be given to terminate contract. Only charges for reasonable business expenses upon successful sale.

RECENT SALES Clients include Peter Ho Davies, Kim Addonizio, Natasha Trethewey, David Sirota, Katie Crouch, Uwen Akpan, Lydia Millet, Tom Perrotta, Jonathan Lopez, Chris Hayes, Caroline Weber.

LKG AGENCY

465 West End Ave., 2A, New York NY 10024. **E-mail:** query@lkgagency.com. **E-mail:** For middle-grade or young adult: middle-gradeya@lkgagency.com. For nonfiction: nonfiction@lkgagency.com. **Website:** lkgagency.com. **Contact:** Lauren Galit, Caitlen Rubino-Bradway. The LKG Agency was founded in 2005 and is based on the Upper West Side of Manhattan. "We are a boutique literary agency that specializes in middle-grade and young adult fiction, as well as nonfiction, both practical and narrative, with a particular interest in women-focused how-to. We invest a great deal of care and

personal attention in each of our authors with the aim of developing long-term relationships that last well beyond the sale of a single book." Estab. 2005.

MEMBER AGENTS Lauren Galit (nonfiction, middle-grade, young adult); **Caitlen Rubino-Bradway** (middle-grade and young adult, some nonfiction).

REPRESENTS nonfiction, juvenile books. **Considers these nonfiction areas:** animals, child guidance, creative nonfiction, diet/nutrition, design, health, how-to, humor, juvenile nonfiction, memoirs, parenting, popular culture, psychology, women's issues, young adult. **Considers these fiction areas:** middle-grade, young adult.

> Actively seeking parenting, beauty, celebrity, dating and relationships, entertainment, fashion, health, diet and fitness, home and design, lifestyle, memoir, narrative, pets, psychology, women's, middle-grade and young adult fiction. Does not want history, biography, true crime, religion, picture books, spirituality, screenplays, poetry, any fiction other than middle-grade or young adult.

HOW TO CONTACT For nonfiction submissions, please send a query letter to nonfiction@lkgagency.com, along with a TOC and 2 sample chapters. The TOC should be fairly detailed, with a paragraph or two overview of the content of each chapter. Please also make sure to mention any publicity you have at your disposal. For middle-grade and young adult submissions, please send a query, synopsis, and 3 chapters, and address all submissions to middlegradeya@lkgagency.com. On a side note, while both Lauren and Caitlen consider young adult and middle-grade, Lauren tends to look more for middle-grade, while Caitlen deals more with young adult fiction. Please note: due to the high volume of submissions, we are unable to reply to every one. If you do not receive a reply, please consider that a rejection. Accepts simultaneous submissions.

STERLING LORD LITERISTIC, INC.

115 Broadway, New York NY 10006. (212)780-6050. **Fax:** (212)780-6095. **E-mail:** info@sll.com. **Website:** www.sll.com. Estab. 1987. Member of AAR. Signatory of WGA.

MEMBER AGENTS Philippa Brophy (represents journalists, nonfiction writers, and novelists, and is most interested in current events, memoir, science, politics, biography, women's issues); **Laurie** Liss (represents authors of commercial and literary fiction and nonfiction whose perspectives are well developed and unique); **Sterling Lord**; **Peter Matson** (abiding interest in storytelling, whether in the service of history, fiction, the sciences); **Douglas Stewart** (primarily fiction for all ages, from the innovatively literary to the unabashedly commercial); **Neeti Madan** (memoir, journalism, popular culture, lifestyle, women's issues, multicultural books, virtually any intelligent writing on intriguing topics); **Robert Guinsler** (literary and commercial fiction [including young adult], journalism, narrative nonfiction with an emphasis on pop culture, science and current events, memoirs, biography); **Jim Rutman**; **Celeste Fine** (expert, celebrity, corporate clients with strong national and international platforms, particularly in the health, science, self-help, food, business, lifestyle fields); **Martha Millard** (fiction and nonfiction, including well-written science fiction and young adult); **Mary Krienke** (literary fiction, memoir, narrative nonfiction [psychology, popular science, cultural commentary]); **Jenny Stephens** (nonfiction: cookbooks, practical lifestyle projects, transportive travel and nature writing, creative nonfiction; fiction: contemporary literary narratives strongly rooted in place); **Alison MacKeen** (idea-driven research books: social scientific, scientific, historical, relationships/parenting, learning and education, sexuality, technology, the life-cycle, health, the environment, politics, economics, psychology, geography, culture; literary fiction, literary nonfiction, memoirs, essays, travel writing); **John Maas** (serious nonfiction, specifically business, personal development, science, self-help, health, fitness, lifestyle); **Sarah Passick** (commercial nonfiction in the celebrity, food, blogger, lifestyle, health, diet, fitness, fashion categories).

REPRESENTS nonfiction, fiction. **Considers these nonfiction areas:** biography, business, cooking, creative nonfiction, current affairs, economics, education, foods, gay/lesbian, history, humor, memoirs, multicultural, parenting, popular culture, politics, psychology, science, technology, travel, women's issues, fitness. **Considers these fiction areas:** commercial, juvenile, literary, middle-grade, picture books, science fiction, young adult.

HOW TO CONTACT Query via snail mail. "Please submit a query letter, a synopsis of the work, a brief proposal or the first 3 chapters of the manuscript, a brief bio or resume, and SASE for reply. Original artwork is not accepted. Enclose sufficient postage if you wish to have your materials returned to you. We do not respond to unsolicited e-mail inquiries." Accepts simultaneous submissions.

TERMS Agent receives 15% commission on domestic sales; 20% commission on foreign sales. Offers written contract.

LOWENSTEIN ASSOCIATES INC.

115 E. 23rd St., Fourth Floor, New York NY 10010. (212)206-1630. **E-mail:** assistant@bookhaven.com. **Website:** www.lowensteinassociates.com. **Contact:** Barbara Lowenstein. Member of AAR.

MEMBER AGENTS Barbara Lowenstein, president (nonfiction: narrative nonfiction, health, money, finance, travel, multicultural, popular culture, memoir; fiction: literary fiction and women's fiction); Mary South (literary fiction, nonfiction: neuroscience, bioengineering, women's rights, design, digital humanities, investigative journalism, essays, memoir).

REPRESENTS nonfiction, fiction, novels, short story collections. **Considers these nonfiction areas:** autobiography, biography, business, creative nonfiction, cultural interests, health, humor, literature, memoirs, money, multicultural, popular culture, science, technology, travel, women's issues. **Considers these fiction areas:** commercial, literary, middle-grade, science fiction, women's, young adult.

- Barbara Lowenstein is currently looking for writers who have a platform and are leading experts in their field, including business, women's issues, psychology, health, science, and social issues, and is particularly interested in strong new voices in fiction and narrative nonfiction. Does not want westerns, textbooks, children's picture books, and books in need of translation.

HOW TO CONTACT "For fiction, please send us a 1-page query letter, along with the first 10 pages pasted in the body of the message by e-mail to assistant@bookhaven.com. If nonfiction, please send a 1-page query letter, a table of contents, and, if available, a proposal pasted into the body of the e-mail. Please put the word 'QUERY' and the title of your project in the subject field of your e-mail and address it to the agent of your choice. Please do not send an attachment, as the message will be deleted without being read and no

reply will be sent." Accepts simultaneous submissions. Responds in 6 weeks to queries. Obtains most new clients through recommendations from others, solicitations, conferences.

TERMS Agent receives 15% commission on domestic sales; 20% commission on foreign sales. Offers written contract. Charges for large photocopy batches, messenger service, international postage.

TIPS "Know the genre you are working in and read!"

DONALD MAASS LITERARY AGENCY

1000 Dean St., Suite 252, Brooklyn NY 11238. (212)727-8383. **Website:** www.maassagency.com. Estab. 1980. Member of AAR, SFWA, MWA, RWA. Represents more than 100 clients.

MEMBER AGENTS Donald Maass (mainstream, literary, mystery/suspense, science fiction, romance); Jennifer Jackson (science fiction and fantasy for both adult and young adult markets, thriller that mine popular and controversial issues, young adult that challenges traditional thinking); Cameron McClure (literary, mystery/suspense, urban, fantasy, narrative nonfiction, and projects with multicultural, international, and environmental themes, gay/lesbian); Amy Boggs (fantasy and science fiction, young adult/Middle-grade, historical fiction about eras that aren't well known); Katie Shea Boutillier (women's fiction/book club, edgy/dark, realistic/contemporary young adult, commercial-scale literary fiction, celebrity memoir); Michael Curry (science fiction and fantasy, near-future thriller); Caitlin McDonald (science fiction and fantasy [young adult/middle-grade/adult], genre-bending/cross-genre fiction, diversity).

REPRESENTS nonfiction, fiction, novels, juvenile books. **Considers these nonfiction areas:** creative nonfiction, memoirs, popular culture. **Considers these fiction areas:** contemporary issues, crime, detective, ethnic, fantasy, feminist, gay, historical, horror, juvenile, lesbian, literary, mainstream, middle-grade, multicultural, mystery, paranormal, police, regional, romance, science fiction, supernatural, suspense, thriller, urban fantasy, westerns, women's, young adult.

- This agency specializes in commercial fiction, especially science fiction, fantasy, thriller, suspense, and women's fiction, for both the adult and young adult markets. Does not want poetry, screenplays, or picture books.

HOW TO CONTACT Query via e-mail only. All the agents have different submission addresses and instructions. See the website and each agent's online profile for exact submission instructions. Accepts simultaneous submissions.

TERMS Agency receives 15% commission on domestic sales; 20% commission on foreign sales.

RECENT SALES *The Aeronaut's Windlass*, by Jim Butcher (Penguin Random House); *City of Blades*, by Robert Jackson Bennett (Crown); *I Am Princess X*, by Cherie Priest (Scholastic); *Treachery at Lancaster Gate*, by Anne Perry (Random House); *Marked in Flesh*, by Anne Bishop (Penguin Random House); *We Are the Ants*, by Shaun David Hutchinson (Simon & Schuster); *The Book of Phoenix*, by Nnedi Okorafor (DAW); *Ninefox Gambit*, by Yoon Ha Lee (Solaris); *The Far End of Happy*, by Kathryn Craft (Sourcebooks); *The Traitor Baru Cormorant*, by Seth Dickinson (Tor).

TIPS "We are fiction specialists, also noted for our innovative approach to career planning. We are always open to submissions from new writers." Works with subagents in all principal foreign countries and for film and television.

GINA MACCOBY LITERARY AGENCY

P.O. Box 60, Chappaqua NY 10514. (914)238-5630. **E-mail:** query@maccobylit.com. **Website:** www.publishersmarketplace.com/members/ginamaccoby. **Contact:** Gina Maccoby. Estab. 1986. Member of AAR, AAR Board of Directors, Royalties and Ethics and Contracts subcommittees, Authors Guild, SCBWI.

REPRESENTS nonfiction, fiction, novels, juvenile books. **Considers these nonfiction areas:** autobiography, biography, cultural interests, current affairs, ethnic, history, juvenile nonfiction, literature, popular culture, women's issues, women's studies, young adult. **Considers these fiction areas:** crime, detective, family saga, juvenile, literary, mainstream, middle-grade, multicultural, mystery, New Adult, thriller, women's, young adult.

HOW TO CONTACT Query by e-mail only. Accepts simultaneous submissions. Owing to volume of submissions, may not respond to queries unless interested. Obtains most new clients through recommendations.

TERMS AGENT RECEIVES 15% commission on domestic sales; 20-25% commission on foreign sales, which includes subagent's commissions. May recover certain costs, such as purchasing books, shipping books overseas by airmail, legal fees for vetting motion picture contracts, bank fees for electronic funds transfers, overnight delivery services..

MANSION STREET LITERARY MANAGEMENT

E-mail: querymansionstreet@gmail.com, querymichelle@mansionstreet.com. **Website:** mansionstreet.com. **Contact:** Jean Sagendorph, Michelle Witte. Member of AAR. Signatory of WGA.

MEMBER AGENTS Jean Sagendorph, querymansionstreet@gmail.com (pop culture, gift books, cookbooks, general nonfiction, lifestyle, design, brand extensions); **Michelle Witte,** querymichelle@mansionstreet.com (young adult, middle-grade, early readers, picture books [especially from author/illustrators], juvenile nonfiction).

REPRESENTS nonfiction, novels. **Considers these nonfiction areas:** cooking, design, popular culture. **Considers these fiction areas:** juvenile, middle-grade, young adult.

> Ms. Sagendorph is not interested in memoirs or medical/reference. Typically sports and self-help are not a good fit; also does not represent travel books. Ms. Witte is not interested in fiction or nonfiction for adults.

HOW TO CONTACT Send a query letter and no more than the first 10 pages of your ms in the body of an e-mail. Query one specific agent at this agency. No attachments. You must list the genre in the subject line. If the genre is not in the subject line, your query will be deleted. Accepts simultaneous submissions. Responds in up to 6 weeks.

RECENT SALES *Shake and Fetch*, by Carli Davidson; *Bleed, Blister, Puke and Purge*, by J. Marin Younker; *Spectrum*, by Ginger Johnson; *I Left You a Present* and *Movie Night Trivia*, by Robb Pearlman; *Open Sesame!*, by Ashley Evanson; *Fox Hunt*, by Nilah Magruder; *ABC Now You See Me*, by Kim Siebold.

MARSAL LYON LITERARY AGENCY, LLC

PMB 121, 665 San Rodolfo Dr. 124, Solana Beach CA 92075. **E-mail:** kevan@marsallyonliteraryagency.com. **Website:** www.marsallyonliteraryagency.com. **Contact:** Kevan Lyon, Jill Marsal. Query e-mails: jill@marsallyonliteraryagency.com, kevan@marsallyonliteraryagency.com, deborah@marsallyonliteraryagency.com, shannon@marsallyonliteraryagency.com, patricia@marsallyonliteraryagency.com. Estab. 2009. Member of RWA

MEMBER AGENTS Kevan Lyon (women's fiction with an emphasis on commercial women's fiction, young adult fiction, all genres of romance); **Jill Marsal** (all types of women's fiction and all types of romance; mystery, cozies, suspense, thriller; nonfiction: current events, business, health, self-help, relationships, psychology, parenting, history, science, narrative nonfiction); **Patricia Nelson** (literary fiction and commercial fiction, all types of women's fiction, contemporary and historical romance, young adult and middle-grade fiction, LGBTQ fiction for both young adult and adult); **Deborah Ritchkin** (lifestyle books: food, design, entertaining; pop culture; women's issues; biography; current events; her niche interest is projects about France, including fiction); **Shannon Hassan** (literary and commercial fiction, young adult and middle-grade fiction, select nonfiction).

REPRESENTS nonfiction, fiction, novels, juvenile books. **Considers these nonfiction areas:** animals, biography, business, cooking, creative nonfiction, current affairs, diet/nutrition, history, investigative, memoirs, parenting, popular culture, politics, psychology, science, self-help, sports, women's issues, women's studies. **Considers these fiction areas:** commercial, juvenile, literary, mainstream, middle-grade, multicultural, mystery, paranormal, romance, suspense, thriller, women's, young adult.

HOW TO CONTACT Query by e-mail. Query only one agent at this agency at a time. "Please visit our website to determine who is best suited for your work. Write 'query' in the subject line of your e-mail. Please allow up to several weeks to hear back on your query." Accepts simultaneous submissions.

TIPS "Our agency's mission is to help writers achieve their publishing dreams. We want to work with authors not just for a book but for a career; we are dedicated to building long-term relationships with our authors and publishing partners. Our goal is to help find homes for books that engage, entertain, and make a difference."

MARTIN LITERARY AND MEDIA MANAGEMENT

914 164th St. SE, Suite B12, #307, Mill Creek WA 98012. **E-mail:** sharlene@martinliterarymanagement.com. **Website:** www.martinlit.com. **Contact:** Sharlene Martin. Estab. 2002.

Prior to becoming an agent, Ms. Martin worked in film/TV production and acquisitions.

MEMBER AGENTS Sharlene Martin (nonfiction); **Clelia Gore** (children's, middle-grade, young adult); **Adria Goetz** (Christian books, Lifestyle books).

REPRESENTS nonfiction. **Considers these nonfiction areas:** autobiography, biography, business, child guidance, creative nonfiction, current affairs, economics, health, history, how-to, humor, inspirational, investigative, medicine, memoirs, parenting, popular culture, psychology, satire, self-help, true crime, war, women's issues, women's studies. **Considers these fiction areas:** juvenile, middle-grade, young adult.

This agency has strong ties to film/TV. Actively seeking nonfiction that is highly commercial and that can be adapted to film. "We are being inundated with queries and submissions that are wrongfully being submitted to us, which only results in more frustration for the writers."

HOW TO CONTACT Query via e-mail . No attachments on queries, place letter in body of e-mail. Accepts simultaneous submissions. Responds in 2 weeks to queries, 3-4 weeks to mss. Obtains most new clients through recommendations from others.

TERMS Agent receives 15% commission on domestic sales. Offers written contract, binding for 1 year; 1-month notice must be given to terminate contract.

RECENT SALES *Taking My Life Back*, by Rebekah Gregory with Anthony Flacco; *Maximum Harm*, by Michele McPhee; *Breakthrough*, by Jack Andraka; *In the Matter of Nikola Tesla: A Romance of the Mind*, by Anthony Flacco; *Honor Bound: My Journey to Hell and Back with Amanda Knox*, by Raffaele Sollecito.

TIPS "Have a strong platform for nonfiction. Please don't call. (I can't tell how well you write by the sound of your voice.) I welcome e-mail. I'm very responsive when I'm interested in a query and work hard to get my clients' materials in the best possible shape before submissions. Do your homework prior to submission and only submit your best efforts. Please review our website carefully to make sure we're a good match for your work. If you read my book, *Publish Your Nonfiction Book: Strategies for Learning the Industry, Selling Your Book and Building a Successful Career* (Writer's Digest Books), you'll know exactly how to charm me."

SEAN MCCARTHY LITERARY AGENCY

E-mail: submissions@mccarthylit.com. **Website:** www.mccarthylit.com. **Contact:** Sean McCarthy. Estab. 2013.

○ Sean McCarthy began his publishing career as an editorial intern at Overlook Press and then moved over to the Sheldon Fogelman Agency prior to his current position.

REPRESENTS Considers these nonfiction areas: juvenile nonfiction, young adult. **Considers these fiction areas:** juvenile, middle-grade, picture books, young adult.

&— Sean is drawn to flawed, multifaceted characters with devastatingly concise writing in young adult, and boy-friendly mystery or adventures in Middle-grade. In picture books, he looks more for unforgettable characters, off-beat humor, and especially clever endings. He is not currently interested in high fantasy, message-driven stories, or query letters that pose too many questions.

HOW TO CONTACT E-query. "Please include a brief description of your book, your biography, and any literary or relevant professional credits in your query letter. If you are a novelist: Please submit the first 3 chapters of your manuscript (or roughly 25 pages) and a 1-page synopsis in the body of the e-mail or as a Word or PDF attachment. If you are a picture book author: Please submit the complete text of your manuscript. We are not currently accepting picture book manuscripts over 1,000 words. If you are an illustrator: Please attach up to 3 JPEGs or PDFs of your work, along with a link to your website." Accepts simultaneous submissions.

○⊘ ANNE MCDERMID & ASSOCIATES, LTD

320 Front St. W., Suite 1105, Toronto ON M5V 3B6 Canada. (647)788-4016. **Fax:** (416)324-8870. **E-mail:** admin@mcdermidagency.com. **E-mail:** info@mcdermidagency.com. **Website:** www.mcdermidagency.com. **Contact:** Anne McDermid. Estab. 1996.

MEMBER AGENTS Anne McDermid, Martha Webb, Monica Pacheco, Chris Bucci.

REPRESENTS novels.

&— The agency represents literary novelists and commercial novelists of high quality, and also writers of nonfiction in the areas of memoir, biography, history, literary travel, narrative science, and investigative journalism. "We also represent a certain number of children's and young adult writers and writers in the fields of science fiction and fantasy."

HOW TO CONTACT Query via e-mail or mail with a brief bio, description, and first 5 pages of project only. Accepts simultaneous submissions. *No unsolicited manuscripts.* Obtains most new clients through recommendations from others.

MCINTOSH & OTIS, INC.

353 Lexington Ave., New York NY 10016. (212)687-7400. **Fax:** (212)687-6894. **E-mail:** info@mcintoshandotis.com. **Website:** www.mcintoshandotis.com. **Contact:** Eugene H. Winick, Esq.. McIntosh & Otis has a long history of representing authors of adult and children's books. The children's department is a separate division. Estab. 1928. Member of AAR. Signatory of WGA. SCBWI

MEMBER AGENTS Elizabeth Winick Rubinstein, ewrquery@mcintoshandotis.com (literary fiction, women's fiction, historical fiction, mystery/suspense, along with narrative nonfiction, spiritual/self-help, history and current affairs); **Shira Hoffman**, shquery@mcintoshandotis.com (young adult, Middle-grade, mainstream commercial fiction, mystery, literary fiction, women's fiction, romance, urban fantasy, fantasy, science fiction, horror, dystopian); **Christa Heschke**, CHquery@mcintoshandotis.com (picture books, middle-grade, young adult New Adult projects); **Adam Muhlig**, AMquery@mcintoshandotis.com (music—from jazz to classical to punk—popular culture, natural history, travel and adventure, sports); **Eugene Winick**.

REPRESENTS Considers these nonfiction areas: creative nonfiction, current affairs, history, popular culture, self-help, spirituality, sports, travel. **Considers these fiction areas:** fantasy, historical, horror, literary, middle-grade, mystery, New Adult, paranormal, picture books, romance, science fiction, suspense, urban fantasy, women's, young adult.

&— Actively seeking "books with memorable characters, distinctive voices, and great plots."

HOW TO CONTACT E-mail submissions only. All agents have their own e-mail address for subs. For fiction, please send a query letter, synopsis, author bio, and the first 3 consecutive chapters (no more than 30 pages) of your novel. For nonfiction, please send a query letter, proposal, outline, author bio, and 3 sample chapters (no more than 30 pages) of the ms. For children's & young adult: Please send a query letter, synopsis and the first 3 consecutive chapters (not to exceed 25 pages) of the ms. Accepts simultaneous submissions. Obtains clients through recommendations from others, editors, conferences and queries.

TERMS Agent receives 15% commission on domestic sales; 20% on foreign sales.

HOWARD MORHAIM LITERARY AGENCY

30 Pierrepont St., Brooklyn NY 11201. (718)222-8400. **Fax:** (718)222-5056. **E-mail:** info@morhaim-literary.com. **Website:** www.morhaimliterary.com. Member of AAR.

MEMBER AGENTS Howard Morhaim, howard@morhaimliterary.com, **Kate McKean**, kmckean@morhaimliterary.com, **DongWon Song**, dongwon@morhaimliterary.com, **Kim-Mei Kirtland**, kimmei@morhaimliterary.com.

REPRESENTS Considers these nonfiction areas: biography, business, cooking, crafts, creative nonfiction, design, economics, foods, health, humor, memoirs, parenting, self-help, sports. **Considers these fiction areas:** fantasy, historical, literary, middle-grade, New Adult, romance, science fiction, women's, young adult, LGBTQ young adult, magical realism, e high fantasy, historical fiction no earlier than the 20th century..

➤ Kate McKean is open to many subgenres and categories of young adult and Middle-grade fiction. Check the website for the most details. Actively seeking fiction, nonfiction, and young adult novels.

HOW TO CONTACT Query via e-mail with cover letter and 3 sample chapters. See each agent's listing for specifics. Accepts simultaneous submissions.

MOVEABLE TYPE MANAGEMENT

244 Madison Ave., Suite 334, New York NY 10016. **E-mail:** achromy@movabletm.com. **Website:** www.movabletm.com. **Contact:** Adam Chromy. Estab. 2002.

REPRESENTS nonfiction, fiction, novels. **Considers these nonfiction areas:** Americana, business, creative nonfiction, current affairs, film, foods, history, how-to, humor, literature, memoirs, military, money, music, popular culture, politics, psychology, satire, science, self-help, sex, sports, technology, theater, true crime, war, women's issues, women's studies. **Considers these fiction areas:** action, commercial, crime, detective, erotica, hi-lo, historical, literary, mainstream, mystery, romance, satire, science fiction, sports, suspense, thriller, women's.

➤ Mr. Chromy is a generalist, meaning that he accepts fiction submissions of virtually any kind (except juvenile books aimed for middle-grade and younger) as well as nonfiction. He has sold books in the following categories: New Adult, women's, romance, memoir, pop culture, young adult, lifestyle, horror, how-to, general fiction, and more.

HOW TO CONTACT E-queries only. Responds if interested. For nonfiction: Send a query letter in the body of an e-mail that precisely introduces your topic and approach, and includes a descriptive bio. For journalists and academics, please also feel free to include a CV. Fiction: Send your query letter and the first 10 pages of your novel in the body of an e-mail. Your subject line needs to contain the word "Query" or your message will not reach the agency. No attachments and no snail mail. Accepts simultaneous submissions.

RECENT SALES *The Wedding Sisters*, by Jamie Brenner (St. Martin's Press); *Sons Of Zeus*, by Noble Smith (Thomas Dunne Books); *World Made by Hand and Too Much Magic*, by James Howard Kunstler (Grove/Atlantic Press); *Dirty Rocker Boys*, by Bobbie Brown (Gallery/S&S).

DEE MURA LITERARY

P.O. Box 131, Massapequa NY 11762. (516)795-1616. **E-mail:** info@deemuraliterary.com. **E-mail:** query@deemuraliterary.com. **Website:** www.deemuraliterary.com. **Contact:** Dee Mura. "We focus on developing our client's' careers from day one through to publication and beyond by providing personalized editorial feedback, social media and platform marketing, and thorough rights management. Both new and experienced authors are welcome to submit." Signatory of WGA. Member of Women's National Book Association, GrubStreet

○ Prior to opening her agency, Mura was a public relations executive with a roster of film and entertainment clients. She is the president and CEO of both Dee Mura Literary and Dee Mura Entertainment.

MEMBER AGENTS Dee Mura, Kimiko Nakamura, Kaylee Davis.

REPRESENTS nonfiction, fiction, novels, short story collections, juvenile books. **Considers these nonfiction areas:** agriculture, Americana, animals, anthropology, archeology, architecture, art, autobiography, biography, business, child guidance, cooking, crafts, creative nonfiction, cultural interests, current affairs, dance, decorating, diet/nutrition, design, economics, education, environment, ethnic, film, foods, gardening, gay/lesbian, government, health, history, hobbies, horticulture, how-to, humor, inspirational, interior design, investigative, juvenile nonfiction, language, law, literature, medicine, memoirs, metaphysics, military, money, multicultural, music, New Age, parenting, photography, popular culture, politics, psychology, recreation, religious, science, self-help, sex, sociology, spirituality, sports, technology, travel, true crime, war, women's issues, women's studies, young adult, Judaism. **Considers these fiction areas:** action, adventure, comic books, commercial, contemporary issues, crime, detective, erotica, ethnic, family saga, fantasy, feminist, frontier, gay, glitz, historical, horror, humor, inspirational, juvenile, lesbian, literary, mainstream, metaphysical, middle-grade, military, multicultural, multimedia, mystery, New Adult, New Age, occult, paranormal, police, psychic, regional, religious, romance, satire, science fiction, short story collections, spiritual, sports, supernatural, suspense, thriller, translation, urban fantasy, war, westerns, women's, young adult, espionage, magical realism, speculative fiction, crossover.

☞ No screenplays, poetry, or children's picture books.

HOW TO CONTACT Query with SASE or e-mail query@deemuraliterary.com (e-mail queries are preferred). Please include the first 25 pages in the body of the e-mail as well as a short author bio and synopsis of the work. Responds to queries in 4-5 weeks. Responds to mss in approximately 8 weeks. Obtains new clients through recommendations, queries, and conferences. Accepts simultaneous submissions. Responds to queries in 3-4 weeks. Responds to mss in approximately 8 weeks. Obtains new clients through recommendations, queries, and conferences.

TERMS Agent receives 15% commission on domestic sales; 20% commission on foreign sales. Offers written contract.

RECENT SALES *An Infinite Number of Parallel Universes*, by Randy Ribay; *The Number 7*, by Jessica Lidh.

⊘ **ERIN MURPHY LITERARY AGENCY**
824 Roosevelt Trail, #290, Windham ME 04062. **Website:** emliterary.com. **Contact:** Erin Murphy, president; Ammi-Joan Paquette, senior agent; Tricia Lawrence, agent; Tara Gonzalez, associate agent. Estab. 1999.

REPRESENTS Considers these fiction areas: middle-grade, picture books, young adult.

☞ Specializes in children's books only.

HOW TO CONTACT Accepts simultaneous submissions.

TERMS Agent receives 15% commission on domestic sales; 20-30% on foreign sales. Offers written contract; 30-days notice must be given to terminate contract.

JEAN V. NAGGAR LITERARY AGENCY, INC.
JVNLA, Inc., 216 E. 75th St., Suite 1E, New York NY 10021. (212)794-1082. **Website:** www.jvnla.com. **Contact:** Jennifer Weltz. Estab. 1978. Member of AAR, Women's Media Group, SCBWI, Pace University's Masters in Publishing Board Member. Represents 450 clients.

MEMBER AGENTS Jennifer Weltz (well researched and original historicals, thriller with a unique voice, wry dark humor, magical realism; enthralling narrative nonfiction; voice driven young adult, middle-grade); **Alice Tasman** (literary, commercial, young adult, middle-grade, nonfiction: narrative, biography, music, pop culture); **Laura Biagi** (literary fiction, magical realism, psychological thriller, young adult, middle-grade, picture books).

REPRESENTS nonfiction, fiction, novels, short story collections, novellas, juvenile books, scholarly books, poetry books.

☞ This agency specializes in mainstream fiction and nonfiction and literary fiction with commercial potential as well as young adult, middle-grade, and picture books. Does not want to receive screenplays.

HOW TO CONTACT "Visit our website to send submissions and see what our individual agents are looking for. No snail mail submissions please!" Accepts simultaneous submissions. Depends on the agent. No responses for queries unless the agent is interested.

TERMS Agent receives 15% commission on domestic sales; 20% commission on foreign sales.

RECENT SALES *Mort(e)*, by Robert Repino; *The Paying Guests*, by Sarah Waters; *Violent Crimes*, by

Phillip Margolin; *An Unseemly Wife*, by E.B. Moore; *The Man Who Walked Away*, by Maud Casey; *Dietland*, by Sarai Walker; *In the Land of Armadillos*, by Helen Maryles Shankman; *Not If I See You First*, by Eric Lindstrom.

TIPS "We recommend courage, fortitude, and patience: the courage to be true to your own vision, the fortitude to finish a novel and polish it again and again before sending it out, and the patience to accept rejection gracefully and wait for the stars to align themselves appropriately for success."

NELSON LITERARY AGENCY

1732 Wazee St., Suite 207, Denver CO 80202. (303)292-2805. **E-mail:** query@nelsonagency.com. **E-mail:** querykristin@nelsonagency.com. **Website:** www.nelsonagency.com. **Contact: Kristin Nelson**, President; **Danielle Burby**, agent; **Joanna MacKenzie**, agent. Kristin Nelson established Nelson Literary Agency, LLC in 2002 and over the last decade of her career, has represented over 35 *New York Times* bestselling titles and many *USA Today* bestsellers. Estab. 2002. Member of AAR, RWA, SCBWI, SFWA. Represents 37 clients.

REPRESENTS fiction, novels, young adult, middle-grade, literary commercial, upmarket women's fiction, single-title romance, science fiction, fantasy. **Considers these fiction areas:** commercial, fantasy, historical, horror, literary, mainstream, middle-grade, romance, science fiction, suspense, thriller, urban fantasy, women's, young adult.

⚬— NLA specializes in representing commercial fiction and high-caliber literary fiction. "We represent many popular genre categories, including historical romance, steampunk, and all subgenres of young adult." Regardless of genre, "we are actively seeking good stories well told." Does not want nonfiction, memoir, stage plays, screenplays, short story collections, poetry, children's picture books, early reader chapter books, or material for the Christian/inspirational market.

HOW TO CONTACT "Please visit our website and carefully read our submission guidelines. We do not accept any queries on Facebook or Twitter. Query by e-mail only. Write the word 'Query' in the e-mail subject line along with the title of your novel. Send no attachments, but please paste the first 10 pages of your novel in the body of the e-mail beneath your query letter." Accepts simultaneous submissions.

Makes best efforts to respond to all queries within 10 business day. Response to full mss requested can take up to 3 months.

NEW LEAF LITERARY & MEDIA, INC.

110 W. 40th St., Suite 2201, New York NY 10018. (646)248-7989. **Fax:** (646)861-4654. **E-mail:** query@newleafliterary.com. **Website:** www.newleafliterary.com. Estab. 2012. Member of AAR.

MEMBER AGENTS Joanna Volpe (women's fiction, thriller, horror, speculative fiction, literary fiction and historical fiction, young adult, middle-grade, art-focused picture books); **Kathleen Ortiz**, Director of Subsidiary Rights and literary agent (new voices in young adult and animator/illustrator talent); **Suzie Townsend** (New Adult, young adult, middle-grade, romance [all subgenres], fantasy [urban fantasy, science fiction, steampunk, epic fantasy] and crime fiction [mystery, thriller]); **Pouya Shahbazian**, Director of Film and Television (no unsolicited queries); **Janet Reid**, janet@newleafliterary.com; **Jaida Temperly** (all fiction: magical realism, historical fiction; literary fiction; stories that are quirky and fantastical; nonfiction: niche, offbeat, a bit strange; middle-grade); **JL Stermer** (nonfiction, smart pop culture, comedy/satire, fashion, health and wellness, self-help, memoir).

REPRESENTS nonfiction, fiction, novels, novellas, juvenile books, poetry books. **Considers these nonfiction areas:** cooking, crafts, creative nonfiction, science, technology, women's issues, young adult. **Considers these fiction areas:** crime, fantasy, historical, horror, literary, mainstream, middle-grade, mystery, New Adult, paranormal, picture books, romance, thriller, women's, young adult.

HOW TO CONTACT Send query via e-mail. Please do not query via phone. The word "Query" must be in the subject line, plus the agent's name—Subject: Query, Suzie Townsend. You may include up to 5 double-spaced sample pages within the body of the e-mail. No attachments, unless specifically requested. Include all necessary contact information. You will receive an auto-response confirming receipt of your query. "We only respond if we are interested in seeing your work." Responds only if interested. All queries read within 1 month.

RECENT SALES *Carve the Mark*, by Veronica Roth (HarperCollins); *Red Queen*, by Victoria Aveyard (HarperCollins); *Lobster Is the Best Medicine*, by Liz Climo (Running Press); *Ninth House*, by Leigh Bardugo (Henry Holt); *A Snicker of Magic*, by Natalie Lloyd (Scholastic).

PARK LITERARY GROUP, LLC

270 Lafayette St., Suite 1504, New York NY 10012. (212)691-3500. **Fax:** (212)691-3540. **E-mail:** info@ parkliterary.com. **E-mail:** queries@parkliterary. com. **Website:** www.parkliterary.com. Estab. 2005. **MEMBER AGENTS** Theresa Park (plot-driven fiction, serious nonfiction); **Abigail Koons** (popular science, history, politics, current affairs, art, women's fiction); **Peter Knapp** (children's, young adult).
REPRESENTS nonfiction, novels. **Considers these nonfiction areas:** art, current affairs, history, politics, science. **Considers these fiction areas:** juvenile, middle-grade, suspense, thriller, women's, young adult.

- The Park Literary Group represents fiction and nonfiction with a boutique approach: an emphasis on servicing a relatively small number of clients, with the highest professional standards and focused personal attention. Does not want to receive poetry or screenplays.

HOW TO CONTACT Please specify the first and last name of the agent to whom you are submitting in the subject line of the e-mail. All materials must be in the body of the e-mail. Responds if interested. For fiction submissions, please include a query letter with short synopsis and the first 3 chapters of your work. Accepts simultaneous submissions.
RECENT SALES This agency's client list is on its website. It includes bestsellers Nicholas Sparks, Soman Chainani, Emily Giffin, Debbie Macomber.

L. PERKINS AGENCY

5800 Arlington Ave., Riverdale NY 10471. (718)543-5344. **E-mail:** submissions@lperkinsagency.com. **Website:** lperkinsagency.com. Estab. 1987. Member of AAR. Represents 150 clients.

- Ms. Perkins has been an agent for 25 years. She is also the author of *The Insider's Guide to Getting an Agent* (Writer's Digest Books), as well as 3 other nonfiction books. She has edited 25 erotic anthologies, and is also the founder and publisher of Riverdale Avenue Books, an award-winning hybrid publisher with 9 imprints.

MEMBER AGENTS Tish Beaty, ePub agent (erotic romance, including paranormal, historical, gay/lesbian/bisexual, light-BDSM fiction; New Adult, young adult); **Sandy Lu**, sandy@lperkinsagency.com (fiction: dark literary and commercial fiction, mystery, thriller, psychological horror, paranormal/urban fantasy, historical fiction, young adult, historical thriller or mystery set in Victorian times; nonfiction: narrative nonfiction, history, biography, pop science, pop psychology, pop culture [music/theatre/film], humor, food writing); **Lori Perkins** (not currently taking new clients); **Leon Husock** (science fiction and fantasy, young adult and middle-grade); **Rachel Brooks** (picture books, all genres of young adult and New Adult fiction, adult romance—especially romantic suspense [NOTE: Rachel is currently closed to unsolicited submissions]); **Maximilian Ximinez** (fiction: science fiction, fantasy, horror, thriller; nonfiction: popular science, true crime, arts, trends in developing fields and cultures).
REPRESENTS nonfiction, fiction, novels, short story collections. **Considers these nonfiction areas:** autobiography, biography, business, creative nonfiction, cultural interests, current affairs, film, foods, gay/lesbian, history, how-to, humor, literature, memoirs, music, popular culture, psychology, science, sex, theater, true crime, women's issues, women's studies, young adult. **Considers these fiction areas:** commercial, crime, detective, erotica, fantasy, feminist, gay, historical, horror, lesbian, literary, middle-grade, mystery, New Adult, paranormal, picture books, romance, science fiction, short story collections, supernatural, thriller, urban fantasy, women's, young adult.
HOW TO CONTACT E-queries only. Include your query, a 1-page synopsis, and the first 5 pages from your novel pasted into the e-mail, or your proposal. No attachments. Submit to only 1 agent at the agency. No snail mail queries. "If you are submitting to one of our agents, please be sure to check the submission status of the agent by visiting our social media accounts listed [on the agency website]." Accepts simultaneous submissions. Obtains most new clients through recommendations from others, solicitations, conferences.
TERMS Agent receives 15% commission on domestic sales; 20% commission on foreign sales. No written contract. Charges clients for photocopying.

RECENT SALES *Arena*, by Holly Jennings; *Taking the Lead*, by Cecilia Tan; *The Girl with Ghost Eyes*, by M. H. Boroson; *Silent Attraction*, by Lauren Brown.

RUBIN PFEFFER CONTENT

648 Hammond St., Chestnut Hill MA 02467. **E-mail:** info@rpcontent.com. **Website:** www.rpcontent.com. **Contact:** Rubin Pfeffer. Rubin Pfeffer Content is a literary agency exclusively representing children's and young adult literature, as well as content that will serve educational publishers and digital developers. Working closely with authors and illustrators, RPC is devoted to producing long-lasting children's literature: work that exemplifies outstanding writing, innovative creativity, and artistic excellence. Estab. 2014. Member of AAR. Signatory of WGA.

○   Rubin has previously worked as the vice-president and publisher of Simon & Schuster Children's Books and as an independent agent at East West Literary Agency.

REPRESENTS Considers these fiction areas: juvenile, middle-grade, picture books, young adult.
HOW TO CONTACT Note: This agent accepts submissions by referral only. Specify the contact information of your reference when submitting. Authors/illustrators should send a query and a 1-3 chapter ms via e-mail (no postal submissions). The query, placed in the body of the e-mail, should include a synopsis of the piece, as well as any relevant information regarding previous publications, referrals, websites, and biography. The ms may be attached as a .doc or a .pdf file. Specifically for illustrators, attach a PDF of the dummy or artwork to the e-mail. If you would like to query Melissa Nasson with your picture book, middle-grade, or young adult ms, query with the first 50 pages to melissa@rpcontent.com. Accepts simultaneous submissions. Responds within 6-8 weeks.

PIPPIN PROPERTIES, INC.

110 W. 40th St., Suite 1704, New York NY 10018. (212)338-9310. **Fax:** (212)338-9579. **E-mail:** info@pippinproperties.com. **Website:** www.pippinproperties.com. **Contact:** Holly McGhee. "Pippin Properties, Inc. opened its doors in 1998, and for the past 17 years we have been privileged to help build careers for authors and artists whose work stands the test of time, many of whom have become household names in their own right, such as Peter H. Reynolds, Kate DiCamillo, Sujean Rim, Doreen Cronin, Renata Liwska, Sarah Weeks, Harry Bliss, Kate and Jim McMullan, Katherine Applegate, David Small, and Kathi Appelt. We also love to launch new careers for amazing authors and artists such as Jason Reynolds, Anna Kang and Chris Weyant, and Jandy Nelson."Estab. 1998.

○   Prior to becoming an agent, Ms. McGhee was an editor for 7 years and in book marketing for 4 years.

MEMBER AGENTS Holly McGhee, Elena Giovinazzo, Heather Alexander, Sara Crowe. Although each of the agents take children's books, you can find in-depth preferences for each agent on the Pippin website.
REPRESENTS juvenile books. **Considers these fiction areas:** middle-grade, picture books, young adult.

o→   "We are strictly a children's literary agency devoted to the management of authors and artists in all media. We are small and discerning in choosing our clientele."

HOW TO CONTACT If you are a writer who is interested in submitting a ms, please query us via e-mail, and within the body of that e-mail please include the first chapter of your novel with a short synopsis of the work or the entire picture book ms. For illustrators interested in submitting their work, please send a query letter detailing your background in illustration and include links to website with a dummy or other examples of your work. Direct all queries to the agent whom you wish to query and please do not query more than one. No attachments, please. Accepts simultaneous submissions. Obtains most new clients through recommendations from others.
TERMS Agent receives 15% commission on domestic sales; 25% commission on foreign sales. Offers written contract; 30-day notice must be given to terminate contract.

PROSPECT AGENCY

551 Valley Rd., PMB 377, Upper Montclair NJ 07043. (718)788-3217. **Fax:** (718)360-9582. **Website:** www.prospectagency.com. Estab. 2005. Member of AAR. Signatory of WGA. Represents 130+ clients.

MEMBER AGENTS Emily Sylvan Kim, esk@prospectagency.com (romance, women's, commercial, young adult, New Adult); **Rachel Orr**, rko@prospectagency.com (picture books, illustrators, middle-grade, young adult); **Becca Stumpf**, becca@prospectagency.com (young adult and middle-grade [all genres, including fantasy/science fiction, literary, mystery, contemporary, historical, horror/suspense], especially middle-grade and young adult novels featuring diverse protagonists and life circumstances. Adult science fiction and fantasy novels with broad appeal, upmarket women's fiction, smart, spicy romance novels); **Carrie Pestritto**, carrie@prospectagency.com (narrative nonfiction, general nonfiction, biography, memoir; commercial fiction with a literary twist, women's fiction, romance, upmarket, historical fiction, high-concept young adult, upper middle-grade); **Linda Camacho**, linda@prospectagency.com (middle-grade, young adult, adult fiction across all genres, especially women's fiction/romance, horror, fantasy/science fiction, graphic novels, contemporary; select literary fiction; fiction featuring diverse/marginalized groups); **Kirsten Carleton**, kcarleton@prospectagency.com (upmarket speculative, thriller, literary fiction for adult and young adult).

REPRESENTS nonfiction, fiction, novels, novellas, juvenile books, scholarly books, textbooks. **Considers these nonfiction areas:** biography, memoirs, popular culture, psychology. **Considers these fiction areas:** commercial, contemporary issues, crime, ethnic, family saga, fantasy, feminist, gay, historical, horror, humor, juvenile, lesbian, literary, mainstream, middle-grade, multicultural, mystery, New Adult, picture books, romance, science fiction, suspense, thriller, urban fantasy, women's, young adult.

 ⌐ "We're looking for strong, unique voices and unforgettable stories and characters."

HOW TO CONTACT All submissions are electronic and must be submitted through the portal at prospectagency.com/submissions. We do not accept any submissions through snail mail. Accepts simultaneous submissions. Obtains new clients through conferences, recommendations, queries, and some scouting.

TERMS Agent receives 15% on domestic sales; 20% on foreign sales sold directly; 25% on sales using a subagent. Offers written contract.

○ **P.S. LITERARY AGENCY**
2010 Winston Park Dr., Second Floor, Oakville ON L6H 5R7 Canada. **E-mail:** query@psliterary.com. **Website:** www.psliterary.com. **Contact:** Curtis Russell, principal agent; Carly Watters, senior agent; Maria Vicente, associate agent; Kurestin Armada, associate agent; Eric Smith; associate agent. Estab. 2005.

MEMBER AGENTS Curtis Russell (literary/commercial fiction, mystery, thriller, suspense, romance, young adult, middle-grade, picture books, business, history, politics, current affairs, memoirs, health/wellness, sports, humor, pop culture, pop science, pop psychology); **Carly Watters** (upmarket/commercial fiction, women's fiction, book club fiction, literary thriller, cookbooks, health/wellness, memoirs, humor, pop science, pop psychology); **Maria Vicente** (young adult, middle-grade, illustrated picture books, pop culture, science, lifestyle, design); **Kurestin Armada** (magic realism, science fiction, fantasy, illustrated picture books, middle-grade, young adult, graphic novels, romance, design, cookbooks, pop psychology, photography, nature, science); **Eric Smith** (young adult, New Adult, literary/commercial fiction, cookbooks, pop culture, humor, essay collections).

REPRESENTS nonfiction, novels, juvenile books. **Considers these nonfiction areas:** art, autobiography, biography, business, cooking, crafts, creative nonfiction, cultural interests, current affairs, decorating, diet/nutrition, design, economics, environment, film, foods, gardening, gay/lesbian, government, health, history, hobbies, how-to, humor, interior design, juvenile nonfiction, literature, memoirs, military, money, music, New Age, photography, popular culture, politics, psychology, science, self-help, sports, technology, true crime, war, women's issues, women's studies, young adult. **Considers these fiction areas:** action, adventure, detective, erotica, ethnic, experimental, family saga, fantasy, feminist, gay, historical, horror, humor, juvenile, lesbian, literary, mainstream, middle-grade, multicultural, mystery, New Adult, picture books, romance, science fiction, sports, thriller, urban fantasy, women's, young adult.

 ⌐ Actively seeking both fiction and nonfiction. Seeking both new and established writers. Does not want to receive poetry or screenplays.

HOW TO CONTACT Query letters should be directed to query@psliterary.com. PSLA does not accept or respond to phone, paper, or social media queries. Responds in 4-6 weeks to queries/proposals. Obtains most new clients through solicitations.

TERMS Agent receives 15% commission on domestic sales; 25% commission on foreign sales. "We offer a written contract, with 30-days notice terminate."

THE PURCELL AGENCY

E-mail: tpaqueries@gmail.com. **Website:** www.thepurcellagency.com. **Contact:** Tina P. Schwartz. This is an agency for authors of children's and teen literature. Estab. 2012. Member of SCBWI Represents 32 clients.

MEMBER AGENTS Tina P. Schwartz, Kim Blair McCollum.

REPRESENTS nonfiction, novels, juvenile books. **Considers these nonfiction areas:** biography, child guidance, creative nonfiction, gay/lesbian, juvenile nonfiction, multicultural, parenting, young adult. **Considers these fiction areas:** juvenile, middle-grade, young adult.

➤ This agency also takes juvenile nonfiction for Middle-grade and young adult markets. At this point, the agency is not considering fantasy, science fiction, or picture book submissions.

HOW TO CONTACT Check the website to see if agency is open to submissions and for submission guidelines. Accepts simultaneous submissions.

RECENT SALES *A Kind of Justice*, by Renee James; *Adventures at Hound Hotel*, by Shelley Swanson Sateren; *Adventures at Tabby Towers*, by Shelley Swanson Sateren; *Keys to Freedom*, by Karen Meade.

RED SOFA LITERARY

P.O. Box 40482, St. Paul MN 55104. (651)224-6670. **E-mail:** dawn@redsofaliterary.com, jennie@redsofaliterary.com, laura@redsofaliterary.com, bree@redsofaliterary.com, amanda@redsofaliterary.com, stacey@redsofaliterary.com, erik@redsofaliterary.com. **Website:** www.redsofaliterary.com. Estab. 2008. Member of the Authors Guild, the MN Publishers Round Table. Represents 125 clients.

MEMBER AGENTS Jennie Goloboy, Laura Zats, Bree Ogden, Amanda Rutter, Stacey Graham, Erik Hane.

REPRESENTS nonfiction, fiction, novels, juvenile books. **Considers these nonfiction areas:** Americana, animals, anthropology, archeology, crafts, creative nonfiction, cultural interests, current affairs, dance, environment, film, gay/lesbian, government, health, history, hobbies, humor, investigative, juvenile nonfiction, multicultural, popular culture, politics, recreation, satire, science, sociology, true crime, war, women's issues, women's studies, young adult, extreme sports. **Considers these fiction areas:** action, adventure, commercial, detective, erotica, ethnic, fantasy, feminist, gay, humor, juvenile, lesbian, literary, mainstream, middle-grade, mystery, picture books, romance, science fiction, suspense, thriller, urban fantasy, young adult.

HOW TO CONTACT Query by e-mail or mail with SASE. No attachments, please. Submit full proposal (for nonfiction especially, for fiction it would be nice) plus 3 sample chapters (or first 50 pages) and any other pertinent writing samples upon request by the specific agent. Do not send within or attached to the query letter. Accepts simultaneous submissions. Obtains new clients through queries, also through recommendations from others, solicitations.

TERMS Agent receives 15% commission on domestic sales; 20% commission on foreign sales. Offers written contract.

RECENT SALES *Semiosis*, Sue Burke (Tor, 2017); *Welcome Home,* edited by Eric Smith (Jolly Fish Press, 2017); *Body Horror: Essays on Misogyny and Capitalism*, by Anne Elizabeth Moore (Curbside Splendor, 2017); *Dr. Potter's Medicine Show*, by Eric Scott Fischl (Angry Robot Books, 2017); *Play Like a Girl: How a Soccer School in Kenya's Slums Started a Revolution,* by Ellie Roscher (Viva Editions, 2017); *Not Now, Not Ever*, by Lily Anderson (St. Martin's 2018).

TIPS "Always remember the benefits of building an author platform, and the accessibility of accomplishing this task in today's industry. Most importantly, research the agents queried. Avoid contacting every literary agent about a book idea. Due to the large volume of queries received, the process of reading queries for unrepresented categories (by the agency) becomes quite the arduous task. Investigate online directories, printed guides (like *Writer's Market*), individual agent websites, and more, before beginning the query process. It's good to remember that each agent has a vision of what he or shee wants to represent and will communicate this information accordingly. We're simply waiting for those specific book ideas to come in our direction."

REES LITERARY AGENCY

14 Beacon St., Suite 710, Boston MA 02108. (617)227-9014. **E-mail:** lorin@reesagency.com. **Website:** reesagency.com. Estab. 1983. Member of AAR. Represents more than 100 clients.

MEMBER AGENTS Ann Collette, agent10702@aol.com (fiction: literary, upscale commercial women's, crime [including mystery, thriller, psychological suspense], upscale western, historical, military and war, horror; nonfiction: narrative, military and war, books on race and class, works set in Southeast Asia, biography, pop culture, books on film and opera, humor, memoir); Lorin Rees, lorin@reesagency.com (literary fiction, memoirs, business books, self-help, science, history, psychology, narrative nonfiction); Rebecca Podos, rebecca@reesagency.com (young adult and middle-grade fiction, particularly books about complex female relationships, beautifully written contemporary, genre novels with a strong focus on character, romance with more at stake than "will they/won't they," LGBTQ books across all genres).

REPRESENTS novels. **Considers these nonfiction areas:** biography, business, film, history, humor, memoirs, military, popular culture, psychology, science, war. **Considers these fiction areas:** commercial, crime, historical, horror, literary, middle-grade, mystery, suspense, thriller, westerns, women's, young adult.

HOW TO CONTACT Consult website for each agent's submission guidelines and e-mail address, as they differ. Accepts simultaneous submissions. Obtains most new clients through recommendations from others, conferences, submissions.

TERMS Agent receives 15% commission on domestic sales; 20% commission on foreign sales.

REGAL HOFFMANN & ASSOCIATES LLC

242 W. 38th St., Second Floor, New York NY 10018. (212)684-7900. **Fax:** (212)684-7906. **E-mail:** submissions@rhaliterary.com. **Website:** www.rhaliterary.com. Estab. 2002. Member of AAR. Represents 70 clients.

MEMBER AGENTS Claire Anderson-Wheeler (nonfiction: memoirs, biography, narrative histories, popular science, popular psychology; adult fiction: primarily character-driven literary fiction, but open to genre fiction, high-concept fiction; all genres of young adult and middle-grade fiction); **Markus Hoffmann** (international and literary fiction, crime, [pop] cultural studies, current affairs, economics, history, music, popular science, travel literature); **Joseph Regal** (literary fiction, international thriller, history, science, photography, music, culture, whimsy); **Stephanie Steiker** (serious and narrative nonfiction, literary fiction, graphic novels, history, philosophy, current affairs, cultural studies, biography, music, international writing); **Grace Ross** (literary fiction, historical fiction, international narratives, narrative nonfiction, popular science, biography, cultural theory, memoir).

REPRESENTS Considers these nonfiction areas: biography, creative nonfiction, current affairs, economics, history, memoirs, music, psychology, science, travel. **Considers these fiction areas:** literary, mainstream, middle-grade, thriller, young adult.

➤ "We represent works in a wide range of categories, with an emphasis on literary fiction, outstanding thriller and crime fiction, and serious narrative nonfiction." Actively seeking literary fiction and narrative nonfiction. Does not want romance, science fiction, poetry, or screenplays.

HOW TO CONTACT Query with SASE or via e-mail to submissions@rhaliterary.com. No phone calls. Submissions should consist of a 1-page query letter detailing the book in question, as well as the qualifications of the author. For fiction, submissions may also include the first 10 pages of the novel or 1 short story from a collection. Accepts simultaneous submissions. Responds in 4-8 weeks if interested.

TERMS Agent receives 15% commission on domestic sales; 20% commission on foreign sales. "We charge no reading fees."

RECENT SALES *Wily Snare*, by Adam Jay Epstein; *Perfectly Undone*, by Jamie Raintree; *A Sister in My House*, by Linda Olsson; *This Is How It Really Sounds*, by Stuart Archer Cohen; *Autofocus*, by Lauren Gibaldi; *We've Already Gone This Far*, by Patrick Dacey; *A Fierce and Subtle Poison*, by Samantha Mabry; *The Life of the World to Come*, by Dan Cluchey; *Willful Disregard*, by Lena Andersson; *The Sweetheart*, by Angelina Mirabella.

TIPS "We are deeply committed to every aspect of our clients' careers, and are engaged in everything from the editorial work of developing a great book proposal or line-editing a fiction manuscript to negotiating state-of-the-art book deals and working to promote and publicize the book when it's published."

⊘ THE RIGHTS FACTORY

P.O. Box 499, Station C, Toronto ON M6J 3P6 Canada. (416)966-5367. **Website:** www.therightsfactory.com. "The Rights Factory is an international literary agency." Estab. 2004. Represents about 150 clients.
MEMBER AGENTS Sam Hiyate (President; fiction, nonfiction, graphic novel); **Kelvin Kong** (Rights Manager; clients by referral only); **Ali McDonald** (Kidlit Agent; young adult, children's literature of all kinds); **Olga Filina** (Associate Agent; commercial and historical fiction, great genre fiction in the area of romance and mystery, nonfiction in the fields of business, wellness, lifestyle, memoir, and young adult and middle-grade novels with memorable characters); **Cassandra Rogers** (Associate Agent; adult literary and commercial women's fiction, historical fiction, nonfiction on politics, history, science, and finance, humorous, heartbreaking, and inspiring memoir); **Lydia Moed** (Associate Agent; science fiction and fantasy, historical fiction, diverse voices; narrative nonfiction on a wide variety of topics, including history, popular science, biography, travel); **Natalie Kimber** (Associate Agent; literary and commercial fiction and creative nonfiction in categories such as memoir, cooking, popculture, spirituality, sustainability); **Harry Endrulat** (Associate Agent; children's literature, especially author/illustrators and Canadian voices); **Haskell Nussbaum** (Associate Agent; literature of all kinds).
REPRESENTS nonfiction, fiction, novels, short story collections, novellas, juvenile books. **Considers these nonfiction areas:** biography, business, cooking, environment, foods, gardening, health, history, inspirational, juvenile nonfiction, memoirs, money, music, popular culture, politics, science, travel, women's issues, young adult. **Considers these fiction areas:** commercial, crime, family saga, fantasy, gay, hi-lo, historical, horror, juvenile, lesbian, literary, mainstream, middle-grade, multicultural, mystery, New Adult, paranormal, picture books, romance, science fiction, short story collections, suspense, thriller, urban fantasy, women's, young adult.

⌐ Plays, screenplays, textbooks.

HOW TO CONTACT There is a submission form on this agency's website. Accepts simultaneous submissions. Responds in 3-6 weeks.

ANN RITTENBERG LITERARY AGENCY, INC.

15 Maiden Lane, Suite 206, New York NY 10038. (212)684-6936. **E-mail:** info@rittlit.com. **Website:** www.rittlit.com. **Contact:** Ann Rittenberg, president. Member of AAR.
REPRESENTS nonfiction, novels, juvenile books.

⌐ Does not want to receive screenplays, poetry, or self-help.

HOW TO CONTACT Query via e-mail or postal mail (with SASE). Submit query letter with 3 sample chapters pasted in the body of the e-mail. "If you query by e-mail, we will only respond if interested." Accepts simultaneous submissions. Obtains most new clients through referrals from established writers and editors.
TERMS Agent receives 15% commission on domestic sales; 20% commission on foreign sales. Offers written contract. This agency charges clients for photocopying only.
RECENT SALES *Since We Fell* by Dennis Lehane, *A Wretched and Precarious Situation* by David Welky, *Knife Creek* by Paul Doiron.

RLR ASSOCIATES, LTD.

420 Lexington Ave., Suite 2532, New York NY 10170. (212)541-8641. **E-mail:** website.info@rlrassociates.net. **Website:** www.rlrassociates.net. **Contact:** Scott Gould. Member of AAR. Represents 50 clients.
REPRESENTS nonfiction, novels. **Considers these nonfiction areas:** biography, creative nonfiction, foods, history, humor, popular culture, sports. **Considers these fiction areas:** commercial, literary, mainstream, middle-grade, picture books, romance, women's, young adult, genre.

⌐ "We provide a lot of editorial assistance to our clients and have connections." Does not want to receive screenplays.

HOW TO CONTACT Query by snail mail. For fiction, send a query and 1-3 chapters (pasted). For nonfiction, send query or proposal. Accepts simultaneous submissions. "If you do not hear from us within 3 months, please assume that your work is out of active consideration." Obtains most new clients through recommendations from others.

TERMS Agent receives 15% commission on domestic sales; 20% commission on foreign sales. Offers written contract.

RECENT SALES Clients include Shelby Foote, The Grief Recovery Institute, Don Wade, David Plowden, Nina Planck, Karyn Bosnak, Gerald Carbone, Jason Lethcoe, Andy Crouch.

TIPS "Please check out our website for more details on our agency."

RODEEN LITERARY MANAGEMENT

3501 N. Southport #497, Chicago IL 60657. **E-mail:** info@rodeenliterary.com. **E-mail:** submissions@rodeenliterary.com. **Website:** www.rodeenliterary.com. **Contact:** Paul Rodeen. Estab. 2009. Member of AAR. Signatory of WGA.

⊙ Paul Rodeen established Rodeen Literary Management in 2009 after 7 years of experience with the literary agency Sterling Lord Literistic, Inc.

REPRESENTS nonfiction, novels, juvenile books, illustrations, graphic novels. **Considers these fiction areas:** juvenile, middle-grade, picture books, young adult, graphic novels, comics.

⊶ Actively seeking "writers and illustrators of all genres of children's literature including picture books, early readers, middle-grade fiction and nonfiction, graphic novels and comic books, as well as young adult fiction and nonfiction." This is primarily an agency devoted to children's books.

HOW TO CONTACT Unsolicited submissions are accepted by e-mail only. Cover letters with synopsis and contact information should be included in the body of your e-mail. An initial submission of 50 pages from a novel or a longer work of nonfiction will suffice and should be pasted into the body of your e-mail. Accepts simultaneous submissions.

ANDY ROSS LITERARY AGENCY

767 Santa Ray Ave., Oakland CA 94610. (510)238-8965. **E-mail:** andyrossagency@hotmail.com. **Website:** www.andyrossagency.com. **Contact:** Andy Ross. Estab. 2008. Member of AAR.

REPRESENTS nonfiction, fiction, novels, juvenile books, scholarly books. **Considers these nonfiction areas:** anthropology, autobiography, biography, child guidance, cooking, creative nonfiction, cultural interests, current affairs, economics, education, environment, ethnic, gay/lesbian, government,

history, investigative, juvenile nonfiction, language, law, literature, memoirs, military, parenting, philosophy, popular culture, politics, psychology, science, sociology, technology, war, women's issues, women's studies, young adult. **Considers these fiction areas:** commercial, contemporary issues, historical, juvenile, literary, middle-grade, picture books, young adult.

⊶ "This agency specializes in general nonfiction, politics and current events, history, biography, journalism, and contemporary culture as well as literary, commercial, and young adult fiction." Does not want to receive poetry.

HOW TO CONTACT Queries should be less than half-page. Please put the word "query" in the title header of the e-mail. In the first sentence, state the category of the project. Give a short description of the book and your qualifications for writing. Accepts simultaneous submissions. Responds in 1 week to queries.

TERMS Agent receives 15% commission on domestic sales; 20% commission on foreign sales or other deals made through a subagent. Offers written contract.

REPRESENTS "This agency specializes in general nonfiction, politics and current events, history, biography, journalism and contemporary culture as well as literary, commercial, and young adult fiction." Does not want to receive poetry.

RECENT SALES See my website.

TERMS Agent receives 15% commission on domestic sales; 20% commission on foreign sales or other deals made through a subagent. Offers written contract.

HOW TO CONTACT Queries should be less than half page. Please put the word "query" in the title header of the e-mail. In the first sentence, state the category of the project. Give a short description of the book and your qualifications for writing. Accepts simultaneous submissions.

JANE ROTROSEN AGENCY LLC

85 Broad St., 28th Floor, New York NY 10004. (212)593-4330. **Fax:** (212)935-6985. **Website:** www.janerotrosen.com. Estab. 1974. Member of AAR, the Authors Guild. Represents more than 100 clients.

MEMBER AGENTS Jane Rotrosen Berkey (not taking on clients); **Andrea Cirillo**, acirillo@

janerotrosen.com (general fiction, suspense, women's fiction); **Annelise Robey**, arobey@janerotrosen.com (women's fiction, suspense, mystery, literary fiction, select nonfiction); **Meg Ruley**, mruley@janerotrosen.com (commercial fiction, including suspense, mystery, romance, general fiction); **Christina Hogrebe**, chogrebe@janerotrosen.com (young adult, New Adult, book club fiction, romantic comedies, mystery, suspense); **Amy Tannenbaum**, atannenbaum@janerotrosen.com (contemporary romance, psychological suspense, thriller, New Adult, as well as women's fiction that falls into that sweet spot between literary and commercial; memoir, narrative and prescriptive nonfiction: health, business, pop culture, humor, popular psychology); **Rebecca Scherer** rscherer@janerotrosen.com (women's fiction, mystery, suspense, thriller, romance, upmarket/literary-leaning fiction); **Jessica Errera** (assistant to Christina and Rebecca). **REPRESENTS** nonfiction, novels. **Considers these nonfiction areas:** business, health, humor, memoirs, popular culture, psychology, narrative nonfiction. **Considers these fiction areas:** commercial, literary, mainstream, mystery, New Adult, romance, suspense, thriller, women's, young adult.

☛ Jane Rotrosen Agency is best known for representing writers of commercial fiction: thriller, mystery, suspense, women's fiction, romance, historical novels, mainstream fiction, young adult, etc. We also work with authors of memoirs and narrative and prescriptive nonfiction.

HOW TO CONTACT Check website for guidelines. Accepts simultaneous submissions. Obtains most new clients through recommendations from others. **TERMS** Agent receives 15% commission on domestic sales; 20% commission on foreign sales. Offers written contract, binding for 3 years; 2-month notice must be given to terminate contract. Charges clients for photocopying, express mail, overseas postage, book purchase.

VICTORIA SANDERS & ASSOCIATES

440 Buck Rd., Stone Ridge NY 12484. (212)633-8811. **E-mail:** queriesvsa@gmail.com. **Website:** www.victoriasanders.com. **Contact:** Victoria Sanders. Estab. 1992. Member of AAR, signatory of WGA. Represents 135 clients.

MEMBER AGENTS Victoria Sanders, Chris Kepner, Bernadette Baker-Baughman. **REPRESENTS** nonfiction, fiction, novels, juvenile books. **Considers these nonfiction areas:** autobiography, biography, cultural interests, current affairs, ethnic, film, gay/lesbian, government, history, humor, law, literature, music, popular culture, politics, psychology, satire, theater, translation, women's issues, women's studies. **Considers these fiction areas:** action, adventure, cartoon, comic books, contemporary issues, crime, detective, ethnic, family saga, feminist, gay, historical, humor, inspirational, juvenile, lesbian, literary, mainstream, middle-grade, multicultural, multimedia, mystery, New Adult, picture books, thriller, women's, young adult.

HOW TO CONTACT Authors who wish to contact us regarding potential representation should send a query letter with the first 3 chapters (or about 25 pages) pasted into the body of the message to queriesvsa@gmail.com. "We will only accept queries via e-mail. Query letters should describe the project and the author in the body of a single, 1-page e-mail that does not contain any attached files. Accepts simultaneous submissions. Responds in 1-4 weeks, although occasionally it will take longer. "We will not respond to e-mails with attachments or attached files." **TERMS** Agent receives 15% commission on domestic sales; 20% commission on foreign and film sales. Offers written contract. **RECENT SALES** Sold 20+ titles in the last year. **TIPS** "Limit query to letter (no calls) and give it your best shot. A good query is going to get a good response."

WENDY SCHMALZ AGENCY

402 Union St., #831, Hudson NY 12534. (518)672-7697. **E-mail:** wendy@schmalzagency.com. **Website:** www.schmalzagency.com. **Contact:** Wendy Schmalz. Estab. 2002. Member of AAR. **REPRESENTS** nonfiction, fiction, novels, juvenile books. **Considers these nonfiction areas:** biography, cultural interests, history, popular culture, young adult. Many nonfiction subjects are of interest to this agency. **Considers these fiction areas:** literary, mainstream, middle-grade, young adult.

☛ Not looking for picture books, science fiction, or fantasy.

HOW TO CONTACT Accepts only e-mail queries. Paste synopsis into the e-mail. Do not attach the ms, sample chapters, or synopsis. Replies to queries only if they want to read the ms. If you do not hear from this agency within 2 weeks, consider that a no. Accepts simultaneous submissions. Obtains clients through recommendations from others.

TERMS Agent receives 15% commission on domestic sales; 20% on foreign sales; 25% for Asian sales.

SUSAN SCHULMAN LITERARY AGENCY, LLC

454 W. 44th St., New York NY 10036. (212)713-1633. **E-mail:** susan@schulmanagency.com. **E-mail:** queries@schulmanagency.com. **Website:** www.publishersmarketplace.com/members/schulman/. **Contact:** Susan Schulman. Estab. 1980. Member of AAR. Signatory of WGA. Other memberships include Dramatists Guild, Writers Guild of America, East, New York Women in Film, Women's Media Group, Agents' Roundtable, League of New York Theater Women.

REPRESENTS nonfiction, fiction, novels, juvenile books, feature film, TV scripts, theatrical stage plays. **Considers these nonfiction areas:** anthropology, archeology, architecture, art, biography, business, child guidance, cooking, creative nonfiction, current affairs, economics, ethnic, government, health, history, juvenile nonfiction, law, money, popular culture, politics, psychology, religious, science, spirituality, women's issues, women's studies, young adult. **Considers these fiction areas:** commercial, contemporary issues, juvenile, literary, mainstream, New Adult, religious, women's, young adult. **Considers these script areas:** theatrical stage play.

&— "We specialize in books for, by, and about women and women's issues including nonfiction self-help books, fiction, and theater projects. We also handle the film, television, and allied rights for several agencies, as well as foreign rights for several publishing houses." Actively seeking new nonfiction. Considers plays. Does not want to receive poetry, television scripts, or concepts for television.

HOW TO CONTACT "For fiction: query letter with outline and 3 sample chapters, resume and SASE. For nonfiction: query letter with complete description of subject, at least 1 chapter, resume, and SASE. Queries may be sent via regular mail or

e-mail. Please do not submit queries via UPS or Federal Express. Please do not send attachments with e-mail queries. Please incorporate the chapters into the body of the e-mail." Accepts simultaneous submissions. Responds in less than 1 week generally to a full query; 6 weeks to a full ms. Obtains most new clients through recommendations from others, solicitations, conferences.

TERMS Agent receives 15% commission on domestic sales; 20% commission on foreign sales. Offers written contract; 30-day notice must be given to terminate contract.

SERENDIPITY LITERARY AGENCY, LLC

305 Gates Ave., Brooklyn NY 11216. **E-mail:** rbrooks@serendipitylit.com; info@serendipitylit.com. **Website:** www.serendipitylit.com; facebook.com/serendipitylit. **Contact:** Regina Brooks. Estab. 2000. Member of AAR. Signatory of WGA. Represents 150 clients.

◯ Prior to becoming an agent, Ms. Brooks was an acquisitions editor for John Wiley & Sons, Inc. and McGraw-Hill Companies.

MEMBER AGENTS Regina Brooks; Dawn Michelle Hardy (nonfiction, including sports, pop culture, blog and trend, music, lifestyle, social science); Folade Bell (literary and commercial women's fiction, young adult, literary mystery and thriller, historical fiction, African-American issues, gay/lesbian, Christian fiction, humor, books that deeply explore other cultures; nonfiction that reads like fiction, including blog-to-book or pop culture); Nadeen Gayle (romance, memoir, pop culture, inspirational/religious, women's fiction, parenting, young adult, mystery, political thriller, all forms of nonfiction); Rebecca Bugger (narrative nonfiction, investigative journalism, memoir, inspirational self-help, religion/spirituality, international, popular culture, current affairs; literary and commercial fiction); Christina Morgan (literary fiction, crime fiction, narrative nonfiction in the categories of pop culture, sports, current events, memoir); Jocquelle Caiby (literary fiction, horror, middle-grade fiction, children's books by authors who have been published in the adult market, athletes, actors, journalists, politicians, musicians).

REPRESENTS nonfiction, fiction, novels. **Considers these nonfiction areas:** Americana, anthropology, architecture, art, autobiography, biography, business, cooking, creative nonfiction, cultural interests, current affairs, inspirational, interior design, memoirs, metaphysics, music, parenting, popular culture, religious, self-help, spirituality, sports, travel, true crime, women's issues, women's studies, young adult. **Considers these fiction areas:** commercial, gay, historical, lesbian, literary, middle-grade, mystery, romance, thriller, women's, young adult, Christian.

HOW TO CONTACT Check the website, as there are online submission forms for fiction, nonfiction and juvenile. Website will also state if they are temporarily closed to submissions to any areas. Accepts simultaneous submissions. Obtains most new clients through conferences, referrals.

TERMS Agent receives 15% commission on domestic sales; 20% commission on foreign sales. Offers written contract; 2-month notice must be given to terminate contract. Charges clients for office fees, which are taken from any advance.

THE SEYMOUR AGENCY

475 Miner St., Canton NY 13617. (315)386-1831. **E-mail:** nicole@theseymouragency.com; julie@theseymouragency.com. **Website:** www.theseymouragency.com. Member of AAR, signatory of WGA, RWA, Authors Guild, HWA. **MEMBER AGENTS** Nicole Rescinti, nicole@theseymouragency.com; **Julie Gwinn**, julie@theseymouragency.com; **Tina Wainscott**, tina@theseymouragency.com; **Jennifer Wills**, jennifer@theseymouragency.com. **REPRESENTS** nonfiction, novels. **Considers these nonfiction areas:** business, health, how-to, Christian books; cookbooks; any well-written nonfiction that includes a proposal in standard format and 1 sample chapter.. **Considers these fiction areas:** action, fantasy, inspirational, middle-grade, mystery, New Adult, religious, romance, science fiction, suspense, thriller, young adult.

HOW TO CONTACT Accepts e-mail queries. Check online for guidelines. Accepts simultaneous submissions. Responds in 1 month to queries; 3 months to mss.

TERMS Agent receives 12-15% commission on domestic sales.

SPEILBURG LITERARY AGENCY

E-mail: info@speilburgliterary.com. **E-mail:** speilburgliterary@gmail.com. **Website:** speilburgliterary.

com. **Contact:** Alice Speilburg. Estab. 2012. Member of SCBWI, MWA, RWA.

◯   Alice Speilburg previously held publishing positions at John Wiley & Sons and Howard Morhaim Literary Agency.

REPRESENTS nonfiction, fiction, novels. **Considers these nonfiction areas:** biography, cultural interests, environment, foods, health, history, investigative, music, popular culture, psychology, science, sports, travel, women's issues, women's studies, young adult. **Considers these fiction areas:** adventure, commercial, detective, fantasy, feminist, historical, horror, mainstream, middle-grade, mystery, police, science fiction, suspense, urban fantasy, westerns, women's, young adult.

☞   Does not want picture books, screenplays, poetry, romance.

HOW TO CONTACT If you are interested in submitting your manuscript or proposal for consideration, please e-mail a query letter along with either 3 sample chapters for fiction or a TOC and proposal for nonfiction. Accepts simultaneous submissions.

THE SPIELER AGENCY

27 W. 20 St., Suite 302, New York NY 10011. (212)757-4439, ext. 1. **Fax:** (212)333-2019. **Website:** thespieleragency.com. **Contact:** Joe Spieler. Represents 160 clients.

◯   Prior to opening his agency, Mr. Spieler was a magazine editor.

MEMBER AGENTS Victoria Shoemaker, victoria@thespieleragency.com (environment and natural history, popular culture, memoir, photography and film, literary fiction and poetry, food and cooking); **John Thornton**, john@thespieleragency.com (nonfiction); **Joe Spieler**, joe@thespieleragency.com (nonfiction and fiction, books for children and young adults); **Helen Sweetland**, helen@thespieleragency.com (children's from board books through young adult fiction; adult general-interest nonfiction including nature, green living, gardening, architecture, interior design, health, popular science). **REPRESENTS** nonfiction, novels, juvenile books. **Considers these nonfiction areas:** architecture, biography, cooking, environment, film, foods, gardening, health, history, memoirs, photography, popular culture, science, sociology, spirituality. **Considers these fiction areas:** literary, middle-grade, New Age, picture books, thriller, young adult.

HOW TO CONTACT "Before submitting projects to the Spieler Agency, check the listings of our individual agents and see if any particular agent shows a general interest in your subject (e.g., history, memoir, young adult). Please send all queries either by e-mail or regular mail. If you query us by regular mail, we can only reply to you if you include a SASE." Accepts simultaneous submissions. Cannot guarantee a personal response to all queries. Obtains most new clients through recommendations, listing in *Guide to Literary Agents*.

TERMS Agent receives 15% commission on domestic sales. Charges clients for messenger bills, photocopying, postage.

PHILIP G. SPITZER LITERARY AGENCY, INC

50 Talmage Farm Lane, East Hampton NY 11937. (631)329-3650. **Fax:** (631)329-3651. **E-mail:** lukas. ortiz@spitzeragency.com; spitzer516@aol.com. **E-mail:** kim.lombardini@spitzeragency.com. **Website:** www.spitzeragency.com. **Contact:** Lukas Ortiz. Estab. 1969. Member of AAR.

○ Prior to opening his agency, Mr. Spitzer served at New York University Press, Mc-Graw-Hill, and the John Cushman Associates Literary Agency.

MEMBER AGENTS Philip G. Spitzer, Lukas Ortiz.

REPRESENTS novels. **Considers these nonfiction areas:** biography, current affairs, history, politics, sports, travel. **Considers these fiction areas:** juvenile, literary, mainstream, suspense, thriller.

☞ This agency specializes in mystery, suspense, literary fiction, sports, and general nonfiction (no how-to).

HOW TO CONTACT E-mail query containing synopsis of work, brief biography, and a sample chapter (pasted into the e-mail). Be aware that this agency openly says its client list is quite full. Accepts simultaneous submissions. Obtains most new clients through recommendations from others.

TERMS Agent receives 15% commission on domestic sales; 20% commission on foreign sales. Charges clients for photocopying.

RECENT SALES *The Jealous Kind*, by James Lee Burke (Simon & Schuster); *The Ex*, by Alafair Burke (HarperCollins); *Townie*, by Andre Dubus III (Norton); *The Wrong Side of Goodbye*, by Michael Con-

nelly (Little, Brown & Co); *The Emerald Lie*, Ken Bruen (Mysterious Press/Grove-Atlantic).

STIMOLA LITERARY STUDIO

308 Livingston Court, Edgewater NJ 07020. **E-mail:** info@stimolaliterarystudio.com. **E-mail:** see submission page on website. **Website:** www.stimolaliterarystudio.com. **Contact:** Rosemary B. Stimola. Estab. 1997. Member of AAR, PEN, Authors Guild, ALA. Represents 50 clients.

○ Prior to opening her agency, Rosemary Stimola was an independent children's bookseller. Erica Rand Silverman, Senior Agent, was a high school teacher and former senior agent at Sterling Lord Literistic.

MEMBER AGENTS Rosemary B. Stimola; Erica Rand Silverman.

REPRESENTS juvenile books. **Considers these nonfiction areas:** cooking. **Considers these fiction areas:** young adult.

☞ Actively seeking remarkable middle-grade, young adult fiction, and debut picture book author/illustrators. No institutional books.

HOW TO CONTACT Query via e-mail as per submission guidelines on website. Author/illustrators of picture books may attach text and sample art. A PDF dummy is preferred. Accepts simultaneous submissions. Responds in 3 weeks to queries "we wish to pursue further;" 2 months to requested mss. While unsolicited queries are welcome, most clients come through editor, agent, client referrals.

TERMS Agent receives 15% commission on domestic sales; 20% (if subagents are employed) commission on foreign sales. Offers written contract, binding for all children's projects; a 60-days notice must be given to terminate contract.

TIPS Agent is hands-on, no-nonsense. May request revisions. Does not line edit but may offer suggestions for improvement before submission. Well-respected by clients and editors. "A firm but reasonable deal negotiator."

STONESONG

270 W. 39th St. #201, New York NY 10018. (212)929-4600. **E-mail:** editors@stonesong.com. **E-mail:** submissions@stonesong.com. **Website:** stonesong.com. Member of AAR. Signatory of WGA.

MEMBER AGENTS Alison Fargis; Ellen Scordato; Judy Linden; Emmanuelle Morgen; Leila Campoli (business, science, technology, self improvement); **Maria Ribas** (cookbooks, self-help, health, diet, home, parenting, humor, all from authors with demonstrable platforms; she's also interested in narrative nonfiction and select memoir); **Melissa Edwards** (children's fiction and adult commercial fiction, select pop-culture nonfiction); **Alyssa Jennette** (children's and adult fiction, picture books, humor and pop culture nonfiction); **Madelyn Burt** (adult and children's fiction, select historical nonfiction). **REPRESENTS** nonfiction, fiction, novels, juvenile books. **Considers these nonfiction areas:** architecture, art, biography, business, cooking, crafts, creative nonfiction, cultural interests, current affairs, dance, decorating, diet/nutrition, design, economics, foods, gay/lesbian, health, history, hobbies, how-to, humor, interior design, investigative, literature, memoirs, money, music, New Age, parenting, photography, popular culture, politics, psychology, science, self-help, sociology, spirituality, sports, technology, women's issues, young adult. **Considers these fiction areas:** action, adventure, commercial, confession, contemporary issues, ethnic, experimental, family saga, fantasy, feminist, gay, historical, horror, humor, juvenile, lesbian, literary, mainstream, middle-grade, military, multicultural, mystery, New Adult, New Age, occult, paranormal, regional, romance, satire, science fiction, supernatural, suspense, thriller, urban fantasy, women's, young adult.

o→ Does not represent plays, screenplays, picture books, or poetry.

HOW TO CONTACT Accepts electronic queries for fiction and nonfiction. Submit query addressed to a specific agent. Include first chapter or first 10 pages of ms. Accepts simultaneous submissions.

RECENT SALES *Sweet Laurel*, by Laurel Gallucci and Claire Thomas; *Terrain: A Seasonal Guide to Nature at Home*, by Terrain; *The Prince's Bane*, by Alexandra Christo; *Deep Listening*, by Jillian Pransky; *Change Resilience*, by Lior Arussy; *A Thousand Words*, by Brigit Young.

ROBIN STRAUS AGENCY, INC.

Wallace Literary Agency, 229 E. 79th St., Suite 5A, New York NY 10075. (212)472-3282. **Fax:** (212)472-3833. **E-mail:** info@robinstrausagency.com. **Website:** www.robinstrausagency.com. **Contact:** Ms. Robin Straus. Estab. 1983. Member of AAR.

○ Prior to becoming an agent, Robin Straus served as a subsidiary rights manager at Ran-

dom House and Doubleday. She began her career in the editorial department of Little, Brown.

REPRESENTS Considers these nonfiction areas: biography, cooking, creative nonfiction, current affairs, environment, foods, health, history, memoirs, multicultural, music, parenting, popular culture, psychology, science, travel, women's issues, mainstream science. **Considers these fiction areas:** commercial, contemporary issues, literary, mainstream, women's.

o→ Does not represent juvenile, young adult, horror, romance, westerns, poetry, or screenplays.

HOW TO CONTACT E-query or query via snail mail with SASE. "Send us a query letter with contact information, an autobiographical summary, a brief synopsis or description of your book project, submission history, and information on competition. If you wish, you may also include the opening chapter of your manuscript (pasted). While we do our best to reply to all queries, you can assume that if you haven't heard from us after 6 weeks, we are not interested." Accepts simultaneous submissions.

TERMS AGENT RECEIVES 15% commission on domestic sales; 20% commission on foreign sales. Offers written contract.

THE STRINGER LITERARY AGENCY, LLC

P.O. Box 770365, Naples FL 34107. **E-mail:** mstringer@stringerlit.com. **Website:** www.stringerlit.com. **Contact:** Marlene Stringer. This agency focuses on commercial fiction for adults and teens.

REPRESENTS This agency specializes in fiction. "We are an editorial agency, and work with clients to make their manuscripts the best they can be in preparation for submission. We focus on career planning, and help our clients reach their publishing goals. We advise clients on marketing and promotional strategies to help them reach their target readership. Because we are so hands-on, we limit the size of our list; however, we are always looking for exceptional voices and stories that demand we read to the end. You never know where the next great story is coming from." This agency is seeking thrillers, crime fiction (not true crime), mystery, women's fiction, single title and category romance, fantasy (all subgenera), earth-based science fiction (no space opera, aliens, etc.), and young adult/teen. Does not want to receive picture books, middle grade, plays, short stories, or poetry. This is not the agency for inspirational romance or erotica. No space opera.

RECENT SALES *The Conqueror's Wife*, by Stephanie Thornton; *When I'm Gone*, by Emily Bleeker; *Magic Bitter, Magic Sweet*, by Charlie N. Holmberg; *Belle Chasse*, by Suzanne Johnson; *Chapel of Ease*, by Alex Bledsoe; *Wilds of the Bayou*, by Susannah Sandlin; *Summit Lake*, by Charlie Donlea; The Jane Doe Series, by Liana Brooks; *The Mermaid's Secret*, by Katie Schickel; *The Sutherland Scandals*, by Anna Bradley; *Fly By Night*, by Andrea Thalasinos; The Joe Gale Mystery Series, by Brenda Buchanan; The Kate Baer Series, by Shannon Baker; Los Nephilim Series, by T. Frohock; The Dragonsworn Series, by Caitlyn McFarland; *The Devious Dr. Jekyll*, by Viola Carr; *The Dragon's Price*, by Bethany Wiggins; The Otter Bite Romance Series, by Maggie McConnell; *Machinations*, by Haley Stone; Film Rights to *Wreckage*, by Emily Bleeker.

TERMS Standard commission. "We do not charge fees."

HOW TO CONTACT Electronic submissions through website submission form only. Please make sure your ms is as good as it can be before you submit. Agents are not first readers. For specific information on what we like to see in query letters, refer to the information at www.stringerlit.com under the heading "Learn." Accepts simultaneous submissions. Obtains new clients through referrals, submissions, conferences.

TIPS "If your ms falls between categories, or you are not sure of the category, query and we'll let you know if we'd like to take a look. We strive to respond as quickly as possible. If you have not received a response in the time period indicated on website, please re-query."

THE STROTHMAN AGENCY, LLC

63 E. 9th St., 10X, New York NY 10003. **E-mail:** info@strothmanagency.com. **E-mail:** strothmanagency@gmail.com. **Website:** www.strothmanagency.com. **Contact:** Wendy Strothman, Lauren MacLeod. Member of AAR, the Authors' Guild. Represents 50 clients.

Prior to becoming an agent, Ms. Strothman was head of Beacon Press (1983-1995) and executive vice president of Houghton Mifflin's Trade & Reference Division (1996-2002).

MEMBER AGENTS **Wendy Strothman** (history, narrative nonfiction, narrative journalism, science and nature, current affairs); **Lauren MacLeod** (young adult fiction and nonfiction, middle-grade novels, highly polished literary fiction and narrative nonfiction, particularly food writing, science, pop culture, history).

REPRESENTS nonfiction, novels, juvenile books. **Considers these nonfiction areas:** business, current affairs, economics, environment, foods, history, language, popular culture, science. **Considers these fiction areas:** literary, middle-grade, young adult.

"The Strothman Agency seeks out scholars, journalists, and other acknowledged and emerging experts in their fields. We specialize in history, science, narrative journalism, nature and the environment, current affairs, narrative nonfiction, business and economics, young adult fiction and nonfiction, middle-grade fiction and nonfiction. We are not signing up projects in romance, science fiction, picture books, or poetry."

HOW TO CONTACT Accepts queries only via e-mail. See submission guidelines online. Accepts simultaneous submissions. "All e-mails received will be responded to with an auto-reply. If we have not replied to your query within 6 weeks, we do not feel that it is right for us." Accepts simultaneous submissions. Obtains most new clients through recommendations from others.

TERMS Agent receives 15% commission on domestic sales; 20% commission on foreign sales. Offers written contract; 30-day notice must be given to terminate contract.

EMMA SWEENEY AGENCY, LLC

245 E 80th St., Suite 7E, New York NY 10075. **E-mail:** queries@emmasweeneyagency.com. **Website:** www.emmasweeneyagency.com. Estab. 2006. Member of AAR, Women's Media Group. Represents 80 clients.

Prior to becoming an agent, Ms. Sweeney was director of subsidiary rights at Grove Press. Since 1990, she has been a literary agent. Ms. Sutherland Brown was an associate editor at St. Martin's Press/Thomas Dunne Books and a freelance editor. Ms. Watson attended Hunter College where she earned a BA in English (with a focus on Creative Writing) and a BA in Russian Language & Culture.

MEMBER AGENTS **Emma Sweeney**, president; **Margaret Sutherland Brown** (commercial and literary fiction, mystery and thriller, narrative nonfiction, lifestyle, cookbooks); **Kira Watson** (children's literature).

REPRESENTS nonfiction, fiction, novels, juvenile books. **Considers these nonfiction areas:** biography, cooking, creative nonfiction, cultural interests, decorating, diet/nutrition, design, foods, gardening, history, how-to, interior design, juvenile nonfiction, literature, memoirs, popular culture, psychology, religious, science, sex, sociology, young adult. **Considers these fiction areas:** commercial, contemporary issues, crime, historical, juvenile, literary, mainstream, middle-grade, mystery, New Adult, suspense, thriller, women's, young adult.

> Does not want erotica.

HOW TO CONTACT "We accept only electronic queries, and ask that all queries be sent to queries@emmasweeneyagency.com rather than to any agent directly. Please begin your query with a succinct (and hopefully catchy) description of your plot or proposal. Always include a brief cover letter telling us how you heard about ESA, your previous writing credits, and a few lines about yourself. We cannot open any attachments unless specifically requested, and ask that you paste the first 10 pages of your proposal or novel into the text of your e-mail." Accepts simultaneous submissions.

TALCOTT NOTCH LITERARY

31 Cherry St., Suite 104, Milford CT 06460. (203)876-4959. **Fax:** (203)876-9517. **E-mail:** editorial@talcottnotch.net. **Website:** www.talcottnotch.net. **Contact:** Gina Panettieri, president. Represents 150 clients.

> Prior to becoming an agent, Ms. Panettieri was a freelance writer and editor. Ms. Munier was Director of Acquisitions for Adams Media Corporation and had previously worked for Disney. Ms. Sulaiman holds degrees from Wellesley and the University of Chicago and had completed an internship with Sourcebooks prior to joining Talcott Notch. Mr. Shalabi holds an MS in Neuroscience and had completed internships with Folio and Veritas, agencies as well as with Talcott Notch, before joining Talcott Notch as a Junior Agent in late 2016.

MEMBER AGENTS Gina Panettieri, gpanettieri@talcottnotch.net (history, business, self-help, science, gardening, cookbooks, crafts, parenting, memoir, true crime, travel, young adult, Middle-grade, women's fiction, paranormal, urban fantasy, horror, science fiction, historical, mystery, thriller and suspense); **Paula Munier**, pmunier@talcottnotch.net (mystery/thriller, SF/fantasy, romance, young adult, memoir, humor, pop culture, health & wellness, cooking, self-help, pop psych, New Age, inspirational, technology, science, writing); **Saba Sulaiman**, ssulaiman@talcottnotch.net (upmarket literary and commercial fiction, romance [all subgenres except paranormal], character-driven psychological thriller, cozy mystery, memoir, young adult [except paranormal and science fiction], middle-grade, nonfiction humor); **Mohamed Shalabi**, mshalabi@talcottnotch (upmarket literary and commercial fiction, psychological thriller, young adult [and subgenres except romance and paranormal], Middle-grade, adult nonfiction).

REPRESENTS nonfiction, fiction, novels, short story collections, novellas, juvenile books. **Considers these nonfiction areas:** biography, business, cooking, crafts, cultural interests, current affairs, diet/nutrition, ethnic, foods, gardening, gay/lesbian, government, health, history, how-to, humor, inspirational, juvenile nonfiction, literature, memoirs, military, multicultural, parenting, popular culture, politics, psychology, science, self-help, sex, sociology, spirituality, technology, travel, true crime, women's issues, women's studies, young adult. **Considers these fiction areas:** action, adventure, commercial, contemporary issues, crime, ethnic, fantasy, feminist, gay, hi-lo, historical, horror, juvenile, lesbian, literary, mainstream, middle-grade, multicultural, multimedia, mystery, New Adult, New Age, paranormal, police, romance, science fiction, short story collections, suspense, thriller, urban fantasy, women's, young adult.

> "We are most actively seeking projects featuring diverse characters and stories that expand the reader's understanding of our society and the wider world we live in."

HOW TO CONTACT Query via e-mail (preferred) with first 10 pages of the ms pasted within the body of the e-mail, not as an attachment. Accepts simultaneous submissions. Responds in 2 weeks to queries, 6-10 weeks to mss.

TERMS Agent receives 15% commission on domestic sales; 20% commission on foreign sales. Offers written contract, binding for 1 year.

RECENT SALES Agency sold 65 titles in the last year, including *The Widower's Wife,* by Cate Holahan

(Crooked Lane Books); *Tier One*, by Brian Andrews and Jeffrey Wilson (Thomas & Mercer) and *Beijing Red*, written as Alex Ryan (Crooked Lane Books); *Firestorm*, by Nancy Holzner (Berkley Ace Science Fiction).

TIPS "Know your market and how to reach them. A strong platform is essential in your book proposal. Can you effectively use social media? Are you a strong networker? Are you familiar with the book bloggers in your genre? Are you involved with the interest-specific groups that can help you? What can you do to break through the 'noise' and help present your book to your readers? Check our website for more tips and information on this topic."

THOMPSON LITERARY AGENCY

115 W. 29th St., Third Floor, New York NY 10001. (347)281-7685. **E-mail:** submissions@thompsonliterary.com. **Website:** thompsonliterary.com. **Contact:** Meg Thompson, founder. Estab. 2014. Member of AAR. Signatory of WGA.

Before her current position, Ms. Thompson was with LJK Literary and the Einstein Thompson Agency.

MEMBER AGENTS Cindy Uh, senior agent; **John Thorn**, affiliate agent; **Sandy Hodgman**, director of foreign rights.

REPRESENTS nonfiction, fiction, novels, juvenile books. **Considers these nonfiction areas:** autobiography, biography, business, cooking, crafts, creative nonfiction, current affairs, diet/nutrition, design, education, foods, health, history, how-to, humor, inspirational, interior design, juvenile nonfiction, memoirs, multicultural, popular culture, politics, science, self-help, sociology, sports, travel, women's issues, women's studies, young adult. **Considers these fiction areas:** commercial, contemporary issues, fantasy, historical, juvenile, literary, middle-grade, multicultural, picture books, women's, young adult.

The agency is always on the lookout for both commercial and literary fiction, as well as young adult and children's books. "Nonfiction, however, is our specialty, and our interests include biography, memoir, music, popular science, politics, blog-to-book projects, cookbooks, sports, health and wellness, fashion, art, and popular culture. Please note that we do not accept submissions for poetry collections or screenplays, and we only consider picture books by established illustrators."

HOW TO CONTACT "For fiction: Please send a query letter, including any salient biographical information or previous publications, and attach the first 25 pages of your manuscript. For nonfiction: Please send a query letter and a full proposal, including biographical information, previous publications, credentials that qualify you to write your book, marketing information, and sample material. You should address your query to whichever agent you think is best suited for your project." Accepts simultaneous submissions. Responds in 6 weeks if interested.

THREE SEAS LITERARY AGENCY

P.O. Box 444, Sun Prairie WI 53590. (608)834-9317. **E-mail:** queries@threeseaslit.com. **Website:** threeseasagency.com. **Contact:** Michelle Grajkowski, Cori Deyoe. Estab. 2000. Member of AAR, RWA, SCBWI. Represents 55 clients.

Since its inception, 3 Seas has sold more than 500 titles worldwide. Ms. Grajkowski's authors have appeared on all the major lists including *The New York Times, USA Today,* and *Publishers Weekly.* Prior to joining the agency in 2006, Ms. Deyoe was a multi-published author. She represents a wide range of authors and has sold many projects at auction.

MEMBER AGENTS Michelle Grajkowski (romance, women's fiction, young adult and middle-grade fiction, select nonfiction projects); **Cori Deyoe** (all sub-genres of romance, women's fiction, young adult, middle-grade, picture books, thriller, mystery select nonfiction); **Linda Scalissi** (women's fiction, thriller, young adult, mystery, romance).

REPRESENTS nonfiction, novels. **Considers these fiction areas:** middle-grade, mystery, picture books, romance, thriller, women's, young adult.

"We represent more than 50 authors who write romance, women's fiction, science fiction/fantasy, thriller, and young adult and middle-grade fiction, as well as select nonfiction titles. Currently, we are looking for fantastic authors with a voice of their own." 3 Seas does not represent poetry or screenplays.

HOW TO CONTACT E-mail queries only; no attachments, unless requested by agents. For fiction, please e-mail the first chapter and synopsis along with a cover letter. Also, be sure to include the genre and the number of words in your manuscript, as well as pertinent writing experience in your query letter. For nonfiction, e-mail a complete proposal, including a query letter and your first chapter. For picture books, query with complete text. Accepts simultaneous submissions. Obtains most new clients through recommendations from others, conferences.

TERMS Agent receives 15% commission on domestic sales; 20% commission on foreign sales. Offers written contract.

RECENT SALES Represents best-selling authors, including Jennifer Brown, Katie MacAlister, Kerrelyn Sparks, C.L. Wilson.

◐ TRANSATLANTIC LITERARY AGENCY

2 Bloor St. E., Suite 3500, Toronto ON M4W 1A8 Canada. (416)488-9214. **E-mail:** info@transatlanticagency.com. **Website:** transatlanticagency.com. The Transatlantic Agency represents adult and children's authors of all genres, including illustrators. We do not handle stage plays, musicals or screenplays. Please review the agency website and guidelines carefully before making any inquiries, as each agent has particular submission guidelines.

MEMBER AGENTS Trena White (upmarket, accessible nonfiction: current affairs, business, culture, politics, technology, the environment); **Amy Tompkins** (adult: literary fiction, historical fiction, women's fiction including smart romance, narrative nonfiction, quirky or original how-to books; children's: early readers, middle-grade, young adult, New Adult); **Stephanie Sinclair** (literary fiction, upmarket women's and commercial fiction, literary thriller and suspense, young adult crossover; narrative nonfiction, memoir, investigative journalism, true crime); **Samantha Haywood** (literary fiction and upmarket commercial fiction, specifically literary thriller and upmarket mystery, historical fiction, smart contemporary fiction, upmarket women's fiction and cross-over novels; narrative nonfiction, including investigative journalism, politics, women's issues, memoirs, environmental issues, historical narratives, sexuality, true crime; graphic novels [fiction and nonfiction]: preferably full length graphic novels, story collections considered, memoirs, biography, travel narratives); **Jesse Finkelstein** (nonfiction: current affairs, business, culture, politics, technology, religion, the environment); **Marie Campbell** (middle-grade fiction); **Shaun Bradley** (referrals only; adult literary fiction and narrative nonfiction, primarily science and investigative journalism); **Sandra Bishop** (fiction; nonfiction: biog-

raphy, memoir, positive or humorous how-to books on advice/relationships, mind/body/spirit, religion, healthy living, finances, life-hacks, traveling, living a better life); **Fiona Kenshole** (children's and young adult; only accepting submissions from referrals or conferences she attends as faculty); **Lynn Bennett** (not accepting submissions or new clients); **David Bennett** (children's, young adult, adult).

REPRESENTS nonfiction, novels, juvenile books.

> ➥ "In both children's and adult literature, we market directly into the US, the UK, and Canada." Represents adult and children's authors of all genres, including illustrators. Does not want to receive picture books, musicals, screenplays or stage plays.

HOW TO CONTACT Always refer to the website, as guidelines will change, and only various agents are open to new clients at any given time. Obtains most new clients through recommendations from others.

TERMS Agent receives 15% commission on domestic sales; 20% commission on foreign sales. Offers written contract; 45-day notice must be given to terminate contract. This agency charges for photocopying and postage when it exceeds $100.

RECENT SALES Sold 250 titles in the last year.

TRIADA US

P.O. Box 561, Sewickley PA 15143. (412)401-3376. **E-mail:** uwe@triadaus.com, brent@triadaus.com. laura@triadaus.com. mallory@triadaus.com. lauren@triadaus.com. **Website:** www.triadaus.com. **Contact:** Dr. Uwe Stender, President. Triada US was founded by Dr. Uwe Stender over 12 years ago. Since then, the agency has built a high-quality list of fiction and nonfiction for kids, teens, and adults. Triada US titles are consistently critically acclaimed and translated into multiple languages. Estab. 2004. Member of AAR.

MEMBER AGENTS Uwe Stender, Brent Taylor, Laura Crockett, Mallory Brown, Lauren Spieller.

REPRESENTS nonfiction, fiction, novels, juvenile books. **Considers these nonfiction areas:** biography, business, cooking, crafts, creative nonfiction, cultural interests, current affairs, diet/nutrition, economics, education, environment, ethnic, foods, gardening, health, history, how-to, juvenile nonfiction, literature, memoirs, music, parenting, popular culture, politics, science, self-help, sports, true crime, women's issues, young adult. **Considers these fiction areas:** action, adventure, comic books, commercial, contemporary issues, crime, detective, ethnic, family saga, fantasy, gay, historical, horror, juvenile, lesbian, literary, mainstream, middle-grade, multicultural, mystery, New Adult, occult, picture books, police, suspense, thriller, urban fantasy, women's, young adult.

☞   Actively seeking fiction and nonfiction across a broad range of categories of all age levels.

HOW TO CONTACT E-mail queries preferred. Please paste your query letter and the first 10 pages of your ms into the body of a message e-mailed to the agent of your choice. Please note: a rejection from one Triada US agent is a rejection from all. Triada US agents personally respond to all queries and requested material and pride themselves on having some of the fastest response times in the industry. Obtains most new clients through submission inbox (query letters and requested mss), client referrals, and conferences.

TERMS Agent receives 15% commission on domestic sales; 20% commission on foreign and translation sales. Offers written contract; 30-day notice must be given prior to termination.

RECENT SALES *Plants You Can't Kill*, by Stacy Tornio (Skyhorse); *Gettysburg Rebels*, by Tom McMillan (Regnery); *The Smart Girl's Guide to Polyamory*, by Dedeker Winston (Skyhorse); *Raised By Animals*, by Jennifer Verdolin (The Experiment); *The Hemingway Thief*, by Shaun Harris (Seventh Street); *The Perfect Fit*, by Summer Heacock (Mira); *Not Perfect*, by Elizabeth LaBan (Lake Union).

TRIDENT MEDIA GROUP

41 Madison Ave., 36th Floor, New York NY 10010. (212)333-1511. **Website:** www.tridentmediagroup. com. **Contact:** Ellen Levine. Member of AAR.
MEMBER AGENTS Kimberly Whalen, ws.assistant@tridentmediagroup (commercial fiction and nonfiction including women's fiction, romance, suspense, paranormal, pop culture); **Alyssa Eisner Henkin** (picture books through young adult fiction, including mystery, period pieces, contemporary school-settings, issues of social justice, family sagas, eerie magical realism, retellings of classics; children's/YA nonfiction: history, STEM/STEAM themes, memoir) **Scott Miller**, smiller@tridentmediagroup.com (commercial fiction including thriller,

crime fiction, women's, book club fiction, middle-grade, young adult; nonfiction including military, celebrity, pop culture, narrative, sports, prescriptive, current events); **Don Fehr**, dfehr@tridentmediagroup.com (literary and commercial fiction, young adult fiction, narrative nonfiction, memoirs, travel, science, health); **John Silbersack**, silbersack. assistant@tridentmediagroup.com (fiction: literary fiction, crime fiction, science fiction and fantasy, children's, thriller/suspense; nonfiction: narrative nonfiction, science, history, biography, current events, memoirs, finance, pop culture); **Erica Spellman-Silverman**; **Ellen Levine**, levine.assistant@tridentmediagroup.com (popular commercial fiction and compelling nonfiction, including memoir, popular culture, narrative nonfiction, history, politics, biography, science, the odd quirky book); **Mark Gottlieb** (fiction: science fiction, fantasy, young adult, graphic novels, historical, middle-grade, mystery, romance, suspense, thriller; nonfiction: business, finance, history, religious, health, cookbooks, sports, African-American, biography, memoir, travel, mind/body/spirit, narrative nonfiction, science, technology); **Alexander Slater**, aslater@tridentmdiagroup.com (children's, middle-grade, young adult fiction); **Amanda O'Connor**, aoconnor@tridentmediagroup.com; **Tara Carberry**, tcarberry@tridentmediagroup.com (women's commercial fiction, romance, New Adult, young adult, select nonfiction); **Alexa Stark**, astark@tridentmediagroup.com (literary fiction, upmarket commercial fiction, young adult, memoir, narrative nonfiction, popular science, cultural criticism, women's issues).

REPRESENTS Considers these nonfiction areas: biography, business, cooking, creative nonfiction, current affairs, economics, health, history, memoirs, military, popular culture, politics, religious, science, sports, technology, travel, women's issues, young adult, middle-grade. **Considers these fiction areas:** commercial, crime, fantasy, historical, juvenile, literary, middle-grade, mystery, New Adult, paranormal, picture books, romance, science fiction, suspense, thriller, women's, young adult.

☞   Actively seeking new or established authors in a variety of fiction and nonfiction genres.

HOW TO CONTACT Submit through the agency's online submission form on the agency website. Query only one agent at a time. If you e-query, include no attachments. Accepts simultaneous submissions.

TIPS "If you have any questions, please check FAQ page before e-mailing us."

⊙ UNITED TALENT AGENCY

142 W. 57th St., 6th Floor, New York NY 10019. (212)581-3100. **Website:** www.theagencygroup.com. **Contact:** Marc Gerald.

○ Prior to becoming an agent, Mr. Gerald owned and ran an independent publishing and entertainment agency.

MEMBER AGENTS Marc Gerald (no queries); **Juliet Mushens**, UK Literary division, juliet.mushens@unitedtalent.com (high-concept novels, thriller, young adult, historical fiction, literary fiction, psychological suspense, reading group fiction, science fiction, fantasy); **Sasha Raskin**, sasah.raskin@unitedtalent.com (popular science, business books, historical narrative nonfiction, narrative and/or literary nonfiction, historical fiction, genre fiction like science fiction but when it fits the crossover space and isn't strictly confined to its genre); **Sarah Manning**, sarah.manning@unitedtalent.com (crime, thriller, historical fiction, commercial women's fiction, accessible literary fiction, fantasy, young adult); **Diana Beaumont**, UK Literary division, diana.beaumont@unitedtalent.com (accessible literary fiction with a strong hook, historical fiction, crime, thriller, women's commercial fiction that isn't too marshmallowy, cookery, lifestyle, celebrity books, memoir with a distinctive voice).

REPRESENTS nonfiction, novels. **Considers these nonfiction areas:** business, cooking, history, memoirs, popular science, narrative nonfiction, literary nonfiction, lifestyle, celebrity. **Considers these fiction areas:** commercial, crime, fantasy, historical, literary, science fiction, suspense, thriller, women's, young adult.

HOW TO CONTACT To query Juliet: Please send your cover letter, first 3 chapters and synopsis by e-mail. Juliet replies to all submissions, and aims to respond within 8-12 weeks of receipt of e-mail. To query Sasha: e-query. To query Sarah: Please send you cover letter in the body of your e-mail with synopsis and first 3 chapters by e-mail. She responds to all submissions within 8-12 weeks. Accepts simultaneous submissions.

THE UNTER AGENCY

23 W. 73rd St., Suite 100, New York NY 10023. (212)401-4068. **E-mail:** jennifer@theunteragency. com. **Website:** www.theunteragency.com. **Contact:** Jennifer Unter. Estab. 2008. Member of AAR, Women Media Group.

○ Ms. Unter began her book publishing career in the editorial department at Henry Holt & Co. She later worked at the Karpfinger Agency while she attended law school. She then became an associate at the entertainment firm of Cowan, DeBaets, Abrahams & Sheppard LLP where she practiced primarily in the areas of publishing and copyright law.

REPRESENTS nonfiction, fiction, novels, short story collections, juvenile books. **Considers these nonfiction areas:** animals, art, autobiography, biography, cooking, creative nonfiction, current affairs, diet/nutrition, environment, foods, health, history, how-to, humor, juvenile nonfiction, law, memoirs, popular culture, politics, spirituality, sports, travel, true crime, women's issues, young adult, nature subjects. **Considers these fiction areas:** action, adventure, cartoon, commercial, family saga, inspirational, juvenile, mainstream, middle-grade, mystery, paranormal, picture books, thriller, women's, young adult.

⚬━ This agency specializes in children's, nonfiction, and quality fiction.

HOW TO CONTACT Send an e-query. There is also an online submission form. If you do not hear back from this agency within 3 months, consider that a no. Accepts simultaneous submissions. Responds in 3 months.

RECENT SALES A full list of recent sales/titles is available on the agency website.

UPSTART CROW LITERARY

244 Fifth Avenue, 11th Floor, New York NY 10001. **E-mail:** danielle.submission@gmail.com. **Website:** www.upstartcrowliterary.com. **Contact:** Danielle Chiotti, Alexandra Penfold. Estab. 2009. Member of AAR. Signatory of WGA.

MEMBER AGENTS Michael Stearns (not accepting submissions); **Danielle Chiotti** (all genres of young adult and middle-grade fiction; adult upmarket commercial fiction [not considering romance, mystery/suspense/thriller, science fiction, horror, or erotica]; nonfiction in the areas of narrative/memoir, lifestyle, relationships, humor, current events, food, wine, and cooking); **Ted Malawer** (not accepting submissions); **Alexandra Penfold** (not accepting submissions); **Susan Hawk** (books for children and teens only).

REPRESENTS Considers these nonfiction areas: cooking, current affairs, foods, humor, memoirs. **Considers these fiction areas:** commercial, mainstream, middle-grade, picture books, young adult.
HOW TO CONTACT Submit a query and 20 pages pasted into an e-mail. Accepts simultaneous submissions.

VERITAS LITERARY AGENCY

601 Van Ness Ave., Opera Plaza, Suite E, San Francisco CA 94102. (415)647-6964. **Fax:** (415)647-6965. **E-mail:** submissions@veritasliterary.com. **Website:** www.veritasliterary.com. **Contact:** Katherine Boyle. Member of AAR, the Author's Guild, SCBWI.
MEMBER AGENTS Katherine Boyle, kboyle@veritasliterary.com (literary fiction, middle-grade, young adult, narrative nonfiction/memoir, historical fiction, crime/suspense, history, pop culture, popular science, business/career); **Michael Carr**, michael@veritasliterary.com (historical fiction, women's fiction, science fiction and fantasy, nonfiction).
REPRESENTS nonfiction, novels. **Considers these nonfiction areas:** business, history, memoirs, popular culture, women's issues. **Considers these fiction areas:** commercial, crime, fantasy, historical, literary, middle-grade, New Adult, science fiction, suspense, women's, young adult.
HOW TO CONTACT This agency accepts short queries or proposals via e-mail only. "Fiction: Please include a cover letter listing previously published work, a 1-page summary and the first 5 pages in the body of the e-mail (not as an attachment). Nonfiction: If you are sending a proposal, please include an author biography, an overview, a chapter-by-chapter summary, and an analysis of competitive titles. We do our best to review all queries within 4-6 weeks; however, if you have not heard from us in 12 weeks, consider that a no." Accepts simultaneous submissions.

WAXMAN LEAVELL LITERARY AGENCY, INC.

443 Park Ave. S, Suite 1004, New York NY 10016. (212)675-5556. **Fax:** (212)675-1381. **Website:** www.waxmanleavell.com.
MEMBER AGENTS Scott Waxman (nonfiction: history, biography, health and science, adventure, business, inspirational sports); **Byrd Leavell** (narrative nonfiction, sports, humor, select commercial fiction); **Larry Kirschbaum** (fiction and nonfiction;

select self-published breakout books); **Rachel Vogel** (nonfiction: subject-driven narratives, memoirs and biography, journalism, popular culture, the occasional humor and gift book; selective fiction); **Cassie Hanjian** (New Adult novels, plot-driven commercial and upmarket women's fiction, historical fiction, psychological suspense, cozy mystery, contemporary romance; for nonfiction, mind/body/spirit, self-help, health and wellness, inspirational memoir, food/wine (narrative and prescriptive), a limited number of accessible cookbooks); **Fleetwood Robbins** (fantasy and speculative fiction—all subgenres); **Molly O'Neill** (middle-grade and young adult fiction and picture book author/illustrators, and—more selectively—narrative nonfiction [including children's/YA/Middle-grade, pop science/pop culture, lifestyle/food/travel/cookbook projects by authors with well-established platforms]).
REPRESENTS nonfiction, novels. **Considers these nonfiction areas:** biography, business, foods, health, history, humor, inspirational, memoirs, popular culture, science, sports, adventure. **Considers these fiction areas:** fantasy, historical, literary, mainstream, middle-grade, mystery, paranormal, romance, science fiction, suspense, thriller, urban fantasy, women's, young adult.
HOW TO CONTACT To submit a project, please send a query letter only via e-mail to one of the addresses included on the website. Do not send attachments, though for fiction you may include 5-10 pages of your manuscript in the body of your e-mail. "Due to the high volume of submissions, agents will reach out to you directly if interested. The typical time range for consideration is 6-8 weeks." "Please do not query more than 1 agent at our agency simultaneously." (To see the types of projects each agent is looking for, refer to the Agent Biography page on website.) Use these e-mails: scottsubmit@waxmanleavell.com, byrdsubmit@waxmanleavell.com, rachelsubmit@waxmanleavell.com, larrysubmit@waxmanleavell.com, cassiesubmit@waxmanleavell.com, mollysubmit@waxmanleavell.com. Accepts simultaneous submissions.
TERMS Agent receives 15% commission on domestic sales; 10% commission on foreign sales. Offers written contract; 2-month notice must be given to terminate contract.

WELLS ARMS LITERARY

New York NY **E-mail:** info@wellsarms.com. **Website:** www.wellsarms.com. Wells Arms Literary represents children's book authors and illustrators to the trade children's book market. Estab. 2013. Member of AAR, SCBWI, Society of Illustrators. Represents 25 clients.

○ Victoria's career began as an editor at Dial Books for Young Readers, then G. P. Putnam's Sons and then as the founding editorial director and Associate Publisher of Bloomsbury USA's Children's Division. She opened the agency in 2013.

REPRESENTS nonfiction, fiction, novels, juvenile books, children's book illustrators. **Considers these nonfiction areas:** juvenile nonfiction, young adult. **Considers these fiction areas:** juvenile, middle-grade, New Adult, picture books, young adult.

✎ "We focus on books for young readers of all ages: board books, picture books, readers, chapter books, middle-grade, and young adult fiction." Actively seeking middle-grade, young adult, magical realism, contemporary, romance, fantasy. "We do not represent to the textbook, magazine, adult romance or fine art markets."

HOW TO CONTACT E-query. Put "query" and your title in your e-mail subject line addressed to info@wellsarms.com. Accepts simultaneous submissions. Tries to respond in a month's time. If no response, assume it's a no.

WERNICK & PRATT AGENCY

E-mail: submissions@wernickpratt.com. **Website:** www.wernickpratt.com. **Contact:** Marcia Wernick, Linda Pratt, Emily Mitchell. Member of AAR, signatory of WGA, SCBWI

○ Prior to co-founding Wernick & Pratt Agency, Ms. Wernick worked at the Sheldon Fogelman Agency, in subsidiary rights, advancing to director of subsidiary rights. Ms. Pratt also worked at the Sheldon Fogelman Agency. Emily Mitchell began her publishing career at Sheldon Fogelman Agency and then spent eleven years as an editor at Charlesbridge Publishing.

MEMBER AGENTS Marcia Wernick, Linda Pratt, Emily Mitchell.

REPRESENTS juvenile books. **Considers these fiction areas:** middle-grade, young adult.

✎ "Wernick & Pratt Agency specializes in children's books of all genres, from picture books through young adult literature and everything in between. We represent both authors and illustrators. We do not represent authors of adult books." Wants people who both write and illustrate in the picture book genre; humorous young chapter books with strong voice, and which are unique and compelling; middle-grade/YA novels, both literary and commercial. No picture book mss of more than 750 words, or mood pieces; work specifically targeted to the educational market; fiction about the American Revolution, Civil War, or World War II unless it is told from a very unique perspective.

HOW TO CONTACT Submit via e-mail only to submissions@wernickpratt.com. "Please indicate to which agent you are submitting." Detailed submission guidelines available on website. "Submissions will only be responded to further if we are interested in them. If you do not hear from us within 6 weeks of your submission, it should be considered declined." Accepts simultaneous submissions. Responds in 6 weeks.

◐ WESTWOOD CREATIVE ARTISTS, LTD.

94 Harbord St., Toronto ON M5S 1G6 Canada. (416)964-3302. **E-mail:** wca_office@wcaltd.com. **Website:** www.wcaltd.com. Represents 350+ clients.

MEMBER AGENTS Jack Babad; Lix Culotti (foreign contracts and permissions); Carolyn Ford (literary fiction, commerical, women's/literary crossover, thriller, serious narrative nonfiction, pop culture); Jackie Kaiser (president and CEO); Michael A. Levine; Linda McKnight; Hilary McMahon (fiction, nonfiction, children's); John Pearce (fiction, nonfiction); Meg Tobin-O'Drowsky; Bruce Westwood.

REPRESENTS nonfiction, fiction, novels. **Considers these nonfiction areas:** biography, current affairs, history, parenting, science, journalism, practical nonfiction. **Considers these fiction areas:** commercial, juvenile, literary, thriller, women's, young adult.

✎ "We take on children's and young adult writers very selectively. The agents bring their diverse interests to their client lists, but are generally looking for authors with a mastery of language, a passionate, expert or original perspective on their subject, and a gift for storytelling. Please note that WCA does not represent screenwriters, and our agents are not currently seeking poetry or children's picture book submissions."

HOW TO CONTACT E-query only. Include credentials, synopsis, and no more than 10 pages. No attachments. Accepts simultaneous submissions.

RECENT SALES *Ellen in Pieces*, by Caroline Adderson (HarperCollins); *Paper Swan*, by Ann Y.K. Choi (Simon & Schuster); *Hope Makes Love*, by Trevor Cole (Cormorant).

TIPS "We will reject outright complete, unsolicited manuscripts, or projects that are presented poorly in the query letter. We prefer to receive exclusive submissions and request that you do not query more than one agent at the agency simultaneously. It's often best if you approach WCA after you have accumulated some publishing credits."

WRITERS HOUSE

21 W. 26th St., New York NY 10010. (212)685-2400. **Fax:** (212)685-1781. **Website:** www.writershouse. com. Estab. 1973. Member of AAR.

MEMBER AGENTS Amy Berkower, Stephen Barr, Susan Cohen, Dan Conaway, Lisa DiMona, Susan Ginsburg, Susan Golomb, Merrilee Heifetz, Brianne Johnson, Daniel Lazar, Simon Lipskar, Steven Malk, Jodi Reamer, Esq., Robin Rue, Rebecca Sherman, Geri Thoma, Albert Zuckerman, Alec Shane, Stacy Testa, Victoria Doherty-Munro, Beth Miller, Andrea Morrison, Soumeya Roberts.

REPRESENTS nonfiction, novels. **Considers these nonfiction areas:** biography, business, cooking, economics, history, how-to, juvenile nonfiction, memoirs, parenting, psychology, science, self-help. **Considers these fiction areas:** commercial, fantasy, juvenile, literary, mainstream, middle-grade, picture books, science fiction, women's, young adult.

☞ This agency specializes in all types of popular fiction and nonfiction, for both adult and juvenile books as well as illustrators. Does not want to receive scholarly, professional, poetry, plays, or screenplays.

HOW TO CONTACT Individual agent e-mail addresses are available on the website. "Please e-mail us a query letter, which includes your credentials, an explanation of what makes your book unique and special, and a synopsis. Some agents within our agency have different requirements. Please consult their individual Publisher's Marketplace (PM) profile for details. We respond to all queries, generally within 6-8 weeks." If you prefer to submit by mail, address it to an individual agent, and please include SASE for our reply. (If submitting to Steven Malk: Writers House, 7660 Fay Ave., #338H, La Jolla, CA 92037.) Accepts simultaneous submissions. "We respond to all queries, generally within 6-8 weeks." Obtains most new clients through recommendations from authors and editors.

TERMS Agent receives 15% commission on domestic sales; 20% commission on foreign sales. Offers written contract, binding for 1 year. Agency charges fees for copying mss/proposals and overseas airmail of books.

TIPS "Do not send mss. Write a compelling letter. If you do, we'll ask to see your work. Follow submission guidelines and please do not simultaneously submit your work to more than one Writers House agent."

JASON YARN LITERARY AGENCY

3544 Broadway, No. 68, New York NY 10031. **E-mail:** jason@jasonyarnliteraryagency.com. **Website:** www.jasonyarnliteraryagency.com. Member of AAR. Signatory of WGA.

REPRESENTS nonfiction, fiction. **Considers these nonfiction areas:** creative nonfiction, current affairs, foods, history, science. **Considers these fiction areas:** commercial, fantasy, literary, middle-grade, science fiction, suspense, thriller, young adult, graphic novels, comics.

HOW TO CONTACT Please e-mail your query to jason@jasonyarnliteraryagency.com with the word "Query" in the subject line, and please paste the first 10 pages of your manuscript or proposal into the text of your e-mail. Do not send any attachments. "Visit the About page for information on what we are interested in, and please note that JYLA does not accept queries for film, TV, or stage scripts." Accepts simultaneous submissions.

CLUBS & ORGANIZATIONS

///

Contacts made through organizations such as the ones listed in this section can be quite beneficial for children's writers and illustrators. Professional organizations provide numerous educational, business, and legal services in the form of newsletters, workshops, or seminars. Organizations can provide tips about how to be a more successful writer or artist, as well as what types of business cards to keep, health and life insurance coverage to carry, and competitions to consider.

An added benefit of belonging to an organization is the opportunity to network with those who have similar interests, creating a support system. As in any business, knowing the right people can often help your career, and important contacts can be made through your peers. Membership in a writer's or artist's organization also shows publishers you're serious about your craft. This provides no guarantee your work will be published, but it gives you an added dimension of credibility and professionalism.

Some of the organizations listed here welcome anyone with an interest, while others are only open to published writers and professional artists. Organizations such as the Society of Children's Book Writers and Illustrators (SCBWI, www.scbwi.org) have varying levels of membership. SCBWI offers associate membership to those with no publishing credits, and full membership to those who have had work for children published. International organizations such as SCBWI also have regional chapters throughout the US and the world. Write or call for more information regarding any group that interests you, or check the websites of the many organizations that list them. Be sure to get information about local chapters, membership qualifications, and services offered.

AMERICAN ALLIANCE FOR THEATRE & EDUCATION

718 7th St. NW, Washington DC 20001. (202)909-1194. **E-mail:** info@aate.com. **Website:** www.aate.com. Purpose of organization: to promote standards of excellence in theatre and drama education. "We achieve this by assimilating quality practices in theatre and theatre education, connecting artists, educators, researchers, and scholars with each other, and by providing opportunities for our members to learn, exchange, and diversify their work, their audiences, and their perspectives." Membership cost: $115 annually for individual in US and Canada, $220 annually for organization, $60 annually for students, and $70 annually for retired people, $310 annually for University Departmental memberships; add $30 outside Canada and US Holds annual conference (July or August). Contests held for unpublished play reading project and annual awards in various categories. Awards plaque and stickers for published playbooks. Publishes list of unpublished plays deemed worthy of performance and stages readings at conference. Contact national office at number above or see website for contact information for Playwriting Network Chairpersons.

AMERICAN SOCIETY OF JOURNALISTS AND AUTHORS

355 Lexington Ave., 15th Floor, New York NY 10017. (212)997-0947. **Website:** www.asja.org. Qualifications for membership: "Need to be a professional freelance nonfiction writer. Refer to website for further qualifications." Membership cost: Application fee—$50; annual dues—$210. Group sponsors national conferences. Professional seminars online and in person around the country. Workshops/conferences open to nonmembers. Publishes a newsletter for members that provides confidential information for nonfiction writers. **Contact:** Holly Koenig, interim executive director.

ARIZONA AUTHORS' ASSOCIATION

6939 East Chaparral Rd., Paradise Valley AZ 85253. (602)510-8076. **E-mail:** azauthors@gmail.com. **Website:** www.azauthors.com. Since 1978, Arizona Authors' Association has served to offer professional, educational and social opportunities to writers and authors and serves as an informational and referral network for the literary community. Members must be authors, writers working toward publication, agents, publishers, publicists, printers, illustrators, etc. Az Authors' publishes a bimonthly newsletter and the renown annual *Arizona Literary Magazine*. The Association sponsors the international Arizona Literary Contest including poetry, essays, short stories, new drama writing, novels, and published books with cash prizes and awards bestowed at a Fall ceremony. Winning entries are published or advertised in the *Arizona Literary Magazine*. First and second place winners in poetry, essay and short story categories are entered in the annual Pushcart Prize. Learn more online. **Contact:** Lisa Aquilina, President.

THE AUTHORS GUILD, INC.

31 E. 32nd St., 7th Floor, New York NY 10016. (212)563-5904. **Fax:** (212)564-5363. **E-mail:** staff@authorsguild.org. **Website:** www.authorsguild.org. Purpose of organization: to offer services and materials intended to help authors with the business and legal aspects of their work, including contract problems, copyright matters, freedom of expression, and taxation. Guild has 8,000 members. Qualifications for membership: Must be book author published by an established American publisher within 7 years or any author who has had 3 works (fiction or nonfiction) published by a magazine or magazines of general circulation in the last 18 months. Associate membership also available. Different levels of membership include: associate membership with all rights except voting available to an author who has a firm contract offer or is currently negotiating a royalty contract from an established American publisher. "The Guild offers free contract reviews to its members. The Guild conducts several symposia each year at which experts provide information, offer advice, and answer questions on subjects of interest and concern to authors. Typical subjects have been the rights of privacy and publicity, libel, wills and estates, taxation, copyright, editors and editing, the art of interviewing, standards of criticism, and book reviewing. Transcripts of these symposia are published and circulated to members. The *Authors Guild Bulletin*, a quarterly journal, contains articles on matters of interest to writers, reports of Guild activities, contract surveys, advice on problem clauses in contracts, transcripts of Guild and League symposia, and information on a variety of professional topics. Subscription included in the cost of the annual dues. **Contact:** Mary Rasenberger, executive director.

☼ CANADIAN SOCIETY OF CHILDREN'S AUTHORS, ILLUSTRATORS AND PERFORMERS

720 Bathurst St., Suite 503, Toronto, Ontario M5S 2R4, Canada. (416)515-1559. **E-mail:** office@canscaip.org. **Website:** www.canscaip.org. Purpose of organization: development of Canadian children's culture and support for authors, illustrators, and performers working in this field. Qualifications for membership: Members: professionals who have been published (not self-published) or have paid public performances/records/tapes to their credit. Friends: share interest in field of children's culture. Sponsors workshops/conferences. Manuscript evaluation services; publishes newsletter: includes profiles of members; news round-up of members' activities countrywide; market news; news on awards, grants, etc; columns related to professional concerns. **Contact:** Helena Aalto, administrative director.

LEWIS CARROLL SOCIETY OF NORTH AMERICA

11935 Beltsville Dr., Beltsville MD 20705. **E-mail:** secretary@lewiscarroll.org. **Website:** www.lewiscarroll.org. "We are an organization of Carroll admirers of all ages and interests and a center for Carroll studies." Qualifications for membership: "An interest in Lewis Carroll and a simple love for Alice (or the Snark for that matter)." Membership cost: $35 (regular membership), $50 (foreign membership), $100 (sustaining membership). The Society meets twice a year—in spring and in fall; locations vary. Publishes a semi-annual journal, *Knight Letter*, and maintains an active publishing program. **Contact:** Sandra Lee Parker, secretary.

GRAPHIC ARTISTS GUILD

32 Broadway, Suite 1114, New York NY 10004. (212)791-3400. **Fax:** 212-791-0333. **E-mail:** admin@gag.org. **Website:** www.graphicartistsguild.org. Purpose of organization: "To promote and protect the economic interests of member artists. It is committed to improving conditions for all creators of graphic arts and raising standards for the entire industry." Qualification for full membership: 50% of income derived from the creation of graphic artwork. Associate members include those in allied fields and students. Initiation fee: $30. Full memberships: $200; student membership: $75/year. Associate membership: $170/year. Publishes *Graphic Artists Guild Handbook*, *Pricing and Ethical Guidelines* (members receive a copy as part of their membership). **Contact:** Patricia McKiernan, executive director.

HORROR WRITERS ASSOCIATION

P.O. Box 56687, Sherman Oaks CA 91413. 1-818-220-3965. **E-mail:** hwa@horror.org; membership@horror.org. **Website:** www.horror.org. Purpose of organization: To encourage public interest in horror and dark fantasy and to provide networking and career tools for members. Qualifications for membership: Complete membership rules online at www.horror.org/memrule.htm. At least one low-level sale is required to join as an affiliate. Nonwriting professionals who can show income from a horror-related field may join as an associate (booksellers, editors, agents, librarians, etc.). To qualify for full active membership, you must be a published, professional writer of horror. Membership cost: $69 annually. Holds annual Stoker Awards Weekend and HWA Business Meeting. Publishes monthly newsletter focusing on market news, industry news, HWA business for members. Sponsors awards. We give the Bram Stoker Awards for superior achievement in horror annually. Awards include a handmade Stoker trophy designed by sculptor Stephen Kirk. Awards open to nonmembers. **Contact:** Brad Hodson, Administrator.

INTERNATIONAL READING ASSOCIATION

P.O. Box 8139, Newark DE 19714. (302)731-1600. **E-mail:** councils@reading.org. **Website:** www.reading.org. The International Reading Association seeks to promote high levels of literacy for all by improving the quality of reading instruction through studying the reading process and teaching techniques; serving as a clearinghouse for the dissemination of reading research through conferences, journals, and other publications; and actively encouraging the lifetime reading habit. Its goals include professional development, advocacy, partnerships, research, and global literacy development. Sponsors annual convention. Publishes a newsletter called "Reading Today." Sponsors a number of awards and fellowships. More information online.

INTERNATIONAL WOMEN'S WRITING GUILD

International Women's Writing Guild, 5 Penn Plaza, 19th Floor, PMB# 19059, New York NY 10001. (917)720-6959. **E-mail:** iwwgquestions@gmail.com. **Website:** www.iwwg.wildapricot.org. IWWG is a network for the personal and professional empowerment of women through writing. Open to any woman connected to the written word regardless of professional portfolio. IWWG sponsors several annual conferences in all areas of the U.S. The major event, held in the summer, is a week-long conference attracting hundreds of women writers from around the globe. **Contact:** Marj Hahne, Interim Director of Operations.

LITERARY MANAGERS AND DRAMATURGS OF THE AMERICAS

P.O. Box 604074, Bayside NY 11360. (800)680-2148. **E-mail:** info@lmda.org. **Website:** www.lmda.org. LMDA is a not-for-profit service organization for the professions of literary management and dramaturgy. Student Membership: $30/year. Open to students in dramaturgy, performing arts and literature programs, or related disciplines. Proof of student status required. Includes national conference, New Dramaturg activities, local symposia, job phone, and select membership meetings. Individual Membership: $75/year. Open to full-time and part-time professionals working in the fields of literary management and dramaturgy. All privileges and services including voting rights and eligibility for office. Institutional Membership: $200/year. Open to theaters, universities, and other organizations. Includes all privileges and services except voting rights and eligibility for office. Publishes a newsletter featuring articles on literary management, dramaturgy, LMDA program updates, and other articles of interest. Spotlight sponsor membership $500/year; Open to theatres, universities, and other organizations; includes all priviledges for up to six individual members, plus additional promotional benefits.

THE NATIONAL LEAGUE OF AMERICAN PEN WOMEN

Pen Arts Building, 1300 17th St. N.W., Washington D.C. 20036-1973. (202)785-1997. **Fax:** (202)452-6868. **E-mail:** contact@nlapw.org. **Website:** www.americanpenwomen.org. Purpose of organization: to promote professional female work in art, letters, and music since 1897. Qualifications for membership: An applicant must show "proof of sale" in each chosen category—art, letters, and music. Levels of membership include: Active, Associate, International Affiliate, Members-at-Large, Honorary Members (in one or more of the following classifications: Art, Letters, and Music). Holds workshops/conferences. Publishes magazine 4 times/year titled *The Pen Woman*. Sponsors various contests in areas of Art, Letters, and Music. Awards made at Biennial Convention. Biannual scholarships awarded to non-Pen Women for mature women. Awards include cash prizes—up to $1,000. Specialized contests open to nonmembers. **Contact:** Nina Brooks, corresponding secretary.

NATIONAL WRITERS ASSOCIATION

10940 S. Parker Rd., #508, Parker CO 80138. **E-mail:** natlwritersassn@hotmail.com. **Website:** www.nationalwriters.com. Association for freelance writers. Qualifications for membership: associate membership—must be serious about writing; professional membership—must be published and paid writer (cite credentials). Sponsors workshops/conferences: TV/screenwriting workshops, NWAF Annual Conferences, Literary Clearinghouse, editing and critiquing services, local chapters, National Writer's School. Open to nonmembers. Publishes industry news of interest to freelance writers; how-to articles; market information; member news and networking opportunities. Sponsors poetry contest; short story contest; article contest; novel contest. Awards cash for top 3 winners; books and/or certificates for other winners; honorable mention certificate places 5-10. Contests open to nonmembers.

NATIONAL WRITERS UNION

256 W. 38th St., Suite 703, New York NY 10018. (212)254-0279. **Fax:** (212)254-0673. **E-mail:** nwu@nwu.org. **Website:** www.nwu.org. Advocacy for freelance writers. Qualifications for membership: "Membership in the NWU is open to all qualified writers, and no one shall be barred or in any manner prejudiced within the Union on account of race, age, sex, sexual orientation, disability, national origin, religion, or ideology. You are eligible for membership if you have published a book, a play, three articles, five poems, one short story, or an equivalent amount of newsletter, publicity, technical, commer-

cial, government, or institutional copy. You are also eligible for membership if you have written an equal amount of unpublished material and you are actively writing and attempting to publish your work." Holds workshops throughout the country. Members only section on website offers rich resources for freelance writers. Skilled contract advice and grievance help for members.

PEN AMERICAN CENTER

588 Broadway, Suite 303, New York NY 10012. (212)334-1660. **E-mail:** info@pen.org. **Website:** www.pen.org. An association of writers working to advance literature, to defend free expression, and to foster international literary fellowship. PEN welcomes to its membership all writers and those belonging to the larger literary community. We ask that writers have at least one book published or be writers with proven records as professional writers; playwrights and screenwriters should have at least one work produced in a professional setting. Others should have achieved recognition in the literary field. Editors, literary agents, literary scouts, publicists, journalists, bloggers, and other literary professionals are all invited to join as Professional Members. If you feel you do not meet these guidelines, please consider joining as an Advocate Member. Candidates for membership may be nominated by a PEN member or they may nominate themselves with the support of two references from the literary community or from a current PEN member. PEN members receive a subscription to the PEN journal, the PEN Annual Report, and have access to medical insurance at group rates. Members living in the New York metropolitan and tri-state area, or near the Branches, are invited to PEN events throughout the year. Membership in PEN American Center includes reciprocal privileges in PEN American Center branches and in foreign PEN Centers for those traveling abroad. Application forms are available online. PEN American Center is the largest of the 141 centers of PEN International, the world's oldest human rights organization and the oldest international literary organization. PEN International was founded in 1921 to dispel national, ethnic, and racial hatreds and to promote understanding among all countries. PEN American Center, founded a year later, works to advance literature, to defend free expression, and to foster international literary fellowship. The Center has a membership of 3,400 distinguished writers, editors, and translators. In addition to defending writers in prison or in danger of imprisonment for their work, PEN American Center sponsors public literary programs and forums on current issues, sends prominent authors to inner-city schools to encourage reading and writing, administers literary prizes, promotes international literature that might otherwise go unread in the United States, and offers grants and loans to writers facing financial or medical emergencies.

PUPPETEERS OF AMERICA, INC.

Sabathani Community Center, 310 East 38th St., Suite 127, Minneapolis MN 55409. (888)568-6235. **E-mail:** membership@puppeteers.org; execdir@puppeteers.org. **Website:** www.puppeteers.org. Purpose of organization: to promote the art and appreciation of puppetry as a means of communications and as a performing art. The Puppeteers of America boasts an international membership. There are 9 different levels of membership, from family to youth to library to senior and more. See the website for all details. Costs are $35-90 per year.

SCIENCE-FICTION AND FANTASY WRITERS OF AMERICA, INC.

P.O. Box 3238, Enfield CT 06083. **Website:** www.sfwa.org. Purpose of organization: to encourage public interest in science fiction literature and provide organization format for writers/editors/artists within the genre. Qualifications for membership: at least 1 professional sale or other professional involvement within the field. Different levels of membership include: active—requires 3 professional short stories or 1 novel published; associate—requires 1 professional sale; or affiliate—which requires some other professional involvement such as artist, editor, librarian, bookseller, teacher, etc. Workshops/conferences: annual awards banquet, usually in April or May. Open to nonmembers. Publishes quarterly journal, the *SFWA Bulletin*. Sponsors Nebula Awards for best published science fiction or fantasy in the categories of novel, novella, novelette, and short story. Awards trophy. Also presents the Damon Knight Memorial Grand Master Award for Lifetime Achievement, and, beginning in 2006, the Andre Norton Award for Outstanding Young Adult Science Fiction or Fantasy Book of the Year.

SOCIETY OF CHILDREN'S BOOK WRITERS AND ILLUSTRATORS

4727 Wilshire Blvd #301, Los Angeles CA 90010. (323)782-1010. **Fax:** (323)782-1892. **E-mail:** scbwi@scbwi.org; membership@scbwi.org. **Website:** www.scbwi.org. Purpose of organization: to assist writers and illustrators working or interested in the field. Qualifications for membership: an interest in children's literature and illustration. Membership cost: $80/year. Plus one time $95 initiation fee. Different levels of membership include: P.A.L. membership—published by publisher listed in SCBWI Market Surveys; full membership—published authors/illustrators (includes self-published); associate membership—unpublished writers/illustrators. Holds 100 events (workshops/conferences) worldwide each year. National Conference open to nonmembers. Publishes bi-monthly magazine on writing and illustrating children's books. Sponsors annual awards and grants for writers and illustrators who are members. **Contact:** Stephen Mooser, president; Lin Oliver, executive director.

SOCIETY OF ILLUSTRATORS

128 E. 63rd St., New York NY 10065. (212)838-2560. **Fax:** (212)838-2561. **E-mail:** info@societyillustrators.org. **Website:** www.societyillustrators.org. "Our mission is to promote the art and appreciation of illustration, its history, and evolving nature through exhibitions, lectures, and education. Annual dues for nonresident illustrator members (those living more than 125 air miles from SI's headquarters): $300. Dues for resident illustrator members: $500 per year; resident associate members: $500. Artist members shall include those who make illustration their profession and earn at least 60% of their income from their illustration. Associate members are those who earn their living in the arts or who have made a substantial contribution to the art of illustration. This includes art directors, art buyers, creative supervisors, instructors, publishers, and like categories. The candidate must complete and sign the application form, which requires a brief biography, a listing of schools attended, other training and a résumé of his or her professional career. Candidates for illustrators membership, in addition to the above requirements, must submit examples of their work." **Contact:** Anelle Miller, executive director.

SOCIETY OF MIDLAND AUTHORS

P.O. Box 10419, Chicago IL 60610. **Website:** www.midlandauthors.com. Purpose of organization: create closer association among writers of the Middle West; stimulate creative literary effort; maintain collection of members' works; encourage interest in reading and literature by cooperating with other educational and cultural agencies. Qualifications for membership: membership by invitation only. Must be author or co-author of a book demonstrating literary style and published by a recognized publisher and be identified through residence with Illinois, Indiana, Iowa, Kansas, Michigan, Minnesota, Missouri, Nebraska, North Dakota, Ohio, South Dakota or Wisconsin. Open to students (if authors). Membership cost: $40/year dues. Different levels of membership include: regular—published book authors; associate, nonvoting—not published as above but having some connection with literature, such as librarians, teachers, publishers and editors. Program meetings held 5 times a year, featuring authors, publishers, editors, or the like individually or on panels. Usually second Tuesday of October, November, February, March, and April. Also holds annual awards dinner in May. Publishes a newsletter focusing on news of members and general items of interest to writers. Sponsors contests. "Annual awards in six categories, given at annual dinner in May. Monetary awards for books published that premiered professionally in previous calendar year. Send SASE to contact person for details." Categories include adult fiction, adult nonfiction, juvenile fiction, juvenile nonfiction, poetry, biography. No picture books. Contest open to nonmembers. **Contact:** Meg Tebo, president.

SOCIETY OF SOUTHWESTERN AUTHORS

Fax: (520)751-7877. **E-mail:** wporter202@aol.com. **Website:** www.ssa-az.org. Purpose of organization: to promote fellowship among professional and associate members of the writing profession, to recognize members' achievements, to stimulate further achievement, and to assist persons seeking to become professional writers. Qualifications for membership: Professional Membership: proof of publication of a book, articles, TV screenplay, etc. Associate Membership: proof of desire to write, and/or become a professional. Self-published authors may receive status of Professional Membership at the discretion of the board of directors. Membership cost: see website. Sometimes this organization hosts writing events, such as its cosponsorship of the Arizona Writing Workshops in Phoenix and Tucson in November 2014.

○ TEXT & ACADEMIC AUTHORS ASSOCIATION (TAA)

TAA, P.O. Box 367, Fountain City WI 54629. (727)563-0020. **E-mail:** info@taaonline.net. **Website:** www.taaonline.net. TAA's overall mission is "To support textbook and academic authors in the creation of top-quality educational and scholarly works that stimulate the love of learning and foster the pursuit of knowledge." Qualifications for membership: all authors and prospective authors are welcome. Membership cost: $20-$200. Workshops/conferences: June each year. Newsletter focuses on all areas of interest to textbook and academic authors.

THEATRE FOR YOUNG AUDIENCES/USA

c/o The Theatre School, 2350 N. Racine Ave., Chicago IL 60614. (773)325-7981. **Fax:** (773)325-7920. **E-mail:** info@tyausa.org. **Website:** tyausa.org. Purpose of organization: to promote theater for children and young people by linking professional theaters and artists together; sponsoring national, international, and regional conferences and providing publications and information. Also serves as US Center for International Association of the Theatre for Children and Young People. Different levels of memberships include: organizations, individuals, students, retirees, libraries. *TYA Today* includes original articles, reviews, and works of criticism and theory, all of interest to theater practitioners (included with membership). Publishes *Marquee*, a directory that focuses on information on members in US.

VOLUNTEER LAWYERS FOR THE ARTS

1 E. 53rd St., 6th Floor, New York NY 10022. (212)319-2787, ext. 1. **Fax:** (212)752-6575. **E-mail:** vlany@vlany.org. **Website:** www.vlany.org. Purpose of organization: Volunteer Lawyers for the Arts is dedicated to providing free arts-related legal assistance to low-income artists and not-for-profit arts organizations in all creative fields. Over 1,000 attorneys in the New York area donate their time through VLA to artists and arts organizations un-

able to afford legal counsel. Everyone is welcome to use VLA's Art Law Line, a legal hotline for any artist or arts organization needing quick answers to arts-related questions. VLA also provides clinics, seminars, and publications designed to educate artists on legal issues that affect their careers. Members receive discounts on publications and seminars as well as other benefits.

○ WRITERS' FEDERATION OF NEW BRUNSWICK

P.O. Box 4528, Rothesay, New Brunswick E2E 5X2, Canada. (506)224-0364. **E-mail:** info@wfnb.ca. **Website:** www.wfnb.ca. Purpose of organization: "to promote New Brunswick writing and to help writers at all stages of their development." Qualifications for membership: interest in writing. Membership cost: $50 basic annual membership; $5, high school students; $50, institutional membership. Holds workshops/conferences. Publishes a newsletter with articles concerning the craft of writing, member news, contests, markets, workshops, and conference listings. Sponsors annual literary competition, $20-$35 entry fee for members, $25-$40 for nonmembers. Categories: fiction, nonfiction, poetry, children's literature. **Contact:** Cathy Fynn, executive director.

○ WRITERS' FEDERATION OF NOVA SCOTIA

1113 Marginal Rd., Halifax, Nova Scotia B3H 4P7, Canada. (902)423-8116. **Fax:** (902)422-0881. **E-mail:** director@writers.ns.ca. **Website:** www.writers.ns.ca. Purpose of organization: "to foster creative writing and the profession of writing in Nova Scotia; to provide advice and assistance to writers at all stages of their careers; and to encourage greater public recognition of Nova Scotian writers and their achievements." Regional organization open to anybody who writes. Currently has 800+ members. Offerings include resource library with over 2,500 titles, promotional services, workshop series, annual festivals, mentorship program. Publishes *Eastword*, a bimonthly newsletter containing "a plethora of information on who's doing what; markets and contests; and current writing events and issues." Members and nationally known writers give readings that are open to the public. Additional information online.

⊙ WRITERS' GUILD OF ALBERTA

11759 Groat Rd. NW, Edmonton, Alberta T5M 3K6, Canada. (780)422-8174. **E-mail:** mail@writersguild. ca. **Website:** writersguild.ca. Purpose of organization: to support, encourage, and promote writers and writing, to safeguard the freedom to write and to read, and to advocate for the well-being of writers in Alberta. Currently has over 1,000 members. Offerings include retreats/conferences; monthly events; bimonthly magazine that includes articles on writing and a market section; weekly electronic bulletin with markets and event listings; and the Stephan G. Stephansson Award for Poetry (Alberta residents only). Holds workshops/conferences. Publishes a newsletter focusing on markets, competitions, contemporary issues related to the literary arts (writing, publishing, censorship, royalties etc.). Sponsors annual literary awards in 5 categories (novel, nonfiction, children's literature, poetry, drama). Awards include $1,500. Open to nonmembers. **Contact:** Carol Holmes.

CONFERENCES & WORKSHOPS

//

Writers and illustrators eager to expand their knowledge of the children's publishing industry should consider attending one of the many conferences and workshops held each year. Whether you're a novice or seasoned professional, conferences and workshops are great places to pick up information on a variety of topics and network with experts in the publishing industry, as well as with your peers.

Listings in this section provide details about what conference and workshop courses are offered, where and when they are held, and the costs. Some of the national writing and art organizations also offer regional workshops throughout the year. Write, call, or visit websites for information.

Members of the Society of Children's Book Writers and Illustrators (SCBWI) can find information on conferences in national and local SCBWI newsletters. Nonmembers may attend SCBWI events as well. (Some SCBWI regional events are listed in this section.) For information on SCBWI's annual national conferences and all of their regional events, check their website (scbwi.org) for a complete calendar of conferences and happenings.

AGENTS & EDITORS CONFERENCE, WRITERS LEAGUE OF TEXAS

Writers' League of Texas, 611 S. Congress Ave., Suite 200 A-3, Austin TX 78704. (512)499-8914. **E-mail:** michael@writersleague.org. **Website:** www.writersleague.org/38/conference. **Contact:** Michael Noll, program director. Annual conference held in summer. 2017 dates: June 30-July 2. "This standout conference gives each attendee the opportunity to become a publishing insider. Meet more than 25 top agents, editors, and industry professionals through one-on-one consultations and receptions. Get tips and strategies for revising and improving your manuscript from keynote speakers and presenters (including award-winning and best-selling writers)." Discounted rates are available at the conference hotel.

COSTS Registration for the 2017 conference opens January 3. Early bird registration: $399 for members and $459 for nonmembers. After April 30, 2017: $439 for members and $499 for nonmembers.

ADDITIONAL INFORMATION Register before March 15 to receive a free consultation with an agent or editor.

ALASKA WRITERS CONFERENCE

Alaska Writers Guild, P.O. Box 670014, Chugiak AK 99567. **E-mail:** alaskawritersguild.awg@gmail.com. **Website:** alaskawritersguild.com. Annual event held in the fall—usually September. Duration: 2 days. There are many workshops and instructional tracks. Sometimes teams up with SCBWI and Alaska Pacific University to offer courses at the event. Literary agents are in attendance each year to hear pitches and meet writers.

- Manuscript critiques available. Note also that the Alaska Writers Guild has many events and meetings each year, not just the annual conference.

AMERICAN CHRISTIAN WRITERS CONFERENCES

P.O. Box 110390, Nashville TN 37222. (800)219-7483 or (615)331-8668. **E-mail:** acwriters@aol.com. **Website:** www.acwriters.com. **Contact:** Reg Forder, director. ACW hosts a dozen annual two-day writers conferences and mentoring retreats across America taught by editors and professional freelance writers. These events provide excellent instruction, networking opportunities, and valuable one-on-one time with editors. Open to all forms of Christian writing

(fiction, nonfiction, and scriptwriting). Conferences are held between March and November during each year. Special rates are available at the host hotel (usually a major chain like Holiday Inn).

COSTS Costs vary and may depend on type of event (conference or mentoring retreat).

ADDITIONAL INFORMATION E-mail or call for conference brochures.

ANNUAL SPRING POETRY FESTIVAL

City College, 160 Convent Ave., New York NY 10031. (212)650-6356. **Website:** www.ccny.cuny.edu/poetry/festival. Workshops geared to all levels. Open to students. Write for more information. Site: Theater B of Aaron Davis Hall.

ANTIOCH WRITERS' WORKSHOP

Antioch Writers' Workshop, c/o Antioch University Midwest, 900 Dayton St., Yellow Springs OH 45387. (937)769-1803. **E-mail:** info@antiochwritersworkshop.com. **Website:** www.antiochwritersworkshop.com. **Contact:** Sharon Short, director. Programs are offered year-round; annual conference held in summer. Average attendance: 80. Workshop concentrations: fiction, poetry, personal essay, and memoir. Site: Antioch University Midwest in the Village of Yellow Springs. Literary agents attend. Writers of all levels (beginner to advanced) are warmly welcomed to discover their next steps on their writing paths—whether that's developing craft or preparing to submit for publication. An agent and an editor will be speaking and available for meetings with attendees. Accommodations are available at local hotels and bed-and-breakfasts.

ADDITIONAL INFORMATION The easiest way to contact this event is through the website's contact form.

ATLANTA WRITERS CONFERENCE

Atlanta Writers Club, Westin Atlanta Airport Hotel, 4736 Best Rd., Atlanta GA 30337. **E-mail:** awconference@gmail.com. **Website:** www.atlantawritersconference.com/about. **Contact:** George Weinstein. Annual conference held in spring. 2017 dates: May 12-13. Literary agents and editors are in attendance to take pitches and critique ms samples and query letters. Conference offers a self-editing workshop, instructional sessions with local authors, and separate question-and-answer panels with the agents and editors. Site: Westin Airport Atlanta Hotel. A block of rooms is reserved at the conference hotel.

instructions will be sent in the registration confirmation e-mail.

COSTS Manuscript critiques are $160 each (2 spots/waitlists maximum). Pitches are $60 each (2 spots/waitlists maximum). There's no charge for waitlists unless a spot opens. Query letter critiques are $60 (1 spot maximum). Other workshops and panels may also cost extra; see website. The "all activities" option is $560 and includes 2 manuscript critiques, 2 pitches, and 1 of each remaining activity.

ADDITIONAL INFORMATION A free shuttle runs between the airport and the hotel.

BIG SUR WRITING WORKSHOP

Henry Miller Library, Hwy. 1, Big Sur CA 93920. (831)667-2574. **E-mail:** writing@henrymiller.org. **Website:** bigsurwriting.wordpress.com. Annual workshop focusing on children's writing (picture books, middle-grade, and young adult). Held every spring in Big Sur Lodge in Pfeiffer State Park. Cost of workshop includes meals, lodging, workshop, and Saturday evening reception. This event is helmed by the literary agents of the Andrea Brown Literary Agency. All attendees meet with at least 2 faculty members to have their work critiqued.

○   Full editorial schedule and much more available online. The Lodge is located 25 miles south of Carmel in Big Sur's Pfeiffer State Park, 47225 Hwy. 1, Big Sur CA 93920.

BOOKS-IN-PROGRESS CONFERENCE

Carnegie Center for Literacy and Learning, 251 W. Second St., Lexington KY 40507. (859)254-4175. **E-mail:** ccll1@carnegiecenterlex.org. **Website:** carnegiecenterlex.org. **Contact:** Laura Whitaker, program director. This is an annual writing conference at the Carnegie Center for Literacy and Learning in Lexington, Kentucky. It typically happens in June. "Each conference will offer writing and publishing workshops and includes a keynote presentation." Literary agents are flown in to meet with writers and hear pitches. Website is updated several months prior to each annual event. See website for list of area hotels.

○   "Personal meetings with faculty (agents and editors) are only available to full conference participants. Limited slots available. Please choose only one agent; only one pitching session per participant."

CAPE COD WRITERS CENTER ANNUAL CONFERENCE

P.O. Box 408, Osterville MA 02655. **E-mail:** writers@capecodwriterscenter.org. **Website:** www.capecodwriterscenter.org. **Contact:** Nancy Rubin Stuart, executive director. Annual conference held in Hyannis, Massachusetts. 2017 dates: August 3-6. Offers workshops in fiction, commercial fiction, creative nonfiction, poetry, memoir, mystery, thrillers, writing for children, social media, screenwriting, promotion, and pitches and queries, as well as agent meetings and ms mentorship with agents and faculty. Resort and Conference Center of Hyannis, Massachusetts.

COSTS Costs vary, depending on the number of courses selected, beginning at $150. Several scholarships are available.

CELEBRATION OF SOUTHERN LITERATURE

Southern Lit Alliance, 301 E. 11th St., Suite 301, Chattanooga TN 37403. (423)267-1218. **Fax:** (866)483-6831. **Website:** www.southernlitalliance.org. Biennial conference held in odd-numbered years. "The Celebration of Southern Literature stands out because of its unique collaboration with the Fellowship of Southern Writers, an organization founded by towering literary figures like Eudora Welty, Cleanth Brooks, Walker Percy, and Robert Penn Warren to recognize and encourage literature in the South. The Fellowship awards 11 literary prizes and inducts new members, making this event the place to discover up-and-coming voices in Southern literature. The Southern Lit Alliance's Celebration of Southern Literature attracts more than 1,000 readers and writers from all over the United States. It strives to maintain an informal atmosphere where conversations will thrive, inspired by a common passion for the written word. The Southern Lit Alliance (formerly the Arts & Education Council) started as one of 12 pilot agencies founded by a Ford Foundation grant in 1952. The Alliance is the only organization of the 12 still in existence. The Southern Lit Alliance celebrates Southern writers and readers through community education and innovative literary arts experiences."

CLARKSVILLE WRITERS CONFERENCE

1123 Madison St., Clarksville TN 37040. (931)551-8870. **E-mail:** artsandheritage@cdelightband.net. **Website:** www.artsandheritage.us/writers. **Contact:**

Ellen Kanervo. Annual conference held in the summer at Austin Peay State University. Features a variety of presentations on fiction, nonfiction, and more. Past presenting authors include Tom Franklin, Frye Gaillard, William Gay, Susan Gregg Gilmore, Will Campbell, John Seigenthaler Sr., Alice Randall, George Singleton, Alanna Nash, and Robert Hicks. "Our presentations and workshops are valuable to writers and interesting to readers."

COSTS Costs available online; prices vary depending on how long attendees stay and if they attend the banquet dinner.

ADDITIONAL INFORMATION Multiple literary agents are flown in to the event every year to meet with writers and take pitches.

CONFERENCE FOR WRITERS & ILLUSTRATORS OF CHILDREN'S BOOKS

Book Passage, 51 Tamal Vista Blvd., Corte Madera CA 94925. (415)927-0960, ext. 234. **E-mail:** lberkler@bookpassage.com. **Website:** www.bookpassage.com. Conference for writers and illustrators geared toward beginner and intermediate levels. Sessions cover such topics as the nuts and bolts of writing and illustrating, publisher's spotlight, market trends, developing characters, finding a voice, and the author-agent relationship.

GOTHAM WRITERS' WORKSHOP

writingclasses.com, 555 Eighth Ave., Suite 1402, New York NY 10018. (212)974-8377. **Fax:** (212)307-6325. **E-mail:** contact@gothamwriters.com. **Website:** www.writingclasses.com. Offers craft-oriented creative writing courses in general creative writing, fiction writing, screenwriting, nonfiction writing, article writing, stand-up comedy writing, humor writing, memoir writing, novel writing, children's book writing, playwriting, poetry, songwriting, mystery writing, science fiction writing, romance writing, television writing, article writing, travel writing, and business writing, as well as classes on freelancing, selling your screenplay, blogging, writing a nonfiction book proposal, and getting published. Also, the workshop offers a teen program, private instruction, and a mentoring program. Classes are held at various schools in New York as well as online. Online classes are held throughout the year. Agents and editors participate in some workshops.

ADDITIONAL INFORMATION See the website for courses, pricing, and instructors.

HAMPTON ROADS WRITERS CONFERENCE

P.O. Box 56228, Virginia Beach VA 23456. **E-mail:** hrwriters@cox.net. **Website:** hamptonroadswriters.org. Annual conference held in September. 2017 dates: September 14-16. Workshops cover fiction, nonfiction, memoir, poetry, and the business of getting published. A bookshop, 3 free contests with cash prizes, free evening networking social, and many networking opportunities will be available. Multiple literary agents are in attendance each year to meet with writers and hear ten-minute pitches. Much more information available on the website.

COSTS Costs vary. There are discounts for members, for early bird registration, for students, and more.

HIGHLAND SUMMER CONFERENCE

P.O. Box 7014, Radford University, Radford VA 24142. **E-mail:** tburriss@radford.edu; rbderrick@radford.edu. **Website:** tinyurl.com/q8z8ej9. **Contact:** Dr. Theresa Burriss; Ruth Derrick. The Highland Summer Writers' Conference is a 4-day lecture-seminar workshop combination conducted by well known guest writers. It offers the opportunity to study and practice creative and expository writing within the context of regional culture. The course is graded on a pass/fail basis for undergraduates and with letter grades for graduate students. It may be taken twice for credit. The evening readings are free and open to the public. Services at a reduced rate for continuing education credits or to simply participate.

HIGHLIGHTS FOUNDATION FOUNDERS WORKSHOPS

814 Court St., Honesdale PA 18431. (877)288-3410. **Fax:** (570)253-0179. **E-mail:** klbrown@highlightsfoundation.org. **Website:** highlightsfoundation.org. 814 Court St.Honesdale PA 18431. (570)253-1192. **Fax:** (570)253-0179. **E-mail:** contact@highlightsfoundation.org. **Website:** www.highlightsfoundation.org. **Contact:** Kent Brown, director. Workshops geared toward those interested in writing and illustrating for children, intermediate and advanced levels. Classes offered include: Writing Novels for Young Adults, Biography, Nonfiction Writing, Writing Historical Fiction, Wordplay: Writing Poetry for Children, Heart of the Novel, Nature Writing for Kids, Visual Art of the Picture Book, The Whole

Novel Workshop, and more (see website for updated list). Workshops held near Honesdale, PA. Workshops limited to between 8 and 14 people. Cost of workshops range from $695 and up. Cost of workshop includes tuition, meals, conference supplies and private housing. Call for application and more information. **Contact:** Kent L. Brown, Jr.. Offers more than three dozen workshops per year. Duration: 3-7 days. Attendance: limited to 10-14. Genre-specific workshops and retreats on children's writing, including fiction, nonfiction, poetry, and promotions. "Our goal is to improve, over time, the quality of literature for children by educating future generations of children's authors." Retreat center location: Highlights Founders' home in Boyds Mills, Pennsylvania. Coordinates pickup at local airport. Offers overnight accommodations. Participants stay in guest cabins on the wooded grounds surrounding Highlights Founders' home adjacent to the house/conference center.

○ "Applications will be reviewed and accepted on a first-come, first-served basis. Applicants must demonstrate specific experience in the writing area of the workshop they are applying for—writing samples are required for many of the workshops."

COSTS Prices vary based on workshop. Check website for details.

ADDITIONAL INFORMATION Some workshops require pre-workshop assignment. Brochure available for SASE, by e-mail, on website, by phone, by fax. Accepts inquiries by phone, fax, e-mail, SASE. Editors attend conference.

HOUSTON WRITERS GUILD CONFERENCE

P.O. Box 42255, Houston TX 77242. (281)736-7168. **E-mail:** info@houstonwritersguild.org. **Website:** houstonwritersguild.org. This annual conference, organized by the Houston Writers Guild, happens in the spring and has concurrent sessions and tracks on the craft and business of writing. Each year, multiple agents are in attendance taking pitches from writers.

COSTS Costs are different for members and nonmembers. Costs depend on how many days and events you sign up for.

ADDITIONAL INFORMATION There is a writing contest at the event. There is also a preconference

workshop the day before the event, for an additional cost.

IOWA SUMMER WRITING FESTIVAL

The University of Iowa, 250 Continuing Education Facility, University of Iowa, Iowa City IA 52242. (319)335-4160. **Fax:** (319)335-4039. **E-mail:** iswfestival@uiowa.edu. **Website:** www.iowasummerwritingfestival.org. Annual festival held in June and July. More than 100 workshops and more than 50 instructors. Workshops are 1 week or a weekend. Attendance is limited to 12 people per class, with more than 1,500 participants throughout the summer. Offers courses across the genres: novel, short story, poetry, essay, memoir, humor, travel, playwriting, screenwriting, writing for children, and women's writing. Held at the University of Iowa campus. Speakers have included Marvin Bell, Lan Samantha Chang, John Dalton, Hope Edelman, Katie Ford, Patricia Foster, Bret Anthony Johnston, and Barbara Robinette Moss. Accommodations available at area hotels. Information on overnight accommodations available by phone or on website.

ADDITIONAL INFORMATION Brochures are available in February. Inquire via e-mail or on website. "Register early. Classes fill quickly."

IWWG SPRING BIG APPLE CONFERENCE

(917)720-6959. **E-mail:** iwwgquestions@gmail.com. **Website:** www.iwwg.wildapricot.org. Annual conference held in New York in spring. 2017 dates: April 8-9. Includes writing workshops, author panel discussing publishing trends, book fair, agent panel, and one-on-one pitch sessions.

JAMES RIVER WRITERS CONFERENCE

2319 E. Broad St., Richmond VA 23223. (804)433-3790. **Fax:** (804)291-1466. **E-mail:** info@jamesriverwriters.org; fallconference@jamesriverwriters.org. **Website:** www.jamesriverwriters.org. Annual conference held in October. The event has master classes, agent pitching, editor pitching, critiques, sessions, panels, and more. Previous attending agents have included Kimiko Nakamura, Kaylee Davis, Peter Knapp, and more.

COSTS Check website for updated pricing.

KENTUCKY WRITERS CONFERENCE

Southern Kentucky Book Fest, Knicely Conference Center, 2355 Nashville Rd., Bowling Green KY 42101. (270)745-4502. **E-mail:** sara.volpi@wku.edu.

Website: www.sokybookfest.org. **Contact:** Sara Volpi. This event is entirely free to the public. 2017 date: April 21. Duration: 1 day. Part of the 2-day Southern Kentucky Book Fest. Authors who will be participating in the Book Fest on Saturday will give attendees at the conference the benefit of their wisdom on Friday. Free workshops on a variety of writing topics will be presented. Sessions run for 75 minutes, and the day begins at 9 a.m. and ends at 3:30 p.m. The conference is open to anyone who would like to attend, including high school students, college students, teachers, and the general public.

○ Since the event is free, interested attendees are asked to register in advance. Information on how to do so is on the website.

KINDLING WORDS EAST

Website: www.kindlingwords.org. Annual retreat held early in the year near Burlington, Vermont. 2017 dates: January 26-29. A retreat with three strands: writer, illustrator, and editor; professional level. Intensive workshops for each strand, and an open schedule for conversations and networking. Registration limited to approximately 70. Hosted by the four-star Inn at Essex (room and board extra). Participants must be published by a CCBC listed publisher, or if in publishing, occupy a professional position. Registration opens August 1 or as posted on the website, and fills quickly. Check website to see if spaces are available, to sign up to be notified when registration opens each year, or for more information. Inquire via contact form on the website.

KINDLING WORDS WEST

Website: www.kindlingwords.org. Annual retreat specifically for children's book writers held in spring out west. 2017 dates: March 21-28. 2017 location: Marble Falls, Texas. Kindling Words West is an artist's colony-style week with workshops by gifted teachers followed by a working retreat. Participants gather just before dinner to have white-space discussions; evenings include fireside readings, star gazing, and songs. Participants must be published by CBC-recognized publisher.

LA JOLLA WRITERS CONFERENCE

P.O. Box 178122, San Diego CA 92177. **E-mail:** akuritz@san.rr.com. **Website:** www.lajollawritersconference.com. **Contact:** Jared Kuritz, director. Annual conference held in fall. 2017 dates: October

27-29. Conference duration: 3 days. Attendance: 200 maximum. The LaJolla Writers Conference covers all genres and both fiction and nonfiction as well as the business of writing. "We take particular pride in educating our attendees on the business aspect of the book industry and have agents, editors, publishers, publicists, and distributors teach classes. There is unprecedented access to faculty. Our conference offers lecture sessions that run for 50 minutes and workshops that run for 110 minutes. Each block period is dedicated to either workshop or lecture-style classes, with 6-8 classes on various topics available each block. For most workshop classes, you are encouraged to bring written work for review. Literary agents from prestigious agencies such as the Andrea Brown Literary Agency, the Dijkstra Agency, the McBride Agency, Full Circle Literary Group, the Zimmerman Literary Agency, the Van Haitsma Literary Agency, the Farris Literary Agency, and more have participated in the past, teaching workshops in which they are familiarized with attendee work. Late night and early bird sessions are also available. The conference creates a strong sense of community, and it has seen many of its attendees successfully published."

COSTS $395 for full 2017 conference registration (doesn't include lodging or breakfast).

LEAGUE OF UTAH WRITERS' ANNUAL WRITER'S CONFERENCE

E-mail: luwriters@gmail.com. **Website:** www.leagueofutahwriters.org. **Contact:** Tim Keller. Annual spring and fall conferences. Faculty includes novelists, screenwriters, agents, and editors. Workshops geared toward beginner, intermediate, and advanced levels.

MIDWEST WRITERS WORKSHOP

(765)282-1055. **E-mail:** midwestwriters@yahoo.com. **Website:** www.midwestwriters.org. **Contact:** Jama Kehoe Bigger, director. Annual workshop held in July in east central Indiana. Writer workshops geared toward writers of all levels, including craft and business sessions. Topics include most genres. Faculty/speakers have included Joyce Carol Oates, George Plimpton, Clive Cussler, Haven Kimmel, William Kent Krueger, William Zinsser, John Gilstrap, Lee Martin, Jane Friedman, Chuck Sambuchino, and numerous best-selling mystery, literary fiction, young adult, and children's authors. Workshop also includes agent pitch sessions, ms evaluation, query letter critiques, and social media tutoring. Registration tentatively limited to 240.

COSTS $155-400. Most meals included.

ADDITIONAL INFORMATION Offers scholarships. See website for more information. Keep in touch with the MWW at facebook.com/midwestwriters and twitter.com/midwestwriters.

MISSOURI WRITERS' GUILD CONFERENCE

St. Louis MO **E-mail:** mwgconferenceinfo@gmail. com. **Website:** www.missouriwritersguild.org. **Contact:** Tricia Sanders, vice president/conference chair. Annual conference held in spring. 2017 dates: May 5-7. Writer and illustrator workshops geared to all levels. Open to students. "Gives writers the opportunity to hear outstanding speakers and to receive information on marketing, research, and writing techniques." Agents, editors, and published authors in attendance.

ADDITIONAL INFORMATION The primary contact individual changes every year, because the conference chair changes every year. See the website for contact info.

MOUNT HERMON CHRISTIAN WRITERS CONFERENCE

P.O. Box 413, Mount Hermon CA 95041. **E-mail:** info@mounthermon.org. **Website:** writers.mounthermon.org. Annual professional conference. 2017 dates: April 7-11. Average attendance: 450. Sponsored by and held at the 440-acre Mount Hermon Christian Conference Center near San Jose, California, in the heart of the coastal redwoods. "We are a broad-ranging conference for all areas of Christian writing, including fiction, nonfiction, fantasy, children's, teen, young adult, poetry, magazines, inspirational, and devotional writing. This is a working, how-to conference, with Major Morning tracks in all genres (including a track especially for teen writers), and as many as 20 optional workshops each afternoon. Faculty-to-student ratio is about 1 to 6. The bulk of our more than 70 faculty members are editors and publisher representatives from major Christian publishing houses nationwide." Speakers have included T. Davis Bunn, Debbie Macomber, Jerry Jenkins, Bill Butterworth, Dick Foth, and others.

MUSE AND THE MARKETPLACE

Grub Street, 162 Boylston St., 5th Floor, Boston MA 02116. (617)695-0075. **E-mail:** info@grubstreet. org. **Website:** museandthemarketplace.com. Grub Street's national conference for writers. Held held in the late spring, such as early May. 2017 dates: May 5-7. Conference duration: 3 days. Average attendance: 400. Dozens of agents are in attendance to meet writers and take pitches. The conference has workshops on all aspects of writing.

The Muse and the Marketplace is designed to give aspiring writers a better understanding of the craft of writing fiction and nonfiction, to prepare them for the changing world of publishing and promotion, and to create opportunities for meaningful networking. On all 3 days, prominent and nationally recognized established and emerging authors lead sessions on the craft of writing—the "muse" side of things—while editors, literary agents, publicists, and other industry professionals lead sessions on the business side—the "marketplace."

NORTH CAROLINA WRITERS' NETWORK FALL CONFERENCE

P.O. Box 21591, Winston-Salem NC 27120. (336)293-8844. **E-mail:** mail@ncwriters.org. **Website:** www.ncwriters.org. Annual conference held in November in different North Carolina venues. Average attendance: 250. This organization hosts 2 conferences: 1 in the spring and 1 in the fall. Each conference is a weekend full of workshops, panels, book signings, and readings (including open mic). There will be a keynote speaker, a variety of sessions on the craft and business of writing, and opportunities to meet with agents and editors. Special rates are usually available at the conference hotel, but attendees must make their own reservations.

COSTS Approximately $250 (includes 4 meals).

NORTHERN COLORADO WRITERS CONFERENCE

407 Cormorant Court, Fort Collins CO 80525. (970)227-5746. **E-mail:** april@northerncoloradowriters.com. **Website:** www.northerncoloradowriters. com. Annual conference held in Fort Collins. 2017 dates: May 5-6. Duration: 2-3 days. The conference features a variety of speakers, agents, and editors. There are workshops and presentations on fiction,

nonfiction, screenwriting, children's books, marketing, magazine writing, staying inspired, and more. Previous agents who have attended and taken pitches from writers include Jessica Regel, Kristen Nelson, Rachelle Gardner, Andrea Brown, Ken Sherman, Jessica Faust, Gordon Warnock, and Taylor Martindale. Each conference features more than 30 workshops from which to choose. Previous keynotes include Chuck Sambuchino, Andrew McCarthy, and Stephen J. Cannell. Conference hotel may offer rooms at a discounted rate.

COSTS Prices vary depending on a number of factors. See website for details.

ODYSSEY FANTASY WRITING WORKSHOP

P.O. Box 75, Mont Vernon NH 03057. (603)673-6234. **E-mail:** jcavelos@sff.net. **Website:** www.odysseyworkshop.org. **Contact:** Jeanne Cavelos. Saint Anselm College, 100 Saint Anselm Dr., Manchester NH 03102 Annual workshop held in June (through July). Conference duration: 6 weeks. Average attendance: 15. A workshop for fantasy, science fiction, and horror writers that combines an intensive learning and writing experience with in-depth feedback on students' mss. Held on the campus of Saint Anselm College in Manchester, New Hampshire. Speakers have included George R.R. Martin, Elizabeth Hand, Jane Yolen, Catherynne M. Valente, Holly Black, and Dan Simmons.

COSTS $2,025 tuition, $870 housing (double room), $1,740 housing (single room), $40 application fee, $600 food (approximate), $750 optional processing fee to receive college credit.

ADDITIONAL INFORMATION Students must apply and include a writing sample. Application deadline: April 8. Students' works are critiqued throughout the 6 weeks. Workshop information available in October. For brochure/guidelines, send SASE, e-mail, visit website, or call.

OHIO KENTUCKY INDIANA CHILDREN'S LITERATURE CONFERENCE

Northern Kentucky University, 405 Steely Library, Highland Heights KY 41099. (859)572-6620. **Fax:** (859)572-5390. **E-mail:** smithjen@nku.edu. **Website:** www.dearbornhighlandsarts.org/oki-conference-registration. **Contact:** Jennifer Smith. Annual conference held in November for writers and illustrators, geared toward all levels. Open to all. Emphasizes multicultural literature for children and young adults. Contact Jennifer Smith for more information.

COSTS $85; includes registration/attendance at all workshop sessions, continental breakfast, lunch, and author/illustrator signings. Manuscript critiques are available for an additional cost. E-mail or call for more information.

OKLAHOMA WRITERS' FEDERATION, INC. ANNUAL CONFERENCE

9800 South Hwy. 137, Miami OK 74354. **Website:** www.owfi.org. Annual conference held first weekend in May, just outside Oklahoma City. Writer workshops geared toward all levels. "The goal of the conference is to create good stories with strong bones. We will be exploring cultural writing and cultural sensitivity in writing." Several literary agents are in attendance each year to meet with writers and hear pitches.

COSTS Costs vary depending on when registrants sign up. Cost includes awards banquet and famous author banquet. Three extra sessions are available for an extra fee. Visit the event website for more information and a complete faculty list.

OUTDOOR WRITERS ASSOCIATION OF AMERICA ANNUAL CONFERENCE

615 Oak St., Suite 201, Missoula MT 59801. (406)728-7434. **E-mail:** info@owaa.org. **Website:** owaa.org. **Contact:** Jessica Seitz, conference and membership coordinator. Outdoor communicator workshops geared toward all levels. Annual three-day conference includes craft improvement seminars and newsmaker sessions. 2017 dates: June 24-26. Site: Duluth, Minnesota. Cost includes attendance at all workshops and meals.

COSTS Before April 28, $225 for members and $425 for nonmembers. After April 28, $249 for members and $449 for nonmembers. Single-day rates are also available.

OZARK CREATIVE WRITERS, INC. CONFERENCE

P.O. Box 9076, Fayetteville AR 72703. **E-mail:** ozarkcreativewriters1@gmail.com. **Website:** www.ozarkcreativewriters.com. The annual event is held in October at the Inn of the Ozarks, in the resort town of Eureka Springs, Arkansas. Approximately 200 writers attend each year; many also enter the creative writing competitions. Open to professional and amateur writers, workshops are geared toward all levels and all forms of the creative process and literary arts; sessions sometimes also include songwriting. Includes presentations by best-selling authors, editors, and agents. Offering writing competitions in all genres.

○ A full list of sessions and speakers is online. The conference usually has agents and/or editors in attendance to meet with writers.

PACIFIC COAST CHILDREN'S WRITERS WHOLE-NOVEL WORKSHOP: FOR ADULTS AND TEENS

P.O. Box 244, Aptos CA 95001. **Website:** www.childrenswritersworkshop.com. Annual conference held in fall. 2017 dates: Sept. 22-24. Offers semi-advanced through published writers an editor and/or agent critique on their full novel or 15-page partial. (The latter may include mid-book and synopsis critiques.) Focus is on craft as a marketing tool. Team-taught master classes (open clinic ms critiques) explore topics such as "Story Architecture and Arcs." Offers continuous close contact with faculty, who have included Andrea Brown (agent, president of Andrea Brown Literary) and Simon Boughton (vice president/executive editor of 3 Macmillan imprints). Attendance: 16 maximum. For the most critique options and early bird discount, submit e-application in May (dates on website); regisgtration is open until all places are filled. Content: character-driven upper middle-grade and young adult novels. Collegial; highly hands-on. Reading peer mss before master class observations and discussions maximizes learning. Usually at least one enrollee lands a book deal with faculty. A concurrent workshop is open to teens, who give adults smart target-reader feedback.

COSTS Visit website for tiered fees (includes lodging, meals), schedule, and more; e-mail Director Nancy Sondel via the contact form.

PENNWRITERS CONFERENCE

P.O. Box 685, Dalton PA 18414. **E-mail:** conferenceco@pennwriters.org; info@pennwriters.org. **Website:** pennwriters.org/conference. The Mission of Pennwriters, Inc., is to help writers of all levels, from the novice to the award-winning and multi-published, improve and succeed in their craft. The annual Pennwriters conference is held every year in May in Pennsylvania, switching between locations—Lancaster in even numbered years and Pittsburgh in odd numbered years. 2017 dates: May 19-21 at the

Pittsburgh Airport Marriott. Literary agents are in attendance to meet with writers. Costs vary. Pennwriters members in good standing get a slightly reduced rate.

○ As the official writing organization of Pennsylvania, Pennwriters has 8 different areas with smaller writing groups that meet. Each of these areas sometimes has their own, smaller event during the year in addition to the annual writing conference.

ADDITIONAL INFORMATION Sponsors contest. Published authors judge fiction in various categories. Agent/editor appointments are available on a first-come, first-served basis.

PHILADELPHIA WRITERS' CONFERENCE

P.O. Box 7171, Elkins Park PA 19027. (215)619-7422. **E-mail:** info@pwcwriters.org. **Website:** pwcwriters. org. Annual conference held in June. Duration: 3 days. Average attendance: 160-200. Conference covers many forms of writing: novel, short story, genre fiction, nonfiction book, magazine writing, blogging, juvenile, poetry. See website for details. Hotel may offer discount for early registration.

○ Offers 14 workshops, usually 4 seminars, several "manuscript rap" sessions, a Friday Roundtable Forum Buffet with speaker, and the Saturday Annual Awards Banquet with speaker. Attendees may submit mss in advance for criticism by the workshop leaders and are eligible to submit entries in more than 10 contest categories. Cash prizes and certificates are given to first and second place winners, plus full tuition for the following year's conference to first place winners.

ADDITIONAL INFORMATION Accepts inquiries by e-mail. Agents and editors attend the conference. Many questions are answered online.

PIKES PEAK WRITERS CONFERENCE

Pikes Peak Writers, P.O. Box 64273, Colorado Springs CO 80962. (719)244-6220. **E-mail:** registrar@pikespeakwriters.com. **Website:** www.pikespeakwriters.com/ppwc. Annual conference held in April. 2017 dates: April 28-30. Conference duration: 3 days. Average attendance: 300. Workshops, presentations, and panels focus on writing and publishing mainstream and genre fiction (romance, science fiction/fantasy, suspense/thrillers, action/adventure, mysteries, children's, young adult). Agents and editors are available for meetings with attendees on Saturday. Speakers have included Jeff Lindsay, Rachel Caine, and Kevin J. Anderson. Marriott Colorado Springs holds a block of rooms at a special rate for attendees until late March.

COSTS $395-465 (includes all 7 meals).

ADDITIONAL INFORMATION Readings with critiques are available on Friday afternoon. Registration forms are online; brochures are available in January. Send inquiries via e-mail.

PNWA SUMMER WRITERS CONFERENCE

Writers' Cottage, 317 NW Gilman Blvd. Suite 8, Issaquah WA 98027. (425)673-2665. **E-mail:** pnwa@pnwa.org. **Website:** www.pnwa.org. Annual conference held in July. 2017 dates: July 20-23. Duration: 4 days. Average attendance: 400. Attendees have the chance to meet agents and editors, learn craft from authors, and uncover marketing secrets. Speakers have included J.A. Jance, Sheree Bykofsky, Kimberley Cameron, Jennie Dunham, Donald Maass, Jandy Nelson, Robert Dugoni, and Terry Brooks.

ROCKY MOUNTAIN FICTION WRITERS COLORADO GOLD CONFERENCE

Rocky Mountain Fiction Writers, P.O. Box 711, Montrose CO 81402, USA. **E-mail:** conference@rmfw.org. **Website:** www.rmfw.org. Annual conference held in September. Duration: 3 days. Average attendance: 400+. Themes include general fiction, genre fiction, contemporary romance, mystery, science fiction/fantasy, mainstream, young adult, screenwriting, short stories, and historical fiction, as well as marketing and career management. 2017 keynote speakers are Diana Gabaldon, Sherry Thomas, and Lori Rader-Day. Past speakers have included Ann Hood, Robert J. Sawyer, Jeffery Deaver, William Kent Krueger, Margaret George, Jodi Thomas, Bernard Cornwell, Terry Brooks, Dorothy Cannell, Patricia Gardner Evans, Diane Mott Davidson, Constance O'Day, and Connie Willis. Approximately 8 editors and 8 agents attend annually. Special rates will be available at conference hotel.

COSTS Available on website.

ADDITIONAL INFORMATION Editor-conducted critiques are limited to 8 participants, with auditing available. Craft workshops include beginner through professional levels. Pitch appointments and book blurb critiques available at no charge. Also available for an extra charge are master classes, pitch coaching, query letter coaching, special critiques, and more.

ROCKY MOUNTAIN RETREATS FOR WRITERS & ARTISTS

Website: http://rmfw.org/writers-retreat/. P.O. Box 711, Montrose, CO 81402. (303) 331-2608. **E-mail:** retreat@rmfw.org. **Website:** http://rmfw.org/writers-retreat/. **Director:** Deborah DeBord. Writers workshops geared to all levels. Open to students. Includes information on releasing creative energy, identifying strengths and interests, balancing busy lives, marketing creative works. Annual conference. Registration limited to 30. Writing studio, weaving studio, private facilities available. Cost of workshop: $389; includes room, meals, materials, instruction. "Treat yourself to a week of mountain air, sun, and personal expression. Flourish with the opportunity for sustained work punctuated by structured experiences designed to release the artist's creative energies. Relax over candlelit gourmet meals followed by fireside discussions of the day's efforts. Discover the rhythm of filling the artistic well and drawing on its abundant resources."

RT BOOKLOVERS CONVENTION

81 Willoughby Street, Suite 701, Brooklyn NY 11201. **E-mail:** tere@rtconvention.com. **Website:** rtconvention.com. **Contact:** Tere Michaels. Annual conference with a varying location. 2017 conference: May 2-7, Atlanta. Features 200 workshops, agent and editor appointments, a Giant Book Fair, and more. More than 1,000 authors attend the event.

COSTS $495 for normal registration; $425 for industry professionals (agents, editors). Special discounted rate for readers, $450. Many other pricing options available. See website.

SAN DIEGO STATE UNIVERSITY WRITERS' CONFERENCE

SDSU College of Extended Studies, 5250 Campanile Dr., San Diego State University, San Diego CA 92182. (619)594-2099. **Fax:** (619)594-8566. **E-mail:** sdsuwritersconference@mail.sdsu.edu. **Website:** ces.sdsu.edu/writers. Annual conference held in January. 2017 dates: January 20-22. Conference duration: 2.5 days. Average attendance: 350. Covers fiction, nonfiction, scriptwriting, and e-books. Held at the San Diego Marriott Mission Valley Hotel. Each year the conference offers a variety of workshops for the beginner and advanced writers. This conference

allows writers to choose which workshops best suit their needs. In addition to the workshops, editor reading appointments and agent/editor consultation appointments are provided so attendees may meet with editors and agents one-on-one to discuss specific questions. A reception is offered Saturday immediately following the workshops, offering attendees the opportunity to socialize with the faculty in a relaxed atmosphere. In previous years, approximately 60 faculty members have attended. Attendees must make their own travel arrangements. A conference rate for attendees is available at the event hotel (Marriott Mission Valley Hotel).
COSTS $495-549. Extra costs for consultations.

SAN FRANCISCO WRITERS CONFERENCE

(415)673-0939. **E-mail:** barbara@sfwriters.org; sf-writerscon@aol.com.. **Website:** sfwriters.org. **Contact:** Barbara Santos, marketing director. 2017 dates: February 16-19. Annual conference held President's Day weekend in February. Average attendance: 700. "More than 100 top authors, respected literary agents, and major publishing houses are at the event so attendees can make face-to-face contact with all the right people. Writers of nonfiction, fiction, poetry, and specialty writing (children's books, cookbooks, travel, etc.) will all benefit from the event. There are important sessions on marketing, self-publishing, technology, and trends in the publishing industry. Plus, there's an optional session called Speed Dating with Agents where attendees can meet with more than 20 agents. Past speakers have included Jane Smiley, Debbie Macomber, Clive Cussler, Guy Kawasaki, Jennifer Crusie, R.L. Stine, Lisa See, Steve Berry, and Jacquelyn Mitchard. More than 20 agents and several editors from traditional publishing houses participate each year, and most will be available for meetings with attendees." The Intercontinental Mark Hopkins Hotel offers a discounted SFWC rate (based on availability). Call directly: (415)392-3434. The Mark is a historic landmark at the top of Nob Hill in San Francisco. The hotel is located so that everyone arriving at the Oakland or San Francisco airport can take the BART to either the Embarcadero or Powell Street exits, then walk or take a cable car or taxi directly to the hotel.

Keynoters for 2017: Heather Graham, William Bernhardt, John Perkins. Educational and social sessions featuring more than 120 presenters from the publishing world. Free editorial and PR consults, exhibitor hall, pitching and networking opportunities available throughout the four-day event. Also several free sessions offered to the public. See website for details or sign up for the SFWC Newsletter for updates.

COSTS Full registration is $795 (as of the 2017 event) with early bird registration discounts through February 1.

ADDITIONAL INFORMATION "Present yourself in a professional manner, and the contacts you will make will be invaluable to your writing career. Fliers, details, and registration information are online."

SANTA BARBARA WRITERS CONFERENCE

27 W. Anapamu St., Suite 305, Santa Barbara CA 93101. (805)568-1516. **E-mail:** info@sbwriters.com. **Website:** www.sbwriters.com. Annual conference held in June. 2017 dates: June 18-23. Average attendance: 200. Covers fiction, nonfiction, journalism, memoir, poetry, playwriting, screenwriting, travel writing, young adult, children's literature, humor, and marketing. Speakers have included Ray Bradbury, William Styron, Eudora Welty, James Michener, Sue Grafton, Charles M. Schulz, Clive Cussler, Fannie Flagg, Elmore Leonard, and T.C. Boyle. Agents will appear on a panel; in addition, there will be an agents and editors day that allows writers to pitch their projects in one-on-one meetings. Hyatt Santa Barbara.
COSTS Early conference registration is $575, and regular registration is $650.
ADDITIONAL INFORMATION Register online or contact for brochure and registration forms.

SCBWI; ANNUAL CONFERENCES ON WRITING AND ILLUSTRATING FOR CHILDREN

E-mail: scbwi@scbwi.org. **Website:** www.scbwi.org. **Contact:** Lin Oliver, conference director. Writer and illustrator workshops geared toward all levels. **Open to students.** Covers all aspects of children's book and magazine publishing—the novel, illustration techniques, marketing, etc. Annual conferences held in Los Angeles in April and in New York in February. Cost of conference includes all 4 days and one banquet meal. Write for more information or visit website.

These are very large events—SCBWI's biggest, and both events draw 50+ publishing professionals (agents and editors) as well as many authors.

SCBWI—ALASKA; EVENTS

Website: https://alaska.scbwi.org. P.O. Box 84988, Fairbanks AK 99708-4988. (907)474-2138. **E-mail:** statalias@icloud.com. **Website:** https://alaska.scbwi.org. **Conference Organizer:** Cherie Stihler. SCBWI Alaska holds an annual conference every year. Visit website for details.

SCBWI—ARIZONA; EVENTS

P.O. Box 26384, Scottsdale AZ 85255-0123. **E-mail:** RegionalAdvisor@scbwi-az.org. **Website:** http://arizona.scbwi.org. **Contact:** Michelle Parker-Rock, regional advisor. SCBWI Arizona will offer a variety of workshops, retreats, intensives, conferences, meetings, and other craft and industry-related events throughout the year. Open to members and nonmembers, published and nonpublished. Registration to major events is usually limited. Pre-registration always required. Visit website, write, or e-mail for more information.

SCBWI—AUSTIN CONFERENCE

E-mail: austin@scbwi.org. **Website:** austin.scbwi.org. **Contact:** Samantha Clark, regional advisor. Annual conference features a faculty of published authors and illustrators. Past years have featured National Book Award winner William Alexander, Caldecott Honors Liz Garton Scanlon and Molly Idle, *New York Times* best-selling author Cynthia Leitich Smith, and more. Editors and agents are in attendance to meet with writers. The schedule consists of keynotes and breakout sessions with tracks for writing (picture book and novel), illustrating, and professional development.

COSTS Costs vary for members, students and nonmembers, and discounted early-bird pricing is available. Visit website for full pricing options.

SCBWI BOLOGNA—BIENNIAL CONFERENCE

E-mail: kathleenahrens@gmail.com. **Website:** bologna.scbwi.org. Biennial conference held in even-numbered years. This is when SCBWI has a booth at the Bologna Book Fair, welcoming vistors from all over the world.

"Our next showcase will be 2018 where we will return with the Duelling Illustrators, the PAL showcase, and much, much more."

SCBWI—BRITISH ISLES; ILLUSTRATOR'S DAY (SPRING)/WRITER'S DAY (FALL)

Website: www.britishscbwi.org. (44)(208)249-9716. **E-mail:** ra@britishscbwi.org. **Website:** www.britishscbwi.org. **Regional Advisor:** Natascha Biebow. SCBWI Illustrator Coordinator: Anne-Marie Perks. Writer and illustrator conference geared toward beginner, intermediate, and advanced levels. Open to students. New Reader's Ahoy! Annual conference. Cost of conference: £220 for SCBWI members/£250 for nonmembers; includes tuition and lunch.

SCBWI—CALIFORNIA (SAN FRANCISCO/SOUTH); GOLDEN GATE CONFERENCE AT ASILOMAR

Website: http://sfsouth.scbwi.org. **Contact:** Naomi Kinsman, regional advisor. Annual conference. Welcomes published and not-yet-published writers and illustrators. Lectures and workshops are geared toward professionals and those striving to become professional. Program topics cover aspects of writing or illustrating, and marketing, from picture books to young adult novels. Past speakers include editors, agents, art directors, Newbery Award-winning authors, and Caldecott Award-winning illustrators. For more information, including exact costs and dates, visit website.

SCBWI—CANADA EAST

E-mail: canadaeast@scbwi.org; almafullerton@almafullerton.com. **Website:** www.canadaeast.scbwi.org. **Contact:** Alma Fullerton, regional advisor. Writer and illustrator events geared toward all levels. Usually offers one event in spring and another in the fall. Check website for updated information.

SCBWI—CAROLINAS; ANNUAL FALL CONFERENCE

P.O. Box 1216, Conover NC 28613. (919)967-2549. **Website:** http://carolinas.scbwi.org. **Website:** http://carolinas.scbwi.org. **E-mail:** scbwicarolinas@earthlink.net. **Regional Advisor:** Teresa Fannin. Annual Conference: The Power of Story. September 30-October 2, 2016 at the Crowne Plaza Hotel, Charlotte, NC. Past speakers included: Alvina Ling, senior editor, Little Brown Publishing; Liz Waniewski, editor, Dial Books for Young Readers; Alan Gratz, author,

The Brooklyn Nine; Chris Richman, agent, Upstart Crow Literary Agency; Steve Watkins, 2009 SCBWI Golden Kite Winner, Down Sand Mountain, 2009 debut Author Fran Slayton, *When the Whistle Blows*. Friday afternoon manuscript and portfolio critiques, workshops focusing on the art and craft of writing and illustrating for children visit https://carolinas.scbwi.org for more information.

➕ SCBWI CAROLINAS— SPRING RETREAT, THE ELEMENTS OF STORY

Website: https://carolinas.scbwi.org/events/from-picture-books-to-chapter-books/. April 4-10, 2016. Past speakers included Jennifer Rees, senior editor, Scholastic Books; Stacey Cantor, editor, Walker Books for Young Readers; Bruce Hale, author, The Chet Gecko series. Join us for a weekend of inspiring and informative talks on story in the peaceful seclusion of the center's woodland setting. For more information and registration visit our website at http://carolinas.scbwi.org

SCBWI—CENTRAL-COASTAL CALIFORNIA; FALL CONFERENCE

P.O. Box 1500, Simi Valley CA 93062. **E-mail:** cencal@scbwi.org. **Website:** cencal.scbwi.org. **Contact:** Mary Ann Fraser, regional advisor. Annual conference held in October. Geared to all levels. Speakers include editors, authors, illustrators, and agents. Fiction and nonfiction picture books, middle-grade, and young adult novels, and magazine submissions addressed. There is an annual writing contest in all genres plus illustration display. For fees and other information, e-mail or visit website.

SCBWI—COLORADO/WYOMING (ROCKY MOUNTAIN); EVENTS

E-mail: rmc@scbwi.org. **Website:** www.rmc.scbwi.org. **Contact:** Todd Tuell and Lindsay Eland, regional advisors. SCBWI Rocky Mountain chapter (Colorado/Wyoming) offers special events, schmoozes, meetings, and conferences throughout the year. Major events: Fall Conference (annual, September); Summer Retreat, "Big Sur in the Rockies" (bi- and tri-annual). More info on website.

SCBWI—EASTERN NEW YORK; FALLING LEAVES MASTER CLASS RETREAT

Silver Bay NY **E-mail:** easternny@scbwi.org. **Website:** easternny.scbwi.org; scbwieasternny.weebly.com/falling-leaves.html. **Contact:** Nancy Castaldo, regional advisor. P.O. Box 159, Valatie NY 12184

Annual master class retreat hosted by SCBWI Eastern New York and held in November in Silver Bay on Lake George. Holds ms and portfolio critiques, question-and-answer and speaker sessions, intensives, and more, with respected authors and editors. Theme varies each year between picture books, novels, and nonfiction. Applications accepted June 15 through August 15. See website for more information.

SCBWI—EASTERN PENNSYLVANIA

E-mail: donnaboock@hotmail.com; easternpascbwi@yahoo.com. **Website:** http://epa.scbwi.org; https://easternpennpoints.wordpress.com/. The Eastern Pennsylvania chapter of SCBWI plans conferences and local events that feature lessons on the craft of writing and illustrating books for children. Active members will have the opportunity to make connections to editors, agents, art directors and authors, and have the pleasure of meeting others who also love writing and/or illustrating for children.

SCBWI—FLORIDA; MID-YEAR WRITING WORKSHOP

12973 SW 112 Ct., Miami FL 33186. (305)382-2677. **E-mail:** lindabernfeld@gmail.com; gabytriana@gmail.com. **Website:** florida.scbwi.org. **Contact:** Linda Bernfeld, co-regional advisor. Annual workshop held in June in Orlando. Workshop is geared toward helping everyone hone their writing skills. Attendees choose one track and spend the day with industry leaders who share valuable information about that area of children's book writing. There are a minimum of 3 tracks, picture book, middle grade, and young adult. The 4th and 5th tracks are variable, covering subjects such as poetry, nonfiction, humor or writing for magazines. E-mail for more information.

SCBWI—FLORIDA; REGIONAL CONFERENCE

12973 SW 112 Ct., Miami FL 33186. (305)382-2677. **E-mail:** lindabernfeld@gmail.com; gabytriana@gmail.com. **Website:** https://florida.scbwi.org/events/2016_regional_conference/. **Contact:** Linda Bernfeld, regional advisor. Annual conference held in January in Miami. Past keynote speakers have included Linda Sue Park, Richard Peck, Bruce Coville, Bruce Hale, Arthur A. Levine, Judy Blume, Kate Dicamillo. The 3-day conference will have workshops

Friday afternoon and a field trip to Books and Books Friday evening.

SCBWI—ILLINOIS; PRAIRIE WRITERS DAY

E-mail: alicebmcginty@gmail.com. **Website:** http://illinois.scbwi.org. **Contact:** Alice McGinty, co-regional advisor. Full day of guest speakers, editors/agents TBD. Ms critiques available as well as breakout sessions on career and craft. See website for complete description. This event is usually held in the early summer.

SCBWI—IOWA CONFERENCES

E-mail: hecklit@aol.com. **Website:** http://iowa.scbwi.org/. **Contact:** Connie Heckert, regional advisor. Writer and illustrator workshops in all genres of children writing. The Iowa Region offers conferences of high quality events usually over a 3-day period with registration options. Holds spring and fall events on a regional level, and network events across that state. Individual critiques and portfolio review offerings vary with the program and presenters. For more information e-mail or visit website. Literary agents and editors are present at the events.

SCBWI—MICHIGAN; CONFERENCES

Website: http://michigan.scbwi.org. Three-day fall conference held in late-April to early-May. Workshops periodically. Speakers TBA. See website for details on all upcoming events.

SCBWI—MID-ATLANTIC; ANNUAL FALL CONFERENCE

P.O. Box 3215, Reston VA 20195. **E-mail:** midatlantic@scbwi.org. **Website:** midatlantic.scbwi.org/. **Contact:** Ellen R. Braaf, regional advisor. For updates and details, visit website. Registration limited to 250. Conference fills quickly. Includes continental breakfast and boxed lunch. Optional craft-focused workshops and individual consultations with conference faculty are available for additional fees.

○ This conference takes place in October. Previous conferences have been held in Sterling, Virginia.

SCBWI—MIDSOUTH FALL CONFERENCE

P.O. Box 396, Cordova TN 38088. **E-mail:** ktubb@comcast.net. **Website:** http://midsouth.scbwi.org. **Contact:** Kristin Tubb, regional advisor. Annual conference for writers and illustrators of all experience. Usually held in the fall (September). In the past, workshops were offered on Plotting Your Nov-

el, Understanding the Language of Editors, Landing an Agent, How to Prepare a Portfolio, Negotiating a Contract, The Basics for Beginners, and many others. Attendees are invited to bring a manuscript and/or art portfolio to share in the optional, no-charge critique group session. Illustrators are invited to bring color copies of their art (not originals) to be displayed in the illustrators' showcase. For an additional fee, attendees may schedule a 15-minute manuscript critique or portfolio critique by the editor, art director, or other expert consultant.

○ Some agents and editors attend to meet with writers.

SCBWI—MISSOURI; CHILDREN'S WRITER'S CONFERENCE

Website: http://missouri.scbwi.org/. **Contact:** Kimberly Piddington, regional advisor. Open to students. Speakers include editors, writers, agents, and other professionals. Topics vary from year to year, but each conference offers sessions for both writers and illustrators as well as for newcomers and published writers. Previous topics included: "What Happens When Your Manuscript is Accepted" by Dawn Weinstock, editor; "Writing—Hobby or Vocation?" by Chris Kelleher; "Mother Time Gives Advice: Perspectives from a 25 Year Veteran" by Judith Mathews, editor; "Don't Be a Starving Writer" by Vicki Berger Erwin, author; and "Words & Pictures: History in the Making," by author-illustrator Cheryl Harness. Annual conference held in Fall. For exact date(s), see the website.

SCBWI—NEW ENGLAND; ANNUAL CONFERENCE

Nashua NH 03063. **E-mail:** nescbwi2015@gmail.com. **Website:** http://newengland.scbwi.org. Conference is for all levels of writers and illustrators. Open to students. Offers many workshops at each conference, and often there is a multiday format. Examples of subjects addressed: manuscript development, revision, marketing your work, productive school visits, picture book dummy formatting, adding texture to your illustrations, etc. Annual conference held in Spring. Registration limited to 450. Check website for updated pricing. Details (additional speakers, theme, number of workshop choices, etc.) will be posted to website as they become available. Registration doesn't start until March. Opportunities for one-on-one manuscript critiques and portfolio reviews will be available at the conference.

⬤ Agents and editors in attendance to meet with writers.

SCBWI—NEW ENGLAND; WHISPERING PINES WRITER'S RETREAT

West Greenwich RI **E-mail:** whisperingpinesretreat@yahoo.com. **Website:** newengland.scbwi.org; www.whisperingpinesretreat.org. **Contact:** Kristin Russo and Pam Vaughan, event codirectors. Three-day retreat (with stays overnight) held annually in mid-to-late March. 2017 dates: March 17-19. Offers the opportunity to work intimately with professionals in an idyllic setting. Attendees will work with others who are committed to quality children's literature in small groups and will benefit from a 30-minute one-on-one critique with a mentor. Also includes mentors' presentations and an intimate question-and-answer session, Team Kid Lit Jeopardy with prizes, and more. Retreat limited to 32 full-time participants.

SCBWI—NEW JERSEY; ANNUAL SUMMER CONFERENCE

New Jersey NJ **Website:** newjersey.scbwi.org. **Contact:** Cathleen Daniels, regional advisor. This weekend conference is held in the summer. Highlights include multiple one-on-one critiques; "how to" workshops for every level; first page sessions; agent pitches; and interaction with the faculty of editors, agents, art director, and authors. On Friday, attendees can sign up for writing intensives or register for illustrators' day with the art directors. Published authors attending the conference can sign up to participate in the bookfair to sell and autograph their books; illustrators have the opportunity to display their artwork. Attendees have the option to participate in group critiques after dinner on Saturday evening and attend a mix-and-mingle with the faculty on Friday night. Meals are included with the cost of admission. Conference is known for its high ratio of faculty to attendees and interaction opportunities.

SCBWI—NEW MEXICO; HANDSPRINGS: A CONFERENCE FOR CHILDREN'S WRITERS AND ILLUSTRATORS

PO Box 1084, Socorro NM **E-mail:** carolinestarr@yahoo.com. **Website:** http://newmexico.scbwi.org.

Contact: Linda Tripp, regional advisor; Caroline Starr, assistant advisor. Annual conference for beginner and intermediate writers and illustrators. Conference features editors, agents, art directors and/or illustrators and authors. Offers intensive craft-based workshops and large-group presentations. See website for details. Monthly offerings include Schmoozes, Critique Groups, and Illustrator Meetings.

SCBWI—NORTHERN OHIO; ANNUAL CONFERENCE

E-mail: vselvaggio@windstream.net. **Website:** http://ohionorth.scbwi.org. **Contact:** Victoria A. Selvaggio, regional advisor. Northern Ohio's conference is crafted for all levels of writers and illustrators of children's literature. "Conference costs will be posted on our website with registration information. SCBWI members receive a discount. Additional fees apply for late registration, critiques, or portfolio reviews. Cost includes an optional Friday evening Opening Banquet from 6-10 p.m. with a keynote speaker; Saturday event from 8:30 a.m. to 5 p.m. which includes breakfast snack, full-day conference with headliner presentations, general sessions, breakout workshops, lunch, panel discussion, bookstore, and autograph session. The Illustrator Showcase is open to all attendees at no additional cost. Grand door prize drawn at the end of the day Saturday, is free admission to the following year's conference. Further information, including Headliner Speakers will be posted on our website."

⬤ Literary agents and acquiring editors are brought in every year.

SCBWI—OREGON CONFERENCES

E-mail: suhligford@gmail.com; oregon@scbwi.org. **Website:** http://oregon.scbwi.org. **Contact:** Sue Ford, co-regional advisor; Judith Gardiner, co-regional advisor. Writer and illustrator workshops and presentations geared toward all levels. Invites editors, art directors, agents, attorneys, authors, illustrators, and others in the business of writing and illustrating for children. Faculty members offer craft presentations, workshops, first-page sessions and individual critiques as well as informal networking opportunities. Critique group network opportunities for local group meetings and regional retreats; see website for details. Two main events per year: Writers and Illustrators Retreat: held near Portland in October; Spring Conference: Held in the Portland area (2 day event in May (one-day attendance is permitted). SCBWI Oregon is a regional chapter of the Society of Children's Book Writers and Illustrators. SCBWI Members receive a discount for all events. Oregon and South Washington members get preference.

SCBWI—POCONO MOUNTAINS RETREAT

E-mail: easternpascbwi@yahoo.com. **Website:** http://easternpennpoints.wordpress.com; http://epa.scbwi.org. Annual retreat held in early May. Faculty addresses craft, web design, school visits, writing, illustration, and publishing. Registration limited to 150. For information, online registration and brochure, visit website.

SCBWI—ROCKY MOUNTAIN; ANNUAL FALL CONFERENCE

Website: http://rmc.scbwi.org. Marriott Denver West, Golden CO. **E-mail:** rmc@scbwi.org. **Website:** http://rmc.scbwi.org.

SCBWI—SOUTHERN BREEZE; SPRINGMINGLE

P.O. Box 26282, Birmingham AL 35260. **Website:** http://southern-breeze.scbwi.org. **Contact:** Kathleen Bradshaw, co-regional advisor. Writer and illustrator conference geared toward intermediate, advanced and professional levels. Speakers typically include agents, editors, authors, art directors, illustrators. Open to SCBWI members, nonmembers, and college students. Annual conference held in Atlanta, Georgia. Usually held in late March. Registration limited. Manuscript critiques and portfolio reviews available for additional fee. Preregistration is necessary. Visit website for more information.

SCBWI—SOUTHERN BREEZE; WRITING AND ILLUSTRATING FOR KIDS

P.O. Box 26282, Birmingham AL 35260. **E-mail:** klbradshaw@kathleenbradshaw.com. **Website:** http://southern-breeze.scbwi.org. **Contact:** Kathleen Bradshaw, co-regional advisor; Claudia Pearson, co-regional advisor. Fall event. Writer and illustrator workshops geared toward all levels. Open to SCBWI members, nonmembers and college students. All sessions pertain specifically to the production and support of quality children's literature. This 1-day conference offers about 30 workshops

on craft and the business of writing. Picture books, chapter books, novels covered. Entry and professional level topics addressed by published writers and illustrators, editors and agents. Annual fall conference is held in early October in the Birmingham, AL, metropolitan area. All workshops are limited to 30 or fewer people. Preregistration is necessary. Some workshops fill quickly. Mss critiques and portfolio reviews are available for an additional fee; mss must be sent early. Registration is by mail ahead of time. Ms and portfolio reviews must be prepaid and scheduled.

⬤ SCBWI—TAIWAN; EVENTS

Website: http://taiwan.scbwi.org. **E-mail:** shunu2100@yahoo.com.tw. **Website:** http://taiwan.scbwi.org. **Regional Advisor:** Shu-Nu (Candy) Yen. Writer and illustrator workshops geared toward intermediate level. Open to students. Topics emphasized: "We regularly hold critiques for writers and for illustrators, and invite authors and illustrators visiting Taipei to give talks. See our website for more information."

SCBWI—WESTERN WASHINGTON STATE; CONFERENCE & RETREAT

E-mail: info@scbwi-washington.org; danajsullivan@comcast.net. **Website:** http://chinookupdate.blogspot.com; http://wwa.scbwi.org. **Contact:** Dana Arnim, co-regional advisor; Dana Sullivan, co-regional advisor. The Western Washington region of SCBWI hosts an annual conference in April, a retreat in November, and monthly meetings and events throughout the year. Visit the website for complete details.

SCBWI WINTER CONFERENCE ON WRITING AND ILLUSTRATING FOR CHILDREN

4727 Wilshire Blvd #301, Los Angeles CA 90010. (323)782-1010. **Fax:** (323)782-1892. **E-mail:** scbwi@scbwi.org. **Website:** www.scbwi.org. **Contact:** Stephen Mooser. Annual conference held in February. Average attendance: 1,000. Conference is to promote writing and illustrating for children (picture books, middle-grade, and young adult) and to give participants an opportunity to network with professionals. Covers financial planning for writers, marketing your book, art exhibitions, and more. The winter conference is held in Manhattan.

COSTS See website for current cost and conference information.

ADDITIONAL INFORMATION SCBWI also holds an annual summer conference in August in Los Angeles.

SCBWI—WISCONSIN; FALL RETREAT FOR WORKING WRITERS

E-mail: scbwijamieswenson@gmail.com;. **Website:** http://wisconsin.scbwi.org. Writer and illustrator conference geared toward all levels. All sessions pertain to children's writing/illustration. Faculty addresses writing/illustrating/publishing. Annual conference held in the fall (usually October). Visit website for information.

SOUTH CAROLINA WRITERS WORKSHOP

4711 Forest Dr., Suite 3, P.M.B. 189, Columbia SC 29206. **E-mail:** scwwliaison@gmail.com. **Website:** www.myscwa.org. Conference held in October at the Metropolitan Conference Center in Columbia. Held almost every year. Conference duration: 3 days. Features critique sessions, open mic readings, and presentations from agents and editors. More than 50 different workshops for writers to choose from, dealing with all subjects of writing craft, writing business, getting an agent, and more. Agents will be in attendance.

SOUTH COAST WRITERS CONFERENCE

Southwestern Oregon Community College, P.O. Box 590, 29392 Ellensburg Ave., Gold Beach OR 97444. (541)247-2741. **Fax:** (541)247-6247. **E-mail:** scwc@socc.edu. **Website:** www.socc.edu/scwriters. **Contact:** Karim Shumaker. Annual conference held Presidents' Day weekend in February. 2017 dates: February 17-18. Conference duration: 2 days. Covers fiction, poetry, children's, nature, screenwriting, songwriting, and marketing. 2017 keynote speaker: Jamie Duclos-Yourdon. Presenters include C. Lill Ahrens, Jennifer Burns Bright, Bill Cameron, Nina Kiriki Hoffman, Rita Hosking, Janet Sumner Johnston, Vinnie Kinsella, Michael Lamanna, and Bruce Holland Rogers. List of local motels that offer discounts to conference participants is available on request.

COSTS Friday workshop cost is $55. Saturday conference cost is $60 before January 31 and $70 after. Fish fry lunch is $14 if purchased in advance, or $15 at the door.

SOUTHEASTERN WRITERS ASSOCIATION— ANNUAL WRITERS WORKSHOP

E-mail: purple@southeasternwriters.org. **Website:** www.southeasternwriters.org. Annual 4-day workshop, held in Epworth By The Sea, St. Simons Island, Georgia. Open to all writers. 2017 dates: June 16-20. Tuition includes 3 free evaluation conferences with instructors (minimum 2-day registration). Offers contests with cash prizes. Manuscript deadlines: May 15 for contests and May 25 for evaluations. Lodging at Epworth and throughout St. Simons Island. Visit website for more information.

Instruction offered for novel writing, nonfiction, young adult, commercial writing, screenwriting, marketing/social media. Includes agent in residence/publisher in residence.

COSTS Cost of workshop: $445 for 4 days or lower prices for daily tuition or early bird special. (See website for tuition pricing.)

SPACE COAST WRITERS GUILD ANNUAL CONFERENCE

P.O. Box 262, Melbourne FL 32902. **E-mail:** stilley@scwg.org. **Website:** www.scwg.org. Conference held along the east coast of central Florida in the last weekend of January, though necessarily every year. Check website for up-to-date information. Conference duration: 2 days. Average attendance: 150+. This conference is hosted in Florida and features a variety of presenters on all topics. Critiques are available for a price, and agents in attendance will take pitches from writers. Previous presenters have included Debra Dixon, Davis Bunn (writer), Ellen Pepus (agent), Jennifer Crusie, Chuck Sambuchino, Madeline Smoot, Mike Resnick, Christina York, Ben Bova, and Elizabeth Sinclair. The conference is hosted in a beachside hotel, with special room rates available.

COSTS Check website for current pricing.

STEAMBOAT SPRINGS WRITERS CONFERENCE

A Day For Writers, Steamboat Springs Arts Council, Eleanor Bliss Center for the Arts at the Depot, P.O. Box 774284, Steamboat Springs CO 80477. (970)879-9008. **E-mail:** info@steamboatwriters.com. **Website:** www.steamboatwriters.com. **Contact:** Barbara Sparks. 1001 13th Street, Steamboat Springs CO 80487. Annual event held on a Saturday.

2017 date: July 22. Workshops geared toward intermediate levels. Open to professionals and amateurs alike. Average attendance: 35-40 (registration limited, conference fills quickly). Optional preconference gathering Friday night. Meet-and-greet buffet social followed by Five Minutes of Fame session for conference participants to share their work. 2017 instructors Laura Resau (young adult author) and Laura DiSilverio (mystery focus) will each lead 2 workshops.

○ "Our conference emphasizes instruction within the seminar format. Novices and polished professionals benefit from the individual attention and camaraderie which can be established within small groups. A pleasurable and memorable learning experience is guaranteed by the relaxed and friendly atmosphere of the old train depot."

COSTS $60 early registration; $75 after May 27. Registration fee includes continental breakfast and luncheon.

☼ SURREY INTERNATIONAL WRITERS' CONFERENCE

SiWC, 151-10090 152 St., Suite 544, Surrey British Columbia V3R 8X8, Canada. **E-mail:** kathychung@siwc.ca. **Website:** www.siwc.ca. **Contact:** Kathy Chung, proposals contact and conference coordinator. Annual professional development writing conference outside Vancouver, Canada, held every October. Writing workshops geared toward beginner, intermediate, and advanced levels. More than 80 workshops and panels, on all topics and genres, plus preconference master classes. Blue Pencil and agent/editor pitch sessions included. Different conference price packages available. Check the conference website for more information. This event has many literary agents in attendance taking pitches. Annual fiction writing contest open to all with $1000 prize for first place. Conference registration opens in early June every year. Register early to avoid disappointment as the conference is likely to sell out.

TEXAS MOUNTAIN TRAIL WRITERS SPRING RETREAT

E-mail: asktmtw@texasmountaintrailwriters.org. **Website:** texasmountaintrailwriters.org. HC 65 Box 20P, Alpine TX 79830. (432)364-2399. **E-mail:** asktmtw@texasmountaintrailwriters.org. **President:** Jackie Siglin. Writer and illustrator work-shops geared toward beginner, intermediate, and advanced levels. Open to students. Topics emphasized include: inside information from editors of children's magazines; children's illustrator hints on collaboration; children's writer tips toward publication. Other genres are also covered. Conference held in April. Registration limited to 30-35. Writing facilities available: large comfortable conference room, nearby dining, mountain tourist attractions. Check website for updated information. "Nearby attractions include McDonald Observatory, Ft. Davis, and Big Bend National Park." Writer and illustrator workshops geared toward beginner, intermediate, and advanced levels.

TEXAS WRITING RETREAT

Navasota TX **E-mail:** paultcuclis@gmail.com. **Website:** www.texaswritingretreat.com. **Contact:** Paul Cuclis, coordinator. The Texas Writing Retreat is an intimate event with a limited number of attendees. 2017 dates: January 11-16. Held on a private residence ranch an hour outside of Houston, the retreat has an agent and editor in attendance teaching. All attendees get to pitch the attending agent. Meals, excursions, and amenities are included. This is a unique event that combines craft sessions, business sessions, time for writing, relaxation, and more. The retreat is not held every year; it's best to check the website.

COSTS Costs vary per event. There are different pricing options for those staying on-site versus commuters.

◑ THE UNIVERSITY OF WINCHESTER WRITERS' FESTIVAL

University of Winchester, Winchester Hampshire S022 4NR, United Kingdom. (44)(0)1962-827238. **E-mail:** judith.heneghan@winchester.ac.uk. **Website:** www.writersfestival.co.uk. **Contact:** Judith Heneghan, festival director. The 36th Winchester Writers' Festival (2017) takes place on June 16-18 at the University of Winchester, offering inspiration, learning, and networking for new and emerging writers working in all forms and genres. Choose from 18 day-long workshops and 28 talks, plus book up to 4 one-to-one appointments per attendee with leading literary agents, commissioning editors, and award-winning authors to help you harness your creative ideas, turn them into marketable work, and pitch to publishing professionals. If you cannot attend, you may still enter one of our nine writing competitions. Enjoy a creative writing weekend in Winchester, the oldest city in England. Only one hour from London. To view festival details, including all the competition details, please go to the official event website. Booking opens in February. Onsite student single ensuite accommodation available. Also, a range of hotels and bed and breakfasts nearby in the city.

COSTS See festival program.

ADDITIONAL INFORMATION Lunch, and tea/coffee/cake included in the booking cost. Dinner can be booked separately. All dietary needs catered for.

TMCC WRITERS' CONFERENCE

Truckee Meadows Community College, 7000 Dandini Blvd., Reno NV 89512. (775)673-7111. **E-mail:** wdce@tmcc.edu. **Website:** wdce.tmcc.edu. Annual conference held in April. 2017 date: April 8. Average attendance: 150. Conference focuses on strengthening mainstream/literary fiction and nonfiction works and how to market them to agents and publishers. Site: Truckee Meadows Community College in Reno. "There is always an array of speakers and presenters with impressive literary credentials, including agents and editors." Speakers have included Chuck Sambuchino, Sheree Bykofsky, Andrea Brown, Dorothy Allison, Karen Joy Fowler, James D. Houston, James N. Frey, Gary Short, Jane Hirschfield, Dorrianne Laux, and Kim Addonizio. Literary agents are on site to take pitches from writers. Contact the conference manager to learn about accommodation discounts.

ADDITIONAL INFORMATION "The conference is open to all writers, regardless of their level of experience. Brochures are available online and mailed in January. Send inquiries via e-mail."

UNICORN WRITERS CONFERENCE

17 Church Hill Rd., Redding CT 06896, USA. (203)938-7405. **E-mail:** unicornwritersconference@gmail.com. **Website:** www.unicornwritersconference.com. **Contact:** Jan L. Kardys, chair. This writers conference draws upon its close proximity to New York and pulls in over 40 literary agents and 15 major New York editors to pitch each year. There are manuscript review sessions (40 pages equals 30 minutes with an agent/editor), query/manuscript review sessions, and 6 different workshops every hour. Cost: $325, includes all workshops and 3 meals.

Held at Reid Castle, Purchase, New York. Directions available on event website.

"The forty pages for manuscript reviews are read in advance by your selected agents/editors, but follow the submission guidelines on the website. Check the genre chart for each agent and editor before you make your selection."

COSTS $325 includes all workshops (6 every hour to select on the day of the conference), gift bag, and 3 meals. Additional cost for manuscript reviews: $60 each.

ADDITIONAL INFORMATION The first self-published authors will be featured on the website, and the bookstore will sell their books at the event.

UNIVERSITY OF WISCONSIN AT MADISON WRITERS INSTITUTE

21 N. Park St., Madison WI 53715. (608)265-3972. **E-mail:** laurie.scheer@wisc.edu. **Website:** uwwritersinstitute.wisc.edu. Annual conference. 2017 dates: March 24-26. Conference on fiction and nonfiction held at the University of Wisconsin at Madison. Guest speakers are published authors and publishing executives. Agents and editors take pitches.

COSTS $195-345, depending on discounts and if you attend one day or multiple days.

WESLEYAN WRITERS CONFERENCE

Wesleyan University, 294 High St., Room 207, Middletown CT 06459. (860)685-3604. **Fax:** (860)685-2441. **E-mail:** agreene@wesleyan.edu. **Website:** www.wesleyan.edu/writing/conference. **Contact:** Anne Greene, director. Annual conference held in June. 2017 dates: June 14-18. Average attendance: 100. Focuses on the novel, fiction techniques, short stories, poetry, screenwriting, nonfiction, literary journalism, memoir, mixed media work, and publishing. The conference is held on the campus of Wesleyan University, in the hills overlooking the Connecticut River. Features a faculty of award-winning writers, seminars, and readings of new fiction, poetry, nonfiction, and mixed media forms—as well as guest lectures on a range of topics including publishing. Both new and experienced writers are welcome. Participants may attend seminars in all genres. Speakers have included Esmond Harmsworth (Zachary Shuster Harmsworth), Daniel Mandel (Sanford J. Greenburger Associates), Amy Williams (ICM and Collins McCormick), and many others. Agents will be speaking and available for meetings with attendees. Participants are often successful in finding agents and publishers for their mss. Wesleyan participants are also frequently featured in the anthology *Best New American Voices*. Meals are provided on campus. Lodging is available on campus or in town.

ADDITIONAL INFORMATION Ms critiques are available but not required.

WINTER POETRY & PROSE GETAWAY

Murphy Writing of Stockton University, 35 S. Dr. Martin Luther King Blvd., Atlantic City NJ 08401, USA. (609)626-3596. **E-mail:** info@murphywriting. com. **Website:** www.stockton.edu/wintergetaway. **Contact:** Amanda Murphy. Annual January conference at the Jersey Shore. January 13-16, 2017. "This is not your typical writers conference. Advance your craft and energize your writing at the Winter Getaway. Enjoy challenging and supportive workshops, insightful feedback, and encouraging community. Choose from small, intensive workshops in memoir, novel, young adult, nonfiction, screenwriting, and poetry." Room packages at the historic Stockton Seaview Hotel are available.

❍   "At most conferences, writers listen to talks and panels and sit in sessions where previously written work is discussed. At the Getaway, they write. Most workshops are limited to 10 or fewer participants. By spending the entire weekend in one workshop, participants will venture deeper into their writing, making more progress than they thought possible."

COSTS See website or call for current fee information.

ADDITIONAL INFORMATION Previous faculty has included Julianna Baggott, Christian Bauman, Laure-Anne Bosselaar, Kurt Brown, Mark Doty (National Book Award winner), Stephen Dunn (Pulitzer Prize winner), Dorianne Laux, Carol Plum-Ucci, James Richardson, Mimi Schwartz, Terese Svoboda, and more.

WRITE-BY-THE-LAKE WRITER'S WORKSHOP & RETREAT

21 N. Park St., 7th Floor, Madison WI 53715. (608)262-3447. **E-mail:** christine.desmet@wisc.edu. **Website:** www.dcs.wisc.edu/lsa/writing. **Contact:** Christine DeSmet, director. Open to all writers and

students; 12 workshops for all levels. Includes classes for full novel critique and one master class for 50 pages. Usually held the third week of June on the University of Wisconsin-Madison campus (fourth week in 2017). Registration limited to 15 each section; fewer in master classes. Writing facilities available; computer labs, wifi in all buildings and on the outdoor lakeside terrace. E-mail for more information. "Registration opens every January for following June."

COSTS $385 before May 15; $435 after that. Additional cost for master classes and college credits. Cost includes instruction, welcome luncheon, and pastry/coffee each day.

❍ WRITE CANADA

The Word Guild, Suite 226, 245 King George Rd., Brantford, Ontario N3R 7N7, Canada. **E-mail:** writecanada@thewordguild.com. **Website:** thewordguild.com/events/write-canada. Annual conference in Ontario for Christian writers of all types and at all stages. Conference duration: 3 days. Offers solid instruction, stimulating interaction, exciting challenges, and worshipful community.

❍   "Write Canada is the nation's largest Christian writers' conference held annually. Each year hundreds of writers and editors—authors, journalists, columnists, bloggers, poets and playwrights—gather to hone their craft. Over the past three decades, Write Canada has successfully equipped writers and editors, beginner to professional, from all across North America."

WRITE IN THE HARBOR

Website: continuingedtacoma.com/writeintheharbor. 3993 Hunt St., Gig Harbor WA 98335. (253)460-2424. **Website:** continuingedtacoma.com/writeintheharbor. Annual conference held in fall. Offers workshops geared toward beginner, intermediate, advanced, and professional levels. Includes welcome reception, keynote speaker, and several presenters. Registration limited to 150. Cost of conference: $129 after August 1; $159 after September 16. Write for more information. Annual conference held in fall. Offers workshops geared toward beginner, intermediate, advanced, and professional levels. Includes welcome reception, keynote speaker, and several presenters. Registration limited to 150.

COSTS $129 after August 1; $159 after September 16.

WRITE ON THE SOUND

WOTS, City of Edmonds Arts Commission, Frances Anderson Center, 700 Main St., Edmonds WA 98020. (425)771-0228. **E-mail:** wots@edmondswa. gov. **Website:** www.writeonthesound.com. **Contact:** Laurie Rose or Frances Chapin. Small, affordable annual conference focused on the craft of writing. Held the first weekend in October. 2017 dates: October 6-8. Conference duration: 2.5 days. Average attendance: 275. Features over 30 presenters, keynote, literary contest, ms critiques, roundtable discussions, book signing reception, on-site bookstore, and opportunity to network with faculty and attendees. Edmonds is located just north of Seattle on the Puget Sound. Best Western Plus/Edmonds Harbor Inn.

Past attendee says, "I came away from every session with ideas to incorporate into my own writer's toolbox. The energy was wonderful because everyone was there for a single purpose: to make the most of a weekend for writers, whatever the level of expertise. I can't thank all the organizers, presenters, and volunteers enough for a wonderful experience."

COSTS $80-155 (not including optional fees).

ADDITIONAL INFORMATION Schedule posted on website late spring/early summer. Registration opens mid-July. Review the schedule and register early. Attendees are required to select the sessions they wish to attend at the time of registration. Registration fills quickly, and day-of, on-site registration is not available. Waiting lists for conference and manuscript appointments are available.

WRITE-TO-PUBLISH CONFERENCE

WordPro Communication Services, 9118 W. Elmwood Dr., Suite 1G, Niles IL 60714. (847)296-3964. **E-mail:** lin@writetopublish.com. **Website:** www. writetopublish.com. **Contact:** Lin Johnson, director. Annual conference. 2017 dates: June 14-17. Average attendance: 175. Conference is focused on the Christian market and includes classes for writers at all levels. Open to high school students. Site: Wheaton College, Wheaton, Illinois (Chicago area). This is not a function of Wheaton College. Campus residence hall rooms available. See the website for current information and costs.

ADDITIONAL INFORMATION Conference information available in January. For details, visit website, or e-mail brochure@writetopublish.com. Accepts inquiries by e-mail, phone.

WRITING AND ILLUSTRATING FOR YOUNG READERS CONFERENCE

1480 E. 9400 S., Sandy UT 84093. **E-mail:** staff@wifyr.com. **Website:** www.wifyr.com. Brigham Young University, 348 Harman Continuing Education Bldg. Provo UT 84602-1532. (801)442-2568. **Fax:** (801)422-0745. **E-mail:** cw348@byu.edu. **Website:** http://wifyr.byu.edu. Annual workshop held in June. Five-day workshop designed for people who want to write for children or teenagers. Participants focus on a single market during daily four-hour morning writing workshops: picture books, book-length fiction (novels), fantasy/science fiction, nonfiction, mystery, beginning writing, or illustration. Afternoon workshop sessions feature a variety of topics of interest to writers for all youth ages. Workshop cost: $439—includes all workshop and breakout sessions plus a banquet on Thursday evening. Afternoon-only registration available; participants may attend these sessions all five days for a fee of $109. Attendance at the Thursday evening banquet is included in addition to the afternoon mingle, plenary, and breakout sessions. Annual workshop held in June. 2017 dates: June 12-16. Duration: 5 days. Average attendance: more than 100. Learn how to write, illustrate, and publish in the children's and young adult markets. Beginning and advanced writers and illustrators are tutored in a small-group workshop setting by published authors and artists and receive instruction from and network with editors, major publishing house representatives, and literary agents. Afternoon attendees get to hear practical writing and publishing tips from published authors, literary agents, and editors. Site: Waterford School in Sandy, UT. Speakers have included John Cusick, Stephen Fraser, Alyson Heller, and Ruth Katcher. A block of rooms is available at the Best Western Cotton Tree Inn in Sandy, UT, at a discounted rate. This rate is good as long as there are available rooms. Guidelines and registration are on the website.

ADDITIONAL INFORMATION There is an online form to contact this event.

WRITING FOR THE SOUL

Jerry B. Jenkins Christian Writers Guild, P.O. Box 88288, Black Forest CO 80908. (866)495-7551. **Fax:** (719)494-1299. **E-mail:** jerry@jerryjenkins.com. **Website:** www.jerryjenkins.com. Conferences as announced, covering fiction, nonfiction, and online writing. Nationally known, best-selling authors as keynote speakers, hosted by Jerry B. Jenkins. See website for pricing, locations, dates, and accommodations.

WYOMING WRITERS CONFERENCE

Cheyenne WY **E-mail:** president@wyowriters.org. **Website:** wyowriters.org. **Contact:** Chris Williams. This is a statewide writing conference for writers of Wyoming and neighboring states. Each year, multiple published authors, editors, and literary agents are in attendance to meet with writers and take pitches.

CONTESTS, AWARDS, & GRANTS

Publication is not the only way to get your work recognized. Contests and awards can also be great ways to gain recognition in the industry. Grants, offered by organizations like the Society of Children's Book Writers and Illustrators (SCBWI), offer monetary recognition to writers, giving them more financial freedom as they work on projects.

When considering contests or applying for grants, be sure to study guidelines and requirements. Regard entry deadlines as gospel and follow the rules to the letter.

Note that some contests require nominations. For published authors and illustrators, competitions provide an excellent way to promote your work. Your publisher may not be aware of local competitions such as state-sponsored awards—if your book is eligible, have the appropriate person at your publishing company nominate or enter your work for consideration.

To select potential contests and grants, read through the listings that interest you, then send for more information about the types of written or illustrated material considered and other important details. A number of contests offer information through websites given in their listings.

If you are interested in knowing who has received certain awards in the past, check your local library or bookstores or consult *Children's Books: Awards & Honors*, compiled and edited by the Children's Book Council (www.cbcbooks.org). Many bookstores have special sections for books that are Caldecott and Newbery Medal winners. Visit the American Library Association website, www.ala.org, for information on the Caldecott, Newbery, Coretta Scott King, and Printz Awards. Visit www.hbook.com for information on The Boston Globe-Horn Book Award. Visit www.scbwi.org/awards.htm for information on The Golden Kite Award.

JANE ADDAMS CHILDREN'S BOOK AWARDS

Jane Addams Peace Association, 777 United Nations Plaza, 6th Floor, New York NY 10017. (212)652-8830. **E-mail:** info@janeaddamspeace.org. **Website:** www.janeaddamspeace.org. **Contact:** Heather Palmer, co-chair. The Jane Addams Children's Book Awards are given annually to the children's books published the preceding year that effectively promote the cause of peace, social justice, world community, and the equality of the sexes and all races as well as meeting conventional standards for excellence. Books eligible for this award may be fiction, poetry, or nonfiction. Books may be any length. Entries should be suitable for ages 2-12. See website for specific details on guidelines and required book themes. Deadline: December 31. Judged by a national committee of WILPF members concerned with children's books and their social values is responsible for making the changes each year.

ALCUIN SOCIETY BOOK DESIGN AWARDS

P.O. Box 3216, Vancouver, British Columbia V6B 3X8, Canada. (604)732-5403. **E-mail:** awards@alcuinsociety.com; info@alcuinsociety.com. **Website:** www.alcuinsociety.com. **Contact:** Leah Gordon. The Alcuin Society Awards for Excellence in Book Design in Canada is the only national competition for book design in Canada. Winners are selected from books designed and published in Canada. Awards are presented annually at appropriate ceremonies held in each year. Winning books are exhibited nationally and internationally at the Tokyo, Frankfurt, and Leipzig Book Fairs, and are Canada's entries in the international competition in Leipzig, "Book Design from all over the World" in the following spring. Submit previously published material from the year before the award's call for entries. Submissions made by the publisher, author or designer (Canadian). Deadline: March 1. **Prizes: 1st, 2nd, and 3rd in each category (at the discretion of the judges).** Judged by professionals and those experienced in the field of book design.

AMERICAN ASSOCIATION OF UNIVERSITY WOMEN AWARD IN JUVENILE LITERATURE

4610 Mail Service Center, Raleigh NC 27699-4610. (919)807-7290. **E-mail:** michael.hill@ncdcr.gov. **Website:** www.ncdcr.gov. **Contact:** Michael Hill, awards coordinator. Annual award. Book must be published during the year ending June 30. Submissions made by author, author's agent, or publisher. SASE for contest rules. Author must have maintained either legal residence or actual physical residence, or a combination of both, in the state of North Carolina for 3 years immediately preceding the close of the contest period. Only published work (books) eligible. Recognizes the year's best work of juvenile literature by a North Carolina resident. Deadline: July 15. **Prize: Awards a cup to the winner and winner's name inscribed on a plaque displayed within the North Carolina Office of Archives and History.** Judged by three-judge panel. Competition receives 10-15 submissions per category.

HANS CHRISTIAN ANDERSEN AWARD

Nonnenweg 12, Postfach Basel CH-4009, Switzerland. **E-mail:** liz.page@ibby.org. **E-mail:** ibby@ibby.org. **Website:** www.ibby.org. **Contact:** Liz Page, director. The Hans Christian Andersen Award, awarded every two years by the International Board on Books for Young People (IBBY), is the highest international recognition given to an author and an illustrator of children's books. The Author's Award has been given since 1956, the Illustrator's Award since 1966. Her Majesty Queen Margrethe II of Denmark is the Patron of the Hans Christian Andersen Awards. The awards are presented at the biennial congresses of IBBY. Awarded to an author and to an illustrator, living at the time of the nomination, who by the outstanding value of their work are judged to have made a lasting contribution to literature for children and young people. The complete works of the author and of the illustrator will be taken into consideration in awarding the medal, which will be accompanied by a diploma. Candidates are nominated by National Sections of IBBY in good standing. **Prize: Awards medals according to literary and artistic criteria.** Judged by the Hans Christian Andersen Jury.

MARILYN BAILLIE PICTURE BOOK AWARD

The Canadian Children's Book Centre, 40 Orchard View Blvd., Suite 217, Toronto, Ontario M4R 1B9, Canada. (416)975-0010, ext. 222. **Fax:** (416)975-8970. **E-mail:** meghan@bookcentre.ca. **Website:** www.bookcentre.ca. **Contact:** Meghan Howe. The

Baillie Picture Book Award honors excellence in the illustrated picture book format. To be eligible, the book must be an original work in English, aimed at children ages 3-8, written and illustrated by Canadians and first published in Canada. Eligible genres include fiction, nonfiction, and poetry. Books must be published between Jan. 1 and Dec. 31 of the previous calendar year. New editions or re-issues of previously published books are not eligible for submission. Send 5 copies of title along with a completed submission form. Deadline: mid-December annually. **Prize: $20,000.**

MILDRED L. BATCHELDER AWARD

Website: http://www.ala.org/alsc/awardsgrants/. The Batchelder Award is given to the most outstanding children's book originally published in a language other than English in a country other than the United States, and subsequently translated into English for publication in the US. Visit website for terms and criteria of award. The purpose of the award, a citation to an American publisher, is to encourage international exchange of quality children's books by recognizing US publishers of such books in translation. Deadline: December 31.

JOHN AND PATRICIA BEATTY AWARD

E-mail: tbronzan@sonoma.lib.ca.us. **Website:** http://www.cla-net.org/?page=113. **Contact:** Tiffany Bronzan, award chair. The California Library Association's John and Patricia Beatty Award, sponsored by Baker & Taylor, honors the author of a distinguished book for children or young adults that best promotes an awareness of California and its people. Must be a children's or young adult books published in the previous year, set in California, and highlight California's cultural heritage or future. Send title suggestiosn to the committee members. Deadline: January 31. **Prize: $500 and an engraved plaque.** Judged by a committee of CLA members, who select the winning title from books published in the US during the preceding year.

⊙ THE GEOFFREY BILSON AWARD FOR HISTORICAL FICTION FOR YOUNG PEOPLE

The Canadian Children's Book Centre, 40 Orchard View Blvd., Suite 217, Toronto, Ontario M4R 1B9, Canada. (416)975-0010, ext. 222. **Fax:** (416)975-8970. **Website:** www.bookcentre.ca. **Contact:** Meghan Howe. Awarded annually to reward excellence in the writing of an outstanding work of his-

torical fiction for young readers, by a Canadian author, published in the previous calendar year. Open to Canadian citizens and residents of Canada for at least 2 years. Books must be published between January 1 and December 31 of the previous year. Books must be first foreign or first Canadian editions. Autobiographies are not eligible. Jury members will consider the following: historical setting and accuracy, strong character and plot development, well-told, original story, and stability of book for its intended age group. Send 5 copies of the title along with a completed submission form. Deadline: mid-December annaully. **Prize: $5,000.**

THE IRMA S. AND JAMES H. BLACK AWARD

Bank Street College of Education, 610 W. 112th St., New York NY 10025-1898. (212)875-4458. **Fax:** (212)875-4558. **E-mail:** kfreda@bankstreet.edu. **Website:** http://bankstreet.edu/center-childrens-literature/irma-black-award/. **Contact:** Kristin Freda. Award give to an outstanding book for young children—a book in which text and illustrations are inseparable, each enhancing and enlarging on the other to produce a singular whole. Entries must have been published during the previous calendar year. Publishers submit books. Submit only one copy of each book. Does not accept unpublished mss. Deadline: mid-December. **Prize: A scroll with the recipient's name and a gold seal designed by Maurice Sendak.** Judged by a committee of older children and children's literature professionals. Final judges are first-, second-, and third-grade classes at a number of cooperating schools.

⊙ ANN CONNOR BRIMER BOOK AWARD

(902)490-2742. **Website:** www.atlanticbookawards. ca/. **Contact:** Laura Carter, Atlantic Book Awards Festival Coordinator. In 1990, the Nova Scotia Library Association established the Ann Connor Brimer Award for writers residing in Atlantic Canada who have made an outstanding contribution to writing for Atlantic Candian young people. Author must be alive and residing in Atlantic Canada at time of nomination. Book intended for youth up to the age of 15. Book in print and readily available. Fiction or nonfiction (except textbooks). Book must have been published within the previous year. **Prize: $2,000. Two shortlisted titles: $250 each.**

BUCKEYE CHILDREN'S BOOK AWARD

Website: www.bcbookaward.info. **Contact:** Christine Watters, president. The Buckeye Childeren's Book Award Program is designed to encourage children to read literature critically, to promote teacher and librarian involvement in children's literature programs, and to commend authors of such literature, as well as to promote the use of libraries. Open to Ohio students. Award offered every year. Students may only nominate books published in the previous 2 years (for paperbacks, check the original hardcover publication date), and the book must be originally published in the US. A book in a series that has previously won the award are not eligible for nonfiction. Deadline: March 10. Nominations for the following year's contest begins on March 15 and continues year-round.

RANDOLPH CALDECOTT MEDAL

50 E. Huron, Chicago IL 60611-2795. (312)944-7680. **Fax:** (312)440-9374. **E-mail:** alsc@ala.org; lschulte@ala.org. **Website:** www.ala.org. **Contact:** Laura Schulte-Cooper, program officer. The Caldecott Medal was named in honor of nineteenth-century English illustrator Randolph Caldecott. It is awarded annually by the Association for Library Service to Children, a division of the American Library Association, to the artist of the most distinguished American picture book for children. Illustrator must be US citizen or resident. Must be published year preceding award. SASE for award rules. Entries are not returned. Honors the artist of the most outstanding picture book for children published in the US. Deadline: December 31.

CALIFORNIA YOUNG PLAYWRIGHTS CONTEST

Playwrights Project, 3675 Ruffin Rd., Suite 330, San Diego CA 92123-1870, USA. (858)384-2970. **Fax:** (858)384-2974. **E-mail:** write@playwrightsproject. org. **Website:** http://www.playwrightsproject.org/programs/contest/. **Contact:** Cecelia Kouma, Executive Director. Annual contest open to Californians under age 19. Annual contest. "Our organization and the contest is designed to nurture promising young writers. We hope to develop playwrights and audiences for live theater. We also teach playwriting." Submissions are required to be unpublished and not produced professionally. Submissions made by the author. SASE for contest rules and entry form.

Scripts must be a minimum of 10 standard typewritten pages; send 2 copies. Scripts will *not* be returned. If requested, entrants receive detailed evaluation letter. Guidelines available online. Deadline: June 1. **Prize: Scripts will be produced in spring at a professional theatre in San Diego. Writers submitting scripts of 10 or more pages receive a detailed script evaluation letter upon request.** Judged by professionals in the theater community, a committee of 5-7; changes somewhat each year.

CASCADE WRITING CONTEST & AWARDS

Oregon Christian Writers, 1075 Willow Lake Road N., Keizer Oregon 97303. **E-mail:** cascade@oregonchristianwriters.org. **E-mail:** cascade@oregonchristianwriters.org. **Website:** http://oregonchristianwriters.org/. **Contact:** Marilyn Rhoads and Julie McDonald Zander. The Cascade Awards are presented at the annual Oregon Christian Writers Summer Conference (held at the Red Lion on the River in Portland, Oregon, each August) attended by national editors, agents, and professional authors. The contest is open for both published and unpublished works in the following categories: contemporary fiction book, historical fiction book, speculative fiction book, nonfiction book, memoir book, young adult/middle grade fiction book, young adult/middle grade nonfiction book, children's chapter book and picture book (fiction and nonfiction), poetry, devotional, article, column, story, or blog post. Two additional special Cascade Awards are presented each year: the Trailblazer Award to a writer who has distinguished him/herself in the field of Christian writing; and a Writer of Promise Award for a writer who demonstrates unusual promise in the field of Christian writing. For a full list of categories, entry rules, and scoring elements, visit website. Guidelines and rules available on the website. Entry forms will be available on the first day for entry. Annual multi-genre competition to encourage both published and emerging writers in the field of Christian writing. Deadline: March 31. Submissions period begins February 14. **Prize: Award certificate and pin presented at the Cascade Awards ceremony during the Oregon Christian Writers Annual Summer Conference. Finalists are listed in the conference notebook and winners are listed online. Cascade Trophies are awarded to the recipients of the Trailblazer and Writer of Promise Awards.** Judged by published authors, editors, librarians, and retail book store owners and employees. Final judging by editors, agents, and published authors from the Christian publishing industry.

CHILDREN'S AFRICANA BOOK AWARD

Outreach Council of the African Studies Association, c/o Rutgers University -Livingston campus, 54 Joyce Kilmer Ave., Piscataway NJ 08854, USA. (703)549-8208; (301)585-9136. **E-mail:** africaaccess@aol.com. **E-mail:** Harriet@AfricaAccess-Review.org. **Website:** www.africaaccessreview. org. **Contact:** Brenda Randolph, chairperson. The Children's Africana Book Awards are presented annually to the authors and illustrators of the best books on Africa for children and young people published or distributed in the US. The awards were created by the Outreach Council of the African Studies Association (ASA) to dispel stereotypes and encourage the publication and use of accurate, balanced children's materials about Africa. The awards are presented in 2 categories: Young Children and Older Readers. Entries must have been published in the calendar year previous to the award. Work submitted for awards must be suitable for children ages 4-18; a significant portion of books' content must be about Africa; must by copyrighted in the calendar year prior to award year; must be published or distributed in the US. Books should be suitable for children and young adults, ages 4-18. A significant portion of the book's content should be about Africa. Deadline: January 31 of the award year. Judged by African Studies and Children's Literature scholars. Nominated titles are read by committee members and reviewed by external African Studies scholars with specialized academic training.

CHILDREN'S BOOK GUILD AWARD FOR NONFICTION

E-mail: theguild@childrensbookguild.org. **Website:** www.childrensbookguild.org. Annual award. "One doesn't enter. One is selected. Our jury annually selects one author for the award." Honors an author or illustrator whose total work has contributed significantly to the quality of nonfiction for children. **Prize: Cash and an engraved crystal paperweight.** Judged by a jury of Children's Book Guild specialists, authors, and illustrators.

CHRISTIAN BOOK AWARD® PROGRAM

Evangelical Christian Publishers Association, 9633 S. 48th St., Suite 195, Phoenix AZ 85044. (480)966-3998. **Fax:** (480)966-1944. **E-mail:** info@ecpa.org. **Website:** www.ecpa.org. **Contact:** Stan Jantz, ED. The Evangelical Christian Publishers Association (ECPA) recognizes quality and encourages excellence by presenting the ECPA Christian Book Awards® (formerly known as Gold Medallion) each year. Categories include Christian Living, Biography & Memoir, Faith & Culture, Children, Young People's Literature, Devotion & Gift, Bibles, Bible Reference Works, Bible Study, Ministry Resources and New Author. All entries must be evangelical in nature and submitted through an ECPA member publisher. Books must have been published in the calendar year prior to the award. Publishing companies submitting entries must be ECPA members in good standing. See website for details. The Christian Book Awards® recognize the highest quality in Christian books and is among the oldest and most prestigious awards program in Christian publishing. Submission period runs September 1-30. Judged by ECPA members, who are experts, authors, and retailers with years of experience in their field.

⚫ Book entries are submitted by ECPA member publishers according to criteria including date of publication and category.

⚫ CLA YOUNG ADULT BOOK AWARD

1150 Morrison Dr., Suite 400, Ottawa, Ontario K2H 8S9, Canada. (613)232-9625. **Fax:** (613)563-9895. **E-mail:** cshea@cbvrsb.ca. **Website:** www.cla.ca. **Contact:** Carmelita Cechetto-Shea, chair. This award recognizes an author of an outstanding English language Canadian book which appeals to young adults between the ages of 13 and 18. To be eligible for consideration, the following must apply: it must be a work of fiction (novel, collection of short stories, or graphic novel), the title must be a Canadian publication in either hardcover or paperback, and the author must be a Canadian citizen or landed immigrant. The award is given annually, when merited, at the Canadian Library Association's annual conference. Deadline: December 31. **Prize: $1,000.**

COLORADO BOOK AWARDS

Colorado Humanities & Center for the Book, 7935 E. Prentice Ave., Suite 450, Greenwood Village CO 80111. (303)894-7951. **Fax:** (303)864-9361. **E-mail:**

bess@coloradohumanities.org. **Website:** www.coloradohumanities.org. **Contact:** Bess Maher. An annual program that celebrates the accomplishments of Colorado's outstanding authors, editors, illustrators, and photographers. Awards are presented in at least ten categories including anthology/collection, biography, children's, creative nonfiction, fiction, history, nonfiction, pictorial, poetry, and young adult. To be eligible for a Colorado Book Award, a primary contributor to the book must be a Colorado writer, editor, illustrator, or photographer. Current Colorado residents are eligible, as are individuals engaged in ongoing literary work in the state and authors whose personal history, identity, or literary work reflect a strong Colorado influence. Authors not currently Colorado residents who feel their work is inspired by or connected to Colorado should submit a letter with his/her entry describing the connection. Deadline: January 9.

CRICKET LEAGUE

P.O. Box 300, Peru IL 61354. **E-mail:** cricket@cricketmedia.com. **Website:** www.cricketmagkids.com. Cricket League contests encourage creativity and give young people an opportunity to express themselves in writing, drawing, painting, or photography. There is a contest in each issue. Possible categories include story, poetry, art, or photography. Each contest relates to a specific theme described on each *Cricket* issue's Cricket League page and on the website. Signature verifying originality, age, and address of entrant and permission to publish required. Entries which do not relate to the current month's theme cannot be considered. Unpublished submissions only. Cricket League rules, contest theme, and submission deadline information can be found in the current issue of *Cricket* and via website. Deadline: The 25th of each month. **Prize: Certificates.** Judged by *Cricket* editors.

CWW ANNUAL WISCONSIN WRITERS AWARDS

Council for Wisconsin Writers, 4964 Gilkeson Rd, Waunakee WI 53597. **E-mail:** karlahuston@gmail.com. **Website:** www.wiswriters.org. **Contact:** Geoff Gilpin, president and annual awards co-chair; Karla Huston, secretary and annual awards co-chair; Sylvia Cavanaugh, annual awards co-chair; Edward Schultz, annual awards co-chair, Erik Richardson, annual awards co-chair. Offered annually for work published by Wisconsin writers during the previous calendar year. Nine awards: Major Achievement (presented in alternate years); short fiction; short nonfiction; nonfiction book; poetry book; fiction book; children's literature; Lorine Niedecker Poetry Award; Christopher Latham Sholes Award for Outstanding Service to Wisconsin Writers (presented in alternate years); Essay Award for Young Writers. Open to Wisconsin residents. Entries may be submitted via postal mail only. See website for guidelines and entry forms. Deadline: January 31. Submissions open on November 1. **Prizes: First place prizes: $500. Honorable mentions: $50.** List of judges available on website.

MARGARET A. EDWARDS AWARD

50 East Huron St., Chicago IL 60611-2795. (312)280-4390 or (800)545-2433. **Fax:** (312)280-5276. **E-mail:** yalsa@ala.org. **Website:** www.ala.org/yalsa/edwards. **Contact:** Nichole O'Connor. Annual award administered by the Young Adult Library Services Association (YALSA) of the American Library Association (ALA) and sponsored by *School Library Journal* magazine. Awarded to an author whose book or books, over a period of time, have been accepted by young adults as an authentic voice that continues to illuminate their experiences and emotions, giving insight into their lives. The book or books should enable them to understand themselves, the world in which they live, and their relationship with others and with society. The book or books must be in print at the time of the nomination. Submissions must be previously published no less than 5 years prior to the first meeting of the current Margaret A. Edwards Award Committee at Midwinter Meeting. Nomination form is available on the YALSA website. Deadline: December 1. **Prize: $2,000.** Judged by members of the Young Adult Library Services Association.

SHUBERT FENDRICH MEMORIAL PLAYWRITING CONTEST

Pioneer Drama Service, Inc., P.O. Box 4267, Englewood CO 80155. (303)779-4035. **Fax:** (303)779-4315. **E-mail:** editors@pioneerdrama.com. **E-mail:** submissions@pioneerdrama.com. **Website:** www.pioneerdrama.com. **Contact:** Lori Conary, submissions editor. Annual competition that encourages the development of quality theatrical material for educational, community and children's theatre markets. Previously unpublished submissions only. Only considers mss with a running time between 20-90 minutes. Open to all writers not currently published by Pioneer Drama Service. Guidelines available online. No entry fee. Cover letter, SASE for return of ms, and proof of production or staged reading must accompany all submissions. Deadline: Ongoing contest; a winner is selected by June 1 each year from all submissions received the previous year. **Prize: $1,000 royalty advance in addition to publication.** Judged by editors.

DOROTHY CANFIELD FISHER CHILDREN'S BOOK AWARD

Midstate Library Service Center, Dorothy Canfield Fisher Book Award Committee, c/o Vermont Department of Libraries, 109 State St., Montpelier VT 05609. (802)828-6954. **E-mail:** grace.greene@state. vt.us. **Website:** www.dcfaward.org. **Contact:** Mary Linney, chair. Annual award to encourage Vermont children to become enthusiastic and discriminating readers by providing them with books of good quality by living American or Canadian authors published in the current year. E-mail for entry rules. Titles must be original work, published in the US, and be appropriate to children in grades 4-8. The book must be copyrighted in the current year. It must be written by an American author living in the US or Canada, or a Canadian author living in Canada or the US. Deadline: December of year book was published. **Prize: Awards a scroll presented to the winning author at an award ceremony.** Judged by children, grades 4-8, who vote for their favorite book.

☯ THE NORMA FLECK AWARD FOR CANADIAN CHILDREN'S NONFICTION

The Canadian Children's Book Centre, 40 Orchard View Blvd., Suite 217, Toronto, Ontario M4R 1B9, Canada. (416)975-0010 ext. 222. **Fax:** (416)975-8970. **E-mail:** meghan@bookcentre.ca. **Website:** www. bookcentre.ca. **Contact:** Meghan Howe. The Norma Fleck Award was established by the Fleck Family Foundation to recognize and raise the profile of exceptional nonfiction books for children. Offered annually for books published between January 1 and December 31 of the previous calendar year. Open to Canadian citizens or landed immigrants. Books must be first foreign or first Canadian editions. Nonfiction books in the following categories are eligible: culture and the arts, science, biography,

history, geography, reference, sports, activities, and pastimes. Deadline: mid-December annually. **Prize: $10,000. The award will go to the author unless 40% or more of the text area is composed of original illustrations, in which case the award will be divided equally between author and illustrator.**

FLICKER TALE CHILDREN'S BOOK AWARD

Morton Mandan Public Library, 609 W. Main St., Mandan ND 58554. **E-mail:** laustin@cdln.info. **Website:** www.ndla.info/flickertale. **Contact:** Linda Austin. Award gives children across the state of North Dakota a chance to vote for their book of choice from a nominated list of 20: 4 in the picture book category; 4 in the intermediate category; 4 in the juvenile category (for more advanced readers); 4 in the upper grade level nonfiction category. Also promotes awareness of quality literature for children. Previously published submissions only. Submissions nominated by librarians and teachers across the state of North Dakota. Deadline: April 1. **Prize: A plaque from North Dakota Library Association and banquet dinner.** Judged by children in North Dakota.

DON FREEMAN ILLUSTRATOR GRANTS

4727 Wilshire Blvd Suite 301, Los Angeles CA 90010. (323)782-1010. **Fax:** (323)782-1892. **E-mail:** grants@ scbwi.org; sarahbaker@scbwi.org. **Website:** www. scbwi.org. **Contact:** Sarah Baker. The grant-in-aid is available to both full and associate members of the SCBWI who, as artists, seriously intend to make picture books their chief contribution to the field of children's literature. Applications and prepared materials are available in October. Grant awarded and announced in August. SASE for award rules and entry forms. SASE for return of entries. Enables picture book artists to further their understanding, training, and work in the picture book genre. Deadline: March 31. Submission period begins March 1. **Prize: Two grants of $1,000 each awarded annually. One grant to a published illustrator and one to a prepublished illustrator.**

THEODOR SEUSS GEISEL AWARD

Association for Library Service to Children, Division of the American Library Association, 50 E. Huron, Chicago IL 60611. (800)545-2433. **E-mail:** alscawards@ala.org. **Website:** www.ala.org. The Theodor Seuss Geisel Award is given annually to the author(s) and illustrator(s) of the most distinguished American book for beginning readers published in English in the United States during the preceding year. The award is to recognize the author(s) and illustrator(s) who demonstrate great creativity and imagination in his/her/their literary and artistic achievements to engage children in reading. Terms and criteria for the award are listed on the website. Entry will not be returned. Deadline: December 31. **Prize: Medal, given at awards ceremony during the ALA Annual Conference.**

GOLDEN KITE AWARDS

Society of Children's Book Writers and Illustrators (SCBWI), SCBWI Golden Kite Awards, 8271 Beverly Blvd., Los Angeles CA 90048-4515. (323)782-1010. **Fax:** (323)782-1892. **E-mail:** bonniebader@sbcwi. org. **Website:** www.scbwi.org. Given annually to recognize excellence in children's literature in 4 categories: fiction, nonfiction, picture book text, and picture book illustration. Books submitted must be published in the previous calendar year. Both individuals and publishers may submit. Submit 4 copies of book. Submit to one category only, except in the case of picture books. Must be a current member of the SCBWI. Deadline: December 1. **Prize: One Golden Kite Award Winner and one Honor Book will be chosen per category. Winners and Honorees will receive a commemorative poster also sent to publishers, bookstores, libraries, and schools; a press release; an announcement on the SCBWI website; and on SCBWI Social Networks.**

☉ GOVERNOR GENERAL'S LITERARY AWARDS

Canada Council for the Arts, 150 Elgin St., P.O. Box 1047, Ottawa, Ontario K1P 5V8, Canada. 1-800-263-5588, ext. 5573. **Website:** ggbooks.ca. The Canada Council for the Arts provides a wide range of grants and services to professional Canadian artists and art organizations in dance, media arts, music, theatre, writing, publishing, and the visual arts. Books must be first edition literary trade books written, translated, or illustrated by Canadian citizens or permanent residents of Canada and published in Canada or abroad in the previous year. In the case of translation, the original work must also be a Canadian-authored title. For complete eligibility criteria, deadlines, and submission procedures, please visit the website at www.canadacouncil.ca. The Governor General's Literary Awards are given annually for the best English-language and French-language work in each of 7 categories, including fiction, non-fiction, poetry, drama, children's literature (text), children's literature (illustrated books), and translation. Deadline: Depends on the book's publication date. See website for details. **Prize: Each GG winner receives $25,000. Nonwinning finalists receive $1,000. Publishers of the winning titles receive a $3,000 grant for promotional purposes.** Evaluated by fellow authors, translators, and illustrators. For each category, a jury makes the final selection.

GUGGENHEIM FELLOWSHIPS

John Simon Guggenheim Memorial Foundation, 90 Park Ave., New York NY 10016. (212)687-4470. **E-mail:** fellowships@gf.org. **Website:** www.gf.org. Often characterized as "midcareer" awards, Guggenheim Fellowships are intended for men and women who have already demonstrated exceptional capacity for productive scholarship or exceptional creative ability in the arts. Fellowships are awarded through two annual competitions: one open to citizens and permanent residents of the US and Canada, and the other open to citizens and permanent residents of Latin America and the Caribbean. Candidates must apply to the Guggenheim Foundation in order to be considered in either of these competitions. The Foundation receives between 3,500 and 4,000 applications each year. Although no one who applies is guaranteed success in the competition, there is no prescreening: all applications are reviewed. Approximately 200 Fellowships are awarded each year. Deadline: September 15.

HACKNEY LITERARY AWARDS

4650 Old Looney Mill Rd, Birmingham AL 35243. **E-mail:** info@hackneyliteraryawards.org. **Website:** www.hackneyliteraryawards.org. **Contact:** Myra Crawford, PhD, executive director. Offered annually for unpublished novels, short stories (maximum 5,000 words), and poetry (50 line limit). Guidelines on website. Deadline: September 30 (novels), November 30 (short stories and poetry). **Prize: $5,000 in annual prizes for poetry and short fiction ($2,500 national and $2,500 state level). 1st Place: $600; 2nd Place: $400; 3rd Place: $250; plus $5,000 for an unpublished novel. Competition winners will be announced on the website each March.**

THE MARILYN HALL AWARDS FOR YOUTH THEATRE

P.O. Box 148, Beverly Hills CA 90213. **Website:** www.beverlyhillstheatreguild.com. **Contact:** Candace Coster, competition coordinator. The Marilyn Hall Awards consist of 2 monetary prizes for plays suitable for grades 6-8 (middle school) or for plays suitable for grades 9-12 (high school). The 2 prizes will be awarded on the merits of the play scripts, which includes its suitability for the intended audience. The plays should be approximately 45-75 minutes in length. There is no production connected to any of the prizes, though a staged reading is optional at the discretion of the BHTG. Unpublished submissions only. Authors must be US citizens or legal residents and must sign entry form personally. Deadline: The last day of February. Submission period begins January 15. **Prize: 1st Prize: $700; 2nd Prize: $300.**

AURAND HARRIS MEMORIAL PLAYWRITING AWARD

The New England Theatre Conference, Inc., 215 Knob Hill Dr., Hamden CT 06518. **Fax:** (203)288-5938. **E-mail:** mail@netconline.org. **E-mail:** mail@netconline.org. **Website:** www.netconline.org. Offered annually for an unpublished full-length play for young audiences. Guidelines available online or for SASE. Open to all. All scripts submitted by email *only*. Deadline: May 1.

HIGHLIGHTS FOR CHILDREN FICTION CONTEST

803 Church St., Honesdale PA 18431-1824. (570)253-1080. **Fax:** (570)251-7847. **E-mail:** eds@highlights-corp.com. **Website:** www.highlights.com. **Contact:** Christine French Cully, editor-in-chief. Unpublished submissions only. Open to any writer 16 years of age or older. Winners announced in May. Length up to 800 words. Stories for beginning readers should not exceed 500 words. Stories should be consistent with Highlights' editorial requirements. No violence, crime or derogatory humor. Send SASE or visit website for guidelines and current theme. Stimulates interest in writing for children and rewards and recognizes excellence. Deadline: January 31. Submission period begins January 1. **Prize: Three prizes of $1,000 or tuition for any Highlights Foundation Founders Workshop.**

ERIC HOFFER AWARD

Hopewell Publications, LLC, P.O. Box 11, Titusville NJ 08560-0011. **Fax:** (609)964-1718. **E-mail:** info@hopepubs.com. **Website:** www.hofferaward.com. **Contact:** Christopher Klim, chair. Annual contest for previously published books. Recognizes excellence in independent publishing in many unique categories: Art (titles capture the experience, execution, or demonstration of the arts); Poetry (all styles); Chapbook (40 pages or less, artistic assembly); General Fiction (nongenre-specific fiction); Commercial Fiction (genre-specific fiction); Children (titles for young children); Young Adult (titles aimed at the juvenile and teen markets); Culture (titles demonstrating the human or world experience); Memoir (titles relating to personal experience); Business (titles with application to today's business environment and emerging trends); Reference (titles from traditional and emerging reference areas); Home (titles with practical applications to home or home-related issues, including family); Health (titles promoting physical, mental, and emotional well-being); Self-help (titles involving new and emerging topics in self-help); Spiritual (titles involving the mind and spirit, including relgion); Legacy Fiction and Nonfiction (titles over 2 years of age that hold particular relevance to any subject matter or form); E-book Fiction; E-book Nonfiction. Open to any writer of published work within the last 2 years, including categories for older books. This contest recognizes excellence in independent publishing in many unique categories. Also awards the Montaigne Medal for most though-provoking book, the Da Vinci Eye for best cover, and the First Horizon Award for best new authors. Results published in the US Review of Books. Deadline: January 21. **Grand Prize: $2,000; honors in each category, including the Montaigne Medal (most thought-provoking), da Vinci Art (cover art), First Horizon (first book), and Best in Press (small, academic, micro, self-published).**

MARILYN HOLLINSHEAD VISITING SCHOLARS FELLOWSHIP

University of Minnesota, 113 Anderson Library, 222 21st Ave. South, Minneapolis MN 55455. **Website:** http://www.lib.umn.edu/clrc/awards-grants-and-fellowships. Marilyn Hollinshead Visiting Scholars Fund for Travel to the Kerlan Collection is available for research study. Applicants may request up to $1,500. Send a letter with the proposed purpose and plan to use specific research materials (manuscripts and art), dates, and budget (including airfare and per diem). Travel and a written report on the project must be completed and submitted in the previous year. Deadline: June 1.

⏀ AMELIA FRANCES HOWARD-GIBBON ILLUSTRATOR'S AWARD

1150 Morrison Drie, Suite 400, Ottawa, Ontario K 2H859, Canada. (613)232-9625. **Fax:** (613)563-9895. **Website:** www.bookcentre.ca. **Contact:** Diana Cauthier. Annually awarded to an outstanding illustrator of a children's book published in Canada during the previous calendar year. The award is bestowed upon books that are suitable for children up to and including age 12. To be eligible for the award, an illustrator must be a Canadian citizen or a permanent resident of Canada, and the text of the book must be worthy of the book's illustrations. Deadline: November 30. **Prize: A plaque and a check for $1,000 (CAD).**

THE JULIA WARD HOWE/BOSTON AUTHORS AWARD

The Boston Authors Club, The Boston Authors Club, 36 Sunhill Lane, Newton Center MA 02459. **E-mail:** bostonauthors@aol.com;. **Website:** www.bostonauthorsclub.org. **Contact:** Alan Lawson. This annual award honors Julia Ward Howe and her literary friends who founded the Boston Authors Club in 1900. It also honors the membership over 110 years, consisting of novelists, biographers, historians, governors, senators, philosophers, poets, playwrights, and other luminaries. There are 2 categories: trade books and books for young readers (beginning with chapter books through young adult books). Authors must live or have lived (college counts) within a 100-mile radius of Boston within the last 5 years. Subsidized books, cook books, and picture books are not eligible. Deadline: January 15. **Prize: $1,000.** Judged by the members.

CAROL OTIS HURST CHILDREN'S BOOK PRIZE

Westfield Athenaeum, 6 Elm St., Westfield MA 01085. (413)568-7833. **Fax:** (413)568-0988. **Website:** www.westath.org. **Contact:** Pamela Weingart. The Carol Otis Hurst Children's Book Prize honors outstanding works of fiction and nonfiction, including biography and memoir, written for children and young adults through the age of eighteen that exemplify the highest standards of research, analysis, and authorship in their portrayal of the New England Experience. The prize will be presented annually to an author whose book treats the region's history as broadly conceived to encompass one or more of the following elements: political experience, social development, fine and performing artistic expression, domestic life and arts, transportation and communication, changing technology, military experience at home and abroad, schooling, business and manufacturing, workers and the labor movement, agriculture and its transformation, racial and ethnic diversity, religious life and institutions, immigration and adjustment, sports at all levels, and the evolution of popular entertainment. The public presentation of the prize will be accompanied by a reading and/or talk by the recipient at a mutually agreed upon time during the spring immediately following the publication year. Books must have been copyrighted in their original format during the calendar year, January 1 to December 31, of the year preceding the year in which the prize is awarded. Any individual, publisher, or organization may nominate a book. See website for details and guidelines. Deadline: December 31. **Prize: $500.**

INSIGHT WRITING CONTEST

Insight Magazine, 55 W. Oak Ridge Dr., Hagerstown MD 21740-7390. **Fax:** (301)393-4055. **E-mail:** insight@rhpa.org. **Website:** www.insightmagazine. org. **Contact:** Omar Miranda, editor. Annual contest for writers in the categories of student short story, general short story, and student poetry. Unpublished submissions only. General category is open to all writers; student categories must be age 22 and younger. Deadline: July 31. **Prizes: Student Short and General Short Story: 1st Prize: $250; 2nd Prize: $200; 3rd Prize: $150. Student Poetry: 1st Prize: $100; 2nd Prize: $75; 3rd Prize: $50.**

INTERNATIONAL LITERACY ASSOCIATION CHILDREN'S AND YOUNG ADULT'S BOOK AWARDS

P.O. Box 8139, 800 Barksdale Rd., Newark DE 19714-8139. (302)731-1600, ext. 221. **E-mail:** kbaughman@reading.org. **E-mail:** committees@reading.org. **Website:** www.literacyworldwide.org. **Contact:** Kathy Baughman. The ILA Children's and

Young Adults Book Awards are intended for newly published authors who show unusual promise in the children's and young adults' book field. Awards are given for fiction and nonfiction in each of three categories: primary, intermediate, and young adult. Books from all countries and published in English for the first time during the previous calendar year will be considered. See website for eligibility and criteria information. Entry should be the author's first or second book. Deadline: January 15. **Prize: $1,000.**

☼ THE IODE JEAN THROOP BOOK AWARD

The Lillian H. Smith Children's Library, 239 College St., 4th St., Toronto, Ontario M5T 1R5, Canada. (905)522-9537. **E-mail:** mcscott@torontopubliclibrary.ca; iodeontario@bellnet.ca. **Website:** www.iodeontario.ca. **Contact:** Martha Scott. Each year, the Municipal Chapter of Toronto IODE presents an award intended to encourage the publication of books for children between the ages of 6-12 years. The award-winner must be a Canadian citizen, resident in Toronto or the surrounding area, and the book must be published in Canada. Deadline: December 31. **Prize: Award and cash prize of $2,000.** Judged by a selected committee.

JEFFERSON CUP AWARD

P.O. Box 56312, Virginia Beach VA 23456. (757)689-0594. **Website:** www.vla.org. **Contact:** Lauri Newell, current chairperson. The Jefferson Cup honors a distinguished biography, historical fiction, or American history book for young people. The Jefferson Cup Committee's goal is to promote reading about America's past; to encourage the quality writing of United States history, biography, and historical fiction for young people; and to recognize authors in these disciplines. Deadline: January 31.

THE EZRA JACK KEATS BOOK AWARD FOR NEW WRITER AND A NEW ILLUSTRATOR

450 14th St., Brooklyn NY 11215-5702. **E-mail:** foundation@ezra-jack-keats.org. **Website:** www.ezra-jack-keats.org. Annual award to an outstanding new author and new illustrator of children's books that portray universal qualities of childhood in our multicultural world. Many past winners have gone on to distinguished careers, creating books beloved by parents, children, librarians, and teachers around the world. Writers and illustrators must

have had no more than 3 books previously published. **Prize: $1,000 honorarium for each winner.** Judged by a distinguished selection committee of early childhood education specialists, librarians, illustrators and experts in children's literature.

EZRA JACK KEATS/KERLAN MEMORIAL FELLOWSHIP

University of Minnesota Libraries, 113 Elmer L. Andersen Library, 222 21st Ave. S, Minneapolis MN 55455. **E-mail:** asc-clrc@umn.edu. **Website:** https://www.lib.umn.edu/clrc/awards-grants-and-fellowships. This fellowship from the Ezra Jack Keats Foundation will provide $1,500 to a talented writer and/or illustrator of children's books who wishes to use the Kerlan Collection for the furtherance of his or her artistic development. Special consideration will be given to someone who would find it difficult to finance a visit to the Kerlan Collection. The Ezra Jack Keats Fellowship recipient will receive transportation costs and a per diem allotment. See website for application deadline and for digital application materials. Winner will be notified in February. Study and written report must be completed within the calendar year. Deadline: January 30.

KENTUCKY BLUEGRASS AWARD

Website: www.kasl.us. The Kentucky Bluegrass Award is a student choice program. The KBA promotes and encourages Kentucky students in kindergarten through grade 12 to read a variety of quality literature. Each year, a KBA committee for each grade category chooses the books for the 4 Master Lists (K-2, 3-5, 6-8 and 9-12). All Kentucky public and private schools, as well as public libraries, are welcome to participate in the program. To nominate a book, see the website for form and details. Deadline: March 1. Judged by students who read books and choose their favorite.

CORETTA SCOTT KING BOOK AWARDS

50 E. Huron St., Chicago IL 60611-2795. (800)545-2433. **E-mail:** olos@ala.org. **Website:** www.ala.org/csk. **Contact:** Office for Diversity, Literacy, and Outreach Services. The Coretta Scott King Book Awards are given annually to outstanding African American authors and illustrators of books for children and young adults that demonstrate an appreciation of African American culture and universal human values. The award commemorates the life and work of Dr. Martin Luther King, Jr., and honors his wife,

Mrs. Coretta Scott King, for her courage and determination to continue the work for peace and world brotherhood. Must be written for a youth audience in one of three categories: preschool-4th grade; 5th-8th grade; or 9th-12th grade. Book must be published in the year preceding the year the award is given, evidenced by the copyright date in the book. See website for full details, criteria, and eligibility concerns. Purpose is to encourage the artistic expression of the African American experience via literature and the graphic arts, including biographical, historical, and social history treatments by African American authors and illustrators. Deadline: December 1. Judged by the Coretta Scott King Book Awards Committee.

☯ THE STEPHEN LEACOCK MEMORIAL MEDAL FOR HUMOUR

149 Peter St. N., Orillia, Ontario L3V 4Z4, Canada. (705)326-9286. **E-mail:** bettewalkerca@gmail.com. **Website:** www.leacock.ca. **Contact:** Bette Walker, award committee, Stephen Leacock Associates. The Leacock Associates awards the prestigious Leacock Medal for the best book of literary humor written by a Canadian and published in the current year. The winning author also receives a cash prize of $15,000 thanks to the generous support of the TD Financial Group. 2 runners-up are each awarded a cash prize of $1,500. Deadline: December 31. **Prize: $15,000.**

LEAGUE OF UTAH WRITERS CONTEST

The League of Utah Writers, The League of Utah Writers, P.O. Box 64, Lewiston UT 84320. (435)755-7609. **E-mail:** luwcontest@gmail.com; luwriters@gmail.com. **Website:** www.luwriters.org. Open to any writer, the LUW Contest provides authors an opportunity to get their work read and critiqued. Multiple categories are offered; see website for details. Entries must be the original and unpublished work of the author. Winners are announced at the Annual Writers Round-Up in September. Those not present will be notified by e-mail. Deadline: June 15. Submissions period begins March 15. **Prize: Cash prizes are awarded.** Judged by professional authors and editors from outside the League.

☯ MARSH AWARD FOR CHILDREN'S LITERATURE IN TRANSLATION

The English-Speaking Union, Dartmouth House, 37 Charles St., London En W1J 5ED, United Kingdom. 020 7529 1590. **E-mail:** emma.coffey@esu.org.

Website: www.marshchristiantrust.org; www.esu. org. **Contact:** Emma Coffey, education officer. The Marsh Award for Children's Literature in Translation, awarded biennially, was founded to celebrate the best translation of a children's book from a foreign language into English and published in the UK. It aims to spotlight the high quality and diversity of translated fiction for young readers. The Award is administered by the ESU on behalf of the Marsh Christian Trust. Submissions will be accepted from publishers for books produced for readers from 5 to 16 years of age. Guidelines and eligibility criteria available online.

MCKNIGHT ARTIST FELLOWSHIPS FOR WRITERS, LOFT AWARD(S) IN CHILDREN'S LITERATURE/CREATIVE PROSE/POETRY

The Loft Literary Center, 1011 Washington Ave. S., Suite 200, Open Book, Minneapolis MN 55415. (612)215-2575. **Fax:** (612)215-2576. **E-mail:** loft@loft. org. **Website:** www.loft.org. **Contact:** Bao Phi. "The Loft administers the McKnight Artists Fellowships for Writers. Five $25,000 awards are presented annually to accomplished Minnesota writers and spoken word artists. Four awards alternate annually between creative prose (fiction and creative nonfiction) and poetry/spoken word. The fifth award is presented in children's literature and alternates annually for writing for ages 8 and under and writing for children older than 8." The awards provide the writers the opportunity to focus on their craft for the course of the fellowship year. **Prize: $25,000.**

☯ THE VICKY METCALF AWARD FOR LITERATURE FOR YOUNG PEOPLE

The Writers' Trust of Canada, 460 Richmond St. W., Suite 600, Toronto, Ontario M5V 1Y1, Canada. (416)504-8222. **E-mail:** info@writerstrust.com. **Website:** www.writerstrust.com. **Contact:** Amanda Hopkins. The Vicky Metcalf Award is presented to a Canadian writer for a body of work in children's literature at The Writers' Trust Awards event held in Toronto each fall. Open to Canadian citizens and permanent residents only. **Prize: $20,000.**

MILKWEED PRIZE FOR CHILDREN'S LITERATURE

Milkweed Editions, 1011 Washington Ave. S., Suite 300, Minneapolis MN 55415. (612)332-3192. **Fax:** (612)215-2550. **E-mail:** editor@milkweed.org. **Website:** www.milkweed.org. Milkweed Editions will award the Milkweed Prize for Children's Literature to the best mss for young readers that Milkweed accepts for publication during the calendar year by a writer not previously published by Milkweed. All mss for young readers submitted for publication by Milkweed are automatically entered into the competition. Seeking full-length fiction between 90-200 pages. Does not consider picture books or poetry collections for young readers. Recognizes an outstanding literary novel for readers ages 8-13 and encourage writers to turn their attention to readers in this age group. **Prize: $10,000 cash prize in addition to a publishing contract negotiated at the time of acceptance.** Judged by the editors of Milkweed Editions.

MINNESOTA BOOK AWARDS

The Friends of the Saint Paul Public Library, 1080 Montreal Avenue, Suite 2, St. Paul MN 55116. (651)222-3242. **Fax:** (651)222-1988. **E-mail:** mnbookawards@thefriends.org; friends@thefriends.org; info@thefriends.org. **Website:** www.mnbookawards.org. A year-round program celebrating and honoring Minnesota's best books, culminating in an annual awards ceremony. Recognizes and honors achievement by members of Minnesota's book and book arts community. All books must be the work of a Minnesota author or primary artistic creator (current Minnesota resident who maintains a year-round residence in Minnesota). All books must be published within the calendar year prior to the Awards presentation. Deadline: Nomination should be submitted by 5:00 p.m. on the first Friday in December.

NATIONAL BOOK AWARDS

The National Book Foundation, 90 Broad St., Suite 604, New York NY 10004. (212)685-0261. **E-mail:** nationalbook@nationalbook.org; agall@nationalbook.org. **Website:** www.nationalbook.org. **Contact:** Amy Gall. The National Book Foundation and the National Book Awards celebrate the best of American literature, expand its audience, and enhance the cultural value of great writing in America. The contest offers prizes in 4 categories: fiction, nonfiction, poetry, and young people's literature. Books should be published between December 1 and November 30 of the past year. Submissions must be previously published and must be entered by the publisher. General guidelines available on website.

Interested publishes should phone or e-mail the Foundation. Deadline: Submit entry form, payment, and a copy of the book by July 1. **Prize: $10,000 in each category. Finalists will each receive a prize of $1,000.** Judged by a category specific panel of 5 judges for each category.

NATIONAL OUTDOOR BOOK AWARDS

921 S. 8th Ave., Stop 8128, Pocatello ID 83209. (208)282-3912. **E-mail:** wattron@isu.edu. **Website:** www.noba-web.org. **Contact:** Ron Watters. Nine categories: History/biography, outdoor literature, instructional texts, outdoor adventure guides, nature guides, children's books, design/artistic merit, natural history literature, and nature and the environment. Additionally, a special award, the Outdoor Classic Award, is given annually to books which, over a period of time, have proven to be exceptionally valuable works in the outdoor field. Application forms and eligibility requirements are available online. Applications for the Awards program become available in early June. Deadline: August 24. **Prize: Winning books are promoted nationally and are entitled to display the National Outdoor Book Award (NOBA) medallion.**

NATIONAL WRITERS ASSOCIATION NONFICTION CONTEST

The National Writers Association, 10940 S. Parker Rd., #508, Parker CO 80134. **E-mail:** natlwritersassn@hotmail.com. **Website:** www.nationalwriters.com. Only unpublished works may be submitted. Judging of entries will not begin until the contest ends. Nonfiction in the following areas will be accepted: articles—submission should include query letter, 1st page of manuscript, separate sheet citing 5 possible markets; essay—the complete essay and 5 possible markets on separate sheet; nonfiction book proposal including query letter, chapter by chapter outline, first chapter, bio, and market analysis. Those unsure of proper manuscript format should request Research Report #35. The purpose of the National Writers Association Nonfiction Contest is to encourage the writing of nonfiction and recognize those who excel in this field. Deadline: December 31. **Prize: 1st-5th place awards. Other winners will be notified by March 31st. 1st Prize: $200 and Clearinghouse representation if winner is book proposal; 2nd Prize: $100; 3rd Prize: $50; 4th-10th places will receive a book. Honorable Mentions receive**

a certificate. Judging will be based on originality, marketability, research, and reader interest. Copies of the judges evaluation sheets will be sent to entrants furnishing an SASE with their entry.

NATIONAL WRITERS ASSOCIATION SHORT STORY CONTEST

10940 S. Parker Rd., #508, Parker CO 80134. **E-mail:** natlwritersassn@hotmail.com. **Website:** www.nationalwriters.com. Any genre of short story manuscript may be entered. All entries must be postmarked by July 1. Contest opens April 1. Only unpublished works may be submitted. All manuscripts must be typed, double-spaced, in the English language. Maximum length is 5,000 words. Those unsure of proper manuscript format should request Research Report #35. The entry must be accompanied by an entry form (photocopies are acceptable) and return SASE if you wish the material and rating sheets returned. Submissions will be destroyed, otherwise. Receipt of entry will not be acknowledged without a return postcard. Author's name and address must appear on the first page. Entries remain the property of the author and may be submitted during the contest as long as they are not published before the final notification of winners. Final prizes will be awarded in June. The purpose of the National Writers Association Short Story Contest is to encourage the development of creative skills, recognize, and reward outstanding ability in the area of short story writing. **Prize: 1st Prize: $250; 2nd Prize: $100; 3rd Prize: $50; 4th-10th places will receive a book. 1st-3rd place winners may be asked to grant one-time rights for publication in *Authorship* magazine. Honorable Mentions receive a certificate.** Judging will be based on originality, marketability, research, and reader interest. Copies of the judges evaluation sheets will be sent to entrants furnishing an SASE with their entry.

NATIONAL YOUNGARTS FOUNDATION

2100 Biscayne Blvd., Miami FL 33137. (305)377-1140. **Fax:** (305)377-1149. **E-mail:** info@nfaa.org; apply@youngarts.org. **Website:** www.youngarts.org. The National YoungArts Foundation (formerly known as the National Foundation for Advancement in the Arts) was established in 1981 by Lin and Ted Arison to identify and support the next generation of artists and to contribute to the cultural vitality of the nation by investing in the artistic development of talented young artists in the visual, literary, design, and performing arts. Each year, there are approximately 11,000 applications submitted to YoungArts from 15-18 year old (or grades 10-12) artists, and from these, approximately 700 winners are selected who are eligible to participate in programs in Miami, New York, Los Angeles, and Washington D.C. (with Chicago and other regions in the works). YoungArts provides these emerging artists with life-changing experiences and validation by renowned mentors, access to significant scholarships, national recognition, and other opportunities throughout their careers to help ensure that the nation's most outstanding emerging artists are encouraged to pursue careers in the arts. See website for details about applying. **Prize: Cash awards up to $10,000.**

JOHN NEWBERY MEDAL

Association for Library Service to Children, Division of the American Library Association, 50 E. Huron, Chicago IL 60611. (800)545-2433, ext. 2153. **Fax:** (312)280-5271. **E-mail:** alscawards@ala.org. **Website:** www.ala.org. The Newbery Medal is awarded annually by the American Library Association for the most distinguished contribution to American literature for children. Previously published submissions only; must be published prior to year award is given. SASE for award rules. Entries not returned. Medal awarded at Caldecott/Newbery banquet during ALA annual conference. Deadline: December 31. Judged by Newbery Award Selection Committee.

NEW ENGLAND BOOK AWARDS

1955 Massachusetts Ave., #2, Cambridge MA 02140. (617)547-3642. **Fax:** (617)547-3759. **E-mail:** nan@neba.org. **Website:** http://www.newenglandbooks.org/BookAwards. **Contact:** Nan Sorenson, administrative coordinator. Annual award. Previously published submissions only. Submissions made by New England booksellers and publishers. Submit written nominations only; actual books should not be sent. Member bookstores receive materials to display winners' books. Award is given to a specific title, fiction, nonfiction, children's. The titles must be either about New England, set in New England or by an author residing in the New England. The titles must be hardcover, paperback original or reissue that was published between September 1 and August 31. Entries must be still in print and available. Deadline:

June 10. **Prize: Winners will receive $250 for literacy to a charity of their choice.** Judged by NEIBA membership.

NEW VOICES AWARD

Website: www.leeandlow.com. Open to students. Annual award. Lee & Low Books is one of the few minority-owned publishing companies in the country and has published more than 100 first-time writers and illustrators. Winning titles include *The Blue Roses*, winner of a Patterson Prize for Books for Young People; *Janna and the Kings*, an IRA Children's Book Award Notable; and *Sixteen Years in Sixteen Seconds*, selected for the Texas Bluebonnet Award Masterlist. Submissions made by author. SASE for contest rules or visit website. Restrictions of media for illustrators: The author must be a writer of color who is a resident of the US and who has not previously published a children's picture book. For additional information, send SASE or visit Lee & Low's website. Encourages writers of color to enter the world of children's books. Deadline: September 30. **Prize: $1,000 and standard publication contract (regardless of whether or not writer has an agent) along with an advance against royalties; New Voices Honor Award: $500 prize.** Judged by Lee & Low editors.

NORTH AMERICAN INTERNATIONAL AUTO SHOW HIGH SCHOOL POSTER CONTEST

Detroit Auto Dealers Association, 1900 W. Big Beaver Rd., Troy MI 48084-3531, USA. (248)643-0250. Fax: (248)283-5148. **E-mail:** sherp@dada.org. **Website:** www.naias.com. **Contact:** Sandy Herp. Open to students. Annual contest. Submissions made by the author and illustrator. Entrants must be Michigan high school students enrolled in grades 10-12. Winning posters may be displayed at the NAIAS and reproduced in the official NAIAS program, which is available to the public, international media, corporate executives, and automotive suppliers. Winning posters may also be displayed on the official NAIAS website at the sole discretion of the NAIAS. Contact Detroit Auto Dealers Association (DADA) for contest rules and entry forms or retrieve rules from website. Deadline: November. **Prize: Chairman's Award: $1,000; State Farm Insurance Award: $1,000; Designer's Best of Show (Digital and Traditional): $500; Best Theme: $250;**

Best Use of Color: $250; Most Creative: $250. A winner will be chosen in each category from grades 10, 11 and 12. Prizes: 1st place in 10, 11, 12: $500; 2nd place: $250; 3rd place: $100.** Judged by an independent panel of recognized representatives of the art community.

NORTHERN CALIFORNIA BOOK AWARDS

Northern California Book Reviewers Association, c/o Poetry Flash, 1450 Fourth St. #4, Berkeley CA 94710. (510)525-5476. **E-mail:** ncbr@poetryflash.org; editor@poetryflash.org. **Website:** www.poetryflash.org. **Contact:** Joyce Jenkins, executive director. Annual Northern California Book Award for outstanding book in literature, open to books published in the current calendar year by Northern California authors. NCBR presents annual awards to Bay Area (northern California) authors annually in fiction, nonfiction, poetry, and children's literature. Previously published books only. Must be published the calendar year prior to spring awards ceremony. Submissions nominated by publishers; author or agent could also nominate published work. Send 3 copies of the book to attention: NCBR. Encourages writers and stimulates interest in books and reading. Deadline: December 28. **Prize: $100 honorarium and award certificate.** Judging by voting members of the Northern California Book Reviewers.

☉ NOVA WRITES COMPETITION FOR UNPUBLISHED MANUSCRIPTS

Writers' Federation of Nova Scotia, 1113 Marginal Rd., Halifax, Nova Scotia B3H 4P7. (902)423-8116. **Fax:** (902)422-0881. **E-mail:** programs@writers.ns.ca. **Website:** www.writers.ns.ca. **Contact:** Robin Spittal, communications and development officer. Annual program designed to honor work by unpublished writers in all 4 Atlantic Provinces. Entry is open to writers unpublished in the category of writing they wish to enter. Prizes are presented in the fall of each year. Categories include: short form creative nonfiction, long form creative nonfiction, novel, poetry, short story, and writing for children/young adult novel. Judges return written comments when competition is concluded. Page lengths and rules vary based on categories. See website for details. Anyone resident in the Atlantic Provinces since September 1st immediately prior to the deadline date is eligible to enter. Only one entry per category is allowed. Each entry requires its own entry form and registration fee. Deadline: December 13. **Prizes vary based on categories. See website for details.**

OHIOANA BOOK AWARDS

Ohioana Library Association, 274 E. First Ave., Suite 300, Columbus OH 43201-3673. (614)466-3831. **Fax:** (614)728-6974. **E-mail:** ohioana@ohioana. org. **Website:** www.ohioana.org. **Contact:** David Weaver, executive director. Writers must have been born in Ohio or lived in Ohio for at least 5 years, but books about Ohio or an Ohioan need not be written by an Ohioan. Finalists announced in May and winners in July. Winners notified by mail in early summer. Offered annually to bring national attention to Ohio authors and their books, published in the last year. (Books can only be considered once.) Categories: Fiction, nonfiction, juvenile, poetry, and books about Ohio or an Ohioan. Deadline: December 31. **Prize: $1,000 cash prize, certificate, and glass sculpture.** Judged by a jury selected by librarians, book reviewers, writers and other knowledgeable people.

OKLAHOMA BOOK AWARDS

200 NE 18th St., Oklahoma City OK 73105. (405)521-2502. **Fax:** (405)525-7804. **E-mail:** connie.armstrong@libraries.ok.gov. **Website:** www. odl.state.ok.us/ocb. **Contact:** Connie Armstrong, executive director. This award honors Oklahoma writers and books about Oklahoma. Awards are presented to best books in fiction, nonfiction, children's, design and illustration, and poetry books about Oklahoma or books written by an author who was born, is living or has lived in Oklahoma. SASE for award rules and entry forms. Winner will be announced at banquet in Oklahoma City. The Arrell Gibson Lifetime Achievement Award is also presented each year for a body of work. Previously published submissions only. Submissions made by the author, author's agent, or entered by a person or group of people, including the publisher. Must be published during the calendar year preceding the award. Deadline: January 10. **Prize: Awards a medal.** Judging by a panel of 5 people for each category, generally a librarian, a working writer in the genre, booksellers, editors, etc.

OREGON BOOK AWARDS

925 SW Washington St., Portland OR 97205. (503)227-2583. **Fax:** (503)241-4256. **E-mail:** la@ literary-arts.org. **Website:** www.literary-arts.org. **Contact:** Susan Denning, director of programs and events. The annual Oregon Book Awards celebrate Oregon authors in the areas of poetry, fiction, nonfiction, drama, and young readers' literature published between August 1 and July 31 of the previous calendar year. Awards are available for every category. See website for details. Entry fee determined by initial print run; see website for details. Entries must be previously published. Oregon residents only. Accepts inquiries by phone and e-mail. Finalists announced in January. Winners announced at an awards ceremony in November. List of winners available in April. Deadline: August 26. **Prize: Grant of $2,500. (Grant money could vary.)** Judged by writers who are selected from outside Oregon for their expertise in a genre. Past judges include Mark Doty, Colson Whitehead, and Kim Barnes.

OREGON LITERARY FELLOWSHIPS

925 S.W. Washington, Portland OR 97205. (503)227-2583. **E-mail:** susan@literary-arts.org. **Website:** www.literary-arts.org. **Contact:** Susan Moore, director of programs and events. Oregon Literary Fellowships are intended to help Oregon writers initiate, develop, or complete literary projects in poetry, fiction, literary nonfiction, drama, and young readers literature. Writers in the early stages of their career are encouraged to apply. The awards are merit-based. Guidelines available in February for SASE. Accepts inquiries by e-mail, phone. Oregon residents only. Recipients announced in January. Deadline: Last Friday in June. **Prize: $3,000 minimum award, for approximately 8 writers and 2 publishers.** Judged by out-of-state writers

THE ORIGINAL ART

128 E. 63rd St., New York NY 10065. (212)838-2560. **Fax:** (212)838-2561. **E-mail:** kim@societyillustrators.org; info@societyillustrators.org. **Website:** www.societyillustrators.org. **Contact:** Kate Feirtag, exhibition director. The Original Art is an annual exhibit created to showcase illustrations from the year's best children's books published in the US. For editors and art directors, it's an inspiration and a treasure trove of talent to draw upon. Previously published submissions only. Request "call for entries" to receive contest rules and entry forms. Works will be displayed at the Society

of Illustrators Museum of American Illustration in New York City October-November annually. Deadline: July 18. Judged by 7 professional artists and editors.

HELEN KEATING OTT AWARD FOR OUTSTANDING CONTRIBUTION TO CHILDREN'S LITERATURE

CSLA, 10157 SW Barbur Blvd. #102C, Portland OR 97219. (503)244-6919. **Fax:** (503)977-3734. **E-mail:** sharper1@kent.edu. **Website:** www.cslainfo. org. **Contact:** S. Meghan Harper, awards chair. Annual award given to a person or organization that has made a significant contribution to promoting high moral and ethical values through children's literature. Recipient is honored in July during the conference. Awards certificate of recognition, the awards banquet, and one-night's stay in the hotel. A nomination for an award may be made by anyone. An application form is available online. Elements of creativity and innovation will be given high priority by the judges.

PATERSON PRIZE FOR BOOKS FOR YOUNG PEOPLE

The Poetry Center at Passaic County Community College, One College Blvd., Paterson NJ 07505. (973)684-6555. **Fax:** (973)523-6085. **E-mail:** mgillan@pccc.edu. **Website:** www.pccc.edu/poetry. **Contact:** Maria Mazziotti Gillan, executive director. Award for a book published in the previous year in each age category (Pre-K-Grade 3, Grades 4-6, Grades 7-12). Deadline: February 1. **Prize: $500.**

THE KATHERINE PATERSON PRIZE FOR YOUNG ADULT AND CHILDREN'S WRITING

Hunger Mountain, Vermont College of Fine Arts, 36 College St., Montpelier VT 05602. (802)828-8517. **E-mail:** hungermtn@vcfa.edu. **Website:** www.hungermtn.org. **Contact:** Samantha Kolber, Managing Editor. The annual Katherine Paterson Prize for Young Adult and Children's Writing honors the best in young adult and children's literature. Submit young adult or middle grade mss, and writing for younger children, short stories, picture books, poetry, or novel excerpts, under 10,000 words. Guidelines available on website. Deadline: March 8. **Prize: $1,000 and publication for the first place winner; $100 each and publication for the three category winners.** Judged by a guest judge every year.

PENNSYLVANIA YOUNG READERS' CHOICE AWARDS PROGRAM

Pennsylvania School Librarians Association, 134 Bisbing Road, Henryville PA 18332. **E-mail:** pyrca. psla@gmail.com. **Website:** www.psla.org. **Contact:** Alice L. Cyphers, co-coordinator. Submissions nominated by a person or group. Must be published within 5 years of the award—for example, books published in 2013 to present are eligible for the 2018-2019 award. Check the Program wiki at pyrca. wikispaces.com for submission information. View information at the Pennsylvania School Librarians' website or the Program wiki. Must be currently living in North America. The purpose of the Pennsylvania Young Reader's Choice Awards Program is to promote the reading of quality books by young people in the Commonwealth of Pennsylvania, to encourage teacher and librarian collaboration and involvement in children's literature, and to honor authors whose works have been recognized by the students of Pennsylvania. Deadline: September 15. **Prize: Framed certificate to winning authors. Four awards are given, one for each of the following grade level divisions: K-3, 3-6, 6-8, YA.** Judged by children of Pennsylvania (they vote).

PEN/PHYLLIS NAYLOR WORKING WRITER FELLOWSHIP

E-mail: awards@pen.org. **Website:** www.pen.org/ awards. **Contact:** Arielle Anema, Literary Awards Coordinator. Offered annually to an author of children's or young-adult fiction. The Fellowship has been developed to help writers whose work is of high literary caliber but who have not yet attracted a broad readership. The Fellowship is designed to assist a writer at a crucial moment in his or her career to complete a book-length work-in-progress. Candidates have published at least one novel for children or young adults which have been received warmly by literary critics, but have not generated sufficient income to support the author. Writers must be nominated by an editor or fellow author. See website for eligibility and nomination guidelines. Deadline: Submissions open during the summer of each year. Visit PEN.org/awards for up-to-date information on deadlines. **Prize: $5,000.**

PLEASE TOUCH MUSEUM BOOK AWARD

Memorial Hall in Fairmount Park, 4231 Avenue of the Republic, Philadelphia PA 19131. (215)578-5153.

Fax: (215)578-5171. **E-mail:** hboyd@pleasetouch-museum.org. **Website:** www.pleasetouchmuseum.org. **Contact:** Heather Boyd. This prestigious award has recognized and encouraged the publication of high quality books. The award was exclusively created to recognize and encourage the writing of publications that help young children enjoy the process of learning through books, while reflecting PTM's philosophy of learning through play. The awards to to books that are imaginative, exceptionally illustrated, and help foster a child's life-long love of reading. To be eligible for consideration, a book must be distinguished in text, illustration, and ability to explore and clarify an idea for young children (ages 7 and under). Deadline: October 1. Books for each cycle must be published within previous calendar year (September-August). Judged by a panel of volunteer educators, artists, booksellers, children's authors, and librarians in conjunction with museum staff.

PNWA LITERARY CONTEST

Pacifc Northwest Writers Association, PMB 2717, 1420 NW Gilman Blvd., Suite 2, Issaquah WA 98027. (452)673-2665. **Fax:** (452)961-0768. **E-mail:** pnwa@pnwa.org. **Website:** www.pnwa.org. Annual literary contest with 12 different categories. See website for details and specific guidelines. Each entry receives 2 critiques. Winners announced at the PNWA Summer Conference, held annually in mid-July. Deadline: February 20. **Prize: 1st Place: $600; 2nd Place: $300; 3rd Place: $100.** Judged by an agent or editor attending the conference.

POCKETS FICTION-WRITING CONTEST

P.O. Box 340004, Nashville TN 37203-0004. (615)340-7333. **Fax:** (615)340-7267. **E-mail:** pockets@upperroom.org. **Website:** www.pockets.upperroom.org. **Contact:** Lynn W. Gilliam, senior editor. Designed for 6- to 12-year-olds, *Pockets* magazine offers wholesome devotional readings that teach about God's love and presence in life. The content includes fiction, scripture stories, puzzles and games, poems, recipes, colorful pictures, activities, and scripture readings. Freelance submissions of stories, poems, recipes, puzzles and games, and activities are welcome. Stories should be 750-1,000 words. Multiple submissions are permitted. Past winners are ineligible. The primary purpose of *Pockets* is to help children grow in their relationship with God and to claim the good news of the gos-pel of Jesus Christ by applying it to their daily lives. *Pockets* espouses respect for all human beings and for God's creation. It regards a child's faith journey as an integral part of all of life and sees prayer as undergirding that journey. Deadline: August 15. Submission period begins March 15. **Prize: $500 and publication in magazine.**

EDGAR ALLAN POE AWARD

1140 Broadway, Suite 1507, New York NY 10001. (212)888-8171. **E-mail:** mwa@mysterywriters.org. **Website:** www.mysterywriters.org. Mystery Writers of America is the leading association for professional crime writers in the United States. Members of MWA include most major writers of crime fiction and nonfiction, as well as screenwriters, dramatists, editors, publishers, and other professionals in the field. Categories include: Best Novel, Best First Novel by an American Author, Best Paperback/E-Book Original, Best Fact Crime, Best Critical/Biographical, Best Short Story, Best Juvenile Mystery, Best Young Adult Mystery, Best Television Series Episode Teleplay, and Mary Higgins Clark Award. Purpose of the award: Honor authors of distinguished works in the mystery field. Previously published submissions only. Submissions should be made by the publisher. Work must be published/produced the year of the contest. Deadline: November 30. **Prize: Awards ceramic bust of "Edgar" for winner; certificates for all nominees.** Judged by active status members of Mystery Writers of America (writers).

MICHAEL L. PRINTZ AWARD

Young Adult Library Services Association, Division of the American Library Association, 50 E. Huron, Chicago IL 60611. (800)545-2433. **Fax:** (312)280-5276. **E-mail:** yalsa@ala.org. **Website:** www.ala.org/yalsa/printz. **Contact:** Nichole O'Connor, program officer for events and conferences. The Michael L. Printz Award annually honors the best book written for teens, based entirely on its literary merit, each year. In addition, the Printz Committee names up to 4 honor books, which also represent the best writing in young adult literature. The award-winning book can be fiction, nonfiction, poetry, or an anthology, and can be a work of joint authorship or editorship. The books must be published between January 1 and December 31 of the preceding year and be designated by its publisher as being either a young adult book or one published for the age range that YALSA defines as young adult, e.g. ages 12 through 18. Deadline: December 1. Judged by an award committee.

PURPLE DRAGONFLY BOOK AWARDS

Story Monsters, LLC, 4696 W Tyson St, Chandler AZ 85226-2903. (480)940-8182. **Fax:** (480)940-8787. **E-mail:** Cristy@StoryMonsters.com; Linda@StoryMonsters.com. **Website:** www.Dragonfly-BookAwards.com. **Contact:** Cristy Bertini, contest coordinator. The Purple Dragonfly Book Awards are designed with children in mind. Awards are divided into 52 distinct subject categories, ranging from books on the environment and cooking to sports and family issues. The Purple Dragonfly Book Awards are geared toward stories that appeal to children of all ages. The awards are open to books published in any calendar year and in any country that are available for purchase. Books entered must be printed in English. Traditionally published, partnership published and self-published books are permitted, as long as they fit the above criteria. Submit materials to: Cristy Bertini, Attn: Five Star Book Awards, 1271 Turkey St., Hardwick, MA 01082. Deadline: May 1. **Prize: Grand Prize winner receives a $300 cash prize, 100 foil award seals, one hour of marketing consultation from Story Monsters, LLC, as well as publicity on Dragonfly Book Awards website and inclusion in a winners' news release sent to a comprehensive list of media outlets. All first-place winners of categories will be put into a drawing for a $100 prize. In addition, each first-place winner in each category receives a certificate commemorating their accomplishment, 25 foil award seals and mention on Dragonfly Book Awards website. All winners are listed in Story Monsters Ink magazine.** Judged by industry experts with specific knowledge about the categories over which they preside.

QUILL AND SCROLL WRITING, PHOTO AND MULTIMEDIA CONTEST AND BLOGGING COMPETITION

School of Journalism, Univ. of Iowa, 100 Adler Journalism Bldg., Iowa City IA 52242-2004. (319)335-3457. **Fax:** (319)335-3989. **E-mail:** quill-scroll@uiowa.edu. **E-mail:** quill-scroll@uiowa.edu. **Website:** quillandscroll.org. **Contact:** Vanessa Shelton, contest director. Entries must have been published in a high school or profesional newspaper or website

during the previous year, and must be the work of a currently enrolled high school student, when published. Open to students. Annual contest. Previously published submissions only. Submissions made by the author or school media adviser. Deadline: February 5. **Prize: Winners will receive *Quill and Scroll*'s National Award Gold Key and, if seniors, are eligible to apply for one of the scholarships offered by *Quill and Scroll*. All winning entries are automatically eligible for the International Writing and Photo Sweepstakes Awards. Engraved plaque awarded to sweepstakes winners.**

THE RED HOUSE CHILDREN'S BOOK AWARD

Red House Children's Book Award, 123 Frederick Road, Cheam, Sutton, Surrey SM1 2HT, United Kingdom. **E-mail:** info@rhcba.co.uk. **Website:** www.redhousechildrensbookaward.co.uk. **Contact:** Sinead Kromer, national coordinator. The Red House Children's Book Award is the only national book award that is entirely voted for by children. A shortlist is drawn up from children's nominations and any child can then vote for the winner of the three categories: Books for Younger Children, Books for Younger Readers, and Books for Older Readers. The book with the most votes is then crowned the winner of the Red House Children's Book Award. Deadline: December 31.

TOMÁS RIVERA MEXICAN AMERICAN CHILDREN'S BOOK AWARD

Dr. Jesse Gainer, Texas State University, 601 University Drive, San Marcos TX 78666-4613. (512)245-2357. **E-mail:** riverabookaward@txstate.edu. **Website:** www.riverabookaward.org. **Contact:** Dr. Jesse Gainer, award director. Texas State University College of Education developed the Tomás Rivera Mexican American Children's Book Award to honor authors and illustrators who create literature that depicts the Mexican American experience. The award was established in 1995 and was named in honor of Dr. Tomás Rivera, a distinguished alumnus of Texas State University. The book will be written for younger children, ages pre-K to 5th grade (awarded in even years), or older children, ages 6th grade to 12 grade (awarded in odd years). The text and illustrations will be of highest quality. The portrayal/representations of Mexican Americans will be accurate and engaging, avoid stereotypes, and reflect rich characterization. The book may be fiction or non-fiction. See website for more details and directions. Deadline: November 1.

☸ ROCKY MOUNTAIN BOOK AWARD: ALBERTA CHILDREN'S CHOICE BOOK AWARD

Box 42, Lethbridge, Alberta T1J 3Y3, Canada. (403)381-0855. **Website:** http://www.rmba.info. **Contact:** Michelle Dimnik, contest director. Annual contest. No entry fee. Awards: Gold medal and author tour of selected Alberta schools. Judging by students. Canadian authors and/or illustrators only. Submit entries to Richard Chase. Previously unpublished submissions only. Submissions made by author's agent or nominated by a person or group. Must be published within the 3 years prior to that year's award. Register before January 20th to take part in the Rocky Mountain Book Award. SASE for contest rules and entry forms. Purpose of contest: "Reading motivation for students, promotion of Canadian authors, illustrators, and publishers."

ROYAL DRAGONFLY BOOK AWARDS

Story Monsters, LLC, 4696 W. Tyson St., Chandler AZ 85226. (480)940-8182. **Fax:** (480)940-8787. **E-mail:** Cristy@StoryMonsters.com; Linda@StoryMonsters.com. **E-mail:** cristy@StoryMonsters.com. **Website:** www.DragonflyBookAwards.com. **Contact:** Cristy Bertini. Offered annually for any previously published work to honor authors for writing excellence of all types of literature—fiction and nonfiction—in 66 categories, appealing to a wide range of ages and comprehensive list of genres. Open to any title published in English. Guidelines available online. Send submissions to Cristy Bertini, Attn: Five Star Book Awards, 1271 Turkey St., Ware, MA 01082. Deadline: October 1. **Prize: Grand Prize winner receives a $300 cash prize, 100 foil award seals, one hour of marketing consultation from Story Monsters, LLC, as well as publicity on Dragonfly Book Awards website and inclusion in a winners' news release sent to a comprehensive list of media outlets. All first-place winners of categories will be put into a drawing for a $100 prize. In addition, each first-place winner in each category receives a certificate commemorating their accomplishment, 25 foil award seals and mention on Dragonfly Book Awards website. All winners are listed in Story Monsters Ink magazine.**

☸ SASKATCHEWAN BOOK AWARDS

315-1102 Eighth Ave., Regina, Saskatchewan S4R 1C9, Canada. (306)569-1585. **E-mail:** director@bookawards.sk.ca. **Website:** www.bookawards.sk.ca. **Contact:** Courtney Bates-Hardy, Administrative Director. Saskatchewan Book Awards celebrates, promotes, and rewards Saskatchewan authors and publishers worthy of recognition through 14 awards, granted on an annual or semiannual basis. Awards: Fiction, Nonfiction, Poetry, Scholarly, First Book, *Prix du Livre Français*, Regina, Saskatoon, Aboriginal Peoples' Writing, Aboriginal Peoples' Publishing, Publishing in Education, Publishing, Children's Literature/Young Adult Literature, Book of the Year. Deadline: Early November. **Prize: $2,000 (CAD) for all awards except Book of the Year, which is $3,000 (CAD).** Juries are made up of writing and publishing professionals from outside of Saskatchewan.

○   Saskatchewan Book Awards is the only provincially focused book award program in Saskatchewan and a principal ambassador for Saskatchewan's literary community. Its solid reputation for celebrating artistic excellence in style is recognized nationally.

SCBWI MAGAZINE MERIT AWARDS

4727 Wilshire Blvd., Suite 301, Los Angeles CA 90010. (323)782-1010. **Fax:** (323)782-1892. **E-mail:** grants@scbwi.org. **Website:** www.scbwi.org. **Contact:** Stephanie Gordon, award coordinator. The SCBWI is a professional organization of writers and illustrators and others interested in children's literature. Membership is open to the general public at large. All magazine work for young people by an SCBWI member—writer, artist, or photographer—is eligible during the year of original publication. In the case of co-authored work, both authors must be SCBWI members. Members must submit their own work. Requirements for entrants: 4 copies each of the published work and proof of publication (may be contents page) showing the name of the magazine and the date of issue. Previously published submissions only. For rules and procedures see website. Must be a SCBWI member. Recognizes outstanding original magazine work for young people published during that year, and having been written or illustrated by members of SCBWI. Deadline: December 15 of the year of publication. Submission period begins January 1. **Prize: Awards plaques and honor certificates for each of 4 categories (fiction, nonfiction, illustration, and poetry).** Judged by a magazine editor and two "full" SCBWI members.

SHEEHAN YA BOOK PRIZE

Elephant Rock Books, P.O. Box 119, Ashford CT 06278. **E-mail:** elephantrockbooksya@gmail.com. **Website:** elephantrockbooks.com/ya.html. **Contact:** Jotham Burrello and Amanda Hurley. Elephant Rock is a small independent publisher. Their first young adult book, *The Carnival at Bray* by Jessie Ann Foley was a Morris Award Finalist, and Printz Honor Book. Runs contest every other year. Check website for details. Guidelines are available on the website: www.elephantrockbooks.com./about.html#submissions. "Elephant Rock Books' teen imprint is looking for a great story to follow our critically acclaimed novel, *The Carnival at Bray*. We're after quality stories with heart, guts, and a clear voice. We're especially interested in the quirky, the hopeful, and the real. We are not particularly interested in genre fiction and prefer standalone novels, unless you've got the next *Hunger Games*. We seek writers who believe in the transformative power of a great story, so show us what you've got." Deadline: July 1. **Prize: $1,000 as an advance.** Judges vary year-to-year.

SKIPPING STONES BOOK AWARDS

E-mail: editor@SkippingStones.org. **Website:** www.skippingstones.org. **Contact:** Arun N. Toke', executive editor. Open to published books, publications/magazines, educational videos, and DVDs. Annual awards. Submissions made by the author or publishers and/or producers. Send request for contest rules and entry forms or visit website. Many educational publications announce the winners of our book awards. The winning books and educational videos/DVDs are announced in the July-September issue of *Skipping Stones* and also on the website. In addition to announcements on social media pages, the reviews of winning titles are posted on website. *Skipping Stones* multicultural magazine has been published for over 28 years. Recognizes exceptional, literary and artistic contributions to juvenile/children's literature, as well as teaching resources and educational audio/video resources in the areas of multicultural awareness, nature and ecology, social issues, peace, and nonviolence. Deadline: February 28. **Prize: Winners receive gold honor award seals, attractive honor certificates, and publicity via multiple outlets.** Judged by a multicultural selection committee of editors, students, parents, teachers, and librarians.

SKIPPING STONES YOUTH AWARDS

P.O. Box 3939, Eugene OR 97403-0939. (541)342-4956. **Fax:** (541)342-4956. **E-mail:** editor@skippingstones.org. **Website:** www.skippingstones.org. **Contact:** Arun N. Toké. Annual awards to promote creativity as well as multicultural and nature awareness in youth. Cover letter should include name, address, phone, and e-mail. Entries must be unpublished. Length: 1,000 words maximum; 30 lines maximum for poems. Open to any writer between 7 and 17 years old. Guidelines available by SASE, e-mail, or on website. Accepts inquiries by e-mail or phone. Results announced in the October-December issue of *Skipping Stones*. Winners notified by mail. For contest results, visit website. Everyone who enters receives the issue which features the award winners. Deadline: June 25. **Prize: Publication in the autumn issue of *Skipping Stones*, honor certificate, subscription to magazine, plus 5 multicultural and/or nature books.** Judged by editors and reviewers at *Skipping Stones* magazine.

SKIPPING STONES YOUTH HONOR AWARDS

P.O. Box 3939, Eugene OR 97403-0939. (541)342-4956. **E-mail:** editor@SkippingStones.org. **Website:** www.SkippingStones.org. **Contact:** Arun N. Toké, editor. Now celebrating its 29th year, *Skipping Stones* is a winner of N.A.M.E.EDPRESS, Newsstand Resources, Writer and Parent's Choice Awards. Open to students. Annual awards. Submissions made by the author. The winners are published in the October-December issue of *Skipping Stones*. Everyone who enters the contest receives the Autumn issue featuring Youth Awards. SASE for contest rules or download from website. Entries must include certificate of originality by a parent and/or teacher and a cover letter that included cultural background information on the author. Submissions can either be mailed or e-mailed. Up to ten awards are given in three categories: (1) Compositions (essays, poems, short stories, songs, travelogues, etc.): Entries should be typed (double-spaced) or neatly handwritten.

Fiction or nonfiction should be limited to 1,000 words; poems to 30 lines. Non-English writings are also welcome. (2) Artwork (drawings, cartoons, paintings or photo essays with captions): Entries should have the artist's name, age, and address on the back of each page. Send the originals with SASE. Black & white photos are especially welcome. Limit: 8 pieces. (3) Youth Organizations: Describe how your club or group works to: (a) preserve the nature and ecology in your area, (b) enhance the quality of life for low-income, minority or disabled or (c) improve racial or cultural harmony in your school or community. Use the same format as for compositions. Recognizes youth, 7 to 17, for their contributions to multicultural awareness, nature and ecology, social issues, peace and nonviolence. Also promotes creativity, self-esteem, and writing skills and to recognize important work being done by youth organizations. Deadline: June 25. Judged by *Skipping Stones* staff.

KAY SNOW WRITING CONTEST

Willamette Writers, Willamette Writers, 2108 Buck St., West Linn OR 97068. (503)305-6729. **Fax:** (503)344-6174. **E-mail:** reg@willamettewriters.com. **Website:** www.willamettewriters.org. Willamette Writers is the largest writers' organization in Oregon and one of the largest writers' organizations in the US. It is a nonprofit, tax-exempt Oregon corporation led by volunteers. Elected officials and directors administer an active program of monthly meetings, special seminars, workshops, and an annual writing conference. Continuing with established programs and starting new ones is only made possible by strong volunteer support. See website for specific details and rules. There are six different categories writers can enter: Adult Fiction, Adult Nonfiction, Poetry, Juvenile Short Story, Screenwriting, and Student Writer. The purpose of this annual writing contest, named in honor of Willamette Writer's founder, Kay Snow, is to help writers reach professional goals in writing in a broad array of categories and to encourage student writers. Deadline: April 23. Submission deadline begins January 15. **Prize: One first prize of $300, one second place prize of $150, and a third place prize of $50 per winning entry in each of the six**

categories. Student first prize is $50, $20 for second place, $10 for third.**

SOCIETY OF MIDLAND AUTHORS AWARD

Society of Midland Authors, Society of Midland Authors, P.O. Box 10419, Chicago IL 60610-0419. **E-mail:** marlenetbrill@comcast.net. **Website:** www.midlandauthors.com. **Contact:** Marlene Targ Brill, awards chair. Since 1957, the Society has presented annual awards for the best books written by Midwestern authors. The Society began in 1915. The contest is open to any title published within the year prior to the contest year. Open to adult and children's authors/poets who reside in, were born in, or have strong ties to a Midland state, which includes Illinois, Indiana, Iowa, Kansas, Michigan, Minnesota, Missouri, Nebraska, North Dakota, South Dakota, Ohio, and Wisconsin. The Society of Midland Authors (SMA) Award is presented to one title in each of six categories: adult nonfiction, adult fiction, adult biography and memoir, children's nonfiction, children's fiction, and poetry. There may be honor book winners as well. Books and entry forms must be mailed to the 3 judges in each category; for a list of judges and the entry and payment forms, visit the SMA website. Do not mail books to the society's P.O. box. The fee can be sent to the SMA P.O. box or paid via Paypal. Deadline: January 7. **Prize: $500 and a plaque that is awarded at the SMA banquet in May in Chicago. Honorary winners receive a plaque.**

SYDNEY TAYLOR MANUSCRIPT COMPETITION

Association of Jewish Libraries, Sydney Taylor Manuscript Award Competition, 204 Park St., Montclair NJ 07042-2903. **E-mail:** stmacajl@aol.com. **Website:** www.jewishlibraries.org/main/Awards/SydneyTaylorManuscriptAward.aspx. **Contact:** Aileen Grossberg. This competition is for unpublished writers of juvenile fiction. Material should be for readers ages 8-13. The manuscript should have universal appeal and reveal positive aspects of Jewish life that will serve to deepen the understanding of Judaism for all children. Download rules and forms from website. Must be an unpublished fiction writer or a student; also, books must range from 64-200 pages in length. "AJL assumes no responsibility for publication, but hopes this cash incentive will serve to encourage new writers of children's stories with Jewish themes for all children." To encourage new fiction of Jewish interest for readers ages 8-13. Deadline: September 30. **Prize: $1,000.** Judging by qualified judges from within the Association of Jewish Libraries.

SYDNEY TAYLOR BOOK AWARD

E-mail: chair@sydneytaylorbookaward.org. **Website:** www.sydneytaylorbookaward.org. **Contact:** Ellen Tilman, chair. The Sydney Taylor Book Award is presented annually to outstanding books for children and teens that authentically portray the Jewish experience. Deadline: November 30. Cannot guarantee that books received after November 30 will be considered. **Prize: Gold medals are presented in 3 categories: younger readers, older readers, and teen readers. Honor books are awarded in silver medals, and notable books are named in each category.** Winners are selected by a committee of the Association of Jewish Libraries. Each committee member must receive an individual copy of each book that is to be considered. Please contact the chair for submission details.

TD CANADIAN CHILDREN'S LITERATURE AWARD

The Canadian Children's Book Centre, 40 Orchard View Blvd., Suite 217, Toronto, Ontario M4R 1B9, Canada. (416)975-0010, ext. 222. **Fax:** (416)975-8970. **E-mail:** meghan@bookcentre.ca. **Website:** www.bookcentre.ca. **Contact:** Meghan Howe. The TD Canadian Children's Literature Award is for the most distinguished book of the year. All books, in any genre, written and illustrated by Canadians and for children ages 1-12 are eligible. Only books first published in Canada are eligible for submission. Books must be published between January 1 and December 31 of the previous calendar year. Open to Canadian citizens and/or permanent residents of Canada. Deadline: mid-December. **Prizes: Two prizes of $30,000, 1 for English, 1 for French. $20,000 will be divided among the Honour Book English titles and Honour Book French titles, to a maximum of 4; $2,500 shall go to each of the publishers of the English and French grand-prize winning books for promotion and publicity.**

TORONTO BOOK AWARDS

City of Toronto c/o Toronto Arts & Culture, Cultural Partnerships, City Hall, 9E, 100 Queen St. W., Toronto, Ontario M5H 2N2, Canada. **E-mail:** shan@toronto.ca. **Website:** www.toronto.ca/book_

awards. The Toronto Book Awards honor authors of books of literary or artistic merit that are evocative of Toronto. There are no separate categories; all books are judged together. Any fiction or nonfiction book published in English for adults and/or children that are evocative of Toronto are eligible. To be eligible, books must be published between January 1 and December 31 of previous year. Deadline: April 30. **Prize: Each finalist receives $1,000 and the winning author receives $10,000 ($15,000 total in prize money available).**

VEGETARIAN ESSAY CONTEST

The Vegetarian Resource Group, P.O. Box 1463, Baltimore MD 21203. (410)366-VEGE. **Fax:** (410)366-8804. **E-mail:** vrg@vrg.org. **Website:** www.vrg.org. Write a 2-3 page essay on any aspect of vegetarianism. Entrants should base their paper on interviewing, research, and/or personal opinion. You need not be a vegetarian to enter. Three different entry categories: age 14-18; age 9-13; and age 8 and under. **Prize: $50.**

VFW VOICE OF DEMOCRACY

Veterans of Foreign Wars of the US, National Headquarters, 406 W. 34th St., Kansas City MO 64111. (816)968-1117. **E-mail:** kharmer@vfw.org. **Website:** www.vfw.org/VOD/. The Voice of Democracy Program is open to students in grades 9-12 (on the Nov. 1 deadline), who are enrolled in a public, private, or parochial high school or home study program in the United States and its territories. Contact your local VFW Post to enter (entry must not be mailed to the VFW National Headquarters, only to a local, participating VFW Post). Purpose is to give high school students the opportunity to voice their opinions about their responsibility to our country and to convey those opinions via the broadcast media to all of America. Deadline: November 1. **Prize: Winners receive awards ranging from $1,000-30,000.**

WESTERN AUSTRALIAN PREMIER'S BOOK AWARDS

State Library of Western Australia, Perth Cultural Centre, 25 Francis St., Perth WA 6000, Australia. (61)(8)9427-3151. **E-mail:** premiersbookawards@slwa.wa.gov.au. **Website:** pba.slwa.wa.gov.au. **Contact:** Karen de San Miguel. Annual competition for Australian citizens or permanent residents of Australia, or writers whose work has Australia as its primary focus. Categories: children's books, digital narrative, fiction, nonfiction, poetry, scripts, writing for young adults, West Australian history, and Western Australian emerging writers. Submit 5 original copies of the work to be considered for the awards. All works must have been published between January 1 and December 31 of the prior year. See website for details and rules of entry. Deadline: January 31. **Prize: Awards $25,000 for Premier's Prize; awards $15,000 each for the Children's Books, Digital Narrative, Fiction, and Nonfiction categories; awards $10,000 each for the Poetry, Scripts, Western Australian History, Western Australian Emerging Writers, and Writing for Young Adults; awards $5,000 for People's Choice Award.**

WESTERN HERITAGE AWARDS

National Cowboy & Western Heritage Museum, 1700 NE 63rd St., Oklahoma City OK 73111-7997. (405)478-2250. **Fax:** (405)478-4714. **Website:** www.nationalcowboymuseum.org. **Contact:** Jessica Limestall. The National Cowboy & Western Heritage Museum Western Heritage Awards were established to honor and encourage the legacy of those whose works in literature, music, film, and television reflect the significant stories of the American West. Accepted categories for literary entries: western novel, nonfiction book, art book, photography book, juvenile book, magazine article, or poetry book. Previously published submissions only; must be published the calendar year before the awards are presented. Requirements for entrants: The material must pertain to the development or preservation of the West, either from a historical or contemporary viewpoint. Literary entries must have been published between December 1 and November 30 of calendar year. Five copies of each published work must be furnished for judging with each entry, along with the completed entry form. Works recognized during special awards ceremonies held annually at the museum. There is an autograph party preceding the awards. Awards ceremonies are sometimes broadcast. The WHA are presented annually to encourage the accurate and artistic telling of great stories of the West through 16 categories of western literature, television, film and music; including fiction, nonfiction, children's books and poetry. See website for details and category definitions. Deadline: November 30. **Prize: Awards a Wrangler** bronze sculpture designed by famed western artist, John Free.** Judged by a panel of judges selected each year with distinction in various fields of western art and heritage.

WESTERN WRITERS OF AMERICA

271CR 219, Encampment WY 82325. (307)329-8942. **Fax:** (307)327-5465 (call first). **E-mail:** wwa.moulton@gmail.com. **Website:** www.westernwriters.org. **Contact:** Candy Moulton, executive director. Seventeen Spur Award categories in various aspects of the American West. Send entry form with your published work. Accepts multiple submissions, each with its own entry form. The nonprofit Western Writers of America has promoted and honored the best in western literature with the annual Spur Awards, selected by panels of judges. Awards, for material published last year, are given for works whose inspirations, image, and literary excellence best represent the reality and spirit of the American West.

JACKIE WHITE MEMORIAL NATIONAL CHILDREN'S PLAY WRITING CONTEST

1800 Nelwood Dr., Columbia MO 65202-1447. (573)874-5628. **E-mail:** jwmcontest@cectheatre.org. **Website:** www.cectheatre.org. **Contact:** Tom Phillips. Annual contest that encourages playwrights to write quality plays for family audiences. Previously unpublished submissions only. Submissions made by author. Play may be performed during the following season. All submissions will be read by at least 3 readers. Author will receive a written evaluation of the script. Guidelines available online. Deadline: June 1. **Prize: $500 with production possible.** Judging by current and past board members of CEC and by nonboard members who direct plays at CEC.

LAURA INGALLS WILDER MEDAL

50 E. Huron, Chicago IL 60611. (800)545-2433. **E-mail:** alscawards@ala.org. **Website:** www.ala.org/alsc/awardsgrants/bookmedia/wildermedal. Award offered every 2 years. The Wilder Award honors an author or illustrator whose books, published in the US, have made, over a period of years, a substantial and lasting contribution to literature for children. The candidates must be nominated by ALSC members. Medal presented at Newbery/Caldecott banquet during annual conference. Judging by Wilder Award Selection Committee.

WILLA LITERARY AWARD

E-mail: anneschroederauthor@gmail.com. **Website:** www.womenwritingthewest.org. **Contact:** Anne Schroeder. The WILLA Literary Award honors the year's best in published literature featuring women's or girls' stories set in the West. Women Writing the West (WWW), a nonprofit association of writers and other professionals writing and promoting the Women's West, underwrites and presents the nationally recognized award annually (for work published between January 1 and December 31). The award is named in honor of Pulitzer Prize winner Willa Cather, one of the country's foremost novelists. The award is given in 7 categories: historical fiction, contemporary fiction, original softcover fiction, creative nonfiction, scholarly nonfiction, poetry, and children's/young adult fiction/nonfiction. Entry forms available on the website. Deadline: November 1–February 1. **Prize: $100 and a trophy. Finalist receives a plaque. Both receive digital and sticker award emblems for book covers. Notice of winning and finalist titles mailed to more than 4,000 booksellers, libraries, and others. Award announcement is in early August, and awards are presented to the winners and finalists at the annual WWW Fall Conference.** Judged by professional librarians not affiliated with WWW.

RITA WILLIAMS YOUNG ADULT PROSE PRIZE CATEGORY

Soul-Making Keats Literary Competition, The Webhallow House, 1544 Sweetwood Drive, Broadmoor Village CA 94015-2029. **E-mail:** SoulKeats@mail.com. **Website:** www.soulmakingcontest.us. **Contact:** Eileen Malone. For writers in grades 9-12 or equivalent age. Up to 3,000 words in prose form of choice. Complete rules and guidelines available online. Deadline: November 30 (postmarked). **Prize: $100 for first place; $50 for second place; $25 for third place.** Judged (and sponsored) by Rita Williams, an Emmy-award winning investigative reporter with KTVU-TV in Oakland, California.

PAUL A. WITTY OUTSTANDING LITERATURE AWARD

P.O. Box 8139, Newark DE 19714-8139. (800)336-7323. **Fax:** (302)731-1057. **Website:** www.reading.org. **Contact:** Marcie Craig Post, executive director. This award recognizes excellence in original poetry or prose written by students. Elementary and secondary students whose work is selected will receive an award. Deadline: February 2. **Prize: Not less than $25 and a citation of merit.**

WORK-IN-PROGRESS GRANT

Society of Children's Book Writers and Illustrators (SCBWI), 8271 Beverly Blvd., Los Angeles CA 90048. (323)782-1010. **E-mail:** grants@scbwi.org; wipgrant@scbwi.org. **Website:** www.scbwi.org. Six grants—one designated specifically for picture book text, chapter book/early readers, middle grade, young adult fiction, nonfiction, and multicultural fiction or nonfiction—to assist SCBWI members in the completion of a specific project. Open to SCBWI members only. Deadline: March 31. Open to submissions on March 1.

WRITE NOW

Indiana Repertory Theatre, 140 W. Washington St., Indianapolis IN 46204. 480-921-5770. **E-mail:** info@writenow.co. **Website:** www.writenow.co. The purpose of this biennial workshop is to encourage writers to create strikingly original scripts for young audiences. It provides a forum through which each playwright receives constructive criticism and the support of a development team consisting of a professional director and dramaturg. Finalists will spend approximately one week in workshop with their development team. At the end of the week, each play will be read as a part of the Write Now convening. Guidelines available online. Deadline: August 15.

WRITER'S DIGEST SELF-PUBLISHED BOOK AWARDS

Writer's Digest, 10151 Carver Road, Suite #200, Blue Ash OH 45242. (715)445-4612, ext. 13430. **E-mail:** WritersDigestSelfPublishingCompetition@fwmedia.com. **Website:** www.writersdigest.com. **Contact:** Nicole Howard. Contest open to all English-language, self-published books for which the authors have paid the full cost of publication, or the cost of printing has been paid for by a grant or as part of a prize. Categories include: Mainstream/Literary Fiction, Genre Fiction, Nonfiction, Inspirational (spiritual/new age), Life Stories (biographies/autobiographies/family histories/memoirs), Children's Books, Reference Books (directories/encyclopedias/guide books), Poetry, and Middle-Grade/Young Adult Books. Judges reserve the right to recategorize entries. Judges reserve the right to withhold prizes in any category. All winners will be notified in October. Entrants must send a printed and bound book. Entries will be evaluated on content, writing quality, and overall quality of production and appearance. No handwritten books are accepted. Books must have been published within the past 5 years from the competition deadline. Books which have previously won awards from *Writer's Digest* are not eligible. Early bird deadline: April 3. **Prizes: Grand Prize: $8,000, a trip to the Writer's Digest Conference, promotion in *Writer's Digest*, 10 copies of the book will be sent to major review houses, and a guaranteed review in *Midwest Book Review*; 1st Place (9 winners): $1,000 and promotion in *Writer's Digest*; Honorable Mentions: $50 worth of Writer's Digest Books and promotion on writersdigest.com. All entrants will receive a brief commentary from one of the judges.**

WRITER'S DIGEST SELF-PUBLISHED E-BOOK AWARDS

Writer's Digest, 10151 Carver Road, Suite #200, Blue Ash OH 45242. (715)445-4612, ext. 13430. **E-mail:** WritersDigestSelfPublishingCompetition@fwmedia.com. **Website:** www.writersdigest.com. **Contact:** Nicole Howard. Contest open to all English-language, self-published e-books for which the authors have paid the full cost of publication, or the cost of publication has been paid for by a grant or as part of a prize. Categories include: Mainstream/Literary Fiction, Genre Fiction, Nonfiction (includes reference books), Inspirational (spiritual/new age), Life Stories (biographies/autobiographies/family histories/memoirs), Children's Books, Poetry, and Middle-Grade/Young Adult Books. Judges reserve the right to re-categorize entries. Judges reserve the right to withhold prizes in any category. All winners will be notified by December 31. Entrants must enter online. Entrants may provide a file of the book or submit entry by the Amazon gifting process. Acceptable file types include: .epub, .mobi, .ipa. Word processing documents will not be accepted. Entries will be evaluated on content, writing quality, and overall quality of production and appearance. Books must have been published within the past 5 years from the competition deadline. Books which have previously won awards from *Writer's Digest* are not eligible. Early bird deadline: August 6; Deadline: September 1. **Prizes: Grand Prize: $5,000, promotion in *Writer's Digest*, $200 worth** of Writer's Digest Books, and more; 1st Place (9 winners): $1,000 and promotion in *Writer's Digest*; Honorable Mentions: $50 worth of Writer's Digest Books and promotion on writersdigest. com. All entrants will receive a brief commentary from one of the judges.

WRITERS-EDITORS NETWORK INTERNATIONAL WRITING COMPETITION

CNW Publishing, P.O. Box A, North Stratford NH 03590-0167. **E-mail:** contestentry@writers-editors. com. **E-mail:** info@writers-editors.com. **Website:** www.writers-editors.com. **Contact:** Dana K. Cassell, executive director. Annual award to recognize publishable talent. New categories and awards for 2016: Nonfiction (unpublished or self-published; may be an article, blog post, essay/opinion piece, column, nonfiction book chapter, children's article or book chapter); fiction (unpublished or self-published; may be a short story, novel chapter, Young Adult [YA] or children's story or book chapter); poetry (unpublished or self-published; may be traditional or free verse poetry or children's verse). Guidelines available online. Open to any writer. Maximum length: 4,000 words. Accepts inquiries by e-mail, phone, and mail. Entry form online. Results announced May 31. Winners notified by mail and posted on website. Results available for SASE or visit website. Deadline: March 15. **Prize: 1st Place: $150 plus one year Writers-Editors membership; 2nd Place: $100; 3rd Place: $75. All winners and Honorable Mentions will receive certificates as warranted. Most Promising entry in each category will receive a free critique by a contest judge.** Judged by editors, librarians, and writers.

○ WRITERS' GUILD OF ALBERTA AWARDS

Writers' Guild of Alberta, Percy Page Centre, 11759 Groat Rd., Edmonton, Alberta T5M 3K6, Canada. (780)422-8174. **Fax:** (780)422-2663. **E-mail:** mail@ writersguild.ca. **Website:** writersguild.ca. **Contact:** Executive Director. Offers the following awards: Wilfrid Eggleston Award for Nonfiction; Georges Bugnet Award for Fiction; Howard O'Hagan Award for Short Story; Stephan G. Stephansson Award for Poetry; R. Ross Annett Award for Children's Literature; Gwen Pharis Ringwood Award for Drama; Jon Whyte Memorial Essay Award; James H. Gray Award for Short Nonfiction. Eligible entries will have been published anywhere in the world between

January 1 and December 31 of the current year. The authors must have been residents of Alberta for at least 12 of the 18 months prior to December 31. Unpublished mss, except in the drama and essay categories, are not eligible. Anthologies are not eligible. Works may be submitted by authors, publishers, or any interested parties. Deadline: December 31. **Prize: Winning authors receive $1,500; short piece prize winners receive $700.**

WRITERS' LEAGUE OF TEXAS BOOK AWARDS

Writers' League of Texas, 611 S. Congress Ave., Suite 200A-3, Austin TX 78704. (512)499-8914. **Fax:** (512)499-0441. **E-mail:** sara@writersleague.org. **E-mail:** sara@writersleague.org. **Website:** www.writersleague.org. Open to Texas authors of books published the previous year. Authors are required to show proof of Texas residency (current or past), but are not required to be members of the Writers' League of Texas. Deadline: February 28. Open to submissions October 7. **Prize: $1,000 and a commemorative award.**

WRITING CONFERENCE WRITING CONTESTS

P.O. Box 664, Ottawa KS 66067-0664. (785)242-2947. **Fax:** (785)242-2473. **E-mail:** jbushman@writing-conference.com. **E-mail:** support@studentq.com. **Website:** www.writingconference.com. **Contact:** John H. Bushman, contest director. Unpublished submissions only. Submissions made by the author or teacher. Purpose of contest: To further writing by students with awards for narration, exposition and poetry at the elementary, middle school, and high school levels. Deadline: January 8. **Prize: Awards plaque and publication of winning entry in The Writers' Slate online, April issue.** Judged by a panel of teachers.

YEARBOOK EXCELLENCE CONTEST

100 Adler Journalism Building, Iowa City IA 52242-2004. (319)335-3457. **Fax:** (319)335-3989. **E-mail:** quill-scroll@uiowa.edu. **Website:** www.quilland-scroll.org. **Contact:** Vanessa Shelton, executive director. High school students who are contributors to or staff members of a student yearbook at any public or private high school are invited to enter the competition. Awards will be made in each of the 18 divisions. There are two enrollment categories: Class A: more than 750 students; Class B: 749 or less. Win-

ners will receive Quill and Scroll's National Award Gold Key and, if seniors, are eligible to apply for one of the Edward J. Nell Memorial or George and Ophelia Gallup scholarships. Open to students whose schools have Quill and Scroll charters. Previously published submissions only. Submissions made by the author or school yearbook adviser. Must be published in the 12-month span prior to contest deadline. Visit website for list of current and previous winners. Purpose is to recognize and reward student journalists for their work in yearbooks and to provide student winners an opportunity to apply for a scholarship to be used freshman year in college for students planning to major in journalism. Deadline: November 1.

🌀 THE YOUNG ADULT FICTION PRIZE

Victorian Premier's Literary Awards, State Government of Victoria, The Wheeler Centre, 176 Little Lonsdale Street, Melbourne VIC 3000, Australia. (61)(3)90947800. **E-mail:** vpla@wheelercentre.com. **Website:** www.wheelercentre.com/projects/victorian-premier-s-literary-awards-2016/about-the-awards. **Contact:** Project Officer. Visit website for guidelines and nomination forms. **Prize: $25,000.**

YOUNG READER'S CHOICE AWARD

E-mail: hbray@missoula.lib.mt.us. **Website:** www.pnla.org. **Contact:** Honore Bray, president. The Pacific Northwest Library Association's Young Reader's Choice Award is the oldest children's choice award in the US and Canada. Nominations are taken only from children, teachers, parents, and librarians in the Pacific Northwest: Alaska, Alberta, British Columbia, Idaho, Montana, and Washington. Nominations will not be accepted from publishers. Nominations may include fiction, nonfiction, graphic novels, anime, and manga. Nominated titles are those published 3 years prior to the award year. Deadline: February 1. Books will be judged on popularity with readers. Age appropriateness will be considered when choosing which of the three divisions a book is placed. Other considerations may include reading enjoyment; reading level; interest level; genre representation; gender representation; racial diversity; diversity of social, political, economic, or religions viewpoints; regional consideration; effectiveness of expression; and imagination. The Pacific Northwest Library Association is committed to intellectual freedom and diversity of ideas.

No title will be excluded because of race, nationality, religion, gender, sexual orientation, political or social view of either the author or the material.

THE YOUTH HONOR AWARDS

Skipping Stones Youth Honor Awards, Skipping Stones Magazine, Skipping Stones Magazine, P.O. Box 3939, Eugene OR 97403, USA. (541)342-4956. **E-mail:** info@skippingstones.org. **E-mail:** editor@skippingstones.org. **Website:** www.skippingstones.org. **Contact:** Arun N. Toke, editor and publisher. *Skipping Stones* is an international, literary, and multicultural, children's magazine that encourages cooperation, creativity, and celebration of cultural and linguistic diversity. It explores stewardship of the ecological and social webs that nurture us. It offers a forum for communication among children from different lands and backgrounds. *Skipping Stones* expands horizons in a playful, creative way. This is a noncommercial, nonprofit magazine with no advertisements. In its 28th year. Original writing and art from youth, ages 7 to 17, should be typed or neatly handwritten. The entries should be appropriate for ages 7 to 17. Prose under 1,000 words; poems under 30 lines. Word limit: 1,000. Poetry: 30 lines. Non-English and bilingual writings are welcome. To promote multicultural, international, and nature awareness. Deadline: June 25. **Prize: An Honor Award Certificate, a subscription to *Skipping Stones* and five nature and/or multicultural books. They are also invited to join the Student Review Board. Everyone who enters the contest receives the autumn issue featuring the 10 winners and other noteworthy entries.** Editors and interns at the *Skipping Stones* magazine

Youth awards are for children only; you must be under 18 years of age to qualify.

ANNA ZORNIO MEMORIAL CHILDREN'S THEATRE PLAYWRITING COMPETITION

University of New Hampshire, Department of Theatre and Dance, PCAC, 30 Academic Way, Durham NH 03824. (603)862-3038. **Fax:** (603)862-0298. **E-mail:** mike.wood@unh.edu. **Website:** http://cola.unh.edu/theatre-dance/program/anna-zornio-childrens-theatre-playwriting-award. **Contact:** Michael Wood. Offered every 4 years for unpublished well-written plays or musicals appropriate for young audiences with a maximum length of 60 minutes. May submit more than 1 play, but not more than 3. Honors the late Anna Zornio, an alumna of The University of New Hampshire, for dedication to and inspiration of playwriting for young people, K-12th grade. Deadline: March 1. **Prize: $500.**

SUBJECT INDEX

ACTIVITY BOOKS
Bess Press 142
Black Rose Writing 143
Chicago Review Press 147
Child's Play (International) Ltd. 197
Farrar, Straus & Giroux for Young
 Readers 154
Gibbs Smith 156
Godine, Publisher, David R. 157
Jewish Lights Publishing 161
Kar-Ben Publishing 163
Kids Can Press 199
Magination Press 165
Master Books 166
Nomad Press 170
Sasquatch Books 179
Sterling Publishing Co., Inc. 184
Windward Publishing 190

ADVENTURE
Advocate, PKA's Publication 207
Amulet Books 138

Bancroft Press 140
Barrons Educational Series 141
Black Rose Writing 143
Bread for God's Children 209
Cadet Quest Magazine 210
Children's Brains are Yummy
 (CBAY) Books 147
Child's Play (International) Ltd. 197
Creative Company 149
Curiosity Quills Press 150
Dial Books for Young Readers 151
Faces 212
Farrar, Straus & Giroux for Young
 Readers 154
Fickling Books, David 198
Fun for Kidz 213
Godine, Publisher, David R. 157
Hachai Publishing 158
Highlights for Children 214
JourneyForth 162
Kaeden Books 162

Kar-Ben Publishing 163

Kids Can Press 199

Little, Brown Books for Young
    Readers 164

Milkweed Editions 167

New Moon Girls 218

OnStage Publishing 170

Orca Book Publishers 201

PageSpring Publishing 171

Pockets 219

Roaring Brook Press 179

Sasquatch Books 179

Seedling Continental Press 181

SHINE brightly 220

Simon & Schuster Books for Young
    Readers 182

Sleeping Bear Press 183

Sparkle 222

Stone Arch Books 184

Thistledown Press Ltd. 203

Tor Books 186

Tradewind Books 203

Tu Books 187

Tyndale House Publishers, Inc. 188

Usborne Publishing 204

Viking Children's Books 188

Whitman, Albert & Company 189

Windward Publishing 190

Wiseman Books, Paula 190

Young Rider 223

ANIMAL

Advocate, PKA's Publication 207

Aquila 208

Bancroft Press 140

Barefoot Books 140

Barrons Educational Series 141

Black Rose Writing 143

Bread for God's Children 209

Candlewick Press 145

Child's Play (International) Ltd. 197

Creative Company 149

Dawn Publications 150

Dial Books for Young Readers 151

Farrar, Straus & Giroux for Young
    Readers 154

Fickling Books, David 198

Fun for Kidz 213

Godine, Publisher, David R. 157

Highlights for Children 214

JourneyForth 162

Kaeden Books 162

Kids Can Press 199

Little, Brown Books for Young
    Readers 164

Little Tiger Press 200

New Moon Girls 218

Orca Book Publishers 201

Orchard Books (US) 171

PageSpring Publishing 171

Pineapple Press, Inc. 175

Roaring Brook Press 179

Sasquatch Books 179

Seedling Continental Press 181

SHINE brightly 220

Simon & Schuster Books for Young
    Readers 182

Sleeping Bear Press 183

Sparkle 222

Tafelberg Publishers 203

Tor Books 186

Tradewind Books 203

Viking Children's Books 188

Windward Publishing 190

Wiseman Books, Paula 190

Young Rider 223

ANIMAL NONFICTION

Advocate, PKA's Publication 207

Aquila 208

Bancroft Press 140

Black Rose Writing 143

Child's Play (International) Ltd. 197

Creative Company 149

Dawn Publications 150

Faces 212

Farrar, Straus & Giroux for Young
    Readers 154

Fun for Kidz 213

Godine, Publisher, David R. 157

Highlights for Children 214

Kaeden Books 162

Kids Can Press 199

Master Books 166

National Geographic Kids 218

New Moon Girls 218

Pineapple Press, Inc. 175

Ronsdale Press 202

Sasquatch Books 179

Scholastic Library Publishing 180

Seedling Continental Press 181

SHINE brightly 220

Skipping Stones: A Multicultural
    Literary Magazine 221

Sparkle 222

Viking Children's Books 188

Whitman, Albert & Company 189

Windward Publishing 190

Wiseman Books, Paula 190

World Book, Inc. 191

Young Rider 223

ANTHOLOGY

Barefoot Books 140

Children's Brains are Yummy
    (CBAY) Books 147

Child's Play (International) Ltd. 197

Creative Company 149

Farrar, Straus & Giroux for Young
    Readers 154

Fickling Books, David 198

Lee & Low Books 164

Tafelberg Publishers 203

Thistledown Press Ltd. 203

Tor Books 186

Wiseman Books, Paula 190

ARTS/CRAFTS

Advocate, PKA's Publication 207

Aquila 208

Brilliant Star 209

Cadet Quest Magazine 210

Carolrhoda Books, Inc. 146

Chicago Review Press 147

Creative Company 149

Dramatics Magazine 211

Faces 212

Farrar, Straus & Giroux for Young
    Readers 154

Fun for Kidz 213

Gibbs Smith 156

Girls' Life 213

Highlights for Children 214

Kar-Ben Publishing 163

Kids Can Press 199

Little, Brown Books for Young
    Readers 164
National Geographic Kids 218
New Moon Girls 218
Scholastic Library Publishing 180
Seedling Continental Press 181
SHINE brightly 220
Sparkle 222
Sterling Publishing Co., Inc. 184
Whitman, Albert & Company 189
World Book, Inc. 191

BIOGRAPHY

Advocate, PKA's Publication 207
Bancroft Press 140
Barrons Educational Series 141
Black Rose Writing 143
Candlewick Press 145
Carolrhoda Books, Inc. 146
Creative Company 149
Darby Creek Publishing 150
Dial Books for Young Readers 151
Dig into History 211
Faces 212
Farrar, Straus & Giroux for Young
    Readers 154
Godine, Publisher, David R. 157
Highlights for Children 214
JourneyForth 162
Kaeden Books 162
Kar-Ben Publishing 163
Kids Can Press 199
Lee & Low Books 164
Master Books 166
Mitchell Lane Publishers, Inc. 168
National Geographic Kids 218

New Moon Girls 218
Pelican Publishing Company 173
Pineapple Press, Inc. 175
Puffin Books 177
Ronsdale Press 202
Scholastic Library Publishing 180
Second Story Press 202
Seedling Continental Press 181
Simon & Schuster Books for Young
    Readers 182
Skipping Stones: A Multicultural
    Literary Magazine 221
Sparkle 222
Viking Children's Books 188
Wiseman Books, Paula 190

CAREERS

Advocate, PKA's Publication 207
CollegeXpress Magazine 211
Creative Company 149
Dramatics Magazine 211
Farrar, Straus & Giroux for Young
    Readers 154
Highlights for Children 214
Kaeden Books 162
Kar-Ben Publishing 163
Kids Can Press 199
New Moon Girls 218
On Course 219
Scholastic Library Publishing 180
Seedling Continental Press 181
Seventeen Magazine 220
SHINE brightly 220
Sparkle 222
Windward Publishing 190
World Book, Inc. 191

Young Rider 223

CONCEPT

Barefoot Books 140

Barrons Educational Series 141

Candlewick Press 145

Child's Play (International) Ltd. 197

Farrar, Straus & Giroux for Young
Readers 154

Fickling Books, David 198

Kaeden Books 162

Kar-Ben Publishing 163

Kids Can Press 199

Lee & Low Books 164

Little Tiger Press 200

Sasquatch Books 179

Sleeping Bear Press 183

Tor Books 186

Whitman, Albert & Company 189

Wiseman Books, Paula 190

CONCEPT NONFICTION

Advocate, PKA's Publication 207

Aquila 208

Bancroft Press 140

Barrons Educational Series 141

Black Rose Writing 143

Candlewick Press 145

Child's Play (International) Ltd. 197

Farrar, Straus & Giroux for Young
Readers 154

Kar-Ben Publishing 163

Kids Can Press 199

Lee & Low Books 164

Puffin Books 177

Sasquatch Books 179

Scholastic Library Publishing 180

Seedling Continental Press 181

Simon & Schuster Books for Young
Readers 182

Sparkle 222

Viking Children's Books 188

Wiseman Books, Paula 190

World Book, Inc. 191

CONTEMPORARY

Advocate, PKA's Publication 207

Amulet Books 138

Aquila 208

Bancroft Press 140

Bread for God's Children 209

Brilliant Star 209

Candlewick Press 145

Child's Play (International) Ltd. 197

Creative Company 149

Farrar, Straus & Giroux for Young
Readers 154

Fickling Books, David 198

Godine, Publisher, David R. 157

Hachai Publishing 158

Highlights for Children 214

JourneyForth 162

Kaeden Books 162

Kids Can Press 199

Lee & Low Books 164

Little, Brown Books for Young
Readers 164

Little Tiger Press 200

Milkweed Editions 167

New Moon Girls 218

On Course 219

OnStage Publishing 170

Orca Book Publishers 201

Orchard Books (US) 171

PageSpring Publishing 171

Pockets 219

Roaring Brook Press 179

Sasquatch Books 179

SHINE brightly 220

Simon & Schuster Books for Young
    Readers 182

Skipping Stones: A Multicultural
    Literary Magazine 221

Sparkle 222

Stone Arch Books 184

Tafelberg Publishers 203

Thistledown Press Ltd. 203

Tor Books 186

Tu Books 187

Usborne Publishing 204

Viking Children's Books 188

Wiseman Books, Paula 190

COOKING

Advocate, PKA's Publication 207

Aquila 208

Faces 212

Farrar, Straus & Giroux for Young
    Readers 154

Fun for Kidz 213

Gibbs Smith 156

Kar-Ben Publishing 163

Kids Can Press 199

National Geographic Kids 218

New Moon Girls 218

Pockets 219

Seventeen Magazine 220

SHINE brightly 220

Skipping Stones: A Multicultural

Literary Magazine 221

Sparkle 222

Sterling Publishing Co., Inc. 184

FANTASY

Advocate, PKA's Publication 207

Amulet Books 138

Aquila 208

Atheneum Books for Young Read-
    ers 139

Bancroft Press 140

Barefoot Books 140

Barrons Educational Series 141

Black Rose Writing 143

Brilliant Star 209

Candlewick Press 145

Carolrhoda Books, Inc. 146

Children's Brains are Yummy
    (CBAY) Books 147

Creative Company 149

Curiosity Quills Press 150

Dial Books for Young Readers 151

Evil Jester PRess 153

Farrar, Straus & Giroux for Young
    Readers 154

Fey Publishing 154

Fickling Books, David 198

Highlights for Children 214

JourneyForth 162

Kids Can Press 199

Leading Edge 216

Milkweed Editions 167

New Moon Girls 218

OnStage Publishing 170

Orca Book Publishers 201

Roaring Brook Press 179

Simon & Schuster Books for Young
    Readers 182
Stone Arch Books 184
Tafelberg Publishers 203
Thistledown Press Ltd. 203
Tor Books 186
Tu Books 187
Usborne Publishing 204
Viking Children's Books 188
Whitman, Albert & Company 189
Wiseman Books, Paula 190

FASHION
Advocate, PKA's Publication 207
Faces 212
Girls' Life 213
SHINE brightly 220
Sparkle 222

FOLKTALES
Advocate, PKA's Publication 207
Aquila 208
Barefoot Books 140
Brilliant Star 209
Children's Brains are Yummy
    (CBAY) Books 147
Child's Play (International) Ltd. 197
Creative Company 149
Dial Books for Young Readers 151
Faces 212
Farrar, Straus & Giroux for Young
    Readers 154
Fickling Books, David 198
Godine, Publisher, David R. 157
Highlights for Children 214
JourneyForth 162
Kar-Ben Publishing 163

Kids Can Press 199
Little, Brown Books for Young
    Readers 164
New Moon Girls 218
Piano Press 174
Pineapple Press, Inc. 175
Pockets 219
Seedling Continental Press 181
Skipping Stones: A Multicultural
    Literary Magazine 221
Sleeping Bear Press 183
Tafelberg Publishers 203
Tradewind Books 203
Tu Books 187
Wiseman Books, Paula 190

GAMES/PUZZLES
Advocate, PKA's Publication 207
Aquila 208
Brilliant Star 209
Cadet Quest Magazine 210
Dig into History 211
Faces 212
Fun for Kidz 213
Highlights for Children 214
National Geographic Kids 218
New Moon Girls 218
Pockets 219
SHINE brightly 220
Skipping Stones: A Multicultural
    Literary Magazine 221
Sparkle 222

GEOGRAPHY
Advocate, PKA's Publication 207
Brilliant Star 209
Candlewick Press 145

Carolrhoda Books, Inc. 146
Click 210
Creative Company 149
Faces 212
Farrar, Straus & Giroux for Young
    Readers 154
Highlights for Children 214
Kaeden Books 162
National Geographic Kids 218
Pineapple Press, Inc. 175
Scholastic Library Publishing 180
Sparkle 222
Tor Books 186
Viking Children's Books 188
World Book, Inc. 191

HEALTH

Advocate, PKA's Publication 207
Aquila 208
Black Rose Writing 143
Farrar, Straus & Giroux for Young
    Readers 154
Fickling Books, David 198
Magination Press 165
SHINE brightly 220
Sparkle 222
Wiseman Books, Paula 190

HEALTH NONFICTION

Aquila 208
Bancroft Press 140
Black Rose Writing 143
CollegeXpress Magazine 211
Creative Company 149
Farrar, Straus & Giroux for Young
    Readers 154
Highlights for Children 214

Kids Can Press 199
Magination Press 165
National Geographic Kids 218
New Moon Girls 218
Scholastic Library Publishing 180
SHINE brightly 220
Sparkle 222
Whitman, Albert & Company 189
World Book, Inc. 191
Young Rider 223

HI-LO

Farrar, Straus & Giroux for Young
    Readers 154
Fickling Books, David 198
Orca Book Publishers 201
PageSpring Publishing 171
Tafelberg Publishers 203
Tu Books 187
Viking Children's Books 188
Wiseman Books, Paula 190

HI-LO NONFICTION

Barrons Educational Series 141
Farrar, Straus & Giroux for Young
    Readers 154
Viking Children's Books 188

HISTORY

Amulet Books 138
Aquila 208
Black Rose Writing 143
Calkins Creek 144
Candlewick Press 145
Creative Company 149
Dial Books for Young Readers 151
Faces 212

Farrar, Straus & Giroux for Young
Readers 154
Fickling Books, David 198
Fun for Kidz 213
Godine, Publisher, David R. 157
Hachai Publishing 158
Hendrick-Long Publishing Co., Inc.
159
Highlights for Children 214
JourneyForth 162
Kaeden Books 162
Kar-Ben Publishing 163
Kids Can Press 199
Lee & Low Books 164
Little, Brown Books for Young
Readers 164
New Moon Girls 218
OnStage Publishing 170
Orca Book Publishers 201
Orchard Books (US) 171
Pelican Publishing Company 173
Pineapple Press, Inc. 175
Roaring Brook Press 179
Ronsdale Press 202
Second Story Press 202
SHINE brightly 220
Simon & Schuster Books for Young
Readers 182
Sleeping Bear Press 183
Tor Books 186
Usborne Publishing 204
Viking Children's Books 188
White Mane Kids 189
Whitman, Albert & Company 189
Wiseman Books, Paula 190

HISTORY NONFICTION

Advocate, PKA's Publication 207
Aquila 208
Bancroft Press 140
Calkins Creek 144
Carolrhoda Books, Inc. 146
Chicago Review Press 147
Creative Company 149
Darby Creek Publishing 150
Dial Books for Young Readers 151
Dig into History 211
Faces 212
Farrar, Straus & Giroux for Young
Readers 154
Friend Magazine, The 213
Fun for Kidz 213
Godine, Publisher, David R. 157
Greenhaven Press 157
Highlights for Children 214
Kaeden Books 162
Kar-Ben Publishing 163
Kids Can Press 199
Lee & Low Books 164
Little, Brown Books for Young
Readers 164
National Geographic Kids 218
New Moon Girls 218
Nomad Press 170
Pelican Publishing Company 173
Pineapple Press, Inc. 175
Puffin Books 177
Ronsdale Press 202
Scholastic Library Publishing 180
Simon & Schuster Books for Young
Readers 182
Skipping Stones: A Multicultural

Literary Magazine 221
Sparkle 222
Tor Books 186
Viking Children's Books 188
White Mane Kids 189
Whitman, Albert & Company 189
Wiseman Books, Paula 190
World Book, Inc. 191

HOBBIES
Advocate, PKA's Publication 207
Cadet Quest Magazine 210
Creative Company 149
Farrar, Straus & Giroux for Young
    Readers 154
Fun for Kidz 213
Girls' Life 213
Highlights for Children 214
Kids Can Press 199
National Geographic Kids 218
New Moon Girls 218
On Course 219
Scholastic Library Publishing 180
Seventeen Magazine 220
SHINE brightly 220
Sparkle 222
Sterling Publishing Co., Inc. 184
Whitman, Albert & Company 189
World Book, Inc. 191

HOW-TO
Advocate, PKA's Publication 207
Aquila 208
Barrons Educational Series 141
Black Rose Writing 143
Brilliant Star 209
Cadet Quest Magazine 210

CollegeXpress Magazine 211
Dramatics Magazine 211
Faces 212
Farrar, Straus & Giroux for Young
    Readers 154
Fun for Kidz 213
Gibbs Smith 156
Highlights for Children 214
Kar-Ben Publishing 163
Kids Can Press 199
Scholastic Library Publishing 180
Seventeen Magazine 220
SHINE brightly 220
Sparkle 222
Sterling Publishing Co., Inc. 184
Tor Books 186
World Book, Inc. 191

HUMOR
Advocate, PKA's Publication 207
Aquila 208
Bancroft Press 140
Black Rose Writing 143
Cadet Quest Magazine 210
Candlewick Press 145
Child's Play (International) Ltd. 197
Dial Books for Young Readers 151
Farrar, Straus & Giroux for Young
    Readers 154
Fickling Books, David 198
Fun for Kidz 213
Highlights for Children 214
JourneyForth 162
Kaeden Books 162
Kar-Ben Publishing 163
Kids Can Press 199

Little, Brown Books for Young
    Readers 164
Little Tiger Press 200
New Moon Girls 218
On Course 219
OnStage Publishing 170
Orchard Books (US) 171
PageSpring Publishing 171
Price Stern Sloan, Inc. 176
Roaring Brook Press 179
Sasquatch Books 179
Seedling Continental Press 181
SHINE brightly 220
Simon & Schuster Books for Young
    Readers 182
Skipping Stones: A Multicultural
    Literary Magazine 221
Sleeping Bear Press 183
Sparkle 222
Stone Arch Books 184
Tafelberg Publishers 203
Thistledown Press Ltd. 203
Tor Books 186
Tu Books 187
Usborne Publishing 204
Viking Children's Books 188
Whitman, Albert & Company 189
Wiseman Books, Paula 190

HUMOR NONFICTION

Advocate, PKA's Publication 207
Black Rose Writing 143
Brilliant Star 209
Cadet Quest Magazine 210
CollegeXpress Magazine 211
Faces 212

Friend Magazine, The 213
Fun for Kidz 213
New Moon Girls 218
Seventeen Magazine 220
SHINE brightly 220
Skipping Stones: A Multicultural
    Literary Magazine 221

INTERVIEW/PROFILE

Advocate, PKA's Publication 207
Aquila 208
Cadet Quest Magazine 210
CollegeXpress Magazine 211
Dramatics Magazine 211
Faces 212
Girls' Life 213
Highlights for Children 214
National Geographic Kids 218
New Moon Girls 218
On Course 219
Seventeen Magazine 220
Skipping Stones: A Multicultural
    Literary Magazine 221
Sparkle 222

MATH

Aquila 208
New Moon Girls 218
Sparkle 222
Multicultural
Aquila 208
Bancroft Press 140
Barefoot Books 140
Barrons Educational Series 141
Brilliant Star 209
Cadet Quest Magazine 210
Candlewick Press 145

Child's Play (International) Ltd. 197
Dial Books for Young Readers 151
Faces 212
Farrar, Straus & Giroux for Young
    Readers 154
Fickling Books, David 198
Fun for Kidz 213
Highlights for Children 214
JourneyForth 162
Kaeden Books 162
Kar-Ben Publishing 163
Kids Can Press 199
Lee & Low Books 164
Little, Brown Books for Young
    Readers 164
Magination Press 165
Milkweed Editions 167
New Moon Girls 218
On Course 219
Orca Book Publishers 201
Orchard Books (US) 171
PageSpring Publishing 171
Pelican Publishing Company 173
Piano Press 174
Pinata Books 174
Pockets 219
Roaring Brook Press 179
Seedling Continental Press 181
SHINE brightly 220
Skipping Stones: A Multicultural
    Literary Magazine 221
Sleeping Bear Press 183
Sparkle 222
Stone Arch Books 184
Tafelberg Publishers 203
Tilbury House Publishers 186

Tor Books 186
Tradewind Books 203
Tu Books 187
Usborne Publishing 204
Viking Children's Books 188
Whitman, Albert & Company 189
Wiseman Books, Paula 190

MULTICULTURAL NONFICTION

Bancroft Press 140
Brilliant Star 209
Chicago Review Press 147
Child's Play (International) Ltd. 197
Creative Company 149
Dramatics Magazine 211
Farrar, Straus & Giroux for Young
    Readers 154
Fulcrum Publishing 156
Highlights for Children 214
Kaeden Books 162
Kar-Ben Publishing 163
Kids Can Press 199
Lee & Low Books 164
Little, Brown Books for Young
    Readers 164
Mitchell Lane Publishers, Inc. 168
National Geographic Kids 218
New Moon Girls 218
On Course 219
Pelican Publishing Company 173
Piano Press 174
Pinata Books 174
Pockets 219
Ronsdale Press 202
Scholastic Library Publishing 180

Seedling Continental Press 181

Seventeen Magazine 220

SHINE brightly 220

Skipping Stones: A Multicultural
    Literary Magazine 221

Sparkle 222

Tilbury House Publishers 186

Tor Books 186

Viking Children's Books 188

Whitman, Albert & Company 189

Wiseman Books, Paula 190

MUSIC/DANCE

Bancroft Press 140

Child's Play (International) Ltd. 197

Creative Company 149

Farrar, Straus & Giroux for Young
    Readers 154

Godine, Publisher, David R. 157

Kaeden Books 162

Kids Can Press 199

Piano Press 174

Viking Children's Books 188

Whitman, Albert & Company 189

NATURE/ENVIRONMENT

Advocate, PKA's Publication 207

Aquila 208

Barefoot Books 140

Barrons Educational Series 141

Black Rose Writing 143

Brilliant Star 209

Candlewick Press 145

Child's Play (International) Ltd. 197

Creative Company 149

Dawn Publications 150

Farrar, Straus & Giroux for Young

Readers 154

Fickling Books, David 198

Fun for Kidz 213

Godine, Publisher, David R. 157

JourneyForth 162

Kids Can Press 199

Lee & Low Books 164

Little, Brown Books for Young
    Readers 164

Milkweed Editions 167

New Moon Girls 218

OnStage Publishing 170

Orca Book Publishers 201

PageSpring Publishing 171

Pineapple Press, Inc. 175

Pockets 219

Roaring Brook Press 179

Sasquatch Books 179

Seedling Continental Press 181

SHINE brightly 220

Skipping Stones: A Multicultural
    Literary Magazine 221

Sleeping Bear Press 183

Sparkle 222

Tafelberg Publishers 203

Tilbury House Publishers 186

Tor Books 186

Tu Books 187

Usborne Publishing 204

Viking Children's Books 188

Windward Publishing 190

Wiseman Books, Paula 190

NATURE/ENVIRONMENT NONFICTION

Advocate, PKA's Publication 207

Aquila 208

Bancroft Press 140

Black Rose Writing 143

Brilliant Star 209

Candlewick Press 145

Carolrhoda Books, Inc. 146

Chicago Review Press 147

Child's Play (International) Ltd. 197

Creative Company 149

Dawn Publications 150

Faces 212

Farrar, Straus & Giroux for Young
 Readers 154

Friend Magazine, The 213

Fulcrum Publishing 156

Gibbs Smith 156

Godine, Publisher, David R. 157

Grosset & Dunlap Publishers 158

Highlights for Children 214

Kaeden Books 162

Kids Can Press 199

Little, Brown Books for Young
 Readers 164

Master Books 166

National Geographic Kids 218

New Moon Girls 218

Pineapple Press, Inc. 175

Sasquatch Books 179

Scholastic Library Publishing 180

Seedling Continental Press 181

SHINE brightly 220

Skipping Stones: A Multicultural
 Literary Magazine 221

Sparkle 222

Tilbury House Publishers 186

Tor Books 186

Viking Children's Books 188

Whitman, Albert & Company 189

Windward Publishing 190

Wiseman Books, Paula 190

World Book, Inc. 191

POETRY

Advocate, PKA's Publication 207

Candlewick Press 145

Child's Play (International) Ltd. 197

Creative Company 149

Dial Books for Young Readers 151

Faces 212

Farrar, Straus & Giroux for Young
 Readers 154

Fickling Books, David 198

Friend Magazine, The 213

Fun for Kidz 213

Godine, Publisher, David R. 157

Kids Can Press 199

Lee & Low Books 164

Orchard Books (US) 171

Piano Press 174

Roaring Brook Press 179

Stone Arch Books 184

Thistledown Press Ltd. 203

Viking Children's Books 188

Wiseman Books, Paula 190

PROBLEM NOVELS

Black Rose Writing 143

PageSpring Publishing 171

PROBLEM-SOLVING

Advocate, PKA's Publication 207

Aquila 208

Black Rose Writing 143

Bread for God's Children 209

Brilliant Star 209

Cadet Quest Magazine 210

Clarion Books 149

Fun for Kidz 213

Highlights for Children 214

New Moon Girls 218

On Course 219

Pockets 219

SHINE brightly 220

Sparkle 222

Tu Books 187

PROBLEM-SOLVING NONFICTION

Advocate, PKA's Publication 207

Black Rose Writing 143

Cadet Quest Magazine 210

CollegeXpress Magazine 211

Fun for Kidz 213

Highlights for Children 214

New Moon Girls 218

SHINE brightly 220

Skipping Stones: A Multicultural
   Literary Magazine 221

Sparkle 222

REFERENCE

Bancroft Press 140

Barrons Educational Series 141

Farrar, Straus & Giroux for Young
   Readers 154

Tor Books 186

World Book, Inc. 191

RELIGIOUS

Aquila 208

Bancroft Press 140

Behrman House Inc. 141

Bread for God's Children 209

Brilliant Star 209

Cadet Quest Magazine 210

Creative Company 149

Faces 212

Farrar, Straus & Giroux for Young
   Readers 154

FCA Magazine 212

Fickling Books, David 198

Friend Magazine, The 213

Hachai Publishing 158

Jewish Lights Publishing 161

JourneyForth 162

Kar-Ben Publishing 163

New Moon Girls 218

On Course 219

Pauline Books & Media 172

Pockets 219

Roaring Brook Press 179

SHINE brightly 220

Skipping Stones: A Multicultural
   Literary Magazine 221

Sleeping Bear Press 183

Sparkle 222

Standard Publishing 184

Tyndale House Publishers, Inc. 188

Viking Children's Books 188

Wiseman Books, Paula 190

ROMANCE

Advocate, PKA's Publication 207

Bread for God's Children 209

Tu Books 187

SCIENCE

Advocate, PKA's Publication 207

Aquila 208
Bancroft Press 140
Cadet Quest Magazine 210
Chicago Review Press 147
Child's Play (International) Ltd. 197
Click 210
Creative Company 149
Darby Creek Publishing 150
Dig into History 211
Farrar, Straus & Giroux for Young
    Readers 154
Gibbs Smith 156
Grosset & Dunlap Publishers 158
Highlights for Children 214
Kaeden Books 162
Kids Can Press 199
Leading Edge 216
Lee & Low Books 164
Little, Brown Books for Young
    Readers 164
Master Books 166
National Geographic Kids 218
New Moon Girls 218
Nomad Press 170
Pineapple Press, Inc. 175
Scholastic Library Publishing 180
Seedling Continental Press 181
Sparkle 222
Sterling Publishing Co., Inc. 184
Tor Books 186
Viking Children's Books 188
Whitman, Albert & Company 189
Windward Publishing 190
World Book, Inc. 191

SCIENCE FICTION

Advocate, PKA's Publication 207

Amulet Books 138
Aquila 208
Atheneum Books for Young Read-
    ers 139
Bancroft Press 140
Black Rose Writing 143
Candlewick Press 145
Carolrhoda Books, Inc. 146
Children's Brains are Yummy
    (CBAY) Books 147
Dial Books for Young Readers 151
Evil Jester PRess 153
Farrar, Straus & Giroux for Young
    Readers 154
Fey Publishing 154
Fickling Books, David 198
Leading Edge 216
New Moon Girls 218
OnStage Publishing 170
Roaring Brook Press 179
Stone Arch Books 184
Tafelberg Publishers 203
Thistledown Press Ltd. 203
Tor Books 186
Tu Books 187
Usborne Publishing 204
Viking Children's Books 188
Wiseman Books, Paula 190

SELF HELP

Bancroft Press 140
Barrons Educational Series 141
Farrar, Straus & Giroux for Young
    Readers 154
Free Spirit Publishing, Inc. 155
Impact Publishers, Inc. 161
Little, Brown Books for Young

Readers 164

Magination Press 165

SOCIAL ISSUES

Advocate, PKA's Publication 207

Brilliant Star 209

Click 210

CollegeXpress Magazine 211

Faces 212

Girls' Life 213

National Geographic Kids 218

New Moon Girls 218

On Course 219

Seventeen Magazine 220

SHINE brightly 220

Skipping Stones: A Multicultural
Literary Magazine 221

Sparkle 222

SPECIAL NEEDS

Black Rose Writing 143

Curiosity Quills Press 150

Tu Books 187

SPECIAL NEEDS NONFICTION

Bancroft Press 140

Black Rose Writing 143

Creative Company 149

Farrar, Straus & Giroux for Young
Readers 154

Free Spirit Publishing, Inc. 155

Kar-Ben Publishing 163

Kids Can Press 199

Magination Press 165

Scholastic Library Publishing 180

Whitman, Albert & Company 189

SPORTS

Advocate, PKA's Publication 207

Amulet Books 138

Aquila 208

Bancroft Press 140

Black Rose Writing 143

Bread for God's Children 209

Cadet Quest Magazine 210

Candlewick Press 145

Creative Company 149

Dial Books for Young Readers 151

Farrar, Straus & Giroux for Young
Readers 154

Fickling Books, David 198

Fun for Kidz 213

Highlights for Children 214

Kaeden Books 162

Kids Can Press 199

Lee & Low Books 164

New Moon Girls 218

On Course 219

PageSpring Publishing 171

Roaring Brook Press 179

SHINE brightly 220

Sleeping Bear Press 183

Sparkle 222

Stone Arch Books 184

Tafelberg Publishers 203

Viking Children's Books 188

Wiseman Books, Paula 190

SPORTS NONFICTION

Advocate, PKA's Publication 207

Aquila 208

Bancroft Press 140

Barrons Educational Series 141

Cadet Quest Magazine 210
Carolrhoda Books, Inc. 146
CollegeXpress Magazine 211
Creative Company 149
Darby Creek Publishing 150
Dial Books for Young Readers 151
Faces 212
Farrar, Straus & Giroux for Young
    Readers 154
FCA Magazine 212
Fun for Kidz 213
Girls' Life 213
Highlights for Children 214
Kids Can Press 199
Lee & Low Books 164
Little, Brown Books for Young
    Readers 164
National Geographic Kids 218
New Moon Girls 218
On Course 219
Scholastic Library Publishing 180
SHINE brightly 220
Skipping Stones: A Multicultural
    Literary Magazine 221
Sparkle 222
Viking Children's Books 188
Whitman, Albert & Company 189
Wiseman Books, Paula 190
Young Rider 223

SUSPENSE/MYSTERY

Advocate, PKA's Publication 207
Amulet Books 138
Aquila 208
Bancroft Press 140
Barrons Educational Series 141

Black Rose Writing 143
Candlewick Press 145
Children's Brains are Yummy
    (CBAY) Books 147
Farrar, Straus & Giroux for Young
    Readers 154
Fickling Books, David 198
Godine, Publisher, David R. 157
Highlights for Children 214
JourneyForth 162
Kaeden Books 162
Kids Can Press 199
Little, Brown Books for Young
    Readers 164
Milkweed Editions 167
New Moon Girls 218
OnStage Publishing 170
Orca Book Publishers 201
PageSpring Publishing 171
Roaring Brook Press 179
Simon & Schuster Books for Young
    Readers 182
Sparkle 222
Stone Arch Books 184
Tafelberg Publishers 203
Thistledown Press Ltd. 203
Tor Books 186
Tu Books 187
Tyndale House Publishers, Inc. 188
Usborne Publishing 204
Viking Children's Books 188
Whitman, Albert & Company 189
Wiseman Books, Paula 190

TEXTBOOKS

Bancroft Press 140

Behrman House Inc. 141
Farrar, Straus & Giroux for Young
    Readers 154
Gryphon House, Inc. 158
Prufrock Press, Inc. 176
Windward Publishing 190
Travel
Advocate, PKA's Publication 207
CollegeXpress Magazine 211
Faces 212
Girls' Life 213
National Geographic Kids 218
New Moon Girls 218
SHINE brightly 220
Skipping Stones: A Multicultural
    Literary Magazine 221
Sparkle 222

EDITOR & AGENT NAMES INDEX

Abell, Whitley (Inklings Literary Agency) 257

Abellera, Lisa (Kimberley Cameron & Associates) 244

Abou, Stephanie (Lippincott Massie McQuilkin) 264

Abkemeier, Laurie (DeFiore & Co. Literary Management, Inc.) 236

Abramo, Lauren (Dystel & Goderich Literary Management) 240

Adams, Josh (Adams Literary) 226

Adams, Tracey (Adams Literary) 226

Agyeman, Janell Walden (Marie Brown Associates Inc.) 231

Alexander, Heather (Pippin Properties, Inc.) 274

Almon, Jessica (Razorbill) 178

Altshuler, Miriam (DeFiore & Co. Literary Management, Inc.) 236

Anderson-Wheeler, Claire (Regal Hoffman & Associates, LLC) 277

Anthony, Jason (Lippincott Massie McQuilkin) 264

Armada, Kurestin (P.S. Literary Agency) 275

Axford, Elizabeth C. (Piano Press) 174

Azantian, Jennifer (Azantian Literary Agency) 226

Bail, Margaret (Inklings Literary Agency) 257

Baker, Sue (Child's Play [International] Ltd.) 197

Baker, T. (Fulcrum Publishing) 156

Baker-Baughman, Bernadette (Victoria Sanders & Associates) 280

Ballard, Noah (Curtis Brown, Ltd.) 230

Barba, Alex (Inklings Literary

Agency) 258

Barbara, Stephen (Inkwell Management, LLC) 248

Barer, Julie (The Book Group) 228

Barnett, Amanda Ayers (Donaghy Literary Group) 238

Barr, Stephen (Writers House) 293

Barr, Wayne (Barron's Educational Series, Inc.) 140

Bassoff, Ethan (Lippincott Massie McQuilkin) 264

Beaty, Tish (L. Perkins Agency) 273

Beaumont, Diana (United Talent Agency 290

Becker, Laney Katz (Lippincott Massie McQuilkin) 264

Bedingfield, Sarah (Levine Greenberg Rostan Literary Agency, Inc.) 263

Bell, Folade (Serendipity Literary Agency, LLC) 281

Bender, Faye (The Book Group) 228

Bennet, David (Transatlantic Literary Agency) 288

Bennet, Lynn (Transatlantic Literary Agency) 288

Bent, Jenny (The Bent Agency) 226

Berkey, Jane Rotrosen (Jane Rotrosen Agency, LLC) 279

Berkower, Amy (Writers House) 293

Berson, Barbara (Helen Heller Agency, Inc.) 255

Biagi, Laura (Jean V. Naggar Literary Agency, Inc.) 271

Bialer, Matt (Sanford J. Greenburger Associates, Inc.) 253

Bilmes, Joshua (Jabberwocky Literary Agency) 259

Bishop, Amy (Dystel & Goderich Literary Management) 240

Bishop, Sandra (Transatlantic Literary Agency) 288

Black, David (David Black Literary Agency) 227

Blasdell, Caitlin (Liza Dawson Associates) 235

Blessing, Lyndsey (Inkwell Management, LLC)

Boggs, Amy (Donald Maass Literary Agency) 266

Bourret, Michael (Dystel & Goderich Literary Management) 240

Bortz, Bruce (Bancroft Press) 140

Boutillier, Katie Shea (Donald Maass Literary Agency) 266

Bowen, Brenda (Sanford J. Greenburger Associates, Inc.) 253

Bowles, Brandi (Foundry Literary + Media) 246

Bowman, Hannah (Liza Dawson Associates) 235

Boyle, Katherine (Veritas Literary Agency) 291

Bradford, Laura (Bradford Literary Agency) 228

Bradley, Shaun (Transatlantic Literary Agency) 288

Bridges, Shirin (Goosebottom

Books) 157

Broder, Amanda (Ripple Grove Press) 178

Broder, Rob (Ripple Grove Press) 178

Brooks, Rachel (L. Perkins Agency) 273

Brooks, Regina (Serendipity Literary Agency, LLC) 281

Brophy, Philippa (Sterling Lord Literistic, Inc.) 265

Brown, Andrea (Andrea Brown literary Agency, Inc.) 230

Brown, Mallory (Triada US Literary Agency, Inc.) 288

Brown, Marie (Marie Brown Associates Inc.) 231

Bucci, Chris (Anne McDermid & Associates Literary, Ltd.) 269

Buck, Bethany (Sanford J. Greenburger Associates, Inc.) 253

Burby, Danielle (Nelson Literary Agency) 272

Burden, Neil (Child's Play [International] Ltd.) 197

Burkot, Rachel (Holloway Literary) 256

Burnes, Sarah (The Gernert Company) 251

Burns, Penelope (Gelfman Schneider/ICM Partners) 250

Burt, Madelyn (Stonesong) 284

Cabot, Stephanie (The Gernert Company) 251

Caiby, Jocquelle (Serendipity Literary Agency, LLC) 281

Caligaris, Michael (Holloway Literary) 256

Callahan, William (Inkwell Management, LLC) 258

Camacho, Linda (Prospect Agency) 274

Cameron, Kimberley (Kimberley Cameron & Associates) 232

Campbell, Marie (Transatlantic Literary Agency) 288

Campoli, Leila (Stonesong) 283

Capron, Elise (Sandra Dijkstra Literary Agency) 237

Carleton, Kirsten (Prospect Agency) 275

Carlisle, Michael V. (Inkwell Management, LLC) 258

Carlson, Jennifer (Dunow, Carlson, & Lerner Agency) 239

Carr, Michael (Veritas Literary Agency) 291

Carson, Lucy (The Friedrich Agency) 248

Carvainis, Maria (Maria Carvainis Agency, Inc.) 232

Chalberg, Terra (Chalberg & Sussman) 233

Chambliss, Jamie (Folio Literary Management, LLC) 245

Chilton, Jamie Weiss (Andrea Brown literary Agency, Inc.) 230

Chinchillo, Melissa (Fletcher & Co.) 245

Chiotti, Danielle (Upstart Crow Literary) 290

Choi, Mink (Fletcher & Co.) 245

Chromy, Adam (Moveable Type Management) 270

Chudney, Steven (The Chudney Agency) 233

Cirillo, Andrea (Jane Rotrosen Agency, LLC) 279

Clark, Ginger (Curtis Brown, Ltd.) 230

Clark, June (Fineprint Literary Management) 244

Cloughley, Amy (Kimberley Cameron & Associates) 232

Cohen, Susan (Writers House) 293

Collette, Ann (Rees Literary Agency) 277

Collier, Harold (White Mane Kids) 189

Collins, Amy (Orca Book Publishers) 201

Collins, JoAnn (International Transactions, Inc.) 259

Collum, Ashely (DeFiore & Co. Literary Management, Inc.) 236

Conaway, Dan (Writers House) 293

Concepcion, Christina (Don Congdon Associates Inc.) 233

Congdon, Michael (Don Congdon Associates Inc.) 233

Contardi, Bill (Brandt & Hochman Literary Agents, Inc.) 229

Coonis, Brandie (Rebecca Friedman Literary Agency) 248

Cooper, Gemma (The Bent Agency) 226

Copps, Elizabeth (Maria Carvainis Agency, Inc.) 232

Corvisiero, Marisa A. (Corvisiero Literary Agency) 234

Coughtrey, Ellen (The Gernert Company) 251

Crockett, Laura (Triada US Liteary Agency, Inc.) 288

Cross, Claudia (Folio Literary Management, LLC) 245

Crowe, Sara (Pippin Properties, Inc.) 274

Curry, Michael (Donald Maass Literary Agency) 266

Cusick, John (Folio Literary Management, LLC) 245

Cussen, June (Pineapple Press, Inc.) 175

Dail, Laura (Laura Dail Literary Agency, Inc.) 235

D'Agostino, Kerry (Curtis Brown, Ltd.) 230

Datz, Arielle (Dunow, Carlson, & Lerner Agency) 239

Davis, Jamie (Evatopia, Inc.) 243

Davie, Mike (Manor House Publishing, Inc.) 200

Davies, Sarah (The Greenhouse Literary Agency) 253

Davis, Kaylee (Dee Mura Literary) 270

Davis, Naomi (Inklings Literary Agency) 257

Davis, Reiko (DeFiore & Co. Literary Management, Inc.) 236

Dawson, Liza (Liza Dawson Associates) 235

Day, Charles (Evil Jester Press) 153

De Chiara, Jennifer (The Jennifer De Chiara Literary Agency) 236

Decker, Stacia (Dunow, Carlson, & Lerner Agency) 239

DeFiore, Brian (DeFiore & Co. Literary Management, Inc.) 236

Delman, Stephanie (Sanford J. Greenburger Associates, Inc.) 253

Derviskadic, Dado (Folio Literary Management, LLC) 245

Detweiler, Katelyn (Jill Grinberg Literary Management) 254

Deyoe, Cori (Three Seas Literary Agency) 287

Diforio, Bob (D4eo Literary Agency) 234

Dijkstra, Sandra (Sandra Dijkstra Literary Agency) 237

DiMona, Lisa (Writers House) 293

Diver, Lucienne (The Knight Agency) 261

Doherty-Munro, Victoria (Writers House) 293

Dominguez, Adriana (Full Circle Literary, LLC) 248

Donaghy, Stacey (Donaghy Literary Group) 238

Draper, Claire (Inkwell Management, LLC) 258

Drayton, Catherine (Inkwell Management, LLC) 258

Drowley, Jamie Bodnar (Inklings Literary Agency) 257

Dunham, Jennie (Dunham Literary, Inc.) 239

Dunow, Henry (Dunow, Carlson, & Lerner Agency) 239

Dunton, David (Harvey Klinger, Inc.) 260

Dystel, Jane (Dystel & Goderich Literary Management) 240

Eckstut, Arielle (Levine Greenberg Rostan Literary Agency, Inc.) 263

Edwards, Melissa (Stonesong) 283

Edgecombe, Lindsay (Levine Greenberg Rostan Literary Agency, Inc.) 263

Ehrlich, Judith (Judith Ehrlich Literary Management, LLC) 241

Einstein, Susanna (Einstein Literary Management) 242

Eisenman, Leigh (HSG Agency) 257

Ekstrom, Rachel (Irene Goodman Literary Agency) 252

Elblonk, Matthew (DeFiore & Co. Literary Management, Inc.) 236

Ellison, Nicholas (Sanford J. Greenburger Associates, Inc.) 253

Ellenberg, Ethan (Ethan Ellenberg Literary Agency) 242

Endrulat, Harry (The Rights Factory) 278

Epstein, Linda (Emerald City Literary Agency) 242

Evans, Stephany (Fineprint Literary Management) 244

Evans, Suzy (Sandra Dijkstra Literary Agency) 237

Faderin, Kemi (Dystel & Goderich Literary Management) 240

Falkoff, Kate (Inkwell Management, LLC) 258

Fargis, Alison (Stonesong) 283

Fausset, Katherine (Curtis Brown, Ltd.) 230

Featherstone, Ann (Pajama Press), 201

Fehr, Don (Trident Media Group) 289

Fergesen, Hannah (KT Literary, Inc.) 262

Filina, Olga (The Rights Factory) 278

Finch, Diana (Diana Finch Literary Agency) 243

Fine, Celeste (Sterling Lord Literistic, Inc.) 265

Finesman, Susan (Rebecca Friedman Literary Agency) 248

Finkelstein, Jesse (Transatlantic Literary Agency) 288

Fishman, Seth (The Gernert Company) 251

Flaherty, Heather (The Bent Agency) 226

Flannery, Jennifer (Flannery Literary) 244

Flashman, Melissa (Janklow & Nesbit Associates) 260

Flegal, Diana (Hartline Literary Agency) 254

Fletcher, Christy (Fletcher & Co.) 245

Flum, Caitie (Liza Dawson Associates) 235

Forland, Emily (Brandt & Hochman Literary Agents, Inc.) 229

Forrer, David (Inkwell Management, LLC) 258

Forrie, Allan (Thistledown Press Ltd.) 203

Foster, Roz (Sandra Dijkstra Literary Agency) 237

Fox, Diana (Fox Literary) 247

Fox, Gráinne (Fletcher & Co.) 245

Franks, Alex (Donaghy Literar Group) 238

Fraser-Bub, MacKenzie (Fraser-Bub Literary, LLC) 247

Fraser, Stephen (The Jennifer De Chiara Literary Agency) 236

Frederick, Holly (Curtis Brown, Ltd.) 230

Freet, Roger (Foundry Literary + Media) 246

Freymann, Sarah Jane (Sarah Jane Freymann Literary Agency) 248

Fried, Rachael Dillon (Sanford J. Greenburger Associates, Inc.) 253

Friedman, Claire (Inkwell Management, LLC) 258

Friedman, Phil (Scholastic Library Publishing) 180

Friedman, Rebecca (Rebecca Friedman Literary Agency) 248

Friedrich, Molly (The Friedrich Agency) 248

Froman, Craig (Master Books) 166

Fuentes, Sarah (Fletcher & Co.) 245

Fury, Louise (The Bent Agency) 226

Galit, Lauren (LKG Agency) 264

Gallagher, Lisa (DeFiore & Co. Literary Management, Inc.) 236

Gallt, Nancy (Gallt and Zacker Literary Agency) 250

Gayle, Nadeen (Serendipity Literary Agency, LLC) 281

Gelfman, Jane (Gelfman Schneider/ICM Partners) 250

Gendell, Yfat Reiss (Foundry Literary + Media) 246

Getzler, Josh (HSG Agency) 257

Gerety, Emily (Pants on Fire Press) 171

Gernert, Jack (The Gernert Company) 251

Ghahremani, Lilly (Full Circle Literary, LLC) 248

Glaz, Linda (Hartline Literary Agency) 254

Ginsberg, Peter (Curtis Brown, Ltd.) 230

Ginsberg, Susan (Writers House) 293

Giovinazzo, Elena (Pippin Properties, Inc.) 274

Glick, Stacy Kendall (Dystel & Goderich Literary Management) 240

Goderich, Miriam (Dystel & Goderich Literary Management) 240

Goldblatt, Barry (Barry Goldblatt Literary, LLC) 251

Goldman, Becca (Pants on Fire Press) 171

Goldsmith, Connor (Fuse Literary) 249

Goldstein, Veronica (Fletcher & Co.) 245

Goloboy, Jennie (Red Sofa Literary) 276

Golomb, Susan (Writers House) 293

Gonzalez, Tara (Erin Murphy Literary Agency) 271

Goodman, Irene (Irene Goodman Literary Agency) 252

Gordon, Hannah Brown (Foundry Literary + Media) 246

Gore, Clelia (Martin Literary and Media Management) 268

Gottlieb, Mark (Trident Media Group) 289

Gould, Scott (RLR Associates, Ltd.) 278

Gradinger, Rebecca (Fletcher & Co.) 245

Graham, Stacey (Red Sofa Literary) 276

Graham, Susan (Einstein Literary Management)

Grajkowski, Michelle (Three Seas Literary Agency) 287

Green, Kathy (Kathryn Green Literary Agency, LLC) 252

Green, Michael (Philomel Books) 174

Greenberg, Daniel (Levine Greenberg Rostan Literary Agency, Inc.) 263

Greenberg, Sylvia (Fletcher & Co.) 245

Greenspan, Shari Dash (Flashlight Press) 155

Gregory, Evan (Ethan Ellenberg Literary Agency) 242

Grimm, Katie (Don Congdon Associates Inc.) 233

Grinberg, Jill (Jill Grinberg Literary Management) 254

Grossman, Loren R. (Paul S. Levine Literary Agency) 263

Grossman, Marissa (Razorbill) 178

Grubka, Lisa (Fletcher & Co.) 245

Guinsler, Robert (Sterling Lord Literistic, Inc.) 265

Gus, Alisa (Curiosity Quills) 150

Gwinn, Julie (The Seymour Agency) 282

Hall, Katie (Arbordale Publishing) 138

Hamilton, Diane (Onstage Publishing) 170

Hamlin, Faith (Sanford J. Greenburger Associates, Inc.) 253

Hane, Erik (Red Sofa Literary) 276

Hanjian, Cassie (Waxman Leavell Literary Agency, Inc.) 291

Hannigan, Carrie (HSG Agency) 257

Harding, Elizabeth (Curtis Brown, Ltd.) 230

Hardy, Dawn Michelle (Serendipity Literary Agency, LLC) 281

Harmon, Dan (Zest Books) 192

Harriot, Michael (Folio Literary Management, LLC) 245

Harris, Bill (The Glencannon Press) 156

Harris, Erin (Folio Literary Management, LLC) 245

Harriss, Helen (Peachtree Children's Books) 172

Hart, Cate (Corvisiero Literary Agency) 234

Hart, Jim (Hartline Literary Agency) 254

Hart, Joyce A. (Hartline Literary Agency) 254

Harty, Pamela (The Knight Agency) 261

Harvey, Sarah (Orca Book Publishers) 201

Hassan, Shannon (Marsal Lyon Literary Agency, LLC) 267

Hatch, Ronald B. (Ronsdale Press) 202

Hatch, Veronica (Ronsdale Press) 202

Hawk, Susan (Upstart Crow Literary) 291

Hawn, Molly Ker (The Bent Agency) 226

Haywood, Samantha (Transatlantic Literary Agency) 288

Heath, David (Redleaf Lane) 178

Heifetz, Merrilee (Writers House) 293

Heller, Helen (Helen Heller Agency, Inc.) 255

Heller, Sarah (Helen Heller Agency, Inc.) 255

Henkin, Alyssa Eisner (Trident Media Group) 289

Herman, Ronnie Ann (Ronnie Ann Herman) 255

Herman, Katia (Ronnie Ann Herman) 255

Hernandez, Saritza (Corvisiero Literary Agency) 234

Herrera, Jenny (David Black Literary Agency) 227

Heschke, Christa (McIntosh & Otis, Inc.) 269

Hibbert, Edward (Donadio & Olson, Inc.) 238

Hiyate, Sam (The Rights Factory) 278

Hinz, Carol (The Millbrook Press) 168

Hochman, Gail (Brandt & Hochman Literary Agents, Inc.) 229

Hodgman, Sandy (The Leshne Agency) 262

Hodgman, Sandy (Thompson Literary Agency) 287

Hoffmann, Markus (Regal Hoffman & Associates, LLC) 277

Hoffman, Scott (Folio Literary Management, LLC) 245

Hoffman, Shira (McIntosh & Otis, Inc.) 269

Hogrebe, Christina (Jane Rotrosen Agency, LLC) 279

Holland, Joyce (D4eo Literary Agency) 234

Hoogland, Michael (Dystel & Goderich Literary Management) 240

Hosier, Erin (Dunow, Carlson, & Lerner Agency) 239

Howell, Pam (D4eo Literary Agency) 234

Howland, Carrie (Donadio & Olson, Inc.) 238

Hubbard, Mandy (Emerald City Literary Agency) 242

Hughes, Amy (Dunow, Carlson, & Lerner Agency) 239

Hunter, Kristy (The Knight Agency) 261

Hurley, Alexis (Inkwell Management, LLC) 258

Husock, Leon (L. Perkins Agency) 273

Hwang, Annie (Folio Literary Management, LLC) 245

Hyde, Dara (Hill Nadell Literary Agency) 256)

Jacks, Nathaniel (Inkwell Management, LLC) 258

Jackson, Eleanor (Dunow, Carlson, & Lerner Agency) 239

Jackson, Jennifer (Donald Maass Literary Agency) 266

James, Nicole (Chalberg & Sussman) 233

Jameson, Amy (A+B Works) 226

Jeglinski, Melissa (The Knight Agency) 261

Jenks, Carolyn (The Carolyn Jenks Agency) 260

Jennette, Alyssa (Stonesong) 284

Johnson, Brianne (Writers House) 293

Johnson, Kaitlyn (Corvisiero Literary Agency) 234

Johnson, Michelle (Inklings Literary Agency) 257

Johnson-Blalock, Jennifer (Liza Dawson Associates) 235

Jones, Jill (Evatopia, Inc.) 243

Kahn, Jody (Brandt & Hochman Literary Agents, Inc.) 229

Kaiser, Cecily (Phaidon Press) 174

Karmatz-Rudy, Caryn (DeFiore & Co. Literary Management, Inc.) 236

Kasdin, Steve (Curtis Brown, Ltd.) 230

Kay, Mary (Evatopia, Inc.) 243

Kean, Taylor Martindale (Full Circle Literary, LLC) 248

Kelly, Shana (Einstein Literary Management) 242

Kenny, Julia (Dunow, Carlson, & Lerner Agency) 239

Kenshole, Fiona (Transatlantic Literary Agency) 288

Kepner, Chris (Victoria Sanders & Associates) 280

Keyes, Emily S. (Fuse Literary) 249

Kim, Emily Sylvan (Prospect Agency) 275

Kim, Jennifer (Sandra Dijkstra Literary Agency) 237

Kimber, Natalie (The Rights Factory) 278

Kirschbaum, Larry (Waxman Leavell Literary Agency, Inc.) 291

Kirtland, Kim-Mei (Howard Morhaim Literary Agency) 270

Kleinman, Jeff (Folio Literary Management, LLC) 245

Klinger, Harvey (Harvey Klinger, Inc.) 260

Knapp, Peter (Park Literary Group, LLC) 273

Knight, Deidre (The Knight Agency) 261

Knowlton, Ginger (Curtis Brown, Ltd.) 230

Knowlton, Timothy (Curtis Brown, Ltd.) 230

Kong, Kelvin (The Rights Factory) 278

Kotchman, Katie (Don Congdon Associates Inc.) 233

Kracht, Elizabeth (Kimberley Cameron & Associates) 232

Krienke, Mary (Sterling Lord Literistic, Inc.) 265

Kriss, Miriam (Irene Goodman Literary Agency) 252

Krysan, Alan E. (Windward Publishing) 190

Kukla, Lauren (Mighty Media Press) 167

Kye-Casella, Maura (Don Congdon Associates Inc.) 233

Lakosil, Natalie (Bradford Literary Agency) 228

Lamba, Marie (The Jennifer De

Chiara Literary Agency) 236

Lamm, Donald (Fletcher & Co.) 245

Lange, Heide (Sanford J. Greenburger Associates, Inc.) 253

LaPolla, Sarah (Bradford Literary Agency) 228

Larson, Ellen (The Poisoned Pencil) 175

Latshaw, Katherine (Folio Literary Management, LLC) 245

Laughran, Jennifer (Andrea Brown literary Agency, Inc.) 230

Lawrence, Tricia (Erin Murphy Literary Agency) 271

Lazar, Daniel (Writers House) 293

Le, Thao (Sandra Dijkstra Literary Agency) 237

Leavell, Byrd (Waxman Leavell Literary Agency, Inc.) 291

Lee, Douglas (Kimberley Cameron & Associates) 232

Leshne, Lisa (The Leshne Agency) 262

Lerner, Betsy (Dunow, Carlson, & Lerner Agency) 239

Levine, Ellen (Trident Media Group) 289

Levine, Jim (Levine Greenberg Rostan Literary Agency, Inc.) 276

Levine, Paul S. (Paul S. Levine Literary Agency) 263

Levinson, Wendy (Harvey Klinger, Inc.) 260

Lewis, Bibi (Ethan Ellenberg Literary Agency) 242

Likoff, Laurie (Facts on File, Inc.) 153

Linden, Judy (Stonesong) 283

Lindman, Chelsea (Sanford J. Greenburger Associates, Inc.) 253

Linka, Ruth (Orca Book Publishers) 201

Lippincott, Will (Lippincott Massie McQuilkin) 264

Lipskar, Simon (Writers House) 293

Liss, Laurie (Sterling Lord Literistic, Inc.) 265

Lohr, Nancy (JourneyForth) 162

Lord, Sterling (Sterling Lord Literistic, Inc.) 265

Lowenstein, Barbara (Lowenstein Associates, Inc.) 266

Lowes, Victoria (The Bent Agency) 227

Lu, Sandy (L. Perkins Agency) 273

Lucas, George (Inkwell Management, LLC) 258

Lupfer, Eric (Fletcher & Co.) 245

Lyon, Kevan (Marsal Lyon Literary Agency, LLC) 267

Lyons, Jonathan (Curtis Brown, Ltd.) 230

Maas, John (Sterling Lord Literistic, Inc.) 265

Maass, Donald (Donald Maass Literary Agency) 266

Maccoby, Gina (Gina Maccoby Literary Agency) 267

MacKeen, Alison (Sterling Lord Literistic, Inc.) 265

MacKenzie, Joanna (Nelson Literary Agency, LLC) 272

MacLeod, Lauren (The Strothman Agency, LLC) 285

Madan, Neeti (Sterling Lord Literistic, Inc.) 265

Malawer, Ted (Upstart Crow Literary) 290

Malk, Steven (Writers House) 293

Malnor, Carol (Dawn Publications) 150

Mandel, Daniel (Sanford J. Greenburger Associates, Inc.) 253

Manning, Sarah (United Talent Agency) 290

Marini, Victoria (Irene Goodman Literary Agency) 252

Marr, Jill (Sandra Dijkstra Literary Agency) 237

Marsal, Jill (Marsal Lyon Literary Agency, LLC) 267

Martin, Betsy (Skinner House Books) 182

Martin, Sharlene (Martin Literary and Media Management) 268

Mason, Simon (David Fickling Books) 198

Matson, Peter (Sterling Lord Literistic, Inc.) 265

Mattero, Anthony (Foundry Literary + Media) 246

Mattson, Jennifer (Andrea Brown literary Agency, Inc.) 230

Maxwell, Ed (Sanford J. Greenburger Associates, Inc.) 253

Maynard, Audrey (Tilbury House Publishers) 186

McCarthy, Jim (Dystel & Goderich Literary Management) 240

McCarthy, Sean (Sean McCarthy Literary Agency) 269

McClellan, Gordon (Splashing Cow Books) 184

McClure, Cameron (Donald Maass Literary Agency) 266

McCollum, Kim Blair (The Purcell Agency) 276

McDermid, Anne (Anne McDermid & Associates Literary, Ltd.) 269

McDonald, Ali (The Rights Factory) 278

McDonald, Caitlin (Donald Maass Literary Agency) 266

McFadden, Erin (Fletcher & Co.) 245

McGhee, Holly (Pippin Properties, Inc.) 274

McGuigan, Peter (Foundry Literary + Media) 246

McGuire, Libby (The Gernert Company) 251

McKean, Kate (Howard Morhaim Literary Agency) 270

McKee, Tammy (Bookish Books) 144

McLean, Laurie (Fuse Literary) 249

McMahon, Hilary (Westwood Creative Artists, Ltd.) 292

McNicholl, Damian (The Jennifer De Chiara Literary Agency) 236

McQuilkin, Rob (Lippincott Massie McQuilkin) 264

McReynolds, Brady (Jabberwocky Literary Agency) 259

Mealing, Lindsay (Emerald City Literary Agency) 242

Megibow, Sara (KT Literary, Inc.) 262

Merola, Marianne (Brandt & Hochman Literary Agents, Inc.) 229

Mileo, Jessica (Inkwell Management, LLC) 258

Millard, Martha (Sterling Lord Literistic, Inc.) 265

Miller, Beth (Writers House) 293

Miller, Scott (Trident Media Group) 289

Miller, Sue (Donaghy Literary Group) 238

Miller-Callihan, Courtney (Sanford J. Greenburger Associates, Inc.) 253

Mitchell, Barbara (Mitchell Lane Publishers, Inc.) 168

Mitchell, Emily (Wernick & Pratt Agency) 292

Mitchell, Heather (Gelfman Schneider/ICM Partners) 250

Moed, Lydia (The Rights Factory) 278

Molinari, Pauline (Walter Foster, Jr.) 155

Monaghan, Leila (Elm Books) 152

Moore, Mary C. (Kimberley Cameron & Associates) 232

Morgan, Sam (Jabberwocky Literary Agency) 259

Morgen, Emmanuelle (Stonesong) 283

Morhaim, Howard (Howard Morhaim Literary Agency) 270

Morris, Gary (David Black Literary Agency) 227

Morrison, Andrea (Writers House) 293

Muhlig, Adam (McIntosh & Otis, Inc.) 269

Mungiello, Michael (Inkwell Management, LLC) 258

Munier, Paula (Talcott Notch Literary) 286

Mura, Dee (Dee Mura Literary) 270

Murphy, Dana (The Book Group) 228

Murphy, Erin (Erin Murphy Literary Agency) 271

Murphy, Jacqueline (Fineprint Literary Management) 244

Murphy, Jacqueline (Inkwell Management, LLC) 258

Mushens, Juliet (United Talent Agency) 290

Nadell, Bonnie (Hill Nadell Literary Agency) 256

Nakamura, Kimiko (Dee Mura Literary) 270

Necarsulmer, Edward IV (Dunow, Carlson, & Lerner Agency) 239

Nelson, Kristin (Nelson Literary

Agency) 285

Nelson, Patricia (Marsal Lyon Literary Agency, LLC) 267

Neuhaus, Kirsten (Foundry Literary + Media) 246

Niumata, Erin (Folio Literary Management, LLC) 245

Noble, Valerie (Donaghy Literary Group) 238

Nolan, Polly (The Greenhouse Literary Agency) 253

Noorda, Rachel (ThunderStone Books) 185

Noyce, Pendred (Tumblehome Learning) 187

Nussbaum, Haskell (The Rights Factory) 278

Nunn, Kate (Scholastic Library Publishing) 180

Nyen, Renee (KT Literary, Inc.) 262

Oberweger, Lorin (Adams Literary) 226

O'Connor, Amanda (Trident Media Group) 289

Odom, Monica (Bradford Literary Agency) 228

Ogden, Bre (Red Sofa Literary) 276

Olson, Charlie (Inkwell Management, LLC) 258

Olson, Neil (Donadio & Olson, Inc.) 238

O'Neil, Marie (Scholastic Library Publishing) 180

O'Neill, Molly (Waxman Leavell Literary Agency, Inc.) 291

Orr, Rachel (Prospect Agency) 274

Ortiz, Kathleen (New Leaf Literary & Media, Inc.) 272

Pacheco, Monica (Anne McDermid & Associates Literary, Ltd.) 269

Panettieri, Gina (Talcott Notch Literary) 286

Papin, Jessica (Dystel & Goderich Literary Management) 240

Paquette, Ammi-Joan (Erin Murphy Literary Agency) 271

Park, Chris (Foundry Literary + Media) 246

Park, Veronica (Corvisiero Literary Agency) 234

Parker, Elana Roth (Laura Dail Literary Agency, Inc.) 235

Parker, Liz (Inkwell Management, LLC) 258

Parris-Lamb, Chris (The Gernert Company) 251

Passick, Sarah (Sterling Lord Literistic, Inc.) 265

Patterson, Emma (Brandt & Hochman Literary Agents, Inc.) 229

Pelletier, Sharon (Dystel & Goderich Literary Management) 240

Penfold, Alexandra (Upstart Crow Literary) 290

Pennington, Travis (The Knight Agency) 261

Perel, Kim (Irene Goodman Literary Agency) 252

Perkins, Lara (Andrea Brown literary Agency, Inc.) 230

Perkins, Lori (L. Perkins Agency) 273

Pestritto, Carrie (Prospect Agency) 274

Peterson, Kelly (Corvisiero Literary Agency) 234

Peterson, Laura Blake (Curtis Brown, Ltd.) 230

Pfeffer, Rubin (Rubin Pfeffer Content) 274

Phelan, Beth (The Bent Agency) 226

Pine, Richard (Inkwell Management, LLC) 258

Plentka, Cheryl (Jill Grinberg Literary Management) 254

Podos, Rebecca (Rees Literary Agency) 277

Poelle, Barbara (Irene Goodman Literary Agency) 252

Pohlen, Jerome (Chicago Review Press) 147

Pomerance, Ruth (Folio Literary Management, LLC) 245

Popovic, Lana (Chalberg & Sussman) 233

Posner, Marcy (Folio Literary Management, LLC) 245

Prasanna, Tanusri (HSG Agency) 257

Pratt, Linda (Wernick & Pratt Agency) 292

Quay, Corus (Kids Can Press) 199

Raihofer, Susan (David Black Literary Agency) 227

Ramer, Susan (Don Congdon Associates Inc.) 233

Ranta, Adriann (Foundry Literary + Media) 246

Raskin, Sasha (United Talent Agency) 290

Reamer, Jodi (Writers House) 293

Reardon, Lisa (Chicago Review Press) 147

Rees, Lorin (Rees Literary Agency) 277

Regal, Joseph (Regal Hoffman & Associates, LLC) 277

Regel, Jessica (Foundry Literary + Media) 246

Regan, Ann (Harmony Ink Press) 159

Reid, Janet (New Leaf Literary & Media, Inc.) 272

Reinke, Engela (Tafelberg Publishers) 203

Rennert, Laura (Andrea Brown literary Agency, Inc.) 230

Resciniti, Nicole (The Seymour Agency) 282

Ribar, Lindsay (Sanford J. Greenburger Associates, Inc.) 253

Ribas, Maria (Stonesong) 283

Richter, Michelle (Fuse Literary) 249

Ridout, Rachel (Harvey Klinger, Inc.) 260

Ritchkin, Deborah (Marsal Lyon Literary Agency, LLC) 267

Rittenberg, Ann (Ann Rittenberg Literary Agency, LLC) 278

Riva, Peter (International Transactions, Inc.) 259

Riva, Sandra (International Transactions, Inc.) 259

Robbins, Fleetwood (Waxman Leavell Literary Agency, Inc.) 291

Roberts, Soumeya (Writers House) 293

Roberts, Will (The Gernert Company) 251

Robey, Annelise (Jane Rotrosen Agency, LLC) 279

Robins, Vanessa (Corvisiero Literary Agency) 234

Robinson, Quressa (D4eo Literary Agency) 234

Rodeen, Paul (Rodeen Literary Management) 279

Rodgers, Lisa (Jabberwocky Literary Agency) 259

Rofé, Jennifer (Andrea Brown literary Agency, Inc.) 230

Rogers, Cassandra (The Rights Factory) 278

Rose, Rie Sheridan (Zumaya Publications, LLC) 192

Rosenfeld, Deborah Leah (Hachai Publishing) 158

Ross, Andy (Andy Ross Literary Agency) 279

Rostan, Stephanie (Levine Greenberg Rostan Literary Agency, Inc.) 263

Rothe, Reagan (Black Rose Writing) 143

Rothstein, Eliza (Inkwell Management, LLC) 258

Rowland, Melissa (Levine Greenberg Rostan Literary Agency, Inc.) 263

Rubie, Peter (Fineprint Literary Management) 244

Rubino-Bradway, Caitlen (LKG Agency) 264

Rubinstein, Elizabeth Winick (McIntosh & Otis, Inc.) 269

Rudolph, John (Dystel & Goderich Literary Management) 240

Rue, Robin (Writers House) 293

Ruley, Meg (Jane Rotrosen Agency, LLC) 279

Rushall, Kathleen (Andrea Brown literary Agency, Inc.) 230

Russell, Curtis (P.S. Literary Agency) 275

Rutman, Jim (Sterling Lord Literistic, Inc.) 265

Rutter, Amanda (Red Sofa Literary) 276

Rydzinski, Tamar (Laura Dail Literary Agency, Inc.) 235

Sagendorph, Jean (Mansion Street Literary Management) 267

Salky, Jesseca (HSG Agency) 257

Sanders, Rayhane (Lippincott Massie McQuilkin) 264

Sanders, Victoria (Victoria Sanders & Associates) 280

Sattersten, Todd (Fletcher & Co.) 245

Savits, Logan Garrison (The

Gernert Company) 251

Schear, Adam (DeFiore & Co. Literary Management, Inc.) 236

Scalissi, Linda (Three Seas Literary Agency) 287

Scheer, Andy (Hartline Literary Agency) 254

Scherer, Rebecca (Jane Rotrosen Agency, LLC) 279

Schneider, Deborah (Gelfman Schneider/ICM Partners) 250

Schneider, Eddie (Jabberwocky Literary Agency) 259

Schmalz, Wendy (Wendy Schmalz Agency) 280

Schulman, Abby (Rebecca Friedman Literary Agency) 248

Schulman, Susan (Susan Schulman Literary Agency, LLC) 281

Schwartz, Steven (Sarah Jane Freymann Literary Agency) 248

Schwartz, Tina P. (The Purcell Agency) 276

Scordato, Ellen (Stonesong) 283

Seidman, Yishai (Dunow, Carlson, & Lerner Agency) 239

Seidner, Sophia (Jill Grinberg Literary Management) 254

Selvaggio, Victoria (The Jennifer De Chiara Literary Agency) 236

Shahbazian, Pouya (New Leaf Literary & Media, Inc.) 272

Shalabi, Mohamed (Talcott Notch Literary) 286

Shane, Alec (Writers House) 293

Sherman, Rebecca (Writers House) 293

Sherry, Cynthia (Chicago Review Press) 147

Shoemaker, Victoria (The Spieler Agency) 282

Silberman, Jeff (Folio Literary Management, LLC) 245

Silbersack, John (Trident Media Group) 289

Silverman, Erica Rand (Stimola Literary Studio) 283

Simonoff, Meredith Kaffel (DeFiore & Co. Literary Management, Inc.) 237

Sinclair, Stephanie (Transatlantic Literary Agency) 288

Sinsheimer, Jessica (Sarah Jane Freymann Literary Agency) 248

Skinner, Tricia (Fuse Literary) 249

Skurnick, Victoria (Levine Greenberg Rostan Literary Agency, Inc.) 263

Slater, Alexander (Trident Media Group) 289

Smith, Bridget (Dunham Literary, Inc.) 239

Smith, David Hale (Inkwell Management, LLC) 258

Smith, Eric (P.S. Literary Agency) 275

Smith, Sarah (David Black Literary Agency) 227

Smitley, Mike (Father's Press) 154

Smoot, Madeline (Children's Brains Are Yummy [CBAY] Books) 147

Soloway, Jennifer March (Andrea Brown literary Agency, Inc.) 230

Somberg, Andrea (Harvey Klinger, Inc.) 260

Song, DongWon (Howard Morhaim Literary Agency) 270

Sonnack, Kelly (Andrea Brown literary Agency, Inc.) 230

South, Mary (Lowenstein Associates, Inc.) 266

Sparks, Kerry (Levine Greenberg Rostan Literary Agency, Inc.) 263

Speilburg, Alice (Speilburg Literary Agency) 282

Spellman-Silverman, Erica (Trident Media Group) 289

Spencer, Elaine (The Knight Agency) 261

Spieler, Joe (The Spieler Agency) 282

Spieller, Lauren (Triada US) 288

Stark, Alexa (Trident Media Group) 289

Stead, Rebecca (The Book Group) 228

Stearns, Michael (Upstart Crow Literary) 290

Steele, Emily (Medallion Press) 167

Steinberg, Peter (Foundry Literary + Media) 246

Stender, Uwe (Triada US Liteary Agency, Inc.) 288

Stephens, Jenny (Sterling Lord Literistic, Inc.) 265

Stermer, J.L. (New Leaf Literary & Media, Inc.) 272

Stewart, Douglas (Sterling Lord Literistic, Inc.) 265

Stevenson, Julie (Lippincott Massie McQuilkin) 264

Stimola, Rosemary B. (Stimola Literary Studio) 283

Storella, Erika (The Gernert Company) 251

Strauss, Rebecca (DeFiore & Co. Literary Management, Inc.) 236

Stringer, Marlene (The Stringer LIterary Agency LLC) 284

Strothman, Wendy (The Strothman Agency, LLC) 285

Stumpf, Becca (Prospect Agency) 274

Sulaiman, Saba (Talcott Notch Literary) 286

Sullivan, Corinne (Inkwell Management, LLC) 258

Sussman, Rachel (Chalberg & Sussman) 233

Svetcov, Danielle (Levine Greenberg Rostan Literary Agency, Inc.) 263

Sweetland, Helen (The Spieler Agency) 282

Tannenbaum, Amy (Jane Rotrosen Agency, LLC) 279

Tasman, Alice (Jean V. Naggar Literary Agency, Inc.) 271

Taylor, Brent (Triada US Liteary Agency, Inc.) 288

Taylor, Yuval (Chicago Review

Press) 147

Tegen, Katherine (Katherine Tegen Books) 185

Temperly, Jaida (New Leaf Literary & Media, Inc.) 272

Tempest, Nephele (The Knight Agency) 261

Terpilowski, Nikki (Holloway Literary) 256

Testa, Stacy (Writers House) 293

Testerman, Kate (KT Literary, Inc.) 262

Thayer, Henry (Brandt & Hochman Literary Agents, Inc.) 229

Thoma, Geri (Writers House) 293

Thompson, Meg (Thompson Literary Agency) 287

Thorn, John (Thompson Literary Agency) 287

Thornton, John (The Spieler Agency) 282

Tompkins, Amy (Transatlantic Literary Agency) 288

Tourtelot, Nicole (DeFiore & Co. Literary Management, Inc.) 237

Townsend, Suzie (New Leaf Literary & Media, Inc.) 272

Tran, Jennifer Chen (Fuse Literary) 249

Troha, Steve (Folio Literary Management, LLC) 245

Tutela, Joy E. (David Black Literary Agency) 227

Tyrrell, Bob (Orca Book Publishers) 201

Udden, Jennifer (Barry Goldblatt Literary, LLC) 251

Uh, Cindy (Thompson Literary Agency) 287

Unter, Jennifer (The Unter Agency) 290

Ursell, Geoffrey (Coteau Books) 198

Van Beek, Emily (Folio Literary Management, LLC) 245

Van Sant, Kelly (D4eo Literary Agency) 234

Verma, Monika (Levine Greenberg Rostan Literary Agency, Inc.) 263

Vicente, Maria (P.S. Literary Agency) 275

Vogel, Rachel (Waxman Leavell Literary Agency, Inc.) 291

Voges, Liza (Eden Street Literary) 241

Volpe, Joanna (New Leaf Literary & Media, Inc.) 272

Von Borstel, Stefanie (Full Circle Literary, LLC) 248

Walters, Maureen (Curtis Brown, Ltd.) 230

Warnock, Gordon (Fuse Literary) 249

Waters, Mitchell (Curtis Brown, Ltd.) 230

Watson, Kira (Emma Sweeney Agency, LLC) 285

Wattawa, Gayle (Heyday Books) 159

Watters, Carly (P.S. Literary Agency) 275

Watterson, Jessica (Sandra Dijkstra Literary Agency) 237

Waxman, Scott (Waxman Leavell Literary Agency, Inc.) 291

Webb, Martha (Anne McDermid & Associates Literary, Ltd.) 269

Weed, Elisabeth (The Book Group) 228

Weimann, Frank (Folio Literary Management, LLC) 245

Weiss, Alexandra (The Jennifer De Chiara Literary Agency) 236

Wells, Justin (Corvisiero Literary Agency) 234

Wells, Roseanne (The Jennifer De Chiara Literary Agency) 236

Weltz, Jennifer (Jean V. Naggar Literary Agency, Inc.) 271

Wernick, Marcia (Wernick & Pratt Agency) 292

Whalen, Kimberly (Trident Media Group) 289

Whelan, Maria (Inkwell Management, LLC) 258

White, Melissa (Folio Literary Management, LLC) 245

White, Trena (Transatlantic Literary Agency) 288

Whitman, Stacy (Tu Books) 187

Wilson, Maer (Ellysian Press) 152

Winick, Eugene H. (McIntosh & Otis, Inc.) 269

Wiseman Caryn (Andrea Brown literary Agency, Inc.) 230

Witherell, Jenny (Inkwell Management, LLC) 258

Witherspoon, Kimberly (Inkwell Management, LLC) 258

Witte, Michelle (Mansion Street Literary Management) 279

Wojcik, Tim (Levine Greenberg Rostan Literary Agency, Inc.) 263

Wolf, Kent D. (The Friedrich Agency) 248

Wolf, Kirsten (Emerald City Literary Management) 242

Wood, Laura (Fineprint Literary Management) 244

Woods, Monika (Curtis Brown, Ltd.) 230

Wooldridge, Andrew (Orca Book Publishers) 201

Worrall, Anna (The Gernert Company) 251

Ximinez, Maximilian (L. Perkins Agency) 273

Yarn, Jason (Jason Yarn Literary Agency) 293

Young, Cyle (Hartline Literary Agency) 254

Young, Erin (Dystel & Goderich Literary Management) 240

Zacker, Marietta (Gallt and Zacker Literary Agency) 250

Zats, Laura (Red Sofa Literary) 276

Zhang, Susan (Strawberries Press) 185

Zuckerman, Albert (Writers House) 293

AGE-LEVEL INDEX

PICTURE

Atheneum Books for Young Readers 139

Bailiwick Press 139

Candlewick Press 145

Capstone Press 145

Children's Brains are Yummy (CBAY) Books 147

Dial Books for Young Readers 151

Grosset & Dunlap Publishers 158

Gryphon House, Inc. 158

JourneyForth 162

McElderry Books, Margaret K. 166

Mitchell Lane Publishers, Inc. 168

National Geographic Children's Books 169

Nature Friend Magazine 218

Pauline Books & Media 172

Pinata Books 174

Puffin Books 177

YOUNG READERS

Atheneum Books for Young Readers 139

Bailiwick Press 139

Candlewick Press 145

Capstone Press 145

Children's Brains are Yummy (CBAY) Books 147

Click 210

Dial Books for Young Readers 151

Grosset & Dunlap Publishers 158

Immedium 160

JourneyForth 162

Keys for Kids Devotional 216

Little, Brown Books for Young Readers 164

McElderry Books, Margaret K. 166

National Geographic Children's Books 169

Nature Friend Magazine 218

Pauline Books & Media 172

Pinata Books 174

Puffin Books 177

Rosen Publishing 179

MIDDLE READERS (MIDDLE-GRADE)

Atheneum Books for Young Readers 139

Bailiwick Press 139

Brilliant Star 209

Candlewick Press 145

Capstone Press 145

Children's Brains are Yummy (CBAY) Books 147

Dial Books for Young Readers 151

Dig into History 211

Grosset & Dunlap Publishers 158

JourneyForth 162

Kaeden Books 162

Keys for Kids Devotional 216

Little, Brown Books for Young Readers 164

Magic Dragon 217

McElderry Books, Margaret K. 166

Milkweed Editions 167

Mitchell Lane Publishers, Inc. 168

National Geographic Children's Books 169

On Course 219

Pauline Books & Media 172

Pelican Publishing Company 173

Pinata Books 174

Puffin Books 177

Rosen Publishing 179

Stone Soup 223

Tu Books 187

YOUNG ADULT

Atheneum Books for Young Readers 139

Bailiwick Press 139

Candlewick Press 145

Children's Brains are Yummy (CBAY) Books 147

Dial Books for Young Readers 151

JourneyForth 162

McElderry Books, Margaret K. 166

Mitchell Lane Publishers, Inc. 168

On Course 219

Pauline Books & Media 172

Pelican Publishing Company 173

Pinata Books 174

Poisoned Pencil, The 175

Puffin Books 177

Skurnick Books, Lizzie 182

Tu Books 187

Stone Soup 223

Tu Books 187

PHOTOGRAPHY INDEX

BOOK PUBLISHERS

Abbeville Family 137

Amulet Books 138

Balzer & Bray 139

Behrman House, Inc. 141

Calkins Creek 144

Chicago Review Press 147

Children's Brains Are Yummy
  (CBAY) Books 147

Christian Focus Publications 197

Chronicle Books 148

Creative Company 149

Edupress, Inc. 151

Fickling Books, David 198

Fitzhenry & Whiteside, Ltd. 199

Frances Lincoln CHildren's Books
  199

Free Spirit Publishing, Inc. 155

Fulcrum Publishing 156

Gryphon House, Inc. 158

Lee & Low Books 164

Little, Brown Books for Young
  Readers 164

Mitchell Lane Publishers, Inc. 168

Piano Press 174

Puffin Books 177

Seedling Continental Press 181

Skinner House Books 182

Sterling Publishing Co., Inc. 184

Tilbury House Publishers 186

Tyndale House Publishers, Inc. 188

Usborne Publishing 204

White Mane Kids 189

Whitecap Books, Ltd. 204

Wordsong 190

World Book, Inc. 191

MAGAZINES

Advocate, PKA's Publication 207

Boys' Life 208

Brillian Star 209

Cadet Quest Magazine 210

Dramatics Magazine 211

FCA Magazine 212

Fun for Kidz 213

Girls' Life 213

Green Teacher 214

Highlights for Children 214

Hunger Mountain 215

National Geographic Kids 218

Nature Friend Magazine 218

New Moon Girls 218

On Course 219

Pockets 219

Seventeen Magazine 220

Shine Brightly 220

Skipping Stones: A Multicultural
    Literary Magazine 221

Sparkle 222

Young Rider 223

ILLUSTRATION INDEX

///

BOOK PUBLISHERS

Abbeville Family 137

Abrams Books for Young Readers 137

Algonquin Young Readers 137

Amulet Books 138

Arbordale Publishing 138

Baliwick Press 139

Balzer & Bray 139

Barefood Books 140

Barrons Educational Series 141

Behrman House, Inc. 141

Black Rose Writing 143

Boyds Mills Press 144

Calkins Creek 144

Candlewick Press 145

Capstone Press 145

Chicago Review Press 147

Children's Brains Are Yummy (CBAY) Books 147

Child's Play (International), Ltd. 197

Chooseco, LLC 148

Christian Focus Publications 197

Chronicle Books 148

Clarion Books 149

Darby Creek Publishing 150

Dawn Publications 150

Dial Books for Young Readers 151

Edupress, Inc. 151

Facts on File, Inc. 153

Farrar, Straus & Giroux for Young Readers 154

Fat Fox Books 198

Fickling Books, David 198

Fitzhenry & Whiteside, Ltd. 199

Frances Lincoln Children's Books 199

Free Spirit Publishing, Inc. 155

Gibbs Smith 156

Godine, Publisher, David R. 157

Goosebottom Books 157

Gryphon House, Inc. 158

Hachai Publishing 158

Holiday House, Inc. 160

Impact Publishers, Inc. 161

Islandport 161

Kaeden Books 162

Kids Can Press 199

Lee & Low Books 164

Little, Brown Books for Young
Readers 164

Little Tiger Press 200

Magination Press 165

Mitchell Lane Publishers, Inc. 168

On the Mark Press 200

Orca Book Publishers 201

Pauline Books & Media 172

Peachtree Children's Books 172

Pelican Publishing Company 173

Philomel Books 174

Piano Press 174

Piñata Books 174

Pineapple Books 175

Pomegranate Kids 176

Puffin Books 177

Random House Children's Books
177

Roaring Brook Press 179

Ronsdale Press 202

Sasquatch Books 179

Scholastic Library Publishing 180

Scholastic Press 181

Seedling Continental Press 181

Simon & Schuster Books for Young
Readers 182

Skinner House Books 182

Spinner Books 183

Sterling Publishing Co., Inc. 184

Sone Arch Books 184

Sweet Cherry Publishing 202

Tafelberg Publishers 203

Thistledown Press, Ltd. 203

Tilbury House Publishers 186

Tradewind Books 203

Tu Books 187

Tyndale House Publishers, Inc. 188

Usborne Publishing 204

Viking Children's Books 188

White Mane Kids 189

Whitecap Books, Ltd. 204

Windward Publishing 190

Wiseman Publishing, Paula 190

Wordsong 190

World Book, Inc. 191

Zest Books 192

MAGAZINES

Advocate, PKA's Publication 207

Boys' Life 209

Bread for God's Children 209

Brilliant Star 209

Cadet Quest Magazine 210

Click 210

Dig Into History 211

Dramatics Magazine 211

Faces 212

Friend Magazine, The 213

Fun for Kidz 213

Green Teacher 214

Leading Edge Magazine 217

New Moon Girls 219

Seventeen Magazine 220

Shine Brightly 220

Skipping Stones: A Multicultural
Literary Magazine 221

Sparkle 222

GENERAL INDEX

Abbeville Family 137

ABDO Publishing Co. 137

Abrams Books for Young Readers 137

Abrams, Harry N., Inc. 137

A+B Works 226

Adams Literary 226

Addams Children's Book Awards, Jane 325

Advocate, PKA's Publication 207

Agents & Editors Conference/ Writers' League of Texas 303

Aladdin 137

Alaska Writers Conference 303

Alcuin Society Book Design Awards 325

Algonquin Young Readers 137

Allen & Unwin 196

Amberjack Publishing 138

American Alliance for Theatre & Education 295

American Association of University Women Award in Juvenile Literature 325

American Christian Writers Conferences 303

American Society of Journalists and Authors 295

Amulet Books 138

Andersen Award, Hans Christian 325

Andersen Press 196

Andrews McMeel Publishing 138

Annick Press, Ltd. 196

Annual Spring Poetry Festival 303

Antioch Writers' Workshop 303

Aquila 208

Arbordale Publishing 138

Arizona Authors' Association 295

Artisan Books 139

Ascent Aspirations 208

Atheneum Books for Young Readers 139

Atlanta Writers Conference 303

Authors Guild, Inc., The 295

Azantian Literary 226

Bailiwick Press 139

Baillie Picture Book Award, Marilyn 325

Balzer & Bray 139

Bancroft Press 140

Bantam Books 140

Barefoot Books 140

Barron's 140

Barrons Educational Series 141

Batchelder Award, Mildred L. 326

Beatty Award, John and Patricia 326

Behrman House Inc. 141

BelleBooks 142

Bent Agency, The 226

Berkley 142

Bess Press 142

Bethany House Publishers 142

Beyond Words Publishing, Inc. 143

Big Sur Writing Workshop 304

Bilson Award for Historical Fiction for Young People, The Geoffrey 326

Black Award, The Irma S. and James H. 326

Black Literary Agency, David 226

Black Rose Writing 143

Bloomsbury Children's Books 143

Bloomsbury Spark 143

Bookfish Books 144

Book Group, The 227

Books-in-Progress Conference 304

Bookstop Literary Agency 228

Boyds Mills Press 144

Boys' Life 208

Bradford Literary Agency 228

Brandt & Hochman Literary Agents, Inc. 229

Bread for God's Children 209

Brilliant Star 209

Brimer Book Award, Ann Connor 326

Brown Literary Agency, Inc., Andrea 230

Brown, Ltd., Curtis 230

Brown Associates, Inc., Marie 231

Brucedale Press, The 196

Buckeye Children's Book Award 327

Buster Books 196

Cadet Quest Magazine 210

Caldecott Medal, Randolph 327

California Young Playwrights Contest 327

Calkins Creek 144

Cameron & Associates, Kimberley 232

Canadian Society of Children's Authors, Illustrators and Performers (CANSCAIP) 296

Candlewick Press 145

Cape Cod Writers Center Annual Conference 304

Capstone Press 145

Capstone Professional 145

Carolrhoda Books, Inc. 146

Carroll Society of North America, Lewis 296

Cartwheel Books 146

Carvainis Agency, Inc., Maria 232

Cascade Writing Contest & Awards 327

Cedar Fort, Inc. 146

Celebration of Southern Literature 304

Chalberg & Sussman 233

Charlesbridge Publishing 146

Chicago Review Press 147

Children's Africana Book Award 328

Children's Book Guild Award for Nonfiction 328

Children's Brains are Yummy (CBAY) Books 147

Child's Play (International) Ltd. 197

Chooseco, LLC 148

Christian Book Award® Program 328

Christian Focus Publications 197

Chronicle Books 148

Chronicle Books for Children 149

Chudney Agency 233

Clarion Books 149

Clarksville Writers Conference 304

CLA Young Adult Book Award 328

Click 210

CollegeXpress Magazine 211

Colorado Book Awards 328

Conference for Writers & Illustra-

tors of Children's Books 305

Congdon Associates, Inc., Don 233

Corvisiero Literary Agency 234

Coteau Books 198

Craigmore Creations 149

Creative Company 149

Creston Books 150

Cricket League 329

Curiosity Quills Press 150

Curious Fox 198

CWW Annual Wisconsin Writers Awards 329

D4eo Literary Agency

Dail Literary Agency, Inc., Laura 235

Darby Creek Publishing 150

Dawn Publications 150

Dawson Associates, Liza 235

De Chiara Literary Agency, The Jennifer 236

DeFiore & Company 236

Delacorte Press 151

Dial Books for Young Readers 151

Dig into History 211

Dijkstra Literary Agency, Sandra 237

Donadio & Olson, Inc. 238

Donaghy Literary Group 238

Dramatics Magazine 211

Dunham Literary, Inc. 239

Dunow, Carlson, & Lerner Agency 239

Dystel, Goderich & Bourret LLC 240

Eden Street Literary 241

Edupress, Inc. 151

Edwards Award, Margaret A. 329

Eerdmans Publishing Co., William B. 152

Ehrlich Literary Management, LLC, Judith 241

Einstein Literary Management 242

Ellysian Press 152

Elm Books 152

Entangled Teen 152

Ethan Ellenberg Literary Agency 242

Emerald City Literary Agency 242

Evatopia, Inc. 243

Evil Jester PRess 153

Faces 212

Facts On File, Inc. 153

Familius 153

Farrar, Straus & Giroux for Young Readers 154

Fat Fox Books 198

Father's Press 154

FCA Magazine 212

Feiwel and Friends 154

Fendrich Memorial Playwriting Contest, Shubert 329

Fey Publishing 154

Fickling Books, David 198

Finch Literary Agency, Dana 243

Fineprint Literary Management 244

First Second 155

Fisher Children's Book Award, Dorothy Canfield 330

Fitzhenry & Whiteside Ltd. 199

Flannery Literary 244

Flashlight Press 155

Fleck Award for Canadian Children's Nonfiction, The Norma 330

Fletcher & Co. 245

Flicker Tale Children's Book Award 330

Flying Eye Books 199

Folio Literary Management, LLC 245

Forward Movement 155

Foster, Jr., Walter 155

Foundry Literary + Media 246

Fox Literary 247

Frances Lincoln Children's Books 199

Franklin Watts 199

Fraser-Bub Literary, Inc. 247

Freeman Illustrator Grants, Don 330

Free Spirit Publishing, Inc. 155

Freymann Literary Agency, Sarah Jane 248

Friedman Literary Agency, Rebecca 248

Friedrich Agency, The

Friend Magazine, The 213

Fulcrum Publishing 156

Full Circle Literary, LLC 248

Fun for Kidz 213

Fuse Literary 249

Gallt and Zacker Literary Agency 250

Geisel Award, Theodor Seuss 330

Gelfman Schneider/ICM Partners 250

Gernert Company, The 251
Gibbs Smith 156
Girls' Life 213
Glencannon Press, The 156
Godine, Publisher, David R. 157
Goldblatt Literary LLC, Barry 251
Golden Books for Young Readers
  Group 157
Golden Kite Awards 331
Goodman Literary Agency, irene
  252
Goosebottom Books 157
Gotham Writers' Workshop 305
Governor General's Literary
  Awards 331
Graphic Artists Guild 296
Green Literary Agency, LLC,
  Kathryn 252
Green Teacher 214
Greenburger Associates, Inc.,
  Sanford J. 253
Greenhaven Press 157
Greenhouse Literary Agency, The
  253
Greenwillow Books 157
Grinberg Literary Management,
  Jill 254
Grosset & Dunlap Publishers 158
Gryphon House, Inc. 158
Guggenheim Fellowships 331
Hachai Publishing 158
Hackney Literary Awards 331
Hall Awards for Youth Theatre,
  The Marilyn 332
Hampton Roads Writers Confer-
  ence 305

Harmony Ink Press 159
HarperCollins Children's Books/
  HarperCollins Publishers 159
Harris Memorial Playwriting
  Award, Aurand 332
Hartline Literary Agency 254
Heller Agency, Inc., Helen 255
Hendrick-Long Publishing Co.,
  Inc. 159
Herman, Ronnie Ann 255
Heyday Books 159
Highland Summer Conference
  305
Highlights for Children 214
Highlights for Children Fiction
  Contest 332
Highlights Foundation Founders
  Workshops 305
Hill Nadell Literary Agency 256
Hoffer Award, Eric 332
Holiday House, Inc. 160
Hollinshead Visiting Scholars Fel-
  lowship, Marilyn 332
Holloway Literary 256
Horror Writers Association 296
Houghton Mifflin Harcourt Books
  for Children 160
Houston Writers Guild Confer-
  ence 306
Howard-Gibbon Illustrator's
  Award, Amelia Frances 333
Howe/Boston Authors Award, The
  Julia Ward 333
HSG Agency 257
Hunger Mountain 215
Hurst Children's Book Prize, Carol

Otis 333
ICM Partners 257
Imagination Café 216
Immedium 160
Impact Publishers, Inc. 161
Inklings Literary Agency 257
Inkwell Management, LLC 258
Insight Writing Contest 333
International Literacy Association
  Children's and Young Adult's
  Book Awards 333
International Reading Association
  296
International Transactions, Inc.
  259
International Women's Writing
  Guild 297
IODE Jean Throop Book Award,
  The 334
Iowa Summer Writing Festival
  306
Islandport 161
IWWG Annual Conference 306
Jabberwocky Literary Agency 259
James River Writers Conference
  306
Janklow & Nesbit Associates 260
Jefferson Cup Award 334
Jenks Agency, The Carolyn 260
Jewish Lights Publishing 161
JourneyForth 162
Just Us Books, Inc. 162
Kaeden Books 162
Kane/Miller Book Publishers 163
Kar-Ben Publishing 163
Keats Book Award for New Writer

& New Illustrator, The Ezra Jack
  334
Keats/Kerlan Memorial Fellow-
  ship, Ezra Jack 334
Kentucky Bluegrass Award 334
Kentucky Writers Conference 306
Keys for Kids Devotional 216
Kids Can Press 199
Kindling Words East 307
Kindling Words West 307
King Book Awards, Coretta Scott
  334
Klinger, Inc., Harvey 260
Knight Agency, The 261
Kregel Publications 163
KT Literary, LLC 262
La Jolla Writers Conference 307
Leacock Memorial Medal for Hu-
  mour, Stephen The 335
Leading Edge 216
League of Utah Writers' Annual
  Writer's Conference 307
League of Utah Writers Contest
  335
Lee & Low Books 164
Leshne Agency, The 262
Levine Books, Arthur A. 164
Levine Greenberg Rostan Literary
  Agency, Inc. 263
Levine Literary Agency, Paul S.
  263
Lippincott Massie McQuilkin 264
Little, Brown Books for Young
  Readers 164
Little Pickle Press 165
Little Simon 165

Little Tiger Press 200
LKG Agency 264
Lord Literistic, Inc., Sterling 265
Louisville Review, The 217
Lowenstein Associates, Inc. 266
Maass Literary Agency, Donald
  266
Maccoby Literary Agency, Gina
  267
Magic Dragon 217
Magination Press 165
Manor House Publishing, Inc. 200
Mansion Street Literary Manage-
  ment 267
Marsal Lyon Literary Agency, LLC
  267
Marsh Award for Children's Litera-
  ture in Translation 335
Martin Literary and Media Man-
  agement 268
Martin Sisters Publishing Com-
  pany, Inc. 165
Master Books 166
McCarthy Literary Agency, Sean
  269
McDermid & Associates, Ltd.,
  Anne 269
McElderry Books, Margaret K.
  166
McIntosh & Otis, Inc. 269
McKnight Artist Fellowships for
  Writers, Loft Award(s) in Children's
  Literature/Creative Prose/Poetry 335
McMeel, Andrew 166
Medallion Press 167
Metcalf Award for Literature for

Young People, The Vicky 335
Midwest Writers Workshop 307
Mighty Media Press 167
Milkweed Editions 167
Milkweed for Young Readers 167
Milkweed Prize for Children's
  Literature 335
Millbrook Press, The 168
Minnesota Book Awards 336
Missouri Writers' Guild Confer-
  ence 308
Mitchell Lane Publishers, Inc. 168
Moody Publishers 168
MoonDance Press 169
Morhaim Literary Agency, How-
  ard 270
Mount Hermon Christian Writers
  Conference 308
Moveable Type Management 270
Mura Literary, Dee 270
Murphy Literary Agency, Erin 271
Muse and the Marketplace 308
Naggar Literary Agency, Inc., Jean
  V. 271
National Book Awards 336
National Geographic Children's
  Books 169
National Geographic Kids 218
National League of American Pen
  Women, The 297
National Outdoor Book Awards
  336
National Writers Association 297
National Writers Association Non-
  fiction Contest 336
National Writers Association

Short Story Contest 337
National Writers Union 297
National YoungArts Foundation 337
Nature Friend Magazine 218
Naturegraph Publishers, Inc. 169
Nelson Literary Agency 272
Nelson, Tommy 169
Newbery Medal, John 337
New England Book Awards 337
New Leaf Literary & Media, Inc. 272
New Moon Girls 218
New Voices Award 338
Nightscape Press 169
Nomad Press 170
North American International Auto Show High School Poster Contest 338
North Carolina Writers' Network Fall Conference 308
Northern California Book Awards 338
Northern Colorado Writers Conference 308
NorthSouth Books 170
Nova Writes Competition for Unpublished Manuscripts 338
Odyssey Fantasy Writing Workshop 309
Ohioana Book Awards 339
Ohio Kentucky Indiana Children's Literature Conference 309
Oklahoma Book Awards 339
Oklahoma Writers' Federation, Inc. Annual Conference 309

On Course 219
OnStage Publishing 170
On The Mark Press 200
Ooligan Press 170
Orca Book Publishers 201
Orchard Books (US) 171
Oregon Book Awards 339
Oregon Literary Fellowships 339
Original Art, The 339
Ott Award for Outstanding Contribution to Children's Literature, Helen Keating 340
Outdoor Writers Association of America Annual Conference 309
Ozark Creative Writers, Inc. Conference 309
Pacific Coast Children's Writers Whole-Novel Workshop: For Adults and Teens 310
PageSpring Publishing 171
Pajama Press 201
Pants On Fire Press 171
Paradise Cay Publications 171
Park Literary Group, LLC 273
Paterson Prize for Books for Young People 340
Paterson Prize for Young Adult and Children's Writing, The Katherine 340
Pauline Books & Media 172
Peachtree Children's Books 172
Pelican Publishing Company 173
PEN American Center 298
Penguin Random House, LLC 173
Pennsylvania Young Readers'

Choice Awards Program 340

Pennwriters Conference 310

PEN/Phyllis Naylor Working Writer Fellowship 340

Perkins Agency, L. 273

Persea Books 173

Pfeffer Content, Rubin 274

Phaidon Press 174

Philadelphia Writers' Conference 310

Philomel Books 174

Piano Press 174

Pikes Peak Writers Conference 310

Pinata Books 174

Pineapple Press, Inc. 175

Pippin Properties, Inc. 274

Please Touch Museum Book Award 340

PNWA Literary Contest 341

PNWA Summer Writers Conference 311

Pockets 219

Pockets Fiction-Writing Contest 341

Poe Award, Edgar Allan 341

Poisoned Pencil, The 175

Polis Books 176

Pomegranate Kids 176

POW! 176

Price Stern Sloan, Inc. 176

Printz Award, Michael L. 341

Prospect Agency 274

Prufrock Press, Inc. 176

P.S. Literary Agency 275

Puffin Books 177

Puppeteers of America, Inc. 298

Purcell Agency, The 276

Purple Dragonfly Book Awards 342

Putnam's Sons Hardcover, GP 177

Quill and Scroll Writing, Photo and Multimedia Contest, and Blogging Competition 342

Quirk Books 177

Random House Children's Books 177

Razorbill 178

Rebelight Publishing, Inc. 201

Red House Children's Book Award, The 342

Red Sofa Literary 276

Redleaf Lane 178

Rees Literary Agency 277

Regal Hoffmann & Associates, LLC 277

Rights Factory, The 278

Ripple Grove Press 178

Rittenberg Literary Agency, Inc., Ann 278

Rivera Mexican American Children's Book Award, Tomás 342

RLR Associates, Ltd. 278

Roaring Brook Press 179

Rocky Mountain Book Award: Alberta Children's Choice Book Award 343

Rocky Mountain Retreats for Writers & Artists 311

Rodeen Literary Management 279

Ronsdale Press 202

Rosen Publishing 179

Ross Literary Agency, Andy 279

Rotrosen Agency, LLC, Jane 279

Royal Dragonfly Book Awards 343

RT Booklovers Convention 311

Saddleback Educational Publishing 179

Salina Bookshelf 179

San Diego State University Writers' Conference 311

San Francisco Writers Conference 312

Sanders & Associates, Victoria 280

Santa Barbara Writers Conference 312

Saskatchewan Book Awards 343

Sasquatch Books 179

SCBWI—Alaska; Events 313

SCBWI; Annual Conferences on Writing and Illustrating for Children 312

SCBWI—Arizona; Events 313

SCBWI—Austin Conference 313

SCBWI Bologna—Biennial Conference 313

SCBWI—British Isles 313

SCBWI—California (San Francisco/South); Golden Gate Conference at Asilomar 313

SCBWI—Canada East 313

SCBWI—Carolinas; Annual Fall Conference 313

SCBWI—Carolinas Spring Retreat, The Elements of Stor 314

SCBWI—Central-Coastal California; Fall Conference 314

SCBWI—Colorado/Wyoming (Rocky Mountain); Events 314

SCBWI—Eastern New York; Falling Leaves Master Class Retreat 314

SCBWI—Eastern Pennsylvania 314

SCBWI—Florida; Mid-Year Writing Workshop 314

SCBWI—Florida; Regional Conference 314

SCBWI—Illinois; Prairie Writers Day 315

SCBWI—Iowa Conferences 315

SCBWI Magazine Merit Awards 343

SCBWI—Michigan; Conferences 315

SCBWI—Mid-Atlantic; Annual Fall Conference 315

SCBWI—Midsouth Fall Conference 315

SCBWI—Missouri; Children's Writer's Conference 315

SCBWI—New England; Annual Conference 315

SCBWI—New England; Whispering Pines Writer's Retreat 316

SCBWI—New Jersey; Annual Summer Conference 316

SCBWI—New Mexico; Handsprings: A Conference for Children's Writers and Illustrators 316

SCBWI—Northern Ohio; Annual Conference 316

SCBWI—Oregon Conferences 316

SCBWI—Pocono Mountains Retreat 317
SCBWI—Rocky Mountain; Annual Fall Conference 317
SCBWI—Southern Breeze; Springmingle 317
SCBWI—Southern Breeze; Writing and Illustrating for Kids 317
SCBWI—Taiwan; Events 317
SCBWI—Western Washington State; Conference & Retreat 317
SCBWI Winter Conference on Writing and Illustrating for Children 317
SCBWI—Wisconsin; Fall Retreat for Working Writers 318
Schmalz Agency, Wendy 280
Scholastic, Inc. 180
Scholastic Library Publishing 180
Scholastic Press 181
Schulman Literary Agency, LLC, Susan 281
Schwartz & Wade Books 181
Science-Fiction and Fantasy Writers of America, Inc. 298
Second Story Press 202
Seedling Continental Press 181
Serendipity Literary Agency, LLC 281
Seventeen Magazine 220
Seymour Agency, The
Sheehan YA Book Prize 344
SHINE brightly 220
Silver Dolphin Books 181
Simon & Schuster Books for Young Readers 182

Simply Read Books 202
Skinner House Books 182
Skipping Stones: A Multicultural Literary Magazine 221
Skipping Stones Book Awards 344
Skipping Stones Youth Awards 344
Skipping Stones Youth Honor Awards 344
Skurnick Books, Lizzie 182
Sky Pony Press 183
Sleeping Bear Press 183
Snow Writing Contest, Kay 345
Society of Children's Book Writers and Illustrators (SCBWI) 299
Society of Illustrators 299
Society of Midland Authors 299
Society of Midland Authors Award 345
Society of Southwestern Authors 299
Sourcebooks Fire 183
South Carolina Writers Workshop 318
South Coast Writers Conference 318
Southeastern Writers Association—Annual Writers Workshop 318
Space Coast Writers Guild Annual Conference 318
Sparkle 222
Speilburg Literary Agency 282
Spencer Hill Press 183
Spieler Agency, The 282
Spinner Books 183
Spitzer Literary Agency, Inc.,

Philip G. 283
Splashing Cow Books 184
Standard Publishing 184
Star Bright Books 184
Steamboat Springs Writers Conference 318
Sterling Publishing Co., Inc. 184
Stimola Literary Studio 283
Stone Arch Books 184
Stone Soup 223
Stonesong 283
Strawberries Press 185
Straus Agency, Inc., Robin 284
Stringer Literary Agency, LLC, The 284
Strothman Agency, LLC, The 285
Sunstone Press 185
Surrey International Writers' Conference 319
Sweeney Agency, LLC, Emma 285
Sweet Cherry Publishing 202
Sydney Taylor Manuscript Competition 345
Tafelberg Publishers 203
Talcott Notch Literary 286
Taylor Book Award, Sydney 346
TD Canadian Children's Literature Award 346
Tegen Books, Katherine 185
Texas Mountain Trail Writers Spring Retreat 319
Texas Writing Retreat 319
Text & Academic Authors Association (TAA) 300
Theatre For Young Audiences/ USA 300

The University of Winchester Writers' Festival 319
Thompson Literary Agency 287
Thistledown Press Ltd. 203
Three Seas Literary Agency 287
ThunderStone Books 185
Tilbury House Publishers 186
Timber press 186
TMCC Writers' Conference 320
Tor Books 186
Toronto Book Awards 346
Tradewind Books 203
Transatlantic Literary Agency 288
Triangle Square 186
Triada US 288
Trident Media Group 289
Tu Books 187
Tumblehome Learning 187
Tuttle Publishing 188
Tyndale House Publishers, Inc. 188
Unicorn Writers Conference 320
United Talent Agency 290
University of Wisconsin at Madison Writers' Institute 320
Unter Agency, The 290
Usborne Publishing 204
Vegetarian Essay Contest 346
Veritas Literary Agency 291
VFW Voice of Democracy 346
Viking Children's Books 188
Volunteer Lawyers for the Arts 300
Waxman Leavell Literary Agency, Inc. 291
Wells Arms Literary 292
Wernick & Pratt Agency 292
Wesleyan Writers Conference 320

Western Australian Premier's Book Awards 346

Western Heritage Awards 347

Western Psychological Services 189

Western Writers of America 347

Westwood Creative Artists, Ltd. 292

Whitecap Books, Ltd. 204

White Mane Kids 189

White Memorial National Children's Playwriting Contest, Jackie 347

Whitman, Albert & Company 189

Wilder Medal, Laura Ingalls 347

WILLA Literary Award 348

Williams Young Adult Prose Prize Category, Rita 348

Windward Publishing 190

Winter Poetry & Prose Getaway 321

Wiseman Books, Paula 190

Witty Outstanding Literature Award, Paul A. 348

Woodbine House 190

Wordsong 190

Work-In-Progress Grant 348

Workman Books 191

World Book, Inc. 191

World Weaver Press 191

WorthyKids/Ideals 192

Write-by-the-Lake Writer's Workshop & Retreat 321

Write Canada 321

Write in the Harbor 321

Write Now 348

Write on the Sound Writers' Conference 322

Writer's Digest Self-Published Book Awards 348

Writer's Digest Self-Published e-Book Awards 349

Writers-Editors Network International Writing Competition 349

Writers' Federation of New Brunswick 300

Writers' Federation of Nova Scotia 300

Writers' Guild of Alberta 301

Writers' Guild of Alberta Awards 349

Writers House 293

Writers' League of Texas Book Awards 350

Write-To-Publish Conference 322

Writing and Illustrating for Young Readers Conference 322

Writing Conference Writing Contests 350

Writing for the Soul 323

Wyoming Writers Conference 323

Yarn Literary Agency, Jason 293

Yearbook Excellence Contest 350

Young Adult Fiction Prize, The 350

Young Reader's Choice Award 350

Young Rider 223

Youth Honor Award Program, The 351

Zest Books 192

Zornio Memorial Children's Theatre Playwriting Competition, Anna 351

Zumaya Publications, LLC 192